THE WORLD BOOK

ENCYCLOPEDIA

U·V

Volume 19

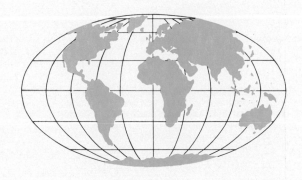

FIELD ENTERPRISES EDUCATIONAL CORPORATION

CHICAGO

LONDON · ROME · STOCKHOLM · SYDNEY · TORONTO

THE WORLD BOOK ENCYCLOPEDIA

COPYRIGHT © 1967, U.S.A.

by FIELD ENTERPRISES EDUCATIONAL CORPORATION

U **u** is the 21st letter of our alphabet. It came from a letter which the Semitic peoples of Syria and Palestine called *waw*. *Waw* was also the source of *F, V, W,* and *Y*. The word *waw* meant hook, and was represented by a symbol of a tenthook. The symbol was probably borrowed from an Egyptian hieroglyphic, or picture symbol. The Greeks borrowed the letter from the Phoenicians and gave it a *Y*-shape. The Romans, when they adopted the letter, dropped its bottom stroke and wrote it as *V*. They used it for the vowel sound, *U,* and the consonant sound, *V*. About A.D. 900, people began to write *U* in the middle of a word and *V* at the beginning. During the Renaissance, it became customary to use *u* as a vowel and *v* as a consonant. See ALPHABET.

Uses. *U* or *u* is about the 12th most frequently used letter in books, newspapers, and other printed material in English. As an abbreviation on report cards, *u* means *unsatisfactory*. In geographic names, it may mean *united*, *union*, or *upper*. It frequently stands for *university*. In chemistry, *U* is the symbol for the element *uranium*.

Pronunciation. *U* is a vowel, and has many sounds in English. The sound we associate with its name, *you*, is really a diphthong. It is made by linking two separate sounds pronounced continuously. A person forms this sound by rounding his lips, with the tip of his tongue below the lower teeth, and raising the back of his tongue. Other sounds of *u* are those in *sun, duty, presume, bull,* and *fur*. A silent *u* may occur after *g*, as in *guard* and *guess*. See PRONUNCIATION.   I. J. GELB and J. M. WELLS

The 21st letter took its shape from an ancient Egyptian symbol for a supporting pole. It was not regularly used for our vowel sound, *you*, until about 500 years ago.

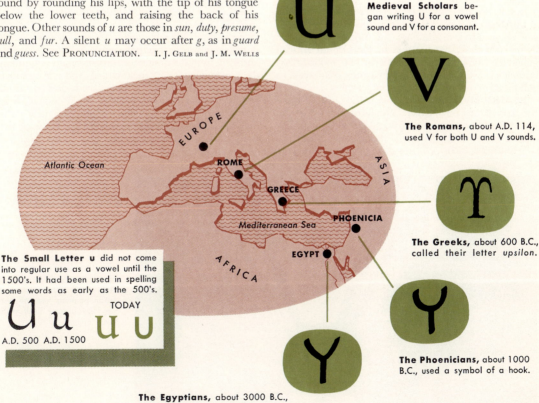

Medieval Scholars began writing U for a vowel sound and V for a consonant.

The Romans, about A.D. 114, used V for both U and V sounds.

The Greeks, about 600 B.C., called their letter *upsilon*.

The Phoenicians, about 1000 B.C., used a symbol of a hook.

The Egyptians, about 3000 B.C., used a symbol of a supporting pole.

The Small Letter u did not come into regular use as a vowel until the 1500's. It had been used in spelling some words as early as the 500's.

A.D. 500   A.D. 1500   TODAY

U-BOAT. See SUBMARINE (During World War I).

U NU. See NU, U.

U THANT. See THANT, U.

U-2, reconnaissance plane. See COLD WAR (Peaceful Coexistence; picture, Spy Flights); UNITED STATES, HISTORY OF (Time for a Change).

U-235 is one of the isotopes present in ordinary uranium. It was the first one used to release atomic energy. U-235 has an atomic number of 92, and an atomic weight of 235. This lighter form of uranium was first identified in 1935 by Arthur J. Dempster at the University of Chicago. U-235 is also formed when an atom of plutonium gives off an alpha particle.

U-235 is fissionable. This means that its atom can easily be split into atoms of new elements. An atom of U-235 can be broken up by bombarding the atom with a neutron. When this happens, such a tremendous explosion takes place that 200 million electron volts of energy are given off. During this bombardment of the neutron, the uranium atom forms two new elements which are lighter in weight. For example, U-235 may break down into barium and krypton, and form two or three neutrons in the process (see ATOMIC ENERGY [illustration, Nuclear Fission]).

A small portion of the energy that binds the neutrons and protons in the uranium atom is given off as radiation. Some of this energy is carried by the neutrons and the new atoms as kinetic energy, and the remainder appears as radiation.   JOHN J. O'NEILL

See also DEMPSTER, ARTHUR J.; URANIUM.

U-238 and **U-239.** See ATOMIC ENERGY (Nuclear Fission); URANIUM.

U.A.R. See UNITED ARAB REPUBLIC.

UBANGI, yoo BANG ee, is a nickname given to women members of the Sara, an African Negro tribe living near the Ubangi River in the Central African Republic. Many of the women wear flat wooden disks in their pierced lips. They begin wearing small disks in childhood and gradually put in larger ones.

UBANGI RIVER, yoo BANG ee, is the chief northern tributary of the Congo River. With its main headstream, the M'Bomu, the Ubangi is about 1,400 miles long. It is formed by the union of the M'Bomu and Uele rivers, and empties into the Congo near Lake Tumba. For about 700 miles, the Ubangi forms the boundary line that separates Congo (Léopoldville) from Congo (Brazzaville) on the west, and Central African Republic on the northwest. During the rainy season, barges and passenger ships can go up the river to Bangui. But larger ships cannot pass the rapids at Zinga. The Ubangi is sometimes called the *Mobangi* in its lower course, and the *Makau* in its upper course.   GEORGE H. T. KIMBLE

UBICO CASTAÑEDA, JORGE. See GUATEMALA (Dictatorship and Progress).

UCAYALI RIVER. See AMAZON RIVER (Its Course).

UCCELLO, oot CHEL loh, **PAOLO** (1397-1475), was one of the first Renaissance painters in Italy. Perspective takes on special emphasis in his work. Its purpose is to bring order into the host of things that people see. Uccello kept it from looking fixed and dead by his bright, almost flat color, and vivid movement. His best-known works include *Noah's Flood* and three scenes of battles. *The Rout of San Romano* appears in color in the PAINTING article. Uccello lived in Florence, and was an apprentice to the sculptor Lorenzo Ghiberti.   CREIGHTON GILBERT

UDALL, STEWART LEE (1920-   ), became Secretary of the Interior under President John F. Kennedy in 1961. He was the first Arizonan named to a Cabinet post. Before his appointment, he served six years as a Democrat in the U.S. House of Representatives.

Udall was born in St. Johns, Ariz. During World War II, he served as a gunner in the army air force in Italy. He received a law degree from the University of Arizona in 1948. Udall practiced law in Tucson until he won election to Congress in 1954. He wrote *Quiet Crisis* (1963), a story of the fight to save the nation's natural resources.   ERIC SEVAREID

UDT. See UNDERWATER DEMOLITION TEAM.

UFFIZI PALACE, oof FEET see, is a famous palace at Florence, Italy. It contains one of the finest art collections in the world. The palace was built between 1560 and 1576 from the designs of Giorgio Vasari. Originally, the Grand Dukes of Tuscany used it as a government office. The second floor of the palace houses part of the art collection of the Medici family, a collection of Dutch and Flemish paintings, and many famous statues. Paintings by Italian artists include some by Fra Angelico, the Lippis, and Michelangelo.   SIBYL MOHOLY-NAGY

Alinari

Uffizi Palace in Florence, Italy, contains classical sculptures and masterpieces of Italian painting from all periods. The palace itself dates from the late 1500's.

UGANDA, *yoo GAN duh*, is an east African country in the Commonwealth of Nations. Formerly the British UGANDA PROTECTORATE, it gained independence in 1962.

The Land. Uganda covers 91,134 square miles, slightly less than Oregon. It straddles the equator and lies about 500 miles from the Indian Ocean.

Kenneth Ingham, the contributor of this article, is Director of Studies at the Royal Military Academy Sandhurst, Camberley, England, and author of The Making of Modern Uganda.

Most of Uganda lies at about 4,000 feet above sea level. *Savannas* (areas covered with tall grass and clumps of low trees) cover most of the land. The Western Great Rift Valley forms a deep trench through Uganda. The Ruwenzori Range stretches for about 75 miles along the country's western border. Margherita Peak rises 16,795 feet there. On the eastern border, Mount Elgon towers 14,178 feet.

Water covers 16,348 square miles of the country. Lake Victoria, Africa's largest lake, extends into southern Uganda from Tanzania and Kenya. Lakes Edward, George, and Albert lie in the Western Great Rift Valley. The headwaters of the White Nile drain Uganda. The Victoria Nile flows north from Lake Victoria. It crosses marshy Lake Kyoga, in central Uganda, then enters Lake Albert. The Albert Nile flows north into Sudan, where it becomes the White Nile.

Uganda has many wild animals, including buffaloes and elephants. Many of these animals live in Queen Elizabeth National Park, along Lake Edward, and in Murchison Falls National Park, along the Victoria Nile.

Uganda lies in the tropics, but its high altitude makes the climate fairly comfortable. Temperatures range from 60° to 80° F. throughout the year. Rainfall averages about 50 inches a year.

The People. Uganda has a population of 7,550,000. Most of the people are Africans. The Baganda, a Bantu group, is the largest of the 28 tribes in Uganda. There are about 76,000 Asians, most of them Indians, and only about 12,000 Europeans.

Kampala (pop. 46,735) is the capital. It has a metropolitan area with over 123,000 persons. Other large towns include Entebbe, Fort Portal, Jinja, Kabale, Lugazi, Mbale, Soroti, and Tororo.

Economic Conditions. Uganda is a prosperous agricultural country. There are few European plantations because the British government developed the protectorate primarily for the Africans. Coffee and cotton are the chief exports. Other cash crops include corn, oilseeds, peanuts, sisal, sugar, tea, and tobacco. The people raise cattle, goats, and sheep, and export hides and skins. Fish form a valuable addition to the people's diet. Uganda exports some hardwoods.

Uganda has many minerals, but mines few of them on a large scale. In 1957, the rich Kilembe copper mines started operating in the Ruwenzori mountain area. The country also exports some gold, lead, phosphates, tin and tungsten. A plant at Tororo makes cement.

The country has few industries. But the opening of

Members of Tribes in Uganda often comb their hair into elaborate styles. The hairdos characterize individual tribes.

Three Lions

by Rand McNally for WORLD BOOK

Missionaries in Uganda have built many churches using local materials. Churches are constructed of palm logs, then thatched with papyrus from swamps. They resemble English village churches of the Middle Ages.

Camera Press, Pix

the Owen Falls Dam on the Victoria Nile in 1954 made power available for future industrial expansion. The hydroelectric plant is one of the largest in Africa.

A 1,081-mile railroad carries mineral exports from the foothills of the Ruwenzori Range to the Indian Ocean port of Mombasa, Kenya. Two branch lines serve the Eastern and Northern provinces. Cargo and passenger ships operate on Lakes Victoria, Kyoga, and Albert and on the Albert Nile. Uganda has about 3,000 miles of all-weather roads and about 8,300 miles of poorer roads. The town of Entebbe has an international airport.

Education. Only about 40 of every 100 adults can read or write. Only 40 of every 100 school-age children go to school. But the government has started a program to educate every child. Makerere University College near Kampala is a college of the University of East Africa.

Government. The National Assembly, a one-house legislature, has a speaker and 91 members. They are elected by the people. The prime minister heads the government. The head of state is the president, elected to a five-year term. In 1966, Prime Minister Obote suspended the constitution and took over the president's

---
FACTS IN BRIEF

Form of Government: Republic.

Capital: Kampala.

Official Language: English.

Head of State: President.

Area: 91,134 square miles. *Greatest distances:* (north-south) about 400 miles; (east-west) about 350 miles.

Population: *1959 census*—6,536,616; distribution, 95 per cent rural, 5 per cent urban. *1967 estimate*--7,550,000; density, 83 persons to the square mile. *1972 estimate*—8,350,000.

Chief Products: *Agriculture*, coffee, corn, cotton, livestock (cattle, goats, sheep), oilseeds, peanuts, sisal, sugar, tea, tobacco. *Mining*, copper, gold, lead, phosphates, tin, tungsten. *Fishing*, fish from lakes, rivers, and fish ponds. *Forestry*, hardwoods.

Flag: A white crested crane is centered on stripes of black (for Africa), yellow (for sunshine), and red (for brotherhood). See FLAG (color picture, Flags of Africa).

Money: *Basic Unit*, shilling. See MONEY (table, Values).

powers. Uganda has four provinces, Buganda, Eastern, Western, and Northern.

History. Little is known of Uganda before the mid-1800's. During the previous 1,000 years, various tribes had migrated to the area. They developed two types of political organization. In the north and east, villages and clans formed tribes. In the south and west, several kingdoms developed, each with a hereditary ruler. Buganda became the leading kingdom.

Arab slave and ivory traders from Africa's east coast reached Buganda about 1850. The British explorers John Speke and James Grant entered the area in 1862 in their search for the source of the Nile. In 1864, Samuel Baker discovered Lake Albert. Henry Stanley visited Buganda in 1875. The reports of these explorers about the partially civilized people in Buganda encouraged the founding of missions there.

In 1889, the Buganda ruler signed a treaty placing the Buganda Kingdom under German protection. But Germany gave up its claim to Uganda to Britain in 1890. The British government authorized the Imperial British East Africa Company to administer Uganda. The company gave up the territory four years later, because of heavy administration costs. Great Britain proclaimed a protectorate over the Buganda Kingdom in 1894 and soon extended the protectorate to the rest of Uganda.

In the early 1900's, the British developed agriculture and built the railroad through Kenya from the Indian Ocean to Lake Victoria.

Executive and legislative councils were established in Uganda in 1921. Uganda, Kenya, and Tanganyika became part of the East Africa High Commission in 1948. The regional body administered such common services as railways and customs. The commission became the East African Common Services Organization in 1961.

After World War II, the British government granted the Africans increasing representation in the Uganda Legislative Council. By March, 1962, the country was self-governing. On Oct. 1, 1962, Uganda became an independent member of the Commonwealth of Nations. A Ugandan president became head of state in October, 1963, replacing the governor-general, who represented Great Britain. In 1964, members of the army revolted for higher wages. But British troops restored peace. In 1966, Prime Minister Milton Obote suspended the constitution and took over the president's powers. He said foreign troops threatened Uganda. Sir Edward Mutesa, the former president, opposed Obote's action. Mutesa's supporters rioted in Kampala, but Obote's forces suppressed them. Mutesa fled to England.   KENNETH INGHAM

Related Articles in WORLD BOOK include:

Coffee (table)	Kampala	Lake Victoria
Entebbe	Lake Albert	Ruwenzori
Family (A Tug of War)	Lake Edward	Range

UHF WAVE. See ULTRAHIGH FREQUENCY WAVE.

UIGUR. See TURKESTAN.

UINTA. See UTAH (Land Regions).

UINTAITE. See ASPHALT.

UITLANDER. See BOER WAR.

UKRAINE, *yoo KRANE,* is one of the leading farming, industrial, and mining regions of Europe. It is the homeland of a Slavic people called Ukrainians. The Ukrainians are not Russians, but Russia controls the Ukraine as one of its political divisions. This division is called the UKRAINIAN SOVIET SOCIALIST REPUBLIC.

The Ukraine's natural wealth has led many nations to fight to control it. Russia has controlled the Ukraine almost continuously since the 1800's.

People. The Ukraine has a population of about 44,900,000. Kiev, in the northern Ukraine, is the capital and the largest city. The Ukrainians have their own language and customs, and most of them belong to the Russian Orthodox Church. But much Ukrainian life is under the strict control of the Russian Communist government.

Land. The Ukrainian Soviet Socialist Republic covers 232,047 square miles. It extends from the Carpathian Mountains east to the Sea of Azov, and north from the Crimean Peninsula for about 500 miles. For location, see RUSSIA (political map).

The Dnepr is the Ukraine's most important river. It divides the region into two parts. West of the Dnepr is a low plateau which rises gradually to the Carpathian Mountains. Part of the Pripyat (Pripet) Marshes lies in the far north. Most of the Ukraine east of the Dnepr is a plain. The coal-rich Donets hills rise in the easternmost portion. Along the shores of the Black Sea and the Sea of Azov in the southern Ukraine, the land is mostly flat. Low mountains rise along the Crimean Peninsula. In addition to the Dnepr, the Ukraine's major rivers include the Bug, Dnestr, and Donets.

Economy. The Ukraine is the major farm area of Russia, and one of that country's leading industrial and mining regions.

Ukrainian farmers raise livestock and produce large crops of barley, corn, rye, and wheat. Other major crops include sugar beets and tobacco. Sunflowers are grown and their seeds are used to make vegetable oil.

The Ukraine is an important source of coal, iron ore, manganese, mercury, natural gas, and salt.

Factories in the Ukraine produce about two-fifths of Russia's iron and steel. Other major industries include the manufacture of chemicals, farm and railroad equipment, and heavy machinery. The main industrial centers are around the Donets Basin in the east, near the hydroelectric power plants on the Dnepr River, and on the shores of the Sea of Azov. Kharkov is an important industrial city in the northern Ukraine.

History. The history of both Russia and the Ukraine began with the establishment of a state at Kiev in the

A.D. 800's. Kiev was an important trading center on the Dnepr River. It became the first state of Russia.

Poland conquered the western part of the Ukraine during the 1400's. During this time, the region became known as the *Ukraine,* meaning *frontier.* Many men of the region did not want to be ruled by the Poles. They fled east and formed a group of soldier-outlaws called *Cossacks.* The Cossacks fought the Poles many times, but they were unable to free the Ukraine from Polish rule.

For the next three hundred years, Poland, Russia, and Turkey fought for control of the Ukraine. During the 1700's, most of the Ukraine came under Russian rule in spite of strong Ukrainian opposition. Ukrainian patriots tried unsuccessfully to oppose the ruling Russians.

In 1917, near the end of World War I, the Ukrainians set up their own short-lived government at Kiev. But by 1921, Russia had restored its control over the Ukraine. The region became one of the original republics when the Union of Soviet Socialist Republics was formed in 1922.

In 1945, after World War II, Russia took over parts of the Ukraine that belonged to Czechoslovakia and Poland. Underground opposition to Russian rule continued for several years after the war. Many Ukrainians still oppose Russian rule.   GEORGE I. KISH

Related Articles in WORLD BOOK include:

Black Sea	Kharkov
Christmas (color picture)	Kiev
Crimea	Lvov
Dnepr River	Mazepa, Ivan S.
Dneproges Dam	Odessa
Dnepropetrovsk	Russia
Dnestr River	Ruthenia
Donetsk	Sevastopol
Easter (In the Ukraine)	Yalta

UKRAINIAN SOVIET SOCIALIST REPUBLIC. See UKRAINE.

UKULELE, *yoo kuh LAY lee,* is a four-stringed musical instrument which was first played in Hawaii. It is patterned after the Portuguese *taropatch fiddle.* The strings

Ukulele-Strumming Arthur Godfrey helped popularize this instrument during his daily radio and television shows.

Wide World

are tuned to A, E, C, and G, or to related pitches. The player *strums* (brushes) the strings with a sweeping motion, and always plays chords. Ukulele music is usually written in chord symbols which indicate finger positions, rather than in notes. The player need not know how to read music. CHARLES B. RIGHTER

See also HAWAII (Dancing and Music).

ULAN BATOR, *OO lahn BAH tohr* (pop. about 195,300; alt. 4,160 ft.), is the capital of Outer Mongolia. For location, see MONGOLIA (map). Its industries produce woolen cloth, felt, saddles, shoes, and meat products. Ulan Bator is a rail center and has a university. Founded in 1649, it has also been called *Urga*.

ULCER, *UL ser*, is an open sore in the skin or mucous membrane. A section of the covering membrane, the *epithelium*, breaks down and dies, leaving a raw area that heals slowly. A wound is not an ulcer.

Ulcers are likely to form on some part of the body which has poor blood circulation. Even a small injury on that part may lead to ulceration. The condition is common on legs with varicose veins. It is important to heal ulcers of the lips or skin, in order to prevent other conditions such as cancer from occurring.

Many persons have *peptic ulcers* (ulcers in the lining structure) in the stomach. Even more have peptic ulcers in the duodenum, the part of the intestine immediately below the stomach. Some of the causes or conditions that may lead to ulcers include heredity, nervous strain, poor circulation, or bad diet. But too much gastric juice is considered the real cause of stomach ulcers. Excess acid in the stomach keeps the ulcer from healing and helps keep it chronic. Ulcers of this kind usually cause pain or distress in the pit of the stomach. They may sometimes bleed, and are most dangerous when they *perforate* (eat through) the organ. This may lead to peritonitis. Stomach ulcers are treated with alkaline drugs and careful diet. Some require surgical treatment.

Ulcers on the eyeball are dangerous. When a tooth ulcerates, an ulcer may form on the gum when pus has gathered around the root.

See also CANCER; CANKER; STOMACH; TYPHOID FEVER.

ULEMA. See SAUDI ARABIA (Courts).

ULITHI, *oo LEE thee*, atoll is one of the western Caroline Islands. It consists of a large atoll, with 183 square miles of lagoon and some detached reefs and islets. The land area totals less than two square miles. About 525 Micronesians live on the islets. They raise food for their own use and make copra for trade. Like the other Caroline Islands, Ulithi is part of the Trust Territory of the Pacific Islands. The U.S. administers Ulithi. See PACIFIC ISLANDS, TRUST TERRITORY OF THE; PACIFIC ISLANDS (color map). EDWIN H. BRYAN, JR.

ULNA, *UL nah.* See ARM.

ULNAR NERVE. See FUNNY BONE.

ULSTER, *UL ster*, was one of the five provinces of early Ireland. It included what is now Northern Ireland, as well as the counties of Cavan, Donegal, and Monaghan. Northern Ireland is often called Ulster. For location, see IRELAND (color map). See also NORTHERN IRELAND.

ULSTERMEN. See NORTHERN IRELAND.

ULTIMA THULE, *UL tih muh THYOO lee*, was the name given in ancient literature to the most northern of known lands. A Greek sailor named Pytheas spoke of it

in the 300's B.C. He said that the days and nights in Ultima Thule lasted for six months, and that the sea there was so thick the rowers could not get through it. Some think that Pytheas was referring to Norway or Iceland. Others believe Ultima Thule was one of the Shetland Islands. Nowadays Ultima Thule is used to mean any distant place or faraway goal. PADRAIC COLUM

ULTIMATUM, *UL tuh MAY tum*, is a final proposition or demand made by one of two negotiating parties. The term is usually used in international affairs. It is a forceful and definite statement of one country's position. It often includes a demand for certain action on the part of the other country within a certain time limit. The rejection of an ultimatum may mean that one nation breaks off peaceful negotiations with the other.

PAYSON S. WILD, JR. Critically reviewed by TELFORD TAYLOR

ULTOR. See MARS (god).

ULTRAFAX is a method for copying and sending printed or written material and photographs by electrical means. A machine, known as the *scanning head*, is moved over small areas of the material that is to be sent. The machine copies the material and changes it into electric waves which can be sent over telephone wires or broadcast by radio to receiving points. At the receiving stations, machines called *recorders* receive the electric waves and reproduce copies of the material originally scanned.

See also MICROWAVE.

ULTRAHIGH FREQUENCY WAVE is a very short radio wave, from .1 to 1 meter long. UHF waves range from 300 million to 3 billion *cycles* (vibrations) a second. In the radio spectrum the ultrahigh frequency waves come between *very high* frequency waves and *super high* or microwaves. All of these high frequency waves have certain characteristics that make them different from standard broadcast waves, which have a lower frequency and a longer wave length. UHF waves, when sent from reflectors or directional antennas, are transmitted in a narrow path and travel through the air in a straight line. Ultrahigh frequency waves can also be reflected, like light waves.

UHF waves, very high frequency waves, and microwaves have been developed to their greatest usefulness in television, radar, "proximity fuses," guided missiles, and radio aircraft equipment. These frequencies are far above the ordinary broadcast band, and can therefore be used without interference. They are similar to light in that they can be projected into a beam in any direction desired. Their reflection from objects allows their use in radar to locate and "track" enemy aircraft and ships. PALMER H. CRAIG

See also GUIDED MISSILE; MICROWAVE; RADAR; TELEVISION (Channels).

ULTRAMARINE, *UL truh muh REEN*, is a blue pigment or coloring matter now prepared by artificial means. It usually has a purplish or greenish tinge. Ultramarine is made by *calcining* (heating) various combinations of China clay, sodium carbonate, silica, carbon, and sulfur until they form a dry powder. Ultramarine was once ground from the rare mineral lapis lazuli. This old method produced a brilliant, durable blue color, which was much prized by artists, but was very expensive. See also LAPIS LAZULI. THOMAS MUNRO

ULTRAMICROSCOPE is an instrument that allows a person to see objects that are much smaller than those he can see under an ordinary microscope. It is a compound microscope with several lenses. But it differs from other compound microscopes, because it uses a strong horizontal beam of light to illuminate the particles to be seen. This light beam can be brought into intense focus. Usually a powerful arc lamp supplies the light. The rays of light are focused by means of a system of condensing lenses. The last lens brings the rays together into very small, intensely brilliant focus.

Scientists often use this microscope to study *colloidal particles*, or bacteria floating in liquid or in the air. They set the microscope so that it receives only the light scattered by the particles themselves. No part of the direct light that illuminates the objects can enter the instrument. Therefore, the particles shine out as bright "stars" against a dark background. However, like the stars in the sky, these particles appear as points of light without structural detail. Objects as small as $\frac{6}{1,000,000}$ of a millimeter can be seen with an ultramicroscope. JOSEPH VALASEK

See also MICROSCOPE.

ULTRASONIC WAVE, *UL truh SAHN ick,* is a sound wave that has such a high frequency that a person cannot hear it. The *frequency* of sound means the number of sound vibrations each second. The band of sound waves with frequencies of more than 15,000 cycles each second is the ultrasonic wave band. Dogs, birds, and other animals can hear sounds of higher frequencies than man can. Manufacturers use ultrasonic waves to find cracks in castings, and to cut quartz radio crystals. Dentists often use drills operated by ultrasonic waves. SAMUEL SEELY

See also SOUND (Ultrasound).

ULTRAVIOLET RAYS are waves of light that lie just beyond the violet end of the visible light spectrum (see LIGHT [Electromagnetic Waves]). They are sometimes known as *invisible light* or *black light*, because they cannot be seen by the human eye.

Sources of Ultraviolet Rays. Sunlight, or *white light*, is a mixture of light of all colors, or wavelengths. When sunlight passes through a glass prism, the colors from red to violet spread out into a rainbowlike spectrum. Each wavelength falls in a different place. The red waves are the longest, and the violet rays are the shortest.

The glass prism absorbs most of the ultraviolet radiation. But if the prism is made of quartz instead of glass, the ultraviolet gets through, and can be detected in the place beyond the violet. The shortest violet rays that we can see are only about sixteen-millionths of an inch long. Ultraviolet rays range from this value down to wavelengths that are about 100 times shorter. See SPECTROSCOPE.

The sun is a strong, natural source of ultraviolet rays, but the air, especially smoke and dust, absorbs much of this radiation. As a result, most of the shortest ultraviolet rays do not reach the earth's surface. This is fortunate, because extremely short waves harm the skin and the tissues of the body. The rays that cause sunburn lie in two portions of the ultraviolet range. One lies just below the shortest violet wavelength, and the other at about three-fourths of this wavelength.

Ultraviolet light, although invisible, can be detected in various ways. It registers better on photographic film than does visible light. Under the influence of ultraviolet rays, various oils, minerals, and chemicals become *fluorescent*, or give off visible light (see FLUORESCENCE).

Uses of Ultraviolet Rays. In fluorescent lamps, an electric current passing through mercury vapor produces ultraviolet light. A coating on the inside of the glass tube absorbs the ultraviolet radiation, and changes it into visible light. Coatings of different types produce various colors. See FLUORESCENT LAMP.

The fluorescent effects of ultraviolet rays have important industrial uses, such as testing materials, identifying ores in mining, and lighting the instrument panels of aircraft. Scholars use the fluorescent effect of ultraviolet rays to examine old documents.

Sunlamps produce ultraviolet light in much the same way as fluorescent lamps. But the glass tube is made of quartz or fluorite to allow the ultraviolet light to pass through readily. Special glasses must be worn in the presence of ultraviolet lamps, because ultraviolet light is extremely harmful to the eyes. Some scientists believe that ultraviolet radiation causes skin cancer.

Certain ranges of ultraviolet rays can kill cells. These rays help sterilize water and milk, or the air in operating rooms. Modern food and drug plants use germicidal lamps to disinfect their products and the containers (see GERMICIDAL LAMP). Ultraviolet rays can also delay, and even change, the growth of cells.

Ultraviolet rays can also have a beneficial effect upon the human body, and have several important medical applications. They serve as a disinfectant. They also help heal wounds, and have been used to treat tuberculosis, rickets, and some skin diseases. Scientists have also found that they can help prevent rickets by treating foods such as milk and cereal with ultraviolet rays. This causes the formation of vitamin D, which is a strong preventive against rickets. Milk and eggs become more nourishing when exposed to ultraviolet rays.

One of the most recent uses of ultraviolet rays is in the field of rocket astronomy. A Geiger counter that is especially sensitive to ultraviolet rays is mounted inside a high-altitude rocket. As the rocket soars above the earth's atmosphere, the Geiger counter scans the skies. The ultraviolet radiation it records shows the presence of clouds of gas in the space between the stars in the galaxy. IRA M. FREEMAN

See also LIGHT (color pictures); RADIATION; SUN LAMP.

ULU, *OO loo,* is an Eskimo knife made of metal or chipped stone. It has a flat blade shaped like a half moon. The curved side is sharp. A handle is on the straight side.

ULYSSES, *yoo LISS eez,* or, in Greek, ODYSSEUS (*o DISS use*), was a king of Ithaca who fought in the Trojan War and wandered for 10 years afterward. He was the son of Laertes and Anticlia. He married Penelope, daughter of Icarus (see PENELOPE). Their son Telemachus was born just before the Trojan War began.

Ulysses did not want to go to war. He pretended to be crazy. He yoked an ox and horse to his plow, and sowed his field with salt. But Palamedes set the infant Telemachus in the plow's path and Ulysses turned aside. This proved to Palamedes that Ulysses was sane, and Ulysses had to go to war.

Ulysses then held a grudge against Palamedes. After

the Greeks reached Troy, Ulysses tricked them into thinking that Palamedes was a traitor, and they stoned Palamedes to death.

The Trojan War. Ulysses was a strong and valiant warrior. But he did more for the Greeks with his brain than with his brawn. He was the cleverest and craftiest man in the Greek army.

Late in the war, Ulysses and Diomedes captured Helenus, a Trojan seer, who told the Greeks what they had to do to win. Ulysses made sure that these things were done. He and Diomedes entered Troy in disguise, and carried off the Palladium, an image of Pallas Athena (see PALLADIUM). As long as the Trojans had it, the city could not be taken. He brought Achilles' son, Pyrrhus, to Troy to take his father's place. He brought Philoctetes with the bow of Hercules to Troy. Without that bow, the Greeks could not take Troy. Ulysses invented the wooden horse, which Epeus built, and he was one of the men inside the horse on the night of Troy's fall (see TROJAN HORSE).

His Travels. When Ulysses and his Ithacan company started home in their ships, a storm blew them off their course. Ulysses did not get home for 10 years, and lost all his men in the meantime. Homer's *Odyssey* tells the story of his adventures: how he escaped death from the Cyclops, the giant Laestrygon, Scylla, and the Sirens; how he outwitted Circe; and how he traveled even to the land of the dead beyond the Ocean Stream (see CIRCE; ODYSSEY; SCYLLA; SIREN).

Finally Ulysses came home to Ithaca. But he had to disguise himself as a beggar, because his house was filled with violent and dangerous men who wanted to marry

Ulysses Bends the Great Bow and sends an arrow through the throat of one of his wife's suitors. Ulysses had returned from the Trojan War disguised as a ragged beggar.

From *The Adventures of Odysseus and the Tale of Troy* by Padraic Colum, illustrated by Willy Pogany, published by the Macmillan Co.

his wife, Penelope. He revealed his identity only to Telemachus and to his faithful swineherd, Eumaeus. His aged dog Argos recognized him and was then content to die. Penelope had held off her suitors as long as she could, hoping always that Ulysses would come back. At last she was forced to set a contest among them. The man who could string Ulysses' bow and shoot an arrow through 12 rings would marry her. All failed, and then the disguised Ulysses took the bow, strung it, and shot an arrow through every ring. Then he suddenly turned the bow against the suitors, and shot an arrow through the throat of the suitor Antinous who had treated him most cruelly. With the help of Telemachus, Eumaeus, and another servant, he killed every one of the suitors. So he recovered his wife and his kingdom. Ulysses lived to be an old man, and died in peace in his own home.   JOSEPH FONTENROSE

See also AJAX; CALYPSO; HECUBA; POLYPHEMUS.

UMBEL. See INFLORESCENCE.

UMBELLIFERAE, UM *buh* LIF *er ee,* is the botanical name for the carrot or parsley family. The word comes from the same root as the word *umbrella.* Most members of the family have flowers arranged in umbrella-like clusters. About 2,700 species of herbaceous plants are included in this family. While they are to be found in all parts of the world, they are most abundant in the North Temperate Zone. Some of the members of the family *Umbelliferae* are poisonous, others have medicinal value, and others are useful food plants. Carrots, celery, and parsnips are edible kinds of *Umbelliferae.*   THEODOR JUST

Related Articles in WORLD BOOK include:

Anise	Cicely	Dill	Herb
Caraway	Coriander	Fennel	Parsley
Carrot	Cow Parsnip	Hemlock	Parsnip
Celery			

UMBER is a brown mineral pigment used to make certain oil and water-color paints. The mineral is ground, washed, and dried to make *raw umber.* When raw umber is heated, it becomes *burnt umber,* which has a deep reddish color. The name comes from Umbria, Italy, where the mineral was first found.

UMBILICAL CORD, um BILL *ih* kuhl, is a rope-like structure that connects the *fetus* (unborn child) to the *placenta* (see EMBRYO [The Placenta]). The cord contains two arteries and one vein. The arteries carry blood containing waste products from the fetus to the placenta. The vein carries blood containing oxygen and food substances obtained from the mother's blood back to the fetus. When the baby is born, the doctor carefully cuts the cord at a point close to the baby's abdomen. The scar, which remains throughout life, is called the *umbilicus,* or *navel.*   CARL C. FRANCIS

UMBRA. See PENUMBRA; SHADOW.

UMBRELLA. The name *umbrella* comes from a Latin word meaning *little shadow.* The first umbrellas originated as sunshades which the slaves of ancient Egypt and Assyria held over their masters. Even today, an umbrella is believed to be a mark of rank by people in some countries.

In ancient Greece and Rome, women carried umbrellas. For a man to do so was regarded as effeminate. Umbrellas began to be used by both sexes in England during the reign of Queen Anne. Today, people in all parts of the world use umbrellas as protection against the rain. The name *parasol* is often applied to umbrellas

The Oriental Institute, University of Chicago

Protection from the Sun was the first use for umbrellas. King Xerxes I of Persia, shown in an ancient carving, had sunshades 2,400 years ago.

Protection from the Rain was first tried in France in the 1500's. The first Englishman to use an umbrella, a London merchant named Jonas Hanway, caused laughter and jeers in the 1750's.

Bettmann Archive

which are carried as sunshades. Large, folding beach umbrellas protect people from the sun.

There are many different kinds of umbrellas. Some are made so that they can be folded and carried in the pocket when not in use. Others may be collapsed and hidden in a cane, which then becomes a walking stick. Women's umbrellas come in many materials and all colors.

See also CAMBODIA (picture, A Cambodian Farmer).

UMBRELLA BIRD lives in the tropical forests of South America. It gets its name from the tuft of plumes which rises from its crown and forms an umbrellalike crest over its head. A flap of skin covered with feathers hangs down from its neck. It looks like an umbrella handle. The umbrella bird is about the size of a crow. It has

New York Zoological Society

The Umbrella Bird of the South American forests has a curious crown of black feathers. The feathers on its head somewhat resemble an umbrella.

black feathers, edged with steel blue. Little is known of the habits of the bird. It lives in the tops of the highest trees, often on islands in the Amazon and other rivers.

Scientific Classification. The umbrella bird belongs to the cotinga family, *Cotingidae*. It is genus *Cephalopterus*, species *C. ornatus*.   RODOLPHE MEYER deSCHAUENSEE

UMBRELLA TREE. See MAGNOLIA.

UMIAK. See ESKIMO (Transportation).

UMPIRE. See BASEBALL (The Umpires); BASKETBALL (The Officials); FOOTBALL (The Officials).

UN. See UNITED NATIONS.

UN-AMERICAN ACTIVITIES COMMITTEE is the common name for two Congressional investigating committees—the House Committee on Un-American Activities and the Senate's Internal Security Subcommittee, part of the Committee on Foreign Relations. The committees investigate subversive activities of such groups as communists in order to determine what federal legislation is needed to protect United States security.

These committees are not courts of law. They cannot sentence anyone who appears before them. They can only inquire to learn the facts at issue. A person who fails to appear at a hearing may be fined or imprisoned for contempt of Congress. Some witnesses have also been charged with perjury in their testimony. Many witnesses have refused to testify, pleading that they might incriminate themselves. The committees can refer testimony to the Department of Justice if they feel that someone may have committed perjury.

The House Committee became a standing committee on Jan. 3, 1945, with nine members. The committee investigates the extent, character, and objectives of un-American propaganda activities in the United States, and hears testimony from persons concerned. It then makes recommendations to Congress and to executive agencies for action. The committee also studies bills relating to internal security and un-American activities, and suggests additions or changes in them.

The Senate Subcommittee also investigates such fields as communist subversion of government employees, anti-American propaganda, and other un-American activities.

History. The House Committee on Un-American Activities grew from a special committee set up in 1938. After 1950, the Senate took the lead in investigating communist activities. The Internal Security Act, passed in 1950, and sponsored by Senator Patrick A. McCarran of Nevada, required communists to be registered. In 1954, the Communist party was outlawed in the United States. Representatives Martin J. Dies of Texas and Richard M. Nixon of California, and Senator Joseph R. McCarthy of Wisconsin won public notice for their leadership of committee investigations.

UNALASKA. See ALEUTIAN ISLANDS.

UNAMUNO Y JUGO, *oo nah MOO noh ee HOO goh*, **MIGUEL DE** (1864-1936), was a Spanish philosopher, novelist, poet, and essayist. He played a large part in overthrowing the Spanish monarchy in 1931. Unamuno, internationally known as an independent thinker, was strongly antimaterialist and anti-intellectualist. He attacked superstition, sham, and the unthinking following of tradition. His ideas are best expressed in *The Tragic Sense of Life* (1913) and in seven volumes of essays (1916-1919). He was born in Bilbao.   EUGENE T. ADAMS

UNAU. See SLOTH.

UNCAS, *UNG kus* (1588?-1683?), was a chief of the Mohican, or Mohegan, Indians in colonial Connecticut. He became noted for his aid and assistance to the English settlers, and his name has been perpetuated in the character Uncas in James Fenimore Cooper's book, *The Last of the Mohicans* (see MOHICAN INDIANS).

Uncas joined the English in a war against the Pequot Indians in 1637. He defeated the Narraganset tribe in 1643, and five years later fought the Mohawk, Narraganset, and other tribes. Uncas helped the English, but opposed Christianity in his tribe.

A monument to Uncas was erected by the citizens of Norwich, Conn., in 1847. Another monument to his name was erected on the site of the home of James Fenimore Cooper, at Cooperstown, N.Y.   WILLIAM H. GILBERT

UNCLE REMUS. See HARRIS, JOEL CHANDLER.

UNCLE SAM is a figure that symbolizes the United States. The term originated as an unfriendly nickname for the United States government during the War of 1812. It was apparently derived from the large initials "U.S." that Samuel Wilson, an army meat inspector, stamped on barrels of salted meat. People in upper New York and Vermont who opposed the war used the nickname. It first appeared in a Troy, N.Y., newspaper in 1813 and spread rapidly. In 1816, the nickname appeared in a book title, *The Adventures of Uncle Sam*.

The costume of Uncle Sam, decorated with stars and stripes, originated in the cartoons of the 1830's. Seba Smith, a humorous political essayist, was cartooned as Uncle Sam, with such a costume. A clown of the 1800's, Dan Rice, made the costume popular.   MERRILL JENSEN

See also BROTHER JONATHAN; UNITED STATES, HISTORY OF (picture, I Want YOU).

Uncle Sam through the years

1834

American Antiquarian Society

1834 Uncle Sam was pictured as a young man without a beard or gray hair in early cartoons.
1869 Uncle Sam is not always popular. A British cartoonist pictured him as a tightwad after the Civil War.
1917 Uncle Sam urged men to enlist in the U.S. Army. James Montgomery Flagg painted this poster of World War I.
1941 Uncle Sam asked men and women to work in World War II defense plants. McClelland Barclay designed this well-known poster.
1961 An elated Uncle Sam received the news that the first American astronaut had successfully flown into outer space and returned safely.

1869   © Punch

1917   United Press, Int.

1941

I WANT YOU FOR U.S. ARMY
NEAREST RECRUITING STATION

Library of Congress

1961

Jensen, *Chicago Daily News*

UNCLE TOM'S CABIN;

OR

LIFE AMONG THE LOWLY.

BY

HARRIET BEECHER STOWE.

VOL. I.

TWENTY-FIFTH THOUSAND.

BOSTON:
JOHN P. JEWETT & COMPANY.
CLEVELAND, OHIO:
JEWETT, PROCTOR & WORTHINGTON.
1852.

Uncle Tom's Cabin, written in 1852 by Harriet Beecher Stowe, describes the evils of slavery. It became a best seller and aroused antislavery feelings. Eliza's escape from slavery, *above*, is one of the most exciting scenes in the book. Though pursued by bloodhounds and carrying her child, she crossed the frozen Ohio River to freedom. This poster was used to advertise a stage version of the story. The title page of the first edition, *right*, shows a humble hut of the kind often used to house slaves.

UNCLE TOM'S CABIN is a famous antislavery novel written by Harriet Beecher Stowe. The book became the most sensational best seller of the 1800's. It was first published in serial form in 1851 and 1852 in the *National Era*, an abolitionist journal. It was published in book form in 1852.

Uncle Tom's Cabin deals with the evils of slavery. Its memorable characters include Uncle Tom, Little Eva, Eliza, and Simon Legree. A play based on the novel won great popularity. To answer attacks made on the accuracy of the book, Mrs. Stowe wrote *A Key to Uncle Tom's Cabin* (1853).   EDWARD WAGENKNECHT

See also STOWE, HARRIET ELIZABETH BEECHER; AMERICAN LITERATURE (Abolition and *Uncle Tom*).

UNCONDITIONAL SURRENDER. See GRANT, ULYSSES S. ("Unconditional Surrender" Grant).

UNCONSCIOUS, in psychology, is the part of the mind that rarely has awareness, or consciousness. It may contain information that has never been conscious. Or the information may at one time have been conscious, but is now unconscious. See also PSYCHOANALYSIS; SUBCONSCIOUS.

UNCONSCIOUSNESS. See FAINTING; FIRST AID.

UNCTION. See ANOINTING OF THE SICK.

UNDERDEVELOPED COUNTRY is one of the world's "have-not" nations. Experts use three standards to determine whether an area is underdeveloped: income, food consumption, and power sources. In an underdeveloped area, the national income per person averages $125 or less a year. The average in a developed area is $1,200. Most of the people in an underdeveloped area average less than 2,500 calories per day. This amount is generally considered the minimum necessary for adequate health. Persons in underdeveloped areas until recently have had a life expectancy of about 35 years, but it is rising as the death rate falls. They make little use of machines and mechanical energy.

In underdeveloped areas, about 7 of every 10 persons depend on farming for their living. But productivity is low. Little new land is available for cultivation. The underdeveloped areas have about three-fourths of the world's population. Too many people live on the land, compared with the amount of natural resources. People lack the knowledge and skills to develop these resources as they have been in other countries. Few of them can read or write. The richer nations have begun to provide aid to underdeveloped areas through technical assistance programs.   C. LANGDON WHITE

See also PEACE CORPS; ECONOMICS (Underdeveloped Economies); TECHNICAL ASSISTANCE; UNESCO.

UNDERGROUND, in political terms, is a secretly conducted movement to overthrow the government or the military occupation forces of a country. Underground tactics have been used since the early days of history, but reached a high point of activity during World War II. Since that time, communist groups have worked underground in their attempts to overthrow many governments.

UNDERGROUND RAILROAD

Adolf Hitler used an underground group called the *fifth column*, especially in the early stages of World War II (see FIFTH COLUMN). German agents worked inside various countries before and during the German invasions of those countries. The agents used espionage, propaganda, and sabotage to aid the German cause and destroy the invaded country's morale.

But once the Germans had conquered a country, the underground of that country's patriots hampered German operations. Underground workers sprang up in France, Belgium, The Netherlands, Denmark, Norway, Yugoslavia, and other conquered countries. They plagued the Germans by blowing up railroad trains and bridges, sabotaging factories, distributing illegal newspapers, rescuing marooned Allied servicemen, and gathering valuable military information.

See also CHETNIK; GUERRILLA; MAQUIS; PARTISANS; WORLD WAR II (Underground Resistance).

UNDERGROUND RAILROAD was a system for helping Negro slaves escape to the northern states and to Canada in the days before the Civil War. It was really neither underground nor a railroad. It was called the underground railroad because of the swift, secret way in which Negroes seemed to escape.

The underground railroad had no formal organization. A large part of its work was done by southern slaves who, though unable to escape themselves, helped runaways with food, clothing, and directions. Free Negroes in both the South and the North frequently assisted the runaways. The most famous Negro "railroader" was Harriet "Moses" Tubman (1821?-1913?). She was a fugitive herself, but she returned to the South 19 times and helped about 300 Negroes escape. A $40,000 reward was offered for her capture.

The work of northern white abolitionists in manning the *stations* (hiding places) of the underground railroad, and in helping the slaves move from one refuge to another, has often been exaggerated. There were few such "agents" and there was little organized activity. But many Quakers and persons of other faiths who felt that slavery was an evil were involved in the underground railroad.

About 50,000 slaves escaped between 1830 and 1860. The underground railroad was most active in Ohio and Pennsylvania. But by the outbreak of the Civil War, runaways were being helped in every northern state from New England to Kansas.

Many fugitive slaves settled in the northern free states. But when Congress passed a strict fugitive slave law as part of the Compromise of 1850, thousands of these settled Negroes fled to Canada for safety. See FUGITIVE SLAVE LAW; COMPROMISE OF 1850.

The underground railroad angered many southerners. This contributed to the sectional ill-feeling that led to the outbreak of the Civil War.   DAVID DONALD

See also ABOLITIONIST; TUBMAN, HARRIET.

UNDERGROUND RAILWAY. See SUBWAY.

UNDERSHOT WHEEL. See WATER WHEEL.

UNDERTAKER. See MORTICIAN.

UNDERTOW. When strong waves beat against a shore, their force causes a current, or undertow, several feet under the surface which flows away from shore to sea. Undertows are dangerous to swimmers.

UNDERWATER DEMOLITION TEAM (UDT) is a highly trained special volunteer unit of the United States Navy that performs dangerous assignments in the water. UDT men are sometimes called *frogmen*.

The primary UDT wartime mission is to find and clear obstacles from assault beaches in preparation for amphibious invasions. Many types of underwater obstacles are used to protect shores from invasion. These obstacles include mines, steel and concrete barriers, sharpened stakes, barbed wire, and log barriers. Nature provides additional obstacles such as coral reefs, sand bars, and underwater rock formations.

On a typical wartime mission, UDT men are assigned to locate obstacles near the assault beach. They approach the beach in small, fast boats called LCPR's. The LCPR's speed toward the *drop line* on a zig-zag course to avoid enemy fire. As the boats approach the drop line, the UDT men put on their swim fins, face masks, and diving equipment. On signals from the boat officers, two swimmers, called a *buddy pair*, roll over the sides of each LCPR into the water at evenly spaced intervals while the boats move at top speed.

Each buddy pair is assigned an area in which to take depth soundings, locate and describe the types and position of obstacles, and note enemy installations.

After the swimmers record the needed information, they swim to the *pick-up line*. On a signal, the LCPR's, speed to the line. Pick-up men ride in rubber boats tied alongside the LCPR's. The pick-up men pull the swimmers into the rubber boats with hard rubber slings that they place over the swimmers' extended arms. All this is done while the LCPR's travel at top speed. When the swimmers have been picked up, the LCPR's return to their ship.

Aboard ship, experts study the information gathered by the frogmen and prepare charts of the beach. After all information has been analyzed, the UDT men prepare packages of high explosives called *demo-packs*. These are used to destroy beach obstacles. The swimmers return to the beach and place the demo-packs on the obstacles. They pull the fuses and swim rapidly to the pick-up line, where they are picked up as before.

UDT men also perform dangerous peacetime tasks, such as ice demolition, channel and harbor clearance, ship and aircraft salvage, and underwater search operations.

Training. UDT volunteers must complete 21 weeks of extremely difficult training. Usually, less than one-third of the candidates complete the course. Training is conducted at the Naval Amphibious Schools at Little Creek, Va., and Coronado, Calif.

The first three weeks of training emphasize physical conditioning. The trainees run, crawl, and climb through obstacle courses, make long forced marches, and take five-mile runs. They learn to use rubber boats and small man-propelled craft in all kinds of surf conditions.

The fourth week, called "Hell Week," eliminates the largest number of candidates. The trainees spend many sleepless hours in cold ocean water, surf, swamps, and mud flats. They paddle in rubber boats for 20 miles. They make all-night forced marches and run through rugged "confidence" courses that contain exploding demolition charges and live machine gun fire.

Those who complete the first four weeks of training

Landing On An Enemy Beach at Wonsan, Korea, *above*, during the Korean War, an Underwater Demolition Team destroyed a North Korean mine field. The success of this Underwater Demolition Team mission enabled a force of United States Marines to make a landing on the beach without suffering any casualties.

Experts With Explosives, UDT members can blow up enemy equipment and installations. Frogmen blew up beach obstacles, *above*, to clear the way for many World War II landings.

Leaving A Submarine under water, UDT men can carry out their assignments, and then re-enter the submarine while it is submerged. UDT units can also drop from airplanes to carry out missions in coastal areas.

spend the next 11 weeks in detailed classroom study and practical field work. They learn demolition techniques, advanced swimming, hand-to-hand combat, water survival, reconnaissance, chart making, and intelligence study. They also become qualified divers, skilled in the use of different types of diving equipment.

The candidates then train in isolated areas. There they perform UDT wartime missions under simulated combat conditions, working from dawn until midnight every day. This training determines which trainees will be assigned to operating units.

Candidates who qualify for UDT units spend their final three weeks of training at the U.S. Army Airborne School at Fort Benning, Ga., where they become qualified military parachutists. Then, they are assigned to operating teams. They must serve a six-month trial period before they earn the right to be called *frogmen*.

History. The first UDT men were not swimmers. They were organized as Naval Combat Demolition Units (NCDU), assigned to clear obstacles from the beaches before Allied landings in North Africa and Europe. In 1944, they cleared thousands of mines and obstacles from Normandy's "Omaha" and "Utah" beaches. Some units suffered over 50 per cent casualties.

The first UDT's were formed in the Pacific area. A disastrous amphibious landing on the island of Tarawa showed the need for swimmers to study beaches and clear obstacles. UDT's played an important role in later island invasions in the Pacific.

Frogmen scouted and cleared beaches during the Korean War. They also made many inland raids and destroyed inland tunnels, dams, and bridges.

The four active UDT units now consist of about 100 men and 15 officers each. Two units are assigned to the U.S. Atlantic Fleet, and two are assigned to the U.S. Pacific Fleet.   WENDELL E. WEBBER

UNDERWOOD, OSCAR WILDER (1862-1929), an Alabama Democrat, served in the U.S. House of Representatives from 1895 to 1896 and 1897 to 1915. He served in the U.S. Senate from 1915 to 1927. In 1913, he sponsored the Underwood Tariff Act. This tariff law lowered rates on imports and removed the duties on milk, sugar, wheat, eggs, raw wool, shoes, and other items. Underwood served as a delegate to the Washington, D.C., Conference from 1921 to 1922. He was born in Louisville, Ky., and moved to Alabama in 1884.

UNDERWOOD TARIFF ACT. See WILSON, WOODROW (Legislative Program).

UNDERWRITING is a term first used in England in the early 1700's. Underwriters, or insurers, wrote their names at the bottom of proposed insurance contracts covering a ship and its cargo. They indicated in this way their willingness to assume part of the risk.

Today, every insurance company has an underwriting department which is important to the success of the firm. Underwriting experts must establish the premium rates for various kinds of policies and the amount and degree of risk to be assumed for each policy.

Underwriters also examine all applications for insurance in order to guard against bad risks and to prevent the company from assuming too many of the same kinds of risks. For example, a fire insurance underwriter may find that several suspicious fires have occurred in the building to be insured, and therefore decide that the risk is bad.

In finance, underwriting is an agreement to purchase a corporation stock or bond issue.   ROBERT D. PATTON

See also INSURANCE; LLOYD'S.

UNDSET, *OON set*, **SIGRID** (1882-1949), was a Norwegian author. Her most widely read book is the trilogy *Kristin Lavransdatter* (1920-1922), a story of medieval life in Norway. The book gives an intimate and powerful insight into a woman's problems in girlhood, marriage, and old age. Sigrid Undset won the 1928 Nobel prize for literature.

She wrote books about young women in contemporary life, and she published her first novel, *Fru Marta Oulie*, in 1907. But she did not become famous until she published *Jenny* in 1911. Her novels about medieval life appeared between 1920 and 1927, and included the four-volume *Master of Hestviken*. She became a Roman Catholic in the 1920's, and wrote from about 1924 on from a Roman Catholic point of view. During this period she wrote such books as *The Burning Bush* (1930) and *The Faithful Wife* (1936). Her other works include *Return to the Future* (1942), an account of her experiences during World War II; and *Happy Days in Norway* (1943).

Alfred A. Knopf
Sigrid Undset

Sigrid Undset was born in Kallundborg, Denmark, on May 20, 1882. She was the daughter of a famous Norwegian archaeologist, who stimulated her first interest in the Middle Ages. Her father died in 1893, and her mother was left poor. Sigrid Undset was sent to a commercial school. She did office work in Christiania (now Oslo) from 1899 to 1909, but then turned to literature. When the Nazis occupied Norway in 1940, she fled, and spent the World War II years in the United States. She returned to Norway in 1945.   EINAR HAUGEN

UNDULANT FEVER, *UN dyoo lunt*, is a disease so named because the fever of the patient *undulates* (varies from time to time). British soldiers seem to have acquired it first on the island of Malta. Therefore, they called it *Malta fever*. It is similar to typhoid, tuberculosis, malaria, and other infectious diseases.

A person may get undulant fever by drinking milk from animals which have the disease, or by handling raw meat from infected animals. Many persons in farm communities still drink unpasteurized milk. Undulant fever is a serious danger in such places.

The first symptoms appear from 10 to 15 days after a person becomes infected. He feels weak, tired, and chilly, loses his appetite, and has general aches and fevers. The disease often develops so slowly that the patient does not realize he is sick. The fever mounts slowly. Only about two out of every 100 cases result in death. But the disease often damages important organs. A combination of streptomycin and sulfa drugs has proved an effective treatment.   PAUL R. CANNON

See also BANG'S DISEASE.

UNEARNED INCREMENT. See SINGLE TAX.

UNEMPLOYMENT is the state of being out of work. It applies to persons who are normally members of the labor force and are able and willing to work full or part time. It applies both to men and women who are looking for work, and to those who are temporarily laid off their jobs and are not looking for work.

Until recent years, many persons believed that any able-bodied person who was out of work was simply lazy and did not want to work. In England and colonial America, the unemployed were divided into two classes: "impotent beggars" and "sturdy beggars." The first group included the aged, the sick, the mentally deficient, and the physically handicapped. These persons were sometimes cared for in poorhouses or supported by charity. The "sturdy beggars" were punished as vagrants or tramps. They were publicly whipped, put into stocks, and sometimes branded or mutilated.

Today it is generally recognized that great numbers of persons may be without work at various times for reasons beyond their control. The unemployed are often persons who would be able to hold jobs if jobs were available. Persons not working because of age, illness, or mental and physical handicaps are considered the *unemployable*, not the *unemployed*.

Causes of Unemployment

There are several causes of unemployment, usually divided into four classes: normal, seasonal, technological, and cyclical.

Normal Unemployment. A small amount of unemployment exists even in times of booming business. Under a free enterprise system, workers can go from one job to another. Workers who are dissatisfied with their jobs or their pay may leave one employer, and may seek employment in a different locality and under different conditions. Normal unemployment seldom affects more than 1 or 2 per cent of the total working population. Normal unemployment presents no special problem to a nation's economy.

Seasonal Unemployment. Many occupations cannot guarantee the worker year-round employment because of weather conditions or seasonal changes. Some jobs in agriculture, lumbering, fishing, and the building industry cannot be carried on during winter months in certain parts of the country. Food canning in some regions is a seasonal industry. Crops must usually be processed as soon as they are harvested, and some crops, such as peaches and cherries, are harvested only once a year. Automobile factories usually shut down for several weeks while the manufacturers *retool*, changing designs for their new models.

Seasonal unemployment affects a large part of the population. Many government agencies have studied the problem, and have encouraged manufacturers in some fields to spread their operations over the entire year. Workers in seasonal industries have been urged to find other work during slack seasons in their chief trade. Many labor leaders regard the supplementary unemployment benefit program, adopted in the auto industry, as one solution to seasonal unemployment.

Technological Unemployment. The introduction of new machinery or of more efficient production methods sometimes creates a problem of unemployment. The introduction of the bottle-making machine in 1903 and the linotype machine in the early 1900's threw many

workers out of work for a time. The cotton picker also displaced millions of workers in the South. Automatic power looms in the textile industry and great improvements in making finished steel also contributed to technological unemployment in many countries. Following World War II, factory production rose 32 per cent, but factory employment rose only 1 per cent, due largely to automatic equipment.

Automatic equipment requires fewer workers to produce more goods, but new machines and methods have also provided new fields for employment. For example, electronic computers and data-processing machines revolutionized "paper work" in business and government offices. But they also created new kinds of jobs and upgraded workers to more interesting jobs.

Before 1956, most of the labor force in the United States was engaged in the production end of manufacturing, mining, farming, and construction. Since that time, the majority of workers are those who are not directly employed in producing goods. They include office workers, service workers, repair workers, and others, including professional people.

Automatic equipment is also doing work that is too dangerous or too precise for man to do, as in atomic fission and the production of nuclear power.

Government and labor experts urge that management, labor, and educators look ahead and plan for technological changes. Fewer manual workers will be required, but more skilled and trained workers will be needed. With proper planning and preparation, tragedies of technological unemployment may be reduced when new methods are adopted. See AUTOMATION.

Cyclical Unemployment. Regular cycles of business depressions are the most serious cause of mass unemployment. There were 14 cycles of business activity in the United States in the 75 years between 1885 and 1960, but there have been other ups and downs in American business activity throughout its history.

In 1873, more than half a million workers were idle. In the panic of 1893, when the unemployed in "Coxey's Army" marched on Washington, D.C., more than a million persons were out of work.

The number of unemployed in the United States rose to a record 14 million in 1933, when more than 25 per cent of the labor force was out of work. There were business slumps again in 1953-1954 and in 1957-1958, when the number of unemployed persons rose once more, but not to such serious levels as in the early 1930's. By the time business picked up in July, 1958, the number of unemployed was over 5 million, or about 7½ per cent of the 1958 labor force.

Unemployment resulting from depressions is far more serious than normal, seasonal, or technological unemployment. As the population increases, the number of workers affected by a business depression also increases. Economists do not agree on the cause of a depression or slump, or on what to do to avoid one, but governments now recognize that they are responsible for helping to maintain employment at as high a level as possible.

Measures to Relieve Unemployment

Relief measures are usually designed chiefly to offset the bad effects of cyclical unemployment. City and

UNEMPLOYMENT

state governments and private charities carried the burden of providing for the unemployed until 1930. The first halting steps the federal government took in meeting unemployment in the 1930's were largely temporary (see NEW DEAL).

In 1931, the federal government formed the National Committee on Unemployment Relief. The Reconstruction Finance Corporation lent $300 million to the states to help them relieve unemployment. New York led the states with its Emergency Relief Administration, and gradually the states took over local relief responsibility. But these actions were not enough to meet the crisis caused by the worst depression in history.

Under President Franklin D. Roosevelt, the Federal Emergency Relief Administration spent $1 billion for direct relief in 1933. In that year, Congress set up the Civilian Conservation Corps to give useful jobs to 500,000 young men. The Civil Works Administration spent another $1 billion in four months to help 4 million unemployed.

The Works Progress Administration gave work on public projects at subsistence wages to 3 million persons by 1935. The National Youth Administration was established to provide jobs and educational opportunities for young people.

The United States took a major step in the direction of a permanent fight against the evils of unemployment with the adoption of the Social Security Act in 1935.

Unemployed Workers line up to register at a state employment office. Employment agencies help workers find jobs, provide counseling and testing, and compile labor-market information. They also take care of claims for unemployment insurance payments.

Arthur Siegel

EMPLOYMENT AND UNEMPLOYMENT IN THE UNITED STATES

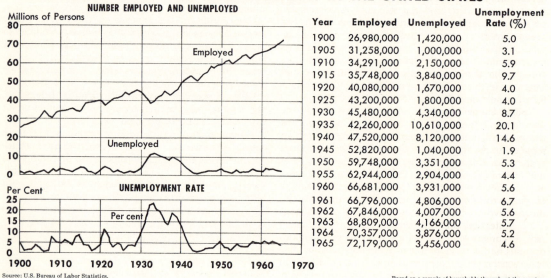

NUMBER EMPLOYED AND UNEMPLOYED

Millions of Persons

UNEMPLOYMENT RATE

Per Cent

Year	Employed	Unemployed	Unemployment Rate (%)
1900	26,980,000	1,420,000	5.0
1905	31,258,000	1,000,000	3.1
1910	34,291,000	2,150,000	5.9
1915	35,748,000	3,840,000	9.7
1920	40,080,000	1,670,000	4.0
1925	43,200,000	1,800,000	4.0
1930	45,480,000	4,340,000	8.7
1935	42,260,000	10,610,000	20.1
1940	47,520,000	8,120,000	14.6
1945	52,820,000	1,040,000	1.9
1950	59,748,000	3,351,000	5.3
1955	62,944,000	2,904,000	4.4
1960	66,681,000	3,931,000	5.6
1961	66,796,000	4,806,000	6.7
1962	67,846,000	4,007,000	5.6
1963	68,809,000	4,166,000	5.7
1964	70,357,000	3,876,000	5.2
1965	72,179,000	3,456,000	4.6

Source: U.S. Bureau of Labor Statistics.

Based on a sample of households throughout the country.

The Social Security Act provided for unemployment insurance, in addition to its old-age and retirement provisions. The act provided for weekly payments to idle workers. The government also set up federal employment agencies, and later turned them over to the states.

Social security and other means of income maintenance are called *built-in stabilizers*. They, together with speeded-up government defense spending and highway programs, were responsible to a large extent for halting the business slump of 1957-1958.

The Fight for Full Employment

Congress adopted the Employment Act in 1946. It defines full employment as "conditions under which there are employment opportunities, including self-employment, for all who are able, willing, and seeking to work." The act commits the federal government to use all its resources for creating and maintaining full employment. The President is directed to report to Congress on the national economy at least once a year.

The Bureau of Employment Security fulfills federal government responsibilities in connection with the public employment service and the unemployment insurance programs. ROBERT D. PATTON

See also DEPRESSION; EMPLOYMENT; EMPLOYMENT AGENCY; INFLATION AND DEFLATION (Deflation); UNEMPLOYMENT INSURANCE.

UNEMPLOYMENT INSURANCE is a means of protecting workers who are out of work, presumably through no fault of their own, and who are looking for employment. These workers receive cash payments, usually each week for a limited period. Most of the industrial countries of the world have unemployment insurance systems. About 30 such programs are in effect in Europe, North America, Australia, and New Zealand.

Trade unions adopted the first plans to help able-bodied wage earners who were temporarily out of work through no fault of their own. In Great Britain, the Journeymen Steam Engine Makers' Society began paying out-of-work benefits as early as 1824. In the late 1800's and early 1900's, Switzerland, Belgium, Denmark, France, Norway, and other European countries began public voluntary unemployment insurance plans. In 1911, Great Britain set up the first compulsory unemployment insurance system. After World War I, it began paying various types of allowances, commonly called the *dole*, to unemployed workers who had used up their unemployment benefits. In 1932, Wisconsin adopted the first U.S. unemployment insurance law. A federal-state unemployment insurance plan was established as part of the Social Security Act of 1935.

United States Plan. The Federal Unemployment Tax Act levies a 3.1 per cent payroll tax on employers who employ four or more workers in each of 20 weeks within a year. No tax is payable on wages over $3,000 a year. But the law provides that in states that have unemployment insurance acts meeting federal standards, the federal government collects only .4 per cent of the payroll tax. This is returned to the states for administrative expenses and, in some cases, for benefits.

The states determine the tax rate each employer must pay for unemployment insurance. The rate usually depends on his unemployment experience. These rates vary generally from as low as zero to more than 2.7 per cent. The national average is about 2 per cent.

In Alabama, Alaska, and New Jersey, employees also contribute a small amount. Each state places the money it collects in the Unemployment Trust Fund of the United States, and withdraws it as needed. The Secretary of the Treasury administers the fund.

Unemployment insurance protection covers most workers in industry and commerce, and includes civilian federal employees. Some state systems cover more workers than the federal law requires, such as employees of small firms and state and local government employees. Some states also tax yearly wages of more than $3,000. Railroad workers have their own separate system. In 1955, several large corporations adopted plans to pay their workers unemployment benefits in addition to the amounts paid by the government.

State Regulations. Each state has different benefit provisions. The unemployed worker must apply at the employment service office both for benefit payments and for getting suitable work. He must also report regularly to receive his benefits and to show that he will take a possible job. To qualify for benefits, a worker must have had a certain amount of covered work in a preceding period, usually a year. In most states, the minimum amount of wages required in this base period ranges from $200 to $600. Most states have a one-week waiting period before benefits are payable. The maximum period for benefit payments varies from a low of about 10 weeks to a high of about 39 weeks.

The amount of the benefit is usually determined from the average wage in the 3 months of the base period that had the highest wages. This average is often adjusted upward to allow for possible unemployment even in that period. The benefit is then computed at half the adjusted average wage, but with certain minimums and maximums. The minimum payment is usually about $10 a week. The maximum is usually from $30 to $45 a week, but several states pay as high as $50 to $55.

A dozen states pay extra benefits for dependents. The benefit is usually a flat amount for each dependent, such as $3 to $6 a week, subject to a maximum total. In these states, the total benefits that workers with dependents can get may be as high as $55 to $70 a week.

During the mid-1960's, the total unemployment insurance benefits paid under state laws ranged from about $2\frac{1}{3}$ billion to about $3\frac{1}{2}$ billion a year. The number of workers receiving weekly benefits ranged from $1\frac{1}{2}$ million to 3 million. Their average benefit totaled about $35 a week. At the same time, the number of workers covered by unemployment insurance averaged about 42 million. The Unemployment Trust Fund had total assets of about $7 billion.

Canadian Plan. The Canadian unemployment insurance plan went into effect in 1941, and applies uniformly in all provinces. All commercial and industrial workers earning less than $5,460 a year are covered, regardless of the size of their firm. The employer and employee each contribute about 1.4 per cent of wages up to about $3,600 a year. Benefits are paid after a one-week waiting period for a total of 52 weeks. They range from $6 to $27 a week, and are increased by about one-third if the worker has dependents. ROBERT J. MYERS

See also EMPLOYMENT SECURITY, BUREAU OF; SOCIAL SECURITY; UNEMPLOYMENT.

UNESCO

UNESCO is a specialized agency of the United Nations. Its full name is UNITED NATIONS EDUCATIONAL, SCIENTIFIC AND CULTURAL ORGANIZATION. UNESCO works for understanding and cooperation among people everywhere. It tries to promote a respect for justice, rule of law, human rights, and basic freedoms for all people. It was established in 1946, and has headquarters in Paris. One hundred countries are members of UNESCO. The agency carries out programs only at the request of members of UNESCO. These nations provide most of the organization's funds.

UNESCO stresses education, the spread of culture, and an increase in scientific knowledge. It stimulates scientific research on such basic problems as the use of arid lands and a knowledge of the world's oceans. UNESCO encourages artists, scientists, teachers, and students to travel, study, and work in other countries. It sponsors model libraries and art exhibits. It advises governments on how to restore and preserve national monuments. It tries to increase the free flow of information. UNESCO works with other United Nations agencies in providing technical aid to underdeveloped areas. UNESCO considers education the first need in improving human conditions in these areas.

How UNESCO Works

Education. UNESCO helps develop education at all levels. It sponsors programs to train teachers, build courses of study, and carry out research in education. UNESCO-trained technicians teach people how to read and write and to improve their living conditions. In 1951, it established a teacher-training center in Pátzcuaro, Mexico. In 1953 it opened a center in Sirs el Laiyana, United Arab Republic. UNESCO sponsors permanent and mobile libraries. Its library in Delhi, India, was the first public library open to all castes and creeds in India.

Science. UNESCO promotes international scientific cooperation. It encourages research in the basic sciences. It develops studies and research on natural resources. In 1952, it helped establish the European Council for Nuclear Research, which carries on research on the peaceful uses of atomic energy. UNESCO maintains science cooperation offices in Latin America, the Middle East, South Asia, and Southeast Asia. These offices help with training programs, scientific conferences, and the distribution of scientific materials.

UNESCO tries to apply the social sciences to special problems of interest to the organization. These problems include race relations, the status of women in society, and the social results of technological changes. In 1956, UNESCO and the government of India established a center to study the effects of industrialization in southern Asia. UNESCO encourages more standardization of statistical data throughout the world. It also stimulates social-science teaching and research.

Culture. UNESCO concentrates on international cultural cooperation. For example it led efforts to save Nile Valley archaeological treasures that might be lost under the lake formed by the Aswân High Dam in Egypt. UNESCO tries to acquaint the public with important works of art and literature, and works for international copyright agreements. It promotes the growth of museums, and advances studies in the humanities. UNESCO produces and distributes reading materials in developing areas. This is done chiefly through the UNESCO regional center in Karachi, Pakistan.

Information. UNESCO works to improve the distribution of information throughout the world. Each month it publishes the *UNESCO Courier* in Arabic,

UNESCO Headquarters, *below,* stands on the left bank of the Seine River near the Eiffel Tower in Paris. It includes the Y-shaped Secretariat Building and the copper-roofed Conference Building, both completed in 1958. The architects were Marcel Breuer of the United States, Pier Luigi Nervi of Italy, and Bernard Zehrfuss of France. UNESCO provides mobile libraries that serve people throughout the world, such as this group of school children in Medellín, Colombia, *right.*

UNESCO

English, French, German, Japanese, Russian, and Spanish. UNESCO provides technical aid for nations in developing newspapers, radio, television, and films.

How UNESCO is Organized

The General Conference of UNESCO consists of delegates appointed by the member nations. It meets every two years. The conference determines UNESCO policies and programs. It approves the budget and passes on financial and staff regulations. The conference selects the Executive Board and appoints the Director-General of UNESCO. It admits new members to UNESCO, and adopts conventions and recommendations for approval by the member nations. General Conference delegates have met in several major cities of the world. But most conferences have been held in Paris.

The Executive Board has 24 members. They serve four-year terms. Half of the members are elected every two years. They are selected from among the delegates to the General Conference. The board meets in regular session at least twice a year. The Executive Board supervises work on UNESCO programs, and prepares the agenda for the General Conference. It recommends new members and nominates the Director-General.

The Secretariat is headed by the Director-General. The chief administrative officer of UNESCO, he has offices at UNESCO headquarters in Paris. More than a thousand persons work in the Secretariat. They come from over half of the member nations. Other employees work in UNESCO field offices.

The Director-General is appointed for a six-year term. He appoints and directs the staff of the Secretariat, and makes regular reports to member nations and the Executive Board on UNESCO activities. He submits work plans and budget estimates to the Executive Board. Sir Julian Huxley of Great Britain, the first

Director-General, served from 1946 to 1948. Jaime Torres Bodet of Mexico succeeded him, serving until 1952. Luther H. Evans of the United States held the post from 1953 to 1958. He was succeeded by Vittorino Veronese of Italy, who was succeeded in 1961 by René Maheu of France.

The National Commissions of the member nations advise their governments. They also assist the delegations to the General Conference. They provide information and help coordinate activities. Most member nations have national commissions to UNESCO. Commission members usually come from national organizations interested in education, science, and culture.

History

After World War I, most of the Allies joined in an international association called the League of Nations (see LEAGUE OF NATIONS). The League recognized the importance of promoting intellectual cooperation among nations. In 1921, it organized the International Institute of Intellectual Cooperation. This committee later founded affiliated national groups in 50 countries.

During World War II, ministers of education of the Allied nations held conferences regularly. They met to consider common problems of education. They were especially concerned with reviving educational systems that had been weakened or destroyed by the war.

The United Nations Charter was signed in San Francisco in June, 1945. In November of that year, the United Nations Conference for the Establishment of an Educational and Cultural Organization met in London. Representatives of 44 countries attended. They drew up the Constitution of UNESCO, and UNESCO officially came into existence on Nov. 4, 1946. By that date, 20 member countries had ratified the constitution.

The UNESCO General Conference session of 1954 became an important milestone. The conference set up five important problems on which UNESCO should concentrate. These problems were (1) illiteracy, (2) primary education, (3) racial, social, and international tensions, (4) mutual appreciation of Eastern and Western cultures, and (5) research on living conditions.

The 1960 General Conference session decided that UNESCO should send more specialists to member countries. It also stressed education for the newly independent nations of Africa. By 1963, membership had reached 107.   L. A. MINNICH, JR.

See also UNITED NATIONS.

UNFEDERATED MALAY STATES. See MALAYA (History).

UNGAVA, *un GAY vuh.* All the peninsula of Labrador, except for a narrow strip along the eastern coast, was once included in the district of Ungava, which covered an area of about 351,800 square miles. But in 1912 Ungava was made part of the province of Quebec.

UNGULATE, *UNG gyoo layt,* is the name given to mammals having the last joint of the toes encased in a hoof or a hooflike nail. It comes from *ungula,* a Latin word meaning *hoof.* Zebras, elephants, hippopotamuses, and deer are wild ungulates. Horses, sheep, goats, cattle, and pigs are domestic ungulates. They may be divided into *odd-toed* ungulates, such as the horse, which has one toe, and the rhinoceros, with three; and the *even-toed,*

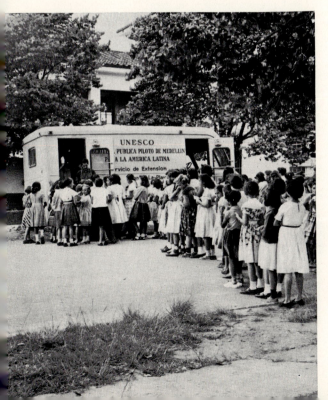

such as the pig, with four. Ungulates are the only horned mammals, but not all have horns. WILLIAM C. BEAVER

Related Articles in WORLD BOOK include:

Alpaca	Caribou	Hippopotamus	Okapi
Antelope	Cashmere Goat	Hog	Peccary
Babirussa	Cattle	Hoof	Rhinoceros
Bighorn	Deer	Horn	Ruminant
Boar, Wild	Dromedary	Horse	Sheep
Brahman	Elephant	Ibex	Vicuña
Buffalo	Giraffe	Karakul	Wart Hog
Camel	Goat	Llama	Yak
Carabao	Guanaco	Musk Ox	

UNICAMERAL LEGISLATURE. See LEGISLATURE; NEBRASKA (Legislature).

UNICEF. See UNITED NATIONS (Aid to Children).

UNICORN, *YOO nuh kawrn,* was a strange animal described in ancient Greek and Roman myths. It was said to look much like a horse, except that on its fore-

head it had a single straight horn with a spiral twist. Its name means *one-horn.* The horn was white at the base, black in the middle, and red at the tip. The unicorn had a white body, a red head, and blue eyes. Its hind legs were like an antelope's, and its tail was like a lion's tail. During the Middle Ages, artists often placed a unicorn beside figures of Christ, the Virgin Mary, and virgin saints, as an emblem of purity. The word *unicorn* appeared in early Bibles, but it is now translated as *wild ox.* NATHAN DANE II

The Unicorn is often used in the design on a coat of arms.

See also TAPESTRY (picture); MIDDLE AGES (picture).

UNIDENTIFIED FLYING OBJECT. See FLYING SAUCER.

UNIFORM is a style of clothing that identifies persons as members of a group or as workers in a particular field. We learn early in life to recognize policemen, firemen, postmen, and nurses by the clothes they wear. The most renowned uniforms are the military uniforms.

United States Air Force. In winter, officers and men wear light blue trousers, light blue coats with silver buttons, and visor caps. They wear blue shirts, black ties, and black shoes. In summer, they wear cotton khaki shirts and trousers. Women wear two-piece wool uniforms in winter and cotton dresses in summer.

United States Army. In winter, men wear light tan shirts with dark green coats and trousers and black ties and shoes. The single-breasted coats have four large gold buttons. Officers' uniforms have black braid on the trousers and coat cuffs. In summer, men wear cotton khaki shirts and trousers. There is narrow braid on the cuffs of officers' coats. Officers wear green visor caps with gold trim. Enlisted men wear visor or overseas caps. Women wear green cotton two-piece summer uniforms and visor or overseas caps.

United States Marine Corps uniforms are of forest-green wool in winter and khaki in summer. For dress occasions, the marines wear dark blue jackets with gold buttons, light blue trousers with scarlet stripes, and

white caps and belts. Women in the marine corps wear wool suits in winter and cotton suits in summer.

United States Navy. In winter, officers and chief petty officers wear navy blue double-breasted suits with six gold buttons. They may wear visor caps. In summer, they may wear single-breasted white or khaki suits. Visor or overseas caps may be worn with the khaki uniform, but only the visor cap is worn with the white uniform. Officers wear gold sleeve braid. In winter, enlisted men wear navy blue jumpers that have three white stripes on their large collars. They wear all-white cotton summer uniforms. Enlisted men wear round white hats.

Women in the navy wear navy blue wool gabardine suits in winter, and gray and white seersucker dresses in summer. They may wear either overseas caps or soft-brim hats with high crowns. THOMAS E. GRIESS

For pictures of uniforms, see AIR FORCE, UNITED STATES; ARMY, UNITED STATES; MARINE CORPS, UNITED STATES; NAVY, UNITED STATES.

UNIFORM CODE OF MILITARY JUSTICE governs the conduct of all members of the United States armed forces. It establishes military courts and procedures for administering military justice. It explains the offenses that are punishable by such courts. Congress enacted the code in 1950, and it went into effect on May 31, 1951. The code replaced the Articles of War of the army and air force, the Articles for the Government of the Navy, and the disciplinary laws of the coast guard. The *Manual of Courts-Martial, United States, 1951,* prescribes the methods for carrying out provisions of the code.

See also COURT-MARTIAL.

UNIFORMITY, ACT OF. See NONCONFORMIST.

UNILEVER is one of the largest industrial corporations in the world. The Unilever organization consists of two holding companies. *Unilever Limited* has headquarters in London. *Unilever N.V.* has headquarters in Rotterdam. Both companies have the same management. Unilever controls more than 500 companies and subsidiaries in more than 50 countries. These companies manufacture oils, fats, soaps, detergents, foodstuffs, prepared foods, and other commodities. Unilever was organized in 1929. For sales, assets, and number of employees, see MANUFACTURING (table, 25 Leading Manufacturers Outside the U.S.). See also LEVERHULME, VISCOUNT. Critically reviewed by LEVER BROTHERS CO.

UNION. See LABOR.

UNION. See FLAG (table, Flag Terms).

UNION, in mathematics. See SET THEORY (Operations with Sets).

UNION, ACT OF, in Canadian history, united the provinces of Upper and Lower Canada. The parliament of Great Britain passed the act in 1840. The British government had set up the two provinces in 1791 to please a group of British colonists called United Empire Loyalists (see UNITED EMPIRE LOYALIST). The creation of two provinces was also intended to please the French-speaking majority in Lower Canada.

The Act of Union of 1840 provided for one governor of the two provinces, and a legislative council of at least 20 members appointed by him. The people of each province elected 42 members to a legislative assembly, which met at least once a year. Its members held office for four years, unless the governor dissolved the assembly. The act also made English the only official language in council and assembly meetings. In 1848, however, French was made the second official language. The Act of Union led to more responsible government. See CANADA, HISTORY OF (Lord Durham's Report).

Act of Union also refers to three other important acts in the history of Great Britain. The first act united England and Wales in 1536. The second act joined England and Scotland as the United Kingdom of Great Britain in 1707. The third made Ireland part of the United Kingdom of Great Britain and Ireland in 1801. For a more detailed description of these events, see WALES (Union); GREAT BRITAIN (Union; Revolt in Ireland); SCOTLAND (Union).   JEAN BRUCHESI

UNION CARBIDE CORPORATION is one of the world's leading producers of synthetic organic chemicals and plastics, atmospheric gases, alloys and metals, and carbon and graphite products. Its products and processes are important to every branch of industry, and to the United States atomic energy and space programs. Union Carbide is one of the largest contractors for the United States Atomic Energy Commission.

The corporation produces a wide variety of products, including aerosol propellants, batteries, carbon textiles, fumigants, liquid hydrogen, industrial solvents, rock-piercing equipment, synthetic gems, and uranium compounds. Union Carbide trade names include *Prestone*, *Eveready*, and *6-12*.

The Union Carbide Corporation was formed in 1917. The corporation has about 360 plants in the United States and Canada. It also has about 50 associated companies doing business in over 100 countries. The corporation operates a plant for refining uranium at Oak Ridge, Tenn. Headquarters are at 270 Park Avenue, New York, N.Y. 10017. For sales, assets, and number of employees of Union Carbide Corporation, see CHEMICAL INDUSTRY (table, 10 Leading U.S. Chemical Companies).   Critically reviewed by UNION CARBIDE CORPORATION

UNION CITY, N.J. (pop. 52,180; alt. 105 ft.), is a manufacturing and residential center just north of Jersey City. The Lincoln Tunnel under the Hudson River links Union City with New York City. For location, see NEW JERSEY (political map).

Union City manufactures clothing and automotive, chemical, electrical, heating, paper, tobacco, and wood products. The city was formed in 1925 through a consolidation of Union and West Hoboken. Union City has a commission form of government.   RICHARD P. MCCORMICK

UNION COLLEGE. See UNIVERSITIES AND COLLEGES (table).

UNION COLLEGE AND UNIVERSITY is a privately controlled school for men at Schenectady, N.Y. It has schools of liberal arts and engineering, and is associated with the Albany (N.Y.) colleges of medicine, law, and pharmacy, and the Dudley Observatory in Albany. Courses lead to B.A., B.S., and M.S. degrees. The college was founded in 1795. Chester Alan Arthur, the twenty-first President of the United States, was graduated from the school. For the enrollment of Union College and University, see UNIVERSITIES AND COLLEGES (table).   CARTER DAVIDSON

See also FRATERNITY (introduction).

UNION JACK is the name sometimes used for the national flag of Great Britain. The flag is officially called the British Union Flag. The United States Jack has been called a union jack.

See also FLAG (Navy Flags).

UNION LABEL is the trademark of organized labor. The label is placed on a finished product to show that members of the union manufactured it. Union labels are registered as trademarks. The purpose of the label is to encourage the use of union-made products. The union label was first used in California during the 1870's. During this time, many Chinese who were willing to work for low wages entered the United States. The unions protested, and used labels to mark their work. The Ford Motor Company made the first automobile to carry a union label in 1940.   ROBERT D. PATTON

UNION LEAGUE. See RECONSTRUCTION (Scalawags and Carpetbaggers).

UNION OF SOUTH AFRICA. See SOUTH AFRICA.

UNION OF SOVIET SOCIALIST REPUBLICS. See RUSSIA.

UNION PACIFIC RAILROAD. See RAILROAD (Leading Railroad Companies).

UNION PARTY. See BORDEN, SIR ROBERT L. (Prime Minister).

UNION SHOP is a form of security given to a union in a collective-bargaining agreement. An employer formally recognizes a union as the sole bargaining agent for a specific group of employees. All these employees must belong to the union, or must join it within a specified period, usually 30 or 60 days following the signing of the contract or of their employment, whichever is later. Usually they must remain members of the union as long as the contract or its union shop provision lasts, or they will lose their jobs.   H. G. HENEMAN, JR.

See also CLOSED SHOP; OPEN SHOP.

UNION THEOLOGICAL SEMINARY is a coeducational graduate school of religion in New York City. It is associated with Columbia University. Its courses lead to degrees in theology, religious education, and sacred music. Union Theological Seminary admits students of all Protestant denominations who wish to become ministers or take up other types of Christian work. The seminary was founded in 1836, and has about 600 students.   EDWIN O. KENNEDY

UNION UNIVERSITY is a coeducational liberal arts school in Jackson, Tenn. It offers preparatory work in engineering, medicine, dentistry, and law. Union was founded in 1825. The Tennessee Baptist Convention owns it. For enrollment, see UNIVERSITIES AND COLLEGES (table).

UNIONS, LABOR. See LABOR.

UNIREME. See GALLEY.

UNIT, in measurement, is a quantity adopted as the standard by which any other quantity of the same kind is measured. The standard units of measure used in science, commerce, and industry have been tabulated in groups called *tables of denominate numbers*. There are units of money, of time, of surface, of volume, of weight, and of many other things. There are two main groups of units, the English and the metric.

Centimeter-Gram-Second System, known as the C.G.S. system, is used in most scientific work. The unit of length is the *centimeter*, the unit of mass is the *gram*, and the unit of time is the *second*. The unit of area is the *square centimeter*, and the unit of volume is the *cubic centimeter*. The unit of force is the *dyne*. The corresponding unit of work is an *erg*.

In Electricity. In electrical calculations, the unit of resistance is the *ohm*. The unit of pressure is the *volt*, which is the force required to maintain a current of one *ampere* through a resistance of one ohm. The *joule*, which is the practical unit of work, equals 10 million ergs, and the *watt* is the corresponding unit of power. The *kilowatt*, 1,000 watts, is a more convenient unit in practice.

Thermal Unit. The quantity of heat required to raise the temperature of a pound of pure water one degree Fahrenheit is known as the *British Thermal Unit* (B.T.U.). In the metric system of measurement, the thermal unit is called a *calorie*.   PHILIP FRANKLIN

See also DENOMINATE NUMBER; MEASUREMENT; METRIC SYSTEM; WEIGHTS AND MEASURES.

UNIT RULE. In a national presidential nominating convention, the roll is called by states. A state delegation may vote as individuals, or it may cast its vote as a bloc. By custom, the Republican party has allowed individual freedom, unless restricted by presidential primaries. Since 1860, Democratic state delegations have voted as a group, or unit, from which comes the term *unit rule*. Unit rule is not required by the national convention, but may be required by a party's state convention, or by the delegation.   ROBERT A. DAHL

UNITARIAN UNIVERSALIST ASSOCIATION is a voluntary association of independent churches and fellowships in the United States and Canada. It was organized in 1961 by merging the American Unitarian Association and the Universalist Church of America.

A Unitarian Universalist Landmark. The First Church in Plymouth, Mass., founded as a Puritan church by the Pilgrims in 1620, became affiliated with Unitarianism in the early 1800's.
American Unitarian Association

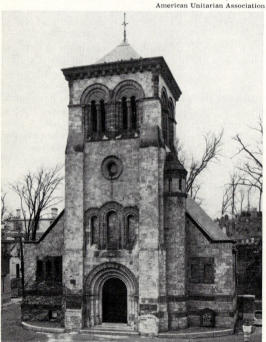

Beliefs. Unitarian Universalists believe an individual should be free to form his own religious beliefs. They hold an optimistic view of the nature of man, and believe him capable of creating a world society based on justice and cooperation. They stress the need to apply religious principles to social problems, and try to integrate scientific findings with their beliefs.

Beginnings. The basic principles of both Unitarianism and Universalism may be traced back to the early days of Christianity. Historically, the word *Unitarian* refers to the idea of the unity of God as opposed to the doctrine of the Trinity (see TRINITY). *Universalism*, or belief in the eventual salvation of all men, stems from the teachings of early Christian writers.

Both Unitarianism and Universalism took on new vigor with the Protestant Reformation of the 1500's. Unitarianism, particularly in Poland and Transylvania, drew support from the writings of the Spanish theologian Michael Servetus and the Italian theologians Laelius and Faustus Socinus. Later, in the 1700's, Unitarianism developed a strong following in England as a result of the teachings of the clergymen Joseph Priestley, Theophilus Lindsey, and others. Universalism, in the 1700's and after, was advocated by various thinkers in Europe and England.

Growth in America. The Universalist and Unitarian movements developed side by side in America.

Universalism, as an organized movement in America, began with John Murray, an English clergyman who came to the colonies in 1770. Murray's efforts paved the way for the first Universalist convention, held at Oxford, Mass., in 1785. Hosea Ballou's *A Treatise on Atonement* (1805) gave the first systematic presentation of Universalist thought. Ballou, a Universalist clergyman, rejected traditional theories of atonement. He taught that Jesus represents God's love for man.

Unitarianism in America grew primarily out of the liberal wing of the Congregational churches in New England. In 1785, King's Chapel (Episcopal) in Boston removed all reference to the Trinity from its prayerbook, and so became the first Unitarian church in America. In 1819, the Unitarian clergyman William Ellery Channing delivered the most notable expression of Unitarian belief in his sermon "Unitarian Christianity." He stressed belief in the unity of God, the humanity of Jesus, and the ability of man to overcome error by reason. In the mid-1800's, the Transcendentalists, led by Ralph Waldo Emerson, absorbed and reaffirmed many Unitarian ideas.

Merger. At first, Unitarians and Universalists were divided by differences in theology and historical development. But, by the 1950's, they had become increasingly alike in their beliefs. Finally, after negotiations for a merger, the Unitarian Universalist Association was established in May, 1961. Headquarters are at 25 Beacon St., Boston, Mass. 02108. For membership in the United States, see RELIGION (table).   ERNEST CASSARA

See also CHANNING, W. E.; TRANSCENDENTALISTS.

UNITED. Many organizations beginning with the word *United* are listed in THE WORLD BOOK ENCYCLOPEDIA under the key word in the name of the organization. Example: STEELWORKERS OF AMERICA, UNITED.

UNITED AIR LINES. See AIRLINE (Major Airlines).

UNITED AIRCRAFT CORPORATION. See AIRPLANE (Leading Airplane Companies).

UNITED ARAB REPUBLIC (U.A.R.) was a union of two independent Middle Eastern countries, Egypt and Syria. It lasted almost four years. President Gamal Abdel Nasser of Egypt and Shukri Al-Kuwatli of Syria proclaimed the union on Feb. 1, 1958. Syrian rebels ended it on Sept. 29, 1961, setting up an independent government for Syria. Egypt continued to use the name United Arab Republic.

In April, 1963, Egypt, Syria, and Iraq agreed to form a new U.A.R. But later that year, the three nations postponed the proposed federation until they could resolve political differences.

Government. The U.A.R. of 1958 had a centralized government, with Cairo as the capital. Egypt and Syria became provinces, with provincial capitals at Cairo for Egypt and Damascus for Syria.

Soon after the merger, the people adopted a provisional constitution and chose Nasser as president. He appointed all members of the national assembly, selecting half from Egypt and half from Syria. The assembly supposedly exercised legislative power, but Nasser made many decisions without consulting it.

History. Before World War I, most of the Middle East was part of the Ottoman Empire. However, western powers had obtained a foothold in the area before 1914. Great Britain gained control of Egypt in the 1880's, and kept it until Egypt became independent in 1922. British troops remained in the Suez Canal Zone until 1956. After World War I, the Middle East was carved into a number of political divisions, one of which was Syria. Along with Lebanon, Syria became a League of Nations mandate of France. Syria remained under French control until after World War II.

Following the war, many Arabs wanted to be united under a single government. Nasser came into power in Egypt during the 1950's, and became the leader of Arab nationalism. Many Arab leaders suspected the West and turned to Russia for assistance. Nasser accepted Russian aid, although he suppressed communism within Egypt. The communists also gained great power in Syria. Arab nationalism, the fear of communist influence in Syria, and Nasser's ambition all contributed to the formation of the United Arab Republic.

United Press Int.

The United Arab Republic was formed in 1958 by merging Egypt and Syria. Egyptian President Gamal Abdel Nasser became president of the new republic by an almost unanimous vote.

Nasser regarded the union of Egypt and Syria as the first step toward uniting all Arab states. On March 8, 1958, Yemen agreed to form a federation with the U.A.R. The union was called the United Arab States, and had Hodeida, Yemen, as the permanent seat of the federation. The United Arab States was not a true federation. Yemen maintained its own membership in the United Nations, as well as separate relations with other countries. Nasser suddenly dissolved the United Arab States in December, 1961. He declared that the federation was no longer of any value.

Nasser quickly made clear that the U.A.R. would be neutral in world affairs. In 1959, he accused Russia of trying to interfere with the internal affairs of the republic, taking the first step toward combating communist influence in Syria. At the same time, he improved relations with the West. During the early 1960's, Nasser continued to accept economic aid from both communist and western countries.

The government introduced many reforms in both provinces. But many Syrians began to feel that Nasser was raising the level of living in Egypt only by lowering it in Syria. Finally, late in 1961, Syrian officers in the U.A.R. army carried out an almost bloodless revolt and proclaimed an independent Syria. The Baath party, the ruling party in Syria and Iraq, blocked a new federation attempt in 1963. The party opposed Nasser's attempt to control the new U.A.R.   CHARLES P. SCHLEICHER

See also EGYPT; IRAQ; NASSER, GAMAL ABDEL; SYRIA; YEMEN.

Egypt and Syria Made Up the United Arab Republic.

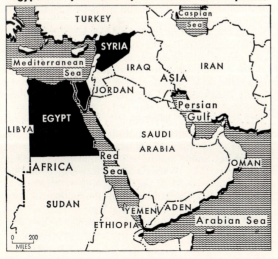

UNITED ARAB STATES. See UNITED ARAB REPUBLIC (History).

UNITED AUTOMOBILE WORKERS (UAW) is a labor union affiliated with the American Federation of Labor and Congress of Industrial Organizations. The UAW has local unions throughout the United States and Canada. Its official name is INTERNATIONAL UNION OF UNITED AUTOMOBILE, AEROSPACE AND AGRICULTURAL IMPLEMENT WORKERS OF AMERICA.

To qualify as a member, a worker must be employed in the manufacture or assembly of automobiles, automobile parts or accessories, aircraft, agricultural implements, electrical, or other allied metalworking trades. Office workers and such salaried employees as draftsmen and engineers in the same field also may become members of the UAW.

The union was organized in Detroit in 1935. It took the place of the National Council of Automobile Workers, which had been affiliated with the American Federation of Labor. In 1937, the federation expelled the union, along with the other AFL international unions which had made up the Committee for Industrial Organization. The UAW later helped develop the Congress of Industrial Organizations, which merged with the AFL in 1955. The UAW adopted its present name in 1941. It maintains headquarters at 8000 E. Jefferson Ave., Detroit, Mich. 48214. For membership, see LABOR (table).   FRANK WINN

See also REUTHER, WALTER P.

UNITED CHURCH OF CANADA became one of the first major Christian groups in the world to be formed by the union of three different denominations. The United Church resulted from the union in 1925 of the Methodist Church in Canada, nearly all the Congregational churches in Canada, and 71 per cent of the Presbyterian churches in Canada. This union was first suggested in 1899 to remedy the overlapping of Protestant missions in western Canada.

Organization. In 1924, the Canadian parliament passed the United Church of Canada Act. It set forth points of universal doctrine, continued the organization of churches already existing, and outlined the organization of those to be formed in the future. For six months after the bill was passed, any church had the privilege of joining or of choosing to remain independent.

The doctrine of the United Church is based on the Bible and the historic creeds. It is found in the Articles of Faith, which are included in the Basis of Union. The United Church follows the Presbyterian form of organization. But it emphasizes and protects congregational rights, and allows both men and women to serve as ministers. All ministers are of equal rank. Each congregation elects church elders. With the minister, the elders are ordained to oversee the spiritual affairs of the congregation. The General Council is the highest court in the church. It meets every two years to legislate for the whole church.

Membership in the United Church has grown from 600,522 in 1925 to about 1,000,000. Some estimates place the total number of people who are adherents of the United Church at about one-fifth of Canada's population, or more than 3 million. The United Church's Sunday schools enroll over 700,000 pupils and teachers,

Duo-Craft Studios, Toronto

The United Church of Canada has headquarters in the United Church House in Toronto, Ont. The church supports three universities and several secondary schools and overseas missions.

and over 245,000 young people share in its 12,000 Christian Education groups.

Services. The United Church maintains three universities, eight theological colleges, several residential secondary schools, a training school for women workers, and four lay training centers.

The United Church maintains a colony of houses at Beamsville, Ont., for retired ministers. The church also runs several homes for the aged and a number of homes for boys and girls. Its program includes hospitals in frontier communities and several boarding schools for Indian children. The United Church has ships on both the Atlantic and Pacific coasts to minister to settlers, lumbermen, and fishermen in remote ports.

The United Church prints and publishes its own materials. The official church publications are the *United Church Observer*, the *United Churchman*, and the *Missionary Monthly*.

The Board of Home Missions is responsible for many of the church's services in Canada. This board also maintains an immigration service to welcome newcomers to Canada and to help them get established in the country. The Woman's Missionary Society and the Board of Overseas Missions administer missions in other countries. These include missions in South Korea, Japan, Hong Kong, Trinidad, Angola, Zambia, and India. The United Church House, at 85 St. Clair Ave. E., Toronto, Ont., Canada, is the headquarters of the church.   ERNEST E. LONG

UNITED CHURCH OF CHRIST is a Protestant religious denomination. It was officially formed on July 4, 1961, when the Congregational Christian Churches and the Evangelical and Reformed Church merged and declared a constitution in force.

The United Church of Christ has a *general synod* (central committee) which directs business affairs, nominates church officials, and performs other duties related to church operations. But individual congregations have the right to govern themselves.

The Congregational movement in the United States dates from the time of the Pilgrims, who landed in America in 1620. In 1931, the Congregational churches merged with a union of three small groups that all used the name Christian. The Evangelical and Reformed Church was formed in 1934 by the union of two American churches of German background.

Church headquarters are at 297 Park Avenue South, New York, N.Y. 10010. For membership in the United States, see RELIGION (table).　　　BEN M. HERBSTER

UNITED COLONIES OF NEW ENGLAND. See NEW ENGLAND CONFEDERATION.

UNITED EMPIRE LOYALIST. Many British colonists in America refused to take up arms against Great Britain in the Revolutionary War in 1775. Between 40,000 and 60,000 of these persons went to Canada. They were known as United Empire Loyalists.

The Loyalists suffered persecutions in the United States from 1775 to 1783. Most of them left the country in 1783 and 1784. Some settled in Nova Scotia and Quebec. Others helped found New Brunswick and Ontario. They soon became the most important single group in Canada, politically and economically.

Many of the Loyalists were among the wealthy people of the 13 colonies. But they left their homes for the sake of their political beliefs. Others left because they hoped to obtain valuable land.　　EDWARD R. ADAIR

UNITED FRUIT COMPANY grows bananas and other tropical crops in eight countries of Central and South America. It operates a steamship line to transport the crops to the United States. The United Fruit Company employs 40,000 persons in Latin America and 10,000 in the United States. It operates 17 hospitals and 150 grade schools in Latin America. It was incorporated in 1899. Headquarters are at 30 St. James Avenue, Boston, Mass. 02116. Critically reviewed by UNITED FRUIT COMPANY

UNITED FUNDS, also called COMMUNITY CHESTS, are local organizations that raise money to support voluntary health and welfare agencies. They combine the fund-raising activities of many independent groups into a single campaign. In the early 1960's, about 34,500 volunteer health and welfare agencies in 2,200 communities in the United States and Canada received aid from one fund-raising campaign. Most drives include the American Red Cross and certain national health causes.

Community Health and Welfare Councils are closely related to the fund-raising organizations. They are composed of persons from voluntary and public agencies, civic groups, and interested citizens. The councils study community problems and recommend action on them. Councils operate in nearly 500 communities.

Nearly 4 million persons served as unpaid volunteers during the 1960's. They raised more than $500 million for voluntary health and welfare services from nearly 31 million contributors each year.

UNITED MINE WORKERS OF AMERICA

United Community Funds and Councils of America is the national organization for united funds, community chests, and community health and welfare councils. It was established in 1918, and is financed by membership dues. It has headquarters at 345 East 46th St., New York, N.Y. 10017.　　　　　LYMAN S. FORD

UNITED JEWISH APPEAL is an organization devoted to raising funds for such Jewish relief agencies as the American Jewish Joint Distribution Committee, the United Israel Appeal, and the New York Association for New Americans. The United Jewish Appeal is constituted on an annual basis by agreement of the participating agencies, and has served continuously since 1939. It aids communities throughout the country in organizing and conducting local campaigns. It has headquarters at 165 W. 46th St., New York, N.Y. 10019.

UNITED KINGDOM, or officially, UNITED KINGDOM OF GREAT BRITAIN AND NORTHERN IRELAND, is a union of four countries: England, Scotland, Wales, and Northern Ireland. The term *Great Britain* is commonly used in place of *United Kingdom* and is the title of the WORLD BOOK article on that country.

King James I used the term United Kingdom as early as 1604 to show that the kingdoms of England and Scotland were joined under his rule. But it was not until 1707 that the Act of Union formed the Kingdom of Great Britain. An act of 1800 formed the United Kingdom of Great Britain and Ireland, with a unified parliament. The term *United Kingdom* became inappropriate when the larger part of Ireland won independence in 1921 and became the Irish Free State (now the Republic of Ireland). Six counties in northeastern Ireland remained with Great Britain. They form Northern Ireland.

The Royal Titles Act of 1927 dropped the words United Kingdom, but the phrase was used again during World War II. In 1945, Britain signed the United Nations charter as the United Kingdom of Great Britain and Northern Ireland. The full title was confirmed in the proclamation following the Royal Titles Act of 1953. By this act, Queen Elizabeth II became "by the grace of God of the United Kingdom of Great Britain and Northern Ireland Queen, Head of the Commonwealth, Defender of the Faith."　　JOHN W. WEBB

See also ENGLAND; GREAT BRITAIN; NORTHERN IRELAND; SCOTLAND; WALES.

UNITED MINE WORKERS OF AMERICA (UMW) is an industrial trade union which represents the workers in most of the coal mines and coal-processing industries of the United States. It also has local unions in Canada.

The union was organized in Columbus, Ohio, in 1890. It was a member of the American Federation of Labor until 1935, when it joined the Committee for Industrial Organization. In 1938, it became a member of the Congress of Industrial Organizations, but withdrew in 1942. It has remained independent, except for a brief reaffiliation with the AFL in 1946 and 1947.

The UMW won fame under John Mitchell in the early 1900's. John L. Lewis served as union president from 1919 until his retirement in 1960. Thomas F. Kennedy, the union's vice-president, succeeded Lewis as president. The UMW has headquarters at 900 15th St. N.W., Washington, D.C. 20005.　　REX W. LAUCK

See also LEWIS, JOHN LLEWELLYN; MITCHELL, JOHN.

The UN General Assembly Has Been Called "The Town Meeting of the World."

THE UNITED NATIONS

UNITED NATIONS (UN) is an organization of nations that works for international peace and security. The UN acts as a meeting place where nations can discuss and try to settle their problems peaceably. If fighting between countries breaks out anywhere, the United Nations meets almost immediately to try to stop it. When the fighting stops, the UN may help work out ways to prevent more bloodshed over the same problem. Its major work is political, social, and economic—not military. The UN has its headquarters in New York City and an office in Geneva, Switzerland. Its agencies have offices in many parts of the world.

The UN is not a world government. Normally, it can only make studies and recommendations. But under certain conditions it can enforce its decisions.

The United Nations was organized in 1945, at the end of World War II. In some ways it resembles the League of Nations, which was established after World War I. But the UN differs from the League in many important ways. For example, the United States never joined the League of Nations, but it was one of the original members of the United Nations. The nations in the League promised to preserve national boundaries exactly as they had been drawn. UN members have no such agreement. In the League, *every* nation had to agree on what was to be done before any action could be taken in most important cases. In the United Nations, *all* member nations do *not* have to agree on some kind of action. With its more flexible rules, the UN has solved problems the League could not have handled.

The United Nations has kept many international disputes and armed conflicts from developing into major wars by acting as mediator between the disagreeing countries. The UN halted fighting in the Arab-Israeli war in 1949, in the Korean War in 1953, and in the Suez Canal dispute in 1956. UN troops restored order in

Lester B. Pearson, the contributor of this article, is Prime Minister of Canada and former president of the United Nations General Assembly. He won the 1957 Nobel peace prize.

Congo (Léopoldville) in 1960. In 1962, the UN helped end the dangerous crisis that arose when Russia built missile bases in Cuba and the United States blockaded all arms shipments to that island.

The main organs, or divisions, of the United Nations are the General Assembly, the Security Council, the Economic and Social Council, the Trusteeship Council, the International Court of Justice, and the Secretariat. Specialized agencies related to the UN deal with such problems as food and agriculture, health, and labor.

Each nation appoints delegates to the United Nations according to its own laws. In the United States, the President nominates men and women to represent the country in the UN. The Senate must confirm his nominations. In Canada, the prime minister and his cabinet choose UN delegates. The United States and Canada, like most other countries, give their chief UN delegate the status of an ambassador.

The United Nations asks all its members to help pay the expenses of the organization. Wealthy countries pay more than poorer ones. The United States pays a little less than one-third of the UN's expenses. The United Nations made a rule in 1957 that no nation should pay more than 30 per cent of the UN budget. By the mid-1960's, the annual budget for the United Nations totaled more than $100,000,000.

A Trip Through UN Headquarters

The 39-story UN Secretariat Building rises majestically as part of the New York City skyline. It towers over the General Assembly, Conference, and Library

MOST COUNTRIES OF THE WORLD BELONG TO THE UNITED NATIONS

United Nations Members

Nonmember Nations

Colonies, Territories, and Mandates of UN Members

The United Nations Flag features the official UN emblem, a map of the world flanked by two olive branches. The olive branches signify the UN's purpose of promoting world peace.

buildings at United Nations Plaza on the east side of Manhattan Island. The 18-acre plaza covers six blocks along the East River between 42nd and 48th streets.

John D. Rockefeller, Jr., of the United States, gave $8,500,000 to the United Nations to buy the site in 1946, after the UN voted to set up headquarters in the United States. New York City donated small adjacent lots to complete the headquarters site. Construction of UN buildings began in 1949, and was completed in the fall of 1952.

The buildings cost $67 million. The UN obtained an interest-free loan of $65 million from the United States to pay for the construction. This loan is being repaid in yearly payments, and must be paid by 1982.

The Secretariat Building has aluminum facing with blue-green glass on its sides, and solid gray Vermont marble on its ends. It houses the offices of many of the more than 4,000 employees of the Secretariat. The UN Post Office Station is below the main lobby of the building. In front of the Secretariat Building, water spouts from a fountain into a circular reflecting pool, designed with alternate serpentines of crushed white marble and black pebbles. The children of the United States and its territorial possessions gave the pool and fountain to the United Nations.

The General Assembly Building is a low, sweeping, marble and limestone structure. Seven nickel-silver doors, donated by Canada, lead to a lobby open to the

THE 119 MEMBERS OF THE UNITED NATIONS

The 51 nations that became charter members of the UN in 1945 do not have dates after their names in the following table. Nations admitted later are listed with their years of admission.

Afghanistan (1946)	Ghana (1957)	Nicaragua
Albania (1955)	Great Britain	Niger (1960)
Algeria (1962)	Greece	Nigeria (1960)
Argentina	Guatemala	Norway
Australia	Guinea (1958)	Pakistan (1947)
Austria (1955)	Guyana (1966)	Panama
Belgium	Haiti	Paraguay
Bolivia	Honduras	Peru
Brazil	Hungary (1955)	Philippines
Bulgaria (1955)	Iceland (1946)	Poland
Burma (1948)	India	Portugal (1955)
Burundi (1962)	Indonesia (1950)	Romania (1955)
Byelorussian S.S.R.	Iran	Russia (U.S.S.R.)
Cambodia (1955)	Iraq	Rwanda (1962)
Cameroon (1960)	Ireland (1955)	Saudi Arabia
Canada	Israel (1949)	Senegal (1960)
Central African	Italy (1955)	Sierra
Republic (1960)	Ivory Coast (1960)	Leone (1961)
Ceylon (1955)	Jamaica (1962)	Singapore (1965)
Chad (1960)	Japan (1956)	Somalia (1960)
Chile	Jordan (1955)	South Africa
China	Kenya (1963)	Spain (1955)
Colombia	Kuwait (1963)	Sudan (1956)
Congo (Brazza-	Laos (1955)	Sweden (1946)
ville) (1960)	Lebanon	Syria
Congo (Léopold-	Liberia	Tanzania (1961)
ville) (1960)	Libya (1955)	Thailand (1946)
Costa Rica	Luxembourg	Togo (1960)
Cuba	Madagascar (Mal-	Trinidad and
Cyprus (1960)	agasy) (1960)	Tobago (1962)
Czechoslovakia	Malawi (1964)	Tunisia (1956)
Dahomey (1960)	Malaysia (1957)	Turkey
Denmark	Maldive Is. (1965)	Uganda (1962)
Dominican Rep.	Mali (1960)	Ukrainian S.S.R.
Ecuador	Malta (1964)	United States
Egypt (U.A.R.)	Mauritania (1961)	Upper
El Salvador	Mexico	Volta (1960)
Ethiopia	Mongolia (1961)	Uruguay
Finland (1955)	Morocco (1956)	Venezuela
France	Nepal (1955)	Yemen (1947)
Gabon (1960)	Netherlands	Yugoslavia
Gambia (1965)	New Zealand	Zambia (1964)

A TRIP THROUGH
UNITED NATIONS HEADQUARTERS

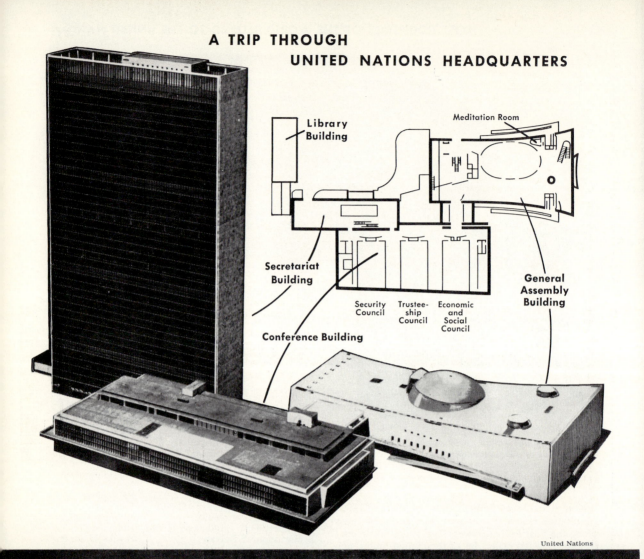

Library Building

Meditation Room

Secretariat Building

Security Council

Trustee-ship Council

Economic and Social Council

General Assembly Building

Conference Building

United Nations

Visitors to UN Headquarters pause in the lobby of the Secretariat Building to look at a special display. Their guided tour takes them through the headquarters buildings, explaining how the UN works. Many of the guides, such as this girl from India, wear the traditional clothing of their homelands.

Conference Rooms stand ready for use by the main committees of the General Assembly. Delegates and observers sit at the curved desks, staff members at the long tables.

The General Assembly is the one main organ of the UN where every member nation is represented and has an equal voice. The president of the Assembly, the Secretary-General, and his top assistant sit below the UN seal, *left*. Interpreters, *above*, translate each speech into the other official languages as it is made. The delegates, *right*, can listen to it in Chinese, English, French, Russian, or Spanish.

75-foot-high roof. In this main lobby are a statue of the god Zeus donated by Greece, a model of Sputnik I donated by Russia, and a pendulum donated by The Netherlands. The pendulum, suspended from the ceiling, illustrates the rotation of the earth. A steep ramp leads from the lobby to the delegates' level of the General Assembly Auditorium. Visitors take elevators to public galleries from which they may watch the proceedings in the General Assembly.

The auditorium is almost half as large as a football field, and has a vaulted ceiling as high as a seven-story building. A skylight, four feet in diameter, admits a shaft of sunlight through the dome. Delegates sit beneath the dome at curved rows of wooden desks, facing the raised speaker's rostrum. On each side wall are two tiers of glass-enclosed booths for interpreters, reporters, cameramen, and radio and television broadcasters. There are about 1,280 seats for delegates, 150 for official observers, 50 for the press, and 800 for the public.

At the west end of the main lobby, a small Meditation Room is open to delegates and to visitors of all faiths. The level below the lobby includes public lounges, several shops, and the United Nations Postal Administration Sales Counter. Visitors may purchase UN stamps there as souvenirs or as postage. Letters and post cards bearing United Nations postage must be mailed from the UN post office.

The Conference Building is a long, low structure of Portland limestone and glass that lies alongside the East River. Corridors link it directly with the General Assembly and Secretariat buildings. On the main level, the building has three chambers of equal area, each larger than a basketball gymnasium. One chamber, designed by Sven Markelius of Sweden, houses the Economic and Social Council. The second chamber, for the Trusteeship Council, was designed by Finn Juhl of Denmark. The Security Council chamber was designed by Arnstein Arneberg of Norway. Each council chamber has seats for visitors and booths for interpreters, radio and television broadcasters, motion picture cameramen, and reporters.

On the level below the council chambers, the main committees of the General Assembly have three large conference halls and six smaller rooms. This level also includes a terrace running the length of the building. It juts out over busy Franklin D. Roosevelt Drive to give delegates and visitors a fine view of the river. On the fourth floor, also overlooking the river, UN delegates and employees have a dining area, a cafeteria, and several private dining rooms.

Below street level, the Conference Building houses maintenance shops, a printing plant, and air conditioning equipment for all the headquarters buildings. This area also contains a fire-fighting unit and a parking garage for about 1,500 cars.

The Library Building at the southwest corner of the UN site was added in 1961. It is dedicated to former Secretary-General Dag Hammarskjöld, who was killed in an airplane crash in 1961. The Ford Foundation contributed $6,200,000 for construction of the six-story building. The library contains collections of UN documents.

Simultaneous Interpretation. All the main meeting rooms are equipped to provide simultaneous interpre-tation for the meetings. The UN has five official languages: Chinese, English, French, Russian, and Spanish. A delegate may speak in any one of these languages, and skilled interpreters translate his remarks into the other four tongues as he talks. Each chair in the meeting rooms has a set of earphones connected to a dial with six numbers. Dial No. 1 always transmits the voice of the speaker. The other numbers are for the five official languages. In this way, anyone who understands one of the five official languages can follow the proceedings.

The United Nations Charter

The Charter is the constitution of the United Nations. It provides laws and a framework for organizing the UN. All members of the UN agree to follow the rules of the Charter. The Charter contains 19 chapters divided into 111 articles that define the purposes, principles, and methods of the UN. The chapters of the Charter were drafted by committees representing all nations present at the San Francisco Conference where the United Nations was created.

Purposes and Principles. Chapter 1 of the Charter consists of two articles, and states the purposes and principles of the UN. The *purposes* are (1) to maintain international peace and security, (2) to develop friendly relations among nations, (3) to achieve international cooperation in solving problems, and (4) to serve as a center for attaining these ends. The *principles* are (1)

THE PREAMBLE TO THE UNITED NATIONS CHARTER

A preamble of about 200 words precedes the chapters of the Charter and expresses the guiding spirit of the organization. Jan Christiaan Smuts of South Africa is credited with drafting the preamble (see SMUTS, JAN C.). The complete preamble states:

"WE THE PEOPLES OF THE UNITED NATIONS DETERMINED

to save succeeding generations from the scourge of war, which twice in our lifetime has brought untold sorrow to mankind, and

to reaffirm faith in fundamental human rights, in the dignity and worth of the human person, in the equal rights of men and women and of nations large and small, and

to establish conditions under which justice and respect for the obligations arising from treaties and other sources of international law can be maintained, and

to promote social progress and better standards of life in larger freedom,

AND FOR THESE ENDS

to practice tolerance and live together in peace with one another as good neighbors, and

to unite our strength to maintain international peace and security, and

to ensure, by the acceptance of principles and the institution of methods, that armed force shall not be used, save in the common interest, and

to employ international machinery for the promotion of the economic and social advancement of all peoples,

HAVE RESOLVED TO COMBINE OUR EFFORTS
TO ACCOMPLISH THESE AIMS.

Accordingly, our respective Governments, through representatives assembled in the city of San Francisco, who have exhibited their full powers found to be in good and due form, have agreed to the present Charter of the United Nations and do hereby establish an international organization to be known as the United Nations."

equality of members, (2) good faith, (3) peace, (4) respect for rights of other nations, (5) cooperation, (6) promotion of UN principles among nonmember nations, and (7) respect by the UN of the right of member nations to govern themselves.

Organizational Chapters. The organizational part of the Charter is in chapters 2 through 17 (articles 3 through 107). These chapters and articles state membership requirements, provide for the creation of the six principal organs of the UN, and state the rights and duties of these organs and of UN member nations.

Article 4 of the Charter declares that membership in the United Nations is open to all "peace-loving states" that accept the obligations stated in the Charter, and are "able and willing to carry out these obligations."

The Security Council may "take such action by air, sea, or land forces as may be necessary to maintain or restore international peace and security," according to article 42 of the Charter. Article 43 states that all member nations should make military forces and supplies available to the Security Council if it calls for them. Thus, although the UN does not have a standing army, it can raise needed troops in an emergency.

Article 51 of the Charter guarantees to nations "the inherent right of individual or collective self-defense," if an armed attack occurs against them. Articles 52, 53, and 54 provide that regional agencies that have purposes similar to those of the UN may help the UN solve matters dealing with particular regions. These articles made it possible for nations to form such regional organizations as the Organization of American States (OAS), the North Atlantic Treaty Organization (NATO), and the Southeast Asia Treaty Organization (SEATO), without causing opposition from the United Nations. Regional organizations must inform the UN Security Council of their activities. See the separate articles on these organizations in WORLD BOOK.

Methods of Amendment. Chapter 18 states the two methods of amending the Charter. An amendment may be proposed if two-thirds of all members vote in the General Assembly to do so. When such a proposed amendment is ratified by two-thirds of the member nations, including all five permanent members of the Security Council, the amendment is adopted. Or, two-thirds of the member nations of the General Assembly and any nine members of the Security Council may decide to have a General Conference of UN members to review the Charter. Each member nation has one vote at the conference. A two-thirds vote of the conference is required to propose an amendment. Then two-thirds of the member nations of the UN, including all five permanent members of the Security Council, must ratify the proposed amendment to adopt it.

The final chapter of the Charter, chapter 19, provides the means for adopting the Charter itself.

The General Assembly

The General Assembly is sometimes called the *Town Meeting of the World*. It is the only principal organ of the UN that includes representatives from every member nation. Each member nation has the same power in the General Assembly as every other member, regardless of its size, population, or wealth. Each member nation may send five delegates, five alternate delegates, and as many advisers as it wishes to the Assembly. But each

member nation has only one vote, and no single nation can *veto* (forbid) any action in the Assembly. A two-thirds majority vote is required in the General Assembly on all important questions. Some of these questions are listed in article 18 of the Charter. A simple majority is required on all other decisions, including the decision to place other questions in the "important" class.

The General Assembly elects its president when it opens its annual session each fall. Assembly presidents serve one annual session. They have used their influence in such cases as (1) easing strained relations between Greece and its northern neighbors in 1948 and (2) helping to find a peaceful solution to the Berlin blockade in 1948 and 1949. See GREECE (After World War II); BERLIN (History).

Powers. The General Assembly may discuss any question that comes under the United Nations Charter. The Assembly may consider some questions because one or more countries ask it to do so. Sometimes it may discuss a question brought up by the Secretary-General, the Security Council, or one of the other principal organs. Some treaties between countries state that if a problem is not settled by a certain date, it will automatically go to the General Assembly for solution.

Regardless of what problem the General Assembly discusses, all United Nations members have the right to speak. After the Assembly has considered a problem, it usually approves a recommendation concerning it. It does not *order* any specific action, and United Nations members may or may not do as the Assembly recommends. But an Assembly recommendation means that a majority of the world's nations have agreed on the action.

Name	Country	Session	Dates
*Paul-Henri Spaak	Belgium	1st	1946-47
Oswaldo Aranha	Brazil	1st S.S.	1947
		2nd	1947-48
José Arce	Argentina	2nd S.S.	1948
Herbert V. Evatt	Australia	3rd	1948-49
*Carlos P. Romulo	Philippines	4th	1949-50
Nasrollah Entezam	Iran	5th	1950-51
Luis Padilla Nervo	Mexico	6th	1951-52
*Lester B. Pearson	Canada	7th	1952-53
*Mme. Vijaya Pandit	India	8th	1953-54
Eelco N. van Kleffens	Netherlands	9th	1954-55
José Maza	Chile	10th	1955-56
Rudecindo Ortega	Chile	1st E.S.S.	1956
		2nd E.S.S.	1956
Prince Wan Waithayakon	Thailand	11th	1956-57
Sir Leslie Munro	New Zealand	12th	1957-58
		3rd E.S.S.	1958
Charles Malik	Lebanon	13th	1958-59
Victor Andrés Belaúnde	Peru	14th	1959-60
		4th E.S.S.	1960
Frederick H. Boland	Ireland	15th	1960-61
		3rd S.S.	1961
Mongi Slim	Tunisia	16th	1961-62
Sir Muhammad Zafrulla Khan	Pakistan	17th	1962-63
		4th S.S.	1963
Carlos Sosa Rodriguez	Venezuela	18th	1963-64
Alex Quaison-Sackey	Ghana	19th	1964-65
Amintore Fanfani	Italy	20th	1965-

───PRESIDENTS OF THE UN GENERAL ASSEMBLY───

*Has a separate biography in WORLD BOOK

S.S. = Special Session
E.S.S. = Emergency Special Session

ECONOMIC AND SOCIAL COUNCIL

Principal Organs of the UN are closely related to the General Assembly, which works out the budget for the organization as a whole. The principal organs submit yearly reports to it on their activities.

SECURITY COUNCIL

SECRETARIAT

Wide World; United Nations

TRUSTEESHIP COUNCIL

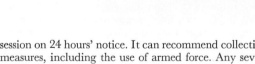

Meetings. The Assembly holds at least one *regular* session each year. This session usually begins on the third Tuesday in September, and lasts about three months. The Assembly may also hold as many *special* sessions as are necessary. Special sessions may be called (1) by the Security Council, (2) by a majority of the members of the United Nations, or (3) by any one member if a majority of the other members agree to the request. Special sessions may last as long as the member nations feel they should.

The Assembly adopted a resolution called "Uniting for Peace" on Nov. 3, 1950. This resolution set up a system for calling *emergency special sessions* of the Assembly. If a member of the Security Council uses its veto to prevent the Council from acting in a serious situation, the Assembly may be called into emergency special

session on 24 hours' notice. It can recommend collective measures, including the use of armed force. Any seven members of the Security Council, or a majority of the UN members, may call such a session.

Delegations sit at their desks in a set order, following the alphabetical order of their country names in English. At the beginning of each regular session of the Assembly, delegates draw lots for the first desk in the front row. The other delegations follow through the alphabet, then start in again at A.

Committees. The Assembly has seven main committees to help it in its work. They are called the First, Second, Third, Fourth, Fifth, and Sixth committees, and the Special Political Committee. The First Committee and the Special Political Committee deal with political problems. The Second Committee deals with

INTERNATIONAL COURT OF JUSTICE

The Specialized Agencies work for advances in such fields as food and medicine. The Economic and Social Council coordinates their jobs to keep several agencies from working on the same tasks.	Food and Agriculture Organization
Inter-Governmental Maritime Consultative Organization	International Bank for Reconstruction and Development
International Civil Aviation Organization	International Development Association
International Finance Corporation	International Labor Organization
International Monetary Fund	International Telecommunication Union
UNESCO	Universal Postal Union
World Health Organization	World Meteorological Organization

economic and financial problems, the Third with social and cultural problems, and the Fourth with problems of countries that do not govern themselves. The Fifth deals with administrative, budget, and personnel problems, and the Sixth with problems of law.

Every General Assembly member has the right to send a delegate to each committee. The committees discuss problems assigned to them by the General Assembly, and recommend action to the Assembly.

The Security Council

The Security Council principally takes up problems concerned with keeping peace in the world. It has 15 members, 5 of which serve permanently. These are France, Great Britain, Nationalist China, Russia, and the United States. The other 10 members serve on the

Security Council for two-year terms. Each year, the General Assembly elects five nonpermanent members to the Security Council. It cannot re-elect a nonpermanent member to the Security Council until at least one year after the nonpermanent member's term has ended.

Powers. The Security Council has greater powers under the Charter than any other organ of the United Nations. It is the only body that can give an order to a member nation. The Security Council can investigate any situation that might cause international friction, and can order the disputing nations to settle their problem by themselves or through the International Court of Justice. If such means fail, the Security Council may ask member nations to furnish troops, and may order them into the area to settle the problem.

The Security Council must approve applications for

31

membership in the United Nations before the General Assembly can act on them. It must agree on a candidate for Secretary-General before the General Assembly can appoint him. All members of the UN must agree, when they sign the Charter, to accept the recommendations of the Security Council in certain given circumstances.

Procedure. Problems may be brought before the Security Council in several ways: (1) any member nation of the UN may ask the Security Council to meet on a question it thinks is serious and may lead to war; (2) the Secretary-General may ask the Security Council to consider a question; or (3) the General Assembly or any other organ of the United Nations may call a matter to the attention of the Security Council.

The Security Council is organized to function continuously. The head of each of the 15 member delegations, or his representative, presides over council meetings for one month. Member nations take turns, in the alphabetical order of their country names in English. Stenographers record every word said in council meetings in the UN's two working languages, English and French. Meetings are also recorded on phonograph records.

The Veto Power. The Security Council is the only organ of the UN in which one member nation can over-

rule the decisions or actions of the group. The five permanent members of the Security Council have a special kind of vote called the veto power. The Security Council must have nine votes in favor of an action to give an order or recommendation. If any permanent member votes against it, the Security Council cannot issue it. In this way, one permanent member can *veto* action approved by the other 14 members. The veto power applies to all Security Council questions except those that deal with the procedures of conducting meetings.

A permanent member of the Security Council can indicate that it disapproves a proposed action without vetoing it. It does this by *abstaining*, or not voting at all. If nine members vote in favor of the action, it is approved, even if six members abstain. President Franklin D. Roosevelt proposed the idea of the veto at the Yalta Conference in 1945.

East-West Deadlock. At the time the veto power was agreed on, the five permanent members of the Security Council were allies in war. After World War II, they drifted apart. Some problems before the United Nations have remained unsolved because the five major countries have been unable to agree upon a solution. Russia has vetoed over 100 Security Council actions since 1946, more than the rest of the Council combined.

The Secretariat

The Secretariat is the service organization of the United Nations. It keeps records, makes studies, handles correspondence, and performs other duties assigned to it by the Charter and by other UN organs. The Secretary-General is the head of the Secretariat.

The Secretary-General of the United Nations holds a unique position. Chapter 15 of the Charter states the Secretary-General shall be the chief administrative officer of the UN. But it also says that he may bring to the attention of the Security Council any matter which in his opinion may threaten international peace and security, and that he shall perform functions entrusted to him by other organs of the UN. Governments confide in the Secretary-General, and he receives information regarding dangerous situations and what might be done to keep the peace. He is a neutral diplomat between nations and is able to help solve many problems without referring them to other UN organs.

The Secretary-General is nominated by the Security Council and appointed by the General Assembly to a term set by the General Assembly. Trygve Lie of Norway served as the first Secretary-General. He was elected to a five-year term in 1946, then elected to continue in office for an additional three years. In 1950, he proposed a 20-year program for achieving peace through the United Nations. Unwillingly caught up in the conflict between East and West, Lie submitted his resignation in November, 1952, and left office early in 1953. See LIE, TRYGVE.

Dag Hammarskjöld of Sweden became Secretary-General in 1953. He made many trips to various parts of the world to relieve tensions or to gain compliance with United Nations orders. His trips included visits to Communist China, the Middle East, and Africa. Under a resolution of the General Assembly, Hammarskjöld organized a UN Emergency Force to keep the peace in the Suez Canal area. He formed another such force to help keep order in the Congo during the disturbances

---------**MEMBERS OF THE UN SECURITY COUNCIL**---------

The Security Council has 15 members. France, Great Britain, Nationalist China, Russia, and the United States are permanent members. The other 10 members are elected to two-year terms, five each year. For the first Security Council, three members served only one-year terms. This table shows the elected members.

1946 Australia, Brazil, Egypt (1-year term), Mexico (1-year term), Netherlands (1-year term), Poland
1947 Australia, Belgium, Brazil, Colombia, Poland, Syria
1948 Argentina, Belgium, Canada, Colombia, Syria, Ukrainian S.S.R.
1949 Argentina, Canada, Cuba, Egypt, Norway, Ukrainian S.S.R.
1950 Cuba, Ecuador, Egypt, India, Norway, Yugoslavia
1951 Brazil, Ecuador, India, Netherlands, Turkey, Yugoslavia
1952 Brazil, Chile, Greece, Netherlands, Pakistan, Turkey
1953 Chile, Colombia, Denmark, Greece, Lebanon, Pakistan
1954 Brazil, Colombia, Denmark, Lebanon, New Zealand, Turkey
1955 Belgium, Brazil, Iran, New Zealand, Peru, Turkey
1956 Australia, Belgium, Cuba, Iran, Peru, Yugoslavia
1957 Australia, Colombia, Cuba, Iraq, Philippines (replacing Yugoslavia), Sweden
1958 Canada, Colombia, Iraq, Japan, Panama, Sweden
1959 Argentina, Canada, Italy, Japan, Panama, Tunisia
1960 Argentina, Ceylon, Ecuador, Italy, Poland, Tunisia
1961 Ceylon, Chile, Ecuador, Liberia, Turkey (replacing Poland), United Arab Republic
1962 Chile, Egypt, Ghana, Ireland, Romania, Venezuela
1963 Brazil, Ghana, Morocco, Norway, Philippines (replacing Romania), Venezuela
1964 Bolivia, Brazil, Czechoslovakia, Ivory Coast, Morocco, Norway
1965 Bolivia, Ivory Coast, Jordan, Malaysia (replacing Czechoslovakia), Netherlands, Uruguay
1966 Argentina, Bulgaria, Japan, Jordan, Mali, Netherlands, New Zealand, Nigeria, Uganda, Uruguay

The Secretary-General holds one of the most important offices in the world. He uses his influence to settle disputes peacefully. Trygve Lie of Norway, *near left,* was the UN's first Secretary-General from 1946 to 1953. After Lie's successor, Dag Hammarskjöld, *far left,* of Sweden, was killed in an airplane crash in the Congo in 1961, U Thant of Burma, *right,* became Secretary-General.

United Nations

United Press Int.

following independence. Hammarskjöld was elected to a second five-year term in 1958, but was killed in an airplane crash in 1961. See HAMMARSKJÖLD, DAG.

U Thant of Burma took over as Acting Secretary-General to fill Hammarskjöld's unexpired term. In 1962, U Thant was officially appointed Secretary-General for a five-year term dating from 1961, when he first assumed the duties of that office. See THANT, U.

Employees. Persons from many countries, and from many occupations and professions, make up the Secretariat. They include accountants, administrators, economists, lawyers, statisticians, translators, typists, and writers. Over 4,000 persons serve in the Secretariat.

The Secretary-General tries to have employees from as many member nations as possible. Employees take orders only from the Secretary-General, never from member nations. Article 100 of the Charter provides that employees shall owe their first allegiance to the United Nations, and that member nations shall not try to influence them in their work.

Most member nations allow their citizens not to pay income taxes if they are employed by the UN. The United States insists that its citizens pay income taxes, even if they are UN employees. The UN adjusts the salaries of its employees so that those who must pay income taxes receive as much take-home pay as those on the same level who are exempt from income taxes.

Other Main UN Organs

The Economic and Social Council studies problems that concern improvements in the way people live. The Council makes recommendations for their solution to the General Assembly, the specialized agencies, and the governments concerned. The Council deals with such problems as communications, economic development, human rights, international trade, narcotics, population, refugees, and transportation. It also helps to coordinate work done by the specialized agencies.

The Economic and Social Council has 27 members. Each year, the General Assembly elects nine members to three-year terms. A retiring member may be re-elected immediately. Each member has 1 vote in the Council, and a simple majority of 14 votes is enough to recommend action. Any member nation or specialized agency that is interested in a problem under discussion by the Council may take part in the discussion without voting.

The Council holds two regular sessions each year, and may also meet in special session. It usually has one regular session at United Nations headquarters and one at the UN European office in Geneva, Switzerland. The Council has four regional economic commissions working for economic development in various parts of the world. They are concerned with increasing economic activity and improving economic relations within their regions. The Council set up economic commissions for Europe and for Asia and the Far East in 1947, for Latin America in 1948, and for Africa in 1958. Members of these commissions include UN members in the regions and interested UN members outside the regions.

The Economic and Social Council carries on other phases of its work through functional commissions. These groups deal with such problems as human rights, narcotics, statistics, transportation and communication, and the status of women. The Council also works with the United Nations Children's Fund (UNICEF) and with a large group of nongovernmental organizations that deal with certain problems or regions of the world.

The Trusteeship Council. The Charter recognizes that certain territories are not yet ready for self-government. It set up the Trusteeship Council to aid in governing territories (1) previously held under League of Nations mandates, (2) taken from Germany, Italy, and Japan after World War II, or (3) voluntarily put in the UN trusteeship system by nations responsible for their administration. Such areas are *trust territories*.

Trusteeships were set up for 11 areas, almost all of them former League of Nations mandates. Only two areas taken from Italy and Japan became trust territories. Italy itself became trustee for Somaliland, with an advisory council made up of representatives from Colombia, the Philippines, and the United Arab Republic to aid it. The U.S. became trustee for several islands taken from Japan in the Pacific Ocean. It governs these islands under a *strategic areas trusteeship,* and reports to the Security Council, as well as the Trusteeship Council, on them. Togoland was the first trust territory to reach independence.

All members administering trust territories and the

World Bank—*India*

The World Bank and other agencies help nations build dams and factories and improve their level of living.

The World Health Organization helps fight disease and provides information on medical and scientific advances.

United Nations—*Turkey*

permanent members of the Security Council not administering trust territories belong to the Trusteeship Council. The General Assembly also elects enough nontrustee members to give the council an equal number of trustee and nontrustee members.

The International Court of Justice is the principal judicial organ of the United Nations. It consists of 15 judges selected for nine-year terms. The General Assembly and the Security Council elect the judges, but they vote independently. No two judges may come from the same country. The judges are selected so that the principal judicial systems of the world are always represented. Judges may be re-elected. The 15 judges choose a president and a vice-president from their number. The court has its seat at The Hague in The Netherlands, but it may decide to meet at other places.

Only governments and certain public international organizations may bring cases before the court. An individual cannot have a case heard unless his government sponsors it. The decision of the court is final and without appeal. When one party in a case fails to fulfill its obligations under a court judgment, the other party may ask the Security Council for action to make the judgment effective. The Security Council may recommend that nations take their legal differences before the court. Some treaties specify that the court will decide any differences of opinion on the meaning of parts of these agreements. See INTERNATIONAL COURT OF JUSTICE.

The Specialized Agencies

The specialized agencies are international organizations related to the UN. They deal with such problems as agriculture, education, and labor. Some of these agencies are older than the United Nations itself. The UN Charter includes provisions for obtaining advice and help from these agencies. The UN makes an agreement with each agency, and the Economic and Social Council acts as a coordinating body to avoid having two or more organizations do the same work.

A number of UN groups are not classified as specialized agencies for various reasons. These groups include

---- **PRESENT AND FORMER UN TRUST TERRITORIES** ----

This table lists the 11 original trust areas, their trustees, and dates for those achieving independence.

Name	Trustee	Status
Cameroons	Great Britain	Independent as parts of Cameroon and Nigeria, 1961
Cameroon	France	Independent, 1960
Nauru	Australia	
New Guinea	Australia	
Pacific Islands (Carolines, Marianas except Guam, Marshalls)	United States	Strategic Area Trusteeship (under the Security Council)
Ruanda-Urundi	Belgium	Independent as Rwanda and Burundi, 1962
Somaliland	Italy	Independent as Somalia, 1960
Tanganyika	Great Britain	Independent, 1961
Togo	France	Independent, 1960
Togoland	Great Britain	Independent as part of Ghana, 1957
Western Samoa	New Zealand	Independent, 1962

United Nations—Guatemala

The United Nations Children's Fund (UNICEF) sends milk and food to hungry children in all parts of the world.

UNESCO teaches people to read and write, and helps them learn more about farming, science, and industry.

tober, 1945, and began working with the UN in December, 1946. It has headquarters in Rome.

Inter-Governmental Maritime Consultative Organization (IMCO) promotes cooperation in matters dealing with international shipping. It is especially concerned with government regulations over shipping, technical matters, and safety at sea. IMCO was founded in March, 1958, and began working with the United Nations later that year. It has headquarters in London.

International Bank for Reconstruction and Development lends money, with repayment guaranteed by governments, to help countries build such projects as irrigation works, power plants, railroads, and steel plants. The bank helped to establish the International Finance Corporation (IFC) in 1956, and the International Development Association (IDA) in 1960. The IFC and the IDA are now separate specialized agencies. The bank began operation in June, 1946, and has been a specialized agency related to the UN since November, 1947. It has headquarters in Washington, D.C.

International Civil Aviation Organization (ICAO) helps governments with aviation problems. It encourages safety measures in air services, and works to standardize laws for planes flying between countries. It tries to make it easier for passengers to enter countries, and promotes the use of new and safer aviation equipment. ICAO began working with the UN in December, 1946, and has headquarters in Montreal.

International Development Association (IDA) is an affiliate of the International Bank for Reconstruction and Development. It provides funds for projects that do not qualify for International Bank or International Finance Corporation loans. It finances projects such as highway development and irrigation programs. Established in September, 1960, it began operations in November, 1960. Headquarters are in Washington, D.C.

International Finance Corporation (IFC), an affiliate of the International Bank for Reconstruction and De-

United Nations—Liberia

the International Atomic Energy Agency (IAEA), the office of the United Nations High Commissioner for Refugees (UNHCR), and the United Nations Children's Fund (UNICEF). The work of these agencies is described in the *Achievements and Problems* section in this article.

One specialized agency, the International Refugee Organization (IRO), has already gone out of existence. Founded in 1946, it took over much of the work of the United Nations Relief and Rehabilitation Administration (UNRRA). It ceased work in 1951, and the office of the UN High Commissioner for Refugees assumed responsibility for dealing with refugees. See UNITED NATIONS RELIEF AND REHABILITATION ADMINISTRATION.

Food and Agriculture Organization (FAO) helps nations obtain more and better products from farms, forests, and fishing waters. It advises governments on improving agriculture, and works to improve the diets of people around the world. FAO was organized in Oc-

The UN Helps Refugees. It helps them find homes, and provides food, medical care, and vocational rehabilitation for handicapped persons.

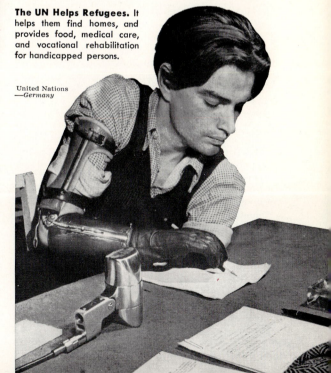

United Nations
—Germany

FOR THE UNITED STATES OF AMERICA:
POUR LES ETATS-UNIS D'AMÉRIQUE:
美利堅合衆國:
За Соединенные Штаты Америки:
POR LOS ESTADOS UNIDOS DE AMÉRICA:

Signing the UN Charter. American delegates, *above*, surrounded Secretary of State Edward R. Stettinius as President Truman looked on. The event took place in San Francisco's Civic Opera House, *below*. Other signers, *left*, were former Secretary of State Cordell Hull, Senators Tom Connally and Arthur Vandenberg, Congressmen Sol Bloom and Charles Eaton, Harold Stassen, and Virginia C. Gildersleeve of Barnard College.

FOUNDING THE UNITED NATIONS

velopment, arranges loans without government guarantee. It encourages private industry to build productive private enterprise, particularly in underdeveloped countries. IFC stimulates smaller, private developments, while the International Bank concentrates on loans for large government projects. Organized in July, 1956, it began working with the UN in February, 1957. It has headquarters in Washington, D.C.

International Labor Organization (ILO) tries to solve labor and manpower problems throughout the world. It helps governments train workers for technical jobs, and advises nations on such problems as social security, paid vacations for workers, and child-labor laws. Founded in 1919, ILO began working with the UN in December, 1946. It has headquarters in Geneva, Switzerland.

International Monetary Fund helps governments set up sound money systems, and sells currencies to members for international trade purposes. The fund began exchange operations in March, 1947, and started working with the United Nations in November of that year. It has headquarters in Washington, D.C.

International Telecommunication Union (ITU) promotes international cooperation in problems dealing with radio, telephone, and telegraph. It helps assign radio frequencies, and seeks to establish the lowest possible rates for radio, telephone, and telegraph messages. ITU was established as the International Telegraph Union in 1865, and began working with the UN in July, 1948. The ITU has headquarters in Geneva.

UNESCO (United Nations Educational, Scientific, and Cultural Organization) promotes better understanding among countries by helping to improve the education of people throughout the world, and by encouraging the development of science. UNESCO's projects include attempts to extend primary education in all parts of the world, and to promote understanding among all peoples. UNESCO began working with the UN in December, 1946. It has headquarters in Paris.

Universal Postal Union (UPU) promotes international postal cooperation. Each member agrees to send the mail of all other members by the best and fastest means it uses for its own mail. The UPU was established in 1875, and started working with the UN in November, 1947. It has its headquarters in Bern, Switzerland.

World Health Organization (WHO) is the world's principal agency for dealing with health problems. It collects and shares information on the latest medical

Temporary Headquarters. The UN moved into this building at Lake Success, N.Y., in 1946. The General Assembly met at Flushing Meadow.

Permanent Headquarters along the East River were completed between 1950 and 1952. John D. Rockefeller, Jr., gave $8,500,000 for the site.

United Nations

and scientific advances, sets up international standards for drugs and vaccines, and helps fight disease. WHO became an official UN agency on April 7, 1948. It has headquarters in Geneva.

World Meteorological Organization (WMO) promotes international cooperation in meteorology by helping establish networks of meteorological stations throughout the world, and by exchanging weather information. It was founded as the International Meteorological Organization in 1878, and started working with the UN in 1951. It has headquarters in Geneva.

Birth of the UN

Nine European governments-in-exile settled in London during the two years after World War II began in 1939. They joined Great Britain and the Commonwealth nations to take the first step toward building a United Nations. They signed the *Inter-Allied Declaration* in June, 1941. This statement declared that the only basis for lasting peace is the willing cooperation of nations free from aggression. These governments declared their intention to work for such cooperation.

The Atlantic Charter, signed in August, 1941, by President Franklin D. Roosevelt and Prime Minister

Winston Churchill, was the next step toward a world organization. It voiced their hope for a better system of security and better economic opportunities for all nations. See ATLANTIC CHARTER.

On Jan. 1, 1942, Roosevelt, Churchill, Foreign Minister T. V. Soong of China, and Maxim Litvinov, the Russian ambassador to the United States, met in Washington. They signed a short document that came to be known as the *Declaration by the United Nations*. It marked the first time that the words *United Nations* were used officially. Roosevelt suggested using them. This document, eventually signed by 47 nations, supported the Atlantic Charter.

The foreign ministers of Great Britain and Russia, the Chinese ambassador to Russia, and U.S. Secretary of State Cordell Hull signed the Moscow Declaration on Oct. 30, 1943. This statement, signed in Moscow, declared that it was necessary to establish an international organization as quickly as possible.

Roosevelt, Churchill, and Premier Joseph Stalin of Russia met in Tehran, Iran, in November and December, 1943. At this meeting, they recognized the responsibility of all the United Nations to achieve a lasting peace that would end war "for many generations." See TEHRAN CONFERENCE.

The Dumbarton Oaks Conference produced the first real steps in setting up a United Nations organization. In talks at an estate in Washington, D.C., from August to October, 1944, delegates from China, Great Britain, Russia, and the United States agreed on plans for the new world organization (see DUMBARTON OAKS). But their proposals did not specify how members of the Security Council would vote. Roosevelt, Churchill, and Stalin settled this problem in their conference at Yalta in February, 1945. They also agreed to call a conference in San Francisco on April 25, 1945, to prepare a charter for the United Nations.

The San Francisco Conference. Four sponsoring nations—China, Great Britain, Russia, and the United States—invited 41 other nations to the San Francisco Conference, and later invited Syria and Lebanon. The conference invited the Byelorussian Soviet Socialist Republic, the Ukrainian Soviet Socialist Republic, Argentina, and Denmark. This made a total of 51 nations. Poland could not attend because its new government had not been formed. It later signed the charter as an original member. Fifty nations were represented when the delegates signed the United Nations Charter on June 26, 1945 (see SAN FRANCISCO CONFERENCE).

On the Move. The United Nations was officially born on Oct. 24, 1945, after China, France, Great Britain, Russia, the United States, and a majority of the other signing nations had ratified the Charter. On Dec. 10, 1945, Congress voted unanimously to invite the UN to establish its permanent home in the United States. The UN accepted the invitation on Feb. 14, 1946, during the first session of the General Assembly in London. The UN headquarters buildings in New York City were completed in the fall of 1952.

Achievements and Problems

Arab-Israeli Armistice. In 1947, Great Britain asked the UN to investigate the disorder and fighting between

UNITED NATIONS

Jews and Arabs in Palestine, which Great Britain ruled. The UN General Assembly sent a special committee to Palestine to study the situation and make recommendations. After studying the committee's report, the General Assembly recommended on November 29 that Palestine be divided into an Arab state and a Jewish state, with international rule for Jerusalem. During early 1948, Great Britain gradually withdrew from Palestine.

The new nation of Israel was born on May 14, 1948, the day Great Britain gave up its control over Palestine. The neighboring Arab states stepped in to support the Arabs in Palestine, and war broke out between Arabs and Israelis. The General Assembly named Count Folke Bernadotte of Sweden as its mediator between Israel and the Arabs. Bernadotte completed proposals for a permanent settlement of the disagreement. But, before he could announce his plan, he was assassinated on Sept. 17, 1948. His assistant, Ralph Bunche of the United States, became acting mediator. Late in 1948, Bunche persuaded Israel and Egypt to begin armistice negotiations. Bunche worked through early 1949 to persuade the combatants to accept UN armistice terms. By June 24, Israel had signed armistice agreements with Egypt, Lebanon, Jordan, and Syria, and peace had been restored. Bunche won the 1950 Nobel peace prize for his efforts. See ISRAEL (History).

After the armistice, the UN cared for more than a million Arab refugees from Palestine. The UN Relief and Works Agency provided food, shelter, and education for them, and the UN tried to resettle them.

Indonesian-Netherlands Dispute. In July, 1947, fighting began in Indonesia between The Netherlands and the Republic of Indonesia over disputed territory in the Netherlands Indies. The Republic of Indonesia wanted to unite all the Netherlands Indies into a United States of Indonesia. The Netherlands and some local rulers opposed the union. On Aug. 1, 1947, the Security Council ordered both governments to stop fighting and to establish a special committee to help settle the question. The parties continued to fight, but the UN arranged a truce on Jan. 17, 1948.

The Netherlands and the Republic of Indonesia tried to set up a new government satisfactory to both sides. But The Netherlands government resumed the war on Dec. 18, 1948, claiming that the Communists would otherwise take over Indonesia. The UN arranged a second truce on Aug. 1, 1949. After a conference at The Hague, The Netherlands granted independence to the United States of Indonesia on Dec. 27, 1949. The new nation included all the Netherlands Indies but western New Guinea. The UN aided in the peaceful transfer of West New Guinea to Indonesia in 1963.

The Korean War. Communist armies of North Korea invaded the Republic of Korea on June 25, 1950. The Security Council met immediately. It asked both sides to stop fighting, and urged North Korea to withdraw its forces. When North Korea had not stopped the attack two days later, the Security Council adopted a resolution recommending that UN member nations send troops to aid South Korea and to restore peace. Russia could not veto the resolution because, shortly before, it had withdrawn its representatives to boycott the UN. The United Nations formed a unified command under the

—————— IMPORTANT DATES IN UN HISTORY ——————

1945 (Apr. 25) The San Francisco Conference opened.
1945 (June 26) The UN Charter was signed by delegates at the San Francisco Conference.
1945 (Oct. 24) The UN was born as the required number of nations ratified the Charter.
1946 (Jan. 10) The 51-member General Assembly met in London, England, to organize.
1946 (Feb. 14) The UN voted to establish headquarters in the United States.
1948 (Jan. 17) The UN negotiated a truce between the Republic of Indonesia and The Netherlands.
1949 (Feb. 24-June 24) UN mediators helped complete an armistice between Israel and the Arab nations.
1949 (Aug. 1) The UN made a new truce in Indonesia.
1950 (June 27) The Security Council approved sending UN troops to Korea to restore peace.
1953 (July 27) North Korea and the UN signed a truce.
1956 (Nov. 4) The General Assembly condemned Russia for using force to suppress uprisings in Hungary.
1956 (Nov. 6) The UN negotiated an Israel-Egypt cease-fire agreement in the Suez Canal dispute.
1956 (Dec. 12) The General Assembly condemned Russia for denying Hungary liberty and independence.
1957 (Mar. 6) The first UN trusteeship came to an end when Togoland became part of independent Ghana.
1957 (July 29) The International Atomic Energy Agency began work on peaceful uses for atomic energy.
1958 (June-Dec.) UN observers prevented the overthrow of the legal governments in Jordan and Lebanon.
1960 (July 14) The Security Council approved sending UN forces to Congo (Léopoldville) to restore order.
1961 (Sept. 18) Secretary-General Dag Hammarskjöld died in a plane crash in Africa while trying to arrange a cease-fire in Congo (Léopoldville).
1962-1963 The United Nations asked member nations to purchase $200 million worth of UN bonds to help the organization pay its debts.
1965 (January) Indonesia became the first country ever to withdraw from the United Nations.

---

leadership of the United States. Of the 60 nations that were members of the UN at that time, 53 expressed general support of the Security Council action. Of these, 41 nations sent supplies to Korea, and 16 sent troops.

Three years later, after many fierce battles, North Korea and the United Nations signed an armistice on July 27, 1953. For the first time, a world organization had recommended and successfully used united military action against aggression. See KOREAN WAR.

The Hungarian Revolt. On Oct. 23, 1956, hundreds of students and workers marched through Budapest demonstrating against Russian control of Hungary's government. Later, Soviet-controlled Hungarian police fired on the crowd. The next day, at a larger meeting, Soviet troops shot down many demonstrators. The Hungarians rebelled. Russian troops and tanks fought the poorly equipped Hungarians. The Security Council could not act because of Russia's veto. The General Assembly, in an emergency session on November 4, gave the Secretary-General power to investigate methods to end the conflict. The Secretary-General tried to send UN observers to Hungary, but the Communists refused to let them enter.

On November 4, the General Assembly passed a resolution condemning Russian military intervention in Hungary. By mid-November, Russian troops had crushed the revolution, and the Communist Hungarian government ordered all captured rebels killed without trial. The Communists had reportedly deported thousands of

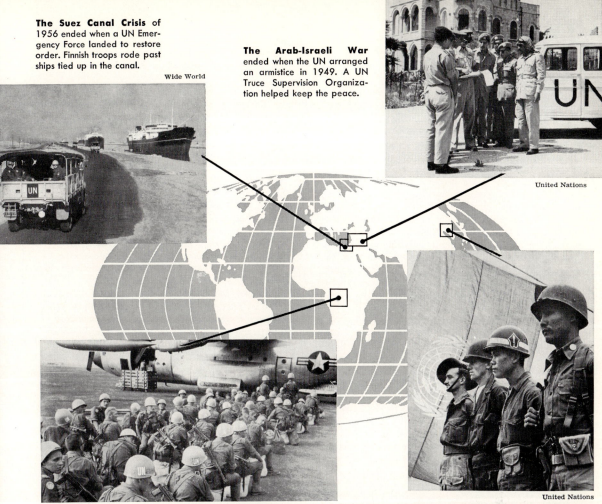

The Suez Canal Crisis of 1956 ended when a UN Emergency Force landed to restore order. Finnish troops rode past ships tied up in the canal.

Wide World

The Arab-Israeli War ended when the UN arranged an armistice in 1949. A UN Truce Supervision Organization helped keep the peace.

United Nations

The Congo Crisis. UN troops helped restore order when riots broke out in 1960. U.S. Air Force planes flew in units from many countries, including this Swedish group.

European

The Korean War brought troops from many nations together under the UN flag. They fought off North Korean and Chinese Communist attacks on South Korea from 1950 to 1953.

United Nations

young Hungarians in sealed trains to Russia. More than 200,000 refugees fled from Hungary to freedom in other lands during the uprising and shortly afterwards. The UN and individual nations throughout the world helped the refugees find new homes. On Dec. 12, 1956, the General Assembly condemned Russia for violating the UN Charter by depriving Hungary of its liberty and independence. The censure was one of the strongest that the UN had ever given to any nation by a resolution. See HUNGARY (Communist Hungary).

Suez Canal Crisis. The 1949 armistice between the Arab nations and Israel failed to keep the peace, and violence flared from time to time. On July 26, 1956, Egypt nationalized the Suez Canal. After private negotiations failed, the Security Council considered the matter on Sept. 26, 1956. On October 29, Israeli forces invaded Egypt, and British and French forces attacked the Suez Canal area of Egypt on October 31.

British and French vetoes kept the Security Council from acting, and, on October 30, the UN General Assembly was called into emergency special session. On November 2, the General Assembly called for a cease-fire in Egypt and the withdrawal of all non-Egyptian forces. On November 2, Lester B. Pearson of Canada, a former President of the General Assembly, recommended that the Secretary-General be asked to set up a UN Emergency Force to end the fighting. The General Assembly accepted a resolution setting up such a force, and appointed Major General E. L. M. Burns of Canada as commander. Twenty-four member nations offered to contribute troops to the UN Emergency Force. With UN troops keeping order, British, French, and Israeli troops moved out. In 1957, the UN helped Egypt clear sunken ships and bombed bridges from the Suez Canal. Pearson won the 1957 Nobel peace prize for his efforts. See ISRAEL (History); SUEZ CANAL (History).

Atomic Energy for Peaceful Uses. The UN sponsored an international conference on the peaceful uses of atomic energy at Geneva, Switzerland, in 1955. Delegates from 73 nations shared their nonmilitary scientific and technical knowledge of atomic energy.

On Oct. 23, 1956, representatives of 82 nations approved the charter of an atoms-for-peace agency, the International Atomic Energy Agency (IAEA). This

39

UN agency was established on July 29, 1957. It has headquarters in Vienna, Austria. IAEA pools non-military atomic information, serves as a bank for atomic material, and works to adapt the atom to peaceful uses.

Technical Assistance programs of the UN and specialized agencies are intended for sharing skills in order to improve levels of living in all countries. The United Nations and some specialized agencies send experts to various countries, and award fellowships to outstanding persons for observation and work in other countries.

In December, 1946, the General Assembly voted to study ways of setting up a plan to give aid on request from governments. It provided that the Secretary-General should administer the program through the Secretariat and finance it from the regular UN budget. In November, 1949, the General Assembly adopted an expanded program of technical assistance, financed by voluntary contributions from governments. It allowed countries to ask either the UN or certain specialized agencies for help. Organizations sharing in the funds for this program include the ILO, FAO, UNESCO, WHO, ICAO, ITU, WMO, UPU, and IAEA.

In 1958, the General Assembly set up a Special Fund to help the economies of developing nations. The fund finances such projects as research, training workers in skills, and surveys of natural resources.

Aid to Refugees. Even before World War II ended, the Allies set up the United Nations Relief and Rehabilitation Administration (UNRRA) to aid refugees. The UN set up a specialized agency, the International Refugee Organization (IRO), to deal with the refugee problem. Then, in December, 1950, the General Assembly established the office of the United Nations High Commissioner for Refugees (UNHCR) to protect and help refugees throughout the world. The office promotes international agreements on the legal status of refugees, protects their rights under these agreements, and coordinates the work of governments in admitting refugees.

In 1954, the office of the High Commissioner established the United Nations Refugee Fund (UNREF) to carry out a four-year program of finding homes for refugees from World War II who were then still living in camps in western and southern Europe. Beginning in 1956, the High Commissioner's office also aided refugees from Hungary. Special UN agencies worked with refugees in war-torn Korea and Palestine.

Aid to Children. The United Nations provides food for millions of mothers and children through its Children's Fund (UNICEF). This agency also helps fight children's diseases, and helps governments set up centers to care for children and mothers. In 1965, UNICEF received the Nobel peace prize for its work.

The General Assembly created UNICEF in 1946. It is not one of the specialized agencies, but it reports to the Economic and Social Council and to the General Assembly. The organization was originally named the United Nations International Children's Emergency Fund. In 1953, the General Assembly shortened its name to the United Nations Children's Fund. School children contribute funds for UNICEF's work.

Disarmament. The United Nations strives to achieve disarmament as a means toward peace, and so that the money, time, and effort that go into arms and armed forces may be used to raise the world's level of living. In January, 1952, the General Assembly set up a 12-member Disarmament Commission under the Security Council to prepare proposals for disarmament treaties. After two years of work, the Commission chose a sub-committee of five members—Canada, France, Great Britain, Russia, and the United States—to speed up disarmament talks. But the five nations could not agree on disarmament terms. The UN Disarmament Commission was enlarged by 14 members in 1957, then expanded in 1959 to include all General Assembly members. Talks in 1961 were limited to the three-power test ban conference and UN General Assembly. An 18-nation Disarmament Committee began talks in 1962.

In 1959, the General Assembly created a permanent 24-nation committee to study the peaceful exploration and uses of outer space.

The UN repeatedly called on all nations to stop testing nuclear weapons. It also gave strong backing to the 12-nation treaty outlawing military activity in Antarctica. This treaty, signed in 1959, specifically banned nuclear weapons from that continent. In August, 1963, Great Britain, Russia, and the United States signed a treaty forbidding nuclear weapons testing in the atmosphere, in outer space, and under water. More than 100 other nations later signed the treaty.

Aid to the Congo. Congo (Léopoldville) gained independence from Belgium on June 30, 1960. A few days later, riots broke out among several tribes. Congolese soldiers mutinied against Belgian officers. Patrice Lumumba, premier of the Congo, appealed to the UN for help in restoring order and in removing Belgian troops. On July 14, the Security Council voted to send aid. On July 15, a UN force began arriving in the Congo. UN troops and negotiators helped keep order until mid-1964, when all UN troops were withdrawn.

The Cuban Crisis became the UN's chief concern in October, 1962. The United States revealed on October 22 that Russia was building missile bases in Cuba that could launch atomic attacks on cities in the Western Hemisphere. Cuba had become a Communist satellite under Fidel Castro. The U.S. set up a *quarantine* (blockade) to turn back ships carrying weapons to Cuba, and demanded that the bases and missiles be taken out of Cuba. Russia accepted these terms on October 28. Acting Secretary-General Thant took a leading part in negotiations on an inspection system that would assure the United States that missiles and other offensive weapons had been removed from Cuba.

Recent Developments. Fighting broke out between Greeks and Turks on the island of Cyprus in 1964. The UN appointed a mediator and sent troops there to control the fighting until a settlement could be reached. UN troops remained on Cyprus in 1965 and 1966.

In January, 1965, Indonesia became the first country ever to withdraw from the UN. Indonesia withdrew in protest against seating Malaysia on the Security Council. But Indonesia returned to the UN in 1966.

A serious showdown involving the U.S., France, and Russia prevented effective UN action in 1965. Russia and France refused to pay their assessments for UN peacekeeping operations in Congo (Léopoldville) and the Middle East. The United States insisted that the General Assembly enforce Article 19 of the UN Charter. Article 19 provides that any member that is two years behind in payments "shall have no vote." To avert a showdown, the General Assembly took no formal votes during the 19th session. In August, 1965, the U.S. withdrew its demand for payment of dues, allowing the General Assembly to resume operations. But financing peacekeeping operations remained a UN problem.

Peacekeeping was among the problems facing the General Assembly when its 20th session began in September, 1965. In August, 1965, fighting broke out between India and Pakistan over the disputed territory of Kashmir. In September, the UN arranged a cease-fire and sent representatives to Kashmir to enforce it.

In November, Rhodesia declared independence from Great Britain. The UN condemned the declaration and urged its members to break off economic relations with Rhodesia. It considered Rhodesia's action a threat to world peace and asked Great Britain to settle the problem.   LESTER B. PEARSON

Related Articles in WORLD BOOK include:

BIOGRAPHIES

Outline

Questions

Why are some UN agencies older than the UN itself?
What are some important differences between the United Nations and the League of Nations?
How did the UN get its name?
How is the UN supported financially?
Who gave the money to buy the building site for the UN headquarters?
What are the duties of the Secretary-General?
Which nations are the five permanent members of the Security Council?
What is the purpose of the veto?
How did the UN try to solve the problem of overcoming a veto in the Security Council?
When does the UN General Assembly meet?

UNITED NATIONS CHILDREN'S FUND. See UNITED NATIONS (Aid to Children).

UNITED NATIONS DAY is October 24. It commemorates the date in 1945 that the required number of nations signed the United Nations Charter, officially establishing the UN. In the United States, the President issues a proclamation. He urges all U.S. citizens, communities, government officials, and organizations to observe UN Day with special programs. In Canada, the prime minister issues a special statement, and many communities plan UN Day observances.

UNITED NATIONS EDUCATIONAL, SCIENTIFIC, AND CULTURAL ORGANIZATION. See UNESCO.

UNITED NATIONS RELIEF AND REHABILITATION ADMINISTRATION (UNRRA) was set up in 1943 by 44 nations to relieve the suffering that came as a result of the destruction caused by World War II. UNRRA began to operate on a large scale in 1944, beginning its work in Italy. It accomplished its greatest work in the two years after the end of the war. UNRRA officials shipped livestock to devastated areas, helped revive agriculture, and rebuilt industries. UNRRA distributed food to millions of needy persons. It officially ended its work in 1947. See also REFUGEE.   FIORELLO H. LaGUARDIA

UNITED PENTECOSTAL CHURCH, INC. See PENTECOSTAL CHURCHES.

UNITED PRESS INTERNATIONAL (UPI) is one of the largest independent news agencies in the world. It distributes news, photographs, television news film, and recorded radio news to more than 6,200 clients. Its clients include newspapers, radio and television stations, and news magazines in more than 100 countries. UPI maintains over 200 news and picture bureaus, including 140 in the United States. It employs a staff of more than 10,000 persons, and leases about 500,000 miles of wires. It sends out dispatches in 48 languages.

Subsidiaries include United Features Syndicate, United Press International of Canada, Ltd., and United Press International (U.K.), Ltd., in Great Britain. It operates a television film service, UPI Newsfilm, Inc.

UPI was formed in May, 1958, when United Press and International News Service merged. E. W. Scripps founded the UP in 1907. William Randolph Hearst formed INS in 1909. The UP covered world news, and was the first North American press association to serve newspapers in Europe, South America, and the Far East.   WILLIAM C. PAYETTE

See also INTERNATIONAL NEWS SERVICE.

UNITED SERVICE ORGANIZATIONS (USO) is a federation of six voluntary agencies. Through these agencies, civilians serve the educational, religious, social, spiritual, and welfare needs of members of the armed forces in the United States and overseas.

The USO maintains recreation centers and organized entertainment for servicemen. There are more than 200 United Service Organizations operations in the United States, and 22 more overseas. More than 42,000 volunteers contribute their time to serve men and women in the armed forces. Service men and women pay more than 36 million visits to USO clubs and centers each year. Founded in 1941, the USO has headquarters at 237 E. 52nd St., New York, N.Y. 10022. Critically reviewed by USO

UNITED SOCIETY OF BELIEVERS. See SHAKERS.

UNITED STATES

UNITED STATES OF AMERICA is the fourth largest country in the world, both in area and population. The United States covers the full width of the North American continent, from the Atlantic Ocean to the Pacific Ocean. It also includes Alaska on the edge of the Arctic, and tropical Hawaii far out in the Pacific.

The land of the United States is as varied as it is vast. It ranges from the warm beaches of Florida to the frozen northlands of Alaska, and from the level Midwest prairies to the snow-capped Rocky Mountains. The United States is the land of the spectacular Grand Canyon, the mighty Mississippi River, and thundering Niagara Falls.

This huge and beautiful country is unbelievably rich in resources. The United States has great stretches of some of the most fertile soils on earth. It has plentiful water supplies. And it has a great treasure house of minerals, including coal, copper, iron, natural gas, and oil.

Until about 300 years ago, what is now the United States was largely a wilderness. People in Europe saw in this great, almost empty land a chance to build new and better lives. They came, thousands upon thousands, from many countries. They brought different skills and different ideas. They also brought the ideals of freedom and equality. They established a government designed to protect the liberty of every man. They wrote a Constitution guaranteeing freedom of speech, of religion, of political belief, and of the press.

The great size and wealth of the land has challenged every generation of Americans since the days of the first colonists. Freedom of thought and action has led each succeeding generation to accept the challenge and make the country advance. When mountains blocked the way, Americans built their roads and railroads around them or through them. When floods threatened their farms and cities, Americans built dams and levees to hold back the waters. In areas where rainfall was too light to raise crops, Americans built great irrigation systems. To reach across their vast country, Americans created huge transportation and communication systems.

Expressway Interchange near Downtown Chicago

Alpha Photo Assoc.

D. Hallinan, FPG

Statue of Liberty in New York Harbor

The United States is still changing and expanding. Its great cities are growing both upward and outward. The towering skylines of the cities change frequently as Americans build, tear down, and rebuild. The nation's busy factories turn out the greatest abundance of goods in the world. The farms of the United States are the most productive on earth.

The arts and sciences have also flourished in this land of enormous wealth. The American way of life inspired the music of George Gershwin, the literature of Mark Twain and Sinclair Lewis, and the architecture of Frank Lloyd Wright. The United States produced atomic energy, the telephone, the hot dog, and Salk vaccine.

The United States has given its people the highest standard of living in the world. But more important, it has tried to give every American freedom and equality of opportunity. The United States is often called the *U.S.*, *U.S.A.*, or *America*.

This article tells of the land and its resources, and of the people and their accomplishments. For detailed discussions of U.S. government and history, see UNITED STATES, GOVERNMENT OF; and UNITED STATES, HISTORY OF.

John Gunther, the contributor of this article, is the author of Inside U.S.A. *The article was critically reviewed by Jewell A. Phelps, Chairman of the Department of Geography at George Peabody College.*

Fertile Fields in California's Imperial Valley
Carlos Elmer, Shostal

FACTS IN BRIEF

Capital: Washington, D.C.

Form of Government: Republic. *Chief of State—* President, elected to a four-year term. *Congress—*Senate, 100 members, 2 from each state, elected to six-year terms; House of Representatives, 435 members, varying number from each state according to population, elected to two-year terms.

Area: 3,675,633 square miles, including 60,422 square miles covered by the U.S. portion of the Great Lakes. *Greatest Distances Excluding Alaska and Hawaii:* (east-west) 2,807 miles; (north-south) 1,598 miles. *Greatest Distances in Alaska:* (north-south) about 1,200 miles; (east-west) about 2,200 miles. *Greatest Distance in Hawaii:* (northwest-southwest) about 1,610 miles. *Extreme Points in the United States Excluding Alaska and Hawaii:* northernmost, Lake of the Woods, Minn.; southernmost, Key West, Fla.; easternmost, West Quoddy Head, Me.; westernmost, Cape Alava, Wash. *Extreme Points in the United States Including Alaska and Hawaii:* northernmost, Point Barrow, Alaska; southernmost, Ka Lae, Hawaii; easternmost, West Quoddy Head, Me.; westernmost, Cape Wrangell, Attu Island, Alaska. *Coastline:* 4,993 miles, excluding Alaska and Hawaii; 12,383 miles, including Alaska and Hawaii.

Elevation: *Highest*, Mount McKinley in Alaska, 20,320 feet above sea level. *Lowest*, Death Valley in California, 282 feet below sea level.

Physical Features: *Longest River*, Mississippi (2,348 miles). *Largest Lake Within the United States*, Michigan (22,400 square miles). *Largest Island*, island of Hawaii (4,021 square miles).

Population: *1960 census—*179,323,175; rank among countries of the world, 4th; distribution, 70 per cent urban, 30 per cent rural. *1967 estimate—*199,765,000; density, 54 persons to the square mile. *1972 estimate—*216,848,000.

Chief Products: *Agriculture*, cattle and calves, corn, cotton, dairy products, feed crops, hogs, poultry and eggs, soybeans, tobacco, wheat. *Manufacturing*, chemicals and related products; clothing; clay, glass, and stone products; food and related products; machinery; metals and metal products; paper and related products; printed matter; textiles; transportation equipment. *Mining*, coal, copper, iron ore, natural gas, petroleum, sand and gravel, stone.

Flag: Adopted June 14, 1777.

Motto: *In God We Trust*, adopted July 30, 1956.

National Anthem: "The Star-Spangled Banner," adopted March 3, 1931.

Bird: Bald Eagle, adopted June 20, 1782.

UNITED STATES

HIGHWAYS

Expressways
Major Roads

⊛ Nat'l. Capitals
★ State Capitals
○ Cities and Towns
-·- State Bdy.

66 U.S. ① Provincial
95 Nat. Interstate
Trans Canada Hys.

1 inch = 220 Statute Miles

Miles 0 25 50   100   150   200

Lambert Conformal Conic Projection

The United States mainland, excluding Alaska, may be divided into seven main geographic regions. The following geographic groupings of states are based on the states' similarities in climate, physical features, economy, people, traditions, and history. Alaska and Hawaii are separate geographic regions. WORLD BOOK has separate articles on each of the 50 states and on the regions listed below.

Middle Atlantic States

New Jersey	New York	Pennsylvania

Midwestern States

Illinois	Kansas	Missouri	Ohio
Indiana	Michigan	Nebraska	South Dakota
Iowa	Minnesota	North Dakota	Wisconsin

New England

Connecticut	Massachusetts	Rhode Island
Maine	New Hampshire	Vermont

Pacific Coast States

California	Oregon	Washington

Rocky Mountain States

Colorado	Montana	Utah
Idaho	Nevada	Wyoming

Southern States

Alabama	Kentucky	South Carolina
Arkansas	Louisiana	Tennessee
Delaware	Maryland	Virginia
Florida	Mississippi	West Virginia
Georgia	North Carolina	

Southwestern States

*Arizona	*New Mexico	Oklahoma	Texas

* Arizona and New Mexico also are often grouped with the Rocky Mountain States.

FACTS IN BRIEF ABOUT

State	Capital	Popular Name	Area (Sq. Mi.)	Rank in Area	Population	Rank in Pop.	Persons per Sq. Mi.
Alabama	Montgomery	Yellowhammer State	51,609	29	3,266,740	19	63
Alaska	Juneau	Last Frontier	586,400	1	226,167	50	0.4
Arizona	Phoenix	Grand Canyon State	113,909	6	1,302,161	35	11
Arkansas	Little Rock	Land of Opportunity	53,104	27	1,786,272	31	34
California	Sacramento	Golden State	158,693	3	15,717,204	2	99
Colorado	Denver	Centennial State	104,247	8	1,753,947	33	17
Connecticut	Hartford	Constitution State	5,009	48	2,535,234	25	506
Delaware	Dover	First State	2,057	49	446,292	46	217
Florida	Tallahassee	Sunshine State	58,560	22	4,951,560	10	85
Georgia	Atlanta	Empire State of the South	58,876	21	3,943,116	16	67
Hawaii	Honolulu	Aloha State	6,424	47	632,772	43	99
Idaho	Boise	Gem State	83,557	13	667,191	42	8
Illinois	Springfield	Land of Lincoln	56,400	24	10,081,158	4	179
Indiana	Indianapolis	Hoosier State	36,291	38	4,662,498	11	128
Iowa	Des Moines	Hawkeye State	56,290	25	2,757,537	24	49
Kansas	Topeka	Sunflower State	82,264	14	2,178,611	28	26
Kentucky	Frankfort	Bluegrass State	40,395	37	3,038,156	22	75
Louisiana	Baton Rouge	Pelican State	48,523	31	3,257,022	20	67
Maine	Augusta	Pine Tree State	33,215	39	969,265	36	29
Maryland	Annapolis	Old Line State	10,577	42	3,100,689	21	293

Name	Acquired	Status
American Samoa	1900	Organized unincorporated territory
Canal Zone	1903	U.S. jurisdiction; Panama sovereignty
Canton and Enderbury Islands	1939	Condominium with Great Britain
Corn Islands	1914	Leased from Nicaragua
Guam	1898	Organized unincorporated territory
Howland, Baker, and Jarvis Islands	1857-58	Unincorporated territory
Johnston Island and Sand Island	1858	Unincorporated territory
Kingman Reef	1922	Unincorporated territory
Midway Islands	1867	Unincorporated territory
Palmyra Island	1898	Unincorporated territory
Puerto Rico	1898	Commonwealth
Trust Territory of the Pacific Islands	1947	UN trust territory (U.S. administration)
Virgin Islands of the United States	1917	Organized unincorporated territory
Wake Island	1898	Unincorporated territory

Geographic Regions of the United States

THE STATES OF THE UNION

State Abbreviation	State Bird	State Flower	State Tree	State Song	Admitted to the Union	Order of Admission	Members of Congress Senate	House
Ala.	Yellow-hammer	Camellia	Southern pine (Longleaf pine)	"Alabama"	1819	22	2	8
Alaska	Willow ptarmigan	Forget-me-not	Sitka spruce	"Alaska's Flag"	1959	49	2	1
Ariz.	Cactus wren	Saguaro (Giant cactus)	Paloverde	"Arizona"	1912	48	2	3
Ark.	Mockingbird	Apple blossom	Pine	"Arkansas"	1836	25	2	4
Calif.	California valley quail	Golden poppy	California redwood	"I Love You, California"	1850	31	2	38
Colo.	Lark bunting	Rocky Mountain columbine	Blue spruce	"Where the Columbines Grow"	1876	38	2	4
Conn.	Robin	Mountain laurel	White oak	None	1788	5	2	6
Del.	Blue hen chicken	Peach blossom	American holly	"Our Delaware"	1787	1	2	1
Fla.	Mockingbird	Orange blossom	Cabbage (Sabal) palm	"Swanee River"	1845	27	2	12
Ga.	Brown thrasher	Cherokee rose	Live oak	"Georgia"	1788	4	2	10
Hawaii	Nene (Hawaiian Goose)	Hibiscus	Kukui	"Hawaii Ponoi"* (Hawaii's Own)	1959	50	2	2
Ida.	Mountain bluebird	Syringa (Mock orange)	Western White pine	"Here We Have Idaho"	1890	43	2	2
Ill.	Cardinal	Violet	Oak	"Illinois"	1818	21	2	24
Ind.	Cardinal	Peony	Tulip tree, or yellow poplar	"On the Banks of the Wabash"	1816	19	2	11
Ia.	Eastern goldfinch	Wild rose	Oak	"The Song of Iowa"	1846	29	2	7
Kans. or Kan.	Western meadow lark	Sunflower	Cottonwood	"Home on the Range"	1861	34	2	5
Ky. or Ken.	Kentucky Cardinal	Goldenrod	Tulip poplar*	"My Old Kentucky Home"	1792	15	2	7
La.	Brown pelican*	Magnolia	Bald cypress	"Song of Louisiana"	1812	18	2	8
Me.	Chickadee	White pine cone and tassel	White pine	"State of Maine Song"	1820	23	2	2
Md.	Baltimore oriole	Black-eyed Susan	White oak	"Maryland, My Maryland"	1788	7	2	8

* Unofficial

State	Capital	Popular Name	Area. (Sq Mi.)	Rank in Area	Population	Rank in Pop.	Persons per Sq. Mi.
Massachusetts	Boston	Bay State	8,257	45	5,148,578	9	624
Michigan	Lansing	Wolverine State	58,216	23	7,823,194	7	134
Minnesota	St. Paul	Gopher State	84,068	12	3,413,864	18	41
Mississippi	Jackson	Magnolia State	47,716	32	2,178,141	29	46
Missouri	Jefferson City	Show Me State	69,686	19	4,319,813	13	62
Montana	Helena	Treasure State	147,138	4	674,767	41	4
Nebraska	Lincoln	Cornhusker State	77,227	15	1,411,330	34	18
Nevada	Carson City	Silver State	110,540	7	285,278	49	3
New Hampshire	Concord	Granite State	9,304	44	606,921	45	65
New Jersey	Trenton	Garden State	7,836	46	6,066,782	8	774
New Mexico	Santa Fe	Land of Enchantment	121,666	5	951,023	37	8
New York	Albany	Empire State	49,576	30	16,782,304	1	339
North Carolina	Raleigh	Tar Heel State	52,712	28	4,556,155	12	86
North Dakota	Bismarck	Flickertail State	70,665	17	632,446	44	9
Ohio	Columbus	Buckeye State	41,222	35	9,706,397	5	235
Oklahoma	Oklahoma City	Sooner State	69,919	18	2,328,284	27	34
Oregon	Salem	Beaver State	96,981	10	1,768,687	32	18
Pennsylvania	Harrisburg	Keystone State	45,333	33	11,319,366	3	250
Rhode Island	Providence	Little Rhody	1,214	50	859,488	39	708
South Carolina	Columbia	Palmetto State	31,055	40	2,382,594	26	77
South Dakota	Pierre	Sunshine State	77,047	16	680,514	40	8
Tennessee	Nashville	Volunteer State	42,244	34	3,567,089	17	84
Texas	Austin	Lone Star State	267,339	2	9,579,677	6	36
Utah	Salt Lake City	Beehive State	84,916	11	890,627	38	10
Vermont	Montpelier	Green Mountain State	9,609	43	389,881	47	41
Virginia	Richmond	Old Dominion	40,815	36	3,966,949	14	97
Washington	Olympia	Evergreen State	68,192	20	2,853,214	23	42
West Virginia	Charleston	Mountain State	24,181	41	1,860,421	30	76
Wisconsin	Madison	Badger State	56,154	26	3,951,777	15	70
Wyoming	Cheyenne	Equality State	97,914	9	330,066	48	3

THE STATES OF THE UNION

State Abbreviation	State Bird	State Flower	State Tree	State Song	Admitted to the Union	Order of Admission	Members of Congress Senate	House
Mass.	Chickadee	Arbutus (Mayflower)	American elm	"Hail Massa- chusetts"*	1788	6	2	12
Mich.	Robin	Apple blossom	White pine	"Michigan, My Michigan"*	1837	26	2	19
Minn.	Common loon	Pink and white lady's-slipper	Norway, or red, pine	"Hail! Minnesota"	1858	32	2	8
Miss.	Mockingbird	Magnolia	Magnolia	"Go, Mis- sis- sip- pi"	1817	20	2	5
Mo.	Bluebird	Hawthorn	Flowering dogwood	"Missouri Waltz"	1821	24	2	10
Mont.	Western meadow lark	Bitterroot	Ponderosa pine	"Montana"	1889	41	2	2
Nebr. or Neb.	Western meadow lark	Goldenrod	American elm	None	1867	37	2	3
Nev.	Mountain bluebird*	Sagebrush*	Single-leaf piñon	"Home Means Nevada"	1864	36	2	1
N.H.	Purple finch	Purple lilac	White birch	"Old New Hamp- shire"	1788	9	2	2
N.J.	Eastern gold- finch	Violet	Red oak	None	1787	3	2	15
N.Mex. or N.M.	Road runner	Yucca	Piñon, or nut pine	"O, Fair New Mexico"	1912	47	2	2
N.Y.	Bluebird*	Rose	Sugar maple	None	1788	11	2	41
N.C.	Cardinal	Flowering dogwood	Pine	"The Old North State"	1789	12	2	11
N.Dak. or N.D.	Western meadow lark	Wild prairie rose	American elm	"North Dakota Hymn"	1889	39	2	2
O.	Cardinal	Scarlet carnation	Buckeye	None	1803	17	2	24
Okla.	Scissor-tailed flycatcher	Mistletoe	Redbud	"Oklahoma!"	1907	46	2	6
Ore. or Oreg.	Western meadow lark	Oregon grape	Douglas fir	"Oregon, My Oregon"	1859	33	2	4
Pa. or Penn.	Ruffed grouse	Mountain laurel	Hemlock	None	1787	2	2	27
R.I.	Rhode Island Red chicken	Violet*	Maple*	"Rhode Island"	1790	13	2	2
S.C.	Carolina wren	Carolina jessamine	Palmetto	"Carolina"	1788	8	2	6
S.Dak. or S.D.	Ring-necked pheasant	American pasqueflower	Black Hills spruce	"Hail, South Dakota"	1889	40	2	2
Tenn.	Mockingbird	Iris	Tulip poplar	"The Tennessee Waltz"	1796	16	2	9
Tex.	Mockingbird	Bluebonnet	Pecan	"Texas, Our Texas"	1845	28	2	23
Ut.	Sea gull	Sego lily	Blue spruce	"Utah, We Love Thee"	1896	45	2	2
Vt.	Hermit thrush	Red clover	Sugar maple	"Hail, Vermont"	1791	14	2	1
Va.	Cardinal	Flowering dogwood	None	"Carry Me Back to Old Virginia"	1788	10	2	10
Wash.	Willow goldfinch	Coast rhodo- dendron	Western hemlock	"Washington, My Home"	1889	42	2	7
W.Va.	Cardinal	Rhododendron	Sugar maple	"The West Virginia Hills"; "This Is My West Virginia"; "West Virginia, My Home Sweet Home"	1863	35	2	5
Wis.	Robin	Violet	Sugar maple	"On, Wisconsin!"	1848	30	2	10
Wyo.	Meadow lark	Indian paint- brush	Cottonwood	"Wyoming"	1890	44	2	1

*Unofficial

49

Ray Atkeson, Devaney from Publix

Hawaiian Fishermen pull in a net of fish. The American people are made up of many racial and national groups.

Americans on the Move. Every year, millions of Americans move, often to different cities and areas of the country.

Aero Mayflower Transit Co.

Population and Ancestry. The 1960 United States census reported that the nation had 179,323,175 persons. The population had increased 18½ per cent over the 1950 figure, 151,325,798 (including Alaska and Hawaii). The U.S. population reached an estimated 196,759,000 by 1966. Only three other countries have larger populations. They are, in order of size, China, India, and Russia.

Every American is an immigrant or a descendant of an immigrant. The Indians, Eskimos, and Hawaiians were the first peoples in what is now the United States. But even their ancestors came from other lands thousands of years ago. Most of the settlers in early colonial America came from England. By the time of the Revolutionary War, large numbers of settlers had arrived from other countries. There were Germans in Pennsylvania, Dutch in New York, French in Louisiana, and Spaniards in Florida and California. There also were Negro slaves, brought from Africa to work on southern plantations. Between 1840 and 1860 about 4,400,000 immigrants came to America. They were drawn by the nation's growing cities and industries, its rich, unsettled land in the West, and its guarantees of individual freedom and opportunities for wealth. Immigrants continued to pour in until the early 1900's. Then, the United States passed laws that limited the number of immigrants. World War II left millions of Europeans homeless. The United States again opened its doors, and received about 2,460,000 more immigrants between 1946 and 1957.

But most Americans now living were born in the United States. Only about 5 of every 100 Americans were born in other countries. About 18 of every 100 are

POPULATION

This map shows the *population density* of the United States and how it varies in different parts of the country. Population density means the average number of persons who live on each square mile. This map also shows how the center of population has moved westward from 1790 to 1960.

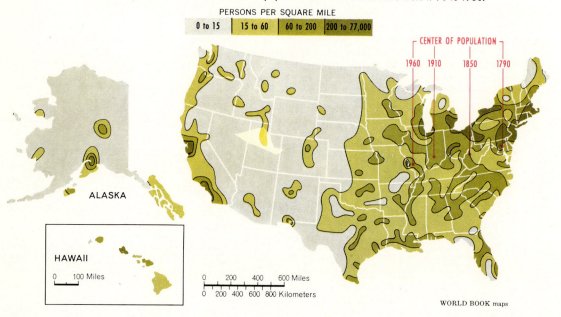

PERSONS PER SQUARE MILE

| 0 to 15 | 15 to 60 | 60 to 200 | 200 to 77,000 |

CENTER OF POPULATION

1960 1910 1850 1790

ALASKA

HAWAII
0   100 Miles

0   200   400   600 Miles
0   200 400 600 800 Kilometers

WORLD BOOK maps

immigrants or children of immigrants. The largest groups born in other countries include, in order of size, Italians, Germans, Poles, Russians, Mexicans, and English and Welsh. See IMMIGRATION AND EMIGRATION.

The United States has long been known as a great *melting pot*. Its people are of all races and have come from many countries. But they have developed a common culture. There are many more similarities than differences among the people of the United States. Most immigrants soon lose the ways of their native land. They quickly learn the language of America, thanks to the public school system. They adopt the nation's customs, follow its traditions, and take part in its politics.

Cities. About 70 of every 100 Americans live in cities. More than 60 of every 100 live in metropolitan areas. The United States has over 200 Standard Metropolitan Statistical Areas as defined by the U.S. Bureau of the Budget (see METROPOLITAN AREA). The three largest metropolitan areas, according to the 1960 census, are the New York City area, with 10,694,633 persons; the Chicago area, with 6,220,913 persons; and the Los Angeles-Long Beach area, with 6,038,771 persons.

New York City, with 7,781,984 persons, is the largest city in the United States. It ranks fourth in the world, after Tokyo, Shanghai, and London. The United States has four other cities with more than a million persons. They are, in order of size, Chicago, Los Angeles, Philadelphia, and Detroit. See the article CITY and the articles on the cities themselves, such as NEW YORK CITY; CHICAGO; and LOS ANGELES.

Farms. In 1850, about 85 of every 100 Americans lived on farms or in farm communities. By 1900, about

FPG

Football Games attract millions of fans each year. The exciting action makes football a leading spectator sport.

Relaxing Under a Shade Tree and swapping stories of the "good old days" is a favorite pastime of America's senior citizens.

WORLD BOOK photo by W. R. Wilson

George Hunter, FPG

Rows of New Houses, such as these near Levittown, Pa., mark the suburban areas that surround many large American cities. About 70 of every 100 Americans live in or near cities.

UNITED STATES

60 of every 100 lived in rural areas. Today, only about 30 per cent of the population is rural—and the percentage continues to fall.

The increasing use of machinery and scientific farming methods has reduced the number of workers needed on farms. Machines and modern methods have also made it possible for farmers to operate larger and larger farms, even with fewer workers. American farms increased in size from an average of 150 acres in 1900 to 325 acres in the 1960's.

The American farmer of today leads a vastly different life from that of his grandfather. Machines have eliminated much backbreaking work. The farmer uses machines to help him plow, plant his seeds, harvest his crops, and deliver his products to market. Some farms have conveyor systems so that the farmer no longer has to shovel feed to his animals. Milking machines make his morning and evening chores easier. In the home, the farmer's wife may have all the comforts and conveniences of a city wife. The automobile, telephone, radio, and television have brought farm families into close contact with the rest of the world. See FARM AND FARMING; RANCHING.

Family Life. The early colonists and pioneers believed strongly in freedom and equality. These ideals were well suited to the new country. There was plenty of room for differences in religion and politics. There was also much work to be done to settle and develop the land. On the frontier, one man's ax was as good as another's, regardless of his beliefs. In various ways, these ideals were written into the laws of the United States.

Families in the United States have an average of 3.65 members. The American ideals of freedom and equality extend into the family. American women are noted for their independence. They participate equally with men in many activities outside the home. About one of every three married women has a job outside the home. Even children share in this equality, and take part in family activities, discussions, and planning.

Grant Heilman

A Town Meeting in Vermont gives all the citizens a chance to take an active, personal part in their local government. Democratic government is the basis of American freedom.

The products of American industry also influence family life. Household appliances make housework easy. Frozen, canned, and concentrated foods make it simple to prepare meals. Such advances help explain how so many American wives find time for so many activities outside the home. Women are active in political parties, community affairs, and charitable and other organizations.

Medical advances through the years have sharply increased the life expectancy of Americans. A baby born in 1900 could be expected to live only to the age of 47. A baby born today can be expected to live to 70. This increase in life expectancy has also increased the percentage of older people in the population. In 1880, only 3 of every 100 Americans were 65 or older. By the 1960's, the number had increased to more than 9 of every 100.

Americans are a people on the move. Every year, about one of every five Americans changes his place of residence. He may simply move from a small house to a larger one. He may be transferred to another town by the company for which he works. Or, like the pioneers before him, he may seek a new life and new opportunities in a different section of the United States.

THE POPULATION OF THE UNITED STATES—1790 to 1960

America's population has risen steadily since the first census. The greatest percentage growth took place in the early years, with increases of more than a third in a 10-year period. The largest total increase took place between 1950 and 1960, when almost 28,000,000 persons were added to the population.

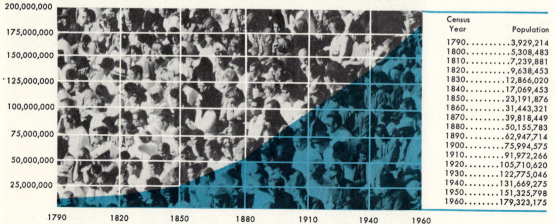

Census Year	Population
1790	3,929,214
1800	5,308,483
1810	7,239,881
1820	9,638,453
1830	12,866,020
1840	17,069,453
1850	23,191,876
1860	31,443,321
1870	39,818,449
1880	50,155,783
1890	62,947,714
1900	75,994,575
1910	91,972,266
1920	105,710,620
1930	122,775,046
1940	131,669,275
1950	151,325,798
1960	179,323,175

Maryland Dept. of Economic Development

A Picnic on the Beach appeals to millions of Americans who enjoy eating outdoors and being near the water. After the meal, swimming and boating are favorite forms of recreation.

Religion. The United States has no laws requiring any person to belong to any religious group. Complete freedom of worship is guaranteed by Amendment 1 to the United States Constitution. Almost two-thirds of the population belong to an organized religious group. About 95 of every 100 members of religious groups are Christians, and almost 5 are Jews. A relatively small number of Americans belong to the Islamic faith or to various Eastern religions, such as Buddhism. About two-thirds of the Christians are Protestants. The largest Protestant groups are the Baptists, Lutherans, and Methodists. The Roman Catholic Church has more members than any single Protestant group. For the memberships of the major religious bodies in the United States, see RELIGION (table).

Recreation. The productivity of America's economic system has earned the people more and more leisure time. In 1900, factory workers spent an average of about 60 hours a week on their jobs, and earned about $13. Today, they spend about 40 hours a week at work, and earn almost $100. To help Americans use their spare time, cities and towns have playgrounds, parks, and swimming pools. The federal and state governments operate large parks and other recreation areas.

Americans spend much of their free time at home. Television has brought motion pictures, plays, and major league baseball into the living room. The high-fidelity stereophonic phonograph has made the home a concert hall. Americans spend many leisure hours reading books and magazines. Entertaining friends at home is another important part of the American way of life. One result of the increase in leisure time is the *do-it-yourselfer*. The head of the household or other members of the family use part of their spare time to make their own household repairs and to do their own redecorating and remodeling.

Millions of Americans are active in bowling, baseball, golf, tennis, and other sports. Many more enjoy watching professional and amateur teams compete in sports contests. Every year, millions of Americans enroll in various kinds of study courses to broaden their education and experience. Others take up such hobbies as music, photography, stamp collecting, or painting. Many Americans spend much of their leisure time taking part in local government activities or in working with community-service groups.

American families eagerly look forward to their annual vacation. During the 1920's, employers began to accept the idea of giving office employees a paid vacation every year. Today, almost all workers—office and factory—receive a two-week vacation annually. Some employees receive three weeks or more. Every summer, millions of Americans pack their suitcases and head for their favorite recreation areas. They travel in comfortable automobiles over paved highways to state and national parks, to summer resorts, or to the large cities. Air travel has made it easier for many Americans to vacation in other countries. Great resort areas in Arizona, California, Florida, Hawaii, and elsewhere attract persons from the North seeking a few days or a few weeks of sunshine in midwinter. The tourist industry plays an important part in the nation's economic life. See HOBBY; RECREATION.

High-Rise Apartments, such as these in Peter Cooper Village in New York City, are the homes of large numbers of city dwellers. Most tall apartment buildings stand near the downtown areas of large cities. Many are part of vast urban renewal projects to rebuild America's cities.

Devaney from Publix

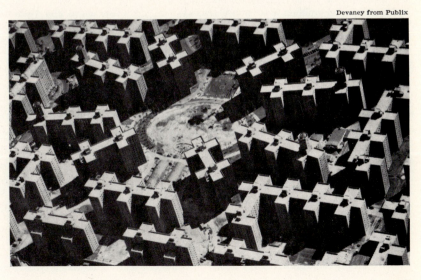

American Schools provide students with instruction in basic skills. Children are also encouraged to develop their own natural interests and abilities. Modern classrooms, such as this one, permit small groups of children to work on special projects.

UNITED STATES /*Education*

Schools. Americans believe that every person should have the opportunity to receive the best possible education to develop his talents and abilities. The ideal of free public schooling for every child began to win increasing support during the early 1800's. More and more educators and statesmen pointed out that America's prosperity and strength depended on widespread systems of public schools. Between 1830 and 1850, such noted educators as Horace Mann and Henry Barnard worked for public control and support of elementary and high schools. In 1852, Massachusetts passed the first law requiring children to attend school.

After the Civil War ended in 1865, many states established public elementary and high schools. There was also a remarkable growth in state universities and agricultural and technical colleges. By the early 1900's, the ideal of a high-school education for everyone was broadly accepted in the United States. The number of students who completed high school and qualified for college increased enormously. A tremendous growth in college and university enrollments followed. See EDUCATION, HISTORY OF.

Today, about 53 million Americans attend some kind of school, college, or university. Another 50 million Americans are enrolled in adult education courses. More than 9 of every 10 children in the United States receive at least an eighth-grade education. About 6 of every 10 are graduated from high school. Almost 2 of every 10 receive a degree from a four-year college or university. This broad program of education in the United States has made Americans among the most schooled people in the world. Only about 2 persons of

every 100 in the United States cannot read or write.

Each state is responsible for its own system of public education. Almost all the states require children to attend school. In most states, they must do so until the age of 16. The states give many educational responsibilities to local boards of education. Most of these boards are elected by the voters in local school districts. Most public schools in the United States are financed and controlled locally. But the federal and state governments are playing an increasing role in financing local school systems.

The states also authorize and accredit private and *parochial* (church-supported) schools that meet certain academic standards. At the elementary level, about 15 of every 100 students attend a private or parochial school. At the high-school level, about 12 of every 100 go to a private or parochial school. About 43 of every 100 college students attend private or parochial schools. See EDUCATION.

Libraries. Public libraries began in the United States. The movement for free public libraries in America began about the same time as the movement for free public schools. By the mid-1800's, an increasing number of cities and towns were supporting libraries as an accepted function of local government. Today, America has over 8,000 public library systems, more than 2,000 university and college libraries, and about 50,000 high-school and elementary-school libraries.

The Library of Congress is the largest library in the United States. This library, founded in 1800, has about 13 million books and pamphlets. More than 30 university libraries in the United States have over 1 million

A College Education helps young Americans enjoy richer, more meaningful lives. Of every 10 children in the United States, 2 will be graduated from college.

Science Museums feature such exhibits as the Möbius Band, *above,* a geometric figure.

volumes each. The largest is that of Harvard University, with more than 7 million volumes.

There are several thousand special libraries in the United States. These libraries limit their collections to certain fields. Outstanding ones include the John Crerar Library of scientific and technical information in Chicago, and the National Library of Medicine in Bethesda, Md. American libraries have pioneered in many fields of service. Many provide audio-visual aids, music rooms, and art rooms. See LIBRARY.

Museums. There are about 5,000 museums in the United States. They include general museums, and special museums of art, history, natural history, and applied science. The first museum in the country, the Charleston Museum, was established by the Charleston (S.C.) Library Society in 1773. It still has a fine collection of items dealing with the history of South Carolina. The nation's oldest art museum is the Pennsylvania Academy of the Fine Arts in Philadelphia, founded in 1805.

Other famous museums include the American Museum of Natural History in New York City; the Art Institute of Chicago; the Field Museum of Natural History in Chicago; the Guggenheim Museum in New York City; the Metropolitan Museum of Art in New York City; the Museum of Modern Art in New York City; the Museum of Science and Industry in Chicago; the National Gallery of Art in Washington, D.C.; the Peabody Museum of Natural History at Yale University in New Haven, Conn.; the Smithsonian Institution in Washington, D.C.; and the William Rockhill Nelson Gallery of Art in Kansas City, Mo. See MUSEUM.

Scientific Research. America's emphasis on the importance of education for everyone has encouraged the growth of scientific research. More Nobel prize-winning scientists have come from the United States than from any other country. Since 1900, Americans have received about 90 Nobel prizes, more than three-fourths of them in the field of science. The great discoveries and achievements credited to Americans by the Nobel awards include the measurement of the speed of light, the effect of X rays on atoms, the function of chromosomes in heredity, and the production of the world's first maser. See NOBEL PRIZES.

In 1957, the Space Age began when Russia launched the first man-made earth satellite. Competition among countries in the exploration of outer space suddenly became intense, especially between the United States and Russia. The opening of the Space Age also marked the beginning of intensified scientific research. In 1957, the U.S. government spent about $4,462,000,000 for research and development in the sciences. In 1964, it spent almost $15 billion. During the late 1950's and the early 1960's, American industry also increased its research programs to produce new and better products and processes.

The tremendous expansion of scientific activity created a new challenge for U.S. colleges and universities, which train scientists and engineers. In addition, college laboratories conduct much of the research financed by government and industry. The emphasis on science has been reflected in the high schools and in some elementary schools, which have broadened their science courses.

THE ARTS IN THE UNITED STATES

Art and Architecture

The individual freedom that marks the American way of life has helped the arts flourish in the United States. The early settlers brought European arts to America, and many of these arts soon took on American features. In architecture, for example, such styles as New England, Dutch Colonial, and Southern Colonial were alterations of European styles, and were created to fit American materials and needs. American sculptors and painters followed European trends for a longer time. Today, the United States is a major influence in world art and architecture. Most American artists have a keen interest in developing new styles, new ways of expressing themselves, and even new forms of art.

Beinecke Rare Book and Manuscript Library at Yale University

American Painting Before 1913 tended to be realistic. *Mrs. Elizabeth Freake* and *Poestenkill*, with their lack of shading and great detail, are fine examples of early primitive art. Many painters of the 1800's, such as James Whistler, were influenced by European styles. Others, including Thomas Eakins, developed individual styles. In the early 1900's, artists began painting everyday life. Charles Marion Russell, for example, painted the West. John Sloan portrayed city life.

Architecture took on distinctly American features early in the country's history. Louis Sullivan helped create the skyscraper in the late 1800's. The imagination of Frank Lloyd Wright influenced architects throughout the world. Today, most American architects use steel, glass, and concrete to create buildings that are striking in their boldness and simplicity.

Mrs. Elizabeth Freake and Baby Mary (artist unknown)

Poestenkill, New York by Joseph H. Hidley

Bronc to Breakfast by Charles Marion Russell

South Beach Bathers by John Sloan

Deacon Samuel Chapin by Augustus Saint-Gaudens

Franklin D. Roosevelt by Jo Davidson

Soldier by Richard Stankiewicz

American Sculpture largely imitated European styles and tastes until the 1900's. Augustus Saint-Gaudens was one of the few American sculptors of the 1800's who showed true imagination in his powerful public monuments. Today, American sculpture is chiefly a personal expression. It takes many forms, and uses a wide variety of materials. For example, Jo Davidson is noted for his lifelike bronze portraits of famous persons. Richard Stankiewicz welds sculptures out of metal to create startling abstract works.

Armory Show of 1913

Premiere by Stuart Davis

Below: Sculpture—*Henry's Piece* by George Segal; Paintings—(ceiling) *Doorstop* by James Rosenquist, (wall) *Great American Nude No. 30* by Tom Wesselman

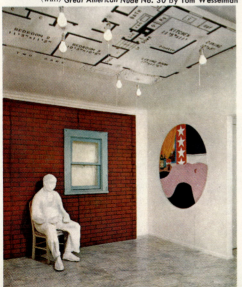

Painting Since 1913. In 1913, an exhibition of modern art was held in an armory in New York City. The Armory Show revolutionized American art. A group of realist painters organized the show to protest against the conservative art galleries that refused to exhibit their pictures. The show also exhibited European art works. These abstract works attracted the most attention. The public found modern European art laughable or shocking. But American artists found it inspiring, and many of them adopted modern European styles. Some American artists of the 1930's, such as Grant Wood, were *regionalists*—painters who portrayed their own states. In the 1940's, some artists, such as Edward Hopper, turned out strikingly realistic American paintings. But by the 1950's, abstract art was firmly established. Today, American painters continually try new styles. In the 1950's, for example, *pop* (popular) art, which looks like posters, or is based on such things as comic strips, first appeared. During the 1960's, *op* art—paintings that are optical illusions—attracted attention.

CREDITS (left to right): *Top Row*—Courtesy Skidmore, Owings & Merrill, and Yale University, photo by Ezra Stoller; Parks Department, City of Springfield, Mass.; Franklin D. Roosevelt Library; William Heller, Inc., New York. *Middle Row*—Worcester Art Museum, gift of Mr. and Mrs. Albert W. Rice; The Metropolitan Museum of Art, New York, gift of Edgar William and Bernice Chrysler Garbisch, 1963; Courtesy The Museum of Modern Art, New York; Los Angeles County Museum of Art. *Bottom Row*—Montana Historical Society; Collection Walker Art Center, Minneapolis; Courtesy of Mr. and Mrs. Robert C. Scull, New York, WORLD BOOK photo by Robert Crandall.

THE ARTS IN THE UNITED STATES

The Performing Arts and Literature

The United States has made important contributions to the performing arts and to literature. Jazz, a new form of music, was created in the United States, and Americans developed the musical comedy into a major art. Americans also pioneered in making motion pictures an art form, especially during the era of silent films. American literature has been translated into almost every language. Early in the country's history, America produced outstanding writers. James Fenimore Cooper, Nathaniel Hawthorne, and Washington Irving described a young and growing America. Later, Herman Melville wrote of the sea and problems of morality. Mark Twain captured the flavor and salty humor of life on the Mississippi River. Six Americans have won Nobel prizes for literature. They are the playwright Eugene O'Neill and the novelists Pearl Buck, William Faulkner, Ernest Hemingway, Sinclair Lewis, and John Steinbeck.

Charlie Chaplin—Culver

Motion Pictures are an American contribution to the arts. The first commercial showing of motion pictures in the United States took place in 1896. Since then, the movies have become a major art form, and provide entertainment for millions of persons throughout the world. Movie actors have become international celebrities since the days of silent motion pictures. One of the first and greatest movie stars was Charlie Chaplin.

Ted Shawn and Ruth St. Denis—John Lindquist

New York City Ballet—Martha Swope

The Dance in the United States reflects Americans' constant desire for change, and their love for new and different things. Such noted dancers as Ted Shawn and Ruth St. Denis helped create the modern dance by bringing new life and new forms to the traditional dance. Americans also brought a fresh approach to classical ballet by stressing natural steps and moves.

Van Cliburn—Jerry Miller, RCA Victor

Leonard Bernstein—Columbia Records

Concert Music. In the early 1900's, American composers began to develop an American musical style. They soon won world acclaim. Conductor-composer Leonard Bernstein and pianist Van Cliburn symbolize the youth and creativity found in U.S. concert music today.

Symphony Hall at Los Angeles Music Center—Welton Becket and Assoc.

Alley Theatre, Houston—WORLD BOOK photo, Bert Brandt

Theater in America means New York City's Broadway to many persons. But professional companies, such as Houston's Alley Theatre, and amateur groups exist throughout the country. Leonard Bernstein's *West Side Story*, with its lively dances and haunting songs, symbolizes America's unique contribution to world theater—the musical comedy.

The Ballad of Baby Doe staged by the Central City Opera—Fred M. Mazzulla

American Opera is based largely on the country's literature, legends, and history. Douglas Moore's *Ballad of Baby Doe*, for example, tells of the rise and fall of a Colorado silver king. The first triumphant American opera was George Gershwin's great folk opera *Porgy and Bess*. It opened in New York City in 1935.

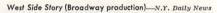

West Side Story (Broadway production)—*N.Y. Daily News*

Porgy and Bess (Broadway production)—*N.Y. Daily News*

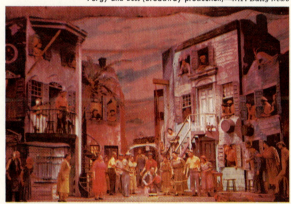

Pete Seeger—Columbia Records

American Folk Music and Jazz—two thoroughly American forms of music—are immensely popular. Noted performers in these fields include folk singer Pete Seeger and jazz musician Dizzy Gillespie.

Dizzy Gillespie—Bert Goldblatt

Die Meistersinger staged by the Metropolitan Opera—Louis Melancon

Grand Opera in the United States is still developing, and has not yet become widely popular. New York City's Metropolitan Opera is the nation's leading opera company. It is noted for its spectacular productions of standard works. Chicago, San Francisco, and several other American cities also have outstanding opera companies.

Specially created for **World Book Encyclopedia** by Rand McNally and World Book editors

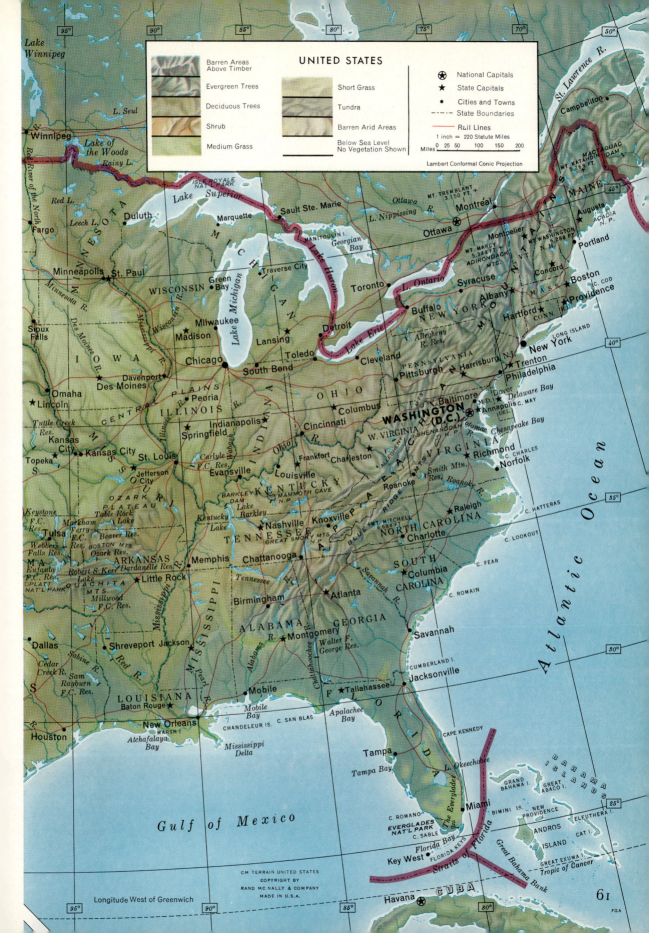

The United States has an area of 3,675,633 square miles, including 60,422 square miles covered by its portion of the Great Lakes. Only Russia, Canada, and China are larger in area.

The U.S. mainland, excluding Alaska, can be divided into seven major land regions. They are: (1) the Appalachian Highlands, (2) the Coastal Lowlands, (3) the Interior Plains, (4) the Ozark-Ouachita Highlands, (5) the Rocky Mountains, (6) the Western Plateaus, Basins, and Ranges, and (7) the Pacific Ranges and Lowlands. For a discussion of the land regions of Alaska and Hawaii, see the articles on these states.

The Appalachian Highlands extend from the northeastern corner of the country southwest into Georgia and Alabama. The region has three main subdivisions, which lie side by side in three long belts. They are, from east to west: (1) the Blue Ridge Mountains area, (2) the Ridge and Valley Region, and (3) the Appalachian Plateau.

The Blue Ridge Mountains Area runs from Pennsylvania south through the Great Smoky and Unaka ranges in the Carolinas, Tennessee, and Georgia. The Green Mountains of Vermont and the White Mountains of New Hampshire form northeastern extensions of the Blue Ridge. The cool summer climate, sparkling streams, and natural beauty of the Blue Ridge Mountains make them a favorite recreation area. Rivers cut through the mountains in steep, forested valleys. These picturesque *water gaps* provide low, level routes for highways and railroads. See BLUE RIDGE MOUNTAINS.

The Ridge and Valley Region. West of the Blue Ridge Mountains, a great series of valleys extends from New York to Tennessee. From north to south, these valleys include the Hudson Valley in New York, the Cumberland Valley in Pennsylvania, the Shenandoah Valley in Virginia, and the Valley of East Tennessee in Tennessee. All these valleys together are known by the general name of the *Great Valley*. The valley bottoms are generally level, except where rivers have cut narrow channels, or where low, rocky hills rise above the valley floors. Prosperous farms and thriving cities, such as Albany and Knoxville, lie in the valleys.

The Appalachian Plateau rises west of the Ridge and Valley Region. This plateau has various local names. It is called the Allegheny Plateau in Pennsylvania, the Kanawha Plateau in West Virginia, and the Cumberland Plateau in eastern Kentucky, eastern Tennessee, and northern Alabama. Rivers have cut deeply into the Appalachian Plateau. In places, the hillsides are so steep that the plateau looks much like a mountain area. A few valleys and some flat areas make good farmland. Rich beds of coal and deposits of petroleum are found beneath parts of the plateau. Some of the nation's greatest industrial centers, such as Pittsburgh, are within the plateau region.

In some parts of Kentucky and West Virginia, the Appalachian Plateau is covered with thin, sandy soil. The sharp, steep hillsides are badly eroded. Only a few farmers attempt to make a living from this poor land. These areas have few good roads, and the hills have almost shut the people off from the rest of the country. Through the years, the people of the hills have clung to old customs and manners of speech. Their traditional folk songs date back to the early days of the nation. See APPALACHIAN MOUNTAINS.

The Coastal Lowlands have three subdivisions: (1) the Atlantic Coastal Plain, (2) the Piedmont, and (3) the Gulf Coastal Plain.

The Atlantic Coastal Plain extends from New England to the southern tip of Florida. The plain is narrow in the north, but widens to about 500 miles in the south. The earliest colonists in America settled along the Atlantic Coast. Ways of making a living differed from place to place. In Virginia, farming was important from the beginning. There, the colonists established the first great southern plantations. But in New England, which

Coastal Islands off South Carolina near Charleston are part of the Coastal Lowlands. This region extends along the coast from New England around southern Florida to Mexico.
Louis Schwartz

MAJOR LAND REGIONS OF THE UNITED STATES*

PACIFIC RANGES AND LOWLANDS

ROCKY MOUNTAINS

WESTERN PLATEAUS, BASINS, AND RANGES

INTERIOR PLAINS

OZARK-OUACHITA HIGHLANDS

APPALACHIAN HIGHLANDS

COASTAL LOWLANDS

*Excluding Alaska and Hawaii.

WORLD BOOK map

has no broad coastal plain for farming, the colonists turned to the sea—to fishing and shipping.

Along the inland edge of the Atlantic Coastal Plain is the fall line. Rivers from the Appalachian Highlands reach the fall line and tumble down to the lower coastal plain in a series of falls or rapids. In the early days, boats sailed up the coastal rivers from the Atlantic Ocean until they reached the fall line. The boats could go no farther inland, and their cargoes were unloaded. In addition, the rapids furnished water power for manufacturing. Industrial cities, such as Raleigh and Richmond, grew up along the fall line.

The rivers that drain the Atlantic Coastal Plain are fairly short, from 100 to 300 miles long. They include the Delaware, Hudson, Potomac, and Susquehanna. Most of the rivers flow into the Atlantic Ocean.

Many of the bays along the Atlantic Coast make excellent harbors. These bays include Boston Bay, Cape Cod Bay, Chesapeake Bay, Delaware Bay, Long Island Sound, and New York Bay. Great cities have grown up beside these bays, including Baltimore, Boston, New York City, Norfolk, and Philadelphia.

The Piedmont is an irregular plain that lies just inland from the *fall line*. This line is where the hard rock of the Piedmont meets the softer rock of the Gulf and Atlantic coastal plains. The Piedmont extends from New England to central Alabama. Rains have washed away most of the topsoil throughout much of the region. Piedmont farmers grow tobacco and apples, and keep herds of dairy cattle. See FALL LINE; PIEDMONT REGION.

The Gulf Coastal Plain borders the Gulf of Mexico from the southern tip of Florida to Mexico. The land is flat, and the climate ranges from warm to hot. Farmers raise rice and subtropical fruits near the gulf. Farther north lies the Cotton Belt of the United States.

The two most important rivers of the Gulf Coastal Plain are the Mississippi and the Rio Grande. The Mis-

Grossman, Alpha
A Fertile Valley in North Carolina lies in the Appalachian Highlands region, which extends from Maine southwest into Alabama.

sissippi and its chief branch, the Missouri, form one of the world's largest river systems. The system drains most of the Interior Plains as well as part of the Gulf Coastal Plain. The Rio Grande rises in the southern Rocky Mountains and flows 1,885 miles across the Southwest United States to the Gulf of Mexico.

Engineers have dredged out the sand and deepened the bays along the Gulf Coast to form harbors for ocean-going ships. These include the harbors at Charleston, Corpus Christi, Galveston, Mobile, and Tampa. Important coastal river ports include Beaumont, Houston, Jacksonville, New Orleans, and Savannah.

The Interior Plains sweep westward from the Appalachian Highlands to the Rocky Mountains. This heart-

Fields of Wheat grow in western Kansas on the Interior Plains. This vast heartland of America stretches over 1,500 miles from the Appalachian Highlands west to the Rockies.
Photography House

GEOGRAPHIC CENTERS OF THE UNITED STATES

This map shows how the geographic center of the United States has moved westward since 1775. The geographic center moves each time new territory is added. As an example, the wide change between 1783 and 1803 was a result of the Louisiana Purchase.

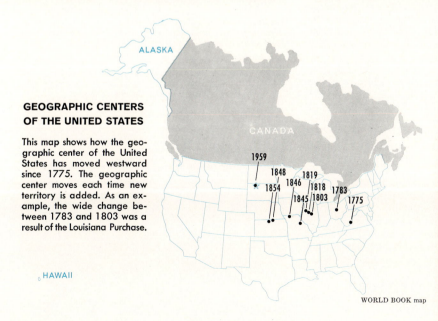

ALASKA

CANADA

1959

1848
1854 1846   1819
      1845 1818   1783
           1803   1775

HAWAII

WORLD BOOK map

UNITED STATES

land of America stretches for seemingly endless miles between the low eastern mountains and the towering snow-capped Rockies. The western part of the Interior Plains is known as the *Great Plains*. Some of the world's most productive farms and many of its greatest manufacturing centers are on the Interior Plains. Several hilly sections rise above the plains, including the Black Hills of South Dakota. Many features of the Interior Plains were created by glaciers which covered parts of the region during the Ice Age. For example, the glaciers left sections of Illinois and Iowa extremely flat, making them ideal for farming. The glaciers also left sections of northern Minnesota, Wisconsin, and Michigan sandy, rough, or swampy.

The mighty Mississippi River cuts through the middle of the Interior Plains. Since the days of earliest settlement, the Mississippi and its branches have provided a water highway through this vast interior region of America. Two of the Mississippi's branches, the Ohio River and the Missouri River, also rank among the most important rivers of the world.

The five Great Lakes have been as important as the rivers in the development of the Interior Plains. These lakes—Erie, Huron, Michigan, Ontario, and Superior —are the world's largest group of fresh-water lakes. They cover a total area of 95,170 square miles, an area greater than that of the six New England states combined. Some lake boats that sail the Great Lakes are larger than ocean ships. The St. Lawrence Seaway connects the Great Lakes with the shipping routes of the world. Such cities as Buffalo, Chicago, Cleveland, Detroit, Duluth, and Milwaukee owe much of their commercial and industrial importance to the Great Lakes.

The Ozark-Ouachita Highlands rise above the Interior Plains. The highlands cover extreme southern Illinois, most of southern Missouri, northwestern Arkansas, and eastern Oklahoma. This region is famous for its rugged beauty, and is a favorite vacationland. There are many swift, clear rivers; big springs; and underground caves. The hills are covered with thick forests and contain rich deposits of coal, iron, and other minerals. Much of the region's soil is too poor for farming, except in the river valleys.

The Rocky Mountains. A traveler approaching the Rocky Mountains from the Interior Plains sees them first as great blue shadows on the horizon. Some persons, in fact, mistake the mountains at first for clouds. As the traveler gets closer, great peaks emerge from the shadows. Some of them are capped with snow. The Rockies extend from northern New Mexico through Canada into Alaska. This great mountain chain forms the high backbone of the North American continent. The *Continental Divide*, or *Great Divide*, passes through the Rockies. This is a line which separates the streams that flow to the Atlantic Ocean from those that flow to the Pacific Ocean. Towns and cities lie on the few small areas of level valley land and around the mineral deposits of the Rockies. But most of the region is thinly settled. The grandeur and wildlife of the Rockies make the region a popular vacationland.

The Western Plateaus, Basins, and Ranges. This region lies west of the Rocky Mountains. It extends from

64

Fred Bond, Publix

Forested Hills and Fertile River Valleys cover the Ozark-Ouachita Highlands. The highlands rise above the Interior Plains, and cover parts of Illinois, Missouri, Arkansas, and Oklahoma.

James H. Roberts, Alpha

The Rugged Rocky Mountains tower high above the city of Boulder in north-central Colorado. The Rockies extend from northern New Mexico through Canada into Alaska.

Death Valley, a desert in east-central California, lies in the Western Plateaus, Basins, and Ranges region. This region extends from northern Washington south to the Mexican border.

Alpha Photo Assoc.

northern Washington south to the Mexican border. The *Columbia Plateau* occupies the northern part of the region. It covers southeastern Washington, eastern Oregon, and southwestern Idaho. The plateau was built up from lava flows that came from cracks in the earth. Deep river canyons cut through the plateau in places. The *Colorado Plateau* of western Colorado, New Mexico, Utah, and Arizona makes up a second section of this land region. The Colorado River has carved deep canyons through the plateau. The most famous is the Grand Canyon. Its jagged forms and brilliant colors make it one of the natural wonders of the world. The *Basin and Range Region* of Arizona, Idaho, Nevada, New Mexico, Oregon, southern California, Utah, and Wyoming forms a third plateau section. This area is generally too dry for farming, except where irrigation projects have been developed.

Within the Basin and Range Region is the *Great Basin*, a desert area. It covers parts of Oregon, California, Idaho, Utah, Wyoming, and Nevada. Occasional violent rainstorms fill the basin's riverbeds with water. The rivers run full and wild for a short time, and then dry up again. The streams empty into mountain-enclosed desert flats called *playas* or *sinks*, where the water soon soaks into the ground.

Many of the lakes in the Great Basin are simply shallow sheets of salty water. Great Salt Lake is the largest of these lakes. It is about 75 miles long and 50 miles wide. The lake's water is from four to seven times as salty as the ocean. Bathers cannot sink in Great Salt Lake because it is so heavy with salt.

The Pacific Ranges and Lowlands. Two mountain ranges—the Sierra Nevada and the Cascade Range—form the eastern boundary of this region. These ranges extend almost the entire length of the Pacific Coast from Canada to Mexico. The mountains are almost as high and rugged as the Rockies. The Columbia River Valley provides the only easy route through the almost unbroken mountain wall. The mountains have great forests and large deposits of minerals, especially gold. They are also a popular recreation area. Many lakes lie high in the mountains, some in the craters of inactive volcanoes.

West of the Sierra Nevada and the Cascade Range is a series of rich valleys. Some of the chief cities of the West lie in these valleys, which are so broad that they seem to be flat plains. The valleys include the San Joaquin-Sacramento River Valley in California, the Willamette River Valley in Oregon, and the lowlands around Puget Sound. Among the important cities that lie in these valleys are Fresno, Portland, Sacramento, Seattle, and Tacoma.

The Coast Ranges rise west of the valleys. At many points, these mountains drop sharply to the Pacific Ocean. But the coastal plain is broad around Los Angeles, one of the great metropolitan areas of the United States. In central California, a break in the Coast Ranges provides an easy route into the San Joaquin-Sacramento River Valley. The cities of San Francisco and Oakland grew up around this break.

The Pacific Coast, unlike the Atlantic Coast, has few bays. The only deep inlets are Columbia River Bay, Grays Harbor, Puget Sound, San Diego Bay, San Francisco Bay, San Pablo Bay, and Willapa Bay. A man-made bay forms a harbor at Los Angeles.

Oregon State Highway Comm.

The Rugged Oregon Coastline near Waldport is part of the Pacific Ranges and Lowlands region. This region extends down the entire length of the Pacific Coast from Canada to Mexico.

Jim Balog, Alpha

Lake Chelatna nestles among slopes of the Alaska Range near Mount McKinley. This range is part of the Pacific Mountain System, which curves from the Aleutian Islands through southern Alaska.

Waipio Valley lies between steep cliffs on the coast of Hawaii in the Hawaiian Islands. The islands have many towering cliffs that rise almost straight up from the water's edge.

Werner Stoy, Camera Hawaii

UNITED STATES / *Climate*

The United States has many kinds of climate because it is such a huge country and has such a great variety of natural features. Some areas are extremely hot, and others are extremely cold. Some areas receive too much rainfall, and others get too little. But most sections of the country have a moderate climate. This moderate climate helped bring about the country's rapid industrial development. The favorable climate also encouraged the growth of the nation's great agricultural economy. Such areas as Arizona, southern California, Florida, and Hawaii have thriving resort industries because of their mild winters.

Precipitation (rain, melted snow, sleet, and hail) is generally well distributed throughout the United States. However, large areas of the West are dry. Nevada, the driest state, has an average of 7.42 inches of precipitation annually. Louisiana, the wettest mainland state, has an average of 56.38 inches. The wettest place in the country is Mount Waialeale on Kauai Island in Hawaii. There, rainfall averages 460 inches yearly. The driest place is Death Valley in California, where the average yearly rainfall is less than 2 inches. Death Valley is also the hottest place in the United States. The highest temperature ever recorded in the country was 134° F., set at Death Valley on July 10, 1913. The lowest recorded temperature was −76° F., registered at Tanana in central Alaska in January, 1886. See NORTH AMERICA (Climate). See also the section on Climate in each state article.

Eric M. Sanford

Rich Spring Pastures in Vermont help support the state's dairy cattle. Late in March, the winter snows begin to melt. Late May is the season of lilacs and apple blossoms in Vermont.

Kabel, Publix

Early Summer Flowers bloom on a plantation near Wilmington, N.C. Flowering azaleas and moss-draped trees are common in this subtropical area, which is warmed by gentle ocean breezes.

Stewart's Photo

Heavy Winter Snow forms a blanket over much of Alaska. Snowplows clear drifts from the Alaska Highway, *above*. Alaska has longer and colder winters than any other state.

Golden Autumn Leaves of Colorado's quaking aspens create a contrast to the snow-capped Rocky Mountains. Hunters come to the area when cold weather forces wildlife down to lower pastures.

O. Roach, Shostal

AVERAGE JANUARY TEMPERATURES

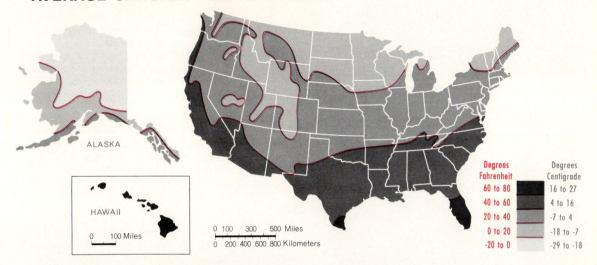

ALASKA

HAWAII

0   100 Miles

0   100   300   500 Miles
0   200 400 600 800 Kilometers

Degrees Fahrenheit	Degrees Centigrade
60 to 80	16 to 27
40 to 60	4 to 16
20 to 40	-7 to 4
0 to 20	-18 to -7
-20 to 0	-29 to -18

AVERAGE JULY TEMPERATURES

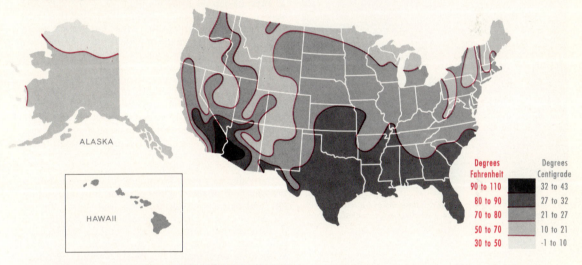

ALASKA

HAWAII

Degrees Fahrenheit	Degrees Centigrade
90 to 110	32 to 43
80 to 90	27 to 32
70 to 80	21 to 27
50 to 70	10 to 21
30 to 50	-1 to 10

AVERAGE YEARLY PRECIPITATION   (Rain, Melted Snow, and Other Moisture)

ALASKA

HAWAII

Inches	Centimeters
64 to 500	163 to 1,270
48 to 64	122 to 163
16 to 48	41 to 122
0 to 16	0 to 41

Source: U.S. Weather Bureau

The United States has vast areas of fertile soil, and most of the minerals required by modern industry. It has plentiful water supplies, deep forests, and an abundance of animal life. These enormous natural resources have helped make the United States one of the richest countries in the world.

Soil. The various regions of the United States have different types of soil. Differences in soil are due to differences in temperature, rainfall, plant life, and the underlying rocks. The soils include the dark-brown soils of the Great Plains, the glacial soils of the Midwest, and the *alluvial* (water-deposited) soils of the lower Mississippi Valley. For a detailed discussion of the soils of the United States, see the section on Soil in each state article.

The abundance of America's rich farmland led the early farmers to form wasteful habits. The settlers planted their fields in the same crops year after year until the land began to wear out. Then the farmers moved to fresh land. They plowed the hillsides with little care to prevent topsoil from washing away. In the early 1900's, the nation finally began to realize that such practices destroy soil fertility. More farmers started to use fertilizers to replace the minerals used up by growing the same crops year after year. Farmers also rotated their crops, and began to control erosion.

Minerals. Four hundred years ago, Spanish adventurers came to America to seek their fortunes. These men had romantic notions about America's mineral riches. In 1540, Francisco Vásquez de Coronado led an expedition through the Southwest in search of seven cities said to be rich in gold. Coronado did not find gold, but it was there—underground. About 300 years later, gold was discovered in California.

But America's greatest mineral treasures are not its precious gold or silver. They are coal, iron ore, natural gas, and petroleum—the minerals that supply the nation's industries. The United States also has bauxite (from which aluminum is made), building stone, copper, lead, phosphorus, potash, uranium, and zinc. Without all these minerals, the nation could never have become the industrial giant that it is.

The United States once could supply most of its own mineral needs. But America's great industrial economy expanded beyond some of its mineral supplies. In addi-

Humble Oil & Refining Co.

Tall Oil Derricks tower above rich deposits of petroleum, which ranks with natural gas and coal as America's leading minerals.

Fontana Dam in North Carolina is part of the nation's network of dams which store water for hydroelectric power.

Tennessee Valley Authority

Irrigated Farmland in Arizona, *right*, supports crops, and creates a striking contrast to unirrigated desert land, *foreground*.

Arizona Photographic Assoc.

tion, some mineral deposits, such as the richer ores in the Lake Superior iron ranges, have been used up. Today, the nation must import large amounts of certain minerals. The United States imports some minerals to supplement its own supply. These include bauxite, copper, iron ore, magnesium, petroleum, and uranium. Other minerals must be imported because the nation lacks them completely or because its supplies are too small. They include antimony, cobalt, industrial diamonds, nickel, and tin. See also the section in this article on *Mining*.

Water. Most places in the United States have enough water to meet the needs of the people. The nation uses more than 342 billion gallons of water a day. About 40 per cent of this water goes to irrigate farmland. Industry uses about 50 per cent of it for air conditioning, for various manufacturing operations, and for the production of electric power. City and rural water systems pump about 10 per cent of it for use in homes and small industries. See WATER SUPPLY.

Irrigation has turned many dry areas of the United States into rich farmland. Water used for irrigation may be stored in lakes or behind dams. Or it may be brought from underground to the surface by powerful pumps. American farmers irrigate more than 33 million acres of land. This total area is about equal to that of the state of New York. Most of the irrigated land lies between the Great Plains and the Pacific Coast Ranges. See IRRIGATION (Irrigation in the United States).

Hydroelectric Power. Hydroelectric plants produce about one-fifth of the electric power in the United States. The country's hydroelectric plants have a capacity of almost 41 million kilowatts of electricity. The United States ranks first in the world in developed hydroelectric power. Both the federal government and private industry have built many high dams to meet the increasing demand for electric power. Some of the dams provide flood control and irrigation as well as power. The nation's largest hydroelectric power stations are at Grand Coulee Dam on the Columbia River and Hoover Dam on the Colorado River. See DAM; ELECTRIC POWER; WATER POWER.

Forests. When the early colonists landed in America during the 1600's, forests covered almost half the land. The pioneers thought the forests were so vast that they would last forever. The settlers chopped down trees to clear land for crops. They destroyed wide forest areas by wasteful lumbering methods.

After the Atlantic Coast forests had been cleared, the lumber industry moved westward. Lumbering was centered in the Great Lakes area until the late 1800's, when it shifted to the South. It moved to the Far West during the 1920's. Today, the Pacific Coast forests produce almost half the nation's lumber. Alaska has many forests, but most of them are difficult to reach.

Some forests that were destroyed have been replanted. An important reforestation program is being carried out in the pine forests of the South. Such programs help increase timber reserves. But the United States still cuts some of its best timber faster than the trees regrow. See FOREST AND FOREST PRODUCTS.

Animal Life. In the pioneer days, wild animals were one of America's chief natural resources. Settlers hunted and trapped them for food, and made clothing from their hides. Frontiersmen pushed far into the interior in search of furs. During the 1800's, buffaloes and much other wildlife were slaughtered recklessly. In the early 1900's, the nation became concerned and began to establish wildlife refuges. Today, there are about 270 federal refuges for animal life. These refuges cover more than 18 million acres. The chief remaining fur-bearing animals of the forests and swamps include beavers, foxes, minks, muskrats, opossums, and raccoons. See WILDLIFE CONSERVATION.

The fish that live in the Great Lakes and off the Atlantic, Pacific, and Gulf coasts are an important natural resource. The coastal waters of New England have excellent fishing grounds, with cod, haddock, herring, mackerel, and other fishes. Menhaden, the nation's greatest single catch, are caught off the South Atlantic and Gulf coasts. Menhaden are used chiefly to make fish oil and meal. The world's largest shrimp fisheries lie off the South Atlantic and Gulf coasts of the United States. The Pacific coastal waters of Alaska have countless salmon. Great numbers of salmon, sardines, tuna, and other fishes are also caught in Pacific waters off the California coast.

American fishermen catch more than 3 million tons of fish and other seafood yearly. The nation has one of the largest commercial fishing industries in the world.

Ray Atkeson

Vast Evergreen Forests blanket the mountainsides near Glacier Peak in northwestern Washington. Trees cover about a third of the land in the United States. Almost half the nation's lumber comes from the Pacific Coast forests. The forest products industry ranks among the 10 largest manufacturing industries in the United States.

In the United States, private business is free to operate for a profit. Under this *free enterprise system*, the American people have reached the highest standard of living in the history of the world. The system has been abused at various times. But it has stimulated the people to develop the resources of their land. And it has encouraged them to find new and better ways of doing things. See FREE ENTERPRISE SYSTEM.

In colonial America, small companies conducted much of the business. Many of these companies were family firms, operated by a father and his sons. Small business still plays a vital role in the American economy. But through the years, some companies have become gigantic. For example, General Motors, one of the nation's largest industrial corporations, has assets of more than $9,640,000,000. The ownership of America's huge industrial and commercial corporations is spread among almost 17 million stockholders. More than 1,130,000 persons own shares in General Motors. The stockholders of corporations elect members of the board of directors, who manage the business. See BUSINESS.

Manufacturing accounts for three-fourths of the value of all goods produced in the United States. Products manufactured in the United States have a *value added by manufacture* of about $190,395,000,000 yearly. This figure represents the value created in products by U.S. industries, not counting such costs as materials, supplies, and fuels.

K. Snyder, FPG

Large Steel Mills, such as this one in Johnstown, Pa., stand near supplies of coal, used in making iron and steel. The United States has the world's largest iron and steel industry.

THE IMPORTANCE OF MANUFACTURING

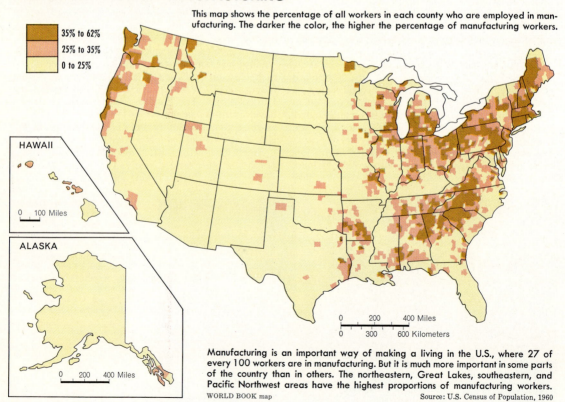

35% to 62%
25% to 35%
0 to 25%

This map shows the percentage of all workers in each county who are employed in manufacturing. The darker the color, the higher the percentage of manufacturing workers.

HAWAII

0   100 Miles

ALASKA

0   200   400 Miles

0   200   400 Miles
0   300   600 Kilometers

Manufacturing is an important way of making a living in the U.S., where 27 of every 100 workers are in manufacturing. But it is much more important in some parts of the country than in others. The northeastern, Great Lakes, southeastern, and Pacific Northwest areas have the highest proportions of manufacturing workers.

WORLD BOOK map   Source: U.S. Census of Population, 1960

70

The United States is the world's leading manufacturing nation. Its factories turn out more than two-fifths of the free world's total industrial production. The United States produces a fourth of the world's steel, the basic metal of industry. It makes about half the world's automobiles. It processes about a fifth of the world's meat, and manufactures about two-fifths of its aluminum. The United States is the free world's leading producer of cheese, clothing, chemicals, paper and paperboard, textiles, and many other products. It ranks first among the countries of the free world in printing and publishing. The nation's biggest manufacturing industry is transportation equipment. Food processing ranks second. Other leading manufacturing industries include chemicals, clothing, electrical machinery, machinery, metal products, paper and allied products, primary metals, and printing and publishing. See MANUFACTURING.

Manufacturing Centers. New York is the nation's leading manufacturing state, followed by California, Ohio, Illinois, Pennsylvania, and Michigan.

America's first manufacturing centers developed along the rivers of New England. Water power from rushing rivers and plunging waterfalls ran the machines of the factories. After coal became the primary source of power, many factories moved closer to coal areas in Pennsylvania and other states. The great industrial cities of Birmingham, Cleveland, and Pittsburgh grew

Giant Industrial Firms are owned by thousands of stockholders. The board of directors of the Du Pont Company reports the corporation's financial condition at the annual stockholders' meeting, *below.*
E. I. Du Pont de Nemours & Co., Inc.

Devaney from Publix

Self-Service Supermarkets offer all kinds of foods in one location. American food stores range from neighborhood groceries to nationwide chains with yearly sales of over $1 billion.

PRODUCTION IN THE UNITED STATES

Total yearly value of goods produced...$251,094,530,000

MANUFACTURED PRODUCTS 76%

AGRICULTURAL PRODUCTS 17%

FISH & MINERAL PRODUCTS 7%

Note: Manufacturing percentage based on value added by manufacture. Other percentages based on value of production. Fish Products are less than 1 per cent.

Source: Latest available U.S. Government statistics

EMPLOYMENT IN UNITED STATES

Average yearly number of persons employed—64,605,000

		Number of Employees
Manufacturing	🧍🧍🧍🧍🧍🧍	17,110,000
Wholesale & Retail Trade	🧍🧍🧍🧍	11,880,000
Government	🧍🧍🧍🧍	9,505,000
Services	🧍🧍🧍	8,348,000
Agriculture	🧍🧍🧍	6,700,000
Transportation & Public Utilities	🧍	3,932,000
Construction	🧍	3,067,000
Finance, Insurance & Real Estate	🧍	2,873,000
Mining	🧍	641,000
Fishing & Forestry	🧍	549,000

Source: Employment statistics supplied by employers to government agencies

Electronics Technicians perform a bonding operation on miniature transistors, which will be installed in television sets. Each worker performs a single task, often with the aid of a machine. Mass production enables industries to produce goods in large quantities at low cost.

Sylvania Electric Products Inc.

Automated Machines permit steelworkers to roll and cool steel by merely pushing buttons on a panel.

International Harvester *Today*

up close to coal fields. As petroleum and electrical power became important, some industries no longer had to remain near coal supplies. Manufacturers could build their factories in areas where workers or raw materials were plentiful.

Transportation facilities have also influenced the location of industry. New York City's outstanding transportation facilities, including its incomparable harbor, helped make it the nation's largest city and greatest manufacturing center. Chicago became the second largest U.S. city partly because it lies at the tip of Lake Michigan and at the crossroads of the continent. The Great Lakes also helped make Buffalo, Detroit, and Milwaukee great industrial centers. See the section on Manufacturing in each state article.

Mass Production. About 1800, two developments occurred that revolutionized industry. One was the invention of *machine tools* (equipment that shapes metal). The second was the use of *interchangeable* (identical) parts. American industry did not link these two developments with the moving assembly line until the 1900's. When it did, the great era of low-cost mass production began. Henry Ford was a pioneer in mass production. By mass-producing Model T automobiles, he made them cheap enough for many persons to buy. Mass production made the United States the industrial giant of the world and raised the nation's standard of living. See ASSEMBLY LINE; MASS PRODUCTION.

Automation has become increasingly important in American industry. Automation is the use of machines that operate with little or no human control. These machines automatically control other machines that manufacture and assemble products. After World War II, the automobile industry became the first to make widespread use of automation. Today, many industries use automatically controlled machines. Automation is reducing the number of unskilled laborers needed in industry. It is making highly trained workers and engineers even more important to society. Automation increases production, but it also creates problems. For example, workers displaced by machines must be retrained for other jobs. See AUTOMATION.

Research and Development. Industry has always been interested in developing new products and discovering better manufacturing techniques. U.S. companies have over 5,000 research laboratories for these purposes. The laboratories employ over 300,000 men and women, and spend almost $5 billion yearly for scientific research. Industrial research is an important part of the nation's research program. It supplements research conducted by government, by universities and colleges, and by private foundations. See RESEARCH.

Agriculture. The United States is one of the world's leading agricultural nations. America's farm products have a value of about $41,737,000,000 yearly. American farmers produce about 50 per cent of the world's corn, 30 per cent of its cotton, 30 per cent of its oats, 25 per cent of its tobacco, 20 per cent of its chickens, 10 per cent of its hogs, and 10 per cent of its wheat.

The Agricultural Revolution. In 1850, about three-fifths of the workers in the United States made their living in agriculture. Today, less than a tenth of the workers—about 4,800,000 persons—make their living on farms. They raise most of the nation's livestock, food crops, and industrial crops. They also produce large quantities for export to other countries.

The increased use of machines and scientific farming methods permits fewer and fewer farmers to feed more and more people. In 1820, each American farmer raised enough food to feed himself and three other persons. Today, each farmer grows enough food to feed himself and more than 30 others. American farmers use tractors, seeders, cultivators, harvesters, and other machines. This equipment makes it possible for only a few persons to operate a large farm. Modern farming methods include the use of improved fertilizers and disease-resistant plants, crop rotation, and scientific breeding and feeding of livestock. American farmers produce so much that finding a market for some products is often a problem.

About four-fifths of the nation's farmers own or partly own the farms on which they live. The rest rent their land. American farms and ranches range from a few acres to several thousand acres. The average size was about 350 acres in the mid-1960's. It is constantly in-

Grant Heilman

Dairy Cattle feed on chopped silage on a farm in Pennsylvania. Dairy and beef cattle are the most important livestock raised on American farms. Many farmers also raise hogs and chickens.

General Motors

Industrial Researchers develop new products and manufacturing methods. Engineers, mathematicians, and scientists work together in solving difficult industrial research problems.

creasing as farms become more and more mechanized.

During the Great Depression of the 1930's, the federal government set up a number of programs to protect the farmer against low prices, to control crop surpluses, and to encourage soil conservation. These goals are still part of the federal farm program.

Crops are raised on about a fifth of the land area of the United States. Crops and farming methods have always differed throughout the country because of differences in climate and soil. On the rocky land of New England, for example, the early farmers raised crops mainly for their own households. Later, their small farms produced dairy products and poultry for the nearby cities. But in the southern colonies, farmers found that the soil, climate, and level land of the coastal plain favored tobacco and cotton. The raising of these crops led to a system of large farms and plantations. In the Midwest, pioneers found the broad, fertile land suited to a variety of grains and hay. Today, this region has more than half the nation's cropland, although it covers only a fifth of the United States.

The most important U.S. crop is corn, both in acreage planted and in dollar value. Other leading crops, in order of value, include hay, cotton, wheat, soybeans, tobacco, and oats. American farmers also raise barley, flaxseed, fruits, peanuts, potatoes and other vegetables, rice, rye, sorghums, and many other crops.

Livestock. More than a fourth of the land area of the United States is used for pasture and grazing. Most of this land is in the Great Plains, where too little rain falls for raising crops. Over 160 million acres of public lands in 11 western states and Alaska are divided into *grazing districts*. These districts are used by private ranchers under permits from the U.S. Department of the Interior. See PUBLIC LANDS.

Dairy and beef cattle are the most important livestock raised on American farms. Farms in the Midwest, and the enormous ranches of the West, raise most of the beef cattle. The great American Dairy Belt extends across the northern United States from New England to Minnesota. Most of the country's hogs come from the Corn Belt of the Midwest. Almost all American farmers

keep small flocks of chickens to supply their families with meat and eggs. Some farmers specialize in raising huge flocks of meat or egg-laying chickens. See AGRICULTURE; FARM AND FARMING.

Mining has an annual value of about $18,585,000,000 in the United States. The value of petroleum output is about 40 per cent of the value of all minerals produced in the country. Natural gas is the second most valuable product, and coal ranks third. The United States produces about 30 per cent of the world's crude petroleum, about 70 per cent of its natural gas, and about 15 per cent of its coal.

Industry's need for more and more minerals is a constant challenge to the mining industry to make new discoveries. Prospectors once located deposits with pick and shovel in a hit-or-miss fashion. Today, mining and drilling firms employ teams of highly trained engineers and geologists to locate new deposits. These experts also work to discover new ways of refining low-grade minerals once considered useless.

The petroleum industry is an outstanding example of the success in using scientific methods of discovery. Since 1900, experts have often predicted that the United States would use up its petroleum reserves in a few years. But new oil fields have continually been discovered. Engineers have also developed better ways of pumping petroleum from the earth, and thus reopened some abandoned fields. In the 1920's, the United States had about 7 billion barrels of known petroleum reserves. Today, the nation has more than 30 billion barrels of known reserves.

The U.S. mining industry has done much to improve the working conditions of miners. At the same time, it has increased their production. In coal mining, for example, machines have replaced much of the backbreaking toil. Better ventilation and other improvements have made the mines safer and more pleasant places in which to work. In the 1960's, miners in America's *bituminous* (soft) coal mines produced almost four tons of coal for every ton they dug in 1920. See MINING.

Petroleum and Natural Gas. The United States produces more petroleum than any other country. Texas is by far the chief petroleum-producing state. It accounts for about a third of the nation's output and about a tenth of the world's production. Louisiana and California are the next most important oil-producing states. Other leading producers include Kansas, New Mexico, Oklahoma, and Wyoming. The United States also produces more natural gas than any other country. Texas supplies almost half the nation's output, and has almost half the total reserves. See GAS; PETROLEUM.

Coal. Only Russia mines more coal than the United States. The nation's largest coal deposits are in Illinois, Montana, North Dakota, and Wyoming. But six states east of the Mississippi River produce more than 85 per cent of all the coal mined. The leading coal-producing states, in order of importance, are West Virginia, Pennsylvania, Kentucky, Illinois, Ohio, Virginia, Indiana, Alabama, Tennessee, and Utah. Pennsylvania has the only large *anthracite* (hard coal) deposits. See COAL.

Iron. More than three-fourths of the nation's iron ore comes from the Lake Superior fields of northern Minnesota, northwestern Wisconsin, and upper Michigan. The soft ore is shipped by large lake boats and railroad cars to such steel centers as Chicago and Pittsburgh. Alabama, New York, Utah, and several other states also have iron-ore deposits. The best grades of ore in the Lake Superior fields have been largely used up. But methods for processing low-grade ores, such as taconite, have been developed. Some steel companies import iron ore from Canada, Venezuela, and other countries. About a third of the iron ore used in the United States is imported. See IRON AND STEEL.

Copper. The United States produces more copper than any other country. The leading copper-mining state is Arizona, which produces half the nation's output. Utah, the second largest copper producer, mines about a fifth of the country's supply. Other copper-producing states include Michigan, Montana, Nevada, and New Mexico. See COPPER.

Aluminum is made from an ore called bauxite. Mines in Arkansas produce about 98 per cent of the bauxite mined in the United States. Bauxite is also mined in Alabama and Georgia. See ALUMINUM.

Zinc and Lead are often found and mined together. The United States is one of the leading zinc-producing countries. Tennessee is the chief zinc-producing state, and Missouri is first in lead production. Other top zinc-producers are Colorado, Idaho, Montana, New Jersey, New Mexico, New York, Pennsylvania, and Utah. Other lead-mining states include Arizona, Colorado, Idaho, Utah, and Washington. See ZINC; LEAD.

Gold and Silver. Arizona, California, Nevada, South Dakota, Utah, and Washington mine most of the nation's gold. The chief silver-producing states are Arizona, Idaho, Montana, and Utah. See GOLD; SILVER.

Construction Industry. During the 1950's and early 1960's, Americans built new homes at a rate of over a million a year. They also erected many new buildings and factories to house their growing business and industrial activities. Over 3 million persons earn their living in the building and construction industry.

To keep pace with the demand for new homes, the building industry has developed new methods of con-

E. I. Du Pont de Nemours & Co., Inc.
Giant Beams and Girders form the steel skeleton of a new industrial plant. Riveters and welders fasten the pieces in place. About 3 million persons work in the U.S. construction industry.

struction. Many builders have erected huge housing projects, which permit economical use of equipment and labor. Such parts as window frames and doorways are often assembled in factories to save on-the-site labor. Many houses are manufactured by sections in factories, and are simply assembled on the building site. They are called *prefabricated* houses. In the mid-1960's, about a fifth of the new homes being constructed were prefabricated. About a tenth of the new homes were *mobile homes* (house trailers). These are popular with workers and military personnel who must often move about the country. See HOUSING.

Trade. The United States has a greater volume of international trade than any other country. And its domestic trade is almost 10 times as great as its trade with other countries. About 12 million Americans earn their living in wholesale and retail trade. The businesses that conduct this trade range from huge wholesale firms and department stores to corner groceries. Each region of the United States produces chiefly the products for which it is best suited. It sells surplus products to other regions that need them. The nation's domestic trade totals about $380 billion annually.

Each year, the United States imports more than $18½ billion worth of goods from other countries and exports over $26 billion worth of goods. The nation's most important trading partner by far is Canada. The United States sends almost a fifth of its exports to Canada. Canada, in turn, supplies the United States with over a fifth of its imports. Other U.S. trading partners, in order of importance, are Japan, Great Britain, and West Germany. The United States also trades with France, India, Italy, Mexico, The Netherlands, Venezuela, and other nations.

The leading exports of the United States, in order of value, include machinery and transportation equipment, foods and beverages, chemicals and related products, and metals. The leading imports, in order of value, include metals, nonmetallic minerals (such as petroleum), foods and beverages, wood and paper, machinery and transportation equipment, and textiles. See BUSINESS; TRADE.

Los Angeles Chamber of Commerce

A Cloverleaf Interchange in Los Angeles connects five California freeways. The U.S. highway system covers more than 3,500,000 miles and is used by over 80,000,000 motor vehicles.

UNITED STATES / *Transportation and Communication*

Transportation. The regions of the United States are linked by an immense system of airlines, railroads, roads and highways, and waterways. The broad country and its transportation system grew up together. The Midwest was only an outpost of the East Coast until waterways linked the two regions. The wild frontier of the West vanished quickly after the first railroad spanned the continent. Modern industrial America grew up along the routes of the railroads. Then automobiles and trucks, traveling on all-weather highways, spread the settlement of America more evenly throughout the country. Finally, the airplane brought almost every community in the United States within a few hours' travel time of every other community. See TRANSPORTATION.

Aviation. About 50 domestic airlines operate in the United States. The leading airlines, flying high-speed jet transports, connect all the large cities. The smaller cities are served by *feeder* lines that connect with a major air center.

Domestic airlines carry more than 77 million passengers yearly. They are also increasingly important in transporting cargo. Domestic airlines fly over 600 million ton-miles of express and freight yearly (a *ton-mile* is one ton carried one mile). Eight American airlines operate international flights. The airlines of many other countries also serve the United States. See AIRLINE; AIRPLANE; AVIATION.

Railroads were largely responsible for the settlement and development of the West. They carried farmers, merchants, and miners across the prairies to the western frontier lands. By 1869, railroads covered much of the eastern half of the United States. That year, the first transcontinental rail route was completed, linking the Atlantic and Pacific coasts. Today, the United States has about 215,000 miles of railroads. Airlines and highways have reduced the importance of railroads in carrying passengers. But the railroads are still the primary means of transporting freight. See RAILROAD.

Roads and Highways. The highway system of the United States covers more than 3,500,000 miles, of which about 2,600,000 miles are surfaced. More than 80 million motor vehicles use this system. Highways are built by local, state, and federal governments. The federal government first took the responsibility of road building in 1811. That year, the government began to build the National, or Cumberland, Road through the Appalachian Mountains. Today, the federal government finances most of the interstate highway system. The states handle construction work on these highways, and have the main responsibility for their own networks of state roads. Most states also help with local road construction. See ROADS AND HIGHWAYS.

Waterways and Ports. America's outstanding network of inland waterways has always been vital to the nation's growth and progress. Early settlers crossed the Appalachian Mountains to the headwaters of the Ohio River. Then they floated down the Ohio and built settlements along its banks. Later, the settlers transported their produce down the Ohio to the Mississippi River, and then on to New Orleans. In 1825, the Erie Canal was completed in New York. It linked the Hudson River with Lake Erie, and spurred the settlement and commercial growth of the entire Great Lakes area.

Today, ocean-going ships can sail up the St. Lawrence Seaway and through the Great Lakes to Chicago. There, the Chicago River and the Chicago Sanitary and Ship Canal form important links in a waterway to the Mississippi River. Thus, the United States has an all-water route from the Atlantic Ocean, through the Midwest, to the Gulf of Mexico. The Missouri River, the great branch of the Mississippi, extends this waterway into much of the western Interior Plains. Agricultural and industrial products are carried on the waterway to coastal cities and to other countries. See INLAND WATERWAY.

Two other important waterways lie along the Atlantic and Gulf coasts. They are the Atlantic Intracoastal Waterway and the Gulf Intracoastal Waterway. Short canals connect many of the lakes, rivers, bays, and lagoons near these coasts, and form protected water routes. See ATLANTIC INTRACOASTAL WATERWAY; GULF INTRACOASTAL WATERWAY.

The United States depends on ocean shipping for most of its trade with other countries. The nation's fleet of merchant ships is the largest in the world in tonnage. The Port of New York is the world's largest and busiest seaport. Other major American ports on the Atlantic include Baltimore, Boston, Norfolk-Newport News, Philadelphia, and Portland. The leading Gulf ports include New Orleans, Houston, and Baton Rouge. Among the major American ports on the Pacific are Los Angeles, Portland, San Francisco, and Seattle. See PORT; SHIP AND SHIPPING.

Communication. The Founding Fathers of the United States believed that a free exchange of ideas was vital to a democracy. As a result, the United States Constitution includes guarantees of freedom of speech and freedom of the press. Upon these freedoms, the

73

Telephones of the Future will include the Picturephone, which permits people to see each other while talking. The United States has one telephone for every two persons.

United States has built a vast communication system. See COMMUNICATION.

Publishing. Publishers in the United States issue almost 2,000 daily newspapers, over 9,000 weeklies, and about 10,000 magazines. Newspaper publishers print about 59 million copies daily—almost one copy for every three persons in the United States.

Every year, the book industry publishes more than 25,000 new books and new editions. The industry sells more than a billion hard-cover and paperbound copies annually. The United States ranks high among the countries of the world in the number of different books published.

The U.S. publishing industry operates without government censorship or license. Individual publishers are regulated only by their own consciences, by libel laws, and by the public that buys their products. The nation's main publishing center is New York City. Other leading publishing cities include Baltimore, Boston, Chicago, Des Moines, Los Angeles, Philadelphia, and St. Louis. See BOOK; MAGAZINE; NEWSPAPER; PUBLISHING.

UNITED STATES / Study Aids

Related Articles. See the separate article on each state with its Related Articles. See also the following:

EDUCATION

Education	School	Universities and Colleges

HISTORY AND GOVERNMENT

City and Local
  Governments
Congress of the
  United States
Democracy
Government
President of the
  United States

State Government
Supreme Court of the
  United States
United States, Government of
United States, History of
United States Constitution
Vice-President of the
  United States

INDUSTRIES AND PRODUCTS

For the rank of the United States among other countries in production, see the following articles:

Agriculture	Fishing	Lumber	Ship and
Aluminum	Industry	Manufacturing	Shipping
Automobile	Flax	Mining	Silver
Barley	Forest and	Oats	Sugar
Cattle	Forest	Orange	Sugar Beet
Cheese	Products	Paper	Sugar Cane
Chemical	Gas	Petroleum	Textile
Industry	Gold	Platinum	Tobacco
Clothing	Horse	Potato	Tuna
Coal	Iron and	Publishing	Tungsten
Copper	Steel	Rubber	Vegetable
Corn	Lead	Rye	Wheat
Cotton	Leather	Salmon	Zinc
Electric Power	Lemon	Salt	

NATIONAL FORESTS, PARKS, AND MONUMENTS

See the tables with the following articles:

National Forest	National Monument	National Park

OUTLYING AREAS

Canton and Ender-	Line Islands	Puerto Rico
bury Islands	Mariana Islands	Samoa
Caroline Islands	Marshall Islands	(American)
Guam	Midway Island	Virgin Islands
Johnston Island	Panama Canal Zone	Wake Island

PHYSICAL FEATURES

See DAM; LAKE; MOUNTAIN; RIVER, with their lists of Related Articles.

REGIONS

Middle Atlantic States	Rocky Mountain States
Midwestern States	Southern States
New England	Southwestern States
Pacific Coast States	

SOCIAL AND CULTURAL LIFE

American Literature	Drama	Music
Architecture	Easter	Painting
Art Museum	Holiday	Recreation
Book	Library	Religion
Christmas	Motion Picture	Sculpture
Dancing	Museum	Theater

OTHER RELATED ARTICLES

Air Force, United States	Flag
Army, United States	Food
Census	Housing
Citizenship	Immigration and
City	Emigration
Clothing	Marine Corps, United
Coast Guard, United	States
States	Money
Communication	Navy, United States
Conservation	Shelter
Farm and Farming	Transportation

Outline

I. People
  A. Population and Ancestry
  B. Cities
  C. Farms
  D. Family Life
  E. Religion
  F. Recreation

II. Education
  A. Schools
  B. Libraries
  C. Museums
  D. Scientific Research

III. The Arts

IV. Land Regions
  A. The Appalachian Highlands
  B. The Coastal Lowlands

Radio, like publishing, is chiefly a private business in the United States. Unlike publishers, however, radio stations are licensed and regulated by the federal government. Individual stations have freedom to operate as they wish, provided they serve the public interest. Radio stations are supported by the money they receive from advertisers who buy time to broadcast sales messages. The United States has almost 5,000 radio stations. More than 90 of every 100 American homes have at least one radio. See RADIO.

Telephone and Telegraph. The United States has one telephone for every two persons. Americans make almost 300 million telephone calls a day, and use about 370 million miles of telephone wires. The telephone system of the United States is efficient as well as huge. A person in New York City can dial a friend in Los Angeles and get him on the phone in less than a minute. See TELEPHONE.

Telephones have replaced the telegraph for many purposes. Since 1935, the mileage of telegraph wires in the United States has been reduced by more than half. Today, the United States has about 625,000 miles of telegraph wires. These wires are used to carry telegraph messages, to transmit photographs, to operate teletype machines, and to carry time signals. See TELEGRAPH.

Television was developed commercially by the radio industry. Radio companies own many television stations. Most television programs are financed in the same manner as radio programs—by the sale of time to advertisers. Some schools and private organizations operate educational television stations on a nonprofit basis. These groups present educational programs on a wide variety of subjects. Some high-school and college courses are presented on television for students in their homes.

The nation's first regular television broadcasts started in 1939 in New York City. Two years later, the first regular commercial broadcasts began. Today, the United States has more than 550 television stations. Almost 90 of every 100 American homes have a television set. See TELEVISION.   JOHN GUNTHER

Critically reviewed by JEWELL A. PHELPS

Questions

How does the United States rank among the countries of the world in population? In area?

Of every 100 homes in the United States, about how many have a television set? A radio?

What country is America's chief trading partner?

How much has the life expectancy of Americans increased since 1900?

Where is the driest place in the United States? The wettest place?

Why is the United States known as a *melting pot*?

How much of the free world's industrial production comes from U.S. factories?

What are the leading crops raised in the United States?

Why has the farm population of the United States declined so sharply since 1850?

What is the most important mineral produced in the United States?

Books for Young Readers

AMERICAN HERITAGE. *The Golden Book of America*. Golden Press. Illustrates ways of American life.

BORDEN, CHARLES A. *Hawaii, Fiftieth State*. Macrae Smith, 1960.

GINIGER, KENNETH S., ed. *America, America, America: Prose and Poetry About the Land, the People, and the Promise*. Watts, 1957.

LINDQUIST, WILLIS. *Alaska, The Forty-Ninth State*. McGraw, 1959.

PATTERSON, LILLIE. *Meet Miss Liberty*. Macmillan, 1962. History and significance of the Statue of Liberty.

SLOANE, ERIC. *ABC Book of Early Americana*. Doubleday, 1963.

SMITH, IRENE. *Washington, D.C.* Rand McNally, 1964.

TOOZE, RUTH. *America*. Viking, 1956. The meaning of America expressed through its land, people, industries, and arts.

Books for Older Readers

BROGAN, DENIS W. *The American Character*. Vintage, 1956.

BRUCKBERGER, RAYMOND L. *Image of America*. Viking, 1959.

BUTCHER, DEVEREUX. *Exploring Our National Parks and Monuments*, 4th ed. Houghton, 1956.

CALLISON, CHARLES H., ed. *America's Natural Resources*. Ronald, 1957. A survey by leading conservationists.

GOWANS, ALAN. *Images of American Living: Four Centuries of Architecture and Furniture as Cultural Expression*. Lippincott, 1964.

GUNTHER, JOHN. *Inside U.S.A.* Rev. ed. Harper, 1951. A guide to modern American life and politics.

LEHNER, ERNST, comp. *American Symbols: A Pictorial History*. Tudor, 1957.

NATIONAL GEOGRAPHIC SOCIETY. *America's Wonderlands: The Scenic National Parks and Monuments of the United States*. The Society, 1959. *America's Historylands: Touring Our Landmarks of Liberty*. 1962.

PEATTIE, DONALD CULROSS. *Parade with Banners*. World Publishing Co., 1957. The American spirit symbolized in the constitution, famous landmarks, and other topics.

TEALE, EDWIN W. *North with the Spring*. Dodd, 1951. *Autumn Across America*. 1956. *Journey into Summer*. 1960. Travels of a naturalist through the United States.

TILDEN, FREEMAN. *The State Parks: Their Meaning in American Life*. Knopf, 1962.

TOCQUEVILLE, ALEXIS DE. *Democracy in America*. There are many editions of this book, which is one of the basic interpretations of American life and its significance.

The Great Seal of the United States

The Declaration of Independence and the Constitution provide the basis for the United States government. These documents are kept in the National Archives Building, Washington, D.C.

UNITED STATES GOVERNMENT

UNITED STATES, GOVERNMENT OF. The government of the United States represents, serves, and protects the American people both at home and abroad. From the nation's capital in Washington, D.C., its activities and influence reach every part of the world.

The three branches of the United States government—executive, legislative, and judicial—are usually represented by the President, Congress, and the Supreme Court, respectively. Generally speaking, the President enforces the laws that Congress passes, and the Supreme Court interprets these laws if any question arises.

United States military forces stationed in many parts of the world support American policy and help preserve peace. Representatives of the government work in international organizations, provide technical assistance, and negotiate with other governments. Millions of civil-service employees and other workers at home and abroad carry out the programs of the government.

The United States government shares governmental powers with the states under the *federal* system established by the United States Constitution. The national governments of most other countries are *unitary*, or centralized. They have final authority in all matters, and grant limited powers to state and local governments.

Government in the United States operates on three levels: national, state, and local. The federal government in Washington cannot abolish the states or rearrange their boundaries. It can exercise only powers that are delegated or implied by the Constitution. The states exercise powers reserved to them or not denied them by the Constitution. In some areas, the federal and state governments have *concurrent* powers. That is, they both have the right to exercise authority. The American judicial system keeps the federal and state governments within their proper fields of power.

The United States government makes and enforces laws, collects taxes, provides services for the people, protects individuals and their property, and works for national and international security. But it is particularly noted for the way it encourages the American people to take part in government, seeks to protect the rights of the people from the government itself, and assures the self-government of the states.

Abraham Lincoln described the United States government in his Gettysburg Address as being "of the people, by the people, for the people."

For a description of the United States, its history, and its Constitution, see UNITED STATES; UNITED STATES, HISTORY OF; UNITED STATES CONSTITUTION.

Government in American Life

The United States government, through its activities, services, and authority, directly affects the lives of the American people in many ways. It collects taxes and customs duties to finance government work. It borrows money and issues bonds. It coins money and prints currency. It establishes uniform weights and measures. It issues patents and copyrights. It controls immigration and emigration, and naturalizes noncitizens. It operates the postal system, and builds roads and highways. It manages a social-security system. It has powers to regulate agriculture, business, and labor through its authority to regulate interstate commerce. It negotiates with other governments, and participates in international organizations to promote peace, health, and education. It has the power to declare war and to conclude peace pacts. It maintains the armed forces and can draft citizens for military service. It admits new states into the union. It governs the District of Columbia and the territories, including American Samoa, Guam, the Panama Canal Zone, and the Virgin Islands. It also governs islands in the Pacific Ocean under a United Nations trusteeship.

The United States seeks not only to govern, but also to protect the liberty of the states and the people. The Bill of Rights in the Constitution guarantees that all persons shall have freedom of speech and of religion, freedom of the press, the right of assembly, and freedom from arbitrary interference by the federal government. It guarantees a person freedom from arbitrary arrest and imprisonment. It also guarantees the right to trial by jury and justice in the federal courts. The government acts to see that no state deprives any person of life, liberty, or property without due process of law, or denies equal protection of the law. See BILL OF RIGHTS.

The Executive Branch

The executive branch of the United States government consists of (1) the Executive Office of the President, (2) the executive departments, and (3) the independent agencies.

The President of the United States is the nation's chief executive and chief of state. He lives in the White House in Washington, D.C., and has offices there. As chief executive, he has the responsibility of enforcing federal laws. He appoints and removes high federal officials. He commands the armed forces. He conducts foreign affairs. He recommends to Congress the laws he would like to have passed. He appoints American representatives to international organizations and to diplomatic missions in other lands. As chief of state, the President performs many ceremonial duties. The people elect the President to a four-year term, and he cannot be elected to more than two terms.

The Executive Office of the President includes: (1) the White House Office, (2) the Bureau of the Budget, (3) the National Security Council, (4) the Office of Emergency Planning, (5) the Council of Economic Advisers, (6) the Office of Science and Technology,

(7) the National Aeronautics and Space Council, (8) the Office of the Special Representative for Trade Negotiations, and (9) the Office of Economic Opportunity. See PRESIDENT OF THE UNITED STATES.

Executive Departments conduct the administration of the national government. These 11 departments are: (1) State, (2) Treasury, (3) Defense, (4) Justice, (5) Post Office, (6) Interior, (7) Agriculture, (8) Commerce, (9) Labor, (10) Health, Education, and Welfare, and (11) Housing and Urban Development. Executive department heads are appointed by the President, with the approval of the Senate. They form the *Cabinet* (see CABINET). Nine heads are called *secretaries*. The attorney general heads the Department of Justice. The postmaster general directs the Post Office Department.

Each executive department has a deputy or under secretary and two or more assistant secretaries. The President appoints these officials, and can remove them without giving any reason. High officials usually resign when a new President takes office, because they help make policy as well as administer it.

Generally, each department is divided into bureaus, bureaus into divisions, divisions into branches, branches into sections, and sections into units. Most officials below the highest level serve under civil-service appointments (see CIVIL SERVICE). All the executive departments have headquarters in Washington, but about 90 of every 100 employees work elsewhere in *field services* (activities that are not a part of headquarters).

Independent Agencies developed with the growth of government regulation. They operate in the fields of aeronautics and space, atomic energy, banking and finance, civil service, communications, farm credit, home loans, information services, interstate commerce, labor mediation and conciliation, labor relations, power, railroad retirement, science, securities and exchange, selective service, small business, tariffs, trade, and veterans affairs.

Administrators or directors head most of the independent agencies. But the regulatory agencies, such as the Interstate Commerce Commission, are headed by several persons of equal rank, although one may be designated as chairman. They usually have legislative, judicial, and administrative duties.

The President appoints the members of these agencies with the approval of the Senate. He has less power to remove these officials than he has with executive officials. He must state reasons for removing them.

The Legislative Branch

The legislative branch of the United States government includes Congress, which consists of the Senate and the House of Representatives. This branch also includes five agencies that perform administrative duties: (1) the Architect of the Capitol, (2) the General Accounting Office, (3) the Government Printing Office, (4) the Library of Congress, and (5) the United States Botanic Garden.

The Senate and the House of Representatives meet in separate chambers in the Capitol in Washington. Congress makes, repeals, and amends federal laws. It levies federal taxes and appropriates funds for the government. See CONGRESS OF THE UNITED STATES.

The Senate has 100 members. Each state, regardless of size or population, has two Senators who serve six-year terms. The Vice-President of the United States presides over the Senate. The Senate has certain exclusive powers. It alone can sit as a court of impeachment to try federal officials impeached by the House of Representatives. It alone has the power to approve the President's nominations for major federal offices. It alone can ratify treaties with other nations. See SENATE.

The House of Representatives consists of 435 members. A state's representation is based on population. It ranges from New York's 41 members to one each from Alaska, Delaware, Nevada, Vermont, and Wyoming. The number of representatives from a state changes as its population changes. Reapportionment takes place every 10 years, after the national census. The House has certain exclusive powers. It alone can bring charges of impeachment against high federal officials. It alone can initiate tax bills. See HOUSE OF REPRESENTATIVES.

The Judicial Branch

The Supreme Court of the United States is the highest court in the land. It has a chief justice and eight associate justices. The President appoints all justices with the approval of the Senate. The justices hold office for life. See SUPREME COURT OF THE UNITED STATES.

Other Federal Courts. About 90 federal *district courts* are located in various cities. Above the district courts are 11 federal *courts of appeals*, often called *circuit courts*. Above the courts of appeals is the Supreme Court. Decisions of a district court may be appealed to an appeals court, and from the appeals court to the Supreme Court. Federal courts decide cases that involve the Constitution and federal laws. Judges of these courts hold office for life. The President appoints them with the approval of the Senate. See COURT.

Principles of American Government

Separation of Powers. The Constitution divides the powers of the United States government among the executive, legislative, and judicial branches. Each branch is generally independent of the other two, and has the authority to check or balance the others. *Checks and balances* give each branch some powers that affect the other two. For example, Congress holds a check over the President with its authority to make government appropriations. It holds a check over the courts with its powers to organize courts and create rules for their procedures. One of the President's checks on Congress is his power to veto bills. He also influences the federal courts by the kind of judges he appoints to them. The courts can check the President and Congress by declaring executive orders and legislative acts unconstitutional.

A Written Constitution provides the basis of government in the United States. It divides powers and duties between the federal and state governments. It specifies the powers of each branch of the national government. A written constitution is one of the unique contributions the American people have made to the art of government. British royal governors had ruled the colonies in America under written charters granted by the king. The idea of adopting a written constitution as the basic law of an independent country was entirely new.

The Constitution not only grants powers, but also

HOW A BILL BECOMES LAW

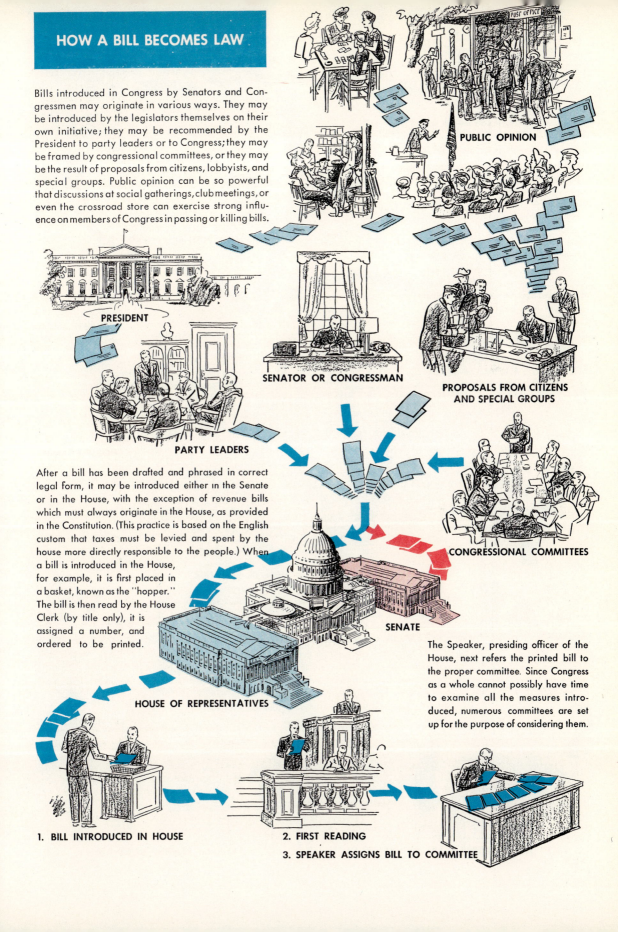

Bills introduced in Congress by Senators and Congressmen may originate in various ways. They may be introduced by the legislators themselves on their own initiative; they may be recommended by the President to party leaders or to Congress; they may be framed by congressional committees, or they may be the result of proposals from citizens, lobbyists, and special groups. Public opinion can be so powerful that discussions at social gatherings, club meetings, or even the crossroad store can exercise strong influence on members of Congress in passing or killing bills.

PUBLIC OPINION

PRESIDENT

SENATOR OR CONGRESSMAN

PROPOSALS FROM CITIZENS AND SPECIAL GROUPS

PARTY LEADERS

After a bill has been drafted and phrased in correct legal form, it may be introduced either in the Senate or in the House, with the exception of revenue bills which must always originate in the House, as provided in the Constitution. (This practice is based on the English custom that taxes must be levied and spent by the house more directly responsible to the people.) When a bill is introduced in the House, for example, it is first placed in a basket, known as the "hopper." The bill is then read by the House Clerk (by title only), it is assigned a number, and ordered to be printed.

CONGRESSIONAL COMMITTEES

SENATE

The Speaker, presiding officer of the House, next refers the printed bill to the proper committee. Since Congress as a whole cannot possibly have time to examine all the measures introduced, numerous committees are set up for the purpose of considering them.

HOUSE OF REPRESENTATIVES

1. BILL INTRODUCED IN HOUSE

2. FIRST READING

3. SPEAKER ASSIGNS BILL TO COMMITTEE

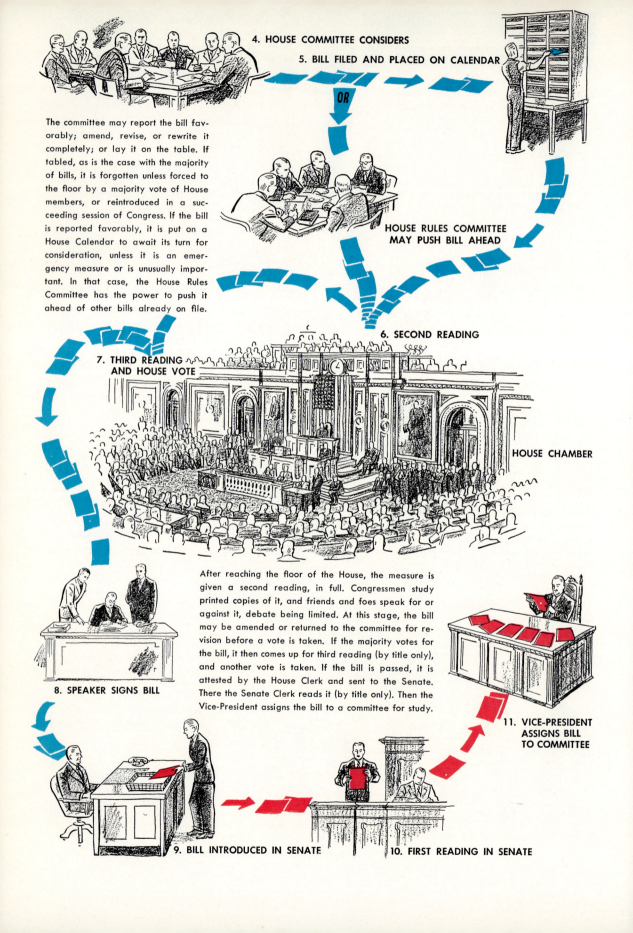

4. HOUSE COMMITTEE CONSIDERS

5. BILL FILED AND PLACED ON CALENDAR

OR

The committee may report the bill favorably; amend, revise, or rewrite it completely; or lay it on the table. If tabled, as is the case with the majority of bills, it is forgotten unless forced to the floor by a majority vote of House members, or reintroduced in a succeeding session of Congress. If the bill is reported favorably, it is put on a House Calendar to await its turn for consideration, unless it is an emergency measure or is unusually important. In that case, the House Rules Committee has the power to push it ahead of other bills already on file.

HOUSE RULES COMMITTEE MAY PUSH BILL AHEAD

6. SECOND READING

7. THIRD READING AND HOUSE VOTE

HOUSE CHAMBER

After reaching the floor of the House, the measure is given a second reading, in full. Congressmen study printed copies of it, and friends and foes speak for or against it, debate being limited. At this stage, the bill may be amended or returned to the committee for revision before a vote is taken. If the majority votes for the bill, it then comes up for third reading (by title only), and another vote is taken. If the bill is passed, it is attested by the House Clerk and sent to the Senate. There the Senate Clerk reads it (by title only). Then the Vice-President assigns the bill to a committee for study.

8. SPEAKER SIGNS BILL

11. VICE-PRESIDENT ASSIGNS BILL TO COMMITTEE

9. BILL INTRODUCED IN SENATE

10. FIRST READING IN SENATE

12. SENATE COMMITTEE CONSIDERS

OR

13. BILL FILED AND PLACED ON CALENDAR

SENATE MAJORITY LEADERS
MAY PUSH BILL AHEAD

Although some committee meetings are not public, open hearings are held for many important bills. When the bill comes out of committee, it is either filed and put on the Senate Calendar to await its turn or is pushed ahead by the Senate majority leaders. After reaching the Senate floor, it is read in full, debated without time limits unless the Senate imposes such limits, and brought to a vote. If it is passed, it is read a third time (by title only) and again put to a vote and passed before it is sent to the Vice-President for his signature.

14. SECOND READING

SENATE CHAMBER

15. THIRD READING AND SENATE VOTE

OR

16. HOUSE DEBATE ON AMENDMENTS

If the Senate amends the bill, it is returned to the House for approval or for further revision.

18. AMENDED BILL APPROVED

When the amendments are not approved by the House, a conference committee, composed of members from both houses, is appointed to reconcile the differences. When agreement is reached, the revised bill is sent back to the House and Senate for their final approval.

HOUSE

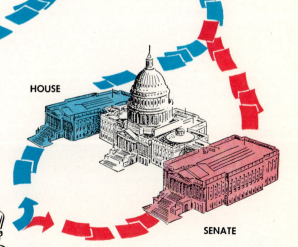

SENATE

17. CONFERENCE COMMITTEE RECONCILES DIFFERENCES

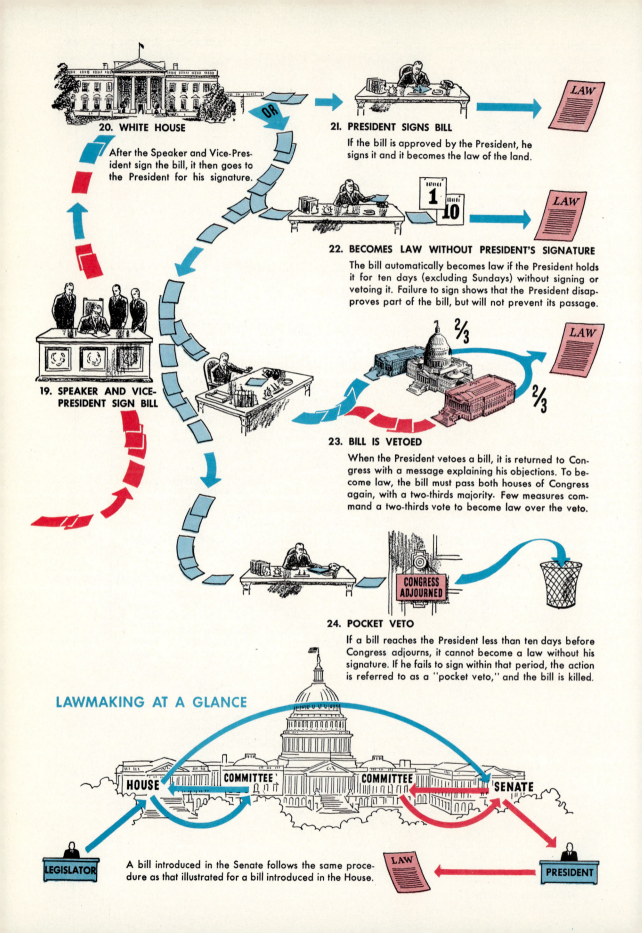

20. WHITE HOUSE

After the Speaker and Vice-President sign the bill, it then goes to the President for his signature.

21. PRESIDENT SIGNS BILL

If the bill is approved by the President, he signs it and it becomes the law of the land.

LAW

LAW

22. BECOMES LAW WITHOUT PRESIDENT'S SIGNATURE

The bill automatically becomes law if the President holds it for ten days (excluding Sundays) without signing or vetoing it. Failure to sign shows that the President disapproves part of the bill, but will not prevent its passage.

19. SPEAKER AND VICE-PRESIDENT SIGN BILL

2/3   *LAW*

2/3

23. BILL IS VETOED

When the President vetoes a bill, it is returned to Congress with a message explaining his objections. To become law, the bill must pass both houses of Congress again, with a two-thirds majority. Few measures command a two-thirds vote to become law over the veto.

CONGRESS ADJOURNED

24. POCKET VETO

If a bill reaches the President less than ten days before Congress adjourns, it cannot become a law without his signature. If he fails to sign within that period, the action is referred to as a "pocket veto," and the bill is killed.

LAWMAKING AT A GLANCE

HOUSE   COMMITTEE   COMMITTEE   SENATE

LEGISLATOR   *LAW*   PRESIDENT

A bill introduced in the Senate follows the same procedure as that illustrated for a bill introduced in the House.

limits them. However, it does not answer all questions. For example, who in the government is to say that a state is trying to use a power that belongs to the federal government? Who is to say that the federal government is attempting to exercise a power that belongs to the states? Who is to say that the President, Congress, or the Supreme Court are acting unconstitutionally?

Judicial Review is the method used to answer the basic question: Who is to say what the Constitution means in cases of dispute? Courts have the power to declare legislative acts and executive orders (1) constitutional, or legal; or (2) unconstitutional, or illegal.

Judicial review confines the state and national governments within their constitutional limits. Generally, the state courts interpret the state constitutions, and federal courts interpret the United States Constitution. The Supreme Court can declare unconstitutional executive orders and legislative acts of the federal or the state governments. The Constitution clearly states that it and all federal laws and treaties are the supreme law of the land.

Popular Sovereignty allows the American people to change the Constitution. Congress initiates amendments to the Constitution. A proposed amendment must have the approval of two thirds of both the Senate and the House of Representatives. It then goes to the states for their approval. Congress may call a national convention to propose amendments, if two thirds of the state legislatures request it. The amendment becomes a part of the Constitution after legislatures or conventions in three fourths of the states have ratified it. The American people may adopt an entirely new constitution by calling a new constitutional convention, like the one at Philadelphia in 1787. If such a convention were held, the constitution it adopted would be sent to the states for approval. It would become effective when ratified in the same way as an amendment.

Political Parties and Elections

The American people have a strong voice in their government. They can exercise their democratic rights by voting in national, state, and local elections, and by working in political parties and campaigns.

The Two-Party System. The United States has two major political parties, the Democratic and the Republican. Both parties receive support from individuals and groups in all parts of the country. Members of these two parties hold almost all the offices in the national, state, and local governments.

Minor political parties of the United States rarely elect candidates to government offices. They serve chiefly to call attention to problems that the major parties may have neglected. Often, one or both of the major parties may then attempt to solve such a problem. Then the third party, which brought attention to the problem, may disappear. See POLITICAL PARTY.

National Elections to elect a President and Vice-President are held every four years on the first Tuesday after the first Monday in November. All members of the House of Representatives and about one-third of the members of the Senate are elected at this same time. Between the presidential elections, all of the representatives and another one-third of the senators are elected. This election is held on the same day in November in even-numbered years.

UNITED STATES, GOVERNMENT OF

Federal and state laws regulate elections and the qualifications of voters. Most states hold *primary* elections in which party members nominate candidates for state and local offices. Some states use the primary to nominate candidates for Congress. National political conventions nominate candidates for President and Vice-President. See POLITICAL CONVENTION; PRIMARY ELECTION.

Presidential elections are held to select electors to the Electoral College (see ELECTORAL COLLEGE). Each state has as many electors as the total of its senators and representatives in Congress. The electors vote for the candidate who receives the most votes in their respective states. A candidate for President must receive a majority of the electoral votes to be elected.

The Development of American Government

English Background. The United States inherited many government practices from the English rulers of colonial days. In England, the people, particularly those in the middle classes, had fought their kings to win the right to representative government. They had also fought successfully for civil rights and liberties that would protect them and their property from arbitrary acts of government.

The English colonists brought with them the ideas of representative government and civil liberties when they came to America. American frontier life produced much individual independence and self-reliance because of the equal opportunity offered each person. Representative government and many civil liberties became even broader than they had been in Great Britain.

Early American Government. The colonies became states after the Declaration of Independence in 1776. They founded the first independent general government in the United States under the *Articles of Confederation* (see ARTICLES OF CONFEDERATION). Under the Articles, the 13 states guarded their individual powers so strictly that they failed to give Congress the power to tax or to regulate interstate and foreign commerce. Congress could not even create an army without asking the state governments for men and money. Such leaders as George Washington, Benjamin Franklin, James Madison, and Alexander Hamilton feared that the weak national government would collapse. They led a constitutional convention in Philadelphia in 1787 that wrote the United States Constitution. The document was ratified by the first nine states by June, 1788, and went into effect in 1789.

The Constitution gave the national government more powers than it had possessed under the Articles of Confederation. The federal government exercises these powers directly over the people, not through the state governments, as it had done under the Articles.

The Growth of American Government. Congress gave the western territories of the United States local representative government as they grew in population. The Northwest Ordinance, passed under the Articles of Confederation in 1787, became a model for future territorial governments (see NORTHWEST ORDINANCE). After a territory had enough people, Congress admitted it into the Union as a state.

The United States purchased Alaska in 1867, and in

CAPITOLS OF THE UNITED STATES

Three Lions
1 CARPENTERS' HALL, PHILADELPHIA (1774)

Bettmann Archive
2 INDEPENDENCE HALL, PHILADELPHIA (1775-1776; 1777; 1778-1783)

The Government met in various cities between 1774 and 1800. The Continental Congress and, later, the Congress of the United States met in the buildings shown here. In 1800, the government moved into the first Capitol in Washington, D.C., which developed by 1863 into the stately, white-domed building we know today.

Hist. Soc. of Pa.
10 CONGRESS HALL, PHILADELPHIA (1790-1800)

Schoenfeld Collection, Three Lions
9 FEDERAL HALL, NEW YORK CITY (1785-1790)

First Trenton National Bank
8 FRENCH ARMS TAVERN, TRENTON, N.J. (1784)

Culver Service
7 STATE HOUSE, ANNAPOLIS, MD. (1783-1784)

1898 it acquired Puerto Rico, Hawaii, and the Philippines. At first, these territories did not receive as democratic and representative a government as the other territories within the borders of the United States. But the Philippines gained full independence in 1946. Puerto Rico became a commonwealth in 1952. Alaska and Hawaii became the 49th and 50th states in 1959.

Problems of Government. Since 1789, all governments—national, state, and local—have taken on more powers and duties. They have been forced to do so by the increase in population, the growth of cities and towns, the development of industries, and the growth of transportation and communications. Problems that were once local, such as conservation and transportation, have become national. The belief has developed that people should use government and other organizations to provide themselves with services, such as social security, made possible by modern wealth and science. As a result, the federal government has grown even faster than the state and local governments.

Many persons object to the expansion of federal authority, particularly over state and local matters. Others insist that public interest demands federal rather than state control in cases that involve more than one state. When conflicts arise, the courts must decide how to balance the rights of the states with the needs of the national government. WILLIAM G. CARLETON

Related Articles in WORLD BOOK include:

EXECUTIVE DEPARTMENTS

Agriculture, Department of
Commerce, Department of
Defense, Department of
Health, Education, and Welfare, Department of
Housing and Urban Development, Department of
Interior, Department of the
Justice, Department of
Labor, Department of
Post Office Department
State, Department of
Treasury, Department of the

EXECUTIVE OFFICE OF THE PRESIDENT

Budget, Bureau of the
Central Intelligence Agency
Economic Advisers, Council of
Economic Opportunity, Office of
National Security Council
President of the United States

INDEPENDENT AGENCIES

American Battle Monuments Commission
Atomic Energy Commission
Civil Aeronautics Board
Civil Service Commission
District of Columbia
Export-Import Bank of Washington
Farm Credit Administration
Federal Aviation Agency
Federal Communications Commission
Federal Deposit Insurance Corporation
Federal Mediation and Conciliation Service
Federal Power Commission
Federal Reserve System
Federal Trade Commission
Fine Arts, Commission of
General Services Administration
Indian Claims Commission

84

Maryland Historical Society
3 CONGRESS HOUSE, BALTIMORE (1776-1777)

4 OLD COURT HOUSE, LANCASTER, PA. (1777)

Historical Society of Pennsylvania

Bettmann Archive
6 NASSAU HALL, PRINCETON, N.J. (1783)

Historical Society of York County
5 YORK COUNTY COURT HOUSE, YORK, PA. (1777-1778)

Interstate Commerce Commission
National Aeronautics and Space Administration and Council
National Labor Relations Board
National Mediation Board
National Science Foundation
National Security Agency
Railroad Retirement Board
Saint Lawrence Seaway Development Corp.

Securities and Exchange Commission
Selective Service System
Small Business Administration
Tariff Commission, United States
Tax Court of the United States
Tennessee Valley Authority
United States Information Agency
Veterans Administration

INTERNATIONAL AGENCIES

Caribbean Organization
Food and Agriculture Organization
International Atomic Energy Agency
International Bank for Reconstruction and Development
International Civil Aviation Organization
International Finance Corporation
International Labor Organization

International Monetary Fund
International Telecommunication Union
Organization of American States
Pan American Union
Postal Union, Universal
UNESCO
United Nations
World Health Organization
World Meteorological Organization

JUDICIAL BRANCH

Court of Appeals   Court of Claims

UNITED STATES, GOVERNMENT OF

Court of Military Appeals
Customs Court, U.S.
District Court

Supreme Court of the United States
Territorial Courts

LEGISLATIVE BRANCH

Congress of the United States
General Accounting Office
Government Printing Office
House of Representatives

Library of Congress
Senate
Vice-President of the United States

SYMBOLS OF GOVERNMENT

Bald Eagle
Columbia
E Pluribus Unum
Flag

Great Seal of the United States
Liberty, Statue of
Liberty Bell

Pledge to the Flag
Star-Spangled Banner
Uncle Sam

OTHER RELATED ARTICLES

Americanization
American's Creed
Ballot
Bill of Rights
Citizenship
City and Local Governments
Civil Service
County
Court
Democracy
Electoral College
Foreign Service
Government
Hoover Commission

Immigration and Emigration
Initiative and Referendum
Law
Law Enforcement
Money
National Debt
Naturalization
Political Party
Presidential Succession
Public Lands
Social Security
Spoils System
State Government

States' Rights
Statuary Hall
Tariff
Taxation
Territory
United States, History of
United States Capitals
United States Constitution
Veto
Voting
Washington, D.C.
White House
Yankee

Outline

I. Government in American Life
II. The Executive Branch
  A. The President
  B. Executive Departments
  C. Independent Agencies
III. The Legislative Branch
  A. The Senate   B. The House of Representatives
IV. The Judicial Branch
  A. The Supreme Court   B. Other Federal Courts
V. Principles of American Government
  A. Separation of Powers   C. Judicial Review
  B. A Written Constitution   D. Popular Sovereignty
VI. Political Parties and Elections
  A. The Two-Party System   B. National Elections
VII. The Development of American Government
  A. English Background   D. Problems of Government
  B. Early American Government
  C. The Growth of American Government

Questions

How does the United States government differ from most other national governments?

What are the three branches of the United States government?

What is *popular sovereignty? Judicial review?* Why are they important in the United States government?

How does each branch of the government exercise its powers of checks and balances?

How does the United States Constitution divide powers among the national and state governments?

What is an *independent agency?* What does it do?

How did the ideas of representative government develop in the colonies?

How may the United States Constitution be amended?

What are two exclusive powers of the House of Representatives?

What are some typical questions of government left unanswered by the United States Constitution?

Daniel Boone Coming Through the Cumberland Gap by George Caleb Bingham

UNITED STATES, HISTORY OF.

UNITED STATES, HISTORY OF. The history of the United States is the story of a great nation created from a vast wilderness in an unbelievably short time. It is the story of a nation founded on the principle that all men have a right to "life, liberty, and the pursuit of happiness."

Five hundred years ago, not a single European settler lived in the land that is now the United States. Three hundred years ago, only a few scattered settlements lay along the Atlantic Coast. Even as recently as 200 years ago, the United States of America did not exist.

But, during those 200 years, the United States has developed its unique culture and grown to maturity. Its Founding Fathers wrote the world's most lasting constitution. Hardy pioneers crossed the continent. Scien-

tists experimented with inventions in every field. Brother fought against brother in a deadly civil war. Businessmen poured millions of dollars into growing industries. Wave after wave of immigrants found a common loyalty in their new homeland without losing their individuality. In more recent years, statesmen turned their attention to world problems, without losing sight of national ones.

The people of the United States found that the ideals of the Founding Fathers were as useful in the atomic age as they had been in the era of powdered wigs and stagecoaches. They developed a strong belief in growth and progress. They were always willing to try new ways of doing things. They proved their faith in "the American experiment," which, by the middle 1900's, placed

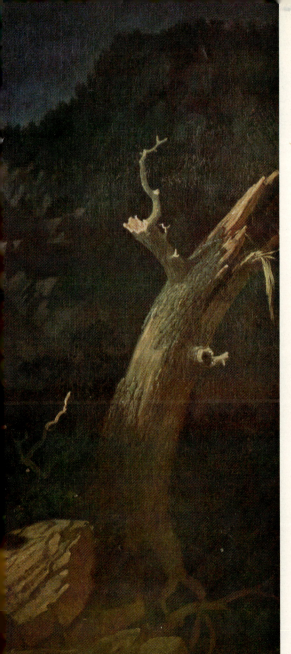

Courtesy of Washington University, St. Louis, Mo.

Carved and gilded wooden eagle.
Courtesy National Gallery of Art,
Index of American Design

HISTORY
of the
UNITED STATES

Americans Explored and Won a Rich New Land.
Armed with gun and ax, plow and Bible, they transformed
a wilderness into one of the world's greatest nations.

the United States first among the countries of the world in freedom, opportunity, wealth, and power.

Finding a New World

For hundreds of years, Europeans knew nothing about the land that was to become the United States. Indian tribes had the land to themselves. They hunted and fished, and set up villages where great cities now stand. For this earliest chapter of American history, see INDIAN, AMERICAN.

American history began when Europeans brought their civilization across the Atlantic Ocean during the 1500's and 1600's. Much earlier, about the year 1000, vikings from Greenland and Iceland had sailed to the American coast. But they did not make permanent

settlements, and people forgot about their trips. Then, in the late 1400's, many Europeans began to talk of sailing westward to reach China. They believed that the world was round. But they thought that it was smaller than it is. They hoped to sail around the world and trade directly with the Orient.

Christopher Columbus sailed westward in 1492, because he believed that Asia lay just across the Atlantic Ocean. When he found land, he thought he had reached the East Indies (now Indonesia). He never knew that he had discovered a new continent. But the Spaniards and Portuguese who came after him realized that they had reached an unexplored land. They called it *The New World*. Hernando Cortes conquered the rich Aztec empire in Mexico between 1519 and 1521. Other

87

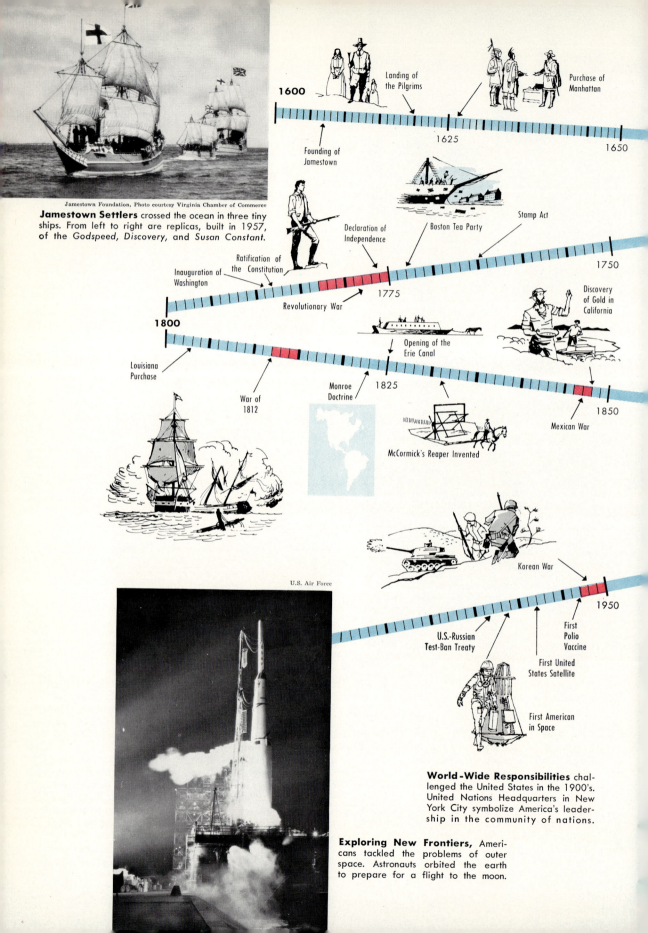

Jamestown Foundation, Photo courtesy Virginia Chamber of Commerce

Jamestown Settlers crossed the ocean in three tiny ships. From left to right are replicas, built in 1957, of the *Godspeed*, *Discovery*, and *Susan Constant*.

1600

Landing of the Pilgrims

Purchase of Manhattan

1625

1650

Founding of Jamestown

Declaration of Independence

Boston Tea Party

Stamp Act

1750

Inauguration of Washington

Ratification of the Constitution

1775

Revolutionary War

1800

Discovery of Gold in California

Opening of the Erie Canal

Louisiana Purchase

War of 1812

Monroe Doctrine

1825

1850

Mexican War

McCormick's Reaper Invented

U.S. Air Force

Korean War

1950

U.S.-Russian Test-Ban Treaty

First Polio Vaccine

First United States Satellite

First American in Space

World-Wide Responsibilities challenged the United States in the 1900's. United Nations Headquarters in New York City symbolize America's leadership in the community of nations.

Exploring New Frontiers, Americans tackled the problems of outer space. Astronauts orbited the earth to prepare for a flight to the moon.

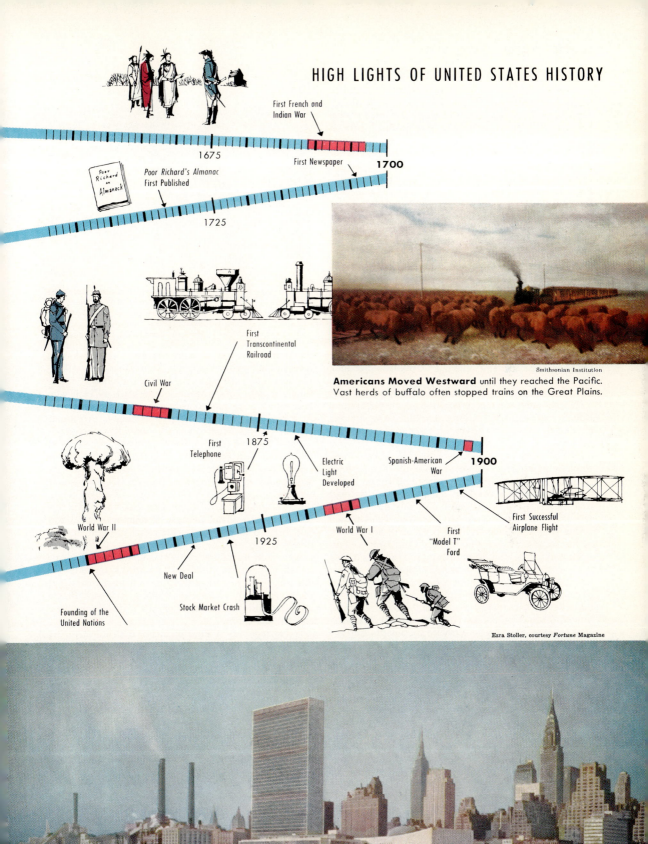

HIGH LIGHTS OF UNITED STATES HISTORY

First French and Indian War

1675

First Newspaper

1700

Poor Richard's Almanac First Published

1725

First Transcontinental Railroad

Civil War

Smithsonian Institution

Americans Moved Westward until they reached the Pacific. Vast herds of buffalo often stopped trains on the Great Plains.

First Telephone

1875

Electric Light Developed

Spanish-American War

1900

First Successful Airplane Flight

World War II

World War I

First "Model T" Ford

New Deal

1925

Stock Market Crash

Founding of the United Nations

Ezra Stoller, courtesy *Fortune* Magazine

Spaniards discovered Florida. In 1565 they founded St. Augustine, the oldest city in what is now the United States. Hernando de Soto and Francisco Coronado led expeditions into the interior of North America. Other nations also entered the race to explore the Americas. John Cabot, sailing under the English flag, discovered the mainland of North America when he landed on the coast of Labrador in 1497. The French explorer Jacques Cartier sailed up the Saint Lawrence River in 1534. For the story of this period, see EXPLORATION AND DISCOVERY.

But all this exploration had little effect on what is now the United States. The bitter winters, fierce Indian tribes, and thick forests along the Atlantic Coast discouraged the Spaniards. The French spread their fur-trading posts from Quebec to the Great Lakes and down the Mississippi River. But they were not interested in colonization on a large scale. The British were the first to settle in North America in large numbers. British settlers came prepared to face any problems. They also had enough money to finance private colonizing and trading ventures. Settlers had many reasons for coming to America. Some hoped to make fortunes. Others sought religious or political freedom.

The Thirteen Colonies

Private enterprise was responsible for all the original British colonies in North America. The king granted charters to joint-stock corporations to found and govern *chartered*, or *commercial*, colonies. Sometimes he gave grants of land to individuals to establish *proprietary* colonies. Most of the colonies eventually became *royal* colonies, ruled by a governor appointed by the king.

Virginia and Maryland. In 1585, Sir Walter Raleigh tried unsuccessfully to establish a colony on Roanoke Island (see LOST COLONY). More than 20 years passed before colonists made the first permanent settlement, at Jamestown in 1607. The London Company, a joint-stock company, sponsored this group of 104 men. For a time, the little band struggled desperately against sickness, Indians, and other misfortunes. Two men rescued the colony. Captain John Smith put the colony under severe military rule. He made the men work and trained them to fight. John Rolfe began experimenting with tobacco. This crop soon became popular in Europe, and the colony grew prosperous from growing and selling it. By 1619, Virginia had its own legislature, the first representative assembly on the mainland of North America. Within 25 years after the first colonists landed, 40,000 persons lived in Virginia. Meanwhile, other colonists came to Maryland. This proprietary colony was established by Lord Baltimore north of Chesapeake Bay.

At first, the region on both sides of Chesapeake Bay was a land of small farms. Many young men and women came as *indentured servants*. They worked for other colonists to repay the cost of their passage. Many of them then received their own grants of land. But the profits from tobacco soon gave Virginia and Maryland a special character. Tobacco growers wanted a steady supply of labor. They needed large plantations, because tobacco growing rapidly wore out the soil. A few Negroes arrived on a Dutch ship in 1619, probably as indentured servants. But in the years that followed, most of the Negroes who came were slaves. After 1660, planters began buying slaves in large numbers. Negroes finally replaced most white laborers. Many men who had small farms moved westward. They became unhappy with the slavery system, and some of them took part in Bacon's Rebellion (see BACON'S REBELLION).

New England. A joint-stock company sent the first permanent settlers to New England. The *Mayflower* carried 102 persons to Plymouth, Mass., in 1620. The settlers had intended to go to Virginia, but storms blew their ship off its course. These colonists called themselves *Pilgrims*. Most of them were Separatist Puritans fleeing from England because of religious persecution (see PILGRIM; PURITAN). Others came to improve their fortunes. On shipboard, the founders of Plymouth Colony drew up the Mayflower Compact, an agreement for self-government under majority rule. They had some difficult years, but friendly Indians helped them, and they had an able leader in William Bradford. Before long they prospered from their trade in furs, lumber, codfish, and grain.

A larger group of Puritans decided to move to the same area after they saw how the God-fearing Pilgrims had prospered. John Endecott led a small group to Salem in 1628. The following year this area received its charter as the Massachusetts Bay Colony. In 1630, a fleet of 18 ships carried nearly 1,000 passengers to Massachusetts Bay, where stern John Winthrop soon rose to power. Most of the newcomers were prosperous, hard-working, middle-class people. Within a dozen years, about 20,000 enterprising and courageous English people came to Massachusetts. They raised large families, pushed the Indians back, and founded new settlements. They spread out in all directions from the first colonies—up the Maine coast, south into Rhode Island, and west into Connecticut and Long Island. In 1691 both Plymouth Colony and settlements in Maine became a part of Massachusetts Bay Colony.

The New Englanders set a high value on freedom. In many matters, each Puritan congregation ruled it-

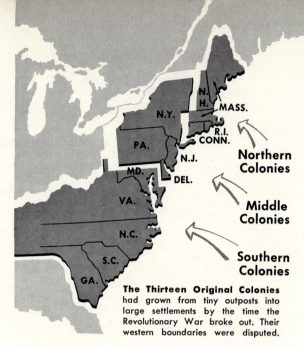

The Thirteen Original Colonies had grown from tiny outposts into large settlements by the time the Revolutionary War broke out. Their western boundaries were disputed.

EARLY DAYS

In New England, stern Puritans at first farmed the rocky land. But trade and industry soon proved more profitable.

In the South, the climate favored tobacco growing. Large plantations shipped the crop in kegs from their own wharves.

Shostal

Colonial Life depended on home manufacture of many necessities. Women spun and wove, and made the family's clothes.

Defending Their Lands, the colonists quickly learned the techniques of wilderness fighting. Rogers' Rangers, shown *below*, gained fame for their daring exploits in the French and Indian War.

self. John Winthrop and other founders of Massachusetts Bay brought the company's charter with them. It gave the *freemen* (stockholders) the power to elect their own governor and legislature. After Roger Williams was expelled from Massachusetts because of his radical religious beliefs, he founded a new colony in Rhode Island where people had complete freedom to think and worship as they pleased. The settlers who moved to Connecticut established their own government in 1639. Several New England settlements formed a confederation to help one another against common dangers (see NEW ENGLAND CONFEDERATION).

The New England people were also democratic in economic matters. There was not enough land to form big plantations. The people had to work their land hard to produce grain and fruits on the rocky soil. Farmers did not need slaves. People lived in villages, and walked out to work on their farms. They built their houses around a central *common*, a village square or meadow often used for pasturing livestock. They governed themselves by town meetings, where every citizen had a vote. Massachusetts was practically independent until the late 1600's. It became a royal colony in 1691. During most of the colonial period, Rhode Island and Connecticut resembled little republics, electing their own governors and other officials. In time, New England developed a spirit of freedom rarely equaled anywhere before in the world.

The Middle Colonies. Great colonies controlled by individual proprietors grew up in the area between New England and Virginia. The Dutch settled New Netherland in 1624, but they could not establish a successful government. The rulers proved so unpopular that the English took over in 1664 almost without resistance. King Charles II gave the province to his brother, the Duke of York, who renamed it New York. The Duke of York made large grants of land to close friends, which encouraged the growth of great estates. The northern parts of the province became noted for aristocratic landholders and their tenants. But New York City quickly developed a brisk shipping and trading business with the other colonies. People of every nationality and religion lived in the city. Tolerance of opinion grew rapidly.

William Penn, who became a Quaker after leaving the Church of England, founded Pennsylvania as a bold liberal experiment. The Quakers believed in peace, industry, freedom of opinion, and universal kindness. The king gave Pennsylvania to Penn in 1681, and Penn planned his colony carefully. He helped poor people settle in it, proclaimed religious freedom, and set up the most humane laws known anywhere in the world. English, Scotch-Irish, and German settlers quickly moved to this attractive colony.

The people did not really govern New York or Pennsylvania. New York soon became a royal province, with a governor appointed by the king. In Pennsylvania, William Penn kept considerable power and passed it on to his sons. Pennsylvania was unusual in its interest in culture. The Quakers promoted science, medicine, and education. They established schools and published newspapers and books. Philadelphia became a center of culture. Young Benjamin Franklin naturally went

there when he left Boston in 1723 to better himself. By 1750, Philadelphia, with nearly 20,000 people, had become the largest city in North America.

New Jersey, originally part of New Netherland, was given to the Duke of York in 1664. That same year, he granted it to two friends. They favored religious freedom, and as a result many English Quakers and New England Puritans settled there. Swedes made the first permanent settlement in Delaware in 1638. New Netherland claimed the region, which passed to the Duke of York in 1664, and to William Penn in 1682. The colony remained part of Pennsylvania until the Revolutionary War.

The Southern Colonies. The great region south of Virginia was divided into three very different colonies: North Carolina, South Carolina, and Georgia. King Charles II gave what was called Carolina to eight of his friends in 1663. This area included both North and South Carolina. North Carolina was difficult to settle from the sea, because islands, sand dunes, and marshes barred the way. Most of the people came by land from the north. They included Virginians trying to escape debts, Quakers and French Huguenots fleeing persecution, and Scotch-Irish and Germans looking for cheap land. The region became a country of small farmers, with hardly any slavery. But South Carolina was easy to reach by sea, and attracted wealthy colonists who set up large rice plantations along the coast. These settlers needed Negroes for labor. Charleston became a rich seaport and a lively social center. In this way, South Carolina developed as an aristocratic colony, while North Carolina was more democratic. The two colonies split apart in 1712.

Georgia, like Pennsylvania, was established as an idealistic experiment. Its founder, James Oglethorpe, felt sorry for poor debtors in England, who usually went to prison when they could not pay their debts. He felt that these and other unfortunate persons should have a chance to improve their lives. Oglethorpe brought the first colonists to Georgia in 1733. He founded Savannah as a town of broad streets and beautiful squares. He prohibited slavery and the importation of rum. He also tried to produce silk and other items not usually produced in North America. Oglethorpe wanted a large number of small, independent farmers. But the land was better suited for large rice plantations. The trustees who ruled the colony prohibited slavery and large land holdings, so the population grew slowly. The British government took over Georgia in 1752, and aided its growth with grants of money.

The Colonists. By 1760, more than 1,500,000 persons lived in the 13 colonies. The colonies grew quickly, because large families were common. The population doubled every 25 years. Most of the people lived fairly comfortably, with few very rich men and few very poor. They lived close to the soil and worked hard.

Almost all the colonists were Protestants, and most of them had a keen interest in religion. But many people in Massachusetts and New Hampshire grumbled when they had to support the Puritan, or Congregational, Church. Many Southerners resented paying money to the Anglican Church. There were few class lines in New England, North Carolina, and Georgia. In the other colonies, barriers clearly separated the rich from the poor, and the well-educated from the ignorant.

People in all the colonies owned slaves, but most slave-owners lived south of Delaware, and many persons opposed slaveholding.

No people on earth were freer, more hopeful, or blessed with a higher general standard of living. The colonists were British subjects. But they did not think and act like their fellow subjects in Great Britain. They were a mixture of peoples—English, Scottish, Welsh, Dutch, German, Swedish, and others—and they had learned many new ways from the Indians and from the wilderness. As one writer said, they had "melted into a new race of men." For a description of their way of life, see COLONIAL LIFE IN AMERICA.

The Movement for Liberty

Friction Increases. For many years, the British government paid little attention to the American colonies. The colonies increased in population and independence. New settlements grew up between the Atlantic Coast and the Appalachian Mountains. All the colonies had their own legislatures. Rhode Island and Connecticut elected their own governors. The Privy Council in London could veto laws passed by the colonial legislatures, but it seldom did so. The colonial legislatures gained more and more power. At the same time, the royal governors (and the proprietary families that ruled Pennsylvania, Delaware, and Maryland) steadily lost authority.

The British let the colonies go their own way politically. But they kept economic control over the colonists. Parliament passed laws that required the colonies to carry goods in British or colonial ships, and to buy most of their goods in Britain. In return, the colonies had a protected market for their products in the mother country. These laws were not one-sided. The British and the colonists each gave up something and gained something. In fact, British trade restrictions on their colonies were much lighter than those that France and Spain imposed on their colonies. But the Americans had become such strong individualists that they resented any controls. They could not even agree to unite among themselves (see ALBANY CONGRESS). Disagreements between colonial legislatures and the royal governors also increased.

A Clash of Empires. The French took possession of the Saint Lawrence River in 1534. Then they sent explorers, trappers, traders, and missionaries westward, and claimed the whole Mississippi River Valley. Frenchmen founded Detroit and New Orleans. By 1700, Father Jacques Marquette and Robert Cavelier, Sieur de la Salle, had explored much of the Mississippi river system. But the French settlements, called *New France*, remained weak. Few Frenchmen wanted to leave France. The French government would not let Protestants become colonists. It also imposed harsh restrictions on Frenchmen who did move. French settlers blundered by making enemies of the powerful Iroquois Indians.

It seemed certain that the British, who also claimed the Mississippi Valley, would soon run into trouble with the French. It also appeared certain that they would finally win, because they outnumbered the French 20 to 1 in America. But it took hard fighting. The four so-called French and Indian Wars grew out of conflicts between France and England in Europe. The

first three—King William's, Queen Anne's, and King George's wars—occurred between 1689 and 1748. These wars had little effect in North America, except that after Queen Anne's War the British took Newfoundland, the Hudson Bay region, and Acadia (Nova Scotia).

The Seven Years' War began in 1756. Fighting had begun two years earlier in America. There it was called the French and Indian War. It was caused mainly by conflicts over forts in the Ohio River Valley. A French force defeated young George Washington in southwestern Pennsylvania. He commanded Virginia militiamen sent by the royal governor to warn the French away from what is now Pittsburgh. The French won several important victories in the early months of the war. Then British and American troops captured the Pittsburgh region and invaded Canada. In 1759, General James Wolfe defeated the French under the Marquis de Montcalm and captured Quebec. This battle practically ended the struggle. In the Treaty of Paris of 1763, France gave the British all Canada and the western country as far as the Mississippi River. See FRENCH AND INDIAN WARS.

By 1763, Britain and Spain ruled almost all North America. But Spain was weak. For more than 100 years, the colonists, fearing their French neighbors, had depended on Britain for protection. Now their fear disappeared.

Approach of War. Great Britain had few statesmen who could handle the vast responsibilities of its new empire. The government made a series of unwise decisions. It tried to tighten and enforce trading restrictions on the colonies. It issued a proclamation that prohibited settlement beyond the Appalachian Mountains. It also decided to keep 10,000 troops in the American colonies as a safeguard against the Indians and a possible renewal of the war with France. All these actions injured American pride and independence.

One British blunder followed another. A law of 1765, the Stamp Act, taxed newspapers, legal papers, and some business documents. The colonists denied that the British government had any right to tax them, because the colonists had no representatives in the British Parliament. They protested strongly against "taxation without representation," and the British had to repeal the law. Parliament then imposed tariffs on various goods imported from Britain. In March, 1770, British troops fired on a Boston mob that attacked them, and killed several persons in the so-called Boston Massacre (see BOSTON MASSACRE). When the English East India Company needed financial help, the government allowed it to ship surplus tea to America at a low cost, and to sell it through its own dealers. The colonists resented this action for two reasons: (1) it tended to give one company control of the tea trade, and (2) it renewed the British government's claim that it had the right to tax the colonies without their consent. Angry Bostonians threw the tea into the harbor in what was later called the *Boston Tea Party* (see BOSTON TEA PARTY).

The British government passed a series of acts to punish Boston harshly. The colonies took steps to unite in self-defense against what they called the Intolerable Acts. On the invitation of Virginia, all the colonies

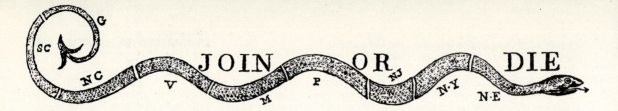

Paul Revere's Cartoon, Based on a Design by Benjamin Franklin, Urged the Colonies to Unite Against Britain.

except Georgia sent representatives to a meeting in Philadelphia. This First Continental Congress met on Sept. 5, 1774, and resolved that America would resist the Intolerable Acts. It sent a friendly petition to King George III, but it also proclaimed a boycott of British goods. The king and parliament refused to make any real concessions. Fighting between the colonists and the British began at Lexington and Concord, near Boston, on April 19, 1775. Colonial troops fortified Breed's Hill in June, 1775, to besiege Boston. But the British routed them in what is called the Battle of Bunker Hill.

Declaring Independence. George Washington's army then besieged the British in Boston for almost a year. But Americans hesitated to declare their independence. Many colonists still felt loyal to Britain, and hoped to settle the conflict peaceably. Meanwhile, the Second Continental Congress met in Philadelphia. It had two distinguished new members, Benjamin Franklin and Thomas Jefferson.

The New England colonies, under John Adams, John Hancock, and others, shared with Virginia the leadership of the movement for independence. The Middle Colonies, especially Pennsylvania with its Quaker love of peace, hung back. The movement received great encouragement early in 1776, when Thomas Paine, a writer from England, published his pamphlet *Common Sense*. This brilliant argument showed that Americans had not only the opportunity to create a free, happy, democratic, and progressive nation, but also every right to do so. In a land of fewer than 2,500,000 people, *Common Sense* sold hundreds of thousands of copies.

On July 2, 1776, every colony in the Continental Congress except New York (which acted a week later) voted for independence. On July 4, the Congress adopted the Declaration of Independence, written by a committee under Thomas Jefferson. The Declaration included many ideas borrowed from writers such as John Locke. But the majesty, earnestness, and grace of its language made it one of the most important documents in the history of human liberty. The Declaration blamed Great Britain for a long list of grievances. But it also emphasized men's natural right to change or overthrow any government that denied their rights. See DECLARATION OF INDEPENDENCE.

Winning Freedom. Americans had declared their independence from Britain, but they still had to fight to win it.

The British left Boston in 1776, and the war then centered chiefly in the Middle Colonies. General William Howe, the British commander, captured New York City in 1776, and Philadelphia the next year. After defeating Washington on Long Island, he almost captured the main American army. For a time in 1777, it seemed that British forces would control a line from

the Hudson River to Canada, cutting the colonies in two. But Howe's troops failed to join forces with another army coming down from Canada, and General John Burgoyne surrendered to General Horatio Gates at Saratoga in October, 1777.

Burgoyne's surrender proved to be the turning point of the war. The Americans took new hope, and France entered the war as an American ally. The fighting then moved to the South. The British captured Charleston, S.C., and defeated General Gates at Camden, S.C. But a French fleet won control of the coast. Moving rapidly, American and French armies penned up a British force under Lord Cornwallis at Yorktown, so he could not escape by land or sea. His surrender to Washington in October, 1781, practically ended the conflict. For a more complete story of the war, see REVOLUTIONARY WAR IN AMERICA.

Making a New Government

Critical Years. The American government that won the Revolutionary War had been set up under the Articles of Confederation, which Congress adopted in 1777 and all the states ratified by 1781 (see ARTICLES OF CONFEDERATION). This government was weak and had little authority. The states insisted on managing their own affairs. The Confederation had little power except that of supervising defense and foreign affairs. It had no real executive head. The Continental Congress, which acted for the Confederation, had no power to impose taxes, control trade, or stop quarrels among

Independence was declared in 1776. This painting shows Thomas Jefferson and his committee, who wrote the Declaration, presenting it to the other delegates. John Hancock, the first to sign, receives it.

the states. The Confederation could not even raise money, except by asking the states for it.

Yet the new nation faced problems that demanded a strong government. It had to protect trade with other countries, and encourage industry at home. As settlers began streaming westward, they came into conflict with Indians. The government had to subdue hostile tribes and distribute public lands. It also had to organize areas to become new states.

The Confederation achieved a few important results. By the Northwest Ordinance of 1787, it created the Northwest Territory, which was to be free of slavery and would some day be divided into five new states. But this success was not enough. An economic depression followed the Revolutionary War. Disorders broke out among debtors and poor farmers. Shays' Rebellion in Massachusetts caused great alarm (see Shays' Rebellion). Trade fell into confusion. Some states printed huge quantities of paper money that soon became worthless.

Virginia finally persuaded five states to send delegates to a convention at Annapolis, Md., in 1786 to discuss interstate commerce. They decided that the Articles of Confederation would have to be revised. Alexander Hamilton, a brilliant young New Yorker, wrote a report calling on the states to join in a new convention. The Continental Congress approved this proposal.

Establishing a More Perfect Union. In the summer of 1787, a group of 55 men from 12 states met in Independence Hall in Philadelphia to frame a new government. Rhode Island did not take part, because it resented "outside interference" in its affairs. George Washington presided, and most of the leading men of the new nation attended.

The convention discussed many plans, and almost all the delegates accepted two main principles. The first principle declared that the powers of the central government should be carefully defined, and that the states should keep all other powers. The second principle stated that the central government should have carefully balanced legislative, executive, and judicial departments. Most delegates favored a strong national authority that would have power to tax, to control interstate and foreign trade, to manage defense and foreign policy, and to enforce order. They wanted a real national government, not a mere league of states. For the story of their work and the results it produced, see United States Constitution.

After the Constitution had been written, the states had to ratify it. At first, many citizens opposed it. Some felt that the states had given up too much power. Others wanted the people to elect the President and senators directly. They opposed the indirect election provisions in the Constitution. But James Madison, Alexander Hamilton, and John Jay wrote an effective set of arguments called *The Federalist*. Washington cast his great influence for the Constitution, and every state finally approved it. Some states urged adding a bill of rights when they ratified the Constitution.

The first 10 amendments to the Constitution became effective in 1791. The first eight amendments, called the Bill of Rights, safeguarded freedom of speech, of the press, of religion, and of petition. They guaranteed jury trial, and protected life, liberty, and property. See Bill of Rights.

The New Nation. A census in 1790 showed that about 4,000,000 persons lived in the United States. Most of them lived along the Atlantic seacoast, either in villages or on farms. Only about 100,000 hardy settlers had ventured west of the Allegheny Mountains. Bad roads and poor communications kept communities isolated. Two stagecoaches and 12 horses carried all the land traffic between New York City and Boston. It took almost a month for news of the Declaration of Independence to travel from Philadelphia to Charleston, S.C.

But the country was growing fast. Vermont became

The Declaration of Independence by Barry Faulkner, courtesy of The National Archives, Washington, D.C.

a state in 1791, and Kentucky in 1792. Settlers began to stream westward. By 1800, Tennessee had more than 100,000 persons and Ohio nearly 50,000. The number of post offices increased from 75 in 1790 to 264 in 1792, and to 453 in 1795. People thought little of hardships so long as they could get ahead in the world. Prosperity grew because land cost so little. After Eli Whitney invented the cotton gin in 1793, cotton growing became a great industry. Jean Boré proved that sugar could be refined successfully near New Orleans, and sugar plantations soon spread throughout much of Louisiana.

The Federalists in Power

Washington

The Rise of Political Parties. The new federal government began its activities in the spring of 1789. The electoral college unanimously chose George Washington as President, and Congress made New York City the temporary capital. Washington appointed Thomas Jefferson as Secretary of State and Alexander Hamilton as Secretary of the Treasury.

Many leaders of the new nation hoped that no political parties would arise. But two parties were already taking shape—the Federalist party and the Democratic-Republican party. Most members of the Democratic-Republican party believed in states' rights and a weak national government, and rallied around Jefferson. He had the general support of farmers and planters. Most Federalists favored a strong central government. They turned to Hamilton, who was backed by merchants, manufacturers, and other businessmen. See DEMOCRATIC-REPUBLICAN PARTY; FEDERALIST PARTY.

Strengthening the Nation required several important measures. Under Hamilton's leadership, the government assumed the responsibility of paying the debts of the Continental Congress, and of the various states. This move strengthened the credit of the new country, although the government was not able to pay the debts at this time. The new Secretary of the Treasury established a national mint, set up the system of coinage, and persuaded Congress to pass a moderate tariff law that encouraged manufacturing. Congress also placed an excise tax on all distilled liquors. Some Scotch-Irish settlers in western Pennsylvania protested the new tax, because whisky was almost the only product they could take to market over rough mountain roads. Hamilton persuaded Washington to call out 15,000 troops to put down the disturbances. Few persons were hurt in the so-called Whisky Rebellion, and the government gained prestige by its firmness (see WHISKY REBELLION).

Hamilton insisted on a broad interpretation of the Constitution in defining the powers of government. Jefferson favored a strict interpretation that would prevent the government from assuming powers not expressly granted to it. For this reason, he opposed the excise tax and the creation of a national bank. But Hamilton had his way, partly because Washington sided with the determined New Yorker and partly because the country really needed these measures. In return, Hamilton gave in to Jefferson, who wanted the permanent capital on the Potomac River, rather than in the North. George Washington chose the site for the city of Washington, which became the capital of the United States in 1800.

Hamilton's plan for a national bank proved especially important. He wanted such a bank to take care of the government's money, to make loans to the government when needed, and to issue bank notes that would provide a sound currency. In 1791, Congress chartered the bank for 20 years. Federalists rejoiced, and Democratic-Republicans grumbled. See BANK OF THE UNITED STATES (The First Bank).

Troubles with Europe tested the strength of the new nation. Great Britain and France went to war in 1793 in a struggle for power. In the United States, the Jeffersonians (Democratic-Republicans) sympathized with France, and the Hamiltonians (Federalists) supported Britain. Washington wisely decided that the United States should remain neutral. But he had great difficulty in keeping it so. The French minister to the United States, Edmond Genêt, tried to use American ports for French warships. He behaved so badly that Washington ordered him sent home.

Additional difficulties with Britain included disputes over the northern boundary of the United States and over British interference with American shipping. The British also refused to give up their forts in the Northwest Territory. In 1794, Washington sent John Jay to London to settle American disputes with Britain. In the resulting Jay Treaty, Great Britain surrendered its western posts, and broadened America's trading privileges with the British Empire. At the same time, Washington's special commissioner to Spain, Thomas Pinckney, completed another important agreement. His treaty gave Americans unlimited use of the Mississippi River. These two treaties greatly benefited the West.

Adams

Keeping the Peace. Washington retired from the presidency in 1797, and John Adams succeeded him. His administration brought more troubles with France, which was still at war in Europe. French cruisers captured American ships, and for a time the two countries carried on an undeclared naval war. The French government insulted three American commissioners in Paris by suggesting that they pay tribute money to France (see XYZ AFFAIR). Hamilton, now a private but influential citizen, favored harsh measures. For a time, war seemed certain. Adams raised troops and appointed generals. He strengthened the navy and appointed the first Secretary of the Navy, who became the fifth member of the President's Cabinet. But then Adams courageously pushed Hamilton aside and sent a new commission to Paris. The two governments arranged a treaty that guaranteed American neutral rights, so that the United States could carry on its affairs without interference.

To silence critics, the Federalists passed the Alien and Sedition Acts (see ALIEN AND SEDITION ACTS). Most Americans felt these acts to be foolish, if not oppressive. Two states adopted resolutions condemning them (see KENTUCKY AND VIRGINIA RESOLUTIONS). The unpopularity of the measures helped the Democratic-Republicans under Jefferson win the election of 1800 by a large majority of the votes cast.

National Unity

Jefferson

Jefferson as President stood for peace, democracy, economy, states' rights, and the promotion of agriculture. His simple ways emphasized the fact that government would now pay more attention to the com-

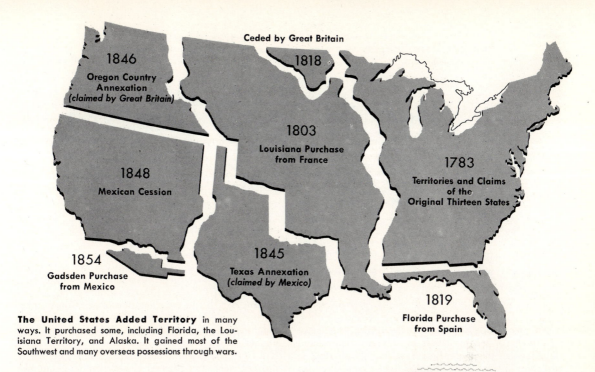

The United States Added Territory in many ways. It purchased some, including Florida, the Louisiana Territory, and Alaska. It gained most of the Southwest and many overseas possessions through wars.

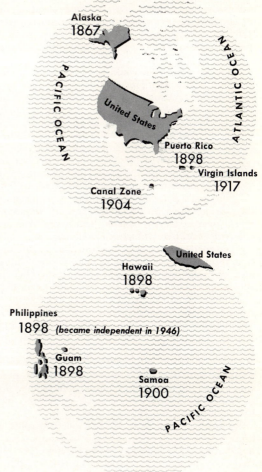

mon man. He cut government expenses, reduced the size of the navy, paid off much of the national debt, and tried hard to avoid war. The government repealed the Alien and Sedition Acts that had not already expired. But the main themes of the Jeffersonian period were national growth and greater national unity.

Jefferson's first great act, the Louisiana Purchase, doubled the size of the United States. Spain had recently ceded the Louisiana territory to France. But Napoleon knew that he could never hold it, and that Great Britain and the United States would seize it at the first opportunity. Jefferson said frankly that Americans could never tolerate French control of the mouth of the Mississippi River. When Napoleon failed to establish a powerful French base in Haiti, he decided to sell the Louisiana area to the United States. For $15,000,000, more than 825,000 square miles came under the American flag. No clause in the Constitution authorized the government to buy foreign territory, so Jefferson had to use the broad interpretation he had once denounced. He admitted that he "stretched the Constitution till it cracked."

A natural sequel to the Louisiana Purchase was the Lewis and Clark expedition. In 1804, Jefferson sent Meriwether Lewis and William Clark to explore the newly purchased territory all the way to the Pacific Ocean. Another sequel was Aaron Burr's conspiracy. Burr, an ambitious man, had been Jefferson's first Vice-President. He had killed Alexander Hamilton in a duel. Burr reportedly planned to establish a nation of his own in the Southwest. Historians are not exactly sure what Burr was trying to do. The government tried him for treason. Though acquitted, he was ruined.

Jefferson was re-elected President in 1804, and spent his second term trying to keep the United States out of the war between Britain and France. Both nations vio-

LESSON IV.

blest	guide	tar'dy	teach'er
learn	wrong	les'sons	school'-boy
haste	i'dler	end'less	knowl'edge

The Newberry Library, Chicago

lated American rights by capturing American ships. Americans particularly resented the British practice of *impressment*, or seizing sailors on American ships and claiming that they were British citizens. From 1804 to 1810, the British impressed more than 4,000 American sailors. In desperation, Congress passed one of the most drastic laws in American history. The Embargo Act of 1807 completely prohibited foreign trade. It ruined most American shipowners and many merchants, particularly in the North. It also harmed Southern and Western farmers, who could not sell their surpluses.

Before Jefferson left office, public protests forced him to drop the Embargo Act and substitute the milder Non-Intercourse Act of 1809. But the nation found it more and more difficult to stay out of European affairs.

The War of 1812. Under James Madison, who was elected President in 1808, the United States drifted rapidly into war with Great Britain. The conflict could probably have been avoided if Madison had shown more of Jefferson's patience. The British announced two days before Congress declared war that they would repeal their Orders in Council, which were America's chief grievance (see ORDER IN COUNCIL).

Madison

The conflict proved futile for both sides. The United States suffered heavy defeats on land, and was humiliated when the British captured Washington, D.C. The British lost many battles at sea, but they easily maintained command of the ocean and blockaded the American coast. The Americans captured what is now Toronto, but could not hold it. The British captured Detroit, but soon lost it. Neither side gained anything, and the war ended in a complete stalemate. The Treaty of Ghent, signed in 1814, said nothing about impressment and neutral rights, supposedly the causes of the war. One of the war's most famous conflicts, the Battle of New Orleans, took place two weeks after the treaty had been signed. See WAR OF 1812.

Nationalism. The War of 1812 failed to solve the country's international problems. It was unpopular in the Northeast. Discontented Federalists from New England sent delegates to Hartford in 1814 to discuss grievances arising from the war (see HARTFORD CON-

VENTION). Their actions seemed suspicious to many Americans, and the Federalist party declined in power. But, in the long run, the war did much to unify the American people and give them self-confidence and pride in their nation. Men from the North, South, East, and West had fought side by side. People throughout the country admired such war heroes as Oliver Hazard Perry and Andrew Jackson. The young nation, remembering its victories and forgetting its defeats, flexed its muscles in a feeling of power.

The Supreme Court became a powerful force in American life during this period. From 1801 to 1835, under Chief Justice John Marshall, the Court decided almost 50 cases involving constitutional issues. The case of *Marbury vs. Madison* fully established the right of the Court to review any federal or state law. The Court's decision in *McCulloch vs. Maryland* upheld Hamilton's doctrine of a broad interpretation of the Constitution. The Court declared that the Constitution gave additional *implied powers* to the national government so that it could carry out the *express powers* specifically granted to it. In these cases and many others, Marshall's leadership not only strengthened the government, but also made the Constitution a living body of principles.

Other factors also unified the country. A national literature had grown up. By 1820, William Cullen Bryant had published his poem *Thanatopsis*, Washington Irving his *Sketch Book*, and James Fenimore Cooper his first novel. Congress passed the Land Act of 1820, which made it easier for small farmers to buy land. The first national bank had expired, and the government created a second one. The Kentucky leader Henry Clay proposed a protective tariff and an "American System" of canals, roads, and other national improvements.

The Era of Good Feeling. James Monroe found few great problems to solve when he succeeded Madison in the White House in 1817. The country was more interested in growth than in political quarrels. Political parties had almost ceased to exist in this "Era of Good Feeling." As one step in national growth, Monroe bought Florida from Spain for only $5,000,000. This purchase helped round out United States territory and made it easier to deal with the Seminole Indians, who had attacked American settlements in the area.

Monroe

Both Monroe and his Secretary of State, John Quincy Adams, deserve credit for the Monroe Doctrine. This great measure made Monroe's administration famous. Latin America was freeing itself from Spanish and Portuguese rule. By 1822, Mexico and many countries in Central and South America had become independent. The United States and Great Britain sympathized with the Latin-American revolts. But Russia, Austria, and Prussia sided with Spain and Portugal. In 1823, they urged France to send troops to help restore Spanish and Portuguese royal government in Latin America. Earlier, in 1821, the Czar of Russia had announced that his claims in Alaska stretched south into western Canada.

The British were alarmed by these moves, and proposed a joint "hands-off" notice to be signed with the United States. But the Monroe administration decided that the

A Love of Nature inspired painters of the "Hudson River School." William Cullen Bryant and the artist Thomas Cole appear in Asher B. Durand's painting *Kindred Spirits*.

United States should act alone. Late in 1823, Monroe announced to the world that the United States would resist any attempt by European nations to colonize or dominate any part of the Western Hemisphere. If European nations had really had any intention of interfering in Latin America, they gave up. But the doctrine owed its effectiveness more to British sea power than to American policy. See MONROE DOCTRINE.

The Problem of Slavery. New settlers poured into the West and Southwest during the early 1800's (see WESTWARD MOVEMENT). Four new states—Indiana, Mississippi, Illinois, and Alabama—joined the Union between 1816 and 1819. At the same time, slavery grew stronger. Cotton planting spread westward into Alabama and Mississippi, and slaveholding became more profitable than ever before. Cotton farming could easily be taught to slaves. It employed women and children as well as men, and used their labor all year round. Sugar plantations in Louisiana, tobacco farms in Kentucky, and hemp fields in Missouri also used Negro slaves. All these crops wore out the soil, and Southern farmers constantly needed new lands.

By 1804, all the states north of Maryland and Delaware had abolished slavery. The states formed from the Northwest Territory were also free. But the South felt that it could not afford to give up slavery, and began to defend it. Most Northerners disliked slavery more and more, and dreaded its growth. Many persons regarded it as a national shame. When Missouri applied to enter the Union in 1819 as a slave state, angry opposition sprang up. The terrible problem of slavery suddenly became a center of national alarm—"like a fire bell in the night," said Jefferson.

In 1819, the Union contained 11 free states and 11 slave states. Maine applied for admission as a free state at the same time that Missouri applied as a slave state. In an obvious compromise, the two states entered the Union together. But this compromise settled only the immediate difficulty. What would happen when other parts of the West asked to become states? Under the leadership of Henry Clay, Congress passed the Missouri Compromise to settle these problems. Missouri entered as a slave state. But the Compromise provided that the rest of the territory in the Louisiana Purchase north of the southern boundary of Missouri would eventually be formed into free states (see MISSOURI COMPROMISE). The country breathed more easily. But farsighted men knew that the slavery issue had only been postponed.

Jacksonian Democracy

The years from 1825 to 1829 under President John Quincy Adams proved uneventful. Adams believed in a strong national government, and proposed a program that included internal improvements and a bigger navy. But much personal bitterness remained after Adams defeated the four other presidential candidates—John C. Calhoun, Henry Clay, William H. Crawford, and Andrew Jackson. This ill feeling, as well as political opposition from sectional interests in Congress, kept Adams from carrying out most of his plans. In 1828, the country turned

Adams

to Andrew Jackson, the hero of the War of 1812. Many of his supporters came from the old Democratic-Republican party and they adopted a new name, the Democratic party (see DEMOCRATIC PARTY).

"Let the People Rule." Americans regarded the election of Jackson as a triumph for the rough, democratic West over the wealthier, more conservative East. New Western states imposed few voting restrictions. Jackson's slogan, "Let the People Rule," symbolized the broad popular movement he led. Jacksonian democracy represented not only western frontiersmen and farmers, but also eastern workingmen and intellectuals. Its program of social reform was designed to benefit the people of all regions. This program included eliminating property qualifications for voting; abolishing both imprisonment for debt and severe sentences for minor crimes; widening the public-school system; encouraging farmers to settle on public lands; and letting workers form labor unions. It stood for a close watch over what Jackson called "the moneyed interest" and "the multitude of corporations with exclusive privileges."

Jackson

Changes in government occurred rapidly under Jackson. Powerful *machines*, or closely knit political organizations, appeared. Martin Van Buren headed one of the strongest machines, in New York. Machine politicians insisted that whenever they won an election, their supporters should get all the available government jobs. As one politician said, "to the victor belong the spoils of the enemy." See SPOILS SYSTEM.

Ships of the Plains by Samuel Colman, Three Lions

Many states changed their constitutions to make more offices elective instead of appointive. After 1824, party leaders in Congress no longer chose presidential candidates. They were chosen in various more democratic ways until 1831 and 1832. In those years, political parties held the first national conventions.

"Our Federal Union—It Must Be Preserved." The chief event of Jackson's first term was the crisis over nullification. In 1828, Congress raised tariff duties in a bill supported by many New Englanders, the Middle Atlantic States, and the states of the Northwest Territory. Southerners opposed this "Tariff of Abominations," which increased the price of goods the South bought, and injured its foreign markets. South Carolina, led by the fiery John C. Calhoun, asserted that each state had the right to *nullify*, or abolish, the law within its own borders. A fierce debate broke out in Congress in 1830, when Senator Robert Hayne set forth South Carolina's views on nullification. Daniel Webster delivered one of the greatest speeches ever heard in the Senate. He argued that the national government had full sovereign powers in its own field, including the tariff, and that any act that weakened the Union was a crime against American liberties.

Jackson did not want a powerful federal government. But he was determined to maintain national authority wherever he thought it legitimate. At a public dinner in 1830, he proposed a toast: "Our Federal Union—it must be preserved." This toast implied that Jackson would use force, if necessary, to preserve national authority. Congress passed a new tariff law in 1832, but the rates remained high. South Carolina called a convention which announced that the state would begin disobeying the law within a few months. Jackson at once had Congress pass an act that gave him the power to use the army and navy against South Carolina. He declared that he would hang Calhoun. At the same time, Congress reduced the tariff. South Carolina said it was satisfied, and dropped the nullification issue. See NULLIFICATION.

Destroying the Bank. During Jackson's second term, he fought a victorious battle with the second national bank. Although the bank had meddled too much in politics, it had served the country well. But Jackson's party included many rising businessmen who resented the privileges that the bank gave to older, established business interests. The President easily aroused popular feeling against what he called "the money monster." He argued that the bank put too much power in the hands of a few men who were not responsible to the people. Jackson had to fight hard to rally his party

behind him. He finally killed the bank in 1836 by refusing to renew its charter. See BANK OF THE UNITED STATES (The Second Bank).

Hundreds of small banks then arose throughout the country. They issued a flood of bank notes, and the country plunged into a great speculative boom. People gambled in stocks, factories, and land. So much money poured into the Treasury that the nation paid off its entire debt for the only time in its history.

Van Buren and the Panic. In 1837, a fearful panic and depression came on the heels of the boom. Hundreds of banks and businesses failed. Prices and wages fell, and jobless men begged and slept in the streets. The blame rested partly on Jackson's rash financial measures, but mostly on the people themselves. Martin Van Buren, elected President on the Democratic ticket in 1836, had to struggle with the problem throughout his term of office. Though he was able and conscientious, people made him a scapegoat for the hard times.

A new party had arisen in the early 1830's. Its members called themselves Whigs, and found their strongest leaders in Henry Clay and Daniel Webster. They saw their chance in 1840, and nominated a military hero, William Henry Harrison, for President. The Whigs won votes by presenting Harrison as a "log-cabin, coonskin, and hard cider candidate," and elected him.

America in the Early 1800's

The United States had grown amazingly in the years after Jefferson took office. Settlement had reached as far west as the Missouri River, and the population had passed 17,000,000. National unity had also been strengthened. Territorial expansion, Andrew Jackson's stern acts, and the speeches of Clay and Webster bolstered feelings of American nationalism. At the same time, improved transportation, industrial development, and reform movements did much to help the nation become a world power.

The Growth of Transportation. It was a great day for America when Robert Fulton's queer-looking boat, the *Clermont*, chugged up the Hudson River in 1807. Steamboats soon traveled upstream at 10 miles an hour or more. In 1818 they appeared on Lake Erie and Long Island Sound. By 1820 more than 60 steamboats were using the Mississippi and its branches, and the number soared to about 1,200 by 1846. River commerce was nearly twice as large as foreign trade.

Steamboats competed with land traffic on *toll roads*, or *turnpikes*, the first hard-surfaced highways. Hundreds of companies built toll roads in New England and the

Political Campaigns carried the issues of the day directly to the people. Young and old alike listen attentively to an earnest orator in George Caleb Bingham's painting *Stump Speaking.*

Henry Clay, according to an 1844 banner, campaigned as "the fearless friend of his country's rights."

The Purchase of Alaska was negotiated with Russia by Secretary of State William Seward, *left,* in 1867.

A Network of Railroads Grew Up to Unite the Country. Train arrivals and departures were exciting events in the quiet towns of the 1800's.

Museum of the City of New York

Middle Atlantic States during the period between Washington's inauguration and the War of 1812. During Madison's administration, the government began building the National Road, often called the Cumberland Road, westward from Cumberland, Md. As Ohio and Indiana developed, stagecoaches, wagons, carts, carriages, and horsemen crowded this road. It finally reached as far as Vandalia, Ill. Branches of the road did much to settle the West.

Canals also helped tie the nation together. The most famous, the Erie Canal, connected the Hudson River with Lake Erie in 1825. The canal helped develop the Great Lakes region, and contributed to the growth of Buffalo, Cleveland, Detroit, and Chicago. It also did much to establish New York City as the principal city on the Atlantic Coast. Grain, meats, and lumber from the West flowed along the lakes, the canal, and the Hudson to New York City. Manufactured goods flowed westward by this route. Other northern states soon built canals, too.

Then came the locomotive. The Baltimore & Ohio operated the first railway in 1830. Peter Cooper won fame by building a locomotive that, until it broke down, far outstripped a stagecoach. By 1835 trains were running from Boston to Worcester, Mass., and by the end of 1848 from Boston to New York City. Railroad cars were little more than wooden boxes, with stiff, uncomfortable seats. They were heated by wood stoves that grew dangerously hot in winter. Passengers never knew when they would arrive at their destinations. They gobbled meals in 10-minute stops along the way. But, by 1850, people could travel by rail from Boston to Baltimore, from New York City to Buffalo, and from Charleston to Chattanooga.

The Industrial Revolution. For 30 years after the Revolutionary War, manufacturing existed only on a small scale. Most of the workshops used hand labor, especially in such industries as weaving and shoemaking. Jefferson's Embargo Act stimulated American manufacturing by shutting off imports. As in England, machinery first appeared on a large scale in the textile industry. Men formed companies to make cotton and

woolen goods, and built mills on swift streams that provided water power. The New England states soon took the lead in textile manufacturing.

Older industries, such as flour milling, began to use improved machinery. In 1798, Eli Whitney built an arms factory in Connecticut with special machinery he had designed. Here he demonstrated the efficiency of separate, standardized parts that could be easily assembled and replaced. Whitney's technique began the era of mass production (see MASS PRODUCTION). Elias Howe made the first practical sewing machine in 1846. Iron foundries and steel mills grew up to supply the expanding transportation and textile industries. The gas industry grew as people began using gas to light homes and city streets. The amount of money invested in American manufacturing in 1850 was 10 times that in 1820. Large corporations, in which many persons held shares, became numerous. They could usually raise more money and operate more efficiently than businesses owned by individuals or families.

The new factories needed workers, and labor problems resulted. At first, factory "hands" came chiefly from northern farms and villages. But, after 1840, countless workers came from other countries. About 1,000,000 came from Ireland alone between 1840 and 1850. Men, women, and children worked long hours—at first 13 to 15 hours a day, later 11 or 12. Children had to perform tasks beyond their strength, and had little chance for schooling. Many factories were hot in summer, cold in winter, and full of accident hazards. Because of keen competition, owners paid the lowest wages they could. Many employees in the North worked under conditions little better than those of southern slaves.

Workers began to form trade unions to protect themselves. In larger cities, they campaigned for free schools, decent government, and the repeal of antiunion laws. But the depression after the Panic of 1837 ended most workers' organizations.

A Surge of Reform. Throughout America and Western Europe, movements for social reform flourished in the early 1800's. Many causes lay behind these movements. The Industrial Revolution had produced many evils, as well as the wealth with which to cure them. A series of revivals had added new vigor to religion. Outstanding idealists wrote essays that contributed to reform. In the United States, the general belief that all men are equal, and should have an equal chance, had a strong influence.

Abolition. The greatest crusade was that against slavery. After the Revolutionary War, more and more people spoke out against it. In 1821, Benjamin Lundy, a Quaker, began publishing a paper called *The Genius of Universal Emancipation.* His ideas did not satisfy a young New Englander named William Lloyd Garrison, who favored a crusade "as harsh as truth." In 1831, Garrison began publishing a fiery weekly called *The Liberator.* He mailed it far and wide from Boston, and the South rang with angry protests.

The abolition crusade quickly became a center of national interest. Georgia offered $5,000 for Garrison's arrest and conviction as a public enemy. A number of church leaders in the North boldly attacked slavery. So did John Quincy Adams, Albert Gallatin, and other political leaders. When Great Britain freed all the slaves in its colonies in 1834, the South realized that it faced a world-wide moral movement.

Public Schools. Another important reform movement favored free public schools. Many Americans had long regarded education as a privilege of the upper classes. Most good schools, especially those outside New England, were expensive private schools. Poor children went to "pauper schools," or did not go at all. But Jacksonian democracy brought a demand that every state should have a free school system. By 1850 the country had 80,000 elementary schools, with 3,500,000 pupils, and had begun to establish free public high schools.

Women's Rights were earnestly championed by another band of reformers. Led by Elizabeth Cady Stanton, they believed that women should be treated as equals of men, not as humble, protected inferiors. Oberlin College became the first coeducational college. The school first admitted women to the full collegiate course in 1837. When Horace Greeley founded the *New York Tribune* in 1841, he named Margaret Fuller literary editor. Another reformer, Amelia Bloomer, became famous mainly for her "sensible costume for females." But the full trousers, or *bloomers*, that she introduced failed to replace in popularity the hoop skirts then in fashion.

Other Reforms. The temperance movement attracted people who saw that liquor often led to crime and poverty. The movement succeeded so well that Maine adopted a prohibition law in 1846, and 12 other states soon followed. Dorothea Dix led a battle to reform insane asylums and prisons. The American Peace Society began an energetic movement in 1828 designed to foster world peace.

Harrison

Slavery Divides the Nation

Tyler

President William Henry Harrison died a month after taking office in 1841. John Tyler succeeded him, and a new era began. The slavery question became so serious that it threatened to split the nation. The annexation of Texas, followed by the Mexican War and the acquisition of the whole Southwest, brought the problem to a head. The new territories would soon have to become states, but the North and South clashed over whether any could have slavery.

The Annexation of Texas. American settlers, chiefly Southerners, had pushed into Texas for many years, and wanted independence from Mexico. They seceded from Mexico in 1835, defeated several Mexican armies, and created the Republic of Texas the following year. From the beginning, they wanted to join the United States. The question of admitting Texas became an issue in the presidential campaign of 1844. The Democrats under James K. Polk favored admitting Texas, and the Whigs under Henry Clay opposed it. Polk won the election in a close contest.

Polk

The new Congress voted to admit Texas to the Union. The new state's boundary was badly defined. Both the United States and Mexico claimed a large area on the Rio Grande. War began when Polk sent General Zachary Taylor and an American force to the disputed region. The fighting at once involved California, a Spanish territory which many Americans also wanted to annex. For the story of the war, see MEXICAN WAR.

Further Expansion. Other new territory became part of the United States as a result of the Mexican War. When peace came in 1848, Americans held Texas, California, and the great area in between. This area included all Nevada and Utah, most of Arizona, and parts of Colorado, New Mexico, and Wyoming.

Polk also peacefully settled the question of the Northwest with Great Britain. The United States gained present-day Idaho, Oregon, and Washington. Great Britain received what is now British Columbia. The Gadsden Purchase from Mexico in 1853 added land to what is now Arizona and New Mexico (see GADSDEN PURCHASE). The country had also gained rich treasures. Prospectors discovered gold in California in 1848. The region asked to become a state, and the slavery dispute suddenly flared again.

The Compromise of 1850. Once more Jefferson's "fire bell in the night" rang fiercely. Slaveholders wanted to expand their territory. They declared that it was the "manifest destiny" of the United States to absorb all North America. They felt that the new lands belonged rightly to them. *Free-soilers*, or Northerners who opposed slavery, insisted that it must be limited and should not gain another state. Texas already had slavery, and came in as a slave state. But California, Utah, and New Mexico did not have it, because Mexico had forbidden slavery. Even during the Mexican War, Congressman David Wilmot of Pennsylvania had offered a measure declaring that slavery should be prohibited forever in any territory gained from Mexico. The House passed this resolution, but Southerners in the Senate angrily defeated it. See WILMOT PROVISO.

California could not be kept waiting for statehood. To meet the crisis, Henry Clay offered a compromise (see COMPROMISE OF 1850). President Zachary Taylor, who had succeeded Polk, opposed the compromise, but Congress approved it. However, John C. Calhoun and his chief follower, Senator Jefferson Davis of Mississippi, denounced the compromise as unfair to the South. "One by one our national ties are breaking," Calhoun said. He warned that if the antislavery movement continued, it would finally "snap every cord,

Taylor

when nothing will be left to hold the states together except force."

Sectional Hatreds Rise. The situation steadily grew worse. During the next 10 years, a series of weak Presidents—Millard Fillmore, Franklin Pierce, and James Buchanan—did not help ease the problem. Both sides grew angrier, and several events made the situation more explosive.

Fillmore

In 1852, Harriet Beecher Stowe published *Uncle Tom's Cabin*, a vivid novel condemning slavery. Northern crowds rescued runaway slaves when federal officers tried to take them back to bondage. The Southern-controlled Supreme Court declared in 1857 that slavery was legal in every territory, but a majority of Northerners rejected the decree (see DRED SCOTT DECISION). In 1859, John Brown, a fanatical abolitionist, led a raid into Virginia to free slaves. He seized the federal arsenal at Harpers Ferry before his little band was captured.

Pierce

Buchanan

Worst of all was the ill feeling aroused by the Kansas-Nebraska Bill in 1854. Settlers had been pushing into the region that now includes Kansas and Nebraska, and began a movement to organize the region into territories. The Missouri Compromise had made this area free soil. But the South opposed organizing the area into free states. Senator Stephen A. Douglas of Illinois then offered a bill allowing settlers to decide for themselves whether the new states should be slave or free. See KANSAS-NEBRASKA ACT.

A storm of anger swept the North. Editors, clergymen, politicians, and businessmen attacked the bill, but Congress passed it. Northern settlers poured into Kansas, and bloody fighting broke out. The Northern free-soilers soon controlled the territory.

Lincoln Emerges. The Whig party fell apart because of a split on the slavery question, and the new Republican party arose in the North (see REPUBLICAN PARTY). Several important Whigs joined the new party. They included Abraham Lincoln. Lincoln had a deliberate but powerful mind, and a marvelous ability to state truths in a way that everyone could understand. In 1858, he argued the slavery issue with Douglas in a series of debates that aroused national interest.

Lincoln

The South and North had become different in many ways. The South remained rural, with New Orleans the only large city. Almost two-thirds of the country's population of about 32,000,000 lived in the North. It had become a busy region of industrial cities. Railroads linked the East and the Middle West.

As Calhoun had predicted, the bonds uniting the North and South were snapping one by one. The last great link to break was the Democratic party. In the 1860 presidential campaign, radical Southern Democrats demanded that the party call for federal protection of slavery in the territories. Northern and Western Democrats under Douglas refused. As a result, the Southerners left the party and nominated John C. Breckinridge on a new ticket. The Constitutional Union party urged national unity, and nominated John Bell. The Republican party nominated Lincoln. Even though he received only about 40 per cent of the votes, Lincoln won more than any of his rivals and became President.

Civil War and Reconstruction

The South Secedes. Southerners had threatened to leave the Union if Lincoln won the election with Northern support alone. Lincoln had stated that he would not try to abolish slavery in the South. But Southerners were angry at the North, bitter over defeat in the election, and fearful of the future. They dreamed of safety and prosperity under a government of their own. South Carolina seceded on Dec. 20, 1860. During the next month, Mississippi, Florida, Alabama, Georgia, and Louisiana also left the Union. In February, 1861, they organized the Confederate States of America at Montgomery, Ala., with Jefferson Davis as president. Texas seceded and joined the Confederacy in March.

Lincoln was firmly opposed to secession. Last-minute efforts to reconcile the North and South proved useless (see CRITTENDEN COMPROMISE).

The Civil War began on April 12, 1861, when Southern troops bombarded Fort Sumter in Charleston harbor. Then, four more states joined the Confederacy: Virginia, Arkansas, Tennessee, and North Carolina. The United States was split into two camps—the 11 Confederate states and the 23 Union states. The war took thousands of lives and ruined millions of dollars worth of property. It also destroyed the "Old South," which had glorified the planter aristocrats and their culture.

Union forces suffered several military defeats early in the war. Confederate Generals Robert E. Lee and "Stonewall" Jackson defended the South against Northern invasions. But Southern forces had less success when they invaded the North, and their losses increased steadily after the Battle of Gettysburg in 1863. General Ulysses S. Grant took over the Union forces in 1864. After many bloody battles, he forced Lee to surrender on April 9, 1865. For a history of the war, see CIVIL WAR.

Lincoln's Presidency was primarily concerned with the war, but it also made other important contributions to the future of the nation. The North needed huge sums of money for the war, and imposed heavy taxes on property, liquor, tobacco, and corporations. Congress passed the first American income-tax law, and raised tariffs to protect manufacturers. Congress also created a great system of national banks. Their bank notes became the common currency of the land. But inflation grew, and the cost of living rose steeply.

The Emancipation Proclamation was perhaps the greatest of Lincoln's measures. It declared free all slaves in areas held by the Confederacy, and showed that the North meant to abolish slavery completely. See EMANCIPATION PROCLAMATION.

The West developed as the war raged. New machinery made farming easier. The corn planter, the improved plow, the thresher, and Cyrus McCormick's new reaper came into widespread use. New laws also helped the West grow. The Homestead Act of 1862 gave free farms to anyone who would settle on a quarter section of land, totaling 160 acres, and live there for five years. The same year, Congress stimulated the growth of state universities by passing an act that set aside large tracts to support agricultural and mechanical colleges. Also in 1862, Congress made generous land grants to the Union Pacific and Central Pacific railroads, which were

The Civil War took a huge toll in lives and property. A cannon on Lookout Mountain commemorates the "Battle Above the Clouds," part of the Battle of Chattanooga in November, 1863.

Ray Houlihan, *American Heritage;* A. M. Wettach

to link the Pacific Coast with the Middle West.

Re-Election. Much opposition to Lincoln arose in 1864. The war had taken the lives of thousands of men, and its outcome still seemed doubtful. The Democrats nominated General George B. McClellan, and urged peace at almost any price. But Generals Ulysses S. Grant and William T. Sherman won great victories in time to aid Lincoln, and he defeated McClellan.

In his second inaugural address, Lincoln, who knew that the war was almost over, pleaded for a kindly peace. "With malice toward none, with charity for all," he urged, "let us press forward to bind up the nation's wounds." Many Northerners wanted to hang Jefferson Davis after the war, but Lincoln opposed severe punishment for Southerners. The assassination of Lincoln on April 14, 1865, was a calamity for both North and South.

Restoring the South. The problems of peace seemed almost overwhelming. Huge areas of the South lay in ruins. Homes had been burned, railroads torn up, bridges destroyed, factories and wharves smashed, and fields left full of weeds. The Negroes, suddenly set free, found themselves penniless, restless, leaderless, and often homeless. The North labored under a heavy debt and an inflated currency. Wartime hatreds complicated the task of rebuilding the nation.

Johnson

Three great difficulties hampered the reconstruction of the Confederacy as a part of the Union. Congress quarreled violently with President Andrew Johnson about the measures to be used. The government had no experience in large-scale social and political planning. Northern desire for revenge, along with Southern bitterness, surrounded the work with a poisonous atmosphere. The Negroes suffered most. Congress made a feeble effort to help them by creating a Freedmen's Bureau under General Oliver O. Howard. But Congress refused to appropriate the money, make the

plans, and enlist the experts needed to put the former slaves on their feet as intelligent, self-supporting, progressive citizens. Congress failed to take proper steps to aid the South.

President Johnson lacked tact and skill. But he was much more generous and farsighted than the Radicals in Congress. He proposed a moderate plan for bringing the Confederate states back into the Union quickly, and the South accepted it. But Congress, led by Representative Thaddeus Stevens of Pennsylvania and Senator Charles Sumner of Massachusetts, insisted on a severe program. Its policies ended in military rule for the South and in the impeachment and trial of Johnson. The Senate acquitted the President, and the Radicals in time admitted that they had been wrong. *Carpetbaggers* from the North and freed Negroes took over Southern state governments. Many Southerners then joined organizations such as the Ku-Klux Klan, which worked to restore control of the state governments to the hands of Southern whites. See RECONSTRUCTION.

The Gilded Age

American life changed rapidly during the 35 years after the Civil War. More and more people moved to cities. The nation's culture matured and became more complex. Mark Twain called this period "The Gilded Age" because of its showy wealth.

Important events in American history between 1865 and 1900 included the industrial development of the North, the taming of the West, and the rise of a new South.

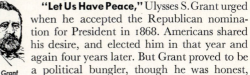

"Let Us Have Peace," Ulysses S. Grant urged when he accepted the Republican nomination for President in 1868. Americans shared his desire, and elected him in that year and again four years later. But Grant proved to be

Grant a political bungler, though he was honest, patriotic, and courageous. His Cabinet, except for Sec-

Giants of Industry helped transform the United States into a great manufacturing nation. Though ruthless in business, many gave away millions for philanthropic purposes.

CORNELIUS VANDERBILT

ANDREW CARNEGIE

JOHN D. ROCKEFELLER

retary of State Hamilton Fish, was made up of mediocre men. Grant took sides with the Radicals on Reconstruction issues. He did his best to keep Republican carpetbaggers in power in the South, and used military force several times without any real excuse. Worst of all, he allowed corruption to cause scandals that blackened his administration.

Scandals in Government under Grant left a permanent blot on American history. Dishonest tax officials and distillers formed the "Whisky Ring" to cheat the government out of taxes (see WHISKY RING). The "Sanborn Contracts" allowed commissions to private individuals who collected certain taxes that the government itself should have collected. A corrupt secretary in the War Department sold traderships at Indian posts in the West, and was forced to resign. Two speculators tried to corner the gold market, and the "Black Friday" affair resulted. Grant let himself be tricked into encouraging speculators, and his last-minute interference came too late to save thousands from ruin. See BLACK FRIDAY.

The war seemed to have coarsened American life. The great Credit Mobilier scandal involved prominent members of the House and Senate (see CREDIT MOBILIER OF AMERICA). Congress also laid itself open to attack by voting its members two years' back pay. In New York City, "Boss" William Tweed ran a political machine that shocked the country with its corruption. State after state had its thefts and scandals, and sharp dealing and graft characterized many businesses.

Foreign Affairs. Fortunately, Hamilton Fish wrote a creditable chapter in foreign affairs. The United States had filed large claims against Great Britain for the damages caused by British cruisers serving the Confederacy during the war (see ALABAMA [ship]). The United States also disputed certain boundaries with Canada. The Treaty of Washington settled all these issues by friendly arbitration in 1871. Fish also avoided war with Spain after the *Virginius* affair (see VIRGINIUS MASSACRE). He made the best of the unhappy situation created when Grant tried to annex Santo Domingo (now the Dominican Republic). The Senate thwarted this move.

Political Battles enlivened the national scene during the late 1800's, but no really grave problems upset the country until the Panic of 1893. Rutherford B. Hayes, a Republican, ran against Democrat Samuel J. Tilden in

Retail Selling, once handled by peddlers and general stores, became big business in the late 1800's. The first 5 & 10¢ store, *right,* opened in Lancaster, Pa., in 1879.

	FARM AND RURAL	CITY
1790		
1850		
1890		
1960		

Americans Moved to Cities in greater and greater numbers. Each symbol represents 10% of the total population.

the presidential election of 1876. At first it seemed that Tilden had won in a close contest. But Reconstruction policies complicated the situation in Florida, Louisiana, and South Carolina. All three states returned two sets of electoral returns, one giving victory to Hayes, the other to Tilden. A Congressional commission finally awarded the disputed votes to Hayes, who became President. Southern Democrats complained bitterly. But Republicans pacified them by promising certain favors, which included restoring political control of the South to its own people. Hayes carried out his end of the bargain by withdrawing the last federal troops from the South in 1877.

Hayes

Hayes was followed by James A. Garfield, another Republican, in 1881. A disappointed office seeker assassinated Garfield a few months after he became President. His Vice-President, Chester A. Arthur, finished out his term. Under Arthur, Congress passed the first Civil Service Act, which put more and more government jobs in the hands of capable men and women, regardless of party.

Garfield

The Rise of Big Business. American energy now concentrated on developing the nation's vast resources, which included (1) petroleum, first pumped commercially in western Pennsylvania in 1859; (2) iron ore, found in a series of *ranges* (beds) around the Great Lakes; (3) copper, mined in Michigan, Montana, and Arizona; (4) coal, which lay in tremendous quantities under the surface of a great part of the country; and (5) timber, which covered much of the South, the Wisconsin-Minnesota region, and the Pacific Northwest.

Arthur

The men who furnished industrial leadership have often been called "Robber Barons," because they seemed to be interested only in making money. Their methods have been criticized, but no one can deny their ability, force, and ingenuity. John D. Rockefeller created a huge federation of oil refiners, the Standard Oil combine. He and his lawyers were trying to find a method of grouping his many companies and plants into one organization. They devised the *trust* which

other groups immediately imitated (see TRUST). Rockefeller worked closely with the railroads, controlled by such industrialists as Jay Gould, Cornelius Vanderbilt, James J. Hill, and Edward H. Harriman. Andrew Carnegie built a vast steel mill near Pittsburgh during the depression after 1873 when prices were low, and soon dominated the steel industry. Philip Armour and Gustavus Swift organized tremendous meat-packing businesses. The Guggenheim interests controlled copper. The success of many of these trusts depended on J. P. Morgan, one of the world's greatest financiers.

The great national industries became possible when the railroads created national markets. Men who packed meats, milled flour, made shoes, built wagons, and marketed kerosene could soon sell their products anywhere from the Atlantic to the Pacific. Eastern rail systems such as the New York Central, the Erie, the Pennsylvania, and the Baltimore & Ohio ran from the Atlantic Coast to the Middle West by 1870. Even before that, in 1869, the tracks of the Union Pacific joined those of the Central Pacific at Promontory Point near Ogden, Utah. They formed the first transcontinental line. Other transcontinental railroads completed early in the 1880's included the Northern Pacific, the Southern Pacific, and the Santa Fe. By 1893, when the Great Northern tracks reached Puget Sound, no other country had such a crisscross of railroads.

Workers and Farmers. The growth of American industry brought difficult new problems that aroused many Americans to action. The labor movement, after years of weakness, began to gain strength. An organization called the Knights of Labor rose and declined in the 1870's and 1880's. It was followed by a stronger group of unions, the American Federation of Labor. Under Samuel Gompers, the AFL gained a membership of more than 500,000 by 1900. See LABOR.

Farmers also formed organizations. The National Grange, founded in 1867, and the Farmers' Alliances of the 1870's and 1880's promoted cooperatives and worked to eliminate railroad abuses. These abuses included high freight and passenger rates, and discrimina-

SAMUEL GOMPERS

LABOR ORGANIZES

JOHN MITCHELL

Leaders of the Labor Movement directed efforts to improve conditions for workers. Samuel Gompers helped organize the American Federation of Labor in 1886. John Mitchell, president of the United Mine Workers, led Pennsylvania coal miners in 1902 in one of the first successful strikes against big business.

tion among shippers. Many farmers joined the Greenback party of the late 1870's. Members of all these groups, together with workers from the Knights of Labor, helped found the Populist party in 1891. This radical movement became strong in both South and West. It demanded that the government regulate railroads, trusts, and finance.

Regulating Industry. The government dealt first with railroad abuses. Several Western states, urged by farmers, had tried to regulate the railroads. But the Supreme Court ruled in 1886 that interstate commerce could be regulated only by the federal government. The people then turned to Congress, which responded with the Interstate Commerce Act of 1887, setting up the Interstate Commerce Commission. Then came the turn of

Harrison

the trusts. The Sherman Antitrust Act of 1890 was passed during the administration of Republican President Benjamin Harrison. It prohibited great combinations that restricted interstate trade. It was a crude law, and accomplished little for several years. The government made no attempt to regulate finance.

These early activities in government regulation did not amount to much. They did not satisfy farmers, workers, or small businessmen. At the end of the 1800's, big business often played a dominant part in local and national affairs. It helped to elect governors and senators, and sometimes even swayed court decisions.

Taming the West. Explorers, fur traders, and missionaries to the Indians did much to open America's Far West in the early 1800's. But the miners of the 1850's and 1860's did even more to open the area to settlement. The 1849 gold rush to California was followed 10 years later by an almost equally exciting rush to Colorado. Then came Nevada's Virginia City, built on the Comstock Lode, a fabulous deposit of gold and silver. Mark Twain described the town with its mansions, banks, saloons, gambling houses, and dance halls. A series of gold and silver discoveries next attracted thousands of prospectors to Montana, Idaho, and the Black Hills of South Dakota. But the mining kingdom fell as swiftly as it had risen. One year the mining camps swarmed with prospectors, bearded miners, card sharps, and desperadoes. Next year the easy riches were gone, a few big corporations took over the mines, and law and order reigned.

The rancher and cowboy had an equally brief era. The great herds of Texas Longhorn cattle that roamed the open range of the Western states had increased during the 1860's. When railroads reached across the plains shortly after the Civil War, ranchers began driving the cattle to such terminal towns as Dodge City, Kan. The so-called "cattle kingdom" flourished until the late 1880's. The "long drive" to the railroads, the annual roundups for branding, the battles against cattle-rustlers, and, above all, the cowboys, made it a colorful era in American history. But farmers soon moved out on the plains, and new inventions such as the windmill and the combine helped them gain a foothold. Their Shorthorn and Hereford cattle displaced the Longhorns, and their barbed-wire fencing ended the open range. For the story of this period, see WESTERN FRONTIER LIFE.

Indian Wars. Settlers and troops faced many sharp battles with the Indians before the West was fully cleared for settlement. Civil War veterans such as Nelson A. Miles and George A. Custer fought Sitting Bull of the Sioux, Chief Joseph of the Nez Percé, and other hostile Indian leaders. The government finally placed all the Indians on reservations. See INDIAN WARS.

New States. Wherever railroads ran, towns and cities sprang up. When the Northern Pacific and Great Northern railroads were planned, their routes lay through wilderness. But settlements soon appeared along these lines, from Duluth and St. Paul to Seattle and Tacoma. Belts of farms spread out from the settlements. Colorado joined the Union in 1876. In 1889 and 1890 six more states came in—the Dakotas, Washington, Montana, Idaho, and Wyoming. The opening of Indian Territory to white settlers dramatically marked the rise of the new West. The federal government bought a large tract of land from the Indians, and threw it open to homesteaders at noon on April 22, 1889. More than 20,000 settlers raced in to scramble for the best sites, and occupied the new Oklahoma Territory almost overnight. An even greater land rush took place in 1893, when the government opened the *Cherokee Strip*, a portion of northwestern Oklahoma.

A New South shared in the general changes, although the region progressed more slowly than other sections of the country. After the Civil War, Southerners had to break up their great plantations, because they had no slaves to work them. The land went to small farmers and tenants, both Negro and white. When the Civil War began, the South had about 700,000 farms. By 1900 there were 2,500,000. Farmers began to plant more than one crop, although they still relied too much on cotton. Southerners found new lands in Texas, and revived old lands with fertilizer. By 1895, the annual cotton crop had grown twice as large as it had been before the Civil War. But cotton farmers suffered from low prices.

More important during this period was the rise of Southern manufacturing, favored by such leaders as Henry Grady, an Atlanta journalist. A rich iron and steel industry grew up at Birmingham, Ala., because deposits of coal, iron ore, and limestone were found nearby. Tobacco men built factories in Virginia and North Carolina, and James B. Duke founded the American Tobacco Company in 1890. Cotton mills provided jobs for many people in the hill country of Alabama, Georgia, and the Carolinas. As in early New England, farm families furnished labor, and workers received low wages for long hours. By 1900, the South produced as much cotton goods every year as New England did. Lumbering also became important in the South.

But the South still lagged behind the North and Middle West in production and profits, because of the Negro problem, war damage, inefficient farming methods, and relatively poor soil. Illiteracy remained high. Malaria and hookworm attacked thousands of Southerners.

Cultural Growth. In the years after the Civil War, great advances took place in education and in the arts. In later years, many Americans looked back especially on the 1890's, "the gay 90's," as one of the happiest periods in American history. The average worker earned little more than $12 a week for 50 or 60 hours of hard labor. But a quart of milk cost only 6¢, and 12¢ bought a pound of round steak. People seemed content with the present and optimistic about the future.

THE TURN OF THE CENTURY

Ornate Homes were built in the Victorian era. The Carson Mansion, typical of the period, is in Eureka, California.

David H. Swanlund, Eureka, Calif.

Women's New Freedom was symbolized by the Gibson Girl.

Expanding Overseas, the United States gained new territory and new responsibilities in the Spanish-American War, which lasted just 113 days.

Mass Production of the "Model T" made it possible for the average American to own a car.

New York Harbor in 1905, Bustling and Energetic, Typified the Optimism with Which America Faced the Future.

The Mariners' Museum, Newport News, Va.

Education. The public-school system expanded swiftly during the late 1800's as the United States sought to become the first nation in the world to educate all its people. Twice as many pupils attended classes in 1900 as in 1870. Colleges and universities also doubled in number between the Civil War and 1900. Johns Hopkins, a Baltimore merchant, founded one of the first true universities in the United States. Older institutions such as Harvard, Yale, and Columbia adopted more advanced teaching methods, and improved their facilities. John D. Rockefeller founded the University of Chicago, and the railway builder Leland Stanford established the university named for his son. Most people now agreed that women were entitled to higher education. Matthew Vassar established Vassar College in 1861. Other women's colleges founded soon afterward included Smith, Wellesley, Bryn Mawr, and Barnard. All the state universities, such as Michigan, Wisconsin, and Illinois, admitted women.

The universities broadened their courses of study to keep up with American needs and the growth of knowledge. Technological schools soon offered courses in all branches of engineering and science. Graduate schools and schools of law and medicine improved. Students everywhere had greater freedom in choosing subjects. University presidents who gained influence throughout the country included Charles W. Eliot of Harvard, Andrew D. White of Cornell, Nicholas Murray Butler of Columbia, and William Rainey Harper of Chicago.

Magazines and Newspapers. Several popular magazines, including *Harper's,* the *Atlantic,* and *Putnam's,* had become famous before the Civil War. Soon after the war, the *Century* and *Scribner's* joined the list. The country also had the *Nation,* one of the period's best magazines of criticism. Near the end of the 1800's, many periodicals built up mass circulations with lower prices, popular features, good illustrations, and modern advertising methods. They included *Cosmopolitan,* the *Ladies' Home Journal, McClure's,* and *Munsey's.* Newspapers increased their circulations by widening news coverage and adding features designed to appeal to the whole family. Joseph Pulitzer, Edward W. Scripps, and William Randolph Hearst founded newspaper chains that included publications throughout the country.

Literature in America broadened in scope after the Civil War. Mark Twain wrote of the Mississippi Valley and the Far West. Bret Harte described the California mining settlements, George W. Cable told of Louisiana after the war, and William Dean Howells wrote about life in Boston and New York City. Henry James portrayed the wealthy Americans who moved between the United States and Europe, belonging to both cultures. Toward the end of the 1800's, many authors used fiction to demand various reforms. Hamlin Garland described the grievances of the farmer, Stephen Crane gave a truthful account of social evils, and Frank Norris attacked corruption in business and industry.

Other Arts also developed and matured in the United States during the Gilded Age. Artists such as Winslow Homer and Thomas Eakins painted the new America. The inventions of Thomas Edison, Alexander Graham Bell, and Henry Ford transformed the whole world. American architecture sank to what was perhaps its lowest level with the "gingerbread" houses of President Grant's time. But later architects such as William Le Baron Jenney, Henry Richardson and Louis Sullivan brought to American buildings a functional beauty they had lost. Clothing also grew more functional, as men and women became interested in sports. Women's bustles and draperies of the 1870's and 1880's gave way to the freer styles inspired by Charles Dana Gibson's "Gibson Girl" of the 1890's. The United States was growing into an adult nation. The World's Columbian Exposition in Chicago in 1893 proved the greatness of many of its achievements, and showed how effectively it could present them to other countries.

"Public Office Is a Public Trust," a slogan adopted by Grover Cleveland, symbolized this strong President's belief in honest government. First chosen in 1884 as the first Democratic President since the Civil War, Cleveland served four quiet years before Harrison replaced

Cleveland him. Cleveland stopped land-grabbing by railroads and pension-grabbing by Civil War veterans. He also tried to lower tariffs. In 1893, he returned to the presidency at the beginning of a great panic, caused by financial disturbances abroad and overexpansion at home.

One trouble followed another. Cleveland called out federal troops to put down riots caused by the Pullman strike in Chicago. He tried once more to cut tariffs, and gained a partial victory. He struggled hard to repress a movement for American intervention in Cuba when the world-wide depression helped cause a rebellion there. A dispute between Great Britain and Venezuela over the boundary of British Guiana prompted Cleveland to send an indignant message to Congress which for a time aroused fear of war. Luckily, a commission soon determined the boundary.

Above all, Cleveland had to face the demands of the new Populist party, and of many Western and Southern congressmen who urged social reforms that included the free coinage of silver. To Cleveland, and to most conservative Americans, this demand meant disaster. He felt that it would sharply reduce the value of the dollar, frighten business, and hurt trade with other nations. The depression had caused national revenues to fall, so that the Treasury was almost empty. But Cleveland's stubborn efforts held back the free-silver movement, and bond issues kept the Treasury solvent.

McKinley's Full Dinner Pail. In the 1896 election, Republican William McKinley defeated William Jennings Bryan, the Democratic candidate. Most people interpreted McKinley's victory as a triumph of conserva-

McKinley tism over radicalism, and of business over farm groups. The traditional gold standard was now safe. The great industries felt secure against government interference, even though the great corporations needed more regulation. Prosperity quickly returned, partly because of this sense of safety, partly because of gold discoveries in Canada and Alaska, and partly because of a boom created by war contracts. Republicans pointed proudly to "the full dinner pail." They returned to high tariffs with the Dingley Act of 1897, and to national expansion with the annexation of Hawaii in 1898.

The Spanish-American War. Many Americans had long disapproved of the Spanish administration in Cuba, charging that it was corrupt, tyrannical, and cruel. High taxes, restrictions on trade and industry, and indifference to education had kept the island poor and backward. In an effort to crush a revolt that began in 1895, Spain sent 200,000 troops to Cuba. The governor, Valeriano Weyler, jammed civilians into concentration camps, where they died in great numbers. Many Americans demanded war with Spain. While the American government urged that Cuba be made self-governing, "jingo" newspapers, especially New York City's *Evening Journal* and *World*, clamored for action (see JINGO). Congress grew anxious to intervene.

Early in February, 1898, newspapers printed a letter from the Spanish minister in Washington that insulted McKinley. Then, on the night of February 15, the battleship *Maine* exploded in Havana harbor, with the loss of 260 lives. War became almost certain. It began on April 21, 1898. If McKinley had shown iron courage, he might have averted war. Spain was at last ready to make far-reaching concessions, amounting to Cuban independence. American business did not really want war. But the Spanish-American War was unquestionably a popular war. The United States won Guam, Puerto Rico, and the Philippines. See SPANISH-AMERICAN WAR.

A World Power. With the Spanish-American War, the United States became a world power. At the same time, the nation adopted a policy of imperialism by extending its authority overseas. Spain wanted to keep all or part of the Philippines, and Germany would also have gladly taken all or part of the islands. Many Americans believed that the United States should not take or govern lands so far away. American tradition had always opposed colonialism. William Jennings Bryan, with the support of such men as Mark Twain, William Dean Howells, and Carl Schurz, took a firm position against imperialism. But the McKinley administration decided to keep both the Philippines and Puerto Rico, and to give Cuba a temporary government.

At the time, this decision seemed wrong to many Americans. The hope that the Philippines would be useful in gaining a rich Asiatic trade soon faded. But time proved McKinley's step right. The new possessions did not corrupt the United States, as some had feared. American rule in both the Philippines and Puerto Rico ended many years later when the islanders proved themselves ready for self-government. American experts in various fields brought benefits to both countries.

The Progressive Period

By 1900, the United States had become one of the greatest economic powers in the world. Its population stood at more than 75,000,000.

A Crusading Spirit inspired many thoughtful Americans at the beginning of the 1900's. They felt that the nation needed many changes to keep up with its growth. Old ideas were becoming outworn, and events called for more planning, courage, and action. Many financiers and monopolists seemed to regard the government with contempt, and often exploited the people. Political bosses and machines corrupted local affairs. Dissatisfaction led to the rise of the Progressive movement. It was built on the foundations laid by the Populist party, the teachings of organized labor, and the ideas of such thinkers as Henry George, William James, and John Dewey. The movement gained prominence in the 1890's. It found leaders such as Tom L. Johnson and "Golden Rule" Jones, the mayors of Cleveland and Toledo, to fight city graft and neglect. The Progressive movement had an even greater fighting leader in Robert M. LaFollette, who battled corruption as governor of Wisconsin. A group of socially conscious writers called *muckrakers* focused public attention on widespread abuses in business and politics.

The Square Deal. President William McKinley was assassinated in 1901, and Theodore Roosevelt succeeded him. The Progressive movement came into its own with Roosevelt. He was an exceptionally well-educated man with a broad knowledge of American life.

Roosevelt

He realized that he had to fight the great monopolies and trusts. He saw that he must end favoritism toward special interests, and stop corruption in government. Roosevelt determined to give the farmer and workingman "a square deal."

In Roosevelt's first annual message to Congress, he outlined a vast program of reforms. He spent his two terms carrying them out. Except for Cleveland, Roosevelt was the first President since Lincoln to exercise strong leadership.

Trust Busting. Roosevelt immediately proved that he meant to enforce the antitrust law. Two powerful railroad men, James J. Hill and E. H. Harriman, formed a combination of lines in the Northwest. Roosevelt immediately began a suit against their Northern Securities Company. As a result, the Supreme Court broke up the combination. Roosevelt had Congress establish the Department of Commerce and Labor, with a Bureau of Corporations to learn the facts about big business. During his administration, the government began 44 antitrust actions. It won major cases that ended Rockefeller's oil trust and James B. Duke's tobacco trust.

But big business often proved more efficient than little business. When the government broke up Standard Oil, for example, the prices of oil products rose. The Supreme Court then drew a line between "reasonable" and "unreasonable" restraint of trade. Roosevelt himself declared that mere bigness was not a reason for government attack. But he did insist on ethical behavior in business, and on the government's right to regulate any corporation, large or small.

Controlling the Railroads came next. The railroads had not always paid attention to the Interstate Commerce Act, and still committed many abuses. In 1903, Congress passed the Elkins Act. This law forbade railroads to give rebates, which favored one shipper over another. Most railroad men supported the measure, because sharp competition had hurt them, as well as the people. But the public still complained about high railroad charges. In 1906, Roosevelt drove the Hepburn Act through Congress. This law broadened the powers of the Interstate Commerce Commission. It also forced the railroads to adopt standard bookkeeping methods, supervised by government officials.

Business Reforms also interested Roosevelt. He intervened dramatically in the great anthracite coal strike of 1902. The United Mine Workers union went on strike for better wages and a nine-hour day, but mineowners stubbornly refused to give these benefits. A prolonged strike threatened to cause great public suffering, because the country depended on coal for fuel. Roosevelt intervened, not to benefit the operators or the workers, but to reach a fair settlement by arbitration. His efforts led to a compromise that ended the strike.

Muckrakers had aroused public interest in the use of harmful ingredients in food and drug products, and in the unsanitary conditions under which they were prepared. In 1906, Congress did much to end these evils by passing the Pure Food and Drugs Act and the Meat Inspection Act.

Conservation, probably Roosevelt's most important reform, made great progress in the early 1900's. No other President had realized that Americans were rapidly wasting their natural wealth, as greedy men seized forests, minerals, and water-power sites. The President put more than 200,000,000 acres of forest, mining, and water-power areas under government control. The time had come to save the nation's wealth and plan its use.

The Big Stick. Under Roosevelt, the United States realized its full responsibility as a world power for the first time. The new President summed up his firm policy in foreign affairs with the phrase, "Speak softly and carry a big stick." During McKinley's presidency, the United States and Great Britain had opposed European plans to split China into colonies. The two countries favored an "open door" for trade in China (see OPEN-DOOR POLICY). Now Roosevelt went much further in extending American power overseas.

The President made a treaty with Panama that allowed the United States to build the Panama Canal to connect the Atlantic and Pacific oceans. Roosevelt also widened the scope of the Monroe Doctrine. In the so-called "Roosevelt Corollary" to the Doctrine, he established the principle that the United States might intervene when any Latin-American country got into trouble that could result in European interference. Under this rule, the United States took charge of finances in Santo Domingo (now the Dominican Republic), and assumed temporary protectorates over Haiti and Nicaragua. Roosevelt also brought about a settlement of the disputed boundary between Alaska and Canada, and helped end the Russo-Japanese War.

Taft's Administration. Roosevelt was so popular that he could name his own successor. He chose William Howard Taft. The Republicans under Taft defeated William Jennings Bryan in 1908. Taft pushed many antitrust cases and obtained another law for railroad legislation, but progressives considered him weak and conservative. He cooperated with such "old-guard" leaders in Congress as Speaker Joseph G. Cannon. He did nothing to spur popular zeal for reform. And he allowed Congress to pass the highest tariff law in history, the Payne-Aldrich Act. Many Republicans, as well as Democrats, denounced this law as an outrage.

Taft

During Taft's term, the states approved a constitutional amendment that permitted Congress to levy an income tax. (The Supreme Court had ruled an earlier law unconstitutional in 1895.) Another amendment provided that the people, rather than the state legislatures, should elect U.S. Senators. But Taft was not responsible for either change. The Republican party

split wide open in 1912. Conservatives renominated Taft, and progressives formed a "Bull Moose" party to re-elect Roosevelt. As a result of the Republican split, the Democratic candidate, Woodrow Wilson, swept to victory. The Democrats also won control of Congress.

The New Freedom. Wilson began at once to urge a program of reforms that he called "the new freedom." He demanded that the tariff laws be rewritten to abolish "everything that bears even the semblance of privilege." The Underwood Act of 1913 brought about the first real tariff reduction in 50 years. The country also needed a more flexible system of credit and currency. Its financial machinery had become creaky, lopsided, and dangerously inefficient. The Federal Reserve Act of 1913 provided proper banking facilities, rescued the West and South from the domination of New York financiers, and furnished a sound currency under federal control (see FEDERAL RESERVE SYSTEM).

Wilson

Wilson also worked to control big business. The Clayton Antitrust Act of 1914 prohibited corporations from grouping themselves together under interlocking boards of directors. The law also helped labor by making it impossible to prosecute unions under antitrust laws. In 1913, Congress set up a separate Department of Labor. Congress also created the Federal Trade Commission, which handles complaints of monopoly and unfair business practices.

Wilson insisted that Congress provide for low-cost loans to farmers. He signed the LaFollette Seamen's Act, which assured decent working conditions for merchant seamen. Another law gave railroad workers an eight-hour day. He vigorously supported conservation, and called for social justice and business honesty.

Wilson struggled constantly with foreign problems. Civil war in Mexico resulted in the death of 18 American marines at Veracruz. War seemed near, but Wilson arranged for three Latin-American nations to settle the dispute by arbitration. In 1916 the Mexican bandit Pancho Villa killed a number of Americans in New Mexico. The President sent troops into Mexico to hunt for Villa, but they failed to capture him. However, a great war in Europe far outweighed all local problems.

"He Kept Us Out of War." Wilson originally tried to keep the United States neutral in World War I, which swept across Europe in 1914. He planned to use America's influence to obtain a fair peace. But the war stirred American feeling tremendously. Strong ties bound the nation to Great Britain, France, and Belgium, although some Americans sympathized with Germany and Austria-Hungary. Economic factors soon strengthened the country's sympathy for the Allies. The United States had developed a profitable trade with the British and French. Americans were equally free to trade with Germany, but ships could not get through the Allied blockade. To counter the blockade, the Germans used submarines to sink Allied ships. In 1915, a German submarine sank the British liner *Lusitania*. Almost 1,200 persons lost their lives, including 128 Americans. The country's anger rose. American and German diplomats exchanged messages for almost a year. Germany finally promised to sink no more merchant ships without warning.

In 1916, the Republicans reunited their progressive and conservative groups into one party, and nominated

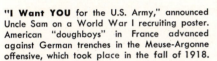

"I Want YOU for the U.S. Army," announced Uncle Sam on a World War I recruiting poster. American "doughboys" in France advanced against German trenches in the Meuse-Argonne offensive, which took place in the fall of 1918.

Library of Congress; U.S. Army

Charles Evans Hughes to oppose Wilson. Both parties stood for neutrality, but also for maintaining American rights. The Democrats used the slogan, "He kept us out of war." But Wilson declared that at any moment he might find that he could not "preserve both the honor and the peace of the United States." He won a close election race, and called for a peace of justice, without victory for either side.

Making the World Safe for Democracy. On Jan. 31, 1917, Germany proclaimed unlimited submarine warfare. The Germans closed the seas to American shipping except for one ship a week to the British Isles. The United States at once broke off diplomatic relations with Germany, and began arming its merchant ships. In March, the Department of State released an intercepted message in which Germany urged Japan and Mexico to attack the United States. German submarines sank five American ships, and the government uncovered German plots for sabotaging American industries. Finally, on April 2, 1917, Wilson asked Congress to declare war. The overwhelming vote in both houses showed that national sentiment strongly favored war.

Fundamentally, Americans went to war believing that they fought "to make the world safe for democracy." The nation united in the war effort and accepted a discipline unknown in any previous conflict. American forces did not reach Europe in large numbers until 1918. But then they did much to repel German advances in France, and played an important part in Allied attacks that won the war. For a history of the United States in the war, see WORLD WAR I.

Boom and Bust

Rejecting the League of Nations. Early in 1918, Wilson sent Congress a message outlining his famous Fourteen Points for a peace settlement. For the text of the Fourteen Points, see WILSON, WOODROW (The Fourteen Points). When the war ended, Wilson seemed to be the leader of a great upheaval of world feeling. Liberal people everywhere looked to him. But much of this idealism proved short-lived.

Wilson first blundered by appealing to the nation in 1918 to elect a Democratic Congress. The people resented such partisanship, and elected Republican majorities in the Senate and House of Representatives. Wilson also made a mistake in the men he chose to go with him to Versailles to help draft a peace treaty. He included no member of Congress and only one Republican.

The people of Europe greeted Wilson enthusiastically. But he found that weariness, war hatreds, and postwar materialism had replaced idealism. The Allied nations thought of 2,000,000 graves and demanded a peace of revenge. Wilson had to negotiate with the experienced David Lloyd George of Britain, stubborn Georges Clemenceau of France, and other leaders with special demands. His supreme desire was to have the peace treaty include a plan for a league of nations. In order to get such a league, he had to compromise on some of his Fourteen Points. The peace treaty had many faults, but Wilson believed the League would correct them all. See LEAGUE OF NATIONS; VERSAILLES, TREATY OF.

When Wilson returned to America, he found strong opposition to both the Versailles Treaty and the Covenant of the League of Nations which it contained. The Senate would have to approve both, and the Republicans had organized the key committee on foreign relations to delay and weaken the treaty. About 40 Senators wanted to adopt the treaty as it stood, about 40 favored acceptance with written reservations, and about 12 opposed the treaty altogether. Party politics, hatred of Wilson, and fear of European entanglements all played a part in the debates that followed.

Wilson could have gained Senate approval for the treaty by accepting the reservations written by Senator Henry Cabot Lodge of Massachusetts. But the President stubbornly refused. He began a nationwide speaking tour to gain support for the League. Wilson's tour ended in September, 1919, when he suffered a paralytic stroke. The Senate later defeated both the treaty and the League, although a large section of the public unquestionably favored both measures.

Harding

Back to Normalcy. In 1920, the Republicans nominated Warren G. Harding for President and Calvin Coolidge for Vice-President. No clear-cut issue appeared, and Harding avoided any plain stand on the League of Nations. The nation's mood had become conservative. Most Americans wanted to avoid international responsibility. They optimistically believed that they could return to prewar "normalcy." Women voted on a nationwide basis for the first time in this election, but their vote had no noticeable effect on the outcome. Harding won an overwhelming victory over Democrat James M. Cox.

During Harding's administration, a satisfied nation shrugged off political corruption as bad as that under Grant. The Secretary of the Interior, A. B. Fall, took bribes to let private oil producers lease valuable federal reserves at Teapot Dome, Wyo. (see TEAPOT DOME). A scandal arising from the sale of pardons and liquor permits involved even Attorney General Harry M. Daugherty, and forced him out of office. The head of the Veterans' Bureau took large sums allocated to federal hospitals and other services.

World War I had raised the national debt from a prewar $1,000,000,000 to more than $26,500,000,000 in 1919. In order to handle fiscal problems more easily, the government provided for the first national budget in 1921, and established the Bureau of the Budget.

Isolationism, the belief that the United States should stay out of foreign affairs altogether, gained many followers during this period. Harding yielded to the

"irreconcilables" and rejected the League of Nations. However, the Washington Naval Conference, under the leadership of Secretary of State Charles Evans Hughes, met in 1921 to discuss disarmament. Five nations agreed to scrap a number of warships, but the gains made by the conference were only temporary.

Coolidge

Later, under President Coolidge, the United States persuaded more than 60 nations to sign the Kellogg-Briand Pact, which was designed to abolish war as a solution to international problems.

Except for these measures, the government aimed for a policy of political isolation in world affairs. The United States wanted to make no commitments to enforce peace or to improve economic cooperation. In 1922, Congress passed the Fordney-McCumber Tariff, which raised duties to the highest level yet known, and shut out most foreign goods from the United States.

Farmer and Labor Hardships. Most American farmers became poor and discontented because of the high tariff and crop surpluses. Between 1920 and 1932, farm income fell from $15,500,000,000 to $5,500,000,000. But Coolidge twice vetoed the McNary-Haugen plan for raising farm prices to a higher level.

Workers' efforts to improve labor conditions suffered many setbacks. Employers organized to defend the open shop, often discriminated against union workers, and established "company unions" which tamely took orders. Federal courts issued injunctions to crush strikes. Many people suspected all reform movements, and frequently attacked liberals and radicals. A revived Ku-Klux Klan enrolled 5,000,000 members for its attacks on Catholics, foreigners, Jews, and Negroes.

The Roaring 20's. In spite of scandals, isolationism, and farmer-labor difficulties, the country as a whole prospered. Stock speculation, riotous spending, and real-estate booms sent prices skyrocketing. Stock gambling soared in the "bull market" of 1928-1929.

During the 1920's, the United States set off on a joy ride in an "era of wonderful nonsense." Americans felt lighthearted after the war. Henry Ford led the way by "putting America on wheels" in his "Model T." People spent more and more money for good roads, travel, and vacation resorts. They announced their revolt from puritanism with jazz bands and a craze for sports and dances. Canned foods, ready-made clothing, and household appliances freed women from much household drudgery. More and more of them worked away from home. Daring young *flappers* shocked their elders with short skirts, bobbed hair, and free use of cosmetics and cigarettes. Newspapers and the growing radio industry featured sensational accounts of "tremendous trifles" and "ballyhoo" about boxing matches, murder trials, and motion-picture stars. Charles A. Lindbergh's solo flight across the Atlantic Ocean in 1927 roused the nation to a fever pitch of excitement. It also did much to stimulate the new aviation industry.

In 1919, Amendment 18 to the Constitution prohibited the manufacture and sale of intoxicating liquor. But many people resented the law, and drank in illegal "clubs" called *speak-easies*. Gangsters took over *bootlegging* (the illegal distribution of liquor), and crime increased. The federal government found it almost impossible to enforce prohibition, mainly because of strong public opinion against it.

"Flaming Youth" of the 1920's revolted against the standards of the prewar era. John Held's flapper wears a "cloche" hat, rolled silk stockings, and open galoshes.

© John Held, Jr.

Depression Hit the nation after the stock market collapsed in 1929. Crowds besieged the New York Stock Exchange, *right*, on October 29. Many unemployed men sold apples.

Under the surface, American life remained fundamentally sound. Education, religion, and science made impressive progress. The average American was still hard-working and serious. The 1920's were a golden period in American literature, distinguished by the works of such writers as Willa Cather, William Faulkner, F. Scott Fitzgerald, Ernest Hemingway, Sinclair Lewis, and Carl Sandburg.

The Great Depression. The future looked bright when Herbert Hoover became President in 1929. He believed staunchly in efficient planning, and seemed admirably qualified to improve the government. But circumstances were too strong for him. His administration

Hoover began unfortunately when Congress, yielding to pressure groups, passed the Smoot-Hawley Tariff Act. This law raised tariffs to extremely steep levels. More than a thousand economists petitioned Hoover to veto the bill, but he signed it. Every important foreign nation protested against the law, and many at once raised their tariffs. The effects on trade were disastrous.

The Hoover administration had hardly begun when the country suffered the worst business crash in its history. The stock market crashed in the fall of 1929. On just one day, October 29, desperate speculators sold 16,400,000 shares of stocks. When the year ended, the government estimated that the stock-market crash had cost investors $40,000,000,000.

Even before the 1929 collapse, business had begun to decline. After the crash, the country sank steadily into the most acute depression in its history. Millions of persons lost every cent they owned. Banks failed, factories shut down, stores closed, and almost every business seemed paralyzed. Empty trains ran between once-busy cities where hardly a wisp of smoke now rose in the air. Local governments could not collect half their taxes. Foreign trade almost came to a stop.

For a while, Hoover and business leaders assured the nation that prosperity was "just around the corner." But conditions grew steadily worse. By the end of 1930, more than 6,000,000 Americans were out of work. The number rose to 12,000,000 a year later. More than 5,000

banks failed, and over 32,000 businesses went bankrupt. Farm prices fell lower than ever before. Desperate men sold apples on street corners, ate in "soup kitchens," and lived in clumps of shacks called "Hoovervilles." Angry farmers prevented mortgage foreclosures with pitchforks, and workmen demanded radical government action.

The Hoover administration did something, but not enough. It began a construction program for roads, public buildings, and airports, and increased the country's credit facilities. Most important, it created the Reconstruction Finance Corporation (RFC), with $2,-000,000,000 for rescuing hard-pressed banks, railroads, factories, and farmers. For the first time, the United States government assumed the responsibility of rescuing the economy by active intervention in business. But the depression continued throughout the nation.

The New Deal

The country urgently demanded changes. The Republicans renominated Hoover. The Democrats turned to Franklin D. Roosevelt, who won an overwhelming victory. His vigorous, optimistic campaign speeches advocated

Roosevelt

a "New Deal" for "the forgotten man." At Roosevelt's inauguration in 1933, he told the people that "The only thing we have to fear is fear itself."

Relief, Recovery, and Reform were Roosevelt's aims when he took office. The country needed immediate relief, recovery from economic collapse, and reform to prevent future depressions. A Democratic Congress stood ready to pass any measures the President urged.

In a 99-day session, Congress passed a history-making number of important bills. Most of them came directly from the White House. One act created a Federal Emergency Relief Administration under Harry L. Hopkins. It eventually paid out about $3,000,000,000 for relief or for wages on public works. Another bill established the Civilian Conservation Corps (CCC), which employed 3,000,000 young men in forestry work, road building, and flood control. Out of these two agencies grew the Works Progress Administration (WPA) of 1935.

One emergency act gave the President the power to regulate banking and to reopen sound banks. Another insured bank deposits up to $5,000 (later $10,000). A new Home Owners' Loan Corporation (HOLC) gave aid to home owners. The government set up the Agricultural Adjustment Administration (AAA) to pay subsidies to farmers who voluntarily reduced the acreage of certain crops. One especially important act created the Tennessee Valley Authority (TVA). This project was authorized to develop the resources of a great river basin with government dams, electric-power plants, and industrial and agricultural planning.

Labor. An important measure of 1933 set up the National Recovery Administration (NRA). This agency tried to put industry on its feet by shortening hours, raising wages, and stopping cutthroat competition. The Supreme Court ruled the NRA unconstitutional in 1935. But most of its provisions about collective bargaining appeared in two later bills. The Wagner Act in 1935 guaranteed workmen the right to negotiate with employers through "unions of their own choice," and set up a Labor Relations Board to handle disputes. This act strengthened the American Federation of Labor, and led to the birth of a new labor movement, the Congress of Industrial Organizations (CIO). The Fair Labor Standards Act of 1938 set a minimum wage of 25 cents an hour and established a 44-hour workweek, with time-and-a-half pay for work over this maximum. The Act provided that the wage would gradually be increased to 40 cents, and the hours decreased to 40. The bill also outlawed child labor under age 16.

Social Welfare. The spirit of the New Deal was as important as its acts. It assumed that the federal government could act in the broadest possible way for human welfare. Beginning in 1935, Congress passed a series of social-security laws that gave pensions to the aged, insurance to the unemployed, and benefit payments to the blind, to crippled children, and to dependent mothers. All these new programs cost money. Government spending rose from $697,000,000 in 1916 to $9,000,000,000 in 1936, an increase of 1,100 per cent. The government adjusted taxation to fall hardest on the rich, who could afford to pay. Conservatives, wealthy persons, and many businessmen bitterly attacked the New Deal. But most of the people stood behind it, and in the election of 1936 every state except Maine and Vermont voted for Roosevelt's re-election. For the story of his political program, see NEW DEAL.

Gathering War Clouds. Like Wilson, Roosevelt saw his domestic program interrupted by a global war. When he took office, the League of Nations had broken down. Germany, Italy, and Japan felt they did not have their share of the world's opportunities and wealth. Germany turned to Nazism under Adolf Hitler; Italy, under Benito Mussolini, adopted Fascism; and military leaders controlled Japan. The leaders of these three countries were aggressive dictators, determined to build great empires by armed force. The peaceful world shuddered when Japan invaded Manchuria in 1931 and Italy marched into Ethiopia in 1935. Japan invaded China in 1937. Germany reoccupied the Rhineland in 1936, and annexed Austria in 1938.

Most Americans tried to ignore the war clouds gathering over Europe. Isolationists thought the United States could remain safe across the broad Atlantic. But neither President Roosevelt nor Secretary of State Cordell Hull sympathized with isolationism. They made repeated efforts to convince the nation that when one country is menaced by an aggressor, all countries are threatened. In the fall of 1937, the President called for action to "quarantine" the aggressive powers. But Congress and most of the public paid little attention.

Between 1935 and 1939, Congress passed several neutrality acts that kept the country from trading with or giving financial credit to any nation involved in a war. These laws actually encouraged aggression, because they meant that if Hitler struck at France or Great Britain, the United States would not furnish them with money or weapons. In 1940 isolationists organized the "America First" Committee to prevent the United States from entering the war. But administration leaders continued to denounce the dictators. They worked to gain the friendship of Latin America and Canada, and took steps to arm the United States. When Hitler seized Czechoslovakia in 1939, many Americans awakened to the fact that if Western Europe fell, the United States might be the next to fall under Hitler's domination.

World War II

World-wide conflict began on September 1, 1939. German forces struck defenseless Poland in a fierce *blitzkrieg*, or *lightning war*, and conquered it with Russia's help (see BLITZKRIEG). Two days later, Great Britain and France declared war on Germany. The following

Tennessee Valley Authority

New Deal Projects such as the TVA represented government planning on a larger scale than ever before. Wheeler Dam in Alabama was the first TVA dam on a main river.

During World War II, civilians on the home front helped the war effort by buying savings bonds and by conducting scrap drives to collect such scarce materials as rubber, metal, and paper.

spring, German armies overran Denmark and Norway. Then they turned west, smashed through The Netherlands and Belgium, and defeated France.

Americans realized that Great Britain stood alone. They saw that if it fell and Hitler continued his advance, the United States would have no allies. In a dramatic series of moves, Congress voted huge sums for arms. The United States allied itself with Canada in a Joint Board on Defense. Peacetime conscription put 1,000,000 men under arms. Roosevelt gave Great Britain 50 destroyers, and the British leased a number of naval bases to the United States.

The United States stood on the brink of war. The international crisis helped Roosevelt defeat Wendell L. Willkie in the 1940 election. He became the first President to win a third term. At Roosevelt's urging, Congress passed the Lend-Lease Act early in 1941. This act allowed the United States to lease or give defense goods or facilities to any nation whose defense was vital to America. A stream of planes, tanks, and foods flowed to Great Britain from "the arsenal of democracy." American forces occupied Greenland and Iceland. American warships patrolled the Atlantic. On Aug. 14, 1941, President Roosevelt and British Prime Minister Winston Churchill proclaimed *The Atlantic Charter* as a set of principles for a better world. The United States seemed to be drifting steadily into war with Germany. Then, on Dec. 7, 1941, Japanese airplanes bombed U.S. bases at Pearl Harbor in Hawaii. Congress declared war on Japan the next day, and on Germany and Italy three days later. For the story of history's biggest war, see WORLD WAR II.

The Atomic Age

Truman Succeeds Roosevelt. As the Allied armies closed in on Germany in the spring of 1945, Roosevelt died suddenly at Warm Springs, Ga. Harry S. Truman, who had been

Truman

elected Vice-President when Roosevelt won a fourth term in 1944, was President during the closing operations of the war. Germany surrendered unconditionally on May 7. Truman then ordered the newly developed atomic bomb dropped on Hiroshima, Japan, on August 6. A second one was dropped on Nagasaki three days later. War in the Pacific ended with the Japanese surrender on August 14, 1945.

Allied statesmen had made preparations for a successor to the League of Nations in meetings at Tehran, Iran; Dumbarton Oaks, in Washington, D.C.; and Yalta, Russia. In April, 1945, representatives of 50 nations attended a conference in San Francisco to draft a charter for the United Nations. The public overwhelmingly favored American membership, and the United States became one of the chief members and supporters of the UN.

The Fair Deal. President Truman proposed a program of progressive measures called "The Fair Deal." His program included federal health insurance and aid to education. Truman fought for his program, but he was less skillful than Roosevelt in dealing with Congress, and less fortunate in choosing his assistants. Investigations of the Reconstruction Finance Corporation and the Bureau of Internal Revenue exposed some corruption in the government. A Senate committee headed by Estes Kefauver of Tennessee reviewed crime in the United States, and found connections between city political machines and crime syndicates. In Congress, Southern Democrats lined up with conservative Republicans to block Truman's chief proposals. Congress also passed the Taft-Hartley Act, which outlawed the closed shop. Labor leaders denounced the law as an effort to destroy collective bargaining. Truman vetoed the bill, but Congress overrode his veto.

Inflation became an acute problem under Truman. United States industry had quickly converted to peacetime production after the war. The country entered a period of prosperity greater than any before in its history. New industries sprang up to supply Americans with plastics, television, frozen foods, and automatic home appliances. The electronics, chemical, natural-gas, and jet-aircraft industries expanded rapidly. But runaway inflation threatened the nation after the government dropped price controls and other wartime restrictions during the first years after the war. Prices spiraled higher and higher. By the middle of 1951, the general price level had risen 85 per cent over the 1935-1939 average.

The Cold War. Truman's greatest troubles and greatest fame came in foreign affairs. The United States emerged from World War II as the leading world power. The nation's importance brought new responsibilities. After the war, a split developed between Russia and

117

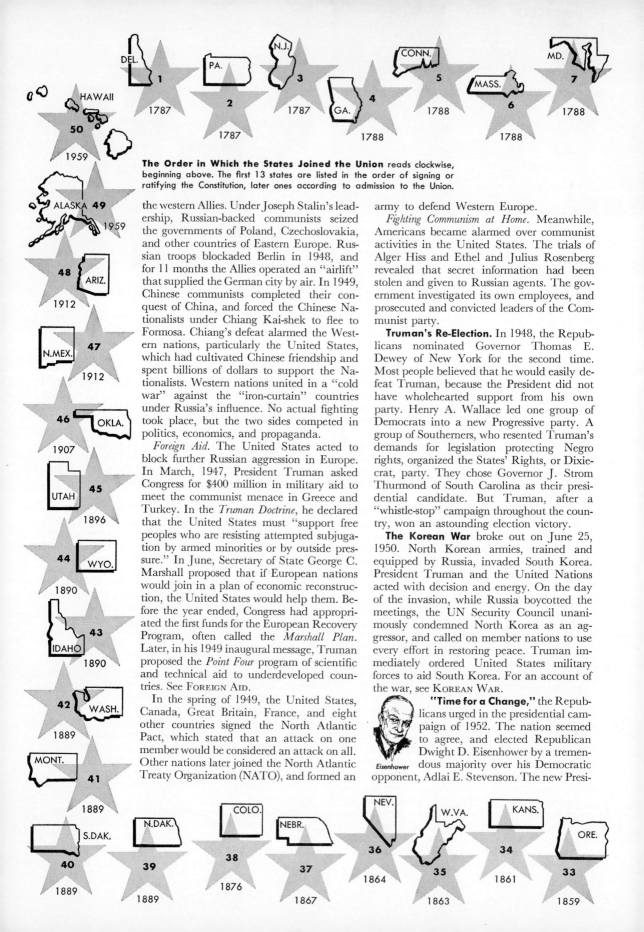

The Order in Which the States Joined the Union reads clockwise, beginning above. The first 13 states are listed in the order of signing or ratifying the Constitution, later ones according to admission to the Union.

the western Allies. Under Joseph Stalin's leadership, Russian-backed communists seized the governments of Poland, Czechoslovakia, and other countries of Eastern Europe. Russian troops blockaded Berlin in 1948, and for 11 months the Allies operated an "airlift" that supplied the German city by air. In 1949, Chinese communists completed their conquest of China, and forced the Chinese Nationalists under Chiang Kai-shek to flee to Formosa. Chiang's defeat alarmed the Western nations, particularly the United States, which had cultivated Chinese friendship and spent billions of dollars to support the Nationalists. Western nations united in a "cold war" against the "iron-curtain" countries under Russia's influence. No actual fighting took place, but the two sides competed in politics, economics, and propaganda.

Foreign Aid. The United States acted to block further Russian aggression in Europe. In March, 1947, President Truman asked Congress for $400 million in military aid to meet the communist menace in Greece and Turkey. In the *Truman Doctrine*, he declared that the United States must "support free peoples who are resisting attempted subjugation by armed minorities or by outside pressure." In June, Secretary of State George C. Marshall proposed that if European nations would join in a plan of economic reconstruction, the United States would help them. Before the year ended, Congress had appropriated the first funds for the European Recovery Program, often called the *Marshall Plan.* Later, in his 1949 inaugural message, Truman proposed the *Point Four* program of scientific and technical aid to underdeveloped countries. See FOREIGN AID.

In the spring of 1949, the United States, Canada, Great Britain, France, and eight other countries signed the North Atlantic Pact, which stated that an attack on one member would be considered an attack on all. Other nations later joined the North Atlantic Treaty Organization (NATO), and formed an army to defend Western Europe.

Fighting Communism at Home. Meanwhile, Americans became alarmed over communist activities in the United States. The trials of Alger Hiss and Ethel and Julius Rosenberg revealed that secret information had been stolen and given to Russian agents. The government investigated its own employees, and prosecuted and convicted leaders of the Communist party.

Truman's Re-Election. In 1948, the Republicans nominated Governor Thomas E. Dewey of New York for the second time. Most people believed that he would easily defeat Truman, because the President did not have wholehearted support from his own party. Henry A. Wallace led one group of Democrats into a new Progressive party. A group of Southerners, who resented Truman's demands for legislation protecting Negro rights, organized the States' Rights, or Dixiecrat, party. They chose Governor J. Strom Thurmond of South Carolina as their presidential candidate. But Truman, after a "whistle-stop" campaign throughout the country, won an astounding election victory.

The Korean War broke out on June 25, 1950. North Korean armies, trained and equipped by Russia, invaded South Korea. President Truman and the United Nations acted with decision and energy. On the day of the invasion, while Russia boycotted the meetings, the UN Security Council unanimously condemned North Korea as an aggressor, and called on member nations to use every effort in restoring peace. Truman immediately ordered United States military forces to aid South Korea. For an account of the war, see KOREAN WAR.

"Time for a Change," the Republicans urged in the presidential campaign of 1952. The nation seemed to agree, and elected Republican Dwight D. Eisenhower by a tremendous majority over his Democratic opponent, Adlai E. Stevenson. The new Presi-

Eisenhower

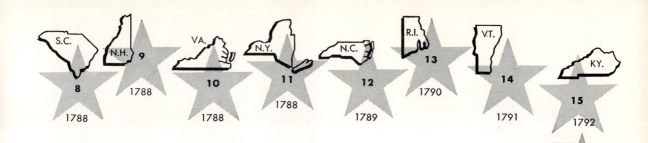

S.C. 8 1788
N.H. 9 1788
VA. 10 1788
N.Y. 11 1788
N.C. 12 1789
R.I. 13 1790
VT. 14 1791
KY. 15 1792

TENN. 16 1796
OHIO 17 1803
LA. 18 1812
IND. 19 1816
MISS. 20 1817
ILL. 21 1818
ALA. 22 1819
ME. 23 1820
MO. 24 1821
ARK. 25 1836

dent kept many New Deal and Fair Deal measures, but followed a moderate path. He believed in a "businessman's government," and stressed teamwork above party disputes.

Foreign Affairs. The nation's dissatisfaction with the Korean War had helped elect Eisenhower. He promised in a campaign speech to visit Korea and try to end the war. His three-day trip in December, 1952, had no immediate results. But United Nations and North Korean leaders signed an armistice in July, 1953. Several other international events also threatened to cause global war. A conflict between the French and Communist Vietminh forces in northern Indochina grew extremely serious in the spring of 1954. France eventually had to surrender northern Vietnam to the communists and grant complete independence to Cambodia, Laos, and Vietnam. Chinese Communist threats to Formosa and nearby islands also alarmed the United States. In 1954, Secretary of State John Foster Dulles helped organize the Southeast Asia Treaty Organization (SEATO).

In the Middle East, Egyptian President Gamal A. Nasser seized the Suez Canal in July, 1956. Three months later, Israeli, British, and French forces invaded Egypt in a "police action" to restore the canal to international control. The United States condemned the use of force, and the United Nations stopped the fighting. In 1957, the President proclaimed his *Eisenhower Doctrine*, aimed at preventing possible communist penetration of the Middle East. This pledge, approved by Congress, committed the United States to send military aid to any Middle Eastern country that requested it. The doctrine served as the basis for United States action in sending a detachment of marines to Lebanon in July, 1958. President Camille Chamoun asked for aid in ending disturbances there.

Events at Home focused attention on changes in administration, communist influence in the United States, and problems of race relations. Early in Eisenhower's first term, Con-

gress established the Department of Health, Education, and Welfare. The secretary of the department became the tenth member of the President's Cabinet. The government also ended most price controls. Eisenhower again defeated Stevenson in 1956. But the Republicans failed to win majorities in either the House of Representatives or the Senate. Eisenhower became the first President in more than 100 years to come into office without a party majority in either house of Congress.

Communist subversive activities continued to alarm Americans. In 1954, Congress passed the Communist Control Act, outlawing the Communist party in the United States. The same year, the Senate censured Senator Joseph R. McCarthy of Wisconsin for disrespect he had shown to Congress during his investigations of communist subversion.

Throughout the 1900's, especially after World War I, both Negroes and whites had worked to increase Negro opportunities in jobs and education, and to lessen discrimination see NEGRO [The Negro Today]). In 1954, the U.S. Supreme Court ruled that public-school segregation, or separation of Negroes from whites, was unconstitutional. The Court recommended that the states end it "with all deliberate speed." Some states began programs to integrate their school systems. But others objected to the ruling.

The Changing Scene. The United States in the mid-1900's found itself stronger and richer than ever before. It grew by two states when Alaska and Hawaii joined the Union in 1959. But its very size and wealth seemed to create new problems.

More than 179 million persons lived in the United States. Their standard of living surpassed that of any other nation. Americans earned more on the average than they ever had before. But prices had also risen to new heights, and inflation worried many economists. A business recession which began in 1957 lowered production, housing, and consumer spending. The number of persons

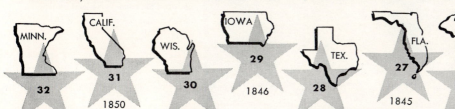

MINN. 32 1858
CALIF. 31 1850
WIS. 30 1848
IOWA 29 1846
TEX. 28 1845
FLA. 27 1845
MICH. 26 1837

AMERICA IN MID-CENTURY

The Space Age opened in 1957. By 1962, American astronaut John Glenn, *left*, and Russian cosmonaut Gherman Titov could compare notes on what it was like to orbit the earth.

The U.S. Population zoomed past 180 million in the 1960's. Growth centered in and around cities. Housing developments sprang up almost overnight in such urban and suburban areas.

California Division of Highways

Compact Cars answered the demand for economy in the late 1950's and revolutionized the U.S. auto industry.

The Jet Age brought distant points within easy reach. Americans traveled faster in the 1960's than ever before as jets replaced piston-engine planes.

The Seattle World's Fair, first in the U.S. in over 20 years, opened in 1962. Its towering Space Needle emphasized the theme—the 21st century.

Century 21 Exposition

without jobs rose to more than 5 million in 1958 to set a postwar record. More and more Americans moved to metropolitan areas, and sprawling suburbs around big cities caused new difficulties in mass transportation and distribution. Automation promised to free men from much of the drudgery of modern industry.

Science became important in many other fields. World War II had shown the vast destructive power of atomic bombs. Men throughout the world wanted to prohibit the use of atomic and hydrogen bombs, and harness the atom for peaceful purposes instead. Soon after President Eisenhower took office in 1953, he proposed an "atoms for peace" plan that would provide power for underdeveloped areas of the world. The United Nations adopted a plan and set up the International Atomic Energy Agency in 1957 to carry it out. The United States launched the *Nautilus*, the world's first atomic-powered submarine, in 1954. In 1957, Shippingport, Pa., opened the first large-scale nuclear reactor in the United States designed to produce electric power for civilian use.

Scientific efforts to explore and conquer outer space had more spectacular appeal. Scientists worked on jet propulsion aircraft, guided missiles, and rockets that reached new heights and speeds. Russia launched the first man-made moon, an artificial satellite called *Sputnik I*, in October, 1957. The United States sent its first satellite, *Explorer I*, into orbit in January, 1958, and others followed (see SPACE TRAVEL [table]). In July, 1958, Congress set up the National Aeronautics and Space Administration to coordinate space efforts.

Space exploration brought home to the United States the importance of education. Many of the nation's schools were overcrowded, understaffed, and poorly equipped. Educators and others urged that the content and quality of U.S. education be improved.

Relations between Russia and the United States became worse in 1960. The Russians shot down a U.S. U-2 reconnaissance plane deep inside Soviet territory. The Russians used the U-2 incident to break up the Paris *summit conference* in May. Leaders of France, Great Britain, Russia, and the United States were to have discussed Cold War differences there.

Kennedy Succeeds Eisenhower. John F. Kennedy, at 43 the youngest man ever elected President, defeated Richard M. Nixon, the Republican nominee, in the 1960 election. For the first time in history, the two major presidential candidates appeared on television Kennedy in face-to-face debates on the issues.

Kennedy served only 34 months before he was assassinated in 1963. During his short administration, Congress failed to pass much of his *New Frontier* program. But President Kennedy established the Peace Corps and the Alliance for Progress in 1961, forced Russia to remove missiles from Cuba in 1962, and arranged a partial nuclear test ban treaty with Russia in 1963.

In World Affairs, Kennedy suffered a great setback soon after he took office. A band of Cuban exiles launched the Bay of Pigs invasion of Cuba in April, 1961, in an attempt to overthrow dictator Fidel Castro. The attack was planned by the U.S. Central Intelligence Agency. The invaders expected support from U.S. aircraft, but it never came. Castro's forces easily crushed the invasion and took nearly 1,200 prisoners.

In June, 1961, Russia renewed threats to sign a separate peace treaty with East Germany unless the Western powers withdrew from West Berlin. Thousands of East Germans fled to West Berlin as tension mounted. In August, 1961, East Germans built a 26-mile border barricade to stop the escapes. Later, they built the infamous Berlin Wall. But Kennedy promised to defend West Berlin, and sent more U.S. troops to the city. See BERLIN (The Wall of Shame).

A second Cuban crisis brought the U.S. and Russia to the brink of all-out atomic war on Oct. 22, 1962. President Kennedy announced that Russia was building missile bases in Cuba and stocking them with missiles capable of launching atomic attacks on U.S. cities. He ordered a naval *quarantine* (blockade) to halt ships carrying offensive arms to Cuba. For a week, war seemed likely. Then Khrushchev ordered the missiles removed. As tension eased, President Kennedy ordered the quarantine lifted. See CUBA (The Cuban Crisis).

In Southeast Asia, the Communists threatened Thailand, Laos, and South Vietnam. Internal problems complicated South Vietnam's war against the Communists. The U.S. severely criticized the South Vietnamese government in 1963 for its repressive policies. Vietnamese military officers overthrew and killed President Ngo Dinh Diem on Nov. 1, 1963. The U.S. supported the new Vietnamese government.

In Latin America, Castro directed Communist attempts to cause revolutions and take over other Latin American countries. To stem his efforts, the U.S. set up in 1961 the Alliance for Progress, a 10-year plan to aid Latin America (see ALLIANCE FOR PROGRESS).

One of Kennedy's greatest achievements in foreign affairs came in 1963. To prevent further atomic fallout and thus protect the health of future generations, the United States, Great Britain, Russia, and more than 100 other countries signed a treaty that banned all except underground atomic test explosions. Many persons felt this treaty marked the beginning of improved international relations in the Cold War.

In Civil Rights, equal rights for Negroes became the leading national issue of the early 1960's. The civil rights movement grew as Negroes demonstrated in the North and the South. The drive toward integration and equal opportunity often resulted in violence. Two persons were killed in rioting in Oxford, Miss., in September, 1962, when James Meredith became the first Negro enrolled at the University of Mississippi. President Kennedy federalized the Mississippi National Guard to help restore order there. In June, 1963, he federalized the Alabama National Guard to enforce integration at the University of Alabama.

About 200,000 persons staged a *Freedom March* in Washington, D.C., in August, 1963, to dramatize Negro demands for equal rights. President Kennedy asked Congress for sweeping civil rights legislation.

In Economic Affairs, the country boomed. For the first time in history, more than 70 million Americans had jobs. However, 5 per cent of the working force remained unemployed. The continued unemployment was blamed on a slow rate of economic growth and increasing automation. Congress refused to heed Kennedy's request for a tax cut to stimulate economic growth.

The Space Age. U.S. astronauts made suborbital flights in space in 1961. In 1962, John H. Glenn, Jr., became the first American to orbit the earth. Project Mercury ended in 1963 after six successful space flights. Kennedy urged an expanded space program to enable a manned U.S. moon flight by 1970. See SPACE TRAVEL.

The Assassination of Kennedy on Nov. 22, 1963, stunned the world. President Kennedy had gone to Texas to heal a split in the state's Democratic party before the 1964 election. Kennedy was shot while riding in an open car through downtown Dallas. Dallas police arrested a Communist sympathizer, Lee Harvey Oswald, and charged him with killing the President. Two days later, Oswald was shot and killed by Dallas nightclub owner Jack Ruby as police were moving Oswald to new jail quarters. See KENNEDY, JOHN FITZGERALD.

Johnson Succeeds Kennedy. President Johnson was sworn in at 2:39 P.M. November 22, aboard the presidential plane in Dallas. He plunged immediately into his new duties. He pledged to a joint session of Congress on November 27 to keep U.S. commitments "from South Vietnam to West Berlin."

Johnson

Johnson won re-election in 1964 by the widest margin in history. He defeated a Republican conservative, Senator Barry M. Goldwater. Johnson proposed a series of federal programs designed for what he called the *Great Society.* The President won the electoral votes of 44 states and the District of Columbia.

In Domestic Affairs, Johnson succeeded in getting Congress to pass the tax cut and civil rights bills Kennedy had proposed. The Civil Rights Act of 1964 provided measures against discrimination in voting, public accommodations, employment, and other fields. Congress also passed the Economic Opportunities Act of 1964, authorizing Johnson's *War on Poverty* program.

The Supreme Court in 1964 hit at unequal representation for rural and urban areas in the House of Representatives and in state legislatures. It said state congressional and legislative districts must be drawn on an equal population, or "one man one vote," basis.

Amendment 24 to the U.S. Constitution was ratified on Jan. 23, 1964. The amendment outlawed poll taxes as a voting requirement in national elections.

Johnson's landslide victory in 1964 increased the Democratic majority in Congress, and ensured passage of many of his legislative programs. These programs included a health plan for the aged called *Medicare,* increased federal aid to education, a cut in excise taxes, and the establishment of the Department of Housing and Urban Development (see HOUSING AND URBAN DEVELOPMENT, DEPARTMENT OF; MEDICARE). A law to guarantee Negro voting rights also passed. Many Negroes in the South had been denied this right.

In the mid-1960's, civil rights activities began to focus on the North as well as the South. Negroes in the North pushed for equal opportunities in housing, education, and employment. Increasing Negro dissatisfaction with life in city slums and white resistance to integrated housing often resulted in violence. Riots by Negroes in the slums of Chicago, Cleveland, Los Angeles, New York, and other cities resulted in deaths, injuries, and property damage. White persons used violence against marchers protesting residential segregation in all-white neighborhoods.

In 1965, astronauts made the first two-man Project Gemini space flights. Gemini astronauts changed the orbit of their spacecraft, walked in space, and *docked* (linked up) with other spacecraft in orbit.

The economy boomed in the mid-1960's and employment rose. But inflation threatened the economy as prices rose. Johnson urged business and labor leaders to limit wage and price rises to help combat inflation.

In World Affairs, Panama provided the first crisis for Johnson. Early in 1964, anti-U.S. riots began in the Canal Zone. Tensions eased when Johnson telephoned Panama's president and agreed to discuss the problems.

In 1964, the U.S., Russia, and Great Britain agreed to reduce production of materials for nuclear weapons.

In mid-1965, a civil war broke out in the Dominican Republic when rebels tried to overthrow the government. Johnson sent U.S. troops there because he feared Communists had gained control of the rebellion. By mid-1966, order had been restored, a new government had been elected, and most troops were withdrawn.

The United States became increasingly involved in defending South Vietnam against Viet Cong rebels backed by Communist North Vietnam. In August, 1964, North Vietnamese torpedo boats attacked U.S. Navy ships in the Gulf of Tonkin. The U.S. then began bombing North Vietnam, and a gradual *escalation* (stepping up) of the war followed. Both sides sent more troops into South Vietnam. The U.S. offered to negotiate for peace, but North Vietnam refused. By late 1966, the U.S. had about 300,000 troops in South Vietnam. A lively debate developed in the United States between supporters and opponents of the U.S. role in the war. See VIETNAM WAR.   ALLAN NEVINS

Related Articles in WORLD BOOK include:

HISTORICAL PERIODS AND WARS

See the separate articles on each President and the History section of each state article. See also:

Civil War	New Deal
Cold War	Pioneer Life
Colonial Life in America	Reconstruction
Exploration and Discovery	Revolutionary War in
French and Indian Wars	America
Gold Rush	Spanish-American War
Immigration and Emigration	War of 1812
Indian Wars	Western Frontier Life
Industrial Revolution	Westward Movement
Korean War	World War I
Mexican War	World War II

IMPORTANT DOCUMENTS

Articles of Confederation	Gettysburg Address
Compromise of 1850	Homestead Act
Declaration of	Kansas-Nebraska Act
Independence	Mayflower Compact
Emancipation Proclamation	Missouri Compromise
Federalist, The	Monroe Doctrine
Four Freedoms	Northwest Ordinance
Fourteen Points	United States Constitution

OTHER RELATED ARTICLES

American Literature	Political Party
Continental Congress	Space Travel
Flag	States' Rights
Indian, American	Trails of Early Days
Lewis and Clark Expedition	United States
Louisiana Purchase	United States,
Money	Government of
Panama Canal	United States Capitals

Outline

Questions

Why did Columbus fail to realize that he had found a new continent?

Why did the first settlers come to North America?

What is the oldest city in the United States?

What was the Boston Tea Party?

What was (1) Impressment? (2) Nullification? (3) The spoils system?

How was American foreign policy shaped by (1) The Monroe Doctrine? (2) The Roosevelt Corollary? (3) The Truman Doctrine?

What President used the slogan "Let the people rule"?

Why did slavery spread in the South, but not in the North?

What Presidents served during (1) The Era of Good Feeling? (2) The Gilded Age? (3) The Roaring 20's? (4) The New Deal?

What was Theodore Roosevelt's "Big Stick" policy?

Who were (1) The Robber Barons? (2) The Muckrakers? (3) The Dixiecrats?

Books for Young Readers

BENÉT, ROSEMARY C. and STEPHEN V. *A Book of Americans*. Rinehart, 1933. Humorous verses about famous men from Columbus to Woodrow Wilson.

COIT, MARGARET L. *The Fight for the Union*. Houghton, 1961. A pre-Civil War history.

COMMAGER, HENRY S. *The First Book of American History*. Watts, 1957.

COY, HAROLD. *The Americans*. Little, Brown, 1958. The people and customs of the United States are the focal points of this informal history.

JOHNSON, GERALD W. *America Is Born*. Morrow, 1959. *America Grows Up*. 1960. *America Moves Forward*. 1960.

LAWSON, ROBERT. *Watchwords of Liberty: A Pageant of American Quotations*. New ed. Little, Brown, 1957.

MIERS, EARL S. *The Rainbow Book of American History*. World Publishing Co., 1955.

PETERSHAM, MAUD F. and MISKA. *An American ABC*. Macmillan, 1941. Each letter of the alphabet is represented by a person, event, or symbol in U.S. history. *The Story of the Presidents of the United States of America*. 1953.

ROGERS, FRANCES, and BEARD, ALICE. *Old Liberty Bell*. Lippincott, 1942. *Birthday of a Nation, July 4, 1776*. 1945.

WIBBERLEY, LEONARD. *John Treegate's Musket*. Farrar, Straus, 1959. *Peter Treegate's War*, 1960. *Sea Captain from Salem*, 1961. *Treegate's Raiders*, 1962. Exciting stories of the American Revolution.

Books for Older Readers

ADAMS, JAMES T. *The Atlas of American History*. 1943. Ed. with R. V. COLEMAN: *The Dictionary of American History*. 2nd ed. rev. Scribner, 1942.

AMERICAN HERITAGE. *The American Heritage Book of Great Historic Places*. Simon & Schuster, 1957. *The American Heritage Book of the Revolution*. 1958.

BAILEY, THOMAS A. *A Diplomatic History of the American People*. 7th ed. Appleton, 1964.

BEARD, CHARLES A. and MARY R. *The Rise of American Civilization*. Macmillan, 1949.

BILLINGTON, RAY A. *Westward Expansion: A History of the American Frontier*. 2nd ed. Macmillan, 1949.

CHANNING, EDWARD. *History of the United States*. 6 vols. Macmillan, 1927-1930. From the colonial period through the Civil War.

COMMAGER, HENRY S., ed. *Documents of American History*. 7th ed. Appleton, 1963.

CURTI, MERLE E. *The Growth of American Thought*. 2nd ed. Harper, 1951.

Harvard Guide to American History. Ed. by OSCAR HANDLIN and others. Harvard Univ. Press, 1954. A detailed and comprehensive bibliography.

HOFSTADTER, RICHARD. *The American Political Tradition and the Men Who Made It*. Vintage, 1954.

LARKIN, OLIVER W. *Art and Life in America*. Rev. & enl. ed. Holt, 1960. A survey of the arts which reflects the development of American ideas.

MORISON, SAMUEL E., and COMMAGER, HENRY S. *The Growth of the American Republic*. 2 vols. 5th ed. rev. & enl. Oxford, 1962.

The Pageant of America. Ed. by RALPH H. GABRIEL. 15 vols. Yale Univ. Press, 1925-1927.

UNITED STATES AIR FORCE. See AIR FORCE, UNITED STATES.

Air Force Cadets drill on the campus of the United States Air Force Academy near Colorado Springs, Colo. The academy trains officers for air-force careers. Its official insignia is at *left*.

UNITED STATES AIR FORCE ACADEMY prepares young men for careers as officers in the United States Air Force. It stands on an 18,000-acre site in the foothills of the Rocky Mountains, near Colorado Springs, Colo. The Air Force Academy is a separate operating agency of the Department of the Air Force.

Students at the academy are called *air force cadets*. A cadet takes four years of academic work leading to a Bachelor of Science degree. He also takes professional military training to earn a regular commission in the United States Air Force. When a student enters the academy, he agrees to serve four years as a cadet and five years as an air force officer.

The United States government provides food, housing, and medical care for the cadets. Each cadet receives $120.60 a month to pay for his uniforms, textbooks, and personal expenses.

Entrance Requirements. Candidates for appointment to the academy must be: (1) male citizens of the United States, (2) at least 17 and not yet 22 years old on July 1 of the year for which they seek appointment, (3) unmarried and never previously married, (4) in good physical condition, and (5) of good moral character. A catalog containing full information may be obtained from the Registrar, United States Air Force Academy, Colorado.

Nomination and Selection of Cadets. Each candidate for the academy must be nominated by one of the legally established nominating sources. He must then pass the qualifying medical examination, the physical aptitude examination, and the college entrance examination board tests in order to qualify for appointment to the academy.

Cadet Life. Cadets live in the cadet dormitory, Vandenberg Hall. A cadet's normal weekday begins with *reveille* at 6:15 A.M. Before classes, he eats breakfast and prepares his room for morning inspection. Classes

—— SELECTION OF CANDIDATES ——

Candidates for the United States Air Force Academy are nominated by the sources listed below. The figures represent the total number of candidates each nominating source may select for the Academy. The figures reflect the Academy strength of 4,417 cadets as authorized by the United States Congress in 1964.

 300 by the President of the United States
  5 by the Vice-President of the United States
 500 by United States Senators
2,175 by United States Congressmen
 600 from qualified alternates selected by Senators and Congressmen
  40 sons of deceased veterans
  5 from the District of Columbia
  1 from Guam, Samoa, and the Virgin Islands
  6 from Puerto Rico
  1 from the Canal Zone
 340 from the regular United States armed forces
 340 from the reserve United States armed forces
  80 from honor military schools
  24 cadets from other countries

An unlimited number of sons of Medal of Honor winners may also attend.

are held from 7:40 A.M. to 11:20 A.M. and from 12:35 P.M. to 3:15 P.M. Most classes are conducted in Fairchild Hall. Cadets may also receive instruction in the aeronautics laboratory or in the planetarium.

After classes, the cadet takes part in sports, drill, or extracurricular activities. After supper, the cadet must study in his room or in the academy library until 10:30 P.M. Taps sounds at 10:45 P.M.

Cadets must attend Sunday or Sabbath services of their faith in the academy chapel. The chapel's 17 towering aluminum spires make it an academy land-

U.S. Air Force

Academic Training. Air Force cadets receive personal help from the instructor in classes limited from 12 to 16 in number.

mark. The chapel is divided into sections for Protestant, Roman Catholic, and Jewish religious services. Cadets may also participate in services in nearby communities.

Social functions for the cadets are held on weekends in Arnold Hall. Privileges to leave the campus on weekends increase as the cadet progresses through the academy. Each year, all cadets receive a 12-day Christmas *leave* (vacation), a 4-day spring leave, and a 4-week summer leave.

The Academy Curriculum consists of the academic program, military training, and physical education. The academic program includes courses in the basic and applied sciences, social sciences, and humanities. The cadet must take certain courses that provide a general background in all subject areas. The cadet also majors in one subject or area of concentration. Cadets who have completed previous college work and cadets with special ability may take graduate-level courses in their major fields. The academy selects a few cadets to attend graduate school at cooperating civilian universities after graduation.

A cadet's work is graded on a percentage basis. The lowest passing grade is 70 per cent. A cadet whose final grades at the end of a term are below passing may be discharged from the academy.

The academy prepares cadets for a role of leadership through military training. This training provides the basic military knowledge required of an air force officer. The training includes flying instruction and field trips. Each summer during their sophomore, junior, and senior years, cadets visit military installations in the United States and overseas.

Cadets develop a high degree of physical fitness through a varied program of physical education and athletics. Each cadet must participate in either intramural or varsity athletic contests.

History. In the 1920's, Brigadier General William "Billy" Mitchell urged that the government set up an air force academy (see MITCHELL, "BILLY," WILLIAM).

In 1949, the Secretary of Defense appointed a service academy board to study the need for another academy. The board recommended that an academy to train future air force officers be established without delay.

On April 1, 1954, Congress authorized the establishment of an air force academy. A site selection committee appointed by the Secretary of the Air Force chose the academy's permanent location. The air force dedicated the academy in 1955. Lt. Gen. Hubert R. Harmon became its first superintendent. The first class of 306 cadets trained at the temporary academy site at Lowry Air Force Base, near Denver, Colo. The academy moved to its permanent site near Colorado Springs in 1958.   Critically reviewed by the AIR FORCE ACADEMY

Practical Training. Cadets service and arm air force jet planes as part of their airmanship training exercises.

UNITED STATES ARMY. See ARMY, UNITED STATES.

UNITED STATES BANK. See BANK OF THE UNITED STATES.

UNITED STATES BORDER PATROL. See BORDER PATROL, UNITED STATES.

UNITED STATES BOTANIC GARDEN in Washington, D.C., exhibits over 10,000 species and varieties of plants, many of them rare. The collection includes products of the United States and other countries.

As a public service, the garden identifies plants and recommends methods of growing them. It also presents special displays and furnishes educational facilities to botanists around the world.

A private organization founded the garden in 1820. In 1842, the government assumed control of the garden to display botanical collections assembled by government expeditions. The Congressional Joint Committee on the Library has supervised the United States Botanic Garden since 1856.   JOHN C. BOLLENS

UNITED STATES CAPITALS. The federal government had no permanent capital from 1776, when the Declaration of Independence was signed, until 1800, when the government took up its residence in Washington, D.C. The Continental Congress, and, later, the Congress authorized under the Articles of Confederation, had many different meeting places. The capitals used by the earliest American Congresses are listed below, with the dates Congress met in each capital.

Philadelphia, September, 1774, to December, 1776.
Baltimore, December 20, 1776, to March, 1777.
Philadelphia, March 4, 1777, to September, 1777.
Lancaster, Pa., September 27, 1777.
York, Pa., September 30, 1777, to July, 1778.
Philadelphia, July 2, 1778, to June 30, 1783.
Princeton, N.J., June 30, 1783, to November 4, 1783.
Annapolis, Md., November 26, 1783, to November 1, 1784.
Trenton, N.J., November 1, 1784, to December 24, 1784.
New York City, January 11, 1785, to June, 1790.

In 1789, the United States Constitution authorized the new Congress to accept a gift of land from the states for the establishment of a new capital. But jealousy among the states blocked every attempt to choose a location. At last, Alexander Hamilton of New York agreed to the selection of Virginia as a site. In return, Congressional delegates from Virginia agreed to support a bill in Congress which Hamilton wanted passed. Finally, both Virginia and Maryland gave land for the new capital. President George Washington chose the site on the Potomac River where the capital was to be built. The commission appointed to survey the ground and plan the city named the capital *The City of Washington* in honor of the President.

The capital was built between 1790 and 1800. During this period, Congress met in Philadelphia. In 1800, the government was established at Washington. After 1801, several attempts were made to change the location of the capital, but all of them failed.   GEORGE E. MOWRY

See also UNITED STATES, GOVERNMENT OF (pictures, Capitols of the United States); DISTRICT OF COLUMBIA; WASHINGTON, D.C.

UNITED STATES CIVIL SERVICE COMMISSION. See CIVIL SERVICE COMMISSION.

UNITED STATES COAST GUARD. See COAST GUARD, UNITED STATES.

UNITED STATES COAST GUARD ACADEMY prepares young men to be commissioned officers in the United States Coast Guard. It covers 65 acres on the banks of the Thames River in New London, Conn. The academy is comparable to those of the other armed forces. But entrance is by annual nationwide competitive test rather than by congressional appointment.

Students at the academy are called *cadets*. The cadet system began in 1876 with the assignment of the cutter *Dobbin* as a training ship. Cadets had their winter quarters at New Bedford, Mass., and later at Arundel Cove, Md. In 1910, the Coast Guard established the academy on shore at New London. The present Georgian-style buildings were built in 1932.

Entrance Requirements. An applicant to be eligible to take the cadet examination must (1) be a citizen of the United States, (2) be between 17 and 22 years of age, and (3) meet the educational and other requirements established by the Commandant of the United States Coast Guard.

The academy has an authorized strength of about 600 cadets. The Corps of Cadets is organized as a regiment for the purpose of military training. Senior cadets act as regimental officers under the supervision of Coast Guard officers.

The Course of Instruction offers a 4-year curriculum in engineering, humanities, mathematics, physical education, professional studies, and science. Specific subjects taught include analytic geometry, calculus, applied atomic physics, navigation, ordnance, seamanship, thermodynamics, economics, English, history, and law. Athletic activities include full schedules of intercollegiate and intramural sports.

During the summer term, cadets usually cruise to European or Atlantic ports in a Practice Squadron. This unit consists of the academy's training bark *Eagle* and one or two modern Coast Guard cutters. Cadets stand bridge, engine room, navigator, and combat-information-center watches. Summer training during the second-class, or junior, year includes aviation courses and gunnery, antisubmarine, and search-and-rescue exercises. Graduates receive bachelor of science degrees and commissions as ensigns.   S. H. EVANS

See also COAST GUARD, UNITED STATES (Training an Officer); CONNECTICUT (color picture, Parading).

UNITED STATES CONGRESS. See CONGRESS OF THE UNITED STATES.

Coast Guard Cadets pass in review on the campus at New London, Conn. Hamilton Hall, the academy's administration building, faces the parade ground. The academy seal is shown, *right*.

UNITED STATES COAST GUARD ACADEMY
1876
SCIENTIÆ CEDIT MARE

Official U.S. Coast Guard Photographs

Shooting the Sun, a Coast Guard cadet learns to use a sextant quickly and accurately.

Aboard the *Eagle,* the academy's training ship, cadets learn to handle all 22 sails. The ship takes a cruise abroad each summer.

Pulling Away, cadets practice handling small boats in the open sea on their cruise.

United States Constitution

Courtesy John M. Haass Litho. Company, N.Y

Signing the Constitution, delegates in Independence Hall approved the summer's work. This painting, by Howard Chandler Christy, hangs in the House wing of the Capitol in Washington.

UNITED STATES CONSTITUTION is the supreme law of the land. It establishes the form of the United States government, and the rights and liberties of the American people. The Constitution made the United States a nation. It is the shield of democracy under which Americans govern themselves as a free people. They respect the Constitution even as they make use of it.

After the United States won its independence in the Revolutionary War, it faced the great problems of peacetime government. It had to enforce law and order, collect taxes, pay what was then a staggering public debt, and regulate and stimulate trade. The new nation also had to deal successfully with the Indian tribes and with other governments.

Most leaders of the infant republic soon became convinced that the Articles of Confederation of 1781 could not solve these problems and perform other tasks of governing a free, active, and expanding country (see ARTICLES OF CONFEDERATION). The confederation government lacked an executive and a system of courts. It could not act directly upon the citizens of the nation, especially to tax them for purposes of diplomacy and defense. The confederation proved to be little more than an assembly of ambassadors from 13 jealous and sovereign states.

Men such as George Washington and Alexander Hamilton viewed the situation with grave concern. As early as 1783, they began to discuss the possibility of creating an entirely new national government under a new constitution. The farseeing Hamilton directed a series of political maneuvers that resulted in the confederation congress calling a convention to meet in

SIGNERS OF THE CONSTITUTION

Signatures on the Constitution included those of Secretary William Jackson and an absentee, John Dickinson, written in by proxy.

1. George Washington
2. Benjamin Franklin
3. James Madison, Jr.
4. Alexander Hamilton
5. Gouverneur Morris
6. Robert Morris
7. James Wilson
8. Charles C. Pinckney
9. Charles Pinckney
10. John Rutledge

11. Pierce Butler
12. Roger Sherman
13. William S. Johnson
14. James McHenry
15. George Read
16. Richard Bassett
17. Richard D. Spaight
18. William Blount
19. Hugh Williamson
20. Dan of St. Thomas Jenifer

21. Rufus King
22. Nathaniel Gorham
23. Jonathan Dayton
24. Daniel Carroll
25. William Few
26. Abraham Baldwin
27. John Langdon
28. Nicholas Gilman
29. William Livingston
30. William Paterson

31. Thomas Mifflin
32. George Clymer
33. Thomas FitzSimons
34. Jared Ingersoll
35. Gunning Bedford, Jr.
36. Jacob Broom
37. John Dickinson
38. John Blair
39. David Brearley
40. William Jackson

UNITED STATES CONSTITUTION

Philadelphia on May 14, 1787, for the "sole and express purpose of revising the Articles of Confederation." The 55 delegates who attended the convention did far more than the congress had intended them to do. They gave up any ideas of fixing the Articles. During that hot, tiresome summer, they wrote a remarkable plan of government, the United States Constitution.

The Supreme Law of the Land

The Constitution consists of a preamble, 7 articles, and 24 amendments. It establishes the federal system of separating powers between the national government and the state governments. And it divides the powers of the national government among the executive, legislative, and judicial branches.

The national government exercises both *delegated powers* (those listed in the Constitution) and *implied powers* (those reasonably implied by the Constitution). Implied powers give the federal government flexibility to expand its delegated powers as conditions change. For example, Congress made paper money "legal tender" under its expressed powers to borrow money. All powers not granted to the federal government and not denied to the states are reserved for the states or for the people. These powers are called *reserved powers*. In some areas, the federal and state governments have *concurrent powers*, and both may exercise authority.

The Supreme Court of the United States has the final authority in interpreting the Constitution. It can set aside any law—federal, state, or local—that conflicts with any provision of the Constitution. See SUPREME COURT OF THE UNITED STATES.

The Need for the Constitution

In 1783, after the Revolutionary War, the nation entered a period of unstable commercial and political conditions. Alexander Hamilton and his friends would have met little success in their campaign for a new constitution if conditions had not been so unsettling for the leading men of trade and finance. Some historians have painted the troubles of the new American republic in much too gloomy colors. But little doubt remains that the situation became steadily worse after 1783. Each state acted almost like an independent country. Each ran its own affairs exactly as it saw fit, with no concern for the broad purposes of the republic. The states circulated a dozen different currencies, most of them inflated to a point where they had practically no value. Neighboring states raised tariff barriers against each other. Great Britain refused to reopen the channels of trade that the colonies had depended on for their economic well-being. The state legislatures declined to pay the debts they had assumed during the Revolutionary War. Many states passed laws that made it possible for debtors to escape paying their obligations.

Worst of all, some men began to think once again of taking up arms in order to solve their problems. In western Massachusetts in 1786, thousands of farmers under Captain Daniel Shays rebelled against the state government in Boston. The militia finally put down Shays' Rebellion (see SHAYS' REBELLION). In Virginia and other states, George Washington and other leaders wondered whether the colonies had rebelled in vain. They felt that it was time to end these troubles and bring peace and order by forming a new national government. This new government would have to be able to act decisively to gain obedience at home and respect abroad.

Representatives from five states met at Annapolis, Md., in 1786. They proposed that the states appoint commissioners to meet in Philadelphia and consider revising the Articles of Confederation (see ANNAPOLIS CONVENTION). Congress agreed to the proposal. It suggested that each state select *deputies*, or delegates, to a constitutional convention.

The Constitutional Convention

The convention was supposed to open on May 14, 1787. But few of the 55 delegates had arrived in Philadelphia by that date. Finally, on May 25, with delegates from a quorum of seven states present, the convention formally opened in Independence Hall. Twelve states had responded to the call for the convention. Rhode Island refused to send delegates, because it feared that a new constitution would remove its power to tax the use of imported supplies by neighboring states.

Of the 55 delegates, 39 stayed to the end and signed the United States Constitution on Sept. 17, 1787. William Jackson, the convention secretary, attested their signatures. The delegates included some of the most experienced and patriotic men in the new republic. George Washington served as a dignified and authoritative presiding officer throughout the sessions. The beloved Benjamin Franklin, at the age of 81, inspired other members by his mere presence. The brilliant Alexander Hamilton expressed views too strongly for the other delegates. The astute James Madison won for himself the title of "Father of the Constitution" with his speeches, negotiations, and attempts at compromise. The delegates were considering a plan that "would decide forever the fate of republican government," he told the convention. Madison kept a record in his *Debates in the Federal Convention of 1787*. Other men who had much to do with writing the new Constitution included John Dickinson, Gouverneur Morris, Edmund Randolph, Roger Sherman, James Wilson, and George Wythe. Morris was probably the most influential delegate, after Madison and Washington. He was given the task of putting all the convention's resolutions and decisions into polished form. Morris actually "wrote the Constitution." The original copy of the document is preserved in the National Archives Building in Washington, D.C.

Several important figures of the time did not attend the convention. John Adams, John Jay, and Thomas Jefferson were absent on other duties. Samuel Adams failed to be appointed a delegate from Massachusetts. Patrick Henry refused to serve after his appointment, because he opposed granting any more power to the national government. Three leading members of the convention—Elbridge Gerry, George Mason, and Luther Martin—declined to sign the Constitution, because they disagreed with some provisions in it.

The Background of the Constitution. The framers of the Constitution relied heavily on past experience as they worked to create a new government. They could look back on all English history since King John granted the Magna Carta in 1215, and all American history since the first representative assembly met at Jamestown in 1619. The fact and theory of American constitutional government emerged from these hundreds of years of trial and error.

The fact of constitutional government came from the colonial governments that had been established in America for many years before the Revolution. They had weaknesses, but they were far advanced over almost all other governments in the world in progressing toward the achievement of liberty under law.

The theory of constitutional government involved the idea of a limited government with balanced executive, legislative, and judicial powers. John Adams became the most eloquent spokesman of this plan of government.

The fact and theory had been brought together successfully by Adams when he wrote the Massachusetts Constitution of 1780. The New York Constitution of 1777, which John Jay helped write, also provided for constitutional government. The delegates in Philadelphia borrowed many techniques and even the words from these two state constitutions to write the plan for the new national government.

The delegates also drew upon their own experiences. Franklin could recall, and learn from the failure of, his Albany plan of 1754 (see ALBANY CONGRESS). Washington remembered his troubles in the Revolution as a strong leader trying to work with a weak legislature. Almost every delegate had served as a soldier or administrator during the Revolution. The framers often disagreed on details. But they were remarkably united in insisting that the new government should be strong enough to meet its obligations, and safe enough to respect the liberties of the people.

The Compromises. The task of creating a new constitutional government was not easily accomplished. On several occasions, arguments over one real point of dispute nearly wrecked the convention: how to protect the interests of both the large and the small states. This issue in turn became a controversy over representation in the proposed national legislature. "The great difficulty lies in the affair of representation," said Madison. "And if this could be adjusted, all others would be surmountable."

The large states favored *the Virginia Plan*, under which population would determine a state's representation in the legislature. The small states supported *the New Jersey Plan*, under which all states would have equal representation. Roger Sherman of Connecticut proposed the compromise that broke the deadlock. His plan provided for equal representation in one house of Congress, and representation in proportion to population in the other house. It became known as *the Connecticut Compromise* or *the Great Compromise*.

Another conflict arose over the question of how to count slaves in determining the number of congressmen a state should have. The Southern States wanted to count all the slaves, even though they would not be allowed to vote. The Northern States opposed this move. The convention finally agreed that three fifths of the slaves should be counted. In another compromise between North and South, the delegates agreed that the foreign slave trade could not be prohibited before 1808.

Ratifying the Constitution

The convention agreed that the new government could be organized after nine states had approved the

Constitution. Less than three months after the Constitution had been signed, Delaware became the first state to ratify it, on Dec. 7, 1787. New Hampshire was the ninth state, on June 21, 1788. But the Founding Fathers could not be sure that the Constitution would be given a fair trial until the key states of New York and Virginia had ratified it. Powerful organized opposition to the Constitution had developed in these two states, and in others. Men such as Elbridge Gerry, Patrick Henry, Richard Henry Lee, and George Mason spoke out against ratification.

Critics objected that a bill of rights had not been included, the President had too much independence, the Senate was too aristocratic, Congress had too many powers, and the national government had too much authority. Friends of the Constitution rallied support for ratification. They became known as *Federalists*. Their opponents were called *Anti-Federalists*. The two factions promoted their causes in newspapers, in pamphlets, and in debates in the ratifying conventions. They developed the first political groupings that became known as *political parties*.

Virginia ratified the Constitution on June 25, 1788, and New York did so on July 26. Early in January, 1789, all ratifying states except New York selected presidential electors in their legislatures or by a direct vote of the people. On February 4, the electors unanimously named George Washington as the first President of the United States. The first Congress under the Constitution met in New York City on March 4. Washington was inaugurated on April 30. But two states—North Carolina and Rhode Island—refused to approve the Constitution and take part in the new government until the first Congress had begun to adopt a bill of rights.

The Bill of Rights

The Federalists might never have obtained ratification in several key states if they had not promised to support amendments to the Constitution. These amendments were designed to protect individual liberties against possible encroachment by the new government. Most state constitutions that were adopted during the Revolution had included a clear declaration of the rights of all persons. Most Americans had come to believe that no constitution could be considered complete without such a declaration. George Mason had been the man most responsible for the first and most famous American bill of rights, the Virginia Declaration of Rights of 1776. His opposition would have been enough to prevent ratification of the Constitution in Virginia, if the Federalists had not agreed to his demands for amendments.

James Madison led the new Congress in proposing 12 amendments to be adopted by the states under the amending process outlined in Article V of the Constitution. By Dec. 15, 1791, enough states had approved 10 of the 12 amendments to make them a permanent addition to the Constitution. These amendments are known as the *Bill of Rights*, although the term usually refers only to the first eight amendments. One of the two rejected amendments dealt with the size of the House of Representatives. It would have allowed Congress to change the proportion of representation from one representative for every 30,000 persons to one representative for every 50,000 persons. The other rejected amendment provided that Congress should not change the salaries of its members until an election of representatives had been held. See BILL OF RIGHTS.

The Development of the Constitution

The Constitution has developed into a charter well suited to the needs of a great industrial nation. Yet it has never been fundamentally revised. In many other countries, constitutions come and go like the leaves of the trees. It was Madison who said, "In framing a system which we wish to last for ages, we should not lose sight of the changes which ages will produce." The Constitution was designed to serve the interests of all the people—rich and poor, Northerners and Southerners, farmers, workers, and businessmen. The farsighted Anti-Federalists accepted defeat when the Constitution was adopted, then set about to win power under its rules (see ANTI-FEDERALIST). Their action set a style for American politics that has never changed. Few Americans have ever had reason to condemn the Constitution or call for a second constitutional convention.

The great principles of the Constitution have been in tune with the beliefs and hopes of an expanding democracy. These principles include the sovereignty of the people, supremacy of the national government, respect for the states, division of power among three equal and independent branches, separation of church and state, and rule by a clear-cut majority.

The framers of the Constitution believed strongly in the rule of the majority. They guaranteed that no majority would have its way unless it could prove itself "persistent and undoubted." They achieved this goal by separating and balancing the powers of government, and by calling for a system of staggered elections, so that all elected officials would not be up for re-election at the same time.

Amendments have expanded the powers and broadened the base of the United States government. But they have not changed its basic structure. Of the 24 amendments, the first 10 took effect in 1791. Amendment 21, adopted in 1933, repealed Amendment 18. Amendments may be proposed by two thirds of each house of Congress, or by national conventions called by Congress. They must then be ratified by the legislatures of three fourths of the states or by conventions in three fourths of the states.

Statutes have also expanded the meaning of the Constitution. For example, Congress has established huge administrative organizations, such as the Federal Aviation Agency and the Interstate Commerce Commission. It has widened the jurisdiction of the Supreme Court of the United States in the matter of appeals from lower courts. Congress has also extended its power to "regulate commerce" into the power to regulate many aspects of the American economy.

Court Decisions. The federal courts have been especially active in fitting the words of the Constitution to new situations. The Supreme Court interprets what the Constitution means in specific cases, and enjoys the power of judicial review. It can also declare laws unconstitutional. The court has these powers largely because of the bold initiative of Chief Justice John Marshall in the case of *Marbury vs. Madison* in 1803 (see MARSHALL, JOHN). More than 70 federal laws and hundreds of state laws have been held unconstitutional since the early 1800's. In every case, the Supreme Court of the United States has interpreted the meaning of the Constitution.

Presidential Actions. Strong Presidents, such as George Washington, Thomas Jefferson, Andrew Jackson, Abraham Lincoln, Theodore Roosevelt, Woodrow Wilson, and Franklin D. Roosevelt, used their authority to expand the few simple words of Article II into a vast reservoir of executive power. This article makes the President commander in chief of the armed forces. It gives him power to grant reprieves and pardons for offenses against the United States, except in cases of impeachment. Washington, for example, made the President the leading figure in foreign affairs. Lincoln used the powers from the article to free the slaves during the Civil War.

Customs have added to the powers of all three branches of the federal government. For example, the President's Cabinet developed from the words in Article II of the Constitution that permit the chief executive to "require the opinion, in writing, of the principal officer in each of the executive departments, upon any subject relating to the duties of their respective offices . . ."

State and Party Actions. The Constitution provides for a general method of electing a President. It does not mention political parties. But state laws and political-party practices have converted the constitutional system of voting into the exciting campaigns and elections of today.

The Constitution has continued to develop in response to the demands of an ever-growing society through all these methods. Yet the spirit and wording of the Constitution have remained constant. Men of each generation have been able to apply its provisions to their own problems in ways that seem reasonable to them.

The British statesman, William E. Gladstone, described the Constitution as "the most wonderful work ever struck off at a given time by the brain and purpose of man." In a world of change and struggle, the American people have no more precious possession than this great document. The story of how the framers wrote the Constitution and how it has met the challenges of American democracy is one that people should never tire of reading.   CLINTON ROSSITER

Related Articles in WORLD BOOK include:

BIOGRAPHIES

There is a biography on each signer of the United States Constitution as listed after Article VII. See also the following articles:

HISTORY

F. State and Party Actions

Questions

Why were the Articles of Confederation of 1781 inadequate for governing the United States?

What compromises were made in forming the Constitution?

What were some major objections against the newly formed Constitution?

How did controversy over the Constitution result in creating the first American political parties?

What government body has the final authority in interpreting the Constitution?

The constitutions of what two states contributed greatly to organizing the United States Constitution?

Why was James Madison called "the Father of the Constitution"?

In what six ways has the Constitution been modified or applied to new situations?

What individual actually "wrote the Constitution"?

What are *delegated powers? Implied powers? Reserved powers? Concurrent powers?*

Outline

I. **The Supreme Law of the Land**
II. **The Need for the Constitution**
III. **The Constitutional Convention**
   A. The Background of the Constitution
   B. The Compromises
IV. **Ratifying the Constitution**
V. **The Bill of Rights**
VI. **The Development of the Constitution**
   A. Amendments
   B. Statutes
   C. Court Decisions
   D. Presidential Actions
   E. Customs

The United States Constitution

The text of the United States Constitution is printed here in boldface type. All words are given their modern spelling and capitalization. Brackets [ ] indicate parts that have been changed or set aside by amendments. The paragraphs printed in lightface type are not part of the Constitution. They explain the meaning of certain passages, or they describe how certain passages in the Constitution have worked in practice. Owen J. Roberts, Associate Justice of the Supreme Court (1930-1945), and William O. Douglas, Associate Justice of the Supreme Court (1939-), authenticated these annotations.

PREAMBLE

We the people of the United States, in order to form a more perfect Union, establish justice, insure domestic tranquility, provide for the common defense, promote the general welfare, and secure the blessings of liberty to ourselves and our posterity, do ordain and establish this Constitution for the United States of America.

ARTICLE I

The Legislative Department

Section 1. All legislative powers herein granted shall be vested in a Congress of the United States, which shall consist of a Senate and House of Representatives.

The small states supported the New Jersey plan. They wanted each state to have the same number of representatives in the legislature. The large states wanted the Virginia plan, representation based on population, so that they would have power in proportion to their size. As a compromise, the two-house Congress was set up, with one house chosen according to each plan. The plan of the large states was carried out in the House of Representatives, and that of the small states in the Senate.

The people were already used to the idea of a two-part legislature. The British Parliament had its House of Commons and House of Lords, and most of the thirteen colonies had set up two-part legislatures.

The House of Representatives

Section 2. (1) The House of Representatives shall be composed of members chosen every second year by the people of the several States, and the electors in each State shall have the qualifications requisite for electors of the most numerous branch of the State legislature.

The "most numerous branch" of the state legislature means the house which has the most members. The question of who shall be allowed to vote for state legislators is entirely up to the state. But if the state lets a person vote for representatives to the lower house of the state legislature, it must let him vote in Congressional elections. Amendment 19 provided that, in fixing qualifications for voters, a state may not discriminate among its inhabitants on account of sex.

(2) No person shall be a Representative who shall not have attained to the age of twenty-five years, and been seven years a citizen of the United States, and who shall not, when elected, be an inhabitant of that State in which he shall be chosen.

Each state decides for itself who is an "inhabitant," by setting up requirements for legal residence. A representative usually lives not only in the state from which he is chosen, but also in the Congressional district which he represents.

(3) Representatives and direct taxes shall be apportioned among the several States which may be included within this Union, according to their respective numbers, [which shall be determined by adding to the whole number of free persons, including those bound to service for a term of years, and excluding Indians not taxed, [three fifths of all other persons]. The actual enumeration shall be made within three years after the first meeting of the Congress of the United States, and within every subsequent term of ten years, in such manner as they shall by law direct. The number of Representatives shall not exceed one for every thirty thousand, but each State shall have at least one representative; [and until such enumeration shall be made, the State of New Hampshire shall be entitled to choose 3, Massachusetts 8, Rhode Island and Providence Plantations 1, Connecticut 5, New York 6, New Jersey 4, Pennsylvania 8, Delaware 1, Maryland 6, Virginia 10, North Carolina 5, South Carolina 5, and Georgia 3].

Historical Documents Co.—Frank H. Fleer Corp.

A Reproduction of the Opening Sections of the Constitution Shows the Preamble and the First Article.

The effect of this paragraph has been greatly changed, both by amendments and by new conditions. It now provides only three things: (a) the number of representatives allotted to each state shall be based on its population; (b) Congress must see that the people of the United States are counted every 10 years; (c) each state gets at least one representative.

The words "and direct taxes" mean poll and property taxes. Amendment 16 gives Congress the right to tax a person according to the size of his own income, rather than according to the population of the state in which he happens to live. But the phrase still forbids Congress to impose any form of direct taxation except by apportioning it.

In the reference to "three fifths of all other persons," the "other persons" meant Negro slaves. Since there are no longer any slaves, this part of the paragraph no longer has any meaning. Indians who pay no taxes and who are wards of the government are still not counted in the apportionment of representatives.

The provision that there shall be no more than one representative for every 30,000 people no longer has any practical force, because there is now about one representative for each 413,000. In 1929 Congress fixed the total number of representatives at 435, and this number still holds today.

(4) When vacancies happen in the representation from any State, the executive authority thereof shall issue writs of election to fill such vacancies.

The Constitution allows each state to decide how the vacancy shall be filled. Most states require the governor to call a special election for this purpose.

(5) The House of Representatives shall choose their Speaker and other officers; and shall have the sole power of impeachment.

The Speaker of the House is its presiding officer (see SPEAKER). The power of impeachment means the power to bring charges against an official. These charges are tried by the Senate (see IMPEACHMENT).

The United States Senate

Section 3. **(1)** The Senate of the United States shall be composed of two Senators from each State, [chosen by the legislature thereof,] for six years; and each Senator shall have one vote.

The Constitution at first provided that each state legislature should pick two Senators. Amendment 17 changed this by allowing the voters in each state to choose their own Senators.

(2) Immediately after they shall be assembled in consequence of the first election, they shall be divided as equally as may be into three classes. The seats of the

Senators of the first class shall be vacated at the expiration of the second year, of the second class at the expiration of the fourth year, and of the third class at the expiration of the sixth year, so that one third may be chosen every second year; [and if vacancies happen by resignation, or otherwise, during the recess of the legislature of any State, the Executive thereof may make temporary appointments until the next meeting of the legislature, which shall then fill such vacancies].

Except in the first two Congresses, all Senators have been elected for a six-year term. This means that at least two thirds of the Senators in each Congress will ordinarily be experienced in the job. The method of filling vacancies is now set forth in Amendment 17.

(3) No person shall be a Senator who shall not have attained to the age of thirty years, and been nine years a citizen of the United States, and who shall not, when elected, be an inhabitant of that State for which he shall be chosen.

Henry Clay of Kentucky was the first person under 30 to be elected to the Senate. He had reached the required age by the time he took the oath of office.

In 1793 Albert Gallatin, who won fame as Secretary of the Treasury, was elected Senator from Pennsylvania. He was barred from taking office because he had not been a citizen for nine years.

Amendment 14 established a qualification for Senators and Representatives that no longer has significance. It provided that no one could be a Senator or Representative who had sided with the Confederacy during the Civil War after taking an oath to support the Constitution. But Congress could remove this disability.

(4) The Vice-President of the United States shall be President of the Senate, but shall have no vote, unless they be equally divided.

The power of the Vice-President to break a tie vote in the Senate has often been important. For example, in 1789 Vice-President John Adams cast the vote which decided that the President could remove members of the Cabinet without the approval of the Senate. In 1899 Vice-President Garret Hobart cast the vote which made possible the ratification of the peace treaty after the Spanish-American War. In 1945 Vice-President Harry S. Truman broke a tie on the extension of Lend-Lease.

(5) The Senate shall choose their other officers, and also a President *pro tempore,* in the absence of the Vice-President, or when he shall exercise the office of President of the United States.

(6) The Senate shall have the sole power to try all impeachments. When sitting for that purpose, they shall be on oath or affirmation. When the President of the United States is tried, the Chief Justice shall preside: and no person shall be convicted without the concurrence of two thirds of the members present.

The provision that the Chief Justice, rather than the Vice-President, shall preside over the Senate when a President is on trial probably grows out of the fact that a conviction would make the Vice-President the President. The phrase "on oath or affirmation" means that Senators are placed under oath when trying impeachment cases, just as jurors are in a regular court trial.

(7) Judgment in cases of impeachment shall not extend further than to removal from office, and disqualification to hold and enjoy any office of honor, trust or profit under the United States: but the party convicted

shall nevertheless be liable and subject to indictment, trial, judgment and punishment, according to law.

In American history, the Senate has convicted only four men, all of them judges. They were removed from office, but none was ever tried before another court.

Organization of Congress

Section 4. (1) The times, places and manner of holding elections for Senators and Representatives, shall be prescribed in each State by the Legislature thereof; but the Congress may at any time by law make or alter such regulations, [except as to the places of choosing Senators].

So long as state legislatures chose the Senators, it would not do to let Congress fix the place of choosing. This would have amounted to giving Congress the power to tell each state where to locate its capital. The words "except as to the places of choosing Senators" are wiped out by the new method of choosing Senators laid down by Amendment 17.

(2) The Congress shall assemble at least once in every year, [and such meeting shall be on the first Monday in December,] unless they shall by law appoint a different day.

In Europe, kings had the power to call legislative bodies into session. They often kept parliaments from meeting, sometimes for many years, simply by not calling them together. This is the reason for the provision that the Congress of the United States must meet at least once a year. Amendment 20 changed the date of the opening day of the session to January 3.

Section 5. (1) Each House shall be the judge of the elections, returns and qualifications of its own members, and a majority of each shall constitute a quorum to do business; but a smaller number may adjourn from day to day, and may be authorized to compel the attendance of absent members, in such manner, and under such penalties as each House may provide.

In judging the qualifications of its members, each House may consider not only the age, citizenship, and residence requirements set forth in the Constitution itself, but any other matters bearing on fitness for the office. The Senate refused to seat one Senator-elect because his campaign was "colored with fraud and corruption" and another because of doubts about his loyalty to the country.

A *quorum* means a group large enough to carry on the business of the House. Discussion and debate can go on whether a quorum is present or not, so long as a quorum comes in to vote.

(2) Each House may determine the rules of its proceedings, punish its members for disorderly behavior, and, with the concurrence of two thirds, expel a member.

The right of each house to make its rules has had important results. For example, the House of Representatives puts strict limit on debate, so as to speed up the transaction of necessary business. In the Senate, debate can go on as long as anyone wishes to speak, and any member may speak as long as he likes. This often delays Senate business. See FILIBUSTERING.

(3) Each House shall keep a journal of its proceedings, and from time to time publish the same, excepting such parts as may in their judgment require secrecy; and the yeas and nays of the members of either House on any question shall, at the desire of one fifth of those present, be entered on the journal.

UNITED STATES CONSTITUTION

The journals of the two houses have been published together in the *Congressional Record* since 1873. The *Record* appears daily while Congress is in session. If either house wants to hold a secret session, it resolves itself into a committee of the whole, and its proceedings are not recorded in the journal.

A member of either house can get leave to insert a speech in the Congressional Record without going to the trouble of delivering it. He can thus give the people at home the impression that he is speaking up in their interests, when he actually has not addressed Congress.

(4) Neither House, during the session of Congress, shall, without the consent of the other, adjourn for more than three days, nor to any other place than that in which the two Houses shall be sitting.

Section 6. **(1) The Senators and Representatives shall receive a compensation for their services, to be ascertained by law, and paid out of the Treasury of the United States. They shall in all cases, except treason, felony and breach of the peace, be privileged from arrest during their attendance at the session of their respective Houses, and in going to and returning from the same; and for any speech or debate in either House, they shall not be questioned in any other place.**

The reason for the provision that congressmen cannot be arrested was that kings had sometimes ordered the arrest of legislators who opposed their policies. Such legislators could be held on trumped-up charges until the legislative session was over. The framers of the Constitution wanted to avoid any risk that a President might do the same thing.

The reason for the provision that a member of Congress shall not be questioned in any other place for any speech or debate in either house is that he may execute his duties without fear of a civil suit or a criminal prosecution for slander, libel, or other cause. Immunity extends to anything said in debate, a report, or a vote.

(2) No Senator or Representative shall, during the time for which he was elected, be appointed to any civil office under the authority of the United States, which shall have been created, or the emoluments whereof shall have been increased during such time; and no person holding any office under the United States, shall be a member of either House during his continuance in office.

These provisions keep congressmen from creating jobs to which they can later be appointed, or from raising salaries of jobs they hope to hold in the future.

In 1909 Senator Philander C. Knox wanted to resign from the Senate in order to become Secretary of State. But the salary of the Secretary of State had been increased during Knox's term as Senator. In order that Knox might accept the post, Congress withdrew the salary increase for the period of Knox's unfinished term.

Section 7. **(1) All bills for raising revenue shall originate in the House of Representatives; but the Senate may propose or concur with amendments as on other bills.**

The tradition that tax bills should start in the House was brought over from England. It now has less meaning, because the Senate can "amend" a money bill by rewriting the whole measure.

(2) Every bill which shall have passed the House of Representatives and the Senate, shall, before it become a law, be presented to the President of the United States; if he approve he shall sign it, but if not he shall return it, with his objections to that House in which it shall have originated, who shall enter the objections at large on their journal, and proceed to reconsider it. If after such reconsideration two thirds of that House shall agree to pass the bill, it shall be sent, together with the objections, to the other House, by which it shall likewise be reconsidered, and if approved by two thirds of that House, it shall become a law. But in all such cases the votes of both Houses shall be determined by yeas and nays, and the names of the persons voting for and against the bill shall be entered on the journal of each House respectively. If any bill shall not be returned by the President within ten days (Sundays excepted) after it shall have been presented to him, the same shall be a law, in like manner as if he had signed it, unless the Congress by their adjournment prevent its return, in which case it shall not be a law.

If the President disapproves of a bill that is sent to him near the close of a session, he will usually hold it for the full 10 days to see if Congress will not adjourn and spare him the trouble of a veto message. If Congress adjourns within 10 days, the bill is killed. This device is known as a "pocket veto."

(3) Every order, resolution, or vote to which the concurrence of the Senate and House of Representatives may be necessary (except on a question of adjournment) shall be presented to the President of the United States; and before the same shall take effect, shall be approved by him, or being disapproved by him, shall be repassed by two thirds of the Senate and House of Representatives, according to the rules and limitations prescribed in the case of a bill.

Powers Vested in Congress

Section 8. **The Congress shall have power:**

(1) To lay and collect taxes, duties, imposts and excises, to pay the debts and provide for the common defense and general welfare of the United States; but all duties, imposts and excises shall be uniform throughout the United States;

Duties are customs taxes on goods brought into the United States. *Excises* are taxes upon sales, use, or production, and sometimes on business procedures or privileges. For example, corporation taxes, cigarette taxes, and amusement taxes are excises. *Imposts* is a general tax term including both duties and excises.

(2) To borrow money on the credit of the United States;

(3) To regulate commerce with foreign nations, and among the several States, and with the Indian tribes;

This "Commerce Clause" grants Congress some of its most important powers. "Commerce" has been interpreted to mean all kinds of traffic and transportation. The commerce power has been construed to cover not only all movements or activities across state lines, but also all activities, even though local, that "affect" those movements or activities.

The word "regulate" may mean to restrain, to prohibit, to protect, to encourage, or to promote. Thus Congress can improve waterways, enforce safety measures, or forbid the shipment of impure goods. It can regulate the movement of trains, people, radio and television programs, electric power, stocks and bonds, lottery tickets, manufactured goods, or raw materials across state lines or national boundaries.

Congress must pass all laws. It cannot delegate the business of lawmaking to any other man or body of men. But in modern times, Congress has found it necessary to pass laws for the regulation of various kinds of business, such as that of railroads and public utility companies. In such cases Congress has, by a law, declared the policy which it desires enforced. It has then conferred on commissions which are part of the Executive Branch of the government the power to make rules and regulations to carry out the declared policy, to conduct investigations to determine whether the declared policy is being obeyed by the business concerns which are subject to regulation, and to compel obedience. See CIVIL AERONAUTICS BOARD; FEDERAL AVIATION AGENCY; FEDERAL COMMUNICATIONS COMMISSION; FEDERAL MARITIME COMMISSION; FEDERAL POWER COMMISSION; FEDERAL TRADE COMMISSION; INTERSTATE COMMERCE COMMISSION; MARITIME ADMINISTRATION; SECURITIES AND EXCHANGE COMMISSION; TARIFF COMMISSION, UNITED STATES.

(4) To establish an uniform rule of naturalization, and uniform laws on the subject of bankruptcies throughout the United States;

(5) To coin money, regulate the value thereof, and of foreign coin, and fix the standard of weights and measures;

From this provision, along with the provision which allows the Congress to regulate commerce and to borrow money, Congress gets its right to charter national banks and to establish the Federal Reserve System. See FEDERAL RESERVE SYSTEM.

(6) To provide for the punishment of counterfeiting the securities and current coin of the United States;

(7) To establish post offices and post roads;

(8) To promote the progress of science and useful arts, by securing for limited times to authors and inventors the exclusive right to their respective writings and discoveries;

Photographs and films may also be copyrighted under this provisions See COPYRIGHT; PATENT.

(9) To constitute tribunals inferior to the Supreme Court;

For examples of federal courts "inferior to the Supreme Court," see COURT (Federal Courts); COURT OF APPEALS; COURT OF CLAIMS.

(10) To define and punish piracies and felonies committed on the high seas, and offenses against the law of nations;

See FELONY; PIRATE.

(11) To declare war, grant letters of marque and reprisal, and make rules concerning captures on land and water;

The war power gives Congress vast powers it does not have in peacetime. To win, the entire nation must mobilize. The war power allows Congress to fix prices, ration commodities, and build factories—acts beyond its power in peacetime. See MARQUE AND REPRISAL.

(12) To raise and support armies, but no appropriation of money to that use shall be for a longer term than two years;

(13) To provide and maintain a navy;

(14) To make rules for the government and regulation of the land and naval forces;

(15) To provide for calling forth the militia to execute

the laws of the Union, suppress insurrections and repel invasions;

The militia is separate from the army and is partly controlled by the states. Congress has given to the President the power to decide when a state of invasion or insurrection exists.

(16) To provide for organizing, arming, and disciplining, the militia, and for governing such part of them as may be employed in the service of the United States, reserving to the States respectively, the appointment of the officers, and the authority of training the militia according to the discipline prescribed by Congress;

Until 1916, the militia was really operated by the states. In that year, the National Defense Act provided for drafting the National Guard into United States service under certain circumstances.

(17) To exercise exclusive legislation in all cases whatsoever, over such district (not exceeding ten miles square) as may, by cession of particular States, and the acceptance of Congress, become the seat of the Government of the United States, and to exercise like authority over all places purchased by the consent of the legislature of the State in which the same shall be for the erection of forts, magazines, arsenals, dockyards, and other needful buildings;—And

This section makes Congress the legislative body not only for the District of Columbia, but for federal property on which forts, naval bases, arsenals, and other federal works or buildings are located.

(18) To make all laws which shall be necessary and proper for carrying into execution the foregoing powers, and all other powers vested by this Constitution in the Government of the United States, or in any department or officer thereof.

The famous "necessary and proper" clause allows Congress to exercise many powers not granted to it in so many words. As a result, the powers of Congress change with changing times. This fact may help to explain why the Constitution of the United States has outlasted any other written constitution in the world.

Restraints, Federal and State

Section 9. (1) The migration or importation of such persons as any of the States now existing shall think proper to admit, shall not be prohibited by the Congress prior to the year one thousand eight hundred and eight, but a tax or duty may be imposed on such importation, not exceeding ten dollars for each person.

This paragraph refers to the slave trade. Dealers in slaves, as well as some slaveholders, wanted to make sure that Congress could not stop anyone from bringing African slaves into the country before the year 1808.

(2) The privilege of the writ of *habeas corpus* shall not be suspended, unless when in cases of rebellion or invasion the public safety may require it.

See HABEAS CORPUS.

(3) No bill of attainder or *ex post facto* law shall be passed.

See ATTAINDER; EX POST FACTO.

(4) No capitation, [or other direct,] tax shall be laid, unless in proportion to the census or enumeration herein before directed to be taken.

The Supreme Court once held that this clause barred the income tax. The decision was wiped out by Amendment 16, which allows Congress to levy taxes on income. See comment under Article I, Section 2, Clause (3).

(5) No tax or duty shall be laid on articles exported from any State.

"Exported" means sent out to other states or to foreign countries. One of the chief reasons for calling the Constitutional Convention together was to pass this provision and thus get rid of tariff barriers between the states.

(6) No preference shall be given by any regulation of commerce or revenue to the ports of one State over those of another: nor shall vessels bound to, or from, one State, be obliged to enter, clear, or pay duties in another.

(7) No money shall be drawn from the Treasury, but in consequence of appropriations made by law; and a regular statement and account of the receipts and expenditures of all public money shall be published from time to time.

It would take forever to authorize every item of government expenditure separately. Congress generally passes appropriations for government funds in lump sums. The Bureau of the Budget accounts for funds after they are spent, and suggests how much should be appropriated for government activities.

(8) No title of nobility shall be granted by the United States: And no person holding any office of profit or trust under them, shall, without the consent of the Congress, accept of any present, emolument, office, or title, of any kind whatever, from any king, prince, or foreign State.

This provision has not always been enforced strictly, for fear of offending the heads of other governments. Presidents accepted gifts from foreign rulers almost from the beginning of the nation. Return gifts have also been made, although Congress could not openly appropriate funds for this purpose. Knightly orders have often been conferred by foreign rulers on high-ranking officers in the armed services of the United States.

Section 10. **(1)** No State shall enter into any treaty, alliance, or confederation; grant letters of marque and reprisal; coin money; emit bills of credit; make anything but gold and silver coin a tender in payment of debts; pass any bill of attainder, *ex post facto* law, or law impairing the obligation of contracts, or grant any title of nobility.

(2) No State shall, without the consent of the Congress, lay any imposts or duties on imports or exports, except what may be absolutely necessary for executing its inspection laws: and the net produce of all duties and imposts, laid by any State on imports or exports, shall be for the use of the Treasury of the United States; and all such laws shall be subject to the revision and control of the Congress.

(3) No State shall, without the consent of Congress, lay any duty of tonnage, keep troops, or ships of war in time of peace, enter into any agreement or compact with another State, or with a foreign power, or engage in war, unless actually invaded, or in such imminent danger as will not admit of delay.

ARTICLE II

The Executive Department

Section 1. **(1)** The executive power shall be vested in a President of the United States of America. He shall hold his office during the term of four years, and, together with the Vice-President, chosen for the same term, be elected, as follows:

(2) Each State shall appoint, in such manner as the legislature thereof may direct, a number of electors, equal to the whole number of Senators and Representatives to which the State may be entitled in the Congress: but no Senator or Representative, or person holding an office of trust or profit under the United States, shall be appointed an elector.

See ELECTORAL COLLEGE.

(3) [The electors shall meet in their respective States, and vote by ballot for two persons, of whom one at least shall not be an inhabitant of the same State with themselves. And they shall make a list of all the persons voted for, and of the number of votes for each; which list they shall sign and certify, and transmit sealed to the seat of the Government of the United States, directed to the President of the Senate. The President of the Senate shall, in the presence of the Senate and House of Representatives, open all the certificates, and the votes shall then be counted. The person having the greatest number of votes shall be the President, if such number be a majority of the whole number of electors appointed; and if there be more than one who have such majority, and have an equal number of votes, then the House of Representatives shall immediately choose by ballot one of them for President; and if no person have a majority, then from the five highest on the list the said House shall in like manner choose the President. But in choosing the President, the votes shall be taken by States, the representation from each State having one vote; a quorum for this purpose shall consist of a member or members from two thirds of the States, and a majority of all the States shall be necessary to a choice. In every case, after the choice of the President, the person having the greatest number of votes of the electors shall be the Vice-President. But if there should remain two or more who have equal votes, the Senate shall choose from them by ballot the Vice-President.]

This procedure made possible a tie between Thomas Jefferson and Aaron Burr, the Republican candidates for President and Vice-President, each of whom got the votes of all the Republican electors in the election of 1800. The House voted 35 times before it elected Jefferson. Amendment 12 corrected this weakness in the Constitution. Electors still vote for President, but the President and Vice-President are voted for separately. See JEFFERSON, THOMAS (The Election of 1800).

(4) The Congress may determine the time of choosing the electors, and the day on which they shall give their votes; which day shall be the same throughout the United States.

(5) No person except a natural-born citizen, or a citizen of the United States at the time of the adoption of this Constitution, shall be eligible to the office of

President; neither shall any person be eligible to that office who shall not have attained to the age of thirty-five years, and been fourteen years a resident within the United States.

(6) In case of the removal of the President from office, or of his death, resignation, or inability to discharge the powers and duties of the said office, the same shall devolve on the Vice-President, and the Congress may by law provide for the case of removal, death, resignation or inability, both of the President and Vice-President, declaring what officer shall then act as President, and such officer shall act accordingly, until the disability be removed, or a President shall be elected.

See PRESIDENTIAL SUCCESSION. Only death has ever cut short the term of a President of the United States.

(7) The President shall, at stated times, receive for his services, a compensation, which shall neither be increased nor diminished during the period for which he shall have been elected, and he shall not receive within that period any other emolument from the United States, or any of them.

The Constitution made it possible for a poor man to become President by providing a salary for that office.

(8) Before he enter on the execution of his office, he shall take the following oath or affirmation:—"I do solemnly swear (or affirm) that I will faithfully execute the office of President of the United States, and will to the best of my ability, preserve, protect and defend the Constitution of the United States."

The Constitution does not say who shall administer the oath to the newly elected President. President George Washington was sworn in by Robert R. Livingston, then a city official in New York City. After that, it became customary for the Chief Justice or an Associate Justice of the Supreme Court to administer the oath. Calvin Coolidge was sworn in by his father, a justice of the peace, at his home in Vermont. He took the oath again before Justice Adolph A. Hoehling of the Supreme Court of the District of Columbia. It is now customary for the Chief Justice to swear in the President.

Section 2. (1) The President shall be commander in chief of the army and navy of the United States, and of the militia of the several States, when called into the actual service of the United States; he may require the opinion, in writing, of the principal officer in each of the executive departments, upon any subject relating to the duties of their respective offices, and he shall have power to grant reprieves and pardons for offenses against the United States, except in cases of impeachment.

The President's powers as Commander in Chief are far-reaching. They have been interpreted to include all powers which may be necessary to wage war effectively. Every war has raised many questions about their extent.

(2) He shall have power, by and with the advice and consent of the Senate, to make treaties, provided two thirds of the Senators present concur; and he shall nominate, and by and with the advice and consent of the Senate, shall appoint ambassadors, other public ministers and consuls, judges of the Supreme Court, and all other officers of the United States, whose appointments are not herein otherwise provided for, and which shall be established by law: but the Congress may by law vest the appointment of such inferior officers, as they

think proper, in the President alone, in the courts of law, or in the heads of departments.

The framers of the Constitution intended that in some matters the Senate should serve as an advisory body for the President, somewhat as the House of Lords advised the king in Great Britain.

The President has the power to make treaties, but two thirds of the Senators must approve before the treaty is ratified. The two-thirds provision, which was taken from the old Articles of Confederation, makes it easy to defeat a treaty.

(3) The President shall have power to fill up all vacancies that may happen during the recess of the Senate, by granting commissions which shall expire at the end of their next session.

This means that when the Senate is not in session, the President can make temporary appointments to offices which require Senate confirmation.

Section 3. He shall from time to time give to the Congress information of the state of the Union, and recommend to their consideration such measures as he shall judge necessary and expedient; he may, on extraordinary occasions, convene both Houses, or either of them, and in case of disagreement between them, with respect to the time of adjournment, he may adjourn them to such time as he shall think proper; he shall receive ambassadors and other public ministers; he shall take care that the laws be faithfully executed, and shall commission all the officers of the United States.

The President gives a message to Congress each year. Presidents George Washington and John Adams delivered their messages in person. For more than 100 years after that, it was customary for the President to send a written message which was read in Congress. President Woodrow Wilson delivered his messages in person, and Presidents Franklin D. Roosevelt, Harry S. Truman, and Dwight D. Eisenhower followed his example.

The President's messages often have great influence on public opinion, and thus on Congress. Famous messages to Congress include the Monroe Doctrine and President Wilson's "Fourteen Points."

The President has often used his power to call Congress into session. He has never used his power to adjourn Congress in case the two houses disagree upon a date for adjournment.

It has been held that the President's power to receive ambassadors and ministers from foreign countries includes the right to dismiss or refuse to receive them.

The responsibility to "take care that the laws be faithfully executed" puts the President at the head of law enforcement in the federal government. Every officer of the United States, civilian or military, draws his authority from the President.

Section 4. The President, Vice-President and all civil officers of the United States, shall be removed from office on impeachment for, and conviction of, treason, bribery, or other high crimes and misdemeanors.

ARTICLE III
The Judicial Department

Section 1. The judicial power of the United States, shall be vested in one Supreme Court, and in such inferior courts as the Congress may from time to time ordain and establish. The judges, both of the Supreme and inferior courts, shall hold their offices during good

UNITED STATES CONSTITUTION

behavior, and shall, at stated times, receive for their services, a compensation, which shall not be diminished during their continuance in office.

The Constitution makes every effort to keep the courts independent of both the legislature and the President. The provision that judges shall hold office during "good behavior" means that, unless they are impeached and convicted, they can hold office for life. This protects a judge from any threat of dismissal by the President who appointed him, or by any other President during the judge's lifetime. The provision that a judge's salary may not be reduced protects him against pressure from Congress, which could otherwise threaten to fix his salary so low that he could be forced to resign. See COURT; SUPREME COURT OF THE UNITED STATES.

Section 2. (1) The judicial power shall extend to all cases, in law and equity, arising under this Constitution, the laws of the United States, and ·treaties made, or which shall be made, under their authority;—to all cases affecting ambassadors, other public ministers and consuls;—to all cases of admiralty and maritime jurisdiction;—to controversies to which the United States shall be a party;—to controversies between two or more States; [between a State and citizens of another State;] between citizens of different States;—between citizens of the same State claiming lands under grants of different States, and between a State, or the citizens thereof, and foreign states, [citizens or subjects].

The right of the federal courts to handle "cases arising under this Constitution" is the basis of the Supreme Court's right to declare laws of Congress unconstitutional. This right of "judicial review" was established by Chief Justice John Marshall's historic decision in the case of *Marbury vs. Madison*. For more information on this famous case, and a brief description of the political and social circumstances surrounding it, see JEFFERSON, THOMAS (The Courts).

The language "between a State and citizens of another State" gave the federal courts the power to hear and decide a case where a state sued a citizen of another state and where a citizen of another state sued a state. Soon after the adoption of the Constitution a citizen of another state sued the state of Georgia, and the Supreme Court held that the suit was authorized by the language of Section 2. Amendment 11 was promptly submitted to the people and adopted, to take away the power of federal courts to hear a suit by a citizen of an outside state against a state. The power to try a suit by a state against a citizen of another state remains.

(2) In all cases affecting ambassadors, other public ministers and consuls, and those in which a State shall be party, the Supreme Court shall have original jurisdiction. In all the other cases before mentioned, the Supreme Court shall have appellate jurisdiction, both as to law and fact, with such exceptions, and under such regulations as the Congress shall make.

The statement that the Supreme Court has "original jurisdiction" in cases affecting the representatives of foreign countries and in cases to which a state is one of the parties means that cases of this kind go *directly* to the Supreme Court. In other kinds of cases, the Supreme Court has "appellate jurisdiction." This means that the cases are tried first in a lower court and may come up to the Supreme Court on appeal, if Congress authorizes an appeal. Congress cannot take away or modify the original jurisdiction of the Supreme Court, but it can

take away the right to appeal to that court or fix the conditions one must meet to present an appeal to that court. Amendment 7 limits the appellate jurisdiction of the Supreme Court by providing that an issue of fact tried by jury may not be re-examined.

(3) The trial of all crimes, except in cases of impeachment, shall be by jury; and such trial shall be held in the State where the said crimes shall have been committed; but when not committed within any State, the trial shall be at such place or places as the Congress may by law have directed.

Section 3. (1) Treason against the United States, shall consist only in levying war against them, or in adhering to their enemies, giving them aid and comfort. No person shall be convicted of treason unless on the testimony of two witnesses to the same overt act, or on confession in open court.

No person can be convicted of treason against the United States unless he confesses in open court, or unless two witnesses testify that he has committed an act of a treasonable nature. Talking or thinking about committing a treasonable act is not considered treason in the United States. See TREASON.

(2) The Congress shall have power to declare the punishment of treason, but no attainder of treason shall work corruption of blood, or forfeiture except during the life of the person attainted.

This provision means that the family of a traitor is not to be punished for his crime unless they aided him in his acts, and that his descendants cannot inherit the burden of his guilt. See ATTAINDER.

ARTICLE IV
Relation of the States to Each Other

Much of this article was taken word for word from the old Articles of Confederation.

Section 1. Full faith and credit shall be given in each State to the public acts, records, and judicial proceedings of every other State. And the Congress may by general laws prescribe the manner in which such acts, records and proceedings shall be proved, and the effect thereof.

Section 2. (1) The citizens of each State shall be entitled to all privileges and immunities of citizens in the several States.

This means that citizens traveling from state to state are entitled to all the privileges and immunities that automatically go to citizens of those states. Some privileges, such as the right to vote do not automatically go with citizenship, but require a period of residence and perhaps other qualifications.

The word *citizen* in this provision does not include corporations.

(2) A person charged in any State with treason, felony, or other crime, who shall flee from justice, and be found in another State, shall on demand of the executive authority of the State from which he fled, be delivered up, to be removed to the State having jurisdiction of the crime.

If a man commits a crime in one state and flees to another state, the governor of the state in which the crime was committed can demand that he be handed over. In some cases, this demand has not been complied with. It is not clear just how the federal government could enforce this provision of the Constitution. See Extradition.

(3) [No person held to service or labor in one State, under the laws thereof, escaping into another, shall, in consequence of any law or regulation therein, be discharged from such service or labor, but shall be delivered up on claim of the party to whom such service or labor may be due.]

A "person held to service or labor" was a slave or an indentured servant. No one is now bound to servitude in the United States, so this part of the Constitution no longer has any force.

Relation of the United States to States and Territories

Section 3. (1) New States may be admitted by the Congress into this Union; but no new State shall be formed or erected within the jurisdiction of any other State; nor any State be formed by the junction of two or more States, or parts of States, without the consent of the legislatures of the States concerned as well as of the Congress.

(2) The Congress shall have power to dispose of and make all needful rules and regulations respecting the territory or other property belonging to the United States; and nothing in this Constitution shall be so construed as to prejudice any claims of the United States, or of any particular State.

Section 4. The United States shall guarantee to every State in this Union a republican form of government, and shall protect each of them against invasion; and on application of the legislature, or of the executive (when the legislature cannot be convened) against domestic violence.

No one knows just what the word "republican" means in this section, for no action has ever been taken under this clause of the Constitution. From time to time, it has been claimed that various state governments are not truly republican in form. The federal courts have held that it is a "political" question whether a state is obeying this section. So the courts cannot decide the question. The decision rests with Congress.

The legislature or the governor of a state can request federal aid in dealing with domestic violence, such as rioting. Federal aid has sometimes been requested to put down strikes, and in one famous case federal troops were sent even though the governor specifically said he did not want them. See Cleveland, Grover (Labor Unrest).

ARTICLE V
Provision for Amending the Constitution

The Congress, whenever two thirds of both Houses shall deem it necessary, shall propose amendments to this Constitution, or, on the application of the legislatures of two thirds of the several States, shall call a convention for proposing amendments, which, in either case, shall be valid to all intents and purposes, as part of this Constitution, when ratified by the legislatures of three fourths of the several States, or by conventions in three fourths thereof, as the one or the other mode of ratification may be proposed by the Congress; provided [that no amendment which may be made prior to the year one thousand eight hundred and eight shall in

UNITED STATES CONSTITUTION

any manner affect the first and fourth clauses in the ninth section of the first Article; and] that no State, without its consent, shall be deprived of its equal suffrage in the Senate.

The framers of the Constitution purposely made it hard to put through an amendment. About 5,400 amendments have been proposed, but only 29 have been passed by Congress and submitted to the states. Of these, only 24 have been ratified. The United States Constitution is harder to amend than any other constitution in history.

State conventions to ratify a constitutional amendment have been used only once—when Amendment 21 was passed to repeal Amendment 18.

The Constitution sets no limit on the time the states shall have to consider an amendment. But Congress, in proposing amendments, has sometimes set a time limit within which the necessary number of states must ratify. Amendment 22 was proposed in 1947 but was not adopted until nearly four years later. This is the longest ratification time on record. The shortest was in 1804, when Amendment 12 was ratified after 229 days. Some persons claim that a proposed amendment cannot remain open for an unreasonable time, but the courts have never had to decide the question.

ARTICLE VI
National Debts

(1) All debts contracted and engagements entered into, before the adoption of this Constitution, shall be as valid against the United States under this Constitution, as under the Confederation.

Supremacy of the National Government

(2) This Constitution, and the laws of the United States which shall be made in pursuance thereof; and all treaties made, or which shall be made, under the authority of the United States, shall be the supreme law of the land; and the judges in every State shall be bound thereby, anything in the constitution or laws of any State to the contrary notwithstanding.

This supremacy clause has been called "the linchpin of the Constitution." It means simply that when state laws conflict with national laws enacted within the powers granted to Congress, the national laws prevail.

(3) The Senators and Representatives before mentioned, and the members of the several State legislatures, and all executive and judicial officers, both of the United States and of the several States, shall be bound by oath or affirmation, to support this Constitution; but no religious test shall ever be required as a qualification to any office or public trust under the United States.

This provision applies only to federal officials. It does not keep any state from imposing religious qualifications either for officeholding or for voting. In the past, some states have actually had such religious qualifications, but they do not exist anywhere in the United States today. For further information, see the note following Section 1 of Amendment 14.

ARTICLE VII

The ratification of the conventions of nine States, shall be sufficient for the establishment of this Constitution between the States so ratifying the same.

Done in Convention by the unanimous consent of the

UNITED STATES CONSTITUTION

States present the seventeenth day of September in the year of our Lord one thousand seven hundred and eighty-seven and of the independence of the United States of America the twelfth. In witness whereof we have hereunto subscribed our names,

George Washington—President and deputy from Virginia

New Hampshire

John Langdon   Nicholas Gilman

Massachusetts

Nathaniel Gorham   Rufus King

Connecticut

William Samuel Johnson   Roger Sherman

New York

Alexander Hamilton

New Jersey

William Livingston   William Paterson
David Brearley   Jonathan Dayton

Pennsylvania

Benjamin Franklin   Thomas FitzSimons
Thomas Mifflin   Jared Ingersoll
Robert Morris   James Wilson
George Clymer   Gouverneur Morris

Delaware

George Read   John Dickinson   Jacob Broom
Gunning Bedford, Jr.   Richard Bassett

Maryland

James McHenry   Daniel Carroll
Dan of St. Thomas Jenifer

Virginia

John Blair   James Madison, Jr.

North Carolina

William Blount   Hugh Williamson
Richard Dobbs Spaight

South Carolina

John Rutledge   Charles Pinckney
Charles Cotesworth Pinckney   Pierce Butler

Georgia

William Few   Abraham Baldwin

The Final Sections of the Constitution Contain the Provisions for Its Ratification and the Signatures.

Historical Document Co.—Frank H. Fleer Corp.

Amendments to the United States Constitution

[*The first 10 Amendments, eight of which are known as "The Bill of Rights," were proposed on Sept. 25, 1789, and have been in force since Dec. 15, 1791.* *Two other amendments proposed at the same time were rejected. All other amendments have been proposed separately. One amendment repealed another one.*]

AMENDMENT 1

Congress shall make no law respecting an establishment of religion, or prohibiting the free exercise thereof; or abridging the freedom of speech, or of the press; or the right of the people peaceably to assemble, and to petition the Government for a redress of grievances.

The Supreme Court has said that the first eight Amendments apply only to the federal government and not to the states. While this is true of Amendment 1, it is now settled by Supreme Court decisions that the command of Amendment 14—that no state shall deprive any person of life, liberty, or property, without due process of law—makes Amendment 1 apply to the states and forbids state action which would violate the rights of religion, speech, press, and assembly, covered by Amendment 1. See the comment under Amendment 14 below.

In many countries, some one religion has been made the official, or "established," church, and has been supported by the government. Congress is forbidden to set up or provide in any way for such an established church in the United States.

None of the rights protected in Amendment 1 can be considered as absolute. For example, Congress cannot prohibit the free exercise of religion, but it could pass legislation against any sect which practiced customs contrary to morality. Some Mormons held that it was entirely proper for a man to take more than one wife. But the clause protecting freedom of religion did not extend to this practice. In the same way, it has been held that Congress may abridge the freedom of speech or of the press in cases of "clear and present danger" to the state. But the rights in Amendment 1 are preferred in the Constitutional scheme, and few actual restrictions on them are allowed. They are, indeed, the very cornerstone of our democratic process.

AMENDMENT 2

A well-regulated militia, being necessary to the security of a free State, the right of the people to keep and bear arms, shall not be infringed.

This Article calls attention to a striking difference between the Constitution and the Declaration of Independence. In the Declaration, many words were used in explaining *why* the colonies were separating from Great Britain. But, in the Constitution, Amendment 2 is the only Article that contains any explanation of why it was passed.

The right to keep and bear arms was exceedingly precious to men who faced dangers of many kinds in their daily lives. Colonial farmers with their muskets had helped to win the Revolutionary War. On the frontier, a gun was usually the pioneer family's only protection against wild animals and prowling Indians.

AMENDMENT 3

No soldier shall, in time of peace be quartered in any house, without the consent of the owner, nor in time of war, but in a manner to be prescribed by law.

This Amendment grew directly out of an old grievance against the British, who had forced people to take soldiers into their homes.

AMENDMENT 4

The right of the people to be secure in their persons, houses, papers, and effects, against unreasonable searches and seizures, shall not be violated, and no warrants shall issue, but upon probable cause, supported by oath or affirmation, and particularly describing the place to be searched, and the persons or things to be seized.

This measure does not prohibit searches and seizures by legal authorities. It simply requires the authorities to obtain a search warrant from a magistrate by showing the need for it, and to conduct themselves according to law. This is an important guarantee of the right of privacy. See SEARCH WARRANT.

AMENDMENT 5

No person shall be held to answer for a capital, or otherwise infamous crime, unless on a presentment or indictment of a grand jury, except in cases arising in the land or naval forces, or in the militia, when in actual service in time of war or public danger; nor shall any person be subject for the same offense to be twice put in jeopardy of life or limb; nor shall be compelled in any criminal case to be a witness against himself, nor be deprived of life, liberty, or property, without due process of law; nor shall private property be taken for public use, without just compensation.

A person cannot be placed in *double jeopardy* (tried twice for the same offense), but he may be *placed on trial* a second time if a jury cannot agree on a verdict, if a mistrial is declared for some other reason, or if a new trial is granted at the defendant's request.

The statement that no person shall be deprived of life, liberty, or property "without due process of law" expresses one of the most important provisions of the Constitution. The same words are found in Amendment 14 as restrictions on the power of the states. They express the idea that man's life, liberty, and property are not subject to the uncontrolled power of the government. This idea can be traced back to the Magna Carta, which provided that the king could not imprison or harm people "save by the lawful judgment of his peers or by the law of the land." That idea grew with the years. The Declaration of Independence expressed it by declaring that all men "are endowed by their Creator with certain unalienable rights; that among these are life, liberty, and the pursuit of happiness." Due process expresses a very vague standard, but it has been given concrete meaning by court decisions over the years. It was once used to stop legislation on such matters as wages, the number of hours that people should work, and the right to join labor unions. Today, the Supreme Court would not use the Due Process Clause to give the courts power to make decisions that are supposed to be made by the other branches of the government. But the court is still prepared to protect people against arbitrary and capricious acts of government. See FIFTH AMENDMENT.

AMENDMENT 6

In all criminal prosecutions, the accused shall enjoy the

right to a speedy and public trial, by an impartial jury of the State and district wherein the crime shall have been committed, which district shall have been previously ascertained by law, and to be informed of the nature and cause of the accusation; to be confronted with the witnesses against him; to have compulsory process for obtaining witnesses in his favor, and to have the assistance of counsel for his defense.

The provision for a speedy public trial grew out of the fact that political trials in England had sometimes been held in secret, and lasted for a number of years. Innocent persons may be punished if courts allow the testimony of unknown persons to be used as evidence. Amendment 6 guarantees the right to confront witnesses. A man on trial has a large measure of protection if he can confront and cross-examine those who accuse him. He may be able to show that his accuser is a liar, is mistaken, is testifying because of spite or an old grudge, or is otherwise unworthy of being believed.

AMENDMENT 7

In suits at common law, where the value in controversy shall exceed twenty dollars, the right of trial by jury shall be preserved, and no fact tried by a jury, shall be otherwise re-examined in any court of the United States, than according to the rules of the common law.

The framers of the Constitution considered the right to jury trial to be of great significance. Experience has shown that juries bring a quality of mercy and good common sense to the administration of the laws when lawyers and judges forget where justice lies. Juries have sometimes inflicted injustice. But for hundreds of years they have been an important safeguard between man and his government.

AMENDMENT 8

Excessive bail shall not be required, nor excessive fines imposed, nor cruel and unusual punishments inflicted.

This amendment applies only to persons held for federal offenses. The courts themselves can say what bail or fine is "excessive" and what punishments are "cruel and unusual." The effect of the Amendment is simply to allow an appeal to the federal courts in cases of this kind.

AMENDMENT 9

The enumeration in the Constitution, of certain rights, shall not be construed to deny or disparage others retained by the people.

This means simply that the Constitution does not pretend to have listed all the specific rights the people have and had before the Constitution and its Amendments were adopted. The courts must therefore consider such claims of right on their merits instead of arguing "if the Constitution had intended to give these rights to the people, it would have done so."

AMENDMENT 10

The powers not delegated to the United States by the Constitution, nor prohibited by it to the States, are reserved to the States respectively, or to the people.

This provision makes it clear that the federal government is limited to certain specific powers. The federal government can do only what the Constitution says it can do, but the states and the people thereof can exercise

any powers not *prohibited* in the Constitution. The state governments are forbidden to act only in cases where the power to act has been placed in the federal government.

AMENDMENT 11

This Amendment was proposed March 4, 1794, and proclaimed in force Jan. 8, 1798.

The judicial power of the United States shall not be construed to extend to any suit in law or equity, commenced or prosecuted against one of the United States by citizens of another State, or by citizens or subjects of any foreign state.

This Amendment modifies Article III, Section 2 (1). See comment above under that paragraph.

AMENDMENT 12

This Amendment was proposed Dec. 9, 1803, and proclaimed as ratified Sept. 25, 1804.

The electors shall meet in their respective States and vote by ballot for President and Vice-President, one of whom, at least, shall not be an inhabitant of the same State with themselves; they shall name in their ballots the person voted for as President, and in distinct ballots the person voted for as Vice-President, and they shall make distinct lists of all persons voted for as President, and of all persons voted for as Vice-President, and of the number of votes for each, which lists they shall sign and certify, and transmit sealed to the seat of the Government of the United States, directed to the President of the Senate;——the President of the Senate shall, in the presence of the Senate and House of Representatives, open all the certificates and the votes shall then be counted;——the person having the greatest number of votes for President, shall be the President, if such number be a majority of the whole number of electors appointed; and if no person have such majority, then from the persons having the highest numbers not exceeding three on the list of those voted for as President, the House of Representatives shall choose immediately, by ballot, the President. But in choosing the President, the votes shall be taken by States, the representation from each State having one vote; a quorum for this purpose shall consist of a member or members from two thirds of the States, and a majority of all the States shall be necessary to a choice. And if the House of Representatives shall not choose a President whenever the right of choice shall devolve upon them, [before the fourth day of March next following,] then the Vice-President shall act as President, as in the case of the death or other constitutional disability of the President.——The person having the greatest number of votes as Vice-President, shall be the Vice-President, if such number be a majority of the whole number of electors appointed, and if no person have a majority, then from the two highest numbers on the list, the Senate shall choose the Vice-President; a quorum for the purpose shall consist of two thirds of the whole number of Senators, and a majority of the whole number shall be necessary to a choice. But no person constitutionally ineligible to the office of President shall be eligible to that of Vice-President of the United States.

This Amendment makes two important changes in the Constitution. It provides for the separate choice of President and Vice-President, and it fixes a time limit on the House of Representatives, in case they are called upon to elect a President. Both changes grew out of the election of 1800, when Burr, the choice of the Electors for Vice-President, had the same number of votes as Jefferson, their choice for President. This tie threw the election into the House of Representatives, and made clear the need for an Amendment to prevent anything of the kind again. The House of Representatives took so long to make its choice that people wondered what would happen if they failed to choose a President before Inauguration Day. Amendment 12 also settled this problem. See Article II, Section I, Clause (3).

AMENDMENT 13

This Amendment was proposed Jan. 31, 1865, and proclaimed Dec. 18, 1865.

Section 1. Neither slavery nor involuntary servitude, except as a punishment for crime whereof the party shall have been duly convicted, shall exist within the United States, or any place subject to their jurisdiction.

Lincoln's Emancipation Proclamation had declared slaves free in the Confederate States. This Amendment completed the abolition of slavery in the United States.

Section 2. Congress shall have power to enforce this article by appropriate legislation.

AMENDMENT 14

This Amendment was proposed June 13, 1866, and proclaimed July 28, 1868.

Section 1. All persons born or naturalized in the United States, and subject to the jurisdiction thereof, are citizens of the United States and of the State wherein they reside. No State shall make or enforce any law which shall abridge the privileges or immunities of citizens of the United States; nor shall any State deprive any person of life, liberty, or property, without due process of law; nor deny to any person within its jurisdiction the equal protection of the laws.

The principal, perhaps the sole, purpose of this Amendment was to make the former slaves citizens and give them full civil rights. A further purpose was to define who is a citizen of the United States. Many had claimed that no one could be a citizen of the United States unless he was a citizen of a state. As all Negroes had recently been made free and were not in many states admitted to state citizenship, the only way to establish their right of citizenship in the United States was to amend the Constitution. Under this provision a person becomes a citizen of the United States if he is born within its borders or, if not, if he has been naturalized according to law. Thus, the children of Chinese or Japanese aliens born in this country are, because they were so born, citizens of the United States. One must reside within a state to become a citizen of it. But it is necessary only that a person should be born or naturalized in the United States to be a citizen of the Union. Thus there are two citizenships which are distinct and depend on different facts.

But while the main purpose of Amendment 14 was to make citizens of former slaves, it has been held that the phrases "all persons" and "any person" are so broad that the Amendment, by repeating the language of Amendment 5, compels the states to afford all persons the rights the Due Process clause of Amendment 5 guaranteed against invasion by the federal government. Among the rights or liberties protected are the right of religious freedom, of free speech, and of freedom of the press, specifically protected against the federal government by the words of Amendment 1. (See comment above, under Amendment 1.) A vast number of cases have been brought to the courts and decided under this

section. Some members of the Supreme Court have argued that Due Process includes all the rights protected against the federal government by the Bill of Rights. But they have never been a majority. As a result, the decisions have attempted, by a process of inclusion and exclusion, to protect persons and corporations from arbitrary state action that would invade either personal or property rights.

Section 2. Representatives shall be apportioned among the several States according to their respective numbers, counting the whole number of persons in each State, excluding Indians not taxed. But when the right to vote at any election for the choice of electors for President and Vice-President of the United States, Representatives in Congress, the executive and judicial officers of a State, or the members of the legislature thereof, is denied to any of the male inhabitants of such State, being twenty-one years of age, and citizens of the United States, or in any way abridged, except for participation in rebellion, or other crime, the basis of representation therein shall be reduced in the proportion which the number of such male citizens shall bear to the whole number of male citizens twenty-one years of age in such State.

This section proposes a penalty for states which refuse to give the vote in federal elections to all adult male citizens. States which restrict voting can have their representation in Congress cut down. This penalty has never been used.

Section 3. No person shall be a Senator or Representative in Congress, or elector of President and Vice-President, or hold any office, civil or military, under the United States, or under any State, who, having previously taken an oath, as a member of Congress, or as an officer of the United States, or as a member of any State legislature, or as an executive or judicial officer of any State, to support the Constitution of the United States, shall have engaged in insurrection or rebellion against the same, or given aid or comfort to the enemies thereof. But Congress may by a vote of two thirds of each House, remove such disability.

This section is of historical interest only. Its purpose was to keep federal officers who joined the Confederacy from becoming federal officers again. Congress could vote to overlook such a record.

Section 4. The validity of the public debt of the United States, authorized by law, including debts incurred for payment of pensions and bounties for services in suppressing insurrection or rebellion, shall not be questioned. But neither the United States nor any State shall assume or pay any debt or obligation incurred in aid of insurrection or rebellion against the United States, or any claim for the loss or emancipation of any slave; but all such debts, obligations and claims shall be held illegal and void.

Section 5. The Congress shall have power to enforce, by appropriate legislation, the provisions of this article.

AMENDMENT 15

This Amendment was proposed Feb. 26, 1869, and proclaimed March 30, 1870.

Section 1. The right of citizens of the United States to vote shall not be denied or abridged by the United

143

UNITED STATES CONSTITUTION

States or by any State on account of race, color, or previous condition of servitude.

Negroes who had been slaves became citizens under the terms of Amendment 14. Amendment 15 did not specifically say that all Negroes must be allowed to vote. States are free to set qualifications for voters. But the Amendment says that a voter cannot be denied the ballot because of his race. Some states have attempted to do this indirectly (see GRANDFATHER CLAUSE). But the Supreme Court quickly struck down such measures, no matter how ingenious they were. See FIFTEENTH AMENDMENT.

Section 2. The Congress shall have power to enforce this article by appropriate legislation.

AMENDMENT 16

This Amendment was proposed July 12, 1909, and proclaimed Feb. 25, 1913.

The Congress shall have power to lay and collect taxes on incomes, from whatever source derived, without apportionment among the several States, and without regard to any census or enumeration.

This Amendment made the federal income tax legal. See comment under Article I, Section 2, Clause (3).

AMENDMENT 17

This Amendment was proposed May 13, 1912, and proclaimed May 31, 1913.

(1) The Senate of the United States shall be composed of two Senators from each State, elected by the people thereof for six years; and each Senator shall have one vote. The electors in each State shall have the qualifications requisite for electors of the most numerous branch of the State legislatures.

(2) When vacancies happen in the representation of any State in the Senate, the executive authority of such State shall issue writs of election to fill such vacancies: *Provided,* That the legislature of any State may empower the executive thereof to make temporary appointments until the people fill the vacancies by election as the legislature may direct.

(3) This Amendment shall not be so construed as to affect the election or term of any Senator chosen before it becomes valid as part of the Constitution.

This Amendment takes the power of electing the Senators of a state from the state legislature and places it in the hands of the people of the state.

AMENDMENT 18

This Amendment was proposed Dec. 18, 1917, and proclaimed Jan. 29, 1919.

Section 1. After one year from the ratification of this article the manufacture, sale, or transportation of intoxicating liquors within, the importation thereof into, or the exportation thereof from the United States and all territory subject to the jurisdiction thereof for beverage purposes is hereby prohibited.

Section 2. The Congress and the several States shall have concurrent power to enforce this article by appropriate legislation.

Section 3. This article shall be inoperative unless it shall have been ratified as an amendment to the Constitution by the legislatures of the several States, as provided in the Constitution, within seven years from the

date of the submission hereof to the States by the Congress.

This is the Prohibition Amendment, repealed by Amendment 21 in 1933.

AMENDMENT 19

This Amendment was proposed June 4, 1919, and proclaimed Aug. 26, 1920.

Section 1. The right of citizens of the United States to vote shall not be denied or abridged by the United States or by any State on account of sex.

Section 2. Congress shall have power to enforce this article by appropriate legislation.

Amendments giving women the right to vote were introduced in Congress one after another for more than 40 years before this one was finally passed.

AMENDMENT 20

This Amendment was proposed March 2, 1932, and proclaimed Feb. 6, 1933.

Section 1. The terms of the President and Vice-President shall end at noon on the 20th day of January, and the terms of Senators and Representatives at noon on the third day of January, of the year in which such terms would have ended if this article had not been ratified; and the terms of their successors shall then begin.

Section 2. The Congress shall assemble at least once in every year, and such meeting shall begin at noon on the third day of January, unless they shall by law appoint a different day.

Section 3. If, at the time fixed for the beginning of the term of the President, the President elect shall have died, the Vice-President elect shall become President. If a President shall not have been chosen before the time fixed for the beginning of his term, or if the President elect shall have failed to qualify, then the Vice-President elect shall act as President until a President shall have qualified; and the Congress may by law provide for the case wherein neither a President elect nor a Vice-President elect shall have qualified, declaring who shall then act as President, or the manner in which one who is to act shall be selected, and such person shall act accordingly until a President or Vice-President shall have qualified.

Section 4. The Congress may by law provide for the case of the death of any of the persons from whom the House of Representatives may choose a President whenever the right of choice shall have devolved upon them, and for the case of the death of any of the persons from whom the Senate may choose a Vice-President whenever the right of choice shall have devolved upon them.

Section 5. Sections 1 and 2 shall take effect on the 15th day of October following the ratification of this article.

Section 6. This article shall be inoperative unless it shall have been ratified as an amendment to the Constitution by the legislatures of three fourths of the several States within seven years from the date of its submission.

This Amendment, called the *Lame Duck Amendment,* moves the term of newly elected Presidents and Congressmen closer to election time. Before it came into force, defeated Congressmen continued to serve for four months. See LAME DUCK AMENDMENT.

AMENDMENT 21

This Amendment was proposed Feb. 20, 1933, and proclaimed Dec. 5, 1933.

Section 1. The Eighteenth Article of Amendment to the Constitution of the United States is hereby repealed.

Section 2. The transportation or importation into any State, Territory, or possession of the United States for delivery or use therein of intoxicating liquors, in violation of the laws thereof, is hereby prohibited.

Section 3. This article shall be inoperative unless it shall have been ratified as an amendment to the Constitution by conventions in the several States, as provided in the Constitution, within seven years from the date of the submission hereof to the States by the Congress.

This Article simply repeals Amendment 18. Section 2 promises federal help to "dry" states in enforcing their own prohibition laws.

AMENDMENT 22

This Amendment was proposed March 24, 1947, and proclaimed March 1, 1951.

Section 1. No person shall be elected to the office of the President more than twice, and no person who has held the office of President, or acted as President, for more than two years of a term to which some other person was elected President shall be elected to the office of the President more than once. But this article shall not apply to any person holding the office of President when this article was proposed by the Congress, and shall not prevent any person who may be holding the office of President, or acting as President, during the term within which this article becomes operative from holding the office of President or acting as President during the remainder of such term.

Section 2. This article shall be inoperative unless it shall have been ratified as an amendment to the Constitution by the legislatures of three fourths of the several States within seven years from the day of its submission to the States by the Congress.

AMENDMENT 23

This Amendment was proposed June 16, 1960, and proclaimed April 3, 1961.

Section 1. The District constituting the seat of Government of the United States shall appoint in such manner as the Congress may direct: A number of electors of President and Vice-President equal to the whole number of Senators and Representatives in Congress to which the District would be entitled if it were a State, but in no event more than the least populous State; they shall be in addition to those appointed by the States, but they shall be considered, for the purposes of the election of President and Vice-President, to be electors appointed by a State; and they shall meet in the District and perform such duties as provided by the twelfth article of amendment.

Section 2. The Congress shall have power to enforce this article by appropriate legislation.

AMENDMENT 24

This Amendment was proposed Aug. 27, 1962, and proclaimed Feb. 4, 1964.

UNITED STATES MARINE CORPS

Section 1. The right of citizens of the United States to vote in any primary or other election for President or Vice-President, for electors for President or Vice-President, or for Senator or Representative in Congress, shall not be denied or abridged by the United States or any State by reason of failure to pay any poll tax or other tax.

Section 2. The Congress shall have power to enforce this article by appropriate legislation.

Annotations by OWEN J. ROBERTS and WILLIAM O. DOUGLAS

UNITED STATES DEPARTMENT may refer to any one of the executive departments of the United States government. Each department has a separate article in WORLD BOOK. For a list of these articles, see the Related Articles at the end of UNITED STATES, GOVERNMENT OF.

UNITED STATES EMPLOYMENT SERVICE. See EMPLOYMENT AGENCY; EMPLOYMENT SECURITY, BUREAU OF.

UNITED STATES FLAG. See FLAG.

UNITED STATES FOREST SERVICE. See FOREST AND FOREST PRODUCTS (Careers); FOREST SERVICE.

UNITED STATES GOVERNMENT. See UNITED STATES, GOVERNMENT OF.

UNITED STATES HISTORY. See UNITED STATES, HISTORY OF.

UNITED STATES INFORMATION AGENCY (USIA) distributes to persons in other countries information about the United States, its culture, its policies, and American life in general. USIA works to "submit evidence to peoples of other nations . . . that the objectives and policies of the United States are in harmony with and will advance their legitimate aspirations for freedom, progress, and peace."

The USIA provides basic materials from its headquarters in Washington, D.C., for information and cultural officers to use in about 100 countries. These officers carry on various USIA programs designed to meet the needs of the countries they serve in. USIA operates abroad as the *United States Information Service* (USIS).

A public affairs officer directs each overseas information post. He works under the United States ambassador to that country. All the information he provides reflects official American foreign policy. But each officer abroad may use techniques best suited to reach the peoples of the country where he works.

The USIA staff employs such communications methods as newspapers, magazines, pamphlets, lectures, films, television, and radio to present a true picture of the United States to other countries. One of the best known means of communication is the *Voice of America*, which broadcasts news, discussions, and music to all parts of the world (see VOICE OF AMERICA).

The USIA was established in 1953. It took over work that had been carried on by the Office of War Information during World War II, and then by the State Department. Its 11,000 employees include about 1,300 Americans overseas and 7,200 local employees in the countries served. Its director is responsible to the President.   LOWELL BENNETT

UNITED STATES MARINE BAND. See BAND.

UNITED STATES MARINE CORPS. See MARINE CORPS, UNITED STATES.

U.S.
MERCHANT MARINE
ACADEMY

U.S. Merchant Marine Academy

U.S. Merchant Marine Academy, *above,* at Kings Point, N.Y., has a 65-acre campus on the shore of Long Island. A regimental color guard, *left,* marches to the parade grounds in full dress uniform. The official insignia of the Merchant Marine Cadet Corps, *inset,* has a border resembling rope to emphasize the sea-faring role played by the merchant marine.

UNITED STATES MERCHANT MARINE ACADEMY trains young men to become officers in the United States Merchant Marine. The academy, often called *Kings Point,* occupies 65 acres on the north shore of Long Island at Kings Point, N.Y., about 20 miles northeast of New York City.

The United States Merchant Marine Cadet Corps was established in 1938. Its academy, founded in 1942, became a permanent, government-sponsored school in 1956, and received equal status with the academies of the armed forces. The Maritime Administration, an agency of the United States Department of Commerce, operates the academy.

Entrance Requirements. Candidates for the school must be unmarried citizens of the United States, not less than 17 and not yet 22 years of age by July 1 of the year in which they seek admission. They must be of good moral character. They must also have 15 high school credits, including 3 units in mathematics, 1 unit in science, and 3 units in English. Competitive examinations are held each year among candidates nominated by United States Senators or Representatives.

Enrollment. Appointments to the academy are governed by a state and territory quota system based on population. The academy has an authorized strength of 900 cadets. They represent every state of the United States, the District of Columbia, the Panama Canal Zone, Puerto Rico, Guam, American Samoa, and the Virgin Islands. In addition, the academy is authorized to admit, for the full period of training, not more than 12 candidates from Central and South America.

The School Program. The academy offers a four-year course of undergraduate study designed to prepare its graduates for the many problems that may confront a merchant marine officer during his career. The cadets study and gain practical experience in an atmosphere of order and discipline. Their practical experience subjects include training aboard a ship. Their academic subjects deal with such fields as marine engineering, navigation, electricity, ship construction, naval science and tactics, economics, business, languages, and history.

The cadets spend their first year as Fourth Classmen at the academy. Their second year, as Third Classmen, is spent aboard a merchant ship. Their third year, as Second Classmen, and fourth year, as First Classmen, are both spent at the academy.

On completion of the four-year program, cadets are examined for their original licenses as third deck, or engineering, officers in the merchant marine. They may then serve on any ship in the United States Merchant Marine. Graduates also receive bachelor of science degrees and commissions as ensigns in the naval reserve. More than 10,000 officers have been graduated from the academy. GORDON McLINTOCK

U.S. Military Academy

Cadets at the United States Military Academy line *The Plain*, the main parade ground. Beautiful Cadet Chapel towers above them. The Academy's seal is *inset*.

A Cadet "Stands Tall," proudly reflecting the traditions of military training for which the Academy is famous. He knows that even the spotless condition of his uniform keeps those traditions alive.

UNITED STATES MILITARY ACADEMY at West Point, N.Y., is the oldest military college in the United States. It prepares young men for careers as military officers. The Academy is supported by the federal government, and is supervised by the Department of the Army.

Students at the Academy are called *cadets*. After four years of training, they earn bachelor of science degrees and commissions in the United States Army.

The Academy is part of a military reservation that occupies 16,000 acres on the west bank of the Hudson River, about 50 miles north of New York City. The superintendent, an army major general, commands the Academy and the military post associated with it.

Entrance Requirements. A candidate for the Academy must be between 17 and 22 years of age; a United States citizen; of good moral character; physically fit; academically qualified; and must never have been married. The Director of Admissions and Registrar, United States Military Academy, West Point, N.Y., handles all inquiries for information on admissions.

A candidate must obtain a nomination to the Academy before he can take the academic, physical aptitude, and medical examinations. About three-fourths of the vacancies for the Academy are filled by nominees of U.S. Senators and Representatives. In addition, qualified men in the regular or reserve components of the armed forces may be nominated under separate quotas. Other candidates may receive nominations from the President or Vice-President of the United States. Quotas also have been established for residents of American terri-

Cadets Take Many Courses in Science and Technology at West Point. A standard course required in atomic and nuclear physics includes work on a nuclear reactor, *above.* Cadets also must learn to operate high-speed digital computers, *below.*

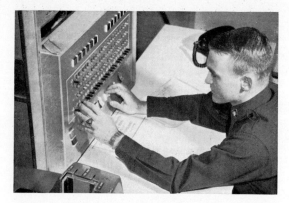

tories, sons of deceased veterans, students at honor military schools, and residents of the District of Columbia.

Cadets are members of the Regular Army. They are paid $147.30 a month. From this amount, they must pay for uniforms, textbooks, and incidental expenses. Housing, meals, and medical care are provided.

SELECTION OF CANDIDATES

Candidates for the United States Military Academy are appointed as follows. These figures reflect the Academy strength of 4,417 cadets, as authorized by the United States Congress in 1964. The figures represent the total number of candidates each nominating source may select for the Academy.

- **300** by the President of the United States
- **5** by the Vice-President of the United States
- **500** by United States Senators
- **2,175** by United States Representatives
- **600** from qualified alternates selected by Senators and Congressmen
- **40** sons of deceased veterans
- **5** from the District of Columbia
- **1** from Guam, Samoa, and the Virgin Islands
- **6** from Puerto Rico
- **1** from the Canal Zone
- **340** from the regular United States armed forces
- **340** from the reserve United States armed forces
- **80** from honor military schools
- **24** cadets from other countries

An unlimited number of sons of Medal of Honor winners may also attend.

The Student Body is called the Corps of Cadets. The Corps follows the army brigade organization. The brigade is broken down into regiments, battalions, and companies.

The Academy Honor Code is a cherished possession of cadets and graduates. Enforced by the cadets themselves, the Code has never outgrown its original and simple meaning—that a cadet will not lie, cheat, or steal. The code requires complete integrity in word and deed. It is strictly enforced, and any intentional violation is a cause for dismissal from the Academy.

The cadet academic year extends from September to June. *June Week* climaxes the year's events for the graduating *First* (senior) class. During graduation exercises in the Academy field house, the President of the United States often presents the cadets with their commissions. Other classes are called the *Fourth* (freshman) class; *Third* (sophomore) class; and *Second* (junior) class.

A Cadet's Day starts with the first call for reveille at 5:50 A.M. All cadets live in barracks, two to a room. They eat their meals in Washington Hall. Classes and study time extend from 7:15 A.M. until 3:15 P.M. From that time until the 6:30 P.M. supper hour, cadets participate in extracurricular activities, parades, or intramural and intercollegiate athletics. The day ends with "Taps" at 10 P.M. Cadets may stay up after taps to study.

Education and Training. The four-year program of military, academic, and physical education is designed to produce military leaders. Because of changes in weapons and techniques of war, the curriculum is often revised. For example, the Academy has increased its emphasis on chemistry, nuclear physics, electronics, and basic astronautics. To prepare students for the demands of complex world affairs, the curriculum also emphasizes geography, history, government, economics, and ideologies of non-Western countries.

During the summer, the cadet takes a one-month *leave* (vacation) and spends the rest of the summer in tactical training, either at West Point, nearby Camp Buckner, or at a military installation in the United States. Tactical training involves instruction in army weapons and actual field maneuvers. Second class and First class cadets spend a month as a junior officer in a U.S. Army division in Europe.

History. George Washington tried to establish a military academy at West Point during his lifetime, but did not succeed. Congress authorized an academy on March 16, 1802. The Academy opened on July 4, 1802. Under Col. Sylvanus Thayer, who served as superintendent from 1817 to 1833, West Point became a military academy of the highest type. Thayer's basic system remains in effect today.

Among the great American military leaders who received their training at West Point were Robert E. Lee, Ulysses S. Grant, Thomas J. "Stonewall" Jackson, Philip Sheridan, John J. Pershing, Douglas MacArthur, and Dwight D. Eisenhower.

The Academy began a major expansion and modernization program in the early 1960's. The building program, which is expected to cost more than $100 million, will be completed by the early 1970's.

Critically reviewed by UNITED STATES MILITARY ACADEMY

See also NEW YORK (picture); THAYER, SYLVANUS.

U.S. News & World Report

The Museum of History and Technology Houses Many Exhibits of the United States National Museum.

UNITED STATES NATIONAL MUSEUM consists of the government's collections of objects relating to natural history, the arts and sciences, and industry. The museum is the largest depository of national collections in the United States. It has over 59 million catalogued items, more than in any other similar collection in the world. Each year, hundreds of thousands of objects are added to the collections. Many of the museum's objects are irreplaceable. For example, the museum displays the original "Star-Spangled Banner" that flew over Fort McHenry in the War of 1812. The museum carries out educational and research work. It issues valuable bulletins dealing with scientific studies of its collections. The museum is a bureau of the Smithsonian Institution (see SMITHSONIAN INSTITUTION). It is maintained by annual grants from Congress.

Museum Collections. The National Museum has two branches, each with its own large building. The branches are the Museum of History and Technology and the Museum of Natural History.

The Museum of History and Technology houses collections of historical objects and technological inventions. The history section includes items that belonged to the Presidents of the United States and to civilian and military leaders. President George Washington's sword, the desk at which Thomas Jefferson wrote the Declaration of Independence, and gowns worn by Presidents' wives are on display. There is also a collection of historic World War I and World War II items. The technology section shows developments in engineering, the graphic arts, medicine, textiles, and woods. The Museum of History and Technology also contains the original "Star-Spangled Banner," the first telegraph instrument, the first sewing machine, and the first automobile. Exhibits in costumes, engineering, medicine, military history, and transportation are housed in separate halls.

The Museum of Natural History contains exhibits on anthropology, botany, entomology, mineralogy, paleontology, and zoology. The museum houses a model of a 92-foot blue whale, and the Fénykövi elephant, the largest land animal ever bagged. The Hall of Gems and Minerals includes the famous 44½-carat Hope Diamond

and the first gold nugget discovered at Sutter's Mill in California in 1848.

History. Congress established the Smithsonian Institution and the United States National Museum in 1846. The museum originally occupied space in the building that housed the institution and its offices. Its collections grew over the years. In 1876, many exhibits of the United States and other countries at the Philadelphia Centennial Exposition were turned over to the museum. Congress then provided a separate building for the museum. Now called the Arts and Industries Building, it was completed in 1881. The white granite Natural History Building was completed in 1909. In 1964, the Museum of History and Technology was built to house the collections that formerly were in the Arts and Industries Building.

Critically reviewed by SMITHSONIAN INSTITUTION

The United States National Museum exhibits animals, such as bighorn sheep, just as they would appear in real life.

Smithsonian Institution

UNITED STATES NAVAL ACADEMY

Caps in the Air, naval academy graduates celebrate the end of four years of training. They will go on to serve in the navy or marines. The academy coat of arms is shown *above*.

Precision Drill gives midshipmen a chance to display their ability at marching in complicated formations. The academy band takes part in the elaborate performances.

U.S. Navy

UNITED STATES NAVAL ACADEMY at Annapolis, Md., is a government-operated military college that educates and trains young men to become officers in the United States Navy and Marine Corps. The academy and adjacent naval activities occupy about 1,100 acres on the banks of the Severn River. George Bancroft, Secretary of the Navy under President James K. Polk, founded the academy in 1845.

Students at the Naval Academy are called *midshipmen*. Their training takes four years. Those who complete the work are awarded a bachelor of science degree, and are commissioned as ensigns in the navy or as second lieutenants in the marine corps.

Entrance Requirements. Candidates for the school must be unmarried citizens of the United States, between 17 and 22 years of age on July 1 of the year of admission, and of good moral character. Candidates are appointed after being nominated by a United States Senator or Representative. Others may be appointed by the President, the Vice-President, and the Secretary of the Navy. Some appointments are approved from the ranks of the navy and naval reserve, from the country at large, and from the District of Columbia.

Candidates for appointment as midshipmen must meet high physical and moral requirements. A candidate is required to have completed a four-year high-school course. He must graduate in the upper 40 per cent of his class. The Secretary of the Navy is authorized to appoint additional midshipmen from among the excess qualified candidates to bring the total enrollment of each class up to its authorized strength of 4,417 midshipmen.

Upon admission to the Naval Academy, all candidates are required to make an entrance deposit of $300 as part payment to cover the cost of uniforms and other clothing, textbooks, and incidental needs. Immediately after admission, each new midshipman is credited with an additional sum of $600 for similar expenses, which is charged against his pay. Every man is allowed a specific sum per mile for traveling expenses from his home to the Naval Academy, which is also credited to his account. Midshipmen are paid $120.60 a month to meet

their essential expenses, plus a food allowance of $1.22 per day.

Information about entering Annapolis is contained in a pamphlet, "Regulations Governing the Admission of Candidates into the United States Naval Academy as Midshipmen." It can be obtained by writing the Office of the Superintendent, United States Naval Academy, Annapolis, Md., or the Bureau of Naval Personnel, Arlington Annex, Arlington, Va.

The Life of a Midshipman. From the time a candidate is accepted, his personal life as well as his school life is under academy control. He spends his last three summer terms at sea or in other practical instruction. During a normal day, the midshipman attends three military formations, recites seven times, and drills or has practical or laboratory work once. He is inspected often, both for personal appearance and for the cleanliness of his quarters. If a midshipman fails to carry out the requirements listed in the *Naval Academy Regulations*, he is reported. As punishment, he is assigned extra duty, which may be several hours of infantry drill during what would normally be a recreation period.

Midshipmen are required to engage in athletics, such as football, baseball, lacrosse, basketball, track, and rowing. Every man must become a qualified swimmer. The best athletes make up the "A" squads from which the members of the varsity teams are chosen. Less experienced men form "B" squads. Academy colors are blue and gold. Navy rowing crews have been famous for years. The "Army-Navy" football game between the U.S. Military Academy at West Point and the U.S. Naval Academy is one of the biggest sports events of the year. The Naval Academy's official mascot, a goat, often accompanies the football team.

Graduates receive their diplomas and commissions at Annapolis in June Week. The President of the United States or another high government official hands out the diplomas. The graduates celebrate their graduation by tossing their midshipmen caps high in the air. One of the academy songs, "Anchors Aweigh," was composed for the June Week of 1907.

The School Program. The Naval Academy offers a four-year course of undergraduate study, with fields of concentration in naval science, mathematics, marine engineering, aeronautical engineering, physics, engineering, social science, foreign languages, and literature. About one-half of the instruction is devoted to engineering and physical sciences. The rest is divided between the social sciences and naval science.

History. Before the United States Naval Academy was established in 1845, midshipmen were trained at sea. Because Annapolis was too close to the battle lines, the academy was moved to Newport, R.I., during the Civil War. Many Southern midshipmen resigned. When the academy came back to Annapolis in 1865, athletics and more recreation were added to the program. The Spanish-American War first brought out the real importance of the school to the navy. Afterward, the course of studies was greatly expanded. New buildings were begun in 1899. Fort Severn, the site of the original naval school; the old chapel; and most other landmarks were torn down. Critically reviewed by the U.S. NAVAL ACADEMY

SELECTION OF CANDIDATES

Candidates for the United States Naval Academy are appointed as follows. These figures reflect the Academy strength of 4,417 midshipmen as authorized by the United States Congress in 1964. The figures represent the total number of candidates each nominating source may select for the Academy.

- **300** by the President of the United States
- **5** by the Vice-President of the United States
- **500** by United States Senators
- **2,175** by United States Congressmen
- **600** from qualified alternates selected by Senators and Congressmen
- **40** sons of deceased veterans
- **5** from the District of Columbia
- **1** from Guam, Samoa, and the Virgin Islands
- **6** from Puerto Rico
- **1** from the Canal Zone
- **340** from the regular United States armed forces
- **340** from the reserve United States armed forces
- **80** from honor military schools
- **24** cadets from other countries

An unlimited number of qualified sons of Medal of Honor winners may also attend.

UNITED STATES NAVAL OBSERVATORY. See NAVAL OBSERVATORY, UNITED STATES.

UNITED STATES NAVAL POSTGRADUATE SCHOOL, at Monterey, Calif., offers graduate courses for naval officers in engineering and science. The school was established by the navy in 1909. For enrollment, see UNIVERSITIES AND COLLEGES (table).

UNITED STATES NAVY. See NAVY, UNITED STATES.

UNITED STATES NOTE. See MONEY (U.S. Money Today).

UNITED STATES OFFICE OF EDUCATION. See EDUCATION, OFFICE OF.

UNITED STATES POST OFFICE. See POST OFFICE.

UNITED STATES PRESIDENT. See PRESIDENT OF THE UNITED STATES.

UNITED STATES RUBBER COMPANY. See RUBBER (Leading Rubber Manufacturers).

UNITED STATES SEAL. See GREAT SEAL OF THE UNITED STATES.

UNITED STATES SENATE HALL OF FAME. See SENATE (Prestige of the Senate).

UNITED STATES SHIPPING BOARD. See MERCHANT MARINE (The United States Merchant Marine).

UNITED STATES STEEL CORPORATION has almost one third of the steel-producing capacity in the United States. For assets and number of employees, see MANUFACTURING (table). The company was incorporated and began business with an authorized capitalization of $1,400,000,000. It was the first billion-dollar corporation in American history.

The chief organizer of the corporation was Elbert H. ("Judge") Gary, a Chicago lawyer, whose aim was more efficient and economical production of steel in large amounts. J. P. Morgan financed the corporation. It included the following original members: Carnegie Company, Federal Steel Company, American Steel and Wire Company, National Tube Company, National Steel Company, American Tin Plate Company, American Steel Hoop Company, and American Sheet Steel Company. Later, the American Bridge Company and the Lake Superior Consolidated Iron Mines became members. These companies and their subsidiaries brought into the new corporation iron and coal properties, steamship facilities, railroads, and steel-producing and fabricating units.

Over the years, the names of most of these companies have disappeared in the evolution of U.S. Steel's operations and corporate structure. As part of a simplifying program, the corporation, on Jan. 1, 1953, became primarily an operating company. It continues to own capital stock of certain subsidiaries not making steel.

U.S. Steel's annual steel-producing capacity increased from 10,600,000 tons in 1901 to 41,900,000 tons in 1960. But its proportion of total national steel-producing capacity dropped from about 50 per cent to about 25 per cent. Headquarters are in New York City and Pittsburgh.   Critically reviewed by UNITED STATES STEEL CORPORATION

See also CHRISTMAS (color picture, Two Aspects); FAIRLESS, BENJAMIN F.; GARY, ELBERT HENRY; HOOD, CLIFFORD F.

UNITED STATES STEEL FOUNDATION, INC., a nonprofit organization, provides grants to support the activities of charitable, educational, and scientific agencies. It makes financial grants to social welfare organizations and others interested in community and public affairs. The United States Steel Foundation also contributes money for higher education, medicine, health, and hospitals.

The foundation's program of aid to higher education includes research, capital, and operating grants. It also offers additional grants to college and university libraries. The foundation gives study aid through graduate fellowships and financial assistance for the advancement of teaching programs.

The members of the foundation and its governing Board of Trustees are all directors of the United States Steel Corporation (see UNITED STATES STEEL CORPORATION). The corporation established the foundation in 1953 with a grant of $12 million. The corporation usually makes annual financial grants to the foundation. The foundation has headquarters at 71 Broadway, New York, N.Y. 10006. For the foundation's assets, see FOUNDATIONS (table).   W. HOMER TURNER

UNITED STATES SUPREME COURT. See SUPREME COURT OF THE UNITED STATES.

UNITED STATES TARIFF COMMISSION. See TARIFF COMMISSION, UNITED STATES.

UNITED STATES WEATHER BUREAU. See WEATHER BUREAU, UNITED STATES.

UNITED STEELWORKERS OF AMERICA. See STEELWORKERS OF AMERICA, UNITED.

UNITED WORKMEN, ANCIENT ORDER OF. See FRATERNAL SOCIETY (History).

UNITY SCHOOL OF CHRISTIANITY is a religious educational institution which aims to give practical application to the teachings of Jesus Christ in daily living. It emphasizes constructive thinking, affirmative prayer, and spiritual healing. It says that the will of God is to give all men health, peace, happiness, and plenty.

Unity is not a denomination. But Unity teachers have formed independent organizations for study in the United States and other countries. These groups, called centers, societies, and churches, are part of the Unity fellowship. Persons who attend Unity are free to belong to other religious organizations.

Charles and Myrtle Fillmore founded the movement in 1889 in Kansas City, Mo. The book, *The Household of Faith*, tells its story. Unity maintains a prayer and healing department called *Silent Unity*. It also publishes books and magazines. Headquarters are at Unity Village, Lee's Summit, Mo.   E. PHARABY BOILEAU

UNIVALVE is the name given to a class of mollusks whose shells are in one piece. The univalves are commonly called *snails*.

See also MOLLUSK; SNAIL.

UNIVERSAL JOINT. See AUTOMOBILE (Major Systems of a Car).

UNIVERSAL LANGUAGE. Language is the main means of communication between peoples. But so many different languages have developed that language has often been a barrier rather than an aid to understanding between peoples. For many years, men have dreamed of setting up an international, universal language which all people could speak and understand.

The arguments in favor of a universal language are simple and obvious. If all peoples spoke the same tongue, cultural and economic ties would be much closer, and good will would increase between countries. But many persons call the promoters of universal languages impractical idealists, and discourage the idea.

In the early 1600's, John Comenius, a Bohemian bishop and educator, originated the idea of a universal language (see COMENIUS, JOHN A.). René Descartes, a French philosopher of the same period, also suggested it. More than 200 languages designed for universal use have been invented since that time.

Volapük was the earliest of these languages to gain much success. The name of the language comes from two of its words meaning *world* and *speak*. Johann Martin Schleyer (1831-1912), a German priest, published the suggested language in 1880. Later, *Idiom Neutral*, a simplified form of Volapük, was suggested. Other proposed international languages include *Spelin*, *Esperanto*, and a revised form of Esperanto called *Ido*. More recently *Interlingua*, *Novial*, and *Interglossa* have received attention.

Some language scholars believe that the world is working by natural processes toward an international tongue. They point out that improved communications are making English almost an international language. To take advantage of this fact, scholars invented *Basic English* (see BASIC ENGLISH).   I. A. RICHARDS

See also ESPERANTO; INTERLINGUA; VOLAPÜK.

UNIVERSAL MILITARY TRAINING. See DRAFT, MILITARY; MILITARY (Selective Service).

UNIVERSAL POSTAL UNION. See POSTAL UNION, UNIVERSAL.

UNIVERSAL SET. See SET THEORY.

UNIVERSALIST CHURCH OF AMERICA is a religious group that believes all mankind will be saved. Universalists believe that truth and righteousness are controlling powers in the universe and that Good must therefore finally triumph over Evil. Their Bond of Fellowship is a common purpose—to do the will of God as Jesus revealed it. They believe in God as Eternal and All-conquering Love, in the spiritual leadership of Jesus, and in the supreme worth of every human being.

Universalism has been taught almost since the founding of the Christian Church. In 1770, John Murray, an English preacher in New Jersey, first established the organized denomination. It was incorporated in 1866. In 1870, the centennial convention adopted its plan of organization. The denomination has local parishes, state conventions, and a General Assembly, the supreme legislative body. In 1953, the Universalists and the Unitarians took a step toward merger by forming The Council of Liberal Churches (Universalist-Unitarian). They completed the merger in May, 1961, and established the Unitarian Universalist Association. Most of the members of the association live in the United States and Canada.   ROBERT CUMMINS

See also UNITARIAN UNIVERSALIST ASSOCIATION.

UNIVERSE. All the works of creation make up the universe. Everything around us is part of the universe, from the chairs in which we are sitting to the most distant stars. Throughout his history, man's ideas about the universe have constantly changed. In ancient times, the known universe was only the small part of the world over which a man had traveled, or which he had heard about. It was also made up of the stars and other heavenly bodies which he could see. Early man thought the stars were the bodies of men and animals which had been placed in the sky. He looked upon the sun and the moon as gods.

Ancient man developed many stories to explain what he knew about the universe. Some ancient people believed that the universe was balanced on the back of a huge tortoise. Most of the ancient peoples thought that the earth was the center of the universe. They believed that the sun and the moon and the stars revolved about the earth. Some persons, but not all, also believed that the earth was flat, and that if one went far enough north, south, east, or west, he would fall off the edge.

Exploring the Universe. Gradually man learned more about the universe. The exploring voyages of the 1400's and the 1500's showed him the general shape of the earth on which he lived. The work of astronomers such as Pythagoras, Copernicus, Galileo, Kepler, and Newton taught man that the earth was not the center of the universe. Man learned that the earth is only one of several planets which revolve around the sun. He learned that the sun itself is a star of only average size and brilliance among a hundred billion stars in the Milky Way galaxy.

Today's astronomers know that the fundamental units of the universe are the stars. The stars cluster together in systems called *galaxies*. We live in a galaxy called the *Milky Way*. But now astronomers know that there are as many galaxies in the universe as there are stars in the Milky Way. All these galaxies together form part of what some astronomers call a *superuniverse*. Its dimensions are almost impossible for the average mind to grasp, as it measures thousands of millions of light years. A light year is the distance that light travels in a year. See ASTRONOMY (Measuring Distances in Space).

A 100-inch telescope on Mount Wilson can "see" as far as 500 million light years into space by means of long-exposure photographs. The 200-inch Hale telescope at the Palomar Observatory can see up to six billion light years in space. Radio telescopes also can penetrate as far as six billion light years. See TELESCOPE; RADIO TELESCOPE.

Size of the Universe. Nobody knows just how large our universe is. Einstein's theory of relativity implies that the superuniverse has a definite size. We cannot see its limits because space itself is curved and, like the surface of the earth, has no definite boundaries. Consequently a light ray from a star does not go out into space and get lost. Instead, it eventually returns to its starting point, like a traveler who journeys around the world.

Einstein also said that our universe is getting bigger all the time. The distant galaxies seem to be moving rapidly away from the sun, the farthest ones fastest, so that it seems just as if the universe were expanding. The speed at which they are traveling indicates to many scientists that some kind of explosion occurred in the universe perhaps 10 or 20 billion years ago.

Some scientists, however, do not believe in the idea of an expanding universe. They look for some law of nature, at present unknown, which will explain the way in which the galaxies seem to be moving away from the sun.   CHARLES ANTHONY FEDERER, JR.

Related Articles in WORLD BOOK include:

Astronomy	Relativity
Cosmos	Solar System
Earth	World
Galaxy	

Michigan State University

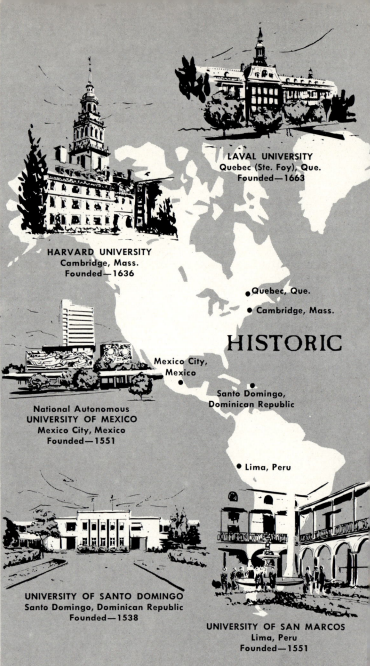

LAVAL UNIVERSITY
Quebec (Ste. Foy), Que.
Founded—1663

HARVARD UNIVERSITY
Cambridge, Mass.
Founded—1636

• Quebec, Que.

• Cambridge, Mass.

HISTORIC

Mexico City,
Mexico

Santo Domingo,
Dominican Republic

National Autonomous
UNIVERSITY OF MEXICO
Mexico City, Mexico
Founded—1551

• Lima, Peru

UNIVERSITY OF SANTO DOMINGO
Santo Domingo, Dominican Republic
Founded—1538

UNIVERSITY OF SAN MARCOS
Lima, Peru
Founded—1551

UNIVERSITIES
and
COLLEGES

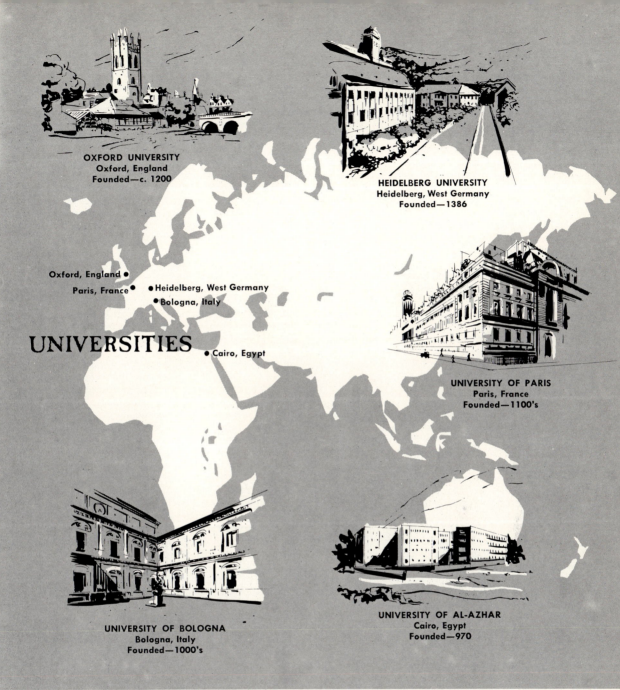

UNIVERSITIES

OXFORD UNIVERSITY
Oxford, England
Founded—c. 1200

HEIDELBERG UNIVERSITY
Heidelberg, West Germany
Founded—1386

UNIVERSITY OF PARIS
Paris, France
Founded—1100's

UNIVERSITY OF BOLOGNA
Bologna, Italy
Founded—1000's

UNIVERSITY OF AL-AZHAR
Cairo, Egypt
Founded—970

Oxford, England ●
Paris, France ● ● Heidelberg, West Germany
● Bologna, Italy

● Cairo, Egypt

UNIVERSITIES AND COLLEGES help young men and women enjoy richer, more meaningful lives. A university or college education enables many persons to earn better salaries, and to participate with greater understanding in the affairs of their communities. A college degree opens the door to many careers. For example, a would-be doctor, lawyer, or teacher must usually receive his training at a university or college. A university or college education also gives a person a better and more complete understanding of such fields of interest as art, literature, and science.

Modern universities developed from European universities of the Middle Ages. These institutions took the name from the Latin word *universitas*. This word referred to the universities' concern with universal, or general, knowledge. Properly speaking, a school that is called a *university* should deal with nearly all fields of learning. But universities today may differ in the variety of their educational programs, and in their specialized fields of study. All universities provide a wide range of graduate programs, and a number of undergraduate schools. They may also have graduate

155

professional schools or colleges. Some universities are known for their work in undergraduate, graduate, and professional schools. Some are noted for certain areas of study. But few universities teach as many branches of learning as the word *university* implies.

The first European colleges were merely groups of students who banded together through common interests. In English universities, colleges were formed to provide living quarters and a dining room for various groups of students. Usually these students took similar studies, and so the word *college* came to refer to a specific field of learning.

Harvard College, the oldest college (and university) in the United States, at first prepared men only for the ministry. Today, we would call it a *college of theology*, or a *seminary* (see SEMINARY). Later, schools broadened their courses to teach the liberal arts (see LIBERAL ARTS). These became known as *colleges of liberal arts*. The first universities in the United States divided their courses into various fields of learning, and called the departments that taught each branch *colleges* or *schools*. In this way, the word *college* has come to have two different meanings in the United States. It may refer to a part of a university that teaches a special branch of knowledge, or to a separate institution which specializes in a single branch of knowledge.

The type of learning available at individual colleges can often be determined from their names. Liberal-arts colleges usually call themselves simply *colleges*. Other schools may be identified by such names as *teachers colleges*, *agricultural colleges*, or *dental colleges*. Modern universities have many kinds of colleges or schools, from liberal arts to law, medicine, theology, dentistry, and fine arts. *Junior colleges* offer only two years of study in liberal arts or semiprofessional or vocational courses.

Going to College

The average high-school student at some time in his studies faces two questions: "Should I attend college?" and "What college will serve my purposes best?" These questions require serious study. The student should take stock of his personal abilities and desires. He must decide whether or not he will receive specific preparation in college that will help him in his lifework. For example, he may find that special vocational training, rather than a college education, will better prepare him for his chosen career (see VOCATIONAL EDUCATION).

Selecting a School. The person who decides he should attend college must choose the school that most nearly fits his needs, his pocketbook, and his personal likes. He can discover many of the facts by talking to his friends and his teachers. He can learn about particular schools by writing to them for information.

There are a number of basic questions a student should ask about any school he is considering.

1. Does the school offer the courses in which I am interested?

2. How well is the school equipped in general buildings, libraries, laboratories, and other property?

3. What teaching methods does the school use? What is the average size of each class?

4. What is the standing of the school? Is it accredited? What is the standing of the particular college

or department of the school in which I intend to do most of my work?

5. How is the school supported or controlled?

6. What are the school's tuition, fees, and living expenses? Does either the school or its community offer opportunities for earning all, or part of, my expenses while I attend school?

7. Does the school offer the *extracurricular*, or nonacademic, activities in which I am interested?

8. How is the school located with regard to transportation, living quarters, and general conveniences?

Entrance Requirements of the various universities and colleges may differ considerably. In general, they require satisfactory completion of a high-school course. Most require that freshmen have taken certain courses in high schools. Many schools will not admit students whose high-school grades are below a certain average. As more and more students attend universities or colleges, entrance requirements tend to become higher.

Many institutions require students to pass an entrance examination. Schools may also give intelligence and aptitude tests for later counseling. For example, a student's adviser may use the test results to help him in his work. See COLLEGE ENTRANCE EXAMINATION.

Colleges and universities state their entrance requirements in their catalogs. They nearly always require a *transcript*, or copy, of an applicant's high-school credits, as well as letters of recommendation. Entrance examinations are generally given several months before the school term begins. Freshmen usually take the intelligence and aptitude tests during an orientation period, frequently called *Freshmen Week* in the United States.

Accrediting. A prospective college student should know the standing of the school he intends to enter. Schools in the United States are accredited by six regional accrediting authorities. These authorities base their judgment on the equipment, financial status, requirements, and teaching standards of the schools.

Professional societies accredit the various professional schools. For example, the American Medical Association accredits medical schools. State boards of education also accredit schools in their states. Credits from approved schools may be used to obtain teaching certificates and professional licenses within the state.

The table with this article includes all universities and colleges fully accredited by one or more of the national and regional accrediting agencies. This list was compiled from the *Education Directory* published by the U.S. Department of Health, Education, and Welfare.

For a complete list of degree-granting universities and colleges in Canada, and a discussion of higher education in Canada, see CANADA (Education).

Size. Universities and colleges in the United States range in enrollment from fewer than a hundred students to more than 100,000. In order of enrollment of all campuses, the ten largest are: University of California; City University of New York; State University of New York; University of Minnesota; University of Wisconsin; University of Illinois; Michigan State University; Indiana University; Ohio State University; and University of Maryland. Canada's largest university, the University of Montreal, has an enrollment of over 25,000.

College Costs vary widely. A year at college, including tuition, books, and living expenses, may cost as

(text continued on page 162n)

Name	Location	Founded	Control	Student Body	Enroll-ment
Abilene Christian College	Abilene, Tex.	1906	Private	Coed.	3,073
Academy of the New Church	Bryn Athyn, Pa.	1876	General Church of the New Jerusalem	Coed.	103
Adams State College	Alamosa, Colo.	1921	State	Coed.	2,242
Adelphi University	Garden City, N.Y.	1896	Private	Coed.	8,322
Adrian College	Adrian, Mich.	1845	Methodist	Coed.	1,403
Agnes Scott College	Decatur, Ga.	1889	Private	Women	744
Agricultural, Mechanical, and Normal College	Pine Bluff, Ark.	1873	State	Coed.	2,957
Air Force Institute of Technology	Wright-Patterson Air Force Base, Ohio	1946	Federal	Men	424
Akron, University of	Akron, Ohio	1870	Municipal	Coed.	12,007
Alabama, University of	Tuscaloosa, Ala.	1831	State	Coed.	17,177
Alabama Agricultural and Mechanical College	Normal, Ala.	1875	State	Coed.	1,646
Alabama College	Montevallo, Ala.	1893	State	Coed.	1,715
Alaska, University of	College, Alaska	1917	State	Coed.	4,140
Alaska Methodist University	Anchorage, Alaska	1957	Methodist	Coed.	458
Albany State College	Albany, Ga.	1903	State	Coed.	1,292
Albertus Magnus College	New Haven, Conn.	1925	Roman Catholic	Women	602
Albion College	Albion, Mich.	1835	Methodist	Coed.	1,557
Albright College	Reading, Pa.	1856	Evangelical United Brethren	Coed.	1,446
Albuquerque, University of	Albuquerque, N.Mex.	1940	Roman Catholic	Coed.	981
Alcorn Agricultural and Mechanical College	Lorman, Miss.	1871	State	Coed.	1,928
Alderson-Broaddus College	Philippi, W.Va.	1871	Baptist	Coed.	591
Alfred University	Alfred, N.Y.	1857	State and Private	Coed.	1,631
Allegheny College	Meadville, Pa.	1815	Private	Coed.	1,461
Alliance College	Cambridge Springs, Pa.	1912	Private	Men; Women	440
Alma College	Alma, Mich.	1886	Presbyterian	Coed.	1,002
Alverno College	Milwaukee, Wis.	1887	Roman Catholic	Women	1,470
American International College	Springfield, Mass.	1885	Private	Coed.	3,402
American University, The	Washington, D.C.	1893	Methodist	Coed.	13,078
Amherst College	Amherst, Mass.	1821	Private	Men	1,206
Anderson College	Anderson, Ind.	1917	Church of God	Coed.	1,394
Andrews University	Berrien Springs, Mich.	1874	Adventist	Coed.	1,947
Anna Maria College for Women	Paxton, Mass.	1946	Roman Catholic	Women	519
Annhurst College	South Woodstock, Conn.	1941	Roman Catholic	Women	330
Antioch College	Yellow Springs, Ohio	1852	Private	Coed.	1,679
Appalachian State Teachers College	Boone, N.C.	1903	State	Coed.	4,653
Aquinas College	Grand Rapids, Mich.	1923	Roman Catholic	Coed.	1,357
Aquinas Institute of Philos-ophy and Theology	River Forest, Ill.	1939	Roman Catholic	Men	139
Arizona, University of	Tucson, Ariz.	1885	State	Coed.	21,430
Arizona State University	Tempe, Ariz.	1885	State	Coed.	22,224
Arkansas, University of	Fayetteville, Ark.	1871	State	Coed.	11,505
Arkansas Agricultural and Mechanical College	College Heights, Ark.	1909	State	Coed.	1,608
Arkansas College	Batesville, Ark.	1872	Presbyterian	Coed.	336
Arkansas Polytechnic College	Russellville, Ark.	1909	State	Coed.	2,219
Arkansas State College	State College, Ark.	1909	State	Coed.	5,349
Arkansas State Teachers College	Conway, Ark.	1907	State	Coed.	3,129
Armstrong College	Berkeley, Calif.	1918	Private	Coed.	502
Art Center College of Design	Los Angeles, Calif.	1930	Private	Coed.	1,097
Asbury College	Wilmore, Ky.	1890	Private	Coed.	1,000
Ashland College	Ashland, Ohio	1878	Brethren	Coed.	2,036
Assumption College	Worcester, Mass.	1904	Roman Catholic	Men	1,215
Athenaeum of Ohio, The	Cincinnati, Ohio	1829	Roman Catholic	Men	566
Athens College	Athens, Ala.	1822	Methodist	Coed.	1,343
Atlanta University	Atlanta, Ga.	1865	Private	Coed.	843
Atlantic Christian College	Wilson, N.C.	1902	Disciples of Christ	Coed.	1,447
Atlantic Union College	South Lancaster, Mass.	1882	Adventist	Coed.	798
Auburn University	Auburn, Ala.	1856	State	Coed.	11,875
Augsburg College	Minneapolis, Minn.	1869	Lutheran	Coed.	1,702
Augustana College	Rock Island, Ill.	1860	Lutheran	Coed.	1,875
Augustana College	Sioux Falls, S.Dak.	1860	Lutheran	Coed.	2,000
Aurora College	Aurora, Ill.	1893	Adventist	Coed.	1,554
Austin College	Sherman, Tex.	1849	Presbyterian	Coed.	1,070
Austin Peay State College	Clarksville, Tenn.	1927	State	Coed.	2,471

Enrollment figures based on *Opening Fall Enrollment in Higher Education*, 1965, U.S. Dept. of Health, Education, and Welfare.

Name	Location	Founded	Control	Student Body	Enroll-ment
Avila College	Kansas City, Mo.	1867	Roman Catholic	Women	325
Azusa Pacific College	Azusa, Calif.	1899	Private	Coed.	602
Babson Institute of Business Administration	Wellesley, Mass.	1919	Private	Men	1,010
Baker University	Baldwin City, Kans.	1858	Methodist	Coed.	892
Baldwin-Wallace College	Berea, Ohio	1845	Methodist	Coed.	2,874
Ball State University	Muncie, Ind.	1918	State	Coed.	11,466
Bank Street College of Education	New York, N.Y.	1916	Private	Coed.	694
Barat College of the Sacred Heart	Lake Forest, Ill.	1919	Roman Catholic	Women	485
Barber-Scotia College	Concord, N.C.	1867	Presbyterian	Coed.	363
Bard College	Annandale-on-Hudson, N.Y.	1860	Private	Coed.	601
Barrington College	Barrington, R.I.	1900	Private	Coed.	653
Barry College	Miami, Fla.	1940	Roman Catholic	Women	1,072
Bates College	Lewiston, Me.	1855	Private	Coed.	900
Baylor University	Waco, Tex.	1845	Baptist	Coed.	7,108
Beaver College	Glenside, Pa.	1853	Presbyterian	Women	777
Belhaven College	Jackson, Miss.	1894	Presbyterian	Coed.	596
Bellarmine College	Louisville, Ky.	1950	Roman Catholic	Men	1,754
Belmont Abbey College	Belmont, N.C.	1876	Roman Catholic	Men; Women	705
Belmont College	Nashville, Tenn.	1951	Baptist	Coed.	1,074
Beloit College	Beloit, Wis.	1846	Private	Coed.	1,172
Bemidji State College	Bemidji, Minn.	1919	State	Coed.	3,410
Benedict College	Columbia, S.C.	1870	Baptist	Coed.	1,100
Bennett College	Greensboro, N.C.	1873	Methodist	Women	642
Bennington College	Bennington, Vt.	1932	Private	Women	385
Berea College	Berea, Ky.	1855	Private	Coed.	1,399
Berry College	Mount Berry, Ga.	1902	Private	Coed.	1,100
Bethany Bible College	Santa Cruz, Calif.	1954	Assemblies of God	Coed.	405
Bethany College	Lindsborg, Kans.	1881	Lutheran	Coed.	478
Bethany College	Bethany, W.Va.	1840	Private	Coed.	1,007
Bethany-Nazarene College	Bethany, Okla.	1920	Nazarene	Coed.	1,678
Bethel College	North Newton, Kans.	1887	Mennonite	Coed.	588
Bethel College	McKenzie, Tenn.	1842	Presbyterian	Coed.	789
Bethel College and Seminary	St. Paul, Minn.	1871	Baptist	Coed.	1,104
Bethune-Cookman College	Daytona Beach, Fla.	1904	Private	Coed.	943
Biola College	La Mirada, Calif.	1906	Private	Coed.	1,102
Birmingham-Southern College	Birmingham, Ala.	1856	Methodist	Coed.	949
Bishop College	Dallas, Tex.	1881	Baptist	Coed.	1,348
Black Hills State College	Spearfish, S.Dak.	1883	State	Coed.	2,507
Blackburn College	Carlinville, Ill.	1857	Private	Coed.	485
Bloomfield College	Bloomfield, N.J.	1868	Presbyterian	Coed.	1,224
Bloomsburg State College	Bloomsburg, Pa.	1839	State	Coed.	3,089
Blue Mountain College	Blue Mountain, Miss.	1873	Baptist	Women	355
Bluefield State College	Bluefield, W.Va.	1895	State	Coed.	1,352
Bluffton College	Bluffton, Ohio	1900	Mennonite	Coed.	680
Borromeo Seminary of Ohio	Wickliffe, Ohio	1953	Roman Catholic	Men	194
Boston College	Newton, Mass.	1863	Roman Catholic	Coed.	9,526
Boston University	Boston, Mass.	1839	Private	Coed.	22,382
Bowdoin College	Brunswick, Me.	1794	Private	Men	891
Bowie State College	Bowie, Md.	1867	State	Coed.	626
Bowling Green State University	Bowling Green, Ohio	1910	State	Coed.	11,293
Bradley University	Peoria, Ill.	1897	Private	Coed.	5,941
Brandeis University	Waltham, Mass.	1948	Private	Coed.	2,090
Brenau College	Gainesville, Ga.	1878	Private	Women	628
Brescia College	Owensboro, Ky.	1925	Roman Catholic	Coed.	1,054
Brevard Engineering College	Melbourne, Fla.	1958	Private	Coed.	1,147
Briar Cliff College	Sioux City, Iowa	1930	Roman Catholic	Women	733
Bridgeport, University of	Bridgeport, Conn.	1927	Private	Coed.	7,938
Bridgewater College	Bridgewater, Va.	1880	Brethren	Coed.	779
Brigham Young University	Provo, Utah	1875	Latter-day Saints	Coed.	19,979
Brooklyn, Polytechnic Institute of	Brooklyn, N.Y.	1854	Private	Men	5,622
Brooks Institute of Photography	Santa Barbara, Calif.	1945	Private	Coed.	277
Brown University	Providence, R.I.	1764	Private	Coordinate	4,808
Bryant College	Providence, R.I.	1916	Private	Coed.	2,749
Bryn Mawr College	Bryn Mawr, Pa.	1880	Private	Women	1,097
Bucknell University	Lewisburg, Pa.	1846	Private	Coed.	2,658
Buena Vista College	Storm Lake, Iowa	1891	Presbyterian	Coed.	1,010
Butler University	Indianapolis, Ind.	1855	Private	Coed.	4,519
Cabrini College	Radnor, Pa.	1957	Roman Catholic	Women	370
Caldwell College for Women	Caldwell, N.J.	1939	Roman Catholic	Women	850

Name	Location	Founded	Control	Student Body	Enrollment
California, University of					
at:	Berkeley, Calif.	1868	State	Coed.	26,834
	Davis, Calif.	1922	State	Coed.	7,907
	Irvine, Calif.	1965	State	Coed.	1,589
	Los Angeles, Calif.	1919	State	Coed.	25,676
	Riverside, Calif.	1954	State	Coed.	3,544
	San Diego, Calif.	1935	State	Coed.	1,438
	San Francisco, Calif.	1864	State	Coed.	3,282
	Santa Barbara, Calif.	1927	State	Coed.	9,570
	Santa Cruz, Calif.	1965	State	Coed.	652
California College of Medicine	Los Angeles, Calif.	1896	State	Coed.	352
San Francisco Art Institute	San Francisco, Calif.	1871	State	Coed.	434
General Extension Division					38,621
California Baptist College	Riverside, Calif.	1950	Baptist	Coed.	593
California College of Arts and Crafts	Oakland, Calif.	1907	Private	Coed.	972
California Institute of Technology	Pasadena, Calif.	1891	Private	Men	1,430
California Institute of the Arts	Los Angeles, Calif.	1957	Private	Coed.	801
California Lutheran College	Thousand Oaks, Calif.	1959	Lutheran	Coed.	863
California Podiatry College	San Francisco, Calif.	1914	Private	Coed.	133
California State College	California, Pa.	1852	State	Coed.	4,433
California State College at Fullerton	Fullerton, Calif.	1959	State	Coed.	6,695
California State College at Hayward	Hayward, Calif.	1957	State	Coed.	4,850
California State College at Long Beach	Long Beach, Calif.	1949	State	Coed.	19,363
California State College at Los Angeles	Los Angeles, Calif.	1947	State	Coed.	21,294
California State College at Palos Verdes	Rolling Hills Estates, Calif.	1965	State	Coed.	53
California State College at San Bernardino	San Bernardino, Calif.	1965	State	Coed.	293
California State Polytechnic College					
at:	Pomona, Calif.	1956	State	Coed.	4,367
	San Luis Obispo, Calif.	1940	State	Coed.	6,825
California Western University	San Diego, Calif.	1924	Methodist	Coed.	1,849
Calvin College	Grand Rapids, Mich.	1876	Reformed Bodies	Coed.	2,942
Campbellsville College	Campbellsville, Ky.	1906	Baptist	Coed.	972
Canisius College	Buffalo, N.Y.	1870	Roman Catholic	Coed.	2,937
Capital University	Columbus, Ohio	1830	Lutheran	Coed.	1,755
Cardinal Glennon College	St. Louis, Mo.	1818	Roman Catholic	Men	241
Cardinal Stritch College	Milwaukee, Wis.	1937	Roman Catholic	Women	528
Carleton College	Northfield, Minn.	1866	Private	Coed.	1,351
Carnegie Institute of Technology	Pittsburgh, Pa.	1900	Private	Coed.	5,162
Carroll College	Helena, Mont.	1909	Roman Catholic	Coed.	906
Carroll College	Waukesha, Wis.	1840	Presbyterian	Coed.	1,041
Carson-Newman College	Jefferson City, Tenn.	1851	Baptist	Coed.	1,699
Carthage College	Kenosha, Wis.	1847	Lutheran	Coed.	1,910
Cascade College	Portland, Ore.	1918	Private	Coed.	335
Case Institute of Technology	Cleveland, Ohio	1880	Private	Coed.	2,615
Castleton State College	Castleton, Vt.	1867	State	Coed.	747
Catawba College	Salisbury, N.C.	1851	United Church of Christ	Coed.	897
Catherine Spalding College	Louisville, Ky.	1920	Roman Catholic	Women	1,594
Catholic University of America	Washington, D.C.	1887	Roman Catholic	Men; Women	6,193
Cedar Crest College	Allentown, Pa.	1867	United Church of Christ	Women	598
Centenary College	Shreveport, La.	1825	Methodist	Coed.	1,490
Central College	Pella, Iowa	1853	Reformed Bodies	Coed.	865
Central Connecticut State College	New Britain, Conn.	1849	State	Coed.	7,046
Central Methodist College	Fayette, Mo.	1854	Methodist	Coed.	935
Central Michigan University	Mount Pleasant, Mich.	1892	State	Coed.	9,781
Central Missouri State College	Warrensburg, Mo.	1870	State	Coed.	9,825
Central State College	Wilberforce, Ohio	1887	State	Coed.	2,255
Central State College	Edmond, Okla.	1890	State	Coed.	8,066
Central Washington State College	Ellensburg, Wash.	1890	State	Coed.	5,567
Centre College of Kentucky	Danville, Ky.	1819	Private	Coed.	662
Chadron State College	Chadron, Nebr.	1911	State	Coed.	1,835
Chaminade College of Honolulu	Honolulu, Hawaii	1955	Roman Catholic	Coed.	549
Chapman College	Orange, Calif.	1861	Disciples of Christ	Coed.	2,057

Name	Location	Founded	Control	Student Body	Enrollment
Charleston, College of	Charleston, S.C.	1770	Private	Coed.	387
Chatham College	Pittsburgh, Pa.	1869	Private	Women	655
Chattanooga, University of	Chattanooga, Tenn.	1886	Private	Coed.	3,059
Chestnut Hill College	Philadelphia, Pa.	1871	Roman Catholic	Women	1,046
Cheyney State College	Cheyney, Pa.	1837	State	Coed.	1,528
Chicago, School of the Art Institute of	Chicago, Ill.	1866	Private	Coed.	1,992
Chicago, University of	Chicago, Ill.	1890	Private	Coed.	9,981
Chico State College	Chico, Calif.	1887	State	Coed.	6,318
Christian Brothers College	Memphis, Tenn.	1854	Roman Catholic	Men	950
Church College of Hawaii	Laie, Oahu, Hawaii	1955	Latter-day Saints	Coed.	985
Cincinnati, University of	Cincinnati, Ohio	1819	Municipal	Coed.	24,512
Citadel, The	Charleston, S.C.	1842	State	Men	2,033
Claflin College	Orangeburg, S.C.	1869	Methodist	Coed.	711
Claremont Graduate School and University Center	Claremont, Calif.	1925	Private	Coed.	1,044
Claremont Men's College	Claremont, Calif.	1947	Private	Men	449
Clarion State College	Clarion, Pa.	1866	State	Coed.	3,028
Clark College	Atlanta, Ga.	1869	Methodist	Coed.	923
Clark University	Worcester, Mass.	1887	Private	Coed.	2,334
Clarke College	Dubuque, Iowa	1843	Roman Catholic	Women	1,018
Clarkson College of Technology	Potsdam, N.Y.	1896	Private	Coed.	2,067
Clemson University	Clemson, S.C.	1889	State	Coed.	5,022
Cleveland State University	Cleveland, Ohio	1923	State	Coed.	5,754
Coe College	Cedar Rapids, Iowa	1851	Private	Coed.	1,284
Coker College	Hartsville, S.C.	1908	Private	Women	348
Colby College	Waterville, Me.	1813	Private	Men; Women	1,450
Colgate University	Hamilton, N.Y.	1819	Private	Men	1,715
College Misericordia	Dallas, Pa.	1924	Roman Catholic	Women	1,301
Colorado, University of	Boulder, Colo.	1861	State	Coed.	23,869
Colorado, Western State College of	Gunnison, Colo.	1901	State	Coed.	2,695
Colorado College	Colorado Springs, Colo.	1874	Private	Coed.	1,551
Colorado School of Mines	Golden, Colo.	1874	State	Coed.	1,442
Colorado State College	Greeley, Colo.	1889	State	Coed.	6,589
Colorado State University	Fort Collins, Colo.	1870	State	Coed.	11,848
Colorado Woman's College	Denver, Colo.	1888	Baptist	Women	950
Columbia College	Columbia, S.C.	1854	Methodist	Women	857
Columbia Union College	Takoma Park, Md.	1904	Adventist	Coed.	1,018
Columbia University:					
Columbia College	New York City	1758	Private	Men	17,496
Barnard College	New York City	1893	Private	Women	1,661
College of Pharmacy	New York City	1905	Private	Coed.	453
Teachers College	New York City	1901	Private	Coed.	5,514
Concord College	Athens, W.Va.	1872	State	Coed.	2,014
Concordia College	Moorhead, Minn.	1891	Lutheran	Coed.	2,101
Concordia College	St. Paul, Minn.	1893	Lutheran	Coed.	635
Concordia Senior College	Fort Wayne, Ind.	1839	Lutheran	Men	452
Concordia Teachers College	River Forest, Ill.	1864	Lutheran	Coed.	1,271
Concordia Teachers College	Seward, Nebr.	1894	Lutheran	Coed.	1,259
Connecticut, University of	Storrs, Conn.	1881	State	Coed.	15,223
Connecticut College	New London, Conn.	1911	Private	Women	1,543
Converse College	Spartanburg, S.C.	1889	Private	Women	782
Cooper Union	New York City	1859	Private	Coed.	1,314
Coppin State College	Baltimore, Md.	1900	State	Coed.	728
Cornell College	Mount Vernon, Iowa	1853	Private	Coed.	961
Cornell University	Ithaca, N.Y.	1865	State and Private	Coed.	14,387
Cranbrook Academy of Art	Bloomfield Hills, Mich.	1942	Private	Coed.	125
Creighton University	Omaha, Nebr.	1878	Roman Catholic	Coed.	3,891
Culver-Stockton College	Canton, Mo.	1853	Disciples of Christ	Coed.	793
Cumberland College	Williamsburg, Ky.	1961	Baptist	Coed.	1,312
Dakota Wesleyan University	Mitchell, S.Dak.	1885	Methodist	Coed.	729
Dallas, University of	Irving, Tex.	1956	Roman Catholic	Coed.	840
Dana College	Blair, Nebr.	1884	Lutheran	Coed.	818
Danbury State College	Danbury, Conn.	1904	State	Coed.	2,195
Dartmouth College	Hanover, N.H.	1769	Private	Men	3,688
David Lipscomb College	Nashville, Tenn.	1891	Church of Christ	Coed.	1,827
Davidson College	Davidson, N.C.	1836	Presbyterian	Men	1,001
Davis and Elkins College	Elkins, W.Va.	1904	Presbyterian	Coed.	689
Dayton, University of	Dayton, Ohio	1850	Roman Catholic	Coed.	9,620
Defiance College	Defiance, Ohio	1850	Private	Coed.	1,024
Delaware, University of	Newark, Del.	1833	State	Coed.	10,031
Delaware State College	Dover, Del.	1891	State	Coed.	814

Name	Location	Founded	Control	Student Body	Enrollment
Delaware Valley College of Science and Agriculture	Doylestown, Pa.	1896	Private	Men	905
Delta State College	Cleveland, Miss.	1924	State	Coed.	1,765
Denison University	Granville, Ohio	1831	Private	Coed.	1,702
Denver, University of	Denver, Colo.	1864	Methodist	Coed.	7,874
DePaul University	Chicago, Ill.	1898	Roman Catholic	Coed.	9,758
DePauw University	Greencastle, Ind.	1837	Private	Coed.	2,426
Detroit, University of	Detroit, Mich.	1877	Roman Catholic	Coed.	9,182
Detroit Institute of Technology	Detroit, Mich.	1891	Private	Men; Women	2,507
Dickinson College	Carlisle, Pa.	1773	Private	Coed.	1,408
Dickinson State College	Dickinson, N.Dak.	1917	State	Coed.	1,333
Dillard University	New Orleans, La.	1869	Private	Coed.	864
District of Columbia Teachers College	Washington, D.C.	1955	Municipal	Coed.	1,444
Doane College	Crete, Nebr.	1858	United Church of Christ	Coed.	542
Dominican College	Racine, Wis.	1863	Roman Catholic	Coed.	634
Dominican College of San Rafael	San Rafael, Calif.	1850	Roman Catholic	Women	832
Drake University	Des Moines, Iowa	1881	Private	Coed.	7,918
Drew University	Madison, N.J.	1867	Methodist	Coed.	1,427
Drexel Institute of Technology	Philadelphia, Pa.	1891	Private	Coed.	9,491
Dropsie College for Hebrew and Cognate Learning	Philadelphia, Pa.	1907	Jewish Congregations	Coed.	160
Drury College	Springfield, Mo.	1873	Private	Coed.	1,358
Dubuque, University of	Dubuque, Iowa	1852	Presbyterian	Coed.	985
Duchesne College of the Sacred Heart	Omaha, Nebr.	1881	Roman Catholic	Women	407
Duke University	Durham, N.C.	1838	Private	Coordinate	6,952
Dunbarton College of Holy Cross	Washington, D.C.	1935	Roman Catholic	Women	544
Duquesne University	Pittsburgh, Pa.	1878	Roman Catholic	Coed.	7,114
D'Youville College	Buffalo, N.Y.	1908	Roman Catholic	Women	975
Earlham College	Richmond, Ind.	1847	Society of Friends	Coed.	1,147
East Carolina College	Greenville, N.C.	1907	State	Coed.	9,172
East Central State College	Ada, Okla.	1907	State	Coed.	2,736
East Stroudsburg State College	East Stroudsburg, Pa.	1893	State	Coed.	2,148
East Tennessee State University	Johnson City, Tenn.	1909	State	Coed.	8,205
East Texas Baptist College	Marshall, Tex.	1912	Baptist	Coed.	666
East Texas State University	Commerce, Tex.	1889	State	Coed.	7,257
Eastern Baptist College	St. Davids, Pa.	1932	Baptist	Coed.	513
Eastern Baptist Theological Seminary	Philadelphia, Pa.	1925	Baptist	Coed.	176
Eastern Illinois University	Charleston, Ill.	1895	State	Coed.	5,569
Eastern Kentucky State College	Richmond, Ky.	1906	State	Coed.	6,949
Eastern Mennonite College	Harrisonburg, Va.	1917	Mennonite	Coed.	708
Eastern Michigan University	Ypsilanti, Mich.	1849	State	Coed.	12,442
Eastern Montana College	Billings, Mont.	1925	State	Coed.	2,644
Eastern Nazarene College	Quincy, Mass.	1900	Nazarene	Coed.	845
Eastern New Mexico University	Portales, N.Mex.	1934	State	Coed.	4,902
Eastern Oregon College	La Grande, Ore.	1929	State	Coed.	1,358
Eastern Washington State College	Cheney, Wash.	1890	State	Coed.	4,323
Edgewood College of the Sacred Heart	Madison, Wis.	1927	Roman Catholic	Women	657
Edinboro State College	Edinboro, Pa.	1857	State	Coed.	3,482
Elizabeth City State College	Elizabeth City, N.C.	1891	State	Coed.	1,013
Elizabethtown College	Elizabethtown, Pa.	1899	Brethren	Coed.	1,800
Elmhurst College	Elmhurst, Ill.	1865	United Church of Christ	Coed.	2,559
Elmira College	Elmira, N.Y.	1855	Private	Women	2,138
Elon College	Elon College, N.C.	1889	Private	Coed.	1,344
Emerson College	Boston, Mass.	1880	Private	Coed.	1,034
Emmanuel College	Boston, Mass.	1919	Roman Catholic	Women	1,329
Emory and Henry College	Emory, Va.	1836	Methodist	Coed.	859
Emory University	Atlanta, Ga.	1836	Methodist	Coed.	5,149
Emporia, College of	Emporia, Kans.	1882	Presbyterian	Coed.	806
Erskine College	Due West, S.C.	1839	Presbyterian	Coed.	773
Eureka College	Eureka, Ill.	1855	Disciples of Christ	Coed.	445
Evangel College	Springfield, Mo.	1955	Assemblies of God	Coed.	753
Evansville College	Evansville, Ind.	1854	Private	Coed.	4,812
Fairfield University	Fairfield, Conn.	1942	Roman Catholic	Men	2,294
Fairleigh Dickinson University	Rutherford, N.J.	1941	Private	Coed.	18,968
Fairmont State College	Fairmont, W.Va.	1867	State	Coed.	2,222

Name	Location	Founded	Control	Student Body	Enrollment
Farmington State College	Farmington, Me.	1864	State	Coed.	615
Fayetteville State College	Fayetteville, N.C.	1877	State	Coed.	1,196
Ferris State College	Big Rapids, Mich.	1884	State	Coed.	6,072
Finch College	New York City	1900	Private	Women	300
Findlay College	Findlay, Ohio	1882	Church of God	Coed.	1,229
Fisk University	Nashville, Tenn.	1865	Private	Coed.	1,027
Florence State College	Florence, Ala.	1830	State	Coed.	2,498
Florida, University of	Gainesville, Fla.	1853	State	Coed.	17,274
Florida Agricultural and Mechanical University	Tallahassee, Fla.	1887	State	Coed.	3,807
Florida Memorial College	St. Augustine, Fla.	1892	Private	Coed.	427
Florida Southern College	Lakeland, Fla.	1885	Methodist	Coed.	2,157
Florida State University	Tallahassee, Fla.	1857	State	Coed.	13,200
Fontbonne College	St. Louis, Mo.	1917	Roman Catholic	Women	953
Fordham University	New York City	1841	Roman Catholic	Coed.	9,980
Fort Hays Kansas State College	Hays, Kans.	1901	State	Coed.	4,768
Fort Lewis College	Durango, Colo.	1911	State	Coed.	1,360
Fort Valley State College	Fort Valley, Ga.	1895	State	Coed.	1,556
Fort Wright College of the Holy Names	Spokane, Wash.	1907	Roman Catholic	Women	493
Francis T. Nicholls State College	Thibodaux, La.	1956	State	Coed.	2,657
Franklin and Marshall College	Lancaster, Pa.	1787	Private	Men	2,136
Franklin College of Indiana	Franklin, Ind.	1834	Baptist	Coed.	665
Fresno State College	Fresno, Calif.	1911	State	Coed.	11,349
Friends University	Wichita, Kans.	1898	Society of Friends	Coed.	715
Frostburg State College	Frostburg, Md.	1902	State	Coed.	2,024
Furman University	Greenville, S.C.	1826	Baptist	Coed.	1,617
Gallaudet College	Washington, D.C.	1864	Private	Coed.	600
Gannon College	Erie, Pa.	1944	Roman Catholic	Men	2,670
General Beadle State College	Madison, S.Dak.	1881	State	Coed.	967
General Motors Institute	Flint, Mich.	1919	Private	Men	2,908
Geneva College	Beaver Falls, Pa.	1848	Presbyterian	Coed.	1,730
George Fox College	Newberg, Ore.	1892	Society of Friends	Coed.	351
George Peabody College for Teachers	Nashville, Tenn.	1875	Private	Coed.	2,117
George Washington University	Washington, D.C.	1821	Private	Coed.	15,813
George Williams College	Downers Grove, Ill.	1890	Private	Coed.	583
Georgetown College	Georgetown, Ky.	1787	Baptist	Coed.	1,408
Georgetown University	Washington, D.C.	1789	Roman Catholic	Men; Women	7,676
Georgia, University of	Athens, Ga.	1785	State	Coed.	17,448
Georgia, Woman's College of	Milledgeville, Ga.	1889	State	Women	1,107
Georgia Institute of Technology	Atlanta, Ga.	1885	State	Coed.	8,542
Georgia Southern College	Statesboro, Ga.	1908	State	Coed.	3,634
Georgia State College	Atlanta, Ga.	1914	State	Coed.	7,467
Georgian Court College	Lakewood, N.J.	1908	Roman Catholic	Women	514
Gettysburg College	Gettysburg, Pa.	1832	Lutheran	Coed.	1,873
Glassboro State College	Glassboro, N.J.	1923	State	Coed.	6,221
Glenville State College	Glenville, W.Va.	1872	State	Coed.	1,313
Goddard College	Plainfield, Vt.	1938	Private	Coed.	550
Golden Gate College	San Francisco, Calif.	1901	Private	Coed.	2,341
Gonzaga University	Spokane, Wash.	1887	Roman Catholic	Coed.	2,605
Good Counsel College	White Plains, N.Y.	1923	Roman Catholic	Women	515
Gordon College	Wenham, Mass.	1889	Private	Coed.	828
Gorham State College	Gorham, Me.	1878	State	Coed.	1,358
Goshen College	Goshen, Ind.	1894	Mennonite	Coed.	1,220
Goucher College	Towson, Md.	1885	Private	Women	1,021
Graceland College	Lamoni, Iowa	1895	Latter Day Saints	Coed.	1,055
Graduate Theological Union	Berkeley, Calif.	1962	Private	Coed.	50
Grambling College	Grambling, La.	1901	State	Coed.	3,784
Great Falls, College of	Great Falls, Mont.	1932	Roman Catholic	Coed.	800
Greensboro College	Greensboro, N.C.	1838	Methodist	Coed.	648
Greenville College	Greenville, Ill.	1892	Methodist	Coed.	783
Grinnell College	Grinnell, Iowa	1846	Private	Coed.	1,168
Grove City College	Grove City, Pa.	1876	Private	Coed.	1,885
Guam, College of	Agana, Guam	1952	Territory	Coed.	1,624
Guilford College	Guilford College, N.C.	1834	Society of Friends	Coed.	2,142
Gustavus Adolphus College	St. Peter, Minn.	1862	Lutheran	Coed.	1,581
Gwynedd-Mercy College	Gwynedd Valley, Pa.	1948	Roman Catholic	Women	1,074
Hamilton College	Clinton, N.Y.	1793	Private	Men	831
Hamline University	St. Paul, Minn.	1854	Methodist	Coed.	1,154

Name	Location	Founded	Control	Student Body	Enroll-ment
Hampden-Sydney College	Hampden-Sydney, Va.	1776	Presbyterian	Men	543
Hampton Institute	Hampton, Va.	1868	Private	Coed.	2,055
Hanover College	Hanover, Ind.	1827	Presbyterian	Coed.	1,062
Hardin-Simmons University	Abilene, Tex.	1891	Baptist	Coed.	1,814
Harding College	Searcy, Ark.	1919	Church of Christ	Coed.	1,582
Harris Teachers College	St. Louis, Mo.	1875	Municipal	Coed.	1,233
Hartford, University of	West Hartford, Conn.	1957	Private	Coed.	11,222
Hartwick College	Oneonta, N.Y.	1928	Lutheran	Coed.	1,336
Harvard University	Cambridge, Mass.	1636	Private	Men; Women	13,411
Harvey Mudd College	Claremont, Calif.	1955	Private	Coed.	286
Hastings College	Hastings, Nebr.	1882	Presbyterian	Coed.	805
Haverford College	Haverford, Pa.	1833	Private	Men	524
Hawaii, University of	Honolulu, Hawaii	1907	State	Coed.	17,486
Hebrew Teachers College	Brookline, Mass.	1921	Private	Coed.	165
Hebrew Union College—Jewish Institute of Religion	Cincinnati, Ohio	1875	Jewish Congregations	Men	800
Heidelberg College	Tiffin, Ohio	1850	United Church of Christ	Coed.	1,110
Henderson State Teachers College	Arkadelphia, Ark.	1890	State	Coed.	2,495
Hendrix College	Conway, Ark.	1884	Methodist	Coed.	767
High Point College	High Point, N.C.	1920	Methodist	Coed.	1,562
Hillsdale College	Hillsdale, Mich.	1844	Private	Coed.	1,213
Hiram College	Hiram, Ohio	1850	Private	Coed.	1,015
Hobart and William Smith Colleges	Geneva, N.Y.	1822	Private	Men; Women	1,414
Hofstra University	New York City	1935	Private	Coed.	11,191
Hollins College	Hollins College, Va.	1842	Private	Women	855
Holy Cross, College of the	Worcester, Mass.	1843	Roman Catholic	Men	2,094
Holy Cross College	Washington, D.C.	1895	Roman Catholic	Men	265
Holy Family College	Torresdale, Pa.	1954	Roman Catholic	Women	577
Holy Family College	Manitowoc, Wis.	1935	Roman Catholic	Women	537
Holy Names, College of the	Oakland, Calif.	1880	Roman Catholic	Women	920
Hood College	Frederick, Md.	1893	Private	Women	742
Hope College	Holland, Mich.	1851	Reformed Bodies	Coed.	1,727
Houghton College	Houghton, N.Y.	1883	Wesleyan Methodist	Coed.	1,092
Houston, University of	Houston, Tex.	1927	State	Coed.	19,588
Howard Payne College	Brownwood, Tex.	1889	Baptist	Coed.	1,364
Howard University	Washington, D.C.	1867	Federal; Private	Coed.	8,059
Humboldt State College	Arcata, Calif.	1913	State	Coed.	3,356
Huntingdon College	Montgomery, Ala.	1854	Methodist	Coed.	1,070
Huntington College	Huntington, Ind.	1897	United Brethren	Coed.	513
Huron College	Huron, S.Dak.	1883	Presbyterian	Coed.	759
Huston-Tillotson College	Austin, Tex.	1877	Private	Coed.	658
Idaho, College of	Caldwell, Idaho	1891	Presbyterian	Coed.	999
Idaho, University of	Moscow, Idaho	1889	State	Coed.	5,996
Idaho State University	Pocatello, Idaho	1901	State	Coed.	5,290
Illinois, University of at:	Urbana, Ill.	1867	State	Coed.	27,941
Chicago Circle	Chicago, Ill.	1965	State	Coed.	8,629
Medical Center	Chicago, Ill.	1881	State	Coed.	2,383
Illinois College	Jacksonville, Ill.	1829	Private	Coed.	739
Illinois Institute of Technology	Chicago, Ill.	1892	Private	Coed.	8,133
Illinois State University	Normal, Ill.	1857	State	Coed.	9,266
Illinois Teachers College Chicago—North	Chicago, Ill.	1961	State	Coed.	3,583
Illinois Teachers College Chicago—South	Chicago, Ill.	1867	State	Coed.	4,541
Illinois Wesleyan University	Bloomington, Ill.	1850	Methodist	Coed.	1,468
Immaculata College	Immaculata, Pa.	1920	Roman Catholic	Women	1,689
Immaculate Conception Seminary	Conception, Mo.	1883	Roman Catholic	Men	411
Immaculate Heart College	Los Angeles, Calif.	1916	Roman Catholic	Women	1,304
Incarnate Word College	San Antonio, Tex.	1881	Roman Catholic	Women	1,326
Indiana Central College	Indianapolis, Ind.	1902	Evangelical United Brethren	Coed.	2,255
Indiana Institute of Technology	Fort Wayne, Ind.	1930	Private	Coed.	1,401
Indiana State College	Indiana, Pa.	1871	State	Coed.	6,331
Indiana State College	Terre Haute, Ind.	1865	State	Coed.	9,336
Indiana University	Bloomington, Ind.	1820	State	Coed.	41,583
Inter American University of Puerto Rico	San German, Puerto Rico	1912	Private	Coed.	8,637
Iona College	New Rochelle, N.Y.	1940	Roman Catholic	Men	2,967

Name	Location	Founded	Control	Student Body	Enrollment
Iowa, State College of	Cedar Falls, Iowa	1876	State	Coed.	6,856
Iowa, University of	Iowa City, Iowa	1847	State	Coed.	16,355
Iowa State University of Science and Technology	Ames, Iowa	1858	State	Coed.	14,014
Iowa Wesleyan College	Mount Pleasant, Iowa	1842	Methodist	Coed.	981
Ithaca College	Ithaca, N.Y.	1892	Private	Coed.	3,255
Jackson State College	Jackson, Miss.	1877	State	Coed.	2,224
Jacksonville State College	Jacksonville, Ala.	1883	State	Coed.	4,055
Jacksonville University	Jacksonville, Fla.	1934	Private	Coed.	2,694
Jamestown College	Jamestown, N.Dak.	1884	Presbyterian	Coed.	508
Jersey City State College	Jersey City, N.J.	1921	State	Coed.	5,100
Jewish Theological Seminary of America	New York City	1887	Jewish Congregations	Coed.	511
John Brown University	Siloam Springs, Ark.	1919	Private	Coed.	650
John Carroll University	Cleveland, Ohio	1886	Roman Catholic	Men	4,559
Johns Hopkins University at:	Baltimore, Md.	1876	Private	Men; Women	9,448
School of Advanced International Studies	Washington, D.C.	1944	Private	Men; Women	168
Johnson C. Smith University	Charlotte, N.C.	1867	Presbyterian	Coed.	1,055
Johnson State College	Johnson, Vt.	1828	State	Coed.	472
Judson College	Marion, Ala.	1838	Baptist	Women	336
Juilliard School of Music	New York City	1926	Private	Coed.	1,021
Juniata College	Huntingdon, Pa.	1876	Brethren	Coed.	1,039
Kalamazoo College	Kalamazoo, Mich.	1833	Baptist	Coed.	1,125
Kansas, University of	Lawrence, Kans.	1864	State	Coed.	14,764
Kansas City Art Institute and School of Design	Kansas City, Mo.	1885	Private	Coed.	409
Kansas State College of Pittsburg	Pittsburg, Kans.	1903	State	Coed.	5,593
Kansas State Teachers College	Emporia, Kans.	1863	State	Coed.	7,162
Kansas State University of Agriculture and Applied Science	Manhattan, Kans.	1863	State	Coed.	10,920
Kansas Wesleyan University	Salina, Kans.	1886	Methodist	Coed.	680
Kearney State College	Kearney, Nebr.	1905	State	Coed.	3,905
Keene State College	Keene, N.H.	1909	State	Coed.	1,828
Kent State University	Kent, Ohio	1910	State	Coed.	21,326
Kentucky, University of	Lexington, Ky.	1865	State	Coed.	18,484
Kentucky State College	Frankfort, Ky.	1886	State	Coed.	1,425
Kentucky Wesleyan College	Owensboro, Ky.	1860	Methodist	Coed.	1,148
Kenyon College	Gambier, Ohio	1824	Private	Men	770
Keuka College	Keuka Park, N.Y.	1892	Baptist	Women	721
King College	Bristol, Tenn.	1867	Presbyterian	Coed.	303
King's College	Wilkes-Barre, Pa.	1946	Roman Catholic	Men	1,466
Knox College	Galesburg, Ill.	1837	Private	Coed.	1,242
Knoxville College	Knoxville, Tenn.	1875	United Presbyterian	Coed.	907
Kutztown State College	Kutztown, Pa.	1860	State	Coed.	3,210
Ladycliff College	Highland Falls, N.Y.	1933	Roman Catholic	Women	527
Lafayette College	Easton, Pa.	1826	Presbyterian	Men	1,840
La Grange College	La Grange, Ga.	1831	Methodist	Coed.	552
Lake Erie College	Painesville, Ohio	1856	Private	Women	1,075
Lake Forest College	Lake Forest, Ill.	1857	Presbyterian	Coed.	1,282
Lakeland College	Sheboygan, Wis.	1862	United Church of Christ	Coed.	573
Lamar State College of Technology	Beaumont, Tex.	1923	State	Coed.	9,063
Lambuth College	Jackson, Tenn.	1843	Methodist	Coed.	834
Lander College	Greenwood, S.C.	1872	Private	Coed.	602
Lane College	Jackson, Tenn.	1882	Methodist	Coed.	734
Langston University	Langston, Okla.	1897	State	Coed.	1,255
La Salle College	Philadelphia, Pa.	1863	Roman Catholic	Men	6,026
La Sierra College	Riverside, Calif.	1922	Adventist	Coed.	1,500
La Verne College	La Verne, Calif.	1891	Brethren	Coed.	695
Lawrence University	Appleton, Wis.	1847	Private	Coed.	1,373
Lebanon Valley College	Annville, Pa.	1866	Evangelical United Brethren	Coed.	1,264
Lehigh University	Bethlehem, Pa.	1865	Private	Men	4,540
Le Moyne College	Memphis, Tenn.	1870	American Missionary Association	Coed.	641
LeMoyne College	Syracuse, N.Y.	1946	Roman Catholic	Coed.	1,490
Lenoir Rhyne College	Hickory, N.C.	1891	Lutheran	Coed.	1,261
Lesley College	Cambridge, Mass.	1909	Private	Coed.	647
Lewis and Clark College	Portland, Ore.	1867	Presbyterian	Coed.	1,679

Name	Location	Founded	Control	Student Body	Enrollment
Lewis College	Lockport, Ill.	1950	Roman Catholic	Coed.	989
Limestone College	Gaffney, S.C.	1845	Private	Women	563
Lincoln Memorial University	Harrogate, Tenn.	1897	Private	Coed.	573
Lincoln University	Jefferson City, Mo.	1866	State	Coed.	1,882
Lincoln University	Lincoln University, Pa.	1854	Private	Coed.	656
Lindenwood College for Women	St. Charles, Mo.	1827	Presbyterian	Women	803
Linfield College	McMinnville, Ore.	1849	Baptist	Coed.	1,138
Little Rock University	Little Rock, Ark.	1927	Private	Coed.	2,851
Livingston State College	Livingston, Ala.	1835	State	Coed.	1,163
Livingstone College	Salisbury, N.C.	1879	Methodist	Coed.	777
Lock Haven State College	Lock Haven, Pa.	1870	State	Coed.	1,659
Loma Linda University	Loma Linda, Calif.	1905	Adventist	Coed.	1,109
Long Island University	Greenvale, N.Y.	1926	Private	Coed.	16,196
Longwood College	Farmville, Va.	1884	State	Women	1,461
Loras College	Dubuque, Iowa	1839	Roman Catholic	Men	1,629
Loretto Heights College	Loretto, Colo.	1918	Roman Catholic	Women	937
Los Angeles College of Optometry	Los Angeles, Calif.	1904	Private	Coed.	163
Louisiana College	Pineville, La.	1906	Baptist	Coed.	1,014
Louisiana Polytechnic Institute	Ruston, La.	1894	State	Coed.	6,534
Louisiana State University at:	Baton Rouge, La.	1860	State	Coed.	16,454
	New Orleans, La.	1958	State	Coed.	5,775
Medical Center	New Orleans, La.	1931	State	Coed.	643
Louisville, University of	Louisville, Ky.	1798	Municipal	Coed.	7,973
Lowell Technological Institute	Lowell, Mass.	1895	State	Coed.	4,377
Loyola College	Baltimore, Md.	1852	Roman Catholic	Men; Women	2,839
Loyola University	Chicago, Ill.	1870	Roman Catholic	Coed.	11,908
Loyola University	New Orleans, La.	1904	Roman Catholic	Coed.	3,306
Loyola University of Los Angeles	Los Angeles, Calif.	1911	Roman Catholic	Men	3,073
Luther College	Decorah, Iowa	1861	Lutheran	Coed.	1,718
Lycoming College	Williamsport, Pa.	1812	Methodist	Coed.	1,744
Lynchburg College	Lynchburg, Va.	1903	Disciples of Christ	Coed.	1,264
Lyndon State College	Lyndon Center, Vt.	1944	State	Coed.	386
Macalester College	St. Paul, Minn.	1885	Private	Coed.	1,863
MacMurray College	Jacksonville, Ill.	1846	Methodist	Coordinate	1,121
Madison College	Harrisonburg, Va.	1908	State	Men; Women	2,348
Madonna College	Livonia, Mich.	1947	Roman Catholic	Women	490
Maine, University of	Orono, Me.	1865	State	Coed.	11,755
Malone College	Canton, Ohio	1957	Society of Friends	Coed.	1,115
Manchester College	North Manchester, Ind.	1889	Brethren	Coed.	1,339
Manhattan College	New York City	1853	Roman Catholic	Men	4,838
Manhattan School of Music	New York City	1920	Private	Coed.	654
Manhattanville College of the Sacred Heart	Purchase, N.Y.	1841	Roman Catholic	Women	1,155
Mankato State College	Mankato, Minn.	1867	State	Coed.	10,113
Mansfield State College	Mansfield, Pa.	1854	State	Coed.	1,935
Marian College	Indianapolis, Ind.	1937	Roman Catholic	Coed.	1,066
Marian College of Fond du Lac	Fond du Lac, Wis.	1936	Roman Catholic	Women	405
Marietta College	Marietta, Ohio	1835	Private	Coed.	2,048
Marillac College	Normandy, Mo.	1954	Roman Catholic	Women	419
Marion College	Marion, Ind.	1920	Private	Coed.	574
Marist College	Poughkeepsie, N.Y.	1946	Roman Catholic-Private	Men	1,631
Marlboro College	Marlboro, Vt.	1947	Private	Coed.	140
Marquette University	Milwaukee, Wis.	1864	Roman Catholic	Coed.	11,320
Marshall University	Huntington, W.Va.	1837	State	Coed.	7,033
Mary Baldwin College	Staunton, Va.	1842	Presbyterian	Women	698
Mary Hardin-Baylor College	Belton, Tex.	1845	Baptist	Coed.	1,024
Mary Immaculate Seminary	Northampton, Pa.	1939	Roman Catholic	Men	62
Mary Manse College	Toledo, Ohio	1873	Roman Catholic	Women	1,503
Mary Rogers College	Maryknoll, N.Y.	1931	Roman Catholic	Women	237
Marycrest College	Davenport, Iowa	1954	Roman Catholic	Women	1,009
Marygrove College	Detroit, Mich.	1905	Roman Catholic	Women	1,498
Maryknoll College	Glen Ellyn, Ill.	1949	Roman Catholic	Men	397
Maryknoll Seminary	Maryknoll, N.Y.	1911	Roman Catholic	Men	168
Maryland, University of at:	College Park, Md.	1807	State	Coed.	38,056
Maryland State College	Princess Anne, Md.	1935	State	Coed.	713
Marylhurst College	Marylhurst, Ore.	1930	Roman Catholic	Women	717
Marymount College	Palos Verdes Estates, Calif.	1948	Roman Catholic	Women	369

Name	Location	Founded	Control	Student Body	Enrollment
Marymount College	Salina, Kans.	1922	Roman Catholic	Women	527
Marymount College	Tarrytown, N.Y.	1907	Roman Catholic	Women	960
Marymount Manhattan College	New York City	1936	Roman Catholic	Women	565
Maryville College	Maryville, Tenn.	1819	Presbyterian	Coed.	812
Maryville College of the Sacred Heart	St. Louis, Mo.	1846	Roman Catholic	Women	484
Marywood College	Scranton, Pa.	1915	Roman Catholic	Women	1,679
Massachusetts, University of	Amherst, Mass.	1863	State	Coed.	9,619
Massachusetts College of Art	Boston, Mass.	1873	State	Coed.	499
Massachusetts Institute of Technology	Cambridge, Mass.	1861	Private	Coed.	7,408
Massachusetts State College at:	Boston, Mass.	1852	State	Coed.	5,533
	Bridgewater, Mass.	1840	State	Coed.	4,388
	Fitchburg, Mass.	1894	State	Coed.	2,164
	Framingham, Mass.	1839	State	Women	1,896
	Lowell, Mass.	1894	State	Coed.	1,083
	North Adams, Mass.	1894	State	Coed.	1,017
	Salem, Mass.	1854	State	Coed.	4,507
	Westfield, Mass.	1839	State	Coed.	2,107
	Worcester, Mass.	1871	State	Coed.	2,214
Mayville State College	Mayville, N.Dak.	1889	State	Coed.	850
McMurry College	Abilene, Tex.	1923	Methodist	Coed.	1,692
McNeese State College	Lake Charles, La.	1939	State	Coed.	3,784
McPherson College	McPherson, Kans.	1887	Brethren	Coed.	757
Medical College of Virginia	Richmond, Va.	1838	State	Coed.	1,419
Memphis Academy of Arts	Memphis, Tenn.	1940	Private	Coed.	415
Memphis State University	Memphis, Tenn.	1909	State	Coed.	13,546
Menlo College	Menlo Park, Calif.	1927	Private	Men	519
Mercer University	Macon, Ga.	1833	Baptist	Coed.	1,845
Mercy College of Detroit	Detroit, Mich.	1941	Roman Catholic	Coed.	1,017
Mercyhurst College	Erie, Pa.	1926	Roman Catholic	Women	645
Meredith College	Raleigh, N.C.	1891	Baptist	Women	885
Merrimack College	North Andover, Mass.	1947	Roman Catholic	Coed.	2,207
Messiah College	Grantham, Pa.	1909	Brethren in Christ	Coed.	369
Miami, University of	Coral Gables, Fla.	1925	Private	Coed.	14,001
Miami University	Oxford, Ohio	1809	State	Coed.	16,817
Michigan, University of	Ann Arbor, Mich.	1817	State	Coed.	34,453
Michigan State University	East Lansing, Mich.	1855	State	Coed.	41,782
Michigan Technological University	Houghton, Mich.	1885	State	Coed.	4,757
Middle Tennessee State University	Murfreesboro, Tenn.	1911	State	Coed.	5,507
Middlebury College	Middlebury, Vt.	1800	Private	Coed.	1,414
Midland Lutheran College	Fremont, Nebr.	1887	Lutheran	Coed.	986
Midwestern University	Wichita Falls, Tex.	1922	Municipal	Coed.	3,369
Millersville State College	Millersville, Pa.	1855	State	Coed.	3,315
Milligan College	Milligan College, Tenn.	1867	Private	Coed.	819
Millikin University	Decatur, Ill.	1901	Presbyterian	Coed.	1,847
Mills College	Oakland, Calif.	1852	Private	Women	760
Mills College of Education	New York City	1909	Private	Women	220
Millsaps College	Jackson, Miss.	1892	Methodist	Coed.	873
Minneapolis School of Art	Minneapolis, Minn.	1886	Private	Coed.	339
Minnesota, University of	Minneapolis, Minn.	1851	State	Coed.	58,274
Minot State College	Minot, N.Dak.	1913	State	Coed.	2,709
Mississippi, University of	University, Miss.	1844	State	Coed.	6,656
Mississippi College	Clinton, Miss.	1826	Baptist	Coed.	1,960
Mississippi State College for Women	Columbus, Miss.	1884	State	Women	2,478
Mississippi State University	State College, Miss.	1878	State	Coed.	7,935
Missouri, University of at:	Columbia, Mo.	1839	State	Coed.	17,740
	Kansas City, Mo.	1933	State	Coed.	6,775
	Rolla, Mo.	1870	State	Coed.	4,756
	St. Louis, Mo.	1963	State	Coed.	4,758
Missouri Valley College	Marshall, Mo.	1889	Presbyterian	Coed.	827
Monmouth College	Monmouth, Ill.	1853	Presbyterian	Coed.	1,145
Monmouth College	West Long Branch, N.J.	1933	Private	Coed.	4,247
Montana, University of	Missoula, Mont.	1893	State	Coed.	6,192
Montana College of Mineral Science and Technology	Butte, Mont.	1893	State	Coed.	603
Montana State University	Bozeman, Mont.	1893	State	Coed.	5,933

Name	Location	Founded	Control	Student Body	Enrollment
Montclair State College	Upper Montclair, N.J.	1908	State	Coed.	5,594
Monterey Institute of Foreign Studies, The	Monterey, Calif.	1955	Private	Coed.	152
Moore College of Art	Philadelphia, Pa.	1844	Private	Women	449
Moorhead State College	Moorhead, Minn.	1887	State	Coed.	3,635
Moravian College	Bethlehem, Pa.	1858	Moravian	Coed.	1,613
Morehead State College	Morehead, Ky.	1922	State	Coed.	4,797
Morehouse College	Atlanta, Ga.	1867	Private	Men	844
Morgan State College	Baltimore, Md.	1867	State	Coed.	3,264
Morningside College	Sioux City, Ia.	1889	Methodist	Coed.	1,769
Morris Brown College	Atlanta, Ga.	1885	Methodist	Coed.	1,001
Morris Harvey College	Charleston, W.Va.	1888	Private	Coed.	3,033
Mount Angel College	Mount Angel, Ore.	1887	Roman Catholic	Coed.	420
Mount Angel Seminary	St. Benedict, Ore.	1889	Roman Catholic	Men	152
Mount Holyoke College	South Hadley, Mass.	1836	Private	Women	1,748
Mount Marty College	Yankton, S.Dak.	1936	Roman Catholic	Women	474
Mount Mary College	Milwaukee, Wis.	1850	Roman Catholic	Women	1,196
Mount Mercy College	Cedar Rapids, Ia.	1928	Roman Catholic	Women	553
Mount Mercy College	Pittsburgh, Pa.	1929	Roman Catholic	Women	1,524
Mount Saint Agnes College	Baltimore, Md.	1890	Roman Catholic	Women	520
Mount Saint Joseph College	Buffalo, N.Y.	1937	Roman Catholic	Women	472
Mount Saint Joseph-on-the-Ohio, College of	Mount St. Joseph, Ohio	1852	Roman Catholic	Women	1,145
Mount Saint Mary College	Hooksett, N.H.	1934	Roman Catholic	Women	303
Mount Saint Mary's College	Los Angeles, Calif.	1925	Roman Catholic	Men; Women	1,610
Mount Saint Mary's College	Emmitsburg, Md.	1808	Roman Catholic	Men	822
Mount Saint Scholastica College	Atchison, Kans.	1863	Roman Catholic	Women	621
Mount Saint Vincent, College of	New York City	1847	Roman Catholic	Women	878
Mount Union College	Alliance, Ohio	1846	Methodist	Coed.	1,312
Muhlenberg College	Allentown, Pa.	1848	Lutheran	Coed.	1,818
Mundelein College	Chicago, Ill.	1930	Roman Catholic	Women	1,418
Murray State College	Murray, Ky.	1922	State	Coed.	6,135
Muskingum College	New Concord, Ohio	1837	Presbyterian	Coed.	1,524
Nasson College	Springvale, Me.	1912	Private	Coed.	615
National College of Education	Evanston, Ill.	1886	Private	Coed.	1,073
Nazareth College	Kalamazoo, Mich.	1897	Roman Catholic	Women	488
Nazareth College of Rochester	Rochester, N.Y.	1924	Roman Catholic	Women	1,308
Nazareth College of Kentucky	Nazareth, Ky.	1814	Roman Catholic	Women	509
Nebraska, University of	Lincoln, Nebr.	1869	State	Coed.	16,634
Nebraska Wesleyan University	Lincoln, Nebr.	1887	Methodist	Coed.	1,480
Nevada, University of	Reno, Nev.	1874	State	Coed.	8,039
New England Conservatory of Music	Boston, Mass.	1867	Private	Coed.	372
New Hampshire, University of	Durham, N.H.	1866	State	Coed.	6,937
New Mexico, University of	Albuquerque, N.Mex.	1889	State	Coed.	12,357
New Mexico Highlands University	Las Vegas, N.Mex.	1893	State	Coed.	1,672
New Mexico Institute of Mining and Technology	Socorro, N.Mex.	1889	State	Coed.	480
New Mexico State University	University Park, N.Mex.	1888	State	Coed.	7,126
New Orleans Baptist Theological Seminary	New Orleans, La.	1917	Southern Baptist	Coed.	681
New Rochelle, College of	New Rochelle, N.Y.	1904	Roman Catholic	Women	895
New School for Social Research	New York City	1919	Private	Coed.	2,187
New York, State University of, College at:	Brockport, N.Y.	1867	State	Coed.	3,353
	Buffalo, N.Y.	1871	State	Coed.	6,610
	Cortland, N.Y.	1869	State	Coed.	3,867
	Fredonia, N.Y.	1868	State	Coed.	2,723
	Geneseo, N.Y.	1871	State	Coed.	3,035
	New Paltz, N.Y.	1886	State	Coed.	4,155
	Oneonta, N.Y.	1863	State	Coed.	3,872
	Oswego, N.Y.	1863	State	Coed.	4,788
	Plattsburgh, N.Y.	1890	State	Coed.	3,122
	Potsdam, N.Y.	1871	State	Coed.	2,537
College of Forestry at Syracuse University	Syracuse, N.Y.	1911	State	Coed.	1,122
Downstate Medical Center	New York City	1950	State	Coed.	831
Maritime College	Fort Schuyler, N.Y.	1847	State	Men	660

Name	Location	Founded	Control	Student Body	Enroll-ment
State University of New York at:	Albany, N.Y.	1844	State	Coed.	5,809
	Binghamton, N.Y.	1946	State	Coed.	2,551
	Buffalo, N.Y.	1846	State	Coed.	20,276
	Stony Brook, N.Y.	1957	State	Coed.	2,837
Upstate Medical Center	Syracuse, N.Y.	1950	State	Coed.	563
New York, The City University of:					
Brooklyn College	New York City	1930	Municipal	Coed.	24,875
City College	New York City	1847	Municipal	Men; Women	29,912
Hunter College	New York City	1870	Municipal	Coed.	26,136
Police Science, College of	New York City	1966	Municipal	Coed.	1,089
Queens College	New York City	1937	Municipal	Coed.	22,464
New York University	New York City	1831	Private	Coed.	31,825
Newark College of Engineering	Newark, N.J.	1881	State; Municipal	Coed.	6,091
Newark State College	Union, N.J.	1855	State	Coed.	7,750
Newberry College	Newberry, S.C.	1856	Lutheran	Coed.	823
Newton College of the Sacred Heart	Newton, Mass.	1946	Roman Catholic	Women	730
Niagara University	Niagara University, N.Y.	1856	Roman Catholic	Coed.	2,159
Nichols College of Business Administration	Dudley, Mass.	1958	Private	Men	663
North Carolina, Agricultural and Technical College of	Greensboro, N.C.	1891	State	Coed.	3,435
North Carolina, University of at:	Chapel Hill, N.C.	1789	State	Coed.	13,130
	Charlotte, N.C.	1963	State	Coed.	1,815
	Greensboro, N.C.	1891	State	Coed.	4,866
North Carolina State University	Raleigh, N.C.	1887	State	Coed.	10,071
North Carolina College at Durham	Durham, N.C.	1910	State	Coed.	2,780
North Central College	Naperville, Ill.	1861	Evangelical United Brethren	Coed.	1,125
North Dakota, University of	Grand Forks, N.Dak.	1883	State	Coed.	6,640
North Dakota State University	Fargo, N.Dak.	1889	State	Coed.	5,006
North Georgia College	Dahlonega, Ga.	1873	State	Coed.	967
North Park College and Theological Seminary	Chicago, Ill.	1891	Evangelical Covenant Church of America	Coed.	1,730
North Texas State University	Denton, Tex.	1890	State	Coed.	14,773
Northeast Louisiana State College	Monroe, La.	1928	State	Coed.	5,140
Northeast Missouri State Teachers College	Kirksville, Mo.	1867	State	Coed.	5,875
Northeastern State College	Tahlequah, Okla.	1846	State	Coed.	4,840
Northeastern University	Boston, Mass.	1898	Private	Coed.	29,131
Northern Arizona University	Flagstaff, Ariz.	1899	State	Coed.	5,779
Northern Baptist Theological Seminary	Oak Brook, Ill.	1913	Baptist	Coed.	66
Northern Illinois University	De Kalb, Ill.	1895	State	Coed.	15,661
Northern Michigan University	Marquette, Mich.	1899	State	Coed.	5,560
Northern Montana College	Havre, Mont.	1929	State	Coed.	1,412
Northern State Teachers College	Aberdeen, S.Dak.	1901	State	Coed.	2,636
Northland College	Ashland, Wis.	1892	Private	Coed.	677
Northrop Institute of Technology	Inglewood, Calif.	1942	Private	Coed.	1,759
Northwest Christian College	Eugene, Ore.	1895	Disciples of Christ	Coed.	433
Northwest Missouri State College	Maryville, Mo.	1905	State	Coed.	3,869
Northwest Nazarene College	Nampa, Idaho	1913	Nazarene	Coed.	1,050
Northwestern College	Orange City, Iowa	1882	Reformed Bodies	Coed.	568
Northwestern State College	Alva, Okla.	1897	State	Coed.	2,040
Northwestern State College of Louisiana	Natchitoches, La.	1884	State	Coed.	4,845
Northwestern University	Evanston, Ill.	1851	Private	Coed.	16,472
Norwich University	Northfield, Vt.	1819	Private	Men	1,221
Notre Dame, College of	Belmont, Calif.	1851	Roman Catholic	Women	543
Notre Dame, University of	Notre Dame, Ind.	1842	Roman Catholic	Men	7,155
Notre Dame College	St. Louis, Mo.	1954	Roman Catholic	Women	424
Notre Dame College	Cleveland, Ohio	1922	Roman Catholic	Women	586
Notre Dame College of Staten Island	New York City	1931	Roman Catholic	Women	478
Notre Dame of Maryland, College of	Baltimore, Md.	1895	Roman Catholic	Women	1,084
Notre Dame Seminary	New Orleans, La.	1923	Roman Catholic	Men	118
Nyack Missionary College	Nyack, N.Y.	1882	Christian and Missionary Alliance	Coed.	577

Name	Location	Founded	Control	Student Body	Enrollment
Oakland University	Rochester, Mich.	1959	State	Coed.	2,458
Oakwood College	Huntsville, Ala.	1896	Adventist	Coed.	488
Oberlin College	Oberlin, Ohio	1833	Private	Coed.	2,465
Occidental College	Los Angeles, Calif.	1887	Private	Coed.	1,603
Oglethorpe College	Atlanta, Ga.	1835	Private	Coed.	691
Ohio Northern University	Ada, Ohio	1871	Methodist	Coed.	2,927
Ohio State University	Columbus, Ohio	1870	State	Coed.	40,470
Ohio University	Athens, Ohio	1804	State	Coed.	19,078
Ohio Wesleyan University	Delaware, Ohio	1842	Methodist	Coed.	2,457
Oklahoma, University of	Norman, Okla.	1890	State	Coed.	17,946
Oklahoma Baptist University	Shawnee, Okla.	1910	Baptist	Coed.	1,536
Oklahoma Christian College	Oklahoma City, Okla.	1962	Private	Coed.	774
Oklahoma City University	Oklahoma City, Okla.	1904	Methodist	Coed.	2,722
Oklahoma College of Liberal Arts	Chickasha, Okla.	1908	State	Coed.	885
Oklahoma State University of Agriculture and Applied Science	Stillwater, Okla.	1890	State	Coed.	18,751
Old Dominion College	Norfolk, Va.	1930	State	Coed.	7,417
Olivet College	Olivet, Mich.	1844	Private	Coed.	682
Olivet Nazarene College	Kankakee, Ill.	1907	Nazarene	Coed.	1,580
Omaha, Municipal University of	Omaha, Nebr.	1908	Municipal	Coed.	9,082
Oregon, University of	Eugene, Ore.	1872	State	Coed.	13,399
Oregon College of Education	Monmouth, Ore.	1856	State	Coed.	2,073
Oregon State University	Corvallis, Ore.	1868	State	Coed.	11,884
Otis Art Institute of Los Angeles County	Los Angeles, Calif.	1918	County	Coed.	291
Ottawa University	Ottawa, Kans.	1865	Baptist	Coed.	961
Otterbein College	Westerville, Ohio	1847	Evangelical United Brethren	Coed.	1,537
Ouachita Baptist University	Arkadelphia, Ark.	1886	Baptist	Coed.	1,785
Our Lady of Cincinnati College	Cincinnati, Ohio	1935	Roman Catholic	Women	1,221
Our Lady of Mercy, College of	Burlingame, Calif.	1952	Roman Catholic	Women	157
Our Lady of the Elms, College of	Chicopee, Mass.	1928	Roman Catholic	Women	925
Our Lady of the Lake College	San Antonio, Tex.	1896	Roman Catholic	Women	1,351
Ozarks, College of the	Clarksville, Ark.	1834	Presbyterian	Coed.	470
Pace College	New York City	1906	Private	Coed.	8,006
Pacific, University of the	Stockton, Calif.	1851	Methodist	Coed.	3,154
Pacific College	Fresno, Calif.	1963	Mennonite Brethren	Coed.	245
Pacific Lutheran University	Tacoma, Wash.	1894	Lutheran	Coed.	2,319
Pacific Oaks College	Pasadena, Calif.	1945	Private	Coed.	92
Pacific Union College	Angwin, Calif.	1882	Adventist	Coed.	1,460
Pacific University	Forest Grove, Ore.	1849	Private	Coed.	1,011
Paine College	Augusta, Ga.	1882	Methodist	Coed.	479
Pan American College	Edinburg, Tex.	1927	County	Coed.	2,861
Panhandle Agricultural and Mechanical College	Goodwell, Okla.	1909	State	Coed.	1,073
Park College	Parkville, Mo.	1875	Presbyterian	Coed.	628
Parsons College	Fairfield, Iowa	1875	Private	Coed.	4,304
Pasadena College	Pasadena, Calif.	1902	Nazarene	Coed.	1,400
Pasadena Playhouse College of Theatre Arts	Pasadena, Calif.	1928	Private	Coed.	240
Paterson State College	Wayne, N.J.	1855	State	Coed.	4,598
Peabody Institute of the City of Baltimore	Baltimore, Md.	1857	Private	Coed.	466
Pembroke State College	Pembroke, N.C.	1887	State	Coed.	1,351
Pennsylvania, University of	Philadelphia, Pa.	1756	Private	Coed.	19,282
Pennsylvania College of Optometry	Philadelphia, Pa.	1919	Private	Coed.	280
Pennsylvania Military College	Chester, Pa.	1821	Private	Men	2,382
Pennsylvania State University	University Park, Pa.	1855	State and Private	Coed.	35,801
Pepperdine College	Los Angeles, Calif.	1937	Private	Coed.	2,354
Peru State College	Peru, Nebr.	1867	State	Coed.	1,129
Pfeiffer College	Misenheimer, N.C.	1885	Methodist	Coed.	917
Philadelphia College of Art	Philadelphia, Pa.	1876	Private	Coed.	1,472
Philadelphia College of Pharmacy and Science	Philadelphia, Pa.	1821	Private	Coed.	837
Philadelphia College of Textiles and Science	Philadelphia, Pa.	1884	Private	Men; Women	1,506
Philander Smith College	Little Rock, Ark.	1868	Methodist	Coed.	628
Phillips University	Enid, Okla.	1906	Disciples of Christ	Coed.	1,395
Piedmont College	Demorest, Ga.	1897	Private	Coed.	328

Name	Location	Founded	Control	Student Body	Enrollment
Pikeville College	Pikeville, Ky.	1889	Presbyterian	Coed.	800
Pittsburgh, University of	Pittsburgh, Pa.	1787	Private	Coed.	17,796
Pitzer College	Claremont, Calif.	1964	Private	Women	348
Plymouth State College	Plymouth, N.H.	1870	State	Coed.	1,546
Pomona College	Claremont, Calif.	1887	Private	Coed.	1,173
Portland, University of	Portland, Ore.	1901	Roman Catholic	Coed.	1,859
Portland State College	Portland, Ore.	1946	State	Coed.	9,089
Pratt Institute	New York City	1887	Private	Coed.	4,238
Presbyterian College	Clinton, S.C.	1880	Presbyterian	Coed.	672
Presbyterian School of Christian Education	Richmond, Va.	1914	Presbyterian	Coed.	103
Princeton University	Princeton, N.J.	1746	Private	Men	4,404
Principia College	Elsah, Ill.	1898	Private	Coed.	649
Providence College	Providence, R.I.	1917	Roman Catholic	Men	3,518
Puerto Rico, Catholic University of	Ponce, P.R.	1948	Roman Catholic	Coed.	5,335
Puerto Rico, University of	Río Piedras, P.R.	1903	Territory	Coed.	26,606
Puget Sound, University of	Tacoma, Wash.	1888	Methodist	Coed.	2,917
Purdue University	Lafayette, Ind.	1869	State	Coed.	27,793
Queens College	Charlotte, N.C.	1857	Presbyterian	Women	933
Quincy College	Quincy, Ill.	1860	Roman Catholic	Coed.	1,518
Quinnipiac College	Hamden, Conn.	1929	Private	Coed.	2,309
Radcliffe College	Cambridge, Mass.	1879	Private	Women	1,191
Radford College	Radford, Va.	1910	State	Coed.	3,122
Randolph-Macon College	Ashland, Va.	1830	Methodist	Men	824
Randolph-Macon Woman's College	Lynchburg, Va.	1891	Methodist	Women	835
Redlands, University of	Redlands, Calif.	1907	Baptist	Coed.	1,625
Reed College	Portland, Ore.	1910	Private	Coed.	1,052
Regis College	Denver, Colo.	1887	Roman Catholic	Men	1,056
Regis College	Weston, Mass.	1927	Roman Catholic	Women	1,260
Rensselaer Polytechnic Institute	Troy, N.Y.	1824	Private	Coed.	5,232
Rhode Island, University of	Kingston, R.I.	1892	State	Coed.	11,861
Rhode Island College	Providence, R.I.	1854	State	Coed.	4,257
Rhode Island School of Design	Providence, R.I.	1877	Private	Coed.	958
Rice University	Houston, Tex.	1891	Private	Coed.	2,488
Richmond, University of	Richmond, Va.	1830	Baptist	Coordinate	4,584
Richmond Professional Institute	Richmond, Va.	1917	State	Coed.	8,076
Rider College	Trenton, N.J.	1865	Private	Coed.	5,559
Ripon College	Ripon, Wis.	1851	Private	Coed.	947
Rivier College	Nashua, N.H.	1933	Roman Catholic	Women	672
Roanoke College	Salem, Va.	1842	Lutheran	Coed.	1,095
Roberts Wesleyan College	North Chili, N.Y.	1866	Methodist	Coed.	600
Rochester, University of	Rochester, N.Y.	1850	Private	Coed.	8,128
Rochester Institute of Technology	Rochester, N.Y.	1829	Private	Coed.	9,737
Rockford College	Rockford, Ill.	1847	Private	Coed.	1,308
Rockhurst College	Kansas City, Mo.	1910	Roman Catholic	Men	2,357
Rocky Mountain College	Billings, Mont.	1883	Private	Coed.	497
Rollins College	Winter Park, Fla.	1885	Private	Coed.	3,241
Roosevelt University	Chicago, Ill.	1945	Private	Coed.	6,579
Rosary College	River Forest, Ill.	1848	Roman Catholic	Women	1,177
Rosary Hill College	Buffalo, N.Y.	1947	Roman Catholic	Women	1,103
Rose Polytechnic Institute	Terre Haute, Ind.	1874	Private	Men	795
Rosemont College	Rosemont, Pa.	1921	Roman Catholic	Women	702
Russell Sage College	Troy, N.Y.	1916	Private	Women	4,128
Rutgers, The State University	New Brunswick, N.J.	1766	State	Men; Women	25,489
Sacramento State College	Sacramento, Calif.	1947	State	Coed.	12,046
Sacred Heart, College of the	Santurce, P.R.	1935	Roman Catholic	Women	445
Sacred Heart Dominican College	Houston, Tex.	1946	Roman Catholic	Women	528
Sacred Heart Seminary	Detroit, Mich.	1919	Roman Catholic	Men	260
St. Albert's College	Oakland, Calif.	1932	Roman Catholic	Men	53
St. Ambrose College	Davenport, Iowa	1882	Roman Catholic	Coordinate	1,219
St. Andrews Presbyterian College	Laurinburg, N.C.	1858	Presbyterian	Coed.	931
St. Anselm's College	Manchester, N.H.	1889	Roman Catholic	Men; Women	1,429
St. Augustine's College	Raleigh, N.C.	1867	Protestant Episcopal	Coed.	818
St. Benedict, College of	St. Joseph, Minn.	1913	Roman Catholic	Women	678
St. Benedict's College	Atchison, Kans.	1858	Roman Catholic	Men	1,007
St. Bernard College	St. Bernard, Ala.	1892	Roman Catholic	Coed.	679
St. Bernardine of Siena College	Loudonville, N.Y.	1937	Roman Catholic	Men; Coed.	2,029
St. Bonaventure University	St. Bonaventure, N.Y.	1856	Roman Catholic	Coed.	2,498
St. Catherine, College of	St. Paul, Minn.	1905	Roman Catholic	Women	1,449

Name	Location	Founded	Control	Student Body	Enrollment
St. Cloud State College	St. Cloud, Minn.	1869	State	Coed.	6,454
St. Edward's University	Austin, Tex.	1881	Roman Catholic	Men	739
St. Elizabeth, College of	Convent Station, N.J.	1899	Roman Catholic	Women	971
St. Francis, College of	Joliet, Ill.	1930	Roman Catholic	Women	723
St. Francis College	Fort Wayne, Ind.	1890	Roman Catholic	Coed.	1,519
St. Francis College	New York City	1858	Roman Catholic	Men	2,139
St. Francis College	Loretto, Pa.	1847	Roman Catholic	Coed.	1,465
St. Francis Seminary	Milwaukee, Wis.	1856	Roman Catholic	Men	282
St. John College of Cleveland	Cleveland, Ohio	1928	Roman Catholic	Women	989
St. John Fisher College, Incorporated	Rochester, N.Y.	1951	Roman Catholic	Men	1,019
St. John's College	Annapolis, Md.	1696	Private	Coed.	487
St. John's College	Camarillo, Calif.	1926	Roman Catholic	Men	376
St. John's University	Collegeville, Minn.	1857	Roman Catholic	Men	1,438
St. John's University	New York City	1870	Roman Catholic	Coed.	13,125
St. Joseph College	West Hartford, Conn.	1925	Roman Catholic	Women	781
St. Joseph College	Emmitsburg, Md.	1809	Roman Catholic	Women	675
St. Joseph College of Orange	Orange, Calif.	1933	Roman Catholic	Women	179
St. Joseph's College	Rensselaer, Ind.	1889	Roman Catholic	Men	2,418
St. Joseph's College	North Windham, Me.	1915	Roman Catholic	Women	387
St. Joseph's College	Philadelphia, Pa.	1851	Roman Catholic	Coed.	6,897
St. Joseph's College for Women	New York City	1916	Roman Catholic	Women	714
St. Joseph's Seminary and College	Yonkers, N.Y.	1833	Roman Catholic	Men	308
St. Joseph's Seminary of Washington, D.C.	Washington, D.C.	1888	Roman Catholic	Men	65
St. Lawrence University	Canton, N.Y.	1856	Private	Coed.	1,886
St. Louis University	St. Louis, Mo.	1818	Roman Catholic	Coed.	10,497
St. Martin's College	Olympia, Wash.	1895	Roman Catholic	Men	572
St. Mary, College of	Omaha, Nebr.	1923	Roman Catholic	Women	636
St. Mary College	Xavier, Kans.	1860	Roman Catholic	Women	618
St. Mary of the Plains College	Dodge City, Kans.	1952	Roman Catholic	Coed.	642
St. Mary of the Springs, College of	Columbus, Ohio	1911	Roman Catholic	Women	948
St. Mary-of-the-Woods College	Saint Mary-of-the-Woods, Ind.	1840	Roman Catholic	Women	669
St. Mary's College	Notre Dame, Ind.	1844	Roman Catholic	Women	1,424
St. Mary's College	Winona, Minn.	1912	Roman Catholic	Men	1,097
St. Mary's College of California	St. Mary's College, Calif.	1863	Roman Catholic	Men	995
St. Mary's Dominican College	New Orleans, La.	1910	Roman Catholic	Women	542
St. Mary's Seminary and University	Baltimore, Md.	1791	Roman Catholic	Men	817
St. Mary's University	San Antonio, Tex.	1852	Roman Catholic	Coed.	3,249
St. Meinrad Seminary	St. Meinrad, Ind.	1854	Roman Catholic	Men	416
St. Michael's College	Winooski, Vt.	1904	Roman Catholic	Men	1,294
St. Norbert College	West De Pere, Wis.	1898	Roman Catholic	Coed.	1,484
St. Olaf College	Northfield, Minn.	1874	Lutheran	Coed.	2,336
St. Patrick's College	Menlo Park, Calif.	1898	Roman Catholic	Men	270
St. Paul Seminary	St. Paul, Minn.	1896	Roman Catholic	Men	256
St. Paul's College	Washington, D.C.	1889	Roman Catholic	Men	73
St. Paul's College	Lawrenceville, Va.	1888	Protestant Episcopal	Coed.	438
St. Peter's College	Jersey City, N.J.	1872	Roman Catholic	Men	2,959
St. Procopius College	Lisle, Ill.	1887	Roman Catholic	Men	815
St. Rose, The College of	Albany, N.Y.	1920	Roman Catholic	Women	1,491
St. Scholastica, College of	Duluth, Minn.	1912	Roman Catholic	Women	540
St. Stephen's College	Dover, Mass.	1955	Roman Catholic	Men	53
St. Teresa, College of	Winona, Minn.	1907	Roman Catholic	Women	1,257
St. Thomas, College of	St. Paul, Minn.	1885	Roman Catholic	Men	2,105
St. Thomas, University of	Houston, Tex.	1947	Roman Catholic	Coed.	872
St. Thomas Seminary	Denver, Colo.	1906	Roman Catholic	Men	275
St. Vincent College	Latrobe, Pa.	1846	Roman Catholic	Men	938
St. Xavier College	Chicago, Ill.	1846	Roman Catholic	Women	1,038
Salem College	Winston-Salem, N.C.	1772	Moravian	Women	544
Salem College	Salem, W.Va.	1888	Baptist	Coed.	1,746
Salisbury State College	Salisbury, Md.	1925	State	Coed.	771
Salve Regina College	Newport, R.I.	1947	Roman Catholic	Women	776
Sam Houston State College	Huntsville, Tex.	1879	State	Coed.	6,524
Samford University	Birmingham, Ala.	1842	Baptist	Coed.	2,780
San Diego, College for Men, University of	San Diego, Calif.	1949	Roman Catholic	Men	393
San Diego, College for Women, University of	San Diego, Calif.	1952	Roman Catholic	Women	734
San Diego State College	San Diego, Calif.	1897	State	Coed.	18,366

Name	Location	Founded	Control	Student Body	Enrollment
San Fernando Valley State College	Northridge, Calif.	1958	State	Coed.	13,399
San Francisco, University of	San Francisco, Calif.	1859	Roman Catholic	Coed.	5,564
San Francisco College for Women	San Francisco, Calif.	1921	Roman Catholic	Women	653
San Francisco Conservatory of Music	San Francisco, Calif.	1917	Private	Coed.	81
San Francisco State College	San Francisco, Calif.	1899	State	Coed.	20,910
San Jose State College	San Jose, Calif.	1857	State	Coed.	23,300
San Luis Rey College	San Luis Rey, Calif.	1940	Roman Catholic	Men	83
Santa Clara, University of	Santa Clara, Calif.	1851	Roman Catholic	Coed.	4,782
Santa Fe, College of	Santa Fe, N.Mex.	1947	Roman Catholic-Private	Men	979
Sarah Lawrence College	Bronxville, N.Y.	1928	Private	Women	629
Savannah State College	Savannah, Ga.	1890	State	Coed.	1,408
Scarritt College for Christian Workers	Nashville, Tenn.	1892	Methodist	Coed.	182
Scranton, University of	Scranton, Pa.	1888	Roman Catholic	Men	2,849
Scripps College	Claremont, Calif.	1926	Private	Women	395
Seattle Pacific College	Seattle, Wash.	1891	Methodist	Coed.	1,920
Seattle University	Seattle, Wash.	1891	Roman Catholic	Coed.	4,174
Seton Hall University	South Orange, N.J.	1856	Roman Catholic	Men; Women	9,173
Seton Hill College	Greensburg, Pa.	1883	Roman Catholic	Women	1,003
Shaw University	Raleigh, N.C.	1865	Baptist	Coed.	766
Shepherd College	Shepherdstown, W.Va.	1871	State	Coed.	1,245
Shimer College	Mount Carroll, Ill.	1853	Private	Coed.	481
Shippensburg State College	Shippensburg, Pa.	1871	State	Coed.	3,093
Shorter College	Rome, Ga.	1873	Baptist	Coed.	833
Siena College	Memphis, Tenn.	1922	Roman Catholic	Women	372
Siena Heights College	Adrian, Mich.	1919	Roman Catholic	Women	803
Simmons College	Boston, Mass.	1899	Private	Women	1,975
Simpson College	Indianola, Iowa	1860	Methodist	Coed.	909
Sioux Falls College	Sioux Falls, S.Dak.	1883	Baptist	Coed.	1,008
Skidmore College	Saratoga Springs, N.Y.	1911	Private	Women	1,448
Slippery Rock State College	Slippery Rock, Pa.	1889	State	Coed.	3,163
Smith College	Northampton, Mass.	1871	Private	Women	2,322
Sonoma State College	Rohnert Park, Calif.	1960	State	Coed.	2,092
South, University of the	Sewanee, Tenn.	1860	Protestant Episcopal	Men	889
South Carolina, University of	Columbia, S.C.	1801	State	Coed.	10,998
South Carolina State College	Orangeburg, S.C.	1895	State	Coed.	1,695
South Dakota, University of	Vermillion, S.Dak.	1882	State	Coed.	4,103
South Dakota School of Mines and Technology	Rapid City, S.Dak.	1885	State	Coed.	1,239
South Dakota State University	Brookings, S.Dak.	1881	State	Coed.	4,779
South Florida, University of	Tampa, Fla.	1960	State	Coed.	7,795
South Texas College	Houston, Tex.	1923	Private	Coed.	3,584
Southeast Missouri State College	Cape Girardeau, Mo.	1873	State	Coed.	5,185
Southeastern Louisiana College	Hammond, La.	1925	State	Coed.	4,581
Southeastern Massachusetts Technological Institute	Dartmouth, Mass.	1949	State	Coed.	3,370
Southeastern State College	Durant, Okla.	1909	State	Coed.	2,239
Southern California, University of	Los Angeles, Calif.	1880	Private	Coed.	18,623
Southern California College	Costa Mesa, Calif.	1920	Assemblies of God	Coed.	445
Southern Colorado State College	Pueblo, Colo.	1963	State	Coed.	5,118
Southern Connecticut State College	New Haven, Conn.	1893	State	Coed.	6,506
Southern Illinois University at:	Carbondale, Ill.	1907	State	Coed.	17,356
	Edwardsville, Ill.	1957	State	Coed.	7,146
Southern Methodist University	Dallas, Tex.	1911	Methodist	Coed.	8,431
Southern Missionary College	Collegedale, Tenn.	1892	Adventist	Coed.	1,125
Southern Mississippi, University of	Hattiesburg, Miss.	1910	State	Coed.	7,637
Southern Oregon College	Ashland, Ore.	1926	State	Coed.	3,202
Southern State College	Magnolia, Ark.	1909	State	Coed.	2,289
Southern State College	Springfield, S.Dak.	1881	State	Coed.	1,114
Southern University and Agricultural and Mechanical College	Baton Rouge, La.	1880	State	Coed.	7,750
Southern Utah, College of	Cedar City, Utah	1964	State	Coed.	1,700
Southwest Missouri State College	Springfield, Mo.	1906	State	Coed.	5,372
Southwest Texas State College	San Marcos, Tex.	1899	State	Coed.	5,579
Southwestern At Memphis	Memphis, Tenn.	1848	Presbyterian	Coed.	993
Southwestern College	Winfield, Kans.	1885	Methodist	Coed.	718
Southwestern Louisiana, The University of	Lafayette, La.	1898	State	Coed.	8,447

Name	Location	Founded	Control	Student Body	Enroll- ment
Southwestern State College	Weatherford, Okla.	1901	State	Coed.	4,074
Southwestern University	Georgetown, Tex.	1840	Methodist	Coed.	815
Spelman College	Atlanta, Ga.	1881	Baptist	Women	723
Spring Arbor College	Spring Arbor, Mich.	1873	Private	Coed.	566
Spring Hill College	Mobile, Ala.	1830	Roman Catholic	Coed.	1,265
Springfield College	Springfield, Mass.	1885	Private	Coed.	2,045
Stanford University	Palo Alto, Calif.	1885	Private	Coed.	11,166
Stanislaus State College	Turlock, Calif.	1957	State	Coed.	1,302
Stephen F. Austin State College	Nacogdoches, Tex.	1923	State	Coed.	5,783
Stephens College	Columbia, Mo.	1833	Private	Women	2,000
Sterling College	Sterling, Kans.	1887	Presbyterian	Coed.	612
Stetson University	De Land, Fla.	1883	Baptist	Coed.	2,475
Steubenville, College of	Steubenville, Ohio	1946	Roman Catholic	Coed.	1,085
Stevens Institute of Technology	Hoboken, N.J.	1870	Private	Men	2,516
Stillman College	Tuscaloosa, Ala.	1876	Presbyterian	Coed.	634
Stonehill College	North Easton, Mass.	1948	Roman Catholic	Coed.	1,218
Stout State University	Menomonie, Wis.	1893	State	Coed.	2,827
Suffolk University	Boston, Mass.	1906	Private	Coed.	2,872
Sul Ross State College	Alpine, Tex.	1917	State	Coed.	1,711
Sulpician Seminary of the Northwest	Kenmore, Wash.	1931	Roman Catholic	Men	83
Susquehanna University	Selinsgrove, Pa.	1858	Lutheran	Coed.	1,141
Swarthmore College	Swarthmore, Pa.	1864	Private	Coed.	1,026
Sweet Briar College	Sweet Briar, Va.	1901	Private	Women	709
Syracuse University	Syracuse, N.Y.	1870	Private	Coed.	21,658
Tabor College	Hillsboro, Kans.	1908	Mennonite	Coed.	383
Talladega College	Talladega, Ala.	1890	United Church of Christ-Private	Coed.	384
Tampa, University of	Tampa, Fla.	1931	Private	Coed.	2,338
Tarkio College	Tarkio, Mo.	1883	Presbyterian	Coed.	580
Taylor University	Upland, Ind.	1846	Private	Coed.	1,016
Temple University	Philadelphia, Pa.	1888	Private-State	Coed.	28,285
Tennessee, University of	Knoxville, Tenn.	1794	State	Coed.	23,862
Tennessee Agricultural and Industrial State University	Nashville, Tenn.	1912	State	Coed.	5,095
Tennessee Technological University	Cookeville, Tenn.	1915	State	Coed.	5,030
Tennessee Wesleyan College	Athens, Tenn.	1857	Methodist	Coed.	829
Texas A&M University System:					
Arlington State College	Arlington, Tex.	1959	State	Coed.	11,849
Prairie View Agricultural and Mechanical College	Prairie View, Tex.	1876	State	Coed.	3,259
Texas A&M University	College Station, Tex.	1876	State	Coed.	9,521
Texas Christian University	Fort Worth, Tex.	1873	Disciples of Christ	Coed.	7,232
Texas College of Arts and Industries	Kingsville, Tex.	1917	State	Coed.	4,851
Texas Lutheran College	Seguin, Tex.	1891	Lutheran	Coed.	926
Texas Southern University	Houston, Tex.	1947	State	Coed.	4,389
Texas Technological College	Lubbock, Tex.	1923	State	Coed.	16,305
Texas Wesleyan College	Fort Worth, Tex.	1891	Methodist	Coed.	1,848
Texas Woman's University	Denton, Tex.	1901	State	Women	3,658
Texas, University of at:	Austin, Tex.	1881	State	Coed.	28,790
Texas Western College	El Paso, Tex.	1914	State	Coed.	7,422
Thiel College	Greenville, Pa.	1870	Lutheran	Coed.	1,174
Tift College	Forsyth, Ga.	1849	Baptist	Women	628
Toledo, University of	Toledo, Ohio	1872	Municipal	Coed.	10,464
Tougaloo College	Tougaloo, Miss.	1869	American Missionary Association and United Christian Mission Society	Coed.	609
Towson State College	Baltimore, Md.	1865	State	Coed.	4,748
Transylvania College	Lexington, Ky.	1780	Private	Coed.	794
Trenton State College	Trenton, N.J.	1855	State	Coed.	7,245
Trinity College	Hartford, Conn.	1823	Private	Men	1,671
Trinity College	Burlington, Vt.	1925	Roman Catholic	Women	483
Trinity College	Washington, D.C.	1897	Roman Catholic	Women	1,034
Trinity University	San Antonio, Tex.	1869	Presbyterian	Coed.	2,677
Tri-State College	Angola, Ind.	1884	Private	Coed.	1,782
Troy State College	Troy, Ala.	1887	State	Coed.	3,487
Tufts University	Medford, Mass.	1852	Private	Coed.	5,015
Tulane University of Louisiana	New Orleans, La.	1834	Private	Coordinate	8,082

Name	Location	Founded	Control	Student Body	Enrollment
Tulsa, University of	Tulsa, Okla.	1894	Private	Coed.	6,170
Tusculum College	Greeneville, Tenn.	1794	Private	Coed.	494
Tuskegee Institute	Tuskegee Institute, Ala.	1881	Private	Coed.	2,751
Union College	Barbourville, Ky.	1879	Methodist	Coed.	937
Union College	Lincoln, Nebr.	1891	Adventist	Coed.	1,077
Union College and University	Schenectady, N.Y.	1795	Private	Men	2,261
Union University	Jackson, Tenn.	1825	Baptist	Coed.	958
U.S. Air Force Academy	Colorado Springs, Colo.	1954	Federal	Men	2,862
U.S. Coast Guard Academy	New London, Conn.	1870	Federal	Men	687
U.S. Merchant Marine Academy	Kings Point, N.Y.	1938	Federal	Men	998
U.S. Military Academy	West Point, N.Y.	1802	Federal	Men	3,094
U.S. Naval Academy	Annapolis, Md.	1845	Federal	Men	4,113
U.S. Naval Postgraduate School	Monterey, Calif.	1909	Federal	Men	1,417
Upper Iowa University	Fayette, Iowa	1857	Private	Coed.	1,170
Upsala College	East Orange, N.J.	1893	Lutheran	Coed.	1,976
Ursinus College	Collegeville, Pa.	1869	Private	Coed.	1,020
Ursuline College	Louisville, Ky.	1921	Roman Catholic	Women	471
Ursuline College for Women	Cleveland, Ohio	1871	Roman Catholic	Women	375
Utah, University of	Salt Lake City, Utah	1850	State	Coed.	17,157
Utah State University	Logan, Utah	1888	State	Coed.	9,347
Valdosta State College	Valdosta, Ga.	1906	State	Coed.	1,657
Valley City State College	Valley City, N.Dak.	1889	State	Coed.	1,252
Valparaiso University	Valparaiso, Ind.	1859	Lutheran	Coed.	4,120
Vanderbilt University	Nashville, Tenn.	1872	Private	Coed.	4,917
Vassar College	Poughkeepsie, N.Y.	1861	Private	Women	1,663
Vermont, University of	Burlington, Vt.	1791	State	Coed.	4,463
Villa Madonna College	Covington, Ky.	1921	Roman Catholic	Coed.	1,756
Villa Maria College	Erie, Pa.	1882	Roman Catholic	Women	810
Villanova University	Villanova, Pa.	1842	Roman Catholic	Men; Women	7,722
Virginia, University of at:	Charlottesville, Va.	1819	State	Men; Women	17,223
Mary Washington College	Fredericksburg, Va.	1919	State	Men; Women	1,976
Virginia Military Institute	Lexington, Va.	1839	State	Men	1,228
Virginia Polytechnic Institute	Blacksburg, Va.	1872	State	Coed.	8,227
Virginia State College	Petersburg, Va.	1882	State	Coed.	5,876
Virginia Union University	Richmond, Va.	1899	Baptist	Coed.	1,382
Viterbo College	La Crosse, Wis.	1931	Roman Catholic	Women	550
Wabash College	Crawfordsville, Ind.	1832	Private	Men	885
Wagner College	New York City	1883	Lutheran	Coed.	2,589
Wake Forest College	Winston-Salem, N.C.	1834	Baptist	Men; Women	2,896
Walla Walla College	College Place, Wash.	1892	Adventist	Coed.	1,706
Warner Pacific College	Portland, Ore.	1937	Church of God	Coed.	338
Wartburg College	Waverly, Iowa	1852	Lutheran	Coed.	1,326
Washburn University of Topeka	Topeka, Kans.	1865	Municipal	Coed.	4,493
Washington, University of	Seattle, Wash.	1861	State	Coed.	28,131
Washington and Jefferson College	Washington, Pa.	1781	Private	Men	907
Washington and Lee University	Lexington, Va.	1782	Private	Men	1,337
Washington College	Chestertown, Md.	1782	Private	Coed.	616
Washington State University	Pullman, Wash.	1890	State	Coed.	10,500
Washington University	St. Louis, Mo.	1853	Private	Coed.	13,725
Wayland Baptist College	Plainview, Tex.	1908	Baptist	Coed.	768
Wayne State College	Wayne, Nebr.	1891	State	Coed.	2,436
Wayne State University	Detroit, Mich.	1868	State	Coed.	29,125
Waynesburg College	Waynesburg, Pa.	1850	Presbyterian	Coed.	1,079
Webb Institute of Naval Architecture	Glen Cove, N.Y.	1889	Private	Men	86
Weber State College	Ogden, Utah	1889	State	Coed.	7,416
Webster College	St. Louis, Mo.	1915	Roman Catholic	Women	1,048
Wellesley College	Wellesley, Mass.	1870	Private	Women	1,765
Wells College	Aurora, N.Y.	1868	Private	Women	567
Wesleyan College	Macon, Ga.	1836	Methodist	Women	709
Wesleyan University	Middletown, Conn.	1831	Private	Men	1,455
West Chester State College	West Chester, Pa.	1871	State	Coed.	5,462
West Coast University	Los Angeles, Calif.	1909	Private	Coed.	1,017
West Georgia College	Carrollton, Ga.	1933	State	Coed.	2,259
West Liberty State College	West Liberty, W.Va.	1837	State	Coed.	2,739
West Texas State University	Canyon, Tex.	1910	State	Coed.	5,328
West Virginia Institute of Technology	Montgomery, W.Va.	1895	State	Coed.	2,009
West Virginia State College	Institute, W.Va.	1891	State	Coed.	2,907
West Virginia University	Morgantown, W.Va.	1867	State	Coed.	12,743

Name	Location	Founded	Control	Student Body	Enroll-ment
West Virginia Wesleyan College	Buckhannon, W.Va.	1890	Methodist	Coed.	1,542
Western Carolina College	Cullowhee, N.C.	1889	State	Coed.	3,317
Western College for Women	Oxford, Ohio	1853	Private	Women	563
Western Illinois University	Macomb, Ill.	1899	State	Coed.	6,466
Western Kentucky State College	Bowling Green, Ky.	1906	State	Coed.	8,272
Western Maryland College	Westminster, Md.	1867	Methodist	Coed.	1,116
Western Michigan University	Kalamazoo, Mich.	1903	State	Coed.	17,672
Western Montana College	Dillon, Mont.	1893	State	Coed.	857
Western New England College	Springfield, Mass.	1919	Private	Coed.	2,112
Western New Mexico University	Silver City, N.Mex.	1893	State	Coed.	1,258
Western Reserve University	Cleveland, Ohio	1826	Private	Coed.	8,805
Western Washington State College	Bellingham, Wash.	1933	State	Coed.	5,745
Westmar College	Le Mars, Iowa	1890	Evangelical United Brethren	Coed.	954
Westminster College	Fulton, Mo.	1851	Presbyterian	Men	675
Westminster College	New Wilmington, Pa.	1852	Presbyterian	Coed.	1,926
Westminster College	Salt Lake City, Utah	1875	Interdenominational	Coed.	602
Westminster Theological Seminary	Philadelphia, Pa.	1929	Private	Men	105
Westmont College	Santa Barbara, Calif.	1940	Private	Coed.	615
Wheaton College	Wheaton, Ill.	1860	Private	Coed.	1,864
Wheaton College	Norton, Mass.	1834	Private	Women	1,090
Wheeling College	Wheeling, W.Va.	1954	Roman Catholic	Coed.	735
Wheelock College	Boston, Mass.	1888	Private	Women	489
Whitman College	Walla Walla, Wash.	1859	Private	Coed.	1,051
Whittier College	Whittier, Calif.	1901	Private	Coed.	1,990
Whitworth College	Spokane, Wash.	1890	Private	Coed.	1,829
Wichita State University	Wichita, Kans.	1895	State	Coed.	10,362
Wilberforce University	Wilberforce, Ohio	1856	Methodist	Coed.	612
Wiley College	Marshall, Tex.	1873	Methodist	Coed.	578
Wilkes College	Wilkes-Barre, Pa.	1933	Private	Coed.	2,335
Willamette University	Salem, Ore.	1842	Methodist	Coed.	1,443
William and Mary, College of	Williamsburg, Va.	1693	State	Coed.	6,538
William Carey College	Hattiesburg, Miss.	1906	Baptist	Coed.	779
William Jewell College	Liberty, Mo.	1849	Baptist	Coed.	1,017
William Penn College	Oskaloosa, Iowa	1873	Society of Friends	Coed.	996
William Woods College	Fulton, Mo.	1870	Private	Women	644
Williams College	Williamstown, Mass.	1793	Private	Men	1,310
Willimantic State College	Willimantic, Conn.	1889	State	Coed.	1,440
Wilmington College	Wilmington, N.C.	1963	State-County	Coed.	1,055
Wilmington College	Wilmington, Ohio	1870	Society of Friends	Coed.	901
Wilson College	Chambersburg, Pa.	1869	Private	Women	674
Winona State College	Winona, Minn.	1858	State	Coed.	2,991
Winston-Salem State College	Winston-Salem, N.C.	1892	State	Coed.	1,242
Winthrop College	Rock Hill, S.C.	1886	State	Women	2,970
Wisconsin, University of at:	Madison, Wis.	1850	State	Coed.	29,299
	Milwaukee, Wis.	1956	State	Coed.	12,818
Extension Division					6,387
Wisconsin State University at:	Eau Claire, Wis.	1916	State	Coed.	4,608
	La Crosse, Wis.	1909	State	Coed.	3,990
	Oshkosh, Wis.	1871	State	Coed.	7,440
	Platteville, Wis.	1866	State	Coed.	3,693
	River Falls, Wis.	1874	State	Coed.	3,404
	Stevens Point, Wis.	1894	State	Coed.	4,915
	Superior, Wis.	1896	State	Coed.	2,476
	Whitewater, Wis.	1868	State	Coed.	6,322
Wittenberg University	Springfield, Ohio	1845	Lutheran	Coed.	3,098
Wofford College	Spartanburg, S.C.	1854	Methodist	Men	989
Woodbury College	Los Angeles, Calif.	1884	Private	Coed.	2,181
Woodstock College	Woodstock, Md.	1869	Roman Catholic	Men	219
Wooster, College of	Wooster, Ohio	1866	Presbyterian	Coed.	1,532
Worcester Polytechnic Institute	Worcester, Mass.	1865	Private	Men	1,643
Wyoming, University of	Laramie, Wyo.	1887	State	Coed.	7,051
Xavier University	Cincinnati, Ohio	1831	Roman Catholic	Men	5,194
Xavier University	New Orleans, La.	1925	Roman Catholic	Coed.	908
Yale University	New Haven, Conn.	1701	Private	Men	8,575
Yankton College	Yankton, S.Dak.	1881	Private	Coed.	611
Yeshiva University	New York, N.Y.	1886	Jewish Congregations	Coordinate	4,867
Youngstown University, The	Youngstown, Ohio	1908	Private	Coed.	11,541

much as $1,500 at a public institution and $2,000 or more at a private one. As enrollments have increased, costs have risen. Most college catalogs list the average living costs for one year, as well as tuition and other fees.

Working Your Way. Many college students earn all or part of their expenses. Many have part-time jobs while they attend school, such as working in stores and restaurants. Most schools offer students jobs, such as waiting on tables in dormitories or working in the library. Schools often operate employment bureaus to help find part-time jobs for their students. Some students work during their summer vacations, and others drop out of college for a time to work. Many wives of students work to help their husbands. Sometimes both husband and wife are students and work part-time.

Other Financial Help. A student may receive all or part of his college expenses through a scholarship or fellowship (see FELLOWSHIP; SCHOLARSHIP). A number of churches have loan funds for college students. The federal government has at times helped college students. During the 1930's, the National Youth Administration provided part-time jobs for deserving students. After World War II and the Korean War, thousands of veterans attended college with funds received through the GI Bill (see GI BILL OF RIGHTS). In 1958, Congress passed the National Defense Education Act, a bill providing loans for students at low interest rates. This bill and other federal programs provide fellowships for graduate study, especially in the biological and physical sciences.

Kinds of Universities and Colleges

Universities and colleges in the United States may be classified as (1) those operating under private sponsorship, and (2) those operating under public sponsorship. Private institutions may be church-related or non-sectarian. Public institutions may be sponsored by local government, state government, or the federal government. The military academies are examples of federally supported institutions. Most private liberal arts colleges are church-related, while most privately sponsored universities are not associated with any church. Most public universities are sponsored by state governments. But most junior or community colleges are sponsored by local governments.

Income. All universities and colleges get their funds from a variety of sources. Private colleges depend primarily upon student fees, endowments, and gifts for their operating income. Church-related institutions sometimes receive money from the church.

Public institutions receive student fees, gifts, and endowments. They also receive local and state tax funds for current operations, and sometimes they get federal funds for research. Public institutions may receive funds for building construction from gifts, borrowing, or from government appropriations. In 1963, the federal government passed legislation providing matching grants to help both public and private institutions build additional classroom facilities.

Governing Boards. Most universities and colleges are controlled by a *board of trustees* or a *board of regents.* Boards of trustees of private institutions usually elect their own members. The church body may elect the trustees of a church-related institution. The alumni association of a private institution often elects some of the trustees. The trustees of public institutions are usually appointed by the chief executive. The voters sometimes elect the trustees or regents.

Boards of trustees or regents approve educational policies. They also appoint the chief administrative officer of the institution. In some states, coordinating committees and boards have been established to exercise supervision over those institutions financially assisted by the state.

Most church-related colleges except seminaries admit students of any religious denomination. Some of them expect all students to attend chapel exercise and to study some religious courses. But some colleges apply these rules only to students of the same religious faith.

In the United States, the federal government has encouraged the development of universities and colleges since the time of the Northwest Ordinance of 1787. The Morrill Act of 1862 provided land grants to all states to support colleges that, among other subjects, would teach agriculture and the mechanical arts. In some instances, these land grants were given to existing state universities. In other cases, new institutions were established. Many are now major universities.

Seven Canadian provinces sponsor and support universities. Some provinces have also founded technical, agricultural, and junior colleges. The first provincial university was the University of Toronto. It was founded in 1827 as the University of King's College.

School Organization

Campus is the land on which a college or university stands. The main buildings on a campus usually include classroom buildings, an administration building, a library, laboratories, a gymnasium, an athletic field and stadium, and dormitories. Many institutions have a building, often called a *union,* where social gatherings, plays, and dances may be held. Many of today's universities have more than one campus.

Administration. The organization of state, province, and city-supported institutions is generally about the

A Campus is a busy place where students rush from class to class. Here students at the University of California at Santa Barbara, above, stop a while to chat, study, or relax.

Department of Health, Education, and Welfare

same as that of other universities and colleges. The public institutions usually offer about the same courses of study, although state institutions often emphasize technical and professional education more than private schools.

In most cases, a *president* or *chancellor* is the chief administrator of a university or college. Other officials handle educational programs, registration, management of funds, and collection of tuition. Most institutions have a *dean of men* and *dean of women* who help direct discipline and advise students.

Each college or separate school of a university generally has an *academic dean* or *director*. He leads the faculty in preparing the course of study of his college or school, and takes part in university planning.

Faculty includes the teachers of a college or university. The faculty of a college is divided into *departments*. Each department deals with one general course of study, such as English, mathematics, or physics. Each department has a *chairman*, who is usually a *professor*. Under him are other professors, *associate professors*, *assistant professors*, and *instructors*. Some departments also have *teaching fellows* or *research fellows*. These are graduate students who teach or do research part time.

Some university faculties include scientists or other research workers who do not teach. Their research is supported by the institution or by funds granted the institution by individuals or groups having specific research interests. During World War II, the armed forces turned to universities and colleges for research assistance. Universities and colleges continue to do much research under government contract.

The Student Body of a university or college is divided into graduates and undergraduates. *Graduates* have already received their bachelor's degrees, while *undergraduates* have not. The undergraduates belong to one of four classes, according to their year of study. These are the *freshman*, *sophomore*, *junior*, and *senior* classes. Most schools also admit *special students* who take a number of courses, but are not working toward a degree. Graduate students work more or less independently.

Student bodies vary considerably from campus to campus. Some institutions are *coeducational*, with both men and women students. Others admit students of only one sex. Most publicly controlled institutions are coeducational. Many private colleges admit only men or only women students. A *coordinate* institution generally has separate men's and women's colleges. They are controlled by the same central authority and are usually located on the same campus or nearby campuses. Most graduate and professional schools are coeducational. See COEDUCATION.

The Calendar is the program of a school year. It is divided according to one of three systems. The most common system divides the calendar into two *semesters* of about 16 weeks each. The first semester begins in September, with a two-week Christmas vacation. The second semester begins about the first of February, with a one-week vacation during the Easter season. The school year ends in June with *commencement*, or graduation exercises (see GRADUATION). Many schools also hold a six- to eight-week summer session.

College calendars may also be arranged according to the *quarter* system. The school year is divided into four quarters of 10, 11, or 12 weeks each. The first quarter

Department of Health, Education, and Welfare

On Registration Day at Stanford University, crowds of students wait in line to sign up for their courses.

begins in the fall. The Christmas holidays come between the first and second quarters, and the spring holidays between the second and third quarters. Many students do not attend the fourth, or summer, quarter, which is followed by a four- or five-week vacation. The popularity of the quarter system increased during World War II, when many men wanted to finish college as quickly as possible before entering the armed forces. The *trimester* system divides the school year into three trimesters of about 15 weeks each. Both the quarter and trimester systems enable students to graduate in three years instead of four if they desire.

Selecting Courses

Curriculum. The courses given by a college or university are called the school's curriculum. The catalog of the institution outlines the complete curriculum. It gives the requirements for taking each course, as well as the credits given for the course. Each course is designated as giving a specified number of *credits*. These usually equal the number of class hours devoted each week to the course. For example, a course that meets three times a week usually gives three credits for graduation. Schools using the semester calendar require about 120 credits for graduation. Between 30 and 40 of the required credits must be in the student's major subject.

Institutions vary considerably in the amount of freedom given students in selecting their courses. Almost all colleges and universities have a certain number of required subjects. Students usually can also choose nonrequired courses called *electives*. Liberal arts colleges usually give a student more opportunity to choose courses than do professional schools. Many institutions have *general education programs* that give courses designed for freshmen and sophomore students. These programs give students a broad range of courses in different fields of knowledge.

When a college freshman registers, he usually indicates the major subject he chooses to study. During the first two years, he takes largely the basic required courses, such as English composition. The last two years are devoted mostly to the student's major. Many schools permit a student to have two major subjects.

Undergraduate Study. The programs of study provided by universities and colleges are divided into un-

M. E. Warren, Photo Researchers

A Lecture Hall at Rutgers has features typical of today's university and college classrooms. Good lighting and almost perfect acoustical conditions allow students to see and hear all instruction.

dergraduate and graduate levels. Colleges generally do not offer graduate programs, although some may offer the master's degree. An undergraduate program usually requires four years to complete. Some engineering programs and all architectural programs require five years to complete. Undergraduate study may be in the arts and sciences, or in a discipline such as English, economics, chemistry, or zoology. Undergraduate programs may also be given in a professional field such as agriculture, teacher education, or business administration.

Graduate Study may also be in the arts and sciences, or in a profession. It ordinarily begins only after a person has completed undergraduate study. Some professional fields will only admit a student who has completed undergraduate study. This is generally true of medicine, law, dentistry, and theology. Graduate study is more intensive and specialized than undergraduate study. It usually involves more reading, and some research experience. The time required to earn a graduate degree varies. It is usually three years in law and theology, and four years in medicine. Some graduate programs may be completed in one or two years.

Degrees. The bachelor of arts or bachelor of science degree is the common degree for completing a four or five year program. One or two years of graduate study are usually required for the master of arts or master of science degree. A doctor's degree signifies more extensive graduate study. Many institutions also award honorary degrees for outstanding achievement in a profession or in public service. See Degree, College.

College Life

College life gives the student a welcome measure of independence. But the student should realize that new responsibilities go with this independence. He must balance hard work with recreation, allow enough time and energy for social activities, and learn to use to the best advantage the opportunities offered by the school.

Residence. Most colleges have *residence halls* or *dormitories*. Dormitory life offers many social advantages and opportunities for friendships. Many schools also have student-controlled residences called *cooperatives*. In these, the students can cut expenses by doing their own housework. Students may often live in private homes approved by the school.

Fraternities and Sororities have houses at many schools. These organizations choose their own members

according to the rules set up by the school. Educators do not agree on the value of the fraternity and sorority system. Some approve the social advantages gained by membership in these organizations. Others believe that they tend to dominate college life, and to become undemocratic. Some colleges prohibit social fraternities and sororities on their campuses. See Fraternity; Sorority.

Instruction. The college freshman finds he has much more time to do as he chooses than he had in high school. His classes generally take up only about 15 hours each week, although he may have additional hours of laboratory work. The rest of the time between classes is free for study or recreation.

Most classes are either lecture or discussion groups. In larger institutions, *lectures* may be given to several hundred students at a time, sometimes with the assistance of closed-circuit television. The student should take careful notes on the information given. *Discussion groups* are much smaller. Students often work on individual projects outside of class and report on them to the group.

For a general discussion of tests and grading, see Grading; Tests and Measurements.

Libraries. University and college libraries are vast storehouses of knowledge. Some hold several million volumes. The library must be used to the fullest extent

Seminars and other discussion groups provide a close relationship between students and instructors. Most seminars offer advanced study and research in specialized areas. This one on international relations is at Wesleyan University, Middletown, Conn.

Tom Hollyman, Photo Researchers

Robert Perron, Photo Researchers

Huge Libraries are important resources of universities and colleges. Visitors to this library at Yale University may view rare books and manuscripts in the display cases, *right.*

if the student is to receive the greatest benefit from his college course. At best, routine classwork can only scratch the surface of any field of knowledge. The student can round out his education only by consistent and intelligent independent reading. See LIBRARY (University and College Libraries).

Research and Laboratory Work. The college teacher tries to do more than merely hand the student facts to memorize. It is far more important for him to develop the student's ability to find information for himself and to learn to think intelligently. For this reason, the teacher tries to direct the student in independent study and research by recommending books for outside reading and by suggesting new avenues of study in his field. Students in the sciences and engineering have laboratories in which to work. World-famous scientists direct some of these laboratories. In them they have made many important discoveries, often with the help of graduate students. For example, much of the original work on the use of atomic energy was done in the laboratories of the University of Chicago and the University of California. See RESEARCH.

Extracurricular Activities outside the normal routine of classes and study help develop the student's personality, and provide a proper balance for his daily routine. Athletics are one of many possible activities (see SPORTS AND SPORTSMANSHIP). Students may also work on the staffs of school newspapers and magazines. They may take part in such activities as dramatics, music, writing, hobbies, debating, politics, religion, and student government (see STUDENT GOVERNMENT). These activities

are valuable, but the wise student remembers that learning is the main purpose of attending college.

History

European Universities. Modern universities had their origin in Europe during the 1100's. But European universities were not the first in the world. The Arabs had universities at earlier dates. The University of Al-Azhar, founded in Cairo in 970, is one of the oldest universities in the world still operating.

European universities developed from the cathedral and monastery schools. Their development took place so slowly that it is difficult to know the point at which they became universities. Many scholars believe the oldest European university is the University of Bologna, Italy. It was founded in the late 1000's, but it had existed as a law school since 890. The University of Paris developed during the 1100's. Many other universities appeared in Europe during the 1200's and 1300's.

These first schools were founded largely to serve the professions. They provided the first unified teaching of law, medicine, and theology. Most of them were modeled on one of two plans—the Bologna plan or the Paris plan. At Bologna, the university was a corporation of the students. They hired the teachers and controlled the school's policies. The University of Paris was a corporation of the teachers. They collected fees from the students and directed the policies of the university.

Control of the schools gradually passed to a permanent body of administrators. The courses of study also broadened. During the Renaissance in the 1400's, the universities helped direct the revival of interest in Greek and Roman learning. From this revival developed the modern concept of the liberal-arts curriculum.

First Universities in the Americas. The first university in the Western Hemisphere, the University of Santo Domingo, was founded in the Dominican Republic in 1538. The University of San Marcos at Lima, Peru, was founded in 1551, as was the National Autonomous University of Mexico. Other universities appeared shortly afterward in the other Spanish colonies.

The first university to be planned in what is now the United States was at Henricopolis, Va. It was authorized in 1619, but plans were dropped after the Indian massacres of 1622. Harvard University is the oldest school of higher education still active in the United States. It was founded as Newtowne College in 1636. The oldest university in Canada, Laval University, was founded as the Seminary of Quebec in 1663. It became a university in 1852. The first English-speaking univer-

THE OLDEST U.S. UNIVERSITIES AND COLLEGES

Name	Location	Founded
Harvard University	Cambridge, Mass.	1636
William and Mary College	Williamsburg, Va.	1693
Saint John's College	Annapolis, Md.	1696
Yale University	New Haven, Conn.	1701
Princeton University	Princeton, N.J.	1746
Columbia University	New York City	1754
University of Pennsylvania	Philadelphia	1756
Brown University	Providence, R.I.	1764
Rutgers University	New Brunswick, N.J.	1766
Dartmouth College	Hanover, N.H.	1769

UNIVERSITIES AND COLLEGES

sity in Canada was established in 1789. It was the University of King's College at Windsor, N.S.

Higher education in the United States began at a time when knowledge was limited. The modern scientific spirit had not yet developed. The early settlers regarded colleges chiefly as a means of training ministers.

Many of the people who came to America came in search of religious freedom. The influence of this fact may be seen in the development of the American system of higher education. Each faith wanted to train its own leaders, and each set up schools to do so. As a result, many small church colleges were founded during the 1700's and 1800's, particularly in the Middle West. These colleges were general rather than specialized. They taught liberal arts rather than technical subjects.

Early in American history, some leaders saw the need for education that went beyond the various religious concerns of the people. The state university was one response to this need.

Another development was the granting of land in new territories for the establishment of schools. In addition, wealthy citizens gave gifts for the founding of nonchurch schools. A number of schools which had been established by churches also passed to private control.

Growth of Specialization. During the 1800's and through the mid-1900's, specialization in knowledge increased. Many colleges were created to train students in such fields as agriculture, medicine, engineering, and commerce. Specialization also resulted in an increased emphasis on advanced study. As a result, graduate schools were established at many larger schools. In turn, professional and research interests came to dominate all other educational interests. Education for professions overshadowed the liberal arts.

Specialization has resulted in the multiplying of the fields of knowledge. Educators have been asked to decide whether the college should become a preparatory school for the professions or whether the professional schools should lengthen their courses. Actually, both have happened. Today there is no set idea of what a college should be.

Another cause of specialization has been the increase in the number of students attending college. In the early days, universities served only a relatively limited group. But the people of the United States insisted that higher education should be available to anyone who wanted it. Obviously, the more the college population grew, the more courses had to be offered to satisfy many different individual interests and abilities.

Recent Developments. During World War II, American colleges contributed to the national effort by developing special programs of study and research. After the war, the typical veteran who entered a university was a young man in a hurry. He wanted to obtain a college education or vocational training as quickly as possible, and start the career that had been interrupted by the war. This development brought into sharp focus the whole problem in modern higher education. An additional factor was Russia's rapid postwar advances in science. Educators agree that the student needs a broad education as a basis for whatever field attracts him.

Some colleges now emphasize the study of classic works of literature. Others have combined campus study with practical training in factories and offices. Some colleges have made special studies of the needs of young people to discover what to emphasize in their programs. State universities generally try to use knowledge in as many ways as possible to serve society.

Another major development in American universities and colleges has been their increasing contribution to the world outside the campus. University laboratories have become important centers of experiment and discovery. College extension services, home study, correspondence courses, and radio and television programs have spread knowledge far beyond the narrow limits of the campus.   JOHN D. MILLETT

Related Articles. See the separate articles on outstanding universities and colleges, such as HARVARD UNIVERSITY; WILLIAM AND MARY, COLLEGE OF. See also the Career section in the various articles on different fields of human knowledge, such as MEDICINE (Careers in Medicine); ENGINEERING (Engineering as a Profession). Other related articles in WORLD BOOK include:

American Association of University Women	Extension Service	Research Scholarship
Caps and Gowns	Fellowship	School
Coeducation	Fraternity	Sorority
College Entrance Examination	Graduate School	Teaching Vocational
Colleges, Association of American	Junior College Land-Grant	Guidance Wilson,
Degree, College	College or	Woodrow
Education	University	(University
Education, History of	Library	President)

Outline

I. Going to College
  A. Selecting a School   E. College Costs
  B. Entrance Requirements F. Working Your Way
  C. Accrediting   G. Other Financial Help
  D. Size

II. Kinds of Universities and Colleges
  A. Privately Controlled Schools
  B. Church-Controlled Schools
  C. Publicly Controlled Schools

III. School Organization
  A. Campus   D. The Student Body
  B. Administration   E. The Calendar
  C. Faculty

IV. Selecting Courses
  A. Curriculum   C. Graduate Study
  B. Preprofessional Courses D. Degrees

V. College Life
  A. Residence
  B. Fraternities and Sororities
  C. Instruction
  D. Libraries
  E. Research and Laboratory Work
  F. Extracurricular Activities

VI. History

Questions

What information should you get when you select a university or college?

How does a university differ from a college?

How is a university faculty usually organized?

In what two ways are school-year programs divided?

In addition to instruction, what opportunities does a university or college offer?

What is the oldest university in the United States? In Canada?

From what sources can a student obtain financial aid?

What kinds of courses did the first universities and colleges in the United States offer? Why?

Why has specialization developed in higher education?

What is the largest university in the United States? In Canada?

UNIVERSITY. For names of universities beginning with University of, see the specific name for entry. For example, for the University of Chicago, see CHICAGO, UNIVERSITY OF.

UNIVERSITY CITY, Mo. (pop. 51,249; alt. 500 ft.), is a residential suburb of St. Louis. It lies just west of St. Louis, near the campus of Washington University. For location, see MISSOURI (political map).

University City received its charter in 1906. It has a council-manager form of government.   NOEL P. GIST

UNIVERSITY EXTENSION. See CORRESPONDENCE SCHOOL; EXTENSION SERVICE.

UNKNOWN NUMBER. See ALGEBRA.

UNKNOWN SOLDIER. After World War I, officials of the Allied countries found that the bodies of many soldiers killed in battle could not be identified. The governments of Belgium, France, Great Britain, Italy, and the United States decided to honor in some special way the memory of these soldiers. Each government chose a symbolic unknown soldier, buried his remains near the national capital, and built a monument in his honor. Belgium placed its unknown soldier in a tomb at the base of the Colonnade of the Congress in Brussels. France buried its unknown soldier beneath the Arc de Triomphe in the center of Paris, and keeps a flame always burning over the grave. Great Britain buried its unknown soldier in Westminster Abbey. Italy's unknown soldier lies in front of the monument to Victor Emmanuel in Rome.

The Unknown Soldier of the United States was one of four war dead taken from American cemeteries in France. An American soldier, Sergeant Edward Younger, selected him from these four. The remains were brought to the United States Capitol to lie in state. On Armistice Day (Nov. 11), 1921, they were buried in Arlington National Cemetery in Virginia, across the Potomac River from Washington, D.C. The tomb, completed 10 years later, has a white marble sarcophagus over the grave bearing the inscription, "Here rests in honored glory an American soldier known but to God."

After World War II and the Korean War, Congress directed that an "Unknown American" from each of these wars be buried near or beside the Tomb of the Unknown Soldier. The World War II Unknown was chosen from two unknowns by an American sailor, Hospitalman William Charette, in a ceremony aboard the cruiser *Canberra* off Norfolk, Va. The Korean War Unknown was chosen by an American soldier, Sergeant Ned Lyle, from the unidentified dead of that war buried in the National Memorial Cemetery of the Pacific at Honolulu, Hawaii. These unknowns lay in state at the Capitol. They were buried in marble-capped crypts at the head of the Tomb of the Unknown Soldier on Memorial Day, 1958. Many persons call the memorial the *Tomb of the Unknowns*.

A memorial amphitheater, built by the Grand Army of the Republic in honor of servicemen killed in battle, stands near the tomb. Memorial Day services are held there each year, and wreaths are placed on the tomb. An honor guard from the Honor Guard Company of the 1st Battle Group, 3rd Infantry, Fort Myer, Va., keeps a sentry on duty at the tomb. The sentry is changed every hour during the day and about every two hours at night. His tour of duty averages about 11 months.

Critically reviewed by the DEPARTMENT OF THE ARMY

See also ARC DE TRIOMPHE DE L'ÉTOILE; ARLINGTON NATIONAL CEMETERY; WASHINGTON, D.C. (picture).

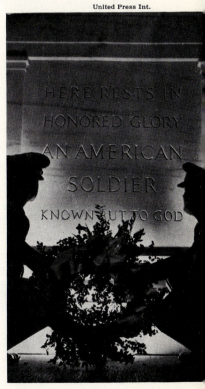

United Press Int.

The Tomb of the Unknown Soldier in Arlington National Cemetery in Virginia is guarded by a sentry 24 hours a day.

UNTERMEYER, LOUIS

Richard L. Simon

Louis Untermeyer

UNTERMEYER, *UN ter MI er*, **LOUIS** (1885-), is an American poet, critic, and editor. He left school at 15, went into the family jewelry company, and for 23 years worked as a businessman by day and as a writer by night. After he became a vice-president of the company, he resigned to write full time. He went to Europe and lived and studied there for three years. Then he published many volumes of poetry and lectured extensively. He is best known, however, as an anthologist of poetry. He edited about 18 collections of poetry, including *Modern British Poetry* (1920), *Modern American Poetry* (1921), and *Stars to Steer By* (1941). Many of these collections are used as school texts. He also wrote an autobiography *From Another World* (1939). He served as consultant in poetry in English for the Library of Congress. Untermeyer was born in New York City.　　　JAMES WOODRESS

UNTOUCHABLE. See CASTE; INDIA (Religion).

UNWRITTEN LAW. See STATUTE.

UNZHA RIVER. See VOLGA RIVER.

UPANISHAD. See VEDA.

UPAS, *YOO puhs*, is the name of a large forest tree that grows in southeastern Asia and Indonesia. It belongs to the mulberry family. Supposedly, tribesmen mixed its poisonous milky sap with other plant poisons to poison their arrows and darts. Tales about the deadliness of this poison terrified early explorers and travelers in the East Indies. Fabulous but false stories started regarding the poison and the plant producing it. People said that nothing could grow in the shade of the tree. They said the tree brought death to birds that perched on it or flew above it. Some people believed that only persons completely covered with clothes could approach the tree without danger.

Scientific Classification. The upas belongs to the mulberry family, *Moraceae*. It is classified as genus *Antiaris*, species *A. toxicaria*.　　　K. A. ARMSON

UPHOLSTERY. Before the 1400's, people made their chairs and couches comfortable by placing loose cushions at the back and on the seat. During the Italian Renaissance, it became the custom to attach cushions to the frames of the furniture. This new part of the furniture craft was called upholstery.

Today, there are many different ways of upholstering chairs and davenports. Cushions and backs may be filled with down, kapok, cotton, or foam rubber, with the arms of the furniture left bare. Or the backs, sides, and arms of the furniture may be spring-filled and overstuffed with padding. Many people prefer to have "overstuffed" furniture in their homes, because it is so comfortable.

Webbing. In upholstering, strips of linen or jute webbing are first stretched both lengthwise and crosswise of the frame, interlacing at the spots where they cross. The number of webbing strips is determined by the number of springs which are to be used. Enough strips are provided to make one crossing for each spring to rest on. The webbing is usually stretched and tacked to the under sides, so that the stretching will not mar the part of the frame which shows. The tacks which fasten the webbing to the frame are fastened out of line, or *staggered*, so as not to split the wood.

Springs. The springs should not be so large as to come in contact with each other when under pressure. But they should be large enough not to leave open spots when the furniture is sat upon. After the springs are placed in position, they are sewed to the webbing to make them secure. Then they are tied down.

Springs are tied down by the row. Twine is passed through the top coils of each row and then fastened to tacks in the frame at either end of the row. The twine is pulled until the springs have been lowered to the desired height above the frame. The less the springs are compressed, the greater the springiness of the upholstery. The springs are then tied with crosswise twines to keep them from tipping from one side to another. Finally, diagonal twines are used to secure the springs even more. The diagonal twines also keep the burlap covering that goes over the springs from slipping.

Stuffing. Burlap is tacked to the furniture frame and sewed to the springs to form a foundation covering for the stuffing which pads the springs. In the best grades of upholstery, curled horsehair or foam rubber forms this padding. The padding is laid evenly over the burlap covering. If the padding is horsehair, it is sewed down securely to keep it from shifting and forming holes or lumps. A muslin first covering is sometimes used to hold the padding in place, so as to prevent any strain on the fine upholstery fabric itself.

Fabric. The final step in upholstering is tacking the upholstery fabric to the finished padding work. The upholstery fabric varies greatly, depending on the type of furniture and the fad of the moment. Chintz, satin, and cotton are popular fabrics for bedroom furniture, while brocade, silk, and linen are preferred for living-room furniture. Leather, nylon, and plastics are also excellent upholstery fabrics.　　　EFFA BROWN

See also FURNITURE..

An Upholsterer Finishes Work on a Lounge Chair.
Baker Furniture, Inc., Holland, Mich.

Karl H. Maslowski

The Upland Plover helps man by killing harmful insects.

UPLAND PLOVER is a North American bird of the sandpiper family. It is usually found on wet prairies or meadows. It is the only member of the tattler group of sandpipers that does not live by the sea.

The upland plover is sometimes known as the Bartramian sandpiper. It is about a foot long, and it has an especially long tail for a sandpiper. Its color is blackish-brown and buff above, and buff with dark streaks on the breast and sides. Its belly is white. The upland plover breeds from Alaska to Montana and Maine. In the fall it migrates to southern Brazil and Argentina. There the upland plover winters on the pampas.

The upland plover makes its nest in clumps of prairie grass or dry leaves on the prairie. The female lays four cream-colored or pale buff eggs, speckled with dark brown. The color of the birds blends with the prairie grass, making the birds difficult to discover. The young birds can fly by midsummer, and start south almost at once.

Upland plovers destroy many harmful insects, such as locusts and cutworms. The birds are protected from hunters by law (see BIRD [Protective Laws]).

Scientific Classification. Upland plovers are in the sandpiper family, *Scolopacidae*, not in the true plover family. Upland plovers are genus *Bartramia*, species *B. longicauda*.　　　　　　GEORGE E. HUDSON

UPOLU. See SAMOA.

UPPER CANADA. See ONTARIO (History).

UPPER CANADA VILLAGE. See ONTARIO (Places to Visit).

UPPER DARBY, Pa. (pop. 44,000; alt. 80 ft.), is one of the most populous U.S. communities that has kept the township form of government rather than changing to the city form. Its development as a residential community began about 1908 and has been most rapid since 1916. It contains about 20 residential centers. Many of the residents of Upper Darby work or have business interests in Philadelphia, which lies about 10 miles north and east. Industrial plants in Upper Darby produce woolen cloth, Turkish towels, chemicals, furniture, communications equipment, and lumber. For location of Upper Darby, see PENNSYLVANIA (political map).　　　　　　S. K. STEVENS

UPPER IOWA UNIVERSITY is a coeducational privately controlled school at Fayette, Iowa. Courses in liberal arts and science lead to B.A. and B.S. degrees. It was founded in 1857. For enrollment, see UNIVERSITIES AND COLLEGES (table).

UPPER PALATINATE. See PALATINATE.

UPPER VOLTA is a landlocked country in western Africa. Formerly a territory in French West Africa, it became independent in 1960 as the REPUBLIC OF UPPER VOLTA. Its name in French, the official language, is RÉPUBLIQUE DE HAUTE-VOLTA.

The Land. Upper Volta covers 105,869 square miles, slightly more than the state of Colorado. The country lies about 625 miles east of the Atlantic Ocean.

The country consists mainly of a huge plateau that gently slopes to the south. The land varies from 650 to 1,000 feet above sea level. Most of Upper Volta is a dry *savanna* (wooded grassland). The Black, White, and Red Volta rivers have cut valleys through the plateau. They flow south into Ghana where they join to form the Volta River. Boats cannot use the rivers because they are either dry or in flood most of the year.

Upper Volta has three distinct seasons. From November through February it is cool and dry. March and

---

FACTS IN BRIEF

Form of Government: Republic.

Capital: Ouagadougou.

Official Language: French.

Head of Government: President.

Legislature: Legislative Assembly (75 members).

Area: 105,869 square miles. *Greatest distances:* (north-south) 400 miles; (east-west) 525 miles.

Population: *1961 census*—4,300,000; distribution, 95 per cent rural, 5 per cent urban. *1967 estimate*—4,805,000; density, 45 persons to the square mile. *1972 estimate*—5,245,000.

Chief Products: *Agriculture,* beans, cassava, corn, cotton, livestock (cattle, donkeys, goats, horses, sheep), millet, peanuts, rice, shea nuts, sorghum, yams. *Fishing,* dried and salted fish. *Mining,* bauxite, copper, gold.

Flag: Three equal horizontal stripes: black, white, and red. They symbolize the main rivers, the Black, White, and Red Voltas. See FLAG (color picture, Flags of Africa).

Money: *Basic unit,* franc. See MONEY (table, Values).

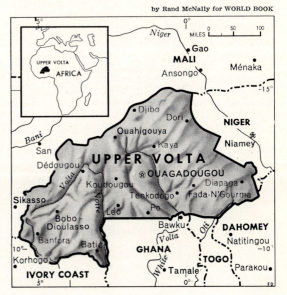

by Rand McNally for WORLD BOOK

168a

Upper Volta Children at Kabourou bush station study in a school that has no desks. They sit on mats on the floor while going over their lessons.

An Ouagadougou Market place has a roof to protect shoppers and vendors from rain and the tropical sun. But many vendors spread out their wares outside the market.

April are hot and dry. The rest of the year is hot and wet. Yearly rainfall varies from about 40 inches in the south to less than 10 inches in the extreme north. The *harmattan*, a hot wind from the desert, adds to the dryness of the north. The average temperature ranges between 68° and 95° F. during the year.

The People. Upper Volta has a population of 4,805,-000, about the same as Florida. Upper Volta has an average of only 45 persons to the square mile, but urban areas are more crowded, with 50 to 125 persons to the square mile. Most of the people live in the central and southern sections of the country.

Almost all the people belong to two main African groups. They are the Voltaic and the Mande. The most numerous of the Voltaic group are the Mossi who make up half the population. They trace their history back to the Moro Naba which ruled the area a thousand years ago. A Mossi "emperor" still holds court in Ouagadougou. The emperor serves as a religious leader, but has little political power. The Mossi farm in the central part of the country. Other Voltaic people include the Bobo, Gourounsi, and Lobi.

The Mande group is only about one-seventh the size of the Voltaic group. The Mande tribes live among the Voltaic people but have preserved their own customs.

They include the Boussance, Dioula, Samo, and Tougan-Marka. Only 3,000 white people live in the country.

Ouagadougou is the capital and largest city of Upper Volta. Other large cities include Banfora, Bobo-Dioulasso, Dedougou, Kaya, Koudougou, and Ouahigouya.

Economic Conditions. Upper Volta is an agricultural land where the people raise livestock and grow food crops. The poor soil, erosion, and lack of water hinder farming. The government has a soil conservation and reclamation program through which it has built many irrigation dams. But many of the people go to Ghana and Ivory Coast to do seasonal farm work because of the scarcity of good farmland in Upper Volta.

The chief wealth of Upper Volta is its livestock. The stock includes 1½ million cattle, 2½ million sheep and goats, and some donkeys, hogs, and horses. Live animals make up more than half of its exports. Dried, salted, and smoked fish are the second most important export. About four-fifths of all exports go to Ghana. Commercial crops include cotton, peanuts, rice, and shea nuts, used as an edible vegetable fat. Food crops include beans, cassava, corn, millet, and sorghum.

Few natural resources have been discovered or developed. Upper Volta mines some gold and gold-bear-

168b

ing quartz, and has deposits of bauxite, copper, and manganese. Its manufactures consist chiefly of processing fats and oils, rice polishing, cotton ginning, and sisal twine production. The well-developed handicrafts include embroidery, bronze figurines, and leather goods.

The Mossi Railroad runs 225 miles through Upper Volta and then another 508 miles in the Ivory Coast. The line links Ouagadougou with the port of Abidjan. The 10,000 miles of road include 1,300 miles of paved highways. Upper Volta has some 30 airfields, including international airports at Ouagadougou and Bobo-Dioulasso.

Education. About 95 of every 100 adults cannot read or write. Only about 7 of every 100 school-age children go to school. But the government has started a program to educate all children. Upper Volta has about 43,000 students enrolled in its public and private schools, including about 300 elementary schools, 6 high schools, and 4 vocational schools. Advanced students attend French universities or the University of Dakar in Senegal.

Government. Under the constitution, the president is the chief executive of Upper Volta. The people elect him for a five-year term. The Legislative Assembly, a one-house legislature, has 75 members elected for five-year terms. In 1966, army chief Sangoule Lamizana suspended the constitution and dissolved the assembly after he took over the government.

History. The feudal Mossi empires dominated the area until the end of the 1800's. They probably came from East Africa in the 1000's. They established kingdoms in what is now northern Ghana and then spread into what is now Upper Volta. Their empire of Moro Naba had its capital first at Tenkodogo and later at Ouagadougou. Kingdoms of the main tribe broke away in the 1200's and 1300's and founded separate empires. But the Moro Naba empire centering around Ouagadougou resisted Moslem invaders. The empire continued until modern times.

The French arrived in 1896 and established a protectorate over the area. The French government created Upper Volta from the colonies of Upper Senegal and Niger in French West Africa in 1919. Upper Volta is named for the upper basin of the Volta River that occupies most of the country.

France divided Upper Volta among the neighboring colonies of Niger, French Sudan, and the Ivory Coast in 1932 because it believed Upper Volta could not become self-supporting. Between 1939 and 1954, the government extended the Mossi Railroad from Bobo-Dioulasso to Ouagadougou to develop the Mossi region.

In 1947, the French reinstated Upper Volta's 1932 boundaries. In 1958, the area became a self-governing state within the French Community called the *Voltaic Republic.* But in 1959, the country changed its name to the *Republic of Upper Volta.* In the same year, Upper Volta joined Dahomey, Ivory Coast, and Niger in the Council of the Entente, a loose economic union.

On Aug. 5, 1960, Upper Volta became an independent republic outside the French Community. It became a member of the United Nations later in 1960.

In January, 1966, trade union members in Ouagadougou called a general strike. They were protesting a government-proposed wage reduction. The strike ended after army chief Sangoule Lamizana took over the government. Lamizana ousted President Maurice Yameogo,

dissolved the Legislative Assembly, and suspended the constitution.   KENNETH ROBINSON

See also FRENCH WEST AFRICA; OUAGADOUGOU.

UPPSALA UNIVERSITY. See SWEDEN (Social and Cultural Achievements).

UPSALA COLLEGE. See UNIVERSITIES AND COLLEGES (table).

UPSTATE MEDICAL CENTER. See UNIVERSITIES AND COLLEGES (table [New York, State University of]).

UR was a city along the Euphrates River in ancient Sumer, a part of Babylonia. For location, see BABYLONIA (map). Sumerians settled the city about 4000 B.C., but excavations have shown traces of earlier village cultures. Its first dynasty, or line of kings, was established about 2800 B.C. As a city-state, Ur became one of the first Sumerian cities to win control over neighboring areas. Archaeologists have found rich grave remains, including jewelry and carvings, that show much technical skill (see ASIA [picture, A Mosaic Panel from Ur]). Ur later came under the control of various other city-states and invaders. It is called *Ur of the Chaldees* (Chaldeans) in the Old Testament, and was said to have been the birthplace of the patriarch Abraham.

URAL MOUNTAINS are probably the richest mountain range of their size in the world. The industrial and mineral development of the Ural Mountains played an important part in supplying the armies of Russia during World War II. These mountains are remarkable in the variety and amount of mineral wealth which they contain. Salt, silver, and gold have been mined in the Ural Mountains since the 1500's. By the 1800's, the Ural region was famous for its gems and semiprecious stones, which include emerald, beryl, amethyst, topaz, and sapphire. Today, mining activities produce coal, iron, copper, gold, platinum, silver, nickel, aluminum, manganese, lead, zinc, magnesium, chromium, potash, salt, building stone, talc, diamonds, and soapstone. Oil is found west of the Ural area, and engineers estimate that the mountains contain $17\frac{1}{2}$ million tons of asbestos.

The Ural Mountains extend for 1,500 miles in a north-south direction, from the Arctic Ocean to near the Aral Sea. Old map makers used this range to mark the continental boundary between Europe and Asia. Many maps continue to show the Urals as the natural division of the two continents, although not all geographers accept the mountains as the boundary mark. For location, see RUSSIA (physical map).

The mountains are geologically old and have been worn down to rounded hills which are from 1,000 to 6,000 feet high. Several peaks in the north and south rise over 5,000 feet above the sea. The highest peak of the Ural Mountains is Mount Narodnaya (6,184 feet), in the northern part of the range.   THEODORE SHABAD

URAL RIVER is a shallow stream that rises on the eastern slopes of the southern Ural Mountains in Russia. For location, see RUSSIA (physical map). The Ural flows generally south for about 1,570 miles and enters the Caspian Sea through several mouths. Salmon and sturgeon fisheries are along the Ural. Railroads cross the river at Orenburg and Ural'sk. The steel center, Magnitogorsk, lies on the upper Ural.   THEODORE SHABAD

URANIA. See MUSE.

URANINITE. See PITCHBLENDE.

Fisher Research Laboratory Inc.

Uranium Prospectors use portable Geiger counters to search in rocks for the valuable uranium ore. The aluminum prospecting stick on this model works well when exploring deep crevices and tunnels.

URANIUM, *yoo RAY nih um* (chemical symbol U), is the main source of atomic energy, produced by the *fission* (splitting) of atoms (see FISSION). It has the highest atomic weight of any element found in nature. Its atomic number is 92 and its atomic weight is 238.03. Uranium is *radioactive* (gives off atomic particles).

Martin Klaproth of Germany discovered an oxide of uranium in the mineral pitchblende in 1789. He named the element in honor of the discovery of the planet Uranus. The element was not isolated until 1842.

Uses of Uranium

The main use of uranium is as a fuel in the production of atomic energy. This energy may be used in weapons such as the atomic bomb. Or it may have peaceful uses, such as the production of electric power. See ATOMIC ENERGY (Uses of Atomic Energy).

Uranium has a number of uses in industry apart from atomic energy production. Steel manufacturers sometimes add uranium to steel to produce steel with special properties. Compounds of uranium with ammonia may be used to color glazes on ceramic products. Uranium carbide acts as a *catalyst*, to increase the rate of chemical reactions in the manufacture of ammonia. Glass containing uranium absorbs X rays. Such glass can shield workers from X rays and *gamma rays* (rays of very high energy) given off by radioactive materials. It is heavy and has a strong yellow color.

Uranium Ores

Uranium is not a rare mineral. It is more common in the earth than such "common" elements as mercury, silver, and iodine. But the concentration of uranium in most rocks is only a few parts in a million.

The richest uranium ore, *pitchblende*, contains uranium oxides. It is a dark bluish-black mineral with a pitchlike luster. The most important ore found in the United States is *carnotite*. It is a complex compound of uranium with vanadium, potassium, and oxygen. See CARNOTITE.

Uranium Deposits. Few high-grade deposits of uranium were known before World War II. The only ones actively mined were the rich pitchblende deposits of the Belgian Congo (now Congo [Léopoldville]) and the Great Bear Lake area in northern Canada. These deposits were mined for the radium, silver, and other valuable metals found together with the uranium.

Due to its importance as a source of atomic energy, supplies of uranium have been vigorously sought since the end of World War II. In the late 1950's, experts estimated that the parts of the world outside Russian control could produce at least 40,000 tons of uranium

LEADING URANIUM MINING STATES AND PROVINCES

Pounds of uranium oxide mined each year

Ontario 12,035,000 lbs.	🛒🛒🛒🛒🛒🛒🛒🛒🛒🛒🛒🛒
New Mexico 9,476,000 lbs.	🛒🛒🛒🛒🛒🛒🛒🛒🛒
Wyoming 6,951,000 lbs.	🛒🛒🛒🛒🛒🛒
Utah 6,029,000 lbs.	🛒🛒🛒🛒🛒🛒
Colorado 3,501,000 lbs.	🛒🛒🛒
Saskatchewan 1,793,000 lbs.	🛒🛒
Washington 864,000 lbs.	🛒
Arizona 759,000 lbs.	🛒
South Dakota 423,000 lbs.	🛒

Based on the latest government statistics.

WHERE URANIUM AND THORIUM COME FROM
(Uranium-233 can be made from thorium)

This map locates the major uranium and thorium deposits in non-Communist countries. No information is available on deposits in Communist countries. Canada, the United States, South Africa, and France have the largest uranium deposits in the non-Communist world. India, Canada, and the United States lead in thorium deposits.

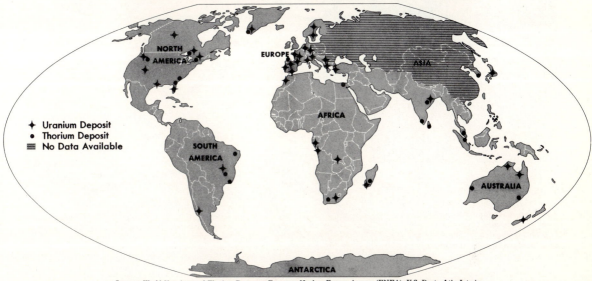

✦ Uranium Deposit
● Thorium Deposit
≡ No Data Available

NORTH AMERICA
EUROPE
ASIA
AFRICA
SOUTH AMERICA
AUSTRALIA
ANTARCTICA

Sources: *World Uranium and Thorium Resources*, European Nuclear Energy Agency (ENEA); U.S. Dept. of the Interior
WORLD BOOK map—FGA

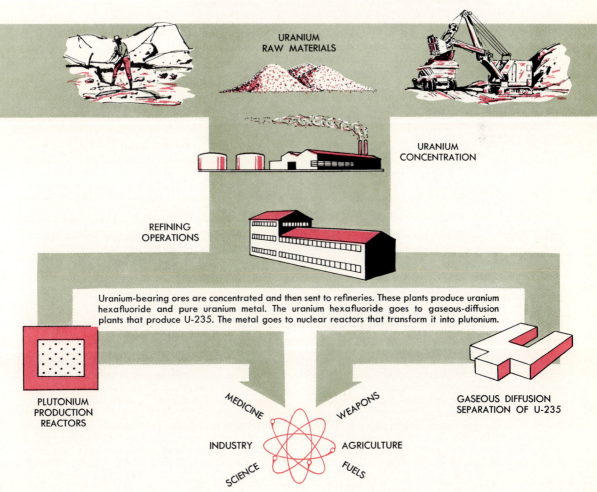

URANIUM RAW MATERIALS

URANIUM CONCENTRATION

REFINING OPERATIONS

Uranium-bearing ores are concentrated and then sent to refineries. These plants produce uranium hexafluoride and pure uranium metal. The uranium hexafluoride goes to gaseous-diffusion plants that produce U-235. The metal goes to nuclear reactors that transform it into plutonium.

PLUTONIUM PRODUCTION REACTORS

GASEOUS DIFFUSION SEPARATION OF U-235

MEDICINE
WEAPONS
INDUSTRY
AGRICULTURE
SCIENCE
FUELS

USES OF URANIUM

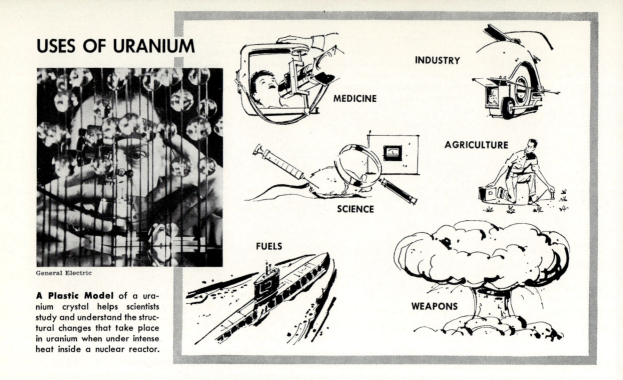

MEDICINE

INDUSTRY

SCIENCE

AGRICULTURE

FUELS

WEAPONS

General Electric

A Plastic Model of a uranium crystal helps scientists study and understand the structural changes that take place in uranium when under intense heat inside a nuclear reactor.

oxide a year. They estimated the total available ore reserves of South America, Canada, the United States, and France at more than 2 million tons. Including estimates of ores in Russia, China, and other countries, the world's total ore reserves in deposits that can be mined probably reaches more than 10 million tons. In addition, enormous quantities of uranium exist in shale and phosphate deposits, in granites, and in the ocean. This uranium cannot be recovered at present at reasonable cost. Technical advances in the future may make some of it available.

In the United States, principal deposits lie in the western states. The leading uranium-producing states are New Mexico, Utah, Colorado, Wyoming, Arizona, and Washington. Many deposits in the United States are not of the highest concentration. But the area has been so thoroughly prospected that the United States ranks as a major uranium-producing country. In the 1950's, many prospectors, both professional and amateur, hunted for uranium in the United States, particularly in the West. They searched among the rocks in many areas with Geiger counters or scintillation counters. These devices indicate the amount of radioactivity in the rocks. Places with high radioactivity may contain uranium ores. In the United States, minerals and ores of uranium may be sold only to the Atomic Energy Commission or with its permission to other users.

In Canada, uranium ores lie in a wide belt running from the Arctic Circle south to Ontario. Ontario leads the provinces in uranium production. It produces more than half of Canada's uranium.

In Other Countries. Deposits in Africa include those in the Congo (Léopoldville) at the rich Shinkolobwe mines. These mines once produced almost pure pitchblende. But the richest deposits are largely used up. The gold mines located in the Witwatersrand region of South Africa rank as another major source of uranium in

Africa. They produce large amounts of uranium as a by-product of gold mining. Substantial deposits also exist in Australia and in France. Deposits in Czechoslovakia, the original source of most of the world's uranium, are still mined. Experts believe that Russia and China have substantial uranium deposits.

Refining and Processing. The uranium ore goes from the mines in the United States and other countries to uranium concentrating plants. There, impurities are removed and the uranium is converted into U_3O_8, an oxide of uranium. Then, in other plants, the uranium oxide is refined to either a metal powder of pure uranium or the compound uranium hexafluoride, UF_6. The uranium metal may be used in nuclear reactors to produce plutonium. The UF_6 goes to *gaseous diffusion* plants. There, the compound is *vaporized* (changed into a gas) and the atoms of uranium of different weight are separated. The highly fissionable uranium is used for weapons and as fuel elements for various reactors. Used fuel elements may be processed to recover any unfissioned uranium. The unfissioned uranium can be returned to the reactor.

Chemical Properties

Pure uranium is a silvery metal, softer than iron. It is a member of the *actinide* series of elements. This series has actinium as its lightest-weight member. Elements of the actinide series have many chemical similarities to the *rare earth*, or *lanthanide*, series. Like other heavy elements, uranium and its compounds are poisonous. See ELEMENT, CHEMICAL; RARE EARTH.

Uranium is very reactive. It combines vigorously with oxygen, and is *pyrophoric*. This means that small chips of the metal may burn spontaneously in air, as magnesium does. Uranium forms several different oxides. The most important in chemistry are uranium dioxide, UO_2, and uranium trioxide, UO_3. Uranium will decompose water. It can combine directly with many gases, including chlorine and hydrogen, at temperatures around 200° C. Metallic uranium reacts with acids to release hydrogen and to form uranium compounds. Metallic uranium may be produced by heating a uranium *halide* with a metal, such as calcium. Uranium halides are compounds of uranium with one of the halogen elements: fluorine, chlorine, bromine, or iodine. In addition to the oxides and halides, uranium forms important compounds with nitrogen, carbon, hydrogen, and many other elements.

Isotopes

As found in nature, uranium consists of a mixture of three isotopes. *Isotopes* are atoms of an element that have the same atomic number but different atomic weights or mass numbers. The uranium isotope with the atomic mass 238, written U^{238}, makes up 99.274 per cent of naturally occurring uranium. The other two isotopes, U^{235} and U^{234}, make up 0.72 per cent and 0.006 per cent, respectively, of the uranium. All of these isotopes are *radioactive*. They decay by giving off alpha particles to form isotopes of the element thorium (see ALPHA RAY; THORIUM). Thorium is also radioactive, and forms radioactive decay products. The decay of these isotopes finally ends in stable isotopes of lead.

Isotope Separation. The main method of separating the various isotopes of uranium is called the *gaseous diffusion* method. In this method, uranium is used in the form of uranium hexafluoride, UF_6, which *vaporizes* (becomes a gas) easily. Since fluorine has only one isotope, any variation in molecular weight depends completely on the weight of the uranium isotope in the molecule. Molecules of lower weight containing U^{235} move slightly faster than heavier molecules, which contain U^{238}. Therefore, the lighter molecules will pass slightly more easily through a very narrow passage, such as the holes in a porous material. Thus, in each passage through a porous barrier, a slight separation of the isotopes occurs. If this is repeated many hundreds of times, the isotopes become separated. Huge factories in the United States and other countries use this method to produce many tons of *enriched* uranium (uranium with a high U^{235} content) each year. The U^{235} isotope is the only naturally occurring uranium isotope that fissions easily.

Artificially Made Isotopes. In addition to the three naturally occurring isotopes, U^{234}, U^{235}, and U^{238}, other isotopes of uranium may be produced in the laboratory. They are all radioactive. These isotopes range in atomic mass from U^{227} to U^{240}. One of them, U^{233}, will fission easily, in the same way as U^{235}.

U^{233} is produced by bombarding thorium-232 atoms (Th^{232}) with neutrons in a nuclear reactor. The Th^{232} captures a neutron to form Th^{233}. Th^{233} then decays by losing a beta particle (an electron) to form protactinium-233. The protactinium is also radioactive, and decays by losing a beta particle to form U^{233}. See BETA RAY; TRANSMUTATION OF ELEMENTS.

Uranium Fission

Fission (splitting) of the uranium atom results in the release of energy. When a neutron hits a uranium atom, the atom breaks up into two smaller atoms, each about half as heavy as the original uranium atom.

Two or three neutrons are released. But the combined weight of the *fission fragments* (smaller atoms) and the neutrons amounts to less than the weight of the original uranium atom and the neutron that hit it. This "lost" mass is converted into energy. In 1905, Albert Einstein explained that mass might be changed into energy according to the formula $E = mc^2$. In this formula, E stands for energy, m stands for mass, and c^2 stands for the speed of light *squared* (multiplied by itself). Thus, a small amount of mass converted into energy results in a huge amount of energy. See ATOMIC ENERGY (Nuclear Fission).

U^{235} is the only naturally occurring isotope of uranium that can fission when bombarded by *slow* (low-energy) neutrons. When a slow neutron hits the U^{235} atom, it is captured by the *nucleus* (core) of the atom. This forms an atom of uranium, with a higher atomic mass—U^{236}. This unstable nucleus becomes deformed, or misshapen, and splits into two smaller nuclei, releasing neutrons and energy. A pound of pure U^{235}, if completely fissioned, would yield energy equal to that of an explosion of 9,000 tons of TNT.

When U^{238} atoms capture slow neutrons, they form atoms of U^{239}. But these atoms do not fission. Bombardment of U^{238} with *fast* (high-energy) neutrons will cause fission.

Chain Reaction. Only one neutron is needed to split an atom of uranium, and each fission releases two or three neutrons. These neutrons can then fission other atoms of uranium. Thus, a *chain reaction* is possible. In a chain reaction, once fission begins it will continue without anything being added to the system. Since U^{238} captures slow neutrons but does not fission, it hinders the chain reaction. Thus it is important to separate the U^{235} from the comparatively inert U^{238} for use in atomic weapons and in many nuclear reactors. But reactors can be designed to use fuels that range from natural uranium to material highly enriched in U^{235}, or in the artificially produced fuels, plutonium-239 (Pu^{239}) and U^{233}. The type of fuel used depends on the type of reactor. See ATOMIC REACTOR; ATOMIC ENERGY (Chain Reactions).

Breeder Reactions in nuclear reactors produce both fissionable material and atomic energy. An efficient breeder reactor may some day produce more fissionable material than it consumes.

In a breeder reactor, the fuel used to operate the atomic power plant is U^{235}. Fission of U^{235} produces energy. Neutrons released from U^{235} fission keep the chain reaction running. But some of them are captured by U^{238} and change it into U^{239}. The U^{239} decays by beta radiation into neptunium-239. The neptunium in turn decays by beta radiation into Pu^{239}, which is fissionable material. In an efficient reactor, the Pu^{239} produced should at least equal the U^{235} used up. U^{238} can be used to produce Pu^{239}, with Pu^{239} used as the fissionable material. Th^{232} can be used to produce U^{233}, also a fissionable material (see ATOMIC REACTOR [Breeder Reactors]).

ROBERT L. THORNTON

Related Articles in WORLD BOOK include:

URANIUM CITY, Sask. (pop. 1,665; alt. 1,042 ft.), lies in the center of some of the world's richest uranium deposits. It is on the north shore of Lake Athabasca. For location, see SASKATCHEWAN (political map). The settlement was laid out by the provincial government in the early 1950's, after uranium was discovered in the area. The provincial government administers the settlement.

URANUS, *YOO ruh nus*, was the name of the oldest god in Greek mythology. His name means heaven. The Greeks believed he gave heat, light, and rain to the earth. Uranus was the husband of Gaea (Earth). He was the father of the Cyclopes, the Titans, Rhea, and of the monsters with 100 hands and 50 heads. His youngest son Saturn killed him. From Uranus' blood the Giants, the Meliai (spirits of ashtrees), and the Furies were born.   JAMES F. CRONIN

URANUS, *YOO ruh nus*, is one of the planets in our solar system. It is the seventh planet from the sun. Sir William Herschel discovered Uranus in March, 1781. Herschel first thought Uranus was a comet. See HERSCHEL (Sir William).

The naked eye can barely see Uranus. The brightness of the planet equals that of a star of the sixth magnitude. It is about 1,782,000,000 miles from the sun, and it revolves around the sun once every 84 years. It rotates on its axis once in about 10 hours and 50 minutes. Peculiarities in its orbit led to the discovery of Neptune.

Astronomers believe Uranus has a diameter of about 32,000 miles, or nearly four times that of the earth. Some authorities believe its diameter is 29,200 miles. Uranus has over 64 times the volume of the earth. Its mass is about $14\frac{1}{2}$ times that of the earth. Its density is about one fourth the density of the earth. Uranus may be in a partially gaseous condition.

Uranus has great power to reflect light, perhaps even greater than Jupiter's. Seen through the telescope, Uranus appears as a pale, greenish disk, marked with faint parallel belts. Its spectrum shows heavy absorption of light in the red end, due to much methane in its atmosphere. Its surface temperature is about $-335°$ F.

Uranus has five satellites, or "moons." They are Miranda, Ariel, Umbriel, Titania, and Oberon, in order outward from Uranus. Their periods of revolution range from 1.4 days for Miranda to 13.2 days for Oberon. Their orbits are almost perpendicular to the orbit of Uranus. But they move from east to west, in the opposite direction from most solar bodies. E. C. SLIPHER

See also SOLAR SYSTEM; PLANET.

URBAN was the name of eight popes of the Roman Catholic Church. Urban II and Urban VIII were the most important. The group, and the years they served, includes:

Urban I, Saint (222-230)	Urban V (1362-1370)
Urban II (1088-1099)	Urban VI (1378-1389)
Urban III (1185-1187)	Urban VII (1590)
Urban IV (1261-1264)	Urban VIII (1623-1644)

Urban II (1042?-1099), a Frenchman, vigorously supported the Cluniac reform movement within the Roman Catholic Church. Pope Urban was opposed by Guibert of Ravenna, the antipope who called himself *Clement III*, a candidate of Emperor Henry IV of Germany. Urban was successful against Clement III and the

emperor. He presided at the Council of Clermont in 1095. There, he gave one of the most effective talks in history, in which he called Christians to a crusade to take the Holy Land from the Turks. The cry, "God wills it!" at the conclusion of his speech inaugurated the First Crusade (see CRUSADES). The Crusaders drove Clement III from Rome, and firmly established Urban on the papal throne before going to Jerusalem.

Under Urban's direction, the Council of Clermont issued a number of strict reform decrees, deposed the emperor's nominee for the see of Cambrai, excommunicated the king of France for adultery, and extended the Truce of God to all Christendom. Urban was born in the province of Champagne, in France.

Urban VIII (1568-1644) was pope during the greater part of the Thirty Years' War (1618-1648). He held foremost the welfare of the church. Urban founded an international seminary to train priests for the missions, and in 1633 he opened China and Japan as mission territory for all religious orders. Urban was born in Florence, Italy.   THOMAS P. NEILL and FULTON J. SHEEN

URBAN LEAGUE is a professional community service agency that promotes better relations among whites and Negroes in the United States. It works for equal opportunities for Negroes in employment and housing, and in educational, health, and welfare services. The group has about 50,000 members in 62 cities and 30 states. It also has a paid staff of nearly 500. The NATIONAL URBAN LEAGUE has headquarters at 14 E. 48th St., New York, N.Y. 10017. WHITNEY M. YOUNG, JR.

URBAN MOVEMENT. See POPULATION (Urban).

URBAN RENEWAL refers to the attempts of local governments to eliminate slums, prevent the growth of blighted areas, and provide better housing and neighborhoods. Some areas may be completely destroyed and rebuilt. The city buys and destroys dilapidated buildings, then builds needed playgrounds, schools, and other facilities. Other areas may need only neighborhood clean-up campaigns or enforcement of housing and health codes. The federal government shares the costs of these local programs. WILLIAM L. C. WHEATON

See also CONSERVATION (Conservation of Human Resources; picture); HOUSING (Public Housing); HOUSING AND URBAN DEVELOPMENT, DEPARTMENT OF.

URBANA. See CHAMPAIGN-URBANA.

URD. See NORNS.

URDU. See PAKISTAN (Language; Arts and Crafts).

UREA, *yoo REE uh*, is an organic compound found in the urine, blood, and lymph of man and other mammals. It is formed in the liver from nitrogen compounds.

Until 1828, chemists thought that only certain life processes could produce organic compounds such as urea. But then, the German chemist Friedrich Wöhler *synthesized* (made artificially) urea from a cyanate and an ammonium salt. His discovery is usually considered the birth of synthetic organic chemistry.

Urea is used in fertilizer and animal feeds, and to make other chemical compounds. The plastics industry uses it to manufacture resins for plastics. Urea is also used as a stabilizer in certain explosives.

Industry prepares urea commercially from liquid ammonia and liquid carbon dioxide. Under high pressure, these chemicals form ammonium carbamate, $NH_4CO_2NH_2$. This decomposes to give urea and water.

Urea occurs as white crystals or powder, and has a

faint odor. It dissolves readily in water. Its chemical formula is NH_2CONH_2, and it melts at 132.7°C. (271°F.). It is also called *carbamide*.   E. CAMPAIGNE

See also LIVER; URINE; WÖHLER, FRIEDRICH.

UREMIA, *yoo RE mih uh*, or uremic poisoning, occurs when there is too much urea in the blood. Uremia comes from the kidney disease called nephritis, and from a kidney weakness of some pregnant women. The waste products normally removed by the kidneys then circulate through the blood and poison the system. Other possible causes are bleeding in the intestines, and tumors.

The symptoms of uremia are headache, dizziness, nausea, drowsiness, constipation, dim vision, and scanty urine. Later symptoms are dry skin, vomiting, fever, convulsions, and coma.

Treatment of uremia is partly through a balanced diet of proteins and carbohydrates. Fluids are given through the mouth or veins. Drugs which increase the urine rid the system of the poisons.   HYMAN S. RUBINSTEIN

See also NEPHRITIS; UREA.

URETER. See KIDNEY.

URETHRA. See BLADDER; KIDNEY.

UREY, *YOO rih*, **HAROLD CLAYTON** (1893-   ), is a leading American chemist and an authority on the structure of the atom. While teaching at Columbia University in 1932, he discovered heavy hydrogen, or deuterium, an isotope of hydrogen which is twice as heavy as ordinary hydrogen (see DEUTERIUM). Urey also separated deuterium from ordinary hydrogen, though it is present only to the extent of 1 part in 7,000. For the discovery and isolation of deuterium, Urey won the 1934 Nobel prize for chemistry. Deuterium is a component of "heavy water," which was a vital material in developing the atomic bomb, because it slowed down neutrons in atomic reactors. Urey was born at Walkerton, Ind.   HERBERT S. RHINESMITH

Jack Hamilton
Harold Urey

URGA. See ULAN BATOR.

URINE, *YOO rin*, is a liquid waste product of the body. The kidneys take urine out of the blood. A healthy person's urine is amber-colored and slightly acid. Urine is a little heavier than water with an average specific gravity of 1.022. It is made up of water, urea, creatinine, uric acid, and inorganic salts. The inorganic salts include sodium, potassium, ammonia, calcium, and magnesium.

Blood reaches the kidneys through the *renal* arteries. Waste matter and water removed from this blood passes from the kidneys to the bladder through two small tubes, the *ureters*. The urine is expelled from the bladder to the outside through another tube, the *urethra*.

The kidneys do not always give off the same amount of urine. During sleep, the amount is smaller and more concentrated. They form less urine when a person perspires freely, and more when he drinks large amounts of liquid. The *antidiuretic hormone*, given off by the pituitary gland, controls the amount of water held by the *nephrons* (tiny kidney tubes). Certain diseases may

also change the amount and strength of urine.

The condition of urine is often an index to a person's health. Sugar in the urine is a symptom of diabetes. Albumin and blood in the urine may mean the kidneys have been damaged.   EWALD E. SELKURT

Related Articles in WORLD BOOK include:

Bladder	Diuretic	Urea
Diabetes	Kidney	Uremia

URIS, *YOO ris*, **LEON MARCUS** (1924-   ), is an American novelist. His best-known work, *Exodus* (1958), tells about Jewish immigration into Palestine and the struggle to establish the state of Israel in the 1940's. It was made into a successful motion picture. Uris also wrote *Mila 18* (1961), a story of the Jewish revolt in the Warsaw ghetto during World War II. His other works include *Battle Cry* (1953), *The Angry Hills* (1955), and *Armageddon* (1964). Uris was born in Baltimore, Md.

UROLOGY. See MEDICINE (table, Kinds of Medical Specialty Fields).

URQUIZA, JUSTO JOSÉ DE. See ARGENTINA (The 1853 Constitution).

URSA MAJOR AND URSA MINOR. See BIG AND LITTLE DIPPERS.

URSINUS COLLEGE is a privately controlled, coeducational school at Collegeville, Pa. It is associated with the Evangelical and Reformed Church. The college offers courses in the sciences and liberal arts, leading to B.A. and B.S. degrees. Ursinus was founded in 1869. For enrollment, see UNIVERSITIES AND COLLEGES (table).

URSULA, *UR suh luh*, **SAINT,** is a saint of the Roman Catholic Church. According to legend, Ursula was a maiden from Britain, who was martyred, together with 11,000 maiden companions. Returning from a pious pilgrimage to Rome, they were attacked by Huns at Cologne, and killed for their faith. Saint Ursula's feast day is October 21. See also URSULINE.   FULTON J. SHEEN

URSULINE, *UR suh lin*, is the name of a Roman Catholic order of women. It was named for Saint Ursula, its patron saint. The order, also called the *Nuns of Saint Ursula*, was established at Brescia, Italy, in 1535, by Saint Angela Merici. The primary work of the Ursulines is the teaching of girls and young women. From the first, the community observed strict discipline. It became a cloistered order through the aid of Saint Charles Borromeo. In 1574 the Ursuline nuns entered France, and a convent was built for them near Paris in 1611. The order spread rapidly to most countries of Europe and to America. Convents were established in Quebec in 1639 and in New Orleans in 1727. The number of Ursuline nuns in all countries totals about 4,500. See also URSULA, SAINT.   FULTON J. SHEEN

URSULINE COLLEGE. See UNIVERSITIES AND COLLEGES (table).

URSULINE COLLEGE FOR WOMEN is a college of liberal arts located at Cleveland, Ohio. It offers B.A. and B.S. degrees. It is conducted by the Roman Catholic Church and was founded in 1871. For enrollment, see UNIVERSITIES AND COLLEGES (table).

URTICARIA. See HIVES.

URUBUPUNGÁ DAM. See BRAZIL (Natural Resources).

URUGUAY

Pan American World Airways; Screen Traveler, Gendreau

The Gauchos Are the Cowboys and Sheepherders Who Developed Uruguay's Rich Livestock Industry.

URUGUAY, *YOO ruh gwy*, is the smallest republic in South America. It has one of the most unusual democratic governments in the world. A nine-man national council heads the government, instead of a president or prime minister. Montevideo is the capital.

Uruguay is an agricultural country of low hills and green pasturelands on the southeast coast of South America. Before Uruguay became a republic, the people in the Spanish colony of Buenos Aires, Argentina, called it *Banda Oriental* (East Bank), because it lay east of them across the Río de la Plata (Silver River). When Uruguayans won independence, they named their country LA REPÚBLICA ORIENTAL DEL URUGUAY, which in Spanish means THE EASTERN REPUBLIC OF URUGUAY.

Uruguay is smaller than Kansas, but it has about 500,000 more people than that state. Nearly half of the people raise sheep and cattle.

Uruguay has made much progress since it became a republic in 1828. The country has a stable government and one of the highest living standards in South America.

The Land and Its Resources

Uruguay covers 72,172 square miles. The *Color Map* shows that it is bounded by Brazil on the north, the Atlantic Ocean on the east, and is separated from Argentina on the south and west by the Río de la Plata and the Uruguay River. It has three land regions: (1) the coastal lowlands, (2) the highlands, and (3) the pasturelands.

The Coastal Lowlands, a narrow belt of sand dunes like those of North and South Carolina, stretches along Uruguay's Atlantic Coast and along the Río de la Plata.

The Highlands. The land rises gradually from the eastern coast to highlands that extend from the Brazilian border almost to the southern coast. Uruguayans call these highlands *Cuchilla Grande* (Big Knife), because

--- FACTS IN BRIEF ---

Form of Government: Republic.

Capital: Montevideo.

Official Language: Spanish.

Area: 72,172 square miles. *Greatest length*, about 340 miles. *Greatest width*, about 300 miles. *Coastline*, about 600 miles.

Population: *1963 census*—2,592,563; distribution, 82 per cent urban; 18 per cent rural. *1967 estimate*—2,788,-000; density, 39 persons to the square mile. *1972 estimate*—2,949,000.

Chief Products: *Agriculture*, linseed, meat, wheat, wool. *Manufacturing and Processing*, canned meat, glass, leather, linseed oil, textiles. *Mining*, granite, gravel, limestone, marble, sand.

Flag: A gold sun on a white canton appears on a field of nine white and blue horizontal stripes. The stripes represent Uruguay's original nine political subdivisions. See FLAG (picture, Flags of the Americas).

National Anthem: "Himno Nacional del Uruguay" ("National Hymn of Uruguay").

National Holiday: Independence Day, August 25.

Money: *Basic unit*, peso. For the value of the peso in dollars, see MONEY (table, Values). See also PESO.

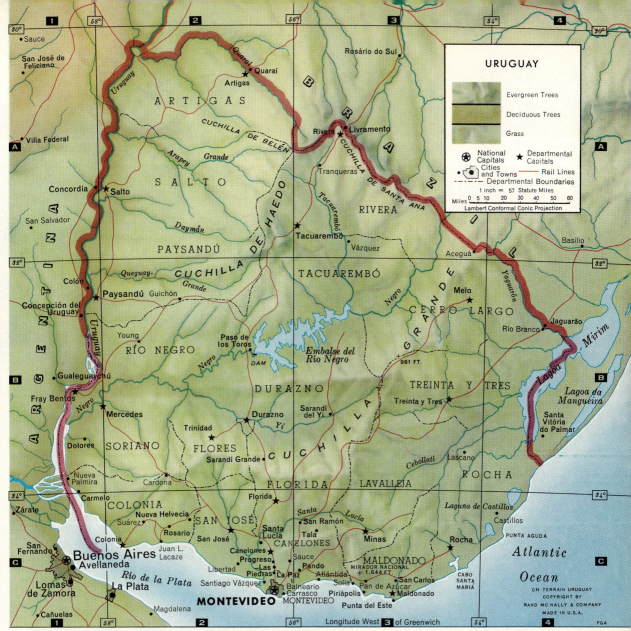

Specially created for **World Book Encyclopedia** by Rand McNally and World Book editors

Departments

ARTIGAS ..52,261..A 2
CANELONES
...........256,200..C 2
CERRO
  LARGO ..71,441..B 3
COLONIA 105,209..C 2
DURAZNO 53,362..B 2
FLORES ..23,550..B 2
FLORIDA ..63,899..B 2
LAVAL-
  LEJA ..65,525..B 3
MALDO-
  NADO ..62,344..C 3
MONTE-
  VIDEO 1,202,890..C 2
PAYSANDÚ 87,229..A 2
RÍO
  NEGRO ..46,852..B 2
RIVERA ..77,496..A 3
ROCHA ..55,523..B 3
SALTO ..92,216..A 2
SAN JOSÉ ..77,300..C 2
SORIANO ..78,234..B 2

TACUAREMBÓ
  ....77,409..B 3
TREINTA Y
  TRES ...43,623..B 3

Cities and Towns

Aceguá ....A 3
Artigas ...23,429..A 2
Atlántida ....C 3
Balneario
  Carrasco ....C 2
Barros
  Blancos* ..4,557..C 3
Canelones ..14,028..C 2
Cardona ...4,110..B 2
Carmelo ..12,705..B 1
Castillos ...5,957..C 4
Colonia ..12,846..C 2
Delta del
  Tigre y
  Villas* ...3,468..C 2
Dolores ..12,480..B 1
Durazno ..22,203..B 2
Florida ..20,934..C 2
Fray Bentos 17,094..B 1
Guichón ...3,683..B 2

Juan L.
  Lacaze ...11,204..C 2
La Paz ..13,226..C 2
Lascano ...5,309..B 3
Las Piedras 40,658..C 2
Libertad ...5,072..C 2
Maldonado ..15,005..C 3
Melo ...33,741..B 3
Mercedes ..31,325..B 2
Minas ..31,256..C 3
Monte-
  video .1,202,890..C 2
Nueva
  Helvecia ..8,012..C 2
Nueva
  Palmira ..6,307..B 1
Pan de
  Azúcar ..4,190..C 3
Pando ..12,876..C 3
Paso de
  Carrasco* ..4,896..C 2
Paso de
  los Toros ..11,359..B 2
Paysandú ..51,645..B 2
Piriápolis ..4,546..C 3
Progreso ...7,018..C 2
Punta
  del Este ...5,272..C 3
Río Branco ..4,023..B 4
Rivera ....41,266..A 3

Rocha ....19,484..C 3
Rosario ...7,705..C 2
Salto ...57,714..A 2
San Carlos 13,695..C 3
San José ..25,392..C 2
San Ramón ..5,672..C 3
Santa Lucía 12,647..C 2
Santiago
  Vázquez ....C 2
Sarandí
  del Yi ....5,882..B 3
Sarandí
  Grande ...5,295..B 2

Sauce ....3,227..C 2
Solís ....C 3
Suárez ....3,052..C 2
Tacuarembó 29,011..A 3
Tala ......3,213..C 3
Tranqueras ..3,658..A 3
Treinta
  y Tres ..21,035..B 3
Trinidad ..15,455..B 2
Vázquez ....A 3
Young .....7,974..B 2

Physical Features

Arapey Grande R. ..A 2
Cabo Santa Mariá
  (Cape) ....C 3
Cebollatí R. ......B 3
Cuchilla de Belén
  (Mts.) ....A 2
Cuchilla de Haedo
  (Mts.) ....B 2
Cuchilla Grande
  (Mts.) ....B 3
Daymán R. ....A 2
Embalse del Río Negro
  (Reservoir) ......B 3
Lagoa Mirim (Lake) B 4

Laguna de Castillos
  (Lake) ....C 4
Mirador Nacional
  (Mtn.) ....C 3
Negro R. ....B 2
Punta Aguda (Pt.) ..C 4
Queguay Grande R. B 2
Río de la Plata
  (Estuary) ......C 2
Santa Lucía R. ...C 3
Tacuarembó R. ...A 3
Uruguay R. ....B 1
Yaguarón R. ......A 3
Yi R. ....B 2

Source: Census figures.

*Not on map; key shows general location.

176a

The Gauchos in Uruguay brand their cattle much like Texas cowboys. Cattle and sheep raising ranks as the country's largest industry.

Montevideo, Uruguay's Capital and Largest City, stands beside the Río de la Plata. Gleaming, modern buildings overlook one of the city's famed beaches.

Pickow, Three Lions

Location Map

knifelike formations of granite jut through the surface soil on many of the ridges. Uruguay's highest point is 1,644-foot Sierra de las Animas in the Cuchilla Grande. Highlands also run along parts of the northern border.

The Pasturelands begin at the highlands in eastern Uruguay and spread across the country to the Uruguay River. They cover about four-fifths of the country.

Rivers. The major rivers are the Uruguay and the Negro. The Río de la Plata is really the bay formed by the Paraná and Uruguay rivers.

Natural Resources. Uruguay's vast pasturelands are its most valuable resource. Pastures, often with 3-foot-high grass, support the sheep and cattle industries. The country has no important forests. The few mineral deposits include limestone, granite, and marble, which is found in a great variety of colors.

Climate. Uruguay's climate resembles that of Virginia. Temperatures range from about 50° F. in winter to about 75° F. in summer. Rain falls throughout the year, although it is heaviest in May and October. Rainfall averages about 45 inches a year, but severe droughts sometimes occur.

Life of the People

About 18 of every 100 persons in Uruguay live in *rural* (farm) areas. About 82 of every 100 live in *urban* (city) areas. Montevideo has almost 45 per cent of the urban population. On the average, there are 39 persons per square mile in Uruguay.

Most of the people speak Spanish and have Spanish or Italian ancestry. Early European settlers drove out nearly all the Charrúas Indians, the original inhabitants. Indians make up less than one-tenth of the population today. Most of them live in farm areas.

Uruguay has complete religious freedom. About two-thirds of the people are Roman Catholics. The rest belong mostly to the Anglican and Methodist churches.

Way of Life. The father of a typical family in Uruguay works on a ranch, in a meat-packing plant, or in a wool warehouse. The mother cares for the home.

1 INCH = 1,200 MILES

Uruguay Covers an Area Slightly Smaller than Kansas.

Shelter. Most people in the cities live in small, tile-roofed houses made of stucco, brick, or concrete, although some live in modern apartment buildings. The houses and apartment buildings often resemble those in Florida and southern California. The government has built numerous low-rent housing developments.

Most ranch owners live in one-story brick houses, plastered on the outside and roofed with tile. Ranch workers and their families usually live near the ranch owner in one- or two-room thatch-roofed houses made of stone, brick, or *adobe* (sun-dried clay brick).

Food. The people eat much meat, particularly beef. Popular dishes include *pavesa*, a type of beef broth, and *asado con cuero*, or beef barbecued in its hide. *Yerba maté*, a South American tea, is a favorite drink.

Clothing. Most Uruguayans wear clothing similar to that worn in the United States and Canada. Men on the ranches sometimes wear the boots, loose trousers, neckerchiefs, and broad-brimmed hats worn by the gauchos more than 100 years ago.

Recreation. Uruguayan soccer teams have won several Olympic championships. Other popular sports include polo, swimming, boating, golf, and tennis.

Uruguayans celebrate their most colorful festival, the *carnaval*, during the three days before Lent. They sing, dance, and parade in masks and colorful costumes.

URUGUAY

City Life. Montevideo is the only city with more than 100,000 people. The cities are clean and modern, with tall buildings, broad streets, beautiful parks and homes, good sewage systems, and electricity. For details on the major cities, see MONTEVIDEO; PAYSANDÚ; SALTO.

Country Life centers around farms, ranches, and small villages. Cattle herded by roving bands of gauchos once roamed over open plains. As the herds increased, cattle owners built fences to keep them separate. This was the beginning of the modern *estancias* (ranches). Gauchos still herd cattle on the larger ranches, which sometimes cover more than 12,000 acres. Small villages stand at many road junctions. These villages usually have one or two stores and a cluster of brick or adobe houses.

Work of the People

About half of Uruguay's people work in agriculture. Ten persons of every 100 make their living in commerce, manufacturing, or government. The rest work in such fields as construction and mining. The government owns all the railroads, power plants, and telephone and telegraph services. Government plants and businesses compete with private companies in many industries. Most Uruguayans earn about $300 a year.

Agriculture, particularly sheep and cattle raising, is the chief industry. Sheep and cattle graze on the vast pasturelands throughout the year, because of the mild, even climate. Farmers cultivate less than one-tenth of the farmland. Most of them live in the south, where their goods can be transported easily to markets in Montevideo. They grow wheat on about half the farm land, and also raise alfalfa, barley, citrus fruits, corn, and oats. Uruguay is a leading flaxseed producer.

The government helps the farmers by paying them subsidies for items such as wheat, dairy products, and cattle. The government often pays part of the cost of shipping cattle to meat-packing plants. Since 1948, the government has bought many large ranches and sold them in smaller parcels to farmers.

Manufacturing and Processing. Meat packing and tanning are the main manufacturing industries. Other industries produce beverages, clothing, foods, furniture, glassware, leather goods, linseed oil, and tobacco.

Electric Power plants provide as much power as is needed by Uruguay's farms and factories. A hydro-electric plant on the Negro River at Rincón del Bonete produces more than half the nation's power.

Trade. Uruguay imports more goods than it exports. Wool and meat account for more than half the exports. Wool shipments, which sometimes total 90,000 tons a year, rank among the largest in the world. Hides make up about 14 per cent of the exports. Uruguay imports raw materials and manufactured goods such as automobiles, cotton, fuel, iron and steel, and machinery. The nation trades mostly with the United States and western European countries. Uruguay joined the Latin-American Free Trade Association in February, 1960.

Transportation. Nearly all transportation centers in Montevideo. Roads, railroads, and airlines connect the main cities. The country has about 1,900 miles of railroad tracks and more than 25,000 miles of roads and highways. Uruguay's section of the Pan American Highway runs from Rio Blanco to Colonia. Ships and airplanes travel to Montevideo from all over the world.

Plaza Libertad Is in the Main Business Section of Montevideo.

Pickow, Three Lions

The Legislative Building in Montevideo Houses Uruguay's General Assembly.

Communication. Montevideo has 15 of the nation's 25 newspapers, and several magazine- and book-publishing firms. Television stations in Montevideo, and radio stations throughout the country, entertain and inform the people. Many cities have telegraph, radio-telegraph, and radio-telephone service.

Education

About 90 of every 100 Uruguayans can read and write. The law requires all children to attend elementary school, starting at the age of 6. The government operates free schools from kindergarten through college.

The University of the Republic in Montevideo was founded in 1849. Students from any country may attend this university without charge. The Technical University consists of 74 different technical schools located throughout the country. Students in these schools learn such subjects as architecture, engineering, and agriculture. There are also several teachers colleges, and schools for the blind and handicapped students.

The Arts

Juan Manuel Blanes (1830-1901), the first important Uruguayan painter, gained fame for his paintings that illustrated the nation's history. The paintings of Pedro Figaro (1861-1938) achieved international fame. The most prominent artists in Uruguay today include the painter José Cúneo (1887-   ) and the sculptor José L. Zorilla de San Martín (1891-   ).

Horacio Quiroga (1878-1937) was one of the earliest Uruguayan writers and poets. Alberto Zum Felde (1889-   ), a writer and critic, is an outstanding literary figure in Uruguay today.

One of Uruguay's best-known musicians is Héctor Tosar Errecart (1923-   ), a pianist and composer who has won world recognition. Much Uruguayan folk music comes from the legends of the gauchos.

What to See and Do in Uruguay

Beaches and resorts at such places as Montevideo, Balneario Carrasco, and Punta del Este make the coun-try a favorite South American vacation spot. People flock to Solís, Santiago Vázquez, Vázquez, Atlántida, and many other river and coastal cities to enjoy fishing and boating.

Uruguayans call Montevideo the *City of Roses*, because of the thousands of roses in its gardens and parks. Museums, theaters, and libraries have made the capital a main cultural center of South America.

Government

Uruguay's constitution provides for a nine-man national council to head the government. The council has duties similar to those of the President of the United States. The General Assembly resembles the U.S. Congress. A supreme court heads the court system.

National Council. The people vote for political parties, and the parties in turn appoint the members of the national council to serve for four years. The party with the majority of votes places six men on the council. The party with the second largest number of votes has three men on the council. The council reaches decisions by a majority vote.

The General Assembly makes the laws in Uruguay. It has two houses, the Senate and the Chamber of Deputies. The people elect the Senate's 31 members from the country at large (without regard to political districts). Senators serve for four years. If the two largest parties together win a majority of the votes cast, each party receives half the Senate seats. Otherwise, seats are divided according to the number of votes received by all parties.

The Chamber of Deputies has 99 members. The voters in each of the country's 19 departments (political districts) elect a certain number of deputies to four-year terms, according to the department's population. Each department has at least two deputies.

Courts. The supreme court controls all the courts. The General Assembly appoints a chief justice and four associate justices to serve 10-year terms. The supreme court appoints judges in the lower courts, and all justices of the peace. Uruguay's laws come from the

URUGUAY

constitution and from laws passed by the federal government and local governments.

Local Government. Uruguay is divided into 19 departments, each governed by a department council of five members. The city of Montevideo makes up one department. The political party that receives the most votes in each department in a national election appoints the majority of members to the council.

Taxation. The government operates many businesses that sell products to the people at low prices. The government must levy many taxes to run these businesses. The people pay taxes of 2 or 3 per cent on motion-picture admissions, matches, rentals, and gasoline.

Politics. The two main political parties are the Colorados and the Blancos. The Colorados believe the government should manage many industries and should break up large estates into small farms. The Blancos represent large landholders who oppose both division of the land and government control of industries.

The law requires every person over 18 who can read and write to vote in all elections.

Armed Forces. The Uruguayan Army has more than 20 regiments, and an air force of about 200 airplanes. The navy has about 1,500 men and several ships. The nation has no compulsory military service.

History

Early Years. In 1516, the Spanish navigator Juan Díaz de Solís (1470-1516) became the first white man to land in Uruguay. But when Solís and part of his crew went ashore, fierce Charrúas Indians killed them.

In 1680, the Portuguese established the first white settlement in Uruguay. They built a fort at Colonia, across the Río de la Plata from Buenos Aires, Argentina. Spain wanted to check Portuguese expansion in Uruguay, so Spanish colonists founded Montevideo in 1726. By the 1770's, the Spaniards had settled most of Uruguay. They attacked Colonia in 1777, and drove the last of the Portuguese out of the country.

José Gervasio Artigas organized an army to fight for independence from Spain in 1810. Artigas, the son of a Uruguayan rancher, had served with the Spanish cavalry. He had almost defeated the Spanish by 1820, when Portuguese troops from Brazil attacked both the Spanish and the Uruguayans. In 1820, the Portuguese seized Uruguay, annexed it to Brazil, and drove Artigas into exile. Artigas never returned to Uruguay. But a group of his followers, called "The Immortal Thirty-three," revolted against Brazil in 1825. Their armies held most of Uruguay within a few months. Uruguay then decided to unite with Argentina for protection against Brazil.

Independence. In 1825, Argentina joined Uruguay in the war against Brazil. Great Britain intervened in 1826 because a Brazilian blockade of Montevideo and Buenos Aires interfered with British trade. In 1828, because of the British intervention, Brazil and Argentina recognized Uruguay as an independent republic. Uruguay adopted its first constitution in 1830.

Civil War. In 1830, the revolutionary leader Fructuoso Rivera (1790-1854) was elected the first president of Uruguay. After his term ended in 1836, he tried to regain power by leading a revolt against his successor, Manuel Oribe (1800-1857). In this civil war, Oribe's

La Carreta Monument in Montevideo is a favorite picture-taking spot. The bronze statue shows oxen drawing a cart, followed by a horseman. The monument honors pioneers who built Uruguay's cattle industry. It stands in a park named for President Ordóñez.

forces called themselves *Blancos* (Whites), and Rivera's men called themselves *Colorados* (Reds). The Colorados won in 1852 after 16 years of fighting.

Struggles for Power. After the civil war, the Colorados took over the government. Uprisings and rebellions marked the next 11 years, as control of the government changed from one party to another. In 1863, the Colorados revolted against the Blancos, who ruled at that time. The Colorados won in 1865, and held power until 1958. But revolutions upset the nation until the 1900's. From 1865 to 1870, Uruguay fought a war with Paraguay. See PARAGUAY (History).

Reforms in the Early 1900's. José Batlle y Ordóñez (1856-1929) was elected president in 1903. He soon put the government in control of the banks, improved the labor laws, and gave credit and aid to farmers. He also encouraged the construction of new harbors, factories, homes, and public buildings.

Batlle thought the great powers of the presidency had caused the country's many revolutions. He worked for a new constitution, which was adopted in 1917. It established a national council. President Gabriel Terra (1873-1942) dissolved the council in 1933.

Recent Events. In 1942, Uruguay severed relations with the Axis powers. Uruguay declared war on Germany and Japan in 1945, but no Uruguayan troops went into battle. The country became a charter member of the United Nations that same year.

In 1951, a new constitution dissolved the presidency, and replaced it with a new national council. The economy suffered in 1957 when foreign trade fell to its lowest point in five years. After ruling for 93 years, the Colorado party lost the 1958 elections to the Nationalist (Blanco) party. In 1961, the Organization of American States met at Punta del Este to sign the charter for the Alliance for Progress, a Latin-American aid program. The OAS met again at Punta del Este in 1962 to expel the Cuban government from the OAS because of its communist activities. In 1964, Uruguay joined other OAS nations in breaking relations with Cuba because of Cuban interference in Venezuela.   JOHN TATE LANNING

Related Articles in WORLD BOOK include:

Agate	Paysandú
Artigas, José Gervasio	Río de la Plata
Batlle y Ordóñez, José	Salto
Gaucho	Uruguay River
Montevideo	

Outline

I. **The Land and Its Resources**
II. **Life of the People**
III. **Work of the People**
IV. **Education**
V. **The Arts**
VI. **What to See and Do in Uruguay**
VII. **Government**
VIII. **History**

Questions

What is Uruguay's most valuable natural resource?
What export ranks among the largest in the world?
What is unusual about the executive branch of Uruguay's government?
Who were the first white men to settle in Uruguay?
Why is José Artigas important in the history of Uruguay?
How does Uruguay rank in size among South American republics?
How much must a student from another country pay to attend the University of the Republic?

URUGUAY RIVER is part of the great Paraná and La Plata river system of South America. The Uruguay rises in the state of Santa Catarina in southern Brazil and flows westward, and then south for about 1,000 miles. The river empties into the bay of the Río de la Plata. The Uruguay forms part of the boundary between Brazil and Argentina, and all the boundary between Uruguay and Argentina. Large vessels can sail up the Uruguay River for more than 150 miles. Before it joins the Río de la Plata, the Uruguay River becomes a lake from 4 to 7 miles wide. For location, see URUGUAY (color map); BRAZIL (color map).   MARGUERITE UTTLEY

U.S. See UNITED STATES.

USEFUL ARTS. From earliest times, men have made their everyday objects beautiful. *Decorative arts* produce objects just for their beauty, but *useful arts* give added beauty to practical items.

Related Articles in WORLD BOOK include:

Bookbinding	Hobby	Pottery
Ceramics	Industrial Design	Printing
Engraving	Mechanical Drawing	Sewing
Handicraft	Photography	Wood Carving

USIA. See UNITED STATES INFORMATION AGENCY.

USMAN ALI, SIR. See HYDERABAD, NIZAM F.

USO. See UNITED SERVICE ORGANIZATIONS.

USPALLATA PASS. See ANDES MOUNTAINS (Transportation).

U.S.S.R. is the abbreviation for Union of Soviet Socialist Republics, the official name of Russia. See RUSSIA.

USURY, *YOO zhoo rih,* is interest at a higher rate than the law allows. The person who charges more than the maximum legal rate is a *usurer.*

In Biblical times, all payments for the use of money were regarded as usury, and were forbidden. Any money lender was then called a usurer. Romans forbade interest charges during the period of the Roman Republic, but permitted them during the time of the Roman Empire. In general, people regarded interest and usury as synonymous until the late Middle Ages, because most of the borrowers were poor persons who needed money in order to obtain the necessities of life.

But the development of modern business, which required the use of large amounts of borrowed funds, made it clear that the borrower used the funds borrowed in productive operations, and thus should expect to pay something for their use. In time, therefore, interest came to be recognized as legitimate.

A difficulty arose from the fact that the risks and costs of making small loans were so great that legitimate dealers would not handle such loans. This gave the illegitimate "loan shark" his opportunity. Eventually people recognized that the government should permit much higher rates on small loans than it permitted on large loans, because of the additional risks and costs involved. The result was a uniform small-loan law, adopted since by many states. It permits licensed lenders to charge as high as $3\frac{1}{2}$ per cent interest per month on an unpaid balance. The interest usually varies with the amount of money borrowed. Service charges and discounts may make the real interest rate much higher than the rate advertised for credit purchases. For the legal rate of interest, see INTEREST; LOAN COMPANY.   JOHN ALAN APPLEMAN

Valley West by Harrison T. Groutage for the Field Enterprises Educational Corporation Collection.

UTAH

The Beehive State

UTAH is an important mining state in the Rocky Mountain region. It also serves as a vital link in the transportation and communications systems of the western United States. Salt Lake City, Utah's capital and largest city, is an industrial and banking center. The city is the headquarters of the Church of Jesus Christ of Latter-day Saints. The members of this church are called *Mormons*. Mormons make up more than 60 per cent of Utah's population.

Utah has rich mineral deposits. Nearly a fifth of the nation's copper comes from Bingham Canyon near Salt Lake City. Utah ranks second only to Arizona in the production of copper, and second to South Dakota in gold production. It stands third in producing lead

and uranium ore. Utah is also among the leading producers of coal, molybdenum, potassium salts, silver, and zinc. It is the only state that produces gilsonite, a solid form of asphalt.

The annual value of Utah's manufacturing is greater than that of its mining and farming combined. But Utah's manufacturing plants depend on the products that are mined and farmed in the state. The smelting and refining of *nonferrous metals* (metals containing no iron), and also the processing of iron and steel are important industries. Also important in the state's economy is the processing of such farm products as fruits, grain, meat, poultry, sugar beets, and vegetables.

Utah has snow-covered mountains and beautifully

colored canyons. The wind and rain have formed rocks into many arches and natural bridges. Great Salt Lake is the largest natural lake west of the Mississippi River. People can easily float in this lake because it is from four to five times as salty as the ocean. Deserts cover much of Utah, but man-made reservoirs provide irrigation water for farmland. The largest reservoirs are Lake Powell, created by Arizona's Glen Canyon Dam, and Flaming Gorge, behind Flaming Gorge Dam. Utah's chief farm products include dairy, livestock, and poultry products.

Mormon pioneers led by Brigham Young settled the Utah region in 1847. They called the region *Deseret*. This Mormon word means *honeybee*, and it stands for hard work and industry. Utah's nickname is the *Beehive State*. Congress organized the region as a territory in 1850, and named it *Utah* for the Ute Indian tribe that lived there. The early white settlers fought several battles against these Indians. In 1861, the first transcontinental telegraph message was sent across wires that met in Salt Lake City. The first transcontinental railroad was completed at Promontory in 1869. Utah was admitted to the Union as the 45th state on Jan. 4, 1896.

For the relationship of Utah to other states in its region, see ROCKY MOUNTAIN STATES.

The contributors of this article are Everett L. Cooley, Director and Editor of the Utah State Historical Society; Robert Layton, Chairman of the Department of Geography at Brigham Young University; and Ernest H. Linford, Chief Editorial Writer of the Salt Lake Tribune.

Lorin D. Wiggins

Statue of Brigham Young in Salt Lake City

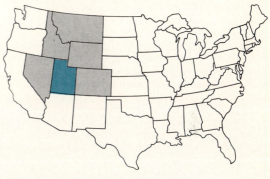

Utah (blue) ranks 11th in size among all the states, and 5th in size among the Rocky Mountain States (gray).

FACTS IN BRIEF

Capital: Salt Lake City.

Government: *Congress*—U.S. Senators, 2; U.S. Representatives, 2. *Electoral Votes*, 4. *State Legislature*—senators, 28; representatives, 69. *Counties*, 29. *Voting Age*, 21 years.

Area: 84,916 square miles (including 2,577 square miles of inland water), 11th in size among the states. *Greatest Distances:* (north-south) 345 mi.; (east-west) 275 mi.

Elevation: *Highest*, Kings Peak, 13,498 feet above sea level; *Lowest*, Beaverdam Creek, in Washington County, 2,000 feet above sea level.

Population: *1960 census*—890,627; rank, 38th among the states; distribution, 75 per cent urban, 25 per cent rural; density, 10 persons to the square mile. *1965 estimate*—998,000.

Chief Products: *Manufacturing and Processing*, meat and dairy products, metal products (especially iron, lead, and steel), missiles, refined copper and oil. *Mining*, coal, copper, gold, iron ore, lead, natural gas, petroleum, sand and gravel, uranium, zinc. *Agriculture*, alfalfa seed, barley, cattle, eggs, fruits, milk, potatoes, poultry, sheep, sugar beets, wheat.

Statehood: Jan. 4, 1896, the 45th state.

State Motto: *Industry*.

State Song: "Utah, We Love Thee." Words and music by Evan Stephens.

Scenic Monument Valley, a Navajo Indian Tribal Park in Southeastern Utah

Hal Rumel, Publix

Constitution. Utah adopted its constitution in 1895, the year before it became a state. Constitutional *amendments* (changes) may be proposed by the state legislature or by a constitutional convention. An amendment proposed by the legislature must receive the approval of two-thirds of the members of each house. The amendment must then be approved in a general election by a majority of the persons voting on the issue. Before a constitutional convention can meet, it must be approved by two-thirds of the members of each house of the legislature. The convention must then be approved by a majority of all the persons voting in a general election. Amendments proposed by a constitutional convention must receive a majority of the total votes cast in a general election.

Executive. The governor of Utah serves a four-year term. He may be re-elected any number of times. The governor receives a yearly salary of $18,000. For a list of all the governors of Utah, see the *History* section of this article.

Other elected state officials include the attorney general, secretary of state, state auditor, and state treasurer. All serve four-year terms and may be re-elected. But the state auditor and state treasurer cannot serve two terms in a row. The secretary of state takes over as governor if the governorship becomes vacant. The governor appoints various state officials who are not elected. They include the adjutant general, department heads, and members of many state boards and agencies. Most of the governor's appointments must be approved by the state senate.

Legislature of Utah consists of a 28-member senate and a 69-member house of representatives. Members of both legislative houses are elected from districts drawn up according to population. The districts for both houses were redrawn in 1965 to give fair representation to all persons in the state. With the new districts, voting power was increased in cities and other urban areas, and reduced in rural areas. State senators serve four-year terms, and state representatives serve for two years. Legislative sessions begin on the second Monday in January of odd-numbered years. They last 60 calendar days. The governor may call special sessions that last up to 30 calendar days.

Courts. Utah's highest court is the state supreme court. This court has five justices, elected to 10-year terms. The justice with the shortest remaining period in office serves as chief justice.

Utah is divided into seven judicial districts. Each district has one or more district court judges, depending on population. District court judges are elected to six-year terms. Other Utah courts include municipal, juvenile, and justice of the peace courts. Municipal judges are elected to six-year terms. Town trustees appoint town justices, who also are municipal judges, to six-year terms. The governor, with the advice of a juvenile court commission, appoints juvenile court judges to six-year terms. Justices of the peace are elected to four-year terms.

Local Government. Each of Utah's 29 counties is managed by a three-member board of county commissioners. Two of the members of each board are elected to four-year terms. The third member is elected for two years. The board is responsible for county affairs and for supervising county departments and officers. All other county officers are elected to four-year terms. They include an assessor, attorney, auditor, clerk, recorder, sheriff, surveyor, and treasurer.

Municipalities in Utah are divided into four classes. First-class cities have 90,000 or more persons. Second-class cities have between 30,000 and 89,999 persons. Third-class cities have from 800 to 29,999 persons. Towns have fewer than 800 persons.

Any city or town may use the council-manager form

Utah Tourist and Publicity Council

Governor's Residence was completed in 1959. It stands about three miles east of the Capitol in Salt Lake City.

The State Seal

Symbols of Utah. On the state seal, the beehive on the shield represents industry. The sego lilies surrounding the beehive symbolize the time when Mormon pioneers ate lily bulbs to avoid starvation. "Industry" is the state motto, and 1847 was the year the Mormons came to Utah. The seal was adopted in 1896 and appears on the state flag. The flag was adopted in 1913.

Flag and bird illustrations, courtesy of Eli Lilly and Company

of government. First- and second-class cities may have the commissioner form. Third-class cities may use the mayor-council form. Towns may be governed by a town board of trustees. The state constitution gives municipalities the right to adopt their own charters. This right is called *home rule*, but no Utah municipality has used it.

Taxation. Sales taxes account for nearly 40 per cent of the state government's income. Other important sources of income include individual income taxes, corporate income taxes, licenses, and property taxes. About 30 per cent of the state government's income comes from federal grants and other U.S. government programs.

Politics. Political strength in Utah has been fairly evenly divided between the Democratic and Republican parties. Republicans gained strength between the late 1940's and early 1960's. But Democrats won most state offices in the 1964 election. For Utah's electoral votes and voting record in presidential elections, see ELECTORAL COLLEGE (table).

The State Capitol is in Salt Lake City, Utah's capital since 1856. Fillmore was the capital from 1851 to 1856.

Utah Tourist and Publicity Council

The State Flag

The State Bird
Sea Gull

The State Flower
Sego Lily

The State Tree
Blue Spruce

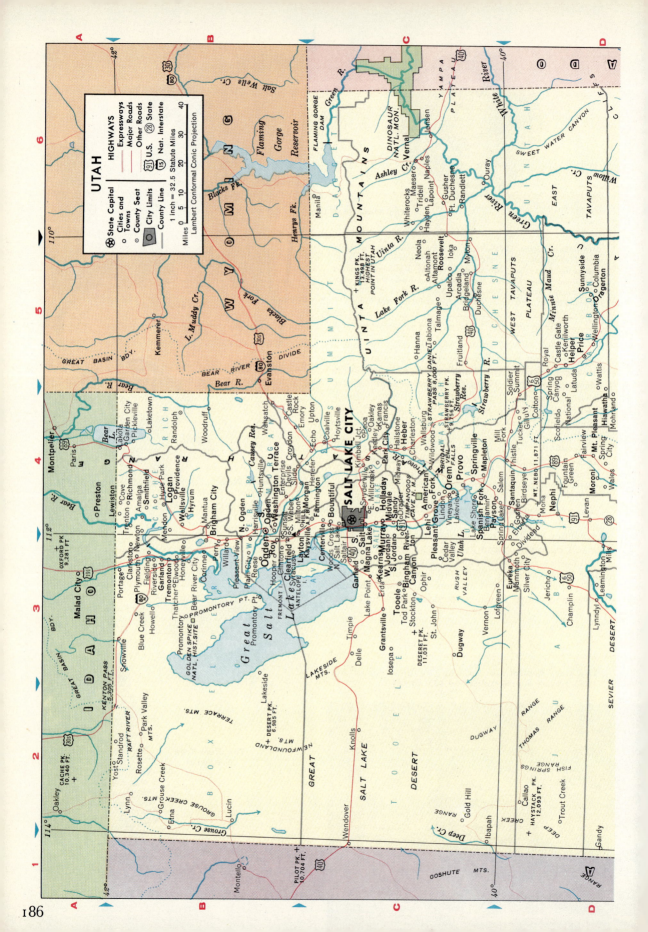

UTAH

HIGHWAYS
- State Capital
- Cities and Towns
- County Seat
- City Limits
- County Line

Expressways
Major Roads
Other Roads
U.S. / State
Nat. Interstate

1 inch = 32.5 Statute Miles
Statute Miles
0 10 20 30 40
Miles
Lambert Conformal Conic Projection

SALT LAKE CITY

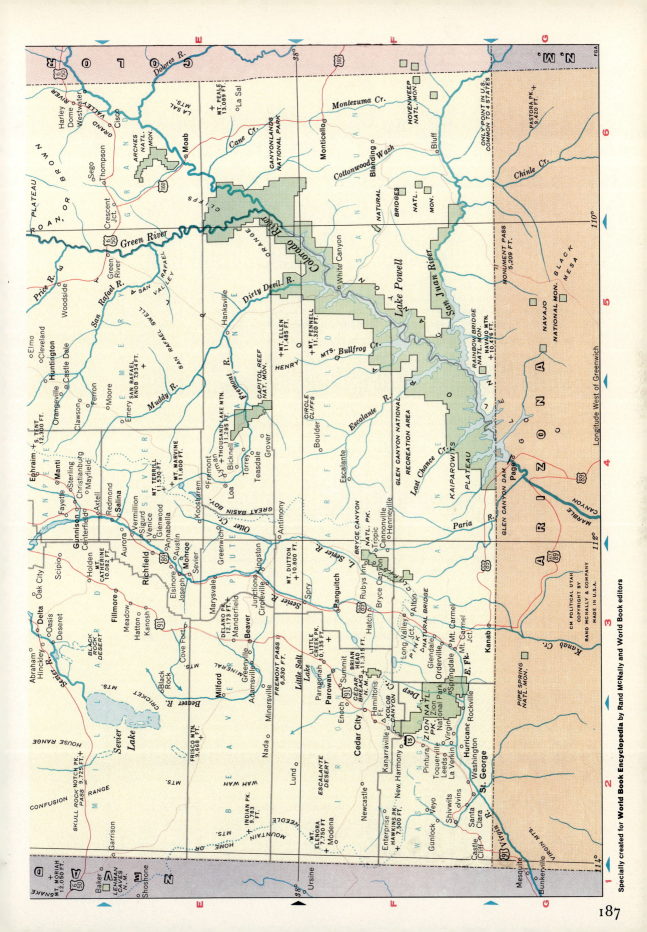

UTAH MAP INDEX

Population

998,000	Estimate 1965
890,627	1960
688,862	1950
550,310	1940
507,847	1930
449,396	1920
373,351	1910
276,749	1900
210,779	1890
143,963	1880
86,786	1870
40,273	1860
11,380	1850

Metropolitan Areas

Ogden	110,744	E 2
Provo-Orem	106,991	B 4
Salt Lake City	447,795	C 6

Counties

Beaver	4,331	E 4
Box Elder	25,061	B 4
Cache	35,788	B 4
Carbon	21,135	C 6
Daggett	1,164	C 5
Davis	64,760	C 3
Duchesne	7,179	C 4
Emery	5,546	D 5
Garfield	3,577	F 3
Grand	6,345	D 6
Iron	10,795	F 2
Juab	4,597	D 3
Kane	2,667	F 3
Millard	7,866	D 2
Morgan	2,837	B 3
Piute	1,164	E 3
Rich	1,436	B 4
Salt Lake	383,035	C 3
San Juan	9,040	F 6
Sanpete	11,053	D 4
Sevier	10,656	E 4
Summit	5,673	C 4
Tooele	17,868	D 2
Uintah	11,582	C 6
Utah	106,991	C 4
Wasatch	5,308	C 4
Washington	10,271	F 2
Wayne	1,728	E 5
Weber	110,744	B 3

Cities and Towns

Alpine*	775	C 4
Altamont	102	C 5
Alton	116	F 3
Amalga	198	B 4
American Fork	6,373	C 4
Annabella	177	E 3
Antimony	161	E 4
Aurora	465	C 4
Austin	100	E 3
Bear River City	447	B 3
Beaver	1,548	E 4
Benjamin	100	C 4
Bennion*	200	C 4
Bicknell	366	E 4
Birdseye		C 4
Brigham Canyon	1,516	C 3
Black Rock	25	D 5
Blanding	1,805	F 6
Bluebell*		C 5
Bluff	100	F 6
Bothwell*	150	B 3
Boulder	302	F 4
Bountiful	17,039	C 3
Brigham City	11,728	B 3
Buena Vista*	200	C 4
Cannonville	153	F 3
Castle Dale	617	D 5
Castle Gate	321	D 5
Cedar City	7,543	F 2
Cedar Valley	150	D 4
Centerfield	475	C 4
Centerville	2,361	C 3
Central*	21	F 2
Champlin		C 4
Charleston	223	C 4
Chesterfield*	500	C 4
Christianburg	478	D 4
Circleville	40	E 4
Cisco	490	D 6
Clarkston	475	B 4
Clawson	130	D 5
Clearfield*	8,833	B 3
Cleveland	483	D 5
Clinton	1,025	B 3
Coalville	907	C 4
Collinston*	75	B 4
Colton	12	D 4
Columbia	300	D 6
Copperton*	850	C 3
Corinne	510	B 3
Cornish*	157	B 4
Cove		E 3
Cove Fort		E 3
Crescent Junction	12	D 6
Croydon	91	C 4
Delle		D 2
Deseret	325	D 3
Devils Slide	250	B 3
Dewyville*	265	B 3
Dividend	10	D 4
Draperton	2,959	B 3
Draper	1,000	C 3
Duchesne	770	C 5
Dugway		D 2
East Layton*	444	B 4
East Millcreek	6,000	C 4
Echo	130	C 4
Edgemont*	300	C 4
Elberta	50	D 4
Elmo	175	D 5
Elsinore	483	E 3
Elwood	345	B 4
Emery	326	E 4
Enoch	465	F 2
Enterprise	859	F 2
Ephraim	1,801	D 4
Erda		D 2
Escalante	702	F 4
Etna		B 2
Eureka	771	D 3
Fairview	1,951	D 4
Farmington	1,951	C 3
Fayette	161	D 4
Ferron	386	D 5
Fielding	270	B 3
Fillmore	1,602	D 3
Fort Duchesne	200	C 6
Fountain Green	544	D 4
Francis	252	C 4
Fremont	125	E 4
Fruit Heights*	175	C 3
Fruitland	10	C 5
Gandy		D 1
Garden City	168	B 4
Garfield		C 3
Garland	1,119	B 3
Garrison	100	D 1
Genola*	380	C 4
Gilluly	12	D 4
Glendale	130	F 3
Glenwood	223	E 4
Gold Hill		C 1
Goshen	426	C 4
Goshute*	75	D 1
Granger*	907	C 3
Granite*	12	C 3
Grantsville	2,166	C 2
Green River	1,075	D 6
Greenville	100	E 4
Greenwich	850	E 4
Grouse Creek	157	B 1
Grover		E 3
Gunlock	90	F 2
Gunnison	1,059	D 4
Gusher	65	C 6
Hailstone	15	C 4
Hamiltons Fort	47	F 2
Hanksville	165	E 5
Hanna	425	C 5
Harrisville	198	B 4
Hatton	99	E 3
Hayden	145	C 6
Heber	2,936	C 4
Helper	2,459	C 6
Henefer	408	C 4
Henrieville	152	F 4
Hermitage*	70	E 3
Hiawatha	439	D 6
Highland Boy*	290	C 3
Hinckley	397	D 3
Holden	388	D 4
Holladay	28,000	C 3
Honeyville	646	B 3
Hooper	75	B 3
Howell	188	B 3
Hoytsville	250	C 4
Huntington	787	D 5
Huntsville	552	B 4
Hurricane	1,251	F 2
Hyde Park	713	B 4
Hyrum	1,728	B 4
Ibapah	25	D 1
Ioka		C 5
Iosepa	15	C 2
Ivins	77	F 2
Jensen	300	C 6
Jericho		D 3
Joseph	117	E 3
Junction	219	E 4
Kamas	749	C 4
Kanarraville	236	F 2
Kanab	1,645	F 3
Kanosh	499	E 3
Kaysville	3,608	C 3
Kearns	17,172	C 3
Keetley	60	C 4
Kenilworth	933	C 6
Kimball Junction	143	C 4
Kingston	100	E 4
Knolls	10	C 2
Koosharem	148	E 4
Lake Point		C 3
Lake Shore	6	C 4
Lakeside	12	C 2
Laketown	211	B 4
Lakeview*		C 4
Lakota		C 6
Lapoint	25	C 6
Lark*	700	C 3
La Sal	200	E 6
Latuda	12	C 6
Layton	9,027	C 3
La Verkin	365	F 2
Leamington	190	D 3
Leeds	109	F 2
Lehi	4,377	C 4
Levan	421	D 4
Lewiston	1,336	B 4
Lindon	1,150	C 4
Loa	359	E 4
Lofgreen		D 3
Logan	18,731	B 4
Long Valley Junction		F 3
Lucin		B 1
Lund	50	E 2
Lyman	255	E 4
Lynndyl	145	D 3
Magna	6,442	C 3
Mammoth	100	D 4
Manderfield	70	E 3
Manila	329	C 6
Manti	1,739	D 4
Mapleton	1,515	C 4
Marysvale	354	E 3
Maxwell*		C 4
Mayfield	329	D 4
Meadow	244	E 3
Mendon	345	B 4
Mexican Hat*	250	F 6
Midvale	5,802	C 3
Midway	713	C 4
Milford	1,471	E 2
Mill Fork	7	D 4
Millville	364	B 4
Milton		C 3
Minersville	580	E 2
Moab	4,682	D 6
Modena	62	F 2
Mohrland		D 5
Mona	347	D 4
Monroe	955	E 3
Monticello	1,845	F 6
Moore	25	D 5
Morgan	1,299	B 3
Moroni	879	D 4
Mount Carmel	100	F 3
Mount Carmel Junction	50	F 3
Mount Pleasant	1,572	D 4
Murray	16,806	C 3
Mutual*	52	D 5
Myton	329	C 5
Nada		E 2
Naples		C 6
Neola		C 5
Nephi	2,566	D 4
New Harmony	105	F 2
Newcastle	68	F 2
Newton	480	B 4
Nibley*		B 4
North Logan*	741	B 4
North Ogden	2,621	B 3
North Salt Lake	1,655	C 3
Oak City	247	D 3
Oakley	421	C 4
Oasis	102	D 3
Ogden	70,197	B 3
Ophir	33	D 3
Orangeville	571	D 5
Orderville	398	F 3
Orem	18,394	C 4
Ouray		C 6
Panguitch	1,435	F 3
Paradise	368	B 4
Paragonah	300	F 2
Park City	1,366	C 4
Park Valley	25	B 2
Parowan	1,486	F 2
Payson	4,237	C 4
Peoa	203	C 4
Perry	587	B 3
Pickleville	94	B 4
Pintura	5	F 2
Plain City	1,152	B 3
Pleasant Grove	4,772	C 4
Pleasant View	927	B 3
Plymouth	189	B 3
Portage		B 3
Price	6,802	D 6
Promontory		B 3
Promontory Point	1,189	B 3
Providence	1,189	B 4
Provo	36,047	C 4
Randlett	10	C 6
Randolph	537	B 4
Redmond	413	E 4
Reese		B 3
Richfield	4,412	E 3
Richmond	1,977	B 4
River Heights*	887	B 4
Riverdale	1,848	B 3
Riverside	150	B 3
Riverton	1,993	C 3
Rockville	142	F 2
Roosevelt	1,812	C 5
Rosette		B 2
Roy	9,239	B 3
Royal	100	D 6
Rubys Inn	50	F 3
St. George	5,130	F 2
St. John		D 3
Salem	920	C 4
Salina	1,618	E 4
Salt Lake City	189,454	C 3
Sandy	3,322	C 3
Santa Clara	1,183	F 2
Santaquin	1,328	C 4
Scipio	328	D 3
Scofield	158	D 5
Sego	20	D 6
Sevier	10	E 4
Shivwits	333	F 2
Sigurd	339	E 4
Silver City	16	D 4
Smithfield	2,512	B 4
Snowville	159	B 3
Snyderville	25	C 4
Soldier Summit	33	D 4
South Jordan	1,354	C 3
South Ogden	7,405	B 3
South Salt Lake	9,520	C 3
South Weber	382	B 3
Spanish Fork	6,472	C 4
Spring Canyon	250	D 6
Spring City	463	D 4
Spring Glen*	500	C 6
Spring Lake		C 4
Springdale	248	F 2
Springdell*	55	C 4
Springville	7,913	C 4
Spry	25	F 3
Standrod	137	B 2
Sterling		D 4
Stockton	362	D 3
Summit	150	F 3
Sunnyside	1,740	D 6
Sunset	4,235	B 3
Syracuse	1,061	B 3
Tabiona	167	C 5
Taylorsville*	500	C 3
Teasdale	200	E 4
Terminal*	65	C 3
Thatcher	160	B 3
Thistle	150	D 4
Thompson	100	D 6
Timpie		C 2
Tod Park	700	C 3
Tooele	9,133	D 3
Toquerville	197	F 2
Torrey	128	E 4
Tremonton	2,115	B 3
Trenton	448	B 4
Tridell	310	C 5
Tropic	385	F 4
Trout Creek		D 1
Tucker	5	D 4
Uintah*	344	B 3
Union*	500	C 3
Upalco	65	C 5
Upton		C 4
Val Verda*	600	C 3
Venice	250	E 4
Vermillion	120	E 4
Vernal	3,655	C 6
Veyo (Onaqui)	511	F 2
Vineyard	60	C 4
Vivian Park	24	C 4
Wahsatch	60	C 4
Wales	180	D 4
Wallsburg	65	C 4
Washakie	339	B 4
Washington	445	F 2
Washington Terrace	6,441	B 3
Wattis		D 5
Wellington	1,066	D 6
Wellsville	1,106	B 4
Wendover	609	C 1
West Bountiful	945	C 3
West Jordan	3,009	C 3
West Point*	599	B 3
Westwater	15	D 6
White Canyon	170	F 5
Whiterocks		C 6
Wildwood		C 4
Willard	814	B 3
Woodruff	169	B 4
Woods Cross	1,098	C 3
Woodside	55	D 6
Yost	87	B 2
Zion National Park	60	F 3

*Does not appear on the map; key shows general location.

°County Seat.
Source: Latest census figures.

UTAH/People

The 1960 United States census reported that Utah had a population of 890,627. This was an increase of about 30 per cent over the 1950 figure of 688,862. The U.S. Bureau of the Census estimated that by 1965 the state's population had grown to about a million.

About three-fourths of Utah's people live in urban areas. That is, they live in or near cities and towns of 2,500 or more persons. The rest of the people live in rural areas. About three-fourths of the people live in the state's three Standard Metropolitan Statistical Areas, as defined by the U.S. Bureau of the Budget (see METRO-POLITAN AREA). For the populations of these metropolitan areas—Ogden, Provo-Orem, and Salt Lake City—see the *Index* to the political map of Utah.

Salt Lake City is the capital and largest city of Utah. Ogden and Provo are the only other incorporated cities with populations of more than 25,000. Holladay, an unincorporated city, also has more than 25,000 persons. See the separate articles on the cities of Utah listed in the *Related Articles* at the end of this article.

More than 95 of every 100 persons living in Utah were born in the United States. The largest groups of persons born in other countries came from Canada, England, Germany, and The Netherlands.

More than 60 per cent of Utah's people are Mormons. Other large church groups in the state include Baptists, Episcopalians, Methodists, Presbyterians, and Roman Catholics.

POPULATION

This map shows the *population density* of Utah, and how it varies in different parts of the state. Population density means the average number of persons who live on each square mile.

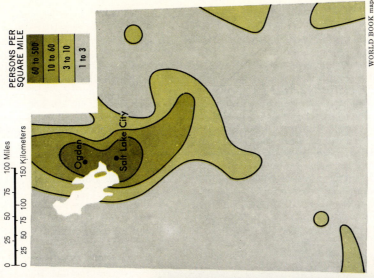

WORLD BOOK map

PERSONS PER SQUARE MILE
60 to 500
10 to 60
3 to 10
1 to 3

The Church of Jesus Christ of Latter-day Saints

Mormons Gather in Salt Lake City's historic Temple Square, the symbolic center of Mormonism. The Sea Gull Monument, left background, honors the sea gulls that saved Utah's crops in 1848. The gulls ate the swarms of crickets that threatened the crops.

Schools. Utah's first school was a tent in the Salt Lake Valley. It was set up in 1847, the year the Mormons first settled in the region. By the mid-1850's, the Utah region had more than 200 schools. Parents had to pay to send their children to these early schools because of a shortage of tax money. The region's first free public school opened in American Fork in 1866. A law passed in 1890 made all public elementary schools free. In 1895, a constitutional convention provided for the establishment and support of free public high schools.

Today, Utah has the highest percentage of high school graduates in the United States—more than 50 per cent of the people. A larger percentage of Utah's population attends college than that of any other state. Utah is second only to Colorado in the percentage of college graduates—nearly 10 per cent of its population.

The state board of education supervises Utah's public school system. The board has nine members, elected to four-year terms. It appoints a superintendent of public instruction as its executive officer. Utah and Ohio require children to attend school longer than do any other states—from age 6 to 18. For the number of teachers and students in Utah, see EDUCATION (table).

Libraries. Utah's first library was established with books hauled to the region by oxen in the 1850's. This library became the Utah State Library. The books from this library are now part of the Utah State Supreme Court of Law Library and the University of Utah Library.

In 1897, a state law provided for free public libraries. The Salt Lake City Public Library opened the next year. The Carnegie Free Library in Ogden was the first

UTAH / A Visitor's Guide

Millions of tourists visit Utah every year. The state's forests, mountains, lakes, and rivers are excellent for fishing, hunting, skiing, swimming, and sightseeing. One of Utah's most popular places to visit is the center of Mormonism—Temple Square in Salt Lake City. Three important Mormon church buildings stand in the square. These are the majestic Mormon Temple, which took 40 years to build; the Salt Lake Tabernacle, famous for its huge organ and choir; and the Assembly Hall. The Temple is not open to the general public.

Bryce Canyon National Park, Land of Brilliant Color
Hal Rumel, Publix

PLACES TO VISIT

Following are brief descriptions of some of Utah's many interesting places to visit.

Beehive House, in Salt Lake City, is the restored home of Brigham Young. This stately, two-story adobe house was built in 1852.

Bingham Canyon Copper Pit, near Salt Lake City, is the largest open-pit copper mine in North America. The mine is nearly half a mile deep, and more than two miles across at its widest point.

Bonneville Speedway, near Wendover, is famous for its summer racing trials. The area has a hundred square miles of flat salt beds that are as hard as cement.

Goosenecks of the San Juan River, near Mexican Hat, form an area where the river winds its way through a 1,200-foot-deep canyon.

Hot Pots, near Midway, are limestone craters in which visitors can swim in water of about 110° F.

Monument Valley, in southeastern Utah, has red sandstone formations that rise several hundred feet from a flat valley floor. In the evening, a formation called the *totem pole* casts a 35-mile-long shadow.

Ruins of Indian Cliff Dwellings line mountain ledges near Blanding, Bluff, Kanab, Parowan, Price, and Vernal. These dwellings were the homes of Indians who lived in the Utah region hundreds of years ago.

National Parks, Monuments, and Forests. Utah has three national parks—Canyonlands, Bryce Canyon, and Zion. The state shares Dinosaur and Hovenweep national monuments with Colorado. Other Utah national monuments are Arches, Capitol Reef, Cedar Breaks, Natural Bridges, Rainbow Bridge, and Timpanogos Cave. The Golden Spike National Historic Site is at Promontory. Utah has two national recreation areas—Glen Canyon, which it shares with Arizona, and Flaming Gorge, which it shares with Wyoming. There are nine national forests in Utah—Ashley, Cache, Caribou, Dixie, Fishlake, Manti-LaSal, Sawtooth, Uinta, and Wasatch. See NATIONAL FOREST (table).

State Parks. Utah has 31 state parks. For information on these parks, write to Director, State Park and Recreation Commission, 19 W. South Temple St., Salt Lake City, Utah 84101.

building in the state to be used only as a library. It opened in 1903. Today, Utah has more than 50 public libraries. Large collections of Mormon literature are owned by Brigham Young University in Provo, the Latter-day Saints Church Historian's Office in Salt Lake City, and the Utah State Historical Society's Morgan Memorial Library in Salt Lake City.

Museums. Utah has about 20 art galleries and museums. Outstanding collections of paintings may be seen at the University of Utah, the Utah Art Center, and the Utah State Institute of Fine Arts—all in Salt Lake City. The Brigham Young University museum in Provo and the Springfield Art Gallery also have excellent collections. The Temple Square Bureau of Information and Museum in Salt Lake City has exhibits describing Mormon pioneer life. Also in Salt Lake City are a museum maintained by the Daughters of Utah Pioneers Association, and a pioneer village operated by the Sons of Utah Pioneers Association.

UNIVERSITIES AND COLLEGES

Utah has five regionally accredited universities and colleges. For enrollments and further information, see UNIVERSITIES AND COLLEGES (table).

Name	Location	Founded
Brigham Young University	Provo	1875
Utah, University of	Salt Lake City	1850
Utah State University of Agriculture and Applied Science	Logan	1888
Weber State College	Ogden	1889
Westminster College	Salt Lake City	1875

ANNUAL EVENTS

Each July, Utahans observe the 1847 arrival of Mormon pioneers in the Salt Lake Valley. Many Utah cities stage celebrations. The symphony season at the Salt Lake Tabernacle extends from November to March.

Other annual events in Utah include the following.

January–April: Statehood Day Celebration in Salt Lake City (January 4); State Art Exhibit in Salt Lake City (February); Ute Tribal Bear Dance in Duchesne (April); Art Exhibit in Springville (April).

May–August: Salt Lake Symphonic Choir Concert in Salt Lake City (May); Ballet Gala in Salt Lake City (May); Utah State Junior Livestock Show in Spanish Fork (May); Re-enactment of the Driving of the Golden Spike at Promontory (May 10); Cache Valley Dairy Festival in Logan (June); University of Utah Theater Summer Festival in Salt Lake City (last week in June, first week in July); Ute Tribal Sun Dance near Whiterocks (July); Shakespearean Drama Festival in Cedar City (second week in July); Mount Timpanogos Hike (July); Bonneville National Speed Trials on Bonneville Speedway (second week in August to September 1).

September–December: Utah State Fair in Salt Lake City (September); Civic Oratorio, *The Messiah*, in the Salt Lake Tabernacle in Salt Lake City (Sunday before Christmas); University Theater Ballet Festival in Salt Lake City (Christmas week).

The Church of Jesus Christ of Latter-day Saints
Brigham Young University Library in Provo

Mormon Temple in Salt Lake City's Temple Square
Lorin D. Wiggins

Pioneer Monument State Park in Salt Lake City
The Church of Jesus Christ of Latter-day Saints

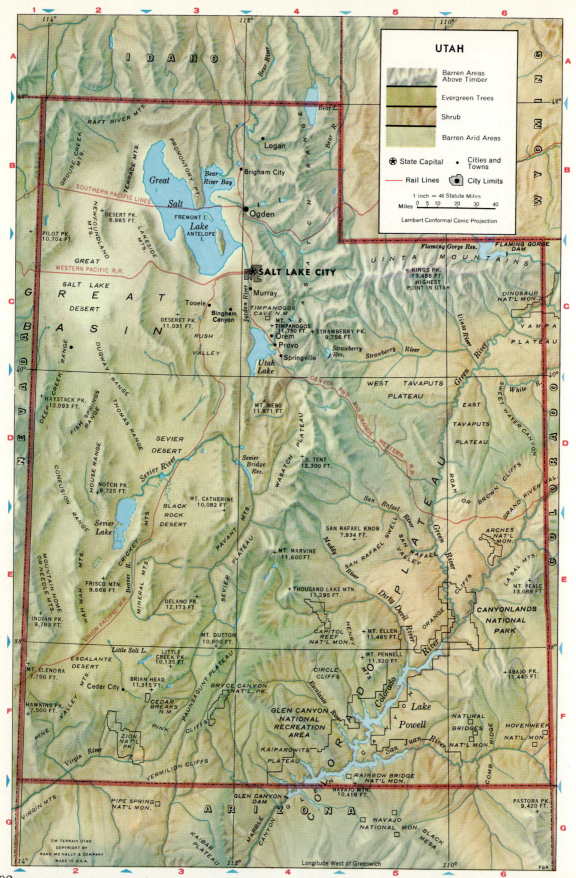

UTAH

Barren Areas
Above Timber

Evergreen Trees

Shrub

Barren Arid Areas

⊛ State Capital   • Cities and Towns

— Rail Lines   City Limits

1 inch = 46 Statute Miles

Miles 0 5 10   20   30   40

Lambert Conformal Conic Projection

IDAHO

Bear River

Logan

Brigham City

Great Salt Lake

Bear River Bay

FREMONT I.

ANTELOPE I.

Ogden

PILOT PK. 10,704 FT.

DESERT PK. 6,985 FT.

SOUTHERN PACIFIC LINES

GREAT WESTERN PACIFIC R.R.

GREAT SALT LAKE DESERT

SALT LAKE CITY

Murray

Tooele

Bingham Canyon

DESERET PK. 11,031 FT.

RUSH VALLEY

TIMPANOGOS CAVE N.M.

MT. TIMPANOGOS 11,750 FT.

Orem

Provo

Springville

STRAWBERRY PK. 9,756 FT.

Strawberry Res.

Strawberry River

Utah Lake

Jordan River

UINTA MOUNTAINS

FLAMING GORGE RES.

FLAMING GORGE DAM

KINGS PK. 13,498 FT. HIGHEST POINT IN UTAH

DINOSAUR NAT'L MON.

YAMPA PLATEAU

Uinta River

Green River

HAYSTACK PK. 12,093 FT.

DEEP CREEK RANGE

FISH SPRINGS RANGE

DUGWAY RANGE

THOMAS RANGE

SEVIER DESERT

Sevier River

MT. NEBO 11,871 FT.

DENVER AND RIO GRANDE WESTERN R.R.

WEST TAVAPUTS PLATEAU

EAST TAVAPUTS PLATEAU

White R.

SWEET WATER CANYON

GRAND RIVER VAL.

NOTCH PK. 9,725 FT.

HOUSE RANGE

CONFUSION RANGE

Sevier Lake

SEVIER BRIDGE RES.

MT. CATHERINE 10,082 FT.

BLACK ROCK DESERT

S. TENT 12,300 FT.

WASATCH PLATEAU

San Rafael River

SAN RAFAEL KNOB 7,934 FT.

Muddy River

San Rafael River

SAN RAFAEL SWELL

SAN RAFAEL VALLEY

Green River

ROAN OR BROWN CLIFFS

ARCHES NAT'L MON.

LA SAL MTS.

MT. PEALE 13,089 FT.

FRISCO MTN. 9,668 FT.

MINERAL MTS.

PAVANT MTS.

Beaver R.

UNION PACIFIC R.R.

MOUNTAIN HOME OR NEEDLE MTS.

INDIAN PK. 9,783 FT.

DELANO PK. 12,173 FT.

SEVIER PLATEAU

MT. MARVINE 11,600 FT.

THOUSAND LAKE MTN. 11,295 FT.

Dirty Devil River

ORANGE CLIFFS

CANYONLANDS NATIONAL PARK

MT. ABAJO PK. 11,445 FT.

MT. DUTTON 10,800 FT.

CAPITOL REEF NAT'L MON.

MT. ELLEN 11,485 FT.

HENRY MTS.

Escalante River

Colorado River

MT. ELENORA 7,750 FT.

Little Salt L.

LITTLE CREEK PK. 10,135 FT.

ESCALANTE DESERT

BRIAN HEAD 11,315 FT.

Cedar City

CEDAR BREAKS N.M.

PAUNSAUGUNT PLATEAU

PINK CLIFFS

BRYCE CANYON NAT'L PK.

CIRCLE CLIFFS

MT. PENNELL 11,320 FT.

Lake Powell

NATURAL BRIDGES NAT'L MON.

HOVENWEEP NAT'L MON.

HAWKINS PK. 7,500 FT.

PINE VALLEY

ZION NAT'L PK.

Virgin River

KAIPAROWITS PLATEAU

GLEN CANYON NATIONAL RECREATION AREA

San Juan River

COMB RIDGE

VERMILION CLIFFS

RAINBOW BRIDGE NAT'L MON.

VIRGIN MTS.

PIPE SPRING NAT'L MON.

GLEN CANYON DAM

NAVAJO MTN. 10,416 FT.

NAVAJO NATIONAL MON. BLACK MESA

PASTORA PK. 9,420 FT.

MARBLE CANYON

KAIBAB PLATEAU

ARIZONA

Longitude West of Greenwich

FGA

CM TERRAIN UTAH COPYRIGHT BY RAND McNALLY & COMPANY MADE IN U.S.A.

192 Specially created for World Book Encyclopedia by Rand McNally and World Book editors

Land Regions.

Utah includes parts of three major land regions: (1) the Rocky Mountains, (2) the Basin and Range Region, and (3) the Colorado Plateau.

The Rocky Mountains extend generally north and south across a large part of western North America. In Utah, two ranges of the Rocky Mountains—the Uinta and the Wasatch—form an angle in the northeast corner of the state. The Uinta Range extends westward from Colorado almost to Salt Lake City. It is the only major range of the Rocky Mountains that runs east and west. Several peaks in the Uinta Range are more than 13,000 feet high. Kings Peak, the highest point in Utah, rises 13,498 feet near the center of the range. Many lakes and flat-bottomed canyons in the Uinta Range were formed by glaciers that once covered the area.

The Wasatch Range extends from Mount Nebo, near Nephi, northward into Idaho. The western side of this rugged range is very steep. It rises 6,000 to 8,000 feet above the valleys that border it. The Wasatch Range also has many canyons. The canyons provide water and serve as recreation areas for the people in Utah's largest cities, just west of the mountains. Some of the canyons were formed by glaciers. The Ogden, Provo, and Weber Canyons were cut by rivers.

The Basin and Range Region covers parts of several states, including the western part of Utah. It is one of the driest regions in the United States. Small mountain ranges and broad basins cover the center of the region. Higher ranges and plateaus border it on the east and the west. Great Salt Lake lies in the northeast part of the region. West and southwest of the lake is a barren area called the Great Salt Lake Desert. The desert has about 4,000 acres of flat salt beds that are as hard as concrete.

The extreme southwestern corner of Utah's Basin and Range region is known as *Utah's Dixie*. The early settlers grew cotton there.

The Colorado Plateau stretches over parts of Utah, Arizona, Colorado, and New Mexico. It covers most of the southern and eastern sections of Utah. This region consists of broad, rough uplands cut by deep canyons and valleys. High plateaus in the western part of the region include the Aquarius, Fish Lake, Markagunt, Paunsagunt, Pavant, Sanpitch, Sevier, and Tushar. These plateaus have elevations of more than 11,000 feet. The famous Bryce, Cedar Breaks, and Zion canyons are in this area. The Henry Mountains rise west of the Colorado River, and the Abajo and La Sal mountains are east of the river. Utah's southeastern corner meets the corners of Arizona, New Mexico, and Colorado. This is the only point in the United States where four states meet (see ARIZONA [picture, Four Corners]).

Rivers and Lakes.

Utah's rivers are used to provide irrigation for thousands of acres of farmland that otherwise would be desert. The Colorado River and its main tributary, the Green River, are the largest rivers in the state. These rivers and their many branches drain the eastern half of Utah. The Snake River of Idaho and its branches drain Utah's northwest corner. The Bear, Provo, and Weber rivers begin in the Uinta Range and flow through the Wasatch Mountains into Great Salt Lake. The Sevier is the chief river of south-central Utah. It begins in the Paunsagunt Plateau and flows north, then bends to the southwest. Most of the Basin and Range Region, which extends across several western states, has no outlet to the sea. It is the largest area of interior drainage in the United States.

Thousands of years ago, a huge body of fresh water

Map Index

Land Regions of Utah

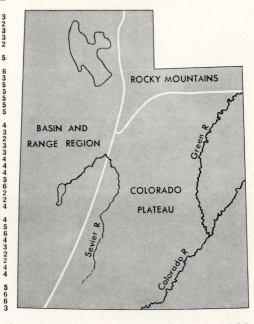

ROCKY MOUNTAINS

BASIN AND RANGE REGION

COLORADO PLATEAU

Green R.

Sevier R.

Colorado R.

UTAH

covered parts of Utah. Scientists have named this ancient sea Lake Bonneville. The Bonneville Salt Flats, in the middle of the Great Salt Lake Desert, cover part of the bed of Lake Bonneville. Great Salt Lake and Utah Lake are also part of what remains of Lake Bonneville. Great Salt Lake is the largest natural lake west of the Mississippi River. It is four to five times as salty as the ocean, and becomes even saltier when the water level drops during dry periods. Great Salt Lake is salty because its waters are not drained by outflowing streams. Instead, some of the water evaporates and leaves salt deposits behind. The Jordan River drains Utah Lake and keeps its waters fresh. Utah Lake and Bear Lake, which Utah shares with Idaho, are important reservoirs in which irrigation waters are stored. Many small lakes lie in the Boulder, Uinta, and Wasatch mountains.

Deserts cover about a third of Utah. Few plants can grow in these deserts because of the lack of rainfall. The Great Salt Lake Desert lies west and south of Great Salt Lake. Other deserts include the Sevier Desert in west-central Utah, and the Escalante Desert in the southwestern part of the state.

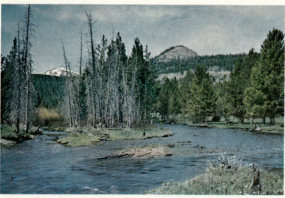

Lorin D. Wiggins

Bear River, fed by melting snow, offers excellent fishing in the Uinta Mountains of Utah's Rocky Mountains region.

W. R. Wilson

Lake Powell, in the Colorado Plateau region, was formed by Glen Canyon Dam on the Colorado River in Arizona.

Great White Throne, *left*, rises nearly half a mile from the canyon floor in Zion National Park. Zion Canyon in the Basin and Range Region is a spectacular example of river erosion.

Union Pacific Railroad

UTAH / Climate

Average July temperatures in Utah range from 60° F. in the northeast to 84° F. in the southwest. January temperatures average 20° F. in the north and 39° F. in the southwest. Utah's record high temperature, 116° F., occurred at St. George on June 28, 1892. The state's lowest temperature was −50° F., at Woodruff on Feb. 6, 1899, and at East Portal on Jan. 5, 1913.

Utah's yearly *precipitation* (rain, melted snow, and other forms of moisture) varies from less than 5 inches in the Great Salt Lake Desert to 40 or 50 inches in the northeastern mountains. Valley areas are generally dry, and mountain areas are wet. Annual snowfall ranges from a few inches in the southwest to more than 400 inches at Alta, a ski area near Salt Lake City.

FPG

A Hot, Dry Climate causes the Great Salt Lake Desert to crack and makes it one of the most desolate regions in the world.

SEASONAL TEMPERATURES

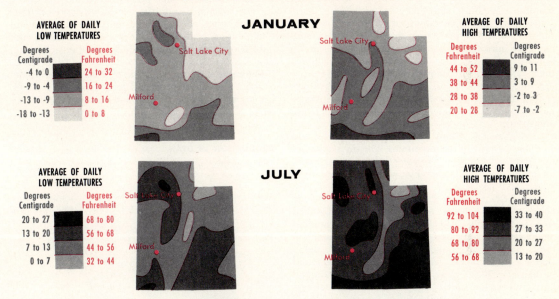

JANUARY

AVERAGE OF DAILY LOW TEMPERATURES

Degrees Centigrade	Degrees Fahrenheit
-4 to 0	24 to 32
-9 to -4	16 to 24
-13 to -9	8 to 16
-18 to -13	0 to 8

AVERAGE OF DAILY HIGH TEMPERATURES

Degrees Fahrenheit	Degrees Centigrade
44 to 52	9 to 11
38 to 44	3 to 9
28 to 38	-2 to 3
20 to 28	-7 to -2

JULY

AVERAGE OF DAILY LOW TEMPERATURES

Degrees Centigrade	Degrees Fahrenheit
20 to 27	68 to 80
13 to 20	56 to 68
7 to 13	44 to 56
0 to 7	32 to 44

AVERAGE OF DAILY HIGH TEMPERATURES

Degrees Fahrenheit	Degrees Centigrade
92 to 104	33 to 40
80 to 92	27 to 33
68 to 80	20 to 27
56 to 68	13 to 20

AVERAGE YEARLY PRECIPITATION
(Rain, Melted Snow, and Other Moisture)

Inches	Centimeters
16 to 32	41 to 81
8 to 16	20 to 41
0 to 8	0 to 20

0   100   200 Miles
0   100   200   300 Kilometers

WORLD BOOK maps

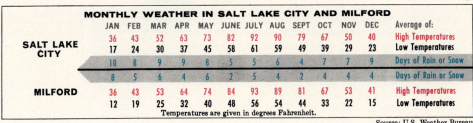

MONTHLY WEATHER IN SALT LAKE CITY AND MILFORD	JAN	FEB	MAR	APR	MAY	JUNE	JULY	AUG	SEPT	OCT	NOV	DEC	Average of:
SALT LAKE CITY	36	43	52	63	73	82	92	90	79	67	50	40	High Temperatures
	17	24	30	37	45	58	61	59	49	39	29	23	Low Temperatures
	10	8	9	9	8	5	5	6	4	7	7	9	Days of Rain or Snow
	8	5	6	4	4	2	5	4	2	4	4	4	Days of Rain or Snow
MILFORD	36	43	53	64	74	84	93	89	81	67	53	41	High Temperatures
	12	19	25	32	40	48	56	54	44	33	22	15	Low Temperatures

Temperatures are given in degrees Fahrenheit.

Source: U.S. Weather Bureau

Utah's economy depends almost entirely on manufacturing, mining, and agricultural activities in the northern and central parts of the state. Most of the irrigated farmland lies in a north-south line across the center of the state.

Natural Resources of Utah include rich mineral deposits, soils, forests, and plant and animal life.

Minerals. Bingham Canyon has rich deposits of copper, gold, lead, molybdenum, silver, and zinc. Coal, natural gas, and oil are found in the Colorado Plateau. North-central and southern Utah have deposits of sand and gravel. Utah has one of the nation's richest deposits of *bituminous sand* (sand containing mineral substances called bitumen). The Escalante Desert in the southwest has large supplies of iron ore. Other Utah minerals include beryllium, clay, gilsonite, gypsum, mineral salts, uranium, vanadium, and stone.

Soils of Utah are generally poor for farming. Most of the mountain soils are poorly developed. Valley soils are often mixtures of sand, gravel, and clay carried down by mountain streams. Where water is available these valley soils can produce good crops.

Forests cover about 16 million acres, or about 30 per cent of the state. The forest land is found in the mountains. Common trees include aspens, firs, junipers, pines, and spruces.

Other Plant Life. Many kinds of grasses, shrubs, and wild flowers grow in the mountains. The dry sections of the state have cactus, creosote bush, greasewood, mesquite, and shadscale. The wetter sections have grasses and sagebrush.

Animal Life. Common small animals in Utah include badgers, foxes, martens, muskrats, rabbits, ring-tailed cats, skunks, and weasels. Among the larger animals are black bears, bobcats, coyotes, lynxes, and mountain lions. The mule deer is the most common game animal. Buffaloes, elks, moose, and pronghorns are also found in the state. Ducks, geese, grouse, pheasants, and quail are common game birds of Utah. The state has such reptiles as lizards, toads, tortoises, and several kinds of snakes. Trout is the most common fish. Others include bass, catfish, graylings, perch, and whitefish.

Manufacturing, including processing, accounts for slightly more than half the value of goods produced in Utah. Goods manufactured there have a *value added by manufacture* of about $685,317,000 annually. This figure represents the value created in products by Utah's industries, not counting such costs as materials, supplies, and fuels. Utah's chief manufactured products, in order of importance, are (1) primary metals, (2) transportation equipment, and (3) foods and related products.

Primary Metals industries in Utah turn out products that have a value added of about $173,509,000 yearly. These industries smelt, refine, and roll metals. They also manufacture nails, bolts, and basic metal products such as castings. Plants near Garfield and Magna and in Tooele are important processors of *nonferrous metals* (metals that do not contain iron). The Provo area is a center for processing coke, pig iron, and steel. Plants in Moab and near Salt Lake City process uranium. The Moab area also has a large potash refinery. Plants in Salt Lake County refine copper and lead.

Transportation Equipment has a value added of about $169,099,000 yearly. This industry developed during the mid-1950's when Utah factories began producing missile engines and parts. Missile production started to fall in the 1960's, when the need for the parts produced in Utah began to decline.

Foods and Related Products in Utah have an annual value added of about $86,650,000. Plants in Salt Lake County process beet sugar, and meat and dairy products. Beet sugar is also processed in Garland and Lewiston. Ogden and Salt Lake City have large flour and feed mills and meat-packing plants. Smithfield has the largest Swiss cheese factory in the United States. Cache Valley in northeastern Utah is an important processor of dairy products. Factories in the state also can, freeze, and preserve fruits and vegetables.

Other Important Industries. The manufacture of stone, clay, and glass products ranks fourth in importance in Utah. Other leading industries include printing and publishing, and the manufacture of fabricated metal products, machinery, and petroleum and coal products.

Mining has an annual value of about $410,412,000, or about a third of the value of goods produced in Utah. Copper is the state's most valuable mineral, and Utah ranks second only to Arizona in copper production.

PRODUCTION IN UTAH

Total yearly value of goods produced—$1,282,629,000

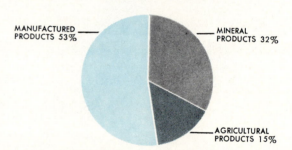

MANUFACTURED PRODUCTS 53%

MINERAL PRODUCTS 32%

AGRICULTURAL PRODUCTS 15%

Note: Manufacturing percentage based on value added by manufacture. Other percentages based on value of production.

Source: Latest available U.S. Government statistics

EMPLOYMENT IN UTAH

Average yearly number of persons employed—332,500

		Number of Employees
Government	🚶🚶🚶🚶🚶🚶	68,700
Wholesale & Retail Trade	🚶🚶🚶🚶🚶🚶	66,500
Manufacturing	🚶🚶🚶🚶🚶	56,600
Services	🚶🚶🚶🚶	39,100
Agriculture	🚶🚶🚶	33,000
Transportation & Public Utilities	🚶🚶	22,400
Construction	🚶🚶	20,800
Finance, Insurance & Real Estate	🚶	12,700
Forestry & Mining	🚶	12,700

Source: Employment statistics supplied by employers to government agencies

Most of Utah's copper is taken from a huge mountain of ore in Bingham Canyon. Most of the state's petroleum, the second most valuable mineral, comes from San Juan County. Utah is among the leading producers of gold, iron ore, lead, uranium, and zinc. It is also the leading coal producer west of the Mississippi River. The Book Cliffs area in Carbon and Emery counties supplies nearly all the state's coal. All Utah's iron ore is mined in Iron County.

Uintah County is the nation's only producer of gilsonite, a solid form of asphalt. The water of Great Salt Lake is used to produce natural salts. Utah is a leading producer of molybdenum, potassium salts, and silver.

Agriculture in Utah provides a yearly gross income of about $186,900,000. Farmland covers more than 12 million acres, or nearly a fourth of the state's land area. About 1,100,000 acres are irrigated by water stored in reservoirs. About 500,000 acres can be farmed without irrigation by using dry farming methods (see DRY FARMING). Utah's 18,000 farms average 712 acres in size. But most of the irrigated farms are under 200 acres. Many dry farms and ranches are much larger. And a few ranches are far above the average.

Livestock and Livestock Products have an annual value of about $129,351,000. Cattle and calves, Utah's leading farm products, earn about $47,781,000 yearly. Milk is the second leading farm product, followed by turkeys, and sheep and lambs. Eggs, hogs, and wool are other important livestock products. Utah is a leading wool-producing state, and the sheep-raising center of the western United States.

Crops have an annual value of about $37,738,000 in Utah. Wheat, the chief crop, earns about $8,588,000 a year. Sugar beets are the second leading crop, and hay is third. Other important crops include alfalfa seed, barley, cherries, greenhouse and nursery products, potatoes, and tomatoes. Most of the wheat and sugar beets come from the northern and central counties. Farmers in the north-central section raise apples, apricots, beans, cherries, corn, peaches, pears, peas, and tomatoes. The largest potato crops are in Beaver, Cache, Iron, Millard, Utah, and Washington counties. Farmers in the extreme southwestern valleys raise almonds, cantaloupes, figs, and melons.

Electric Power. Most of Utah's generating plants are powered by coal or other fuels. Hydroelectric utilities generate the rest. Generators began producing power at Flaming Gorge in 1963 and at Glen Canyon in 1964. For Utah's kilowatt-hour production, see ELECTRIC POWER (table).

Transportation. The first transcontinental railroad in the United States was completed in Utah on May 10, 1869. On that date, the Central Pacific and Union Pacific railroads were joined at Promontory.

Today, Utah has more than 1,700 miles of railroad track. It also has more than 36,000 miles of roads, and about 70 airports and airfields. The largest commercial airport is in Salt Lake City.

Communication. Utah's first newspaper, the *Deseret News*, was established in Salt Lake City in 1850. Today, the state has 65 newspapers and 27 periodicals. The largest newspapers are the *Deseret News* and the *Tribune*, both of Salt Lake City. The state's first radio station, KZN (now KSL), began broadcasting in Salt Lake City in 1922. In 1948, Utah's first television station, KTVT (now KCPX-TV) began operating. Today, Utah has 33 radio stations, 3 commercial television stations, and 5 educational television stations.

FARM AND MINERAL PRODUCTS

This map shows where the state's leading farm and mineral products are produced. The major urban areas (shown on the map in red) are the state's important manufacturing centers.

WORLD BOOK map

Bingham Canyon Copper Mine is the largest open-pit copper mine in North America. Copper is Utah's most important mineral.

W. R. Wilson

HISTORIC UTAH

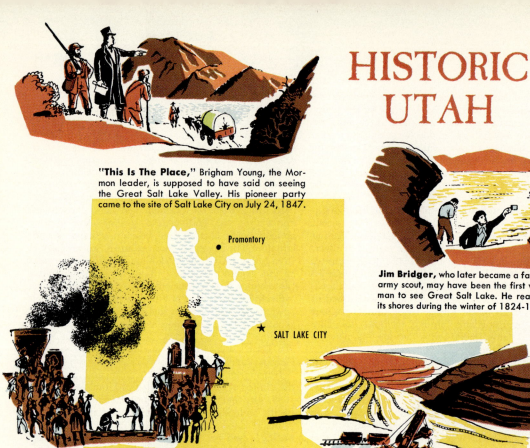

"This Is The Place," Brigham Young, the Mormon leader, is supposed to have said on seeing the Great Salt Lake Valley. His pioneer party came to the site of Salt Lake City on July 24, 1847.

Jim Bridger, who later became a famous army scout, may have been the first white man to see Great Salt Lake. He reached its shores during the winter of 1824-1825.

The First Transcontinental Railroad in America was completed at Promontory, Utah, on May 10, 1869. California Governor Stanford drove in the final spike, made of gold.

The Bingham Canyon Mine supplies nearly a fifth of U.S. copper. The mine boomed after surface mining began in 1906.

The Sugar Beet Industry began in Utah in the 1850's when the Mormons first planted beet seeds. The Lehi plant, opened in 1890, was the third in the country to succeed in beet-sugar manufacture.

The Discovery of Uranium near Moab in 1952 touched off a uranium rush. People came to Utah from all over the country hoping to "strike it rich."

The Mormons Began Irrigation of the land in Utah in 1847, the year of their arrival. They diverted City Creek, now in Salt Lake City, to flood the hard ground before plowing.

The Bonneville Speedway stretches over hard salt beds of the Great Salt Lake Desert. Here, in 1947, John Cobb, a British driver, was the first to travel more than 400 miles an hour on land.

Promontory

★ SALT LAKE CITY

Moab

Indian Days. Indians probably lived in the Utah region several thousand years ago. These early Indians made their homes in pueblos and in cliff dwellings. White explorers who came to the region in 1776 found four major tribes—the Gosiute, Paiute, Shoshoni (Snake), and Ute. Navaho Indians arrived during the 1860's, and now occupy large areas in southwestern Utah.

Early Exploration. In 1540, Spanish explorers discovered the Grand Canyon in what is now Arizona. They may have traveled into the Utah region, although many historians doubt that they did. More than 235 years passed before white men again came to Utah. In 1776, while American colonists were fighting for their independence from Great Britain, two Spanish Franciscan friars led an expedition into the Utah region. They were Silvestre Velez de Escalante and Francisco Atanasio Domínguez. The friars explored the region and discovered Utah Lake. Later, a few other Spaniards visited the region. But Spain was not interested in setting up colonies there. The first Americans to visit the region probably crossed what is now northern Utah in 1811-1812. They were members of a fur trading expedition.

Jim Bridger, a famous scout, was probably the first white man to see Great Salt Lake. He reached its shores during the winter of 1824-1825. Bridger tasted the salty water, and thought he had found an ocean. Hundreds of fur trappers and traders soon came to the Great Salt Lake area. By 1830, travelers were crossing central Utah to get from Santa Fe, in New Mexico, to Los Angeles.

The Mormons were Utah's first permanent settlers. This religious group belonged to the Church of Jesus

--------- **IMPORTANT DATES IN UTAH** ---------

1776 Silvestre Velez de Escalante and Francisco Atanasio Domínguez made the first far-reaching exploration of the Utah region.

1824-1825 Jim Bridger probably was the first white man to see Great Salt Lake.

1847 Brigham Young and the first Mormon pioneers arrived in the Great Salt Lake region.

1848 The United States won the Utah area from Mexico.

1849 The Mormons created the State of Deseret, and adopted their first constitution.

1850 Congress established the Utah Territory.

1860-1861 The pony express crossed Utah.

1861 Telegraph lines met at Salt Lake City, providing the first transcontinental telegraph service.

1869 The first transcontinental railroad was completed at Promontory.

1890 The Mormons in Utah prohibited polygamy.

1896 Utah became the 45th state on January 4.

1913 The U.S. Bureau of Reclamation completed the Strawberry River reservoir, the state's first large reclamation project.

1952 Rich uranium deposits were found near Moab.

1959 Utah became an important missile-producing state.

1963 Flaming Gorge and Glen Canyon dams were completed.

1964 Canyonlands National Park was established in southeast Utah.

Christ of Latter-day Saints. Joseph Smith established the church in Fayette, N.Y., in 1830. Brigham Young became leader of the Mormons after Smith's death in 1844. The Mormons were persecuted nearly everywhere they went. They traveled to Ohio, Missouri, and Illinois in search of religious freedom. In 1846, Young led a group of his people west. They reached the Great Salt Lake region in 1847, and Young settled there. He planned communities for all his followers. See MORMONS.

Many groups of Mormons settled in the valleys of north-central Utah. They irrigated the valleys and made farming productive. In 1848, swarms of grasshoppers invaded the valleys and threatened to ruin the settlers' crops. But sea gulls from Great Salt Lake wiped out the grasshoppers. The sea gull later became the state bird, and a monument was built in Salt Lake City to honor the gulls. The kind of grasshopper that attacked the settlers' crops became known as the Mormon cricket.

In 1849, the Mormons established their Perpetual Emigrating Fund. This fund helped bring to Utah many Mormons who could not pay for the trip. The fund operated for about 40 years. It brought about 50,-000 Mormons to Utah, including many from Denmark, England, Norway, Scotland, Sweden, and Wales.

Indian Troubles. Relations between the Mormons and the Indians were peaceful at first. But some of the Indians resented the settlers who had taken their land. Beginning in 1853, a Ute chief named Walker led attacks against several Mormon settlements. These attacks were known as the *Walker War*. In 1854, Brigham Young persuaded Walker to end the attacks. For several years, the settlers and Indians lived peacefully. Another Ute chief, Black Hawk, led an uprising against the Mormon settlers in 1865. The attack started the Black Hawk War. Other tribes joined in the fighting. About 50 Mormons were killed, and the settlers suffered losses of more than $1 million. In 1867, talks between the Indians and the Mormons at Mount Pleasant in Sanpete County ended the war. Most of the Ute settled on a reservation in the Uinta Basin.

Territorial Days and Statehood. The Utah region belonged to Mexico when the Mormons first arrived in 1847. At the time, the United States and Mexico were fighting the Mexican War (1846-1848). The United States won the war and acquired from Mexico a large area of land, including the Utah region.

In 1849, the Mormons established the *State of Deseret*. They set up a temporary government with Brigham Young as governor. Church leaders filled other government offices. The settlers adopted a constitution and asked to be admitted to the Union. But Congress was engaged in a bitter debate over the question of slavery in the United States. This debate resulted in a series of acts called the *Compromise of 1850*. Part of the compromise established the Utah Territory, with Young as the first territorial governor. The territory extended far to the east and west of present-day Utah. See COMPROMISE OF 1850.

Between 1849 and 1895, Utah asked several times to be admitted to the Union. But Congress refused each time because of the Mormon practice of *polygamy* (one man having more than one wife). Actually, only a small number of the Mormon men had more than one wife. But Utah was refused statehood as long as the Mormons practiced polygamy.

President James Buchanan wanted to take control of the Utah Territory away from the Mormons. In 1857, he appointed Alfred Cumming of Georgia as territorial governor, in place of Brigham Young. Buchanan sent federal troops to enforce the appointment. This period became known as the *Utah*, or *Mormon*, *War*. The soldiers marched toward Utah, stopping along the way during the winter of 1857-1858. In September, 1857, a group of Utahans and Indians, nervously awaiting the federal troops, attacked a party of travelers passing through Utah. Most of the 140 travelers were murdered. Only a few small children were permitted to live. The incident became known as the *Mountain Meadows Massacre*. John D. Lee, who took part in the massacre, was later convicted and executed.

The federal troops, guided by Jim Bridger, arrived in Utah in the spring of 1858. They stayed three years. Bad feeling between the Mormons and the troops existed throughout the period, although little actual fighting occurred. Brigham Young was no longer territorial governor, but he remained the real leader of the Mormons. The troops left Utah when the Civil War began in 1861.

During the 1860's, Utah's boundaries were changed several times. Parts of the territory were given to Nevada, Colorado, and Wyoming. Congress established Utah's present boundaries in 1868.

The pony express began carrying mail on April 3, 1860. Pony express riders crossed Utah on their journeys from St. Joseph, Mo., to Sacramento, Calif. The pony express ended on Oct. 24, 1861. On that date, telegraph lines from Washington, D.C., and from San Francisco met in Salt Lake City. The nation's first transcontinental telegraph service started, providing a link between the eastern and western United States. The pony express was no longer needed.

In 1862, Congress passed a law forbidding polygamy. That same year, federal troops were again sent to Utah, under the command of Colonel Patrick E. Conner. Conner was interested in mining, and he encouraged his troops to prospect for minerals. In 1863, gold and silver were discovered in Bingham Canyon. Conner sent out word of the discovery. He hoped that a mining boom would bring a flood of non-Mormons into Utah and reduce Mormon control of the territory. But profits from Utah's minerals were small during the 1860's, mostly because of transportation problems. Few prospectors came to the territory. By the 1870's, however, many mining companies were operating in Utah.

Plans for a transcontinental railroad had first been made during the 1850's. In 1863, the Central Pacific Railroad began building eastward from Sacramento, and the Union Pacific built westward, starting near Omaha, Neb. The two lines met at Promontory, Utah, on May 10, 1869. A railroad-building boom soon began in Utah.

During the 1880's, federal courts began enforcing federal laws against polygamy. Hundreds of Mormons were fined and sent to prison. A law passed in 1887 permitted the U.S. government to seize church property of the Mormons for use by public schools. In 1890, Wilford Woodruff, the church president, advised the Mormons to give up polygamy. In October of that year, the church officially prohibited polygamy.

In 1895, Utah submitted a new constitution to Congress. This constitution outlawed polygamy and prevented control of the state by any church. Utah was admitted to the Union as the 45th state on Jan. 4, 1896. The people elected Heber M. Wells, a Republican, as their first governor.

The Early 1900's brought expansion of the railroad construction that had begun after the Civil War. The railroads opened new markets for Utah's farm and mining products. Utah farmers increased livestock operations, and beef cattle and sheep became important prod-

Deseret Store in Salt Lake City accepted grain from Mormons as payment for goods in the 1800's.
Culver

First Transcontinental U.S. Railroad was completed in 1869 in Promontory. Central Pacific and Union Pacific railroad officials drove in the last spike.
Union Pacific Railroad

ucts. Surface mining methods were introduced in Bingham Canyon in 1906. The state's copper production increased greatly. A huge federal irrigation project on the Strawberry River, completed in 1913, increased the amount of Utah's irrigated farmland.

Large smelters were built in the Salt Lake Valley during the early 1900's, and Utah's smelting industry grew. After the United States entered World War I in 1917, Utah mines supplied the Allies with large supplies of *nonferrous metals* (metals containing no iron).

Utah was hit hard by the Great Depression of the 1930's. The mining industry suffered. Farm prices dropped. Utah had one of the nation's highest percentages of unemployed workers. The state's economy began to improve in the late 1930's when the depression eased.

The 1940's and 1950's. Utah's manufacturing and mining industries prospered during World War II (1939-1945). The state's value of manufacturing nearly tripled during the war years. Utah became one of the leading producers of copper, gold, lead, silver, and zinc. Early in the war, the U.S. government established the Wendover Bombing Range in the western part of the Great Salt Lake Desert. The range was one of the largest practice bombing sites in the United States.

Industrial growth continued after the war. The manufacture of steel products became an important industry. Oil production and refining prospered. A rich uranium deposit was discovered near Moab in 1952. One of the nation's largest uranium mines was completed near this deposit in 1956. The mine is now a leading producer of uranium. In the middle and late 1950's, missile plants were built in Brigham City, Ogden, and Salt Lake City. By 1959, the state had become a missile-producing center for the United States government.

Utah Today relies heavily on the federal government. About 70 per cent of the state's land area is federally owned and administered. Most of Utah's water comes from streams and lakes in national forests. About 10 of every 100 persons in the state work for federal agencies. Many of Utah's manufacturers, miners, and farmers depend on government contracts. Utah receives more money from the federal government than its people pay in taxes.

Many of the state's industries are still growing. But the Utah economy suffered a series of setbacks in the early 1960's. During the late 1950's and early 1960's, Utah's missile industry brought many professional and technical workers to the state. A state-wide program of training skilled missile workers was set up. By the early 1960's, the industry employed nearly 15,000 persons. But in 1963, the nation's needs for the missile parts produced in Utah declined. The value of Utah's missile industry fell, and employment dropped.

The value of mineral production, which had climbed steadily in Utah during the 1950's, also fell off in the early 1960's. This decline resulted from a slump in the price of minerals.

The operating expenses of Utah schools increased greatly between the late 1940's and early 1960's. In 1963, Utah educators requested an additional $25 million in state aid to education. The legislature provided $11 million—the largest increase in state school funds in Utah's history. Governor George D. Clyde appointed

Thiokol Chemical Corporation

Testing Station for Large Rocket Nozzles operates in Brigham City. The giant motor uses solid fuel. Utah became a leading U.S. missile-producing center in the late 1950's.

--- THE GOVERNORS OF UTAH ---

		Party	Term
1.	Heber M. Wells	Republican	1896-1905
2.	John C. Cutler	Republican	1905-1909
3.	William Spry	Republican	1909-1917
4.	Simon Bamberger	Democratic	1917-1921
5.	Charles R. Mabey	Republican	1921-1925
6.	George H. Dern	Democratic	1925-1933
7.	Henry H. Blood	Democratic	1933-1941
8.	Herbert B. Maw	Democratic	1941-1949
9.	J. Bracken Lee	Republican	1949-1957
10.	George D. Clyde	Republican	1957-1965
11.	Calvin L. Rampton	Democratic	1965-

a special commission to examine the state's educational needs. In the spring of 1964, the commission recommended that aid to education be increased by another $6 million. Clyde refused to approve the increase, which he felt would cripple the state's economy. Utah teachers, led by the Utah Education Association, staged a protest. They stayed away from classes for two days and refused to sign contracts for the coming school year. The National Education Association (NEA) urged teachers throughout the nation not to accept employment in Utah until the problem was solved. It was the first time in history that U.S. educators had staged an organized protest against an entire state. Clyde did not run for re-election in 1964. In 1965, the legislature increased school aid by $25½ million over a two-year period. The NEA then ended its protest.

To help solve its financial problems, Utah is improving its tourist industry. The Great Salt Lake Authority hopes to attract more vacationers to Great Salt Lake. Fishing and other water sports have become popular on Utah's many reservoirs and man-made lakes. Lake Powell is the largest and most promising recreation site in the state. In 1963, work was completed on the Glen Canyon and Flaming Gorge dams. In 1964, the federal government established Canyonlands National Park in a wilderness area of southeast Utah. This park is one of the largest remaining areas of its kind in the United States.

EVERETT L. COOLEY, ROBERT LAYTON, and ERNEST H. LINFORD

UTAH / Study Aids

Outline

I. Government
  A. Constitution
  B. Executive
  C. Legislature
  D. Courts
  E. Local Government
  F. Taxation
  G. Politics
II. People
III. Education
  A. Schools
  B. Libraries
  C. Museums
IV. A Visitor's Guide
  A. Places to Visit
  B. Annual Events

V. The Land
  A. Land Regions
  B. Rivers and Lakes
  C. Deserts
VI. Climate
VII. Economy
  A. Natural Resources
  B. Manufacturing
  C. Mining
  D. Agriculture
  E. Electric Power
  F. Transportation
  G. Communication
VIII. History

Questions

What percentage of Utah's people are high school graduates? How does this percentage compare with that of the other states?

Where is the nation's largest Swiss cheese factory?

What lake once covered most of present-day Utah? What two lakes are remnants of that body of water? How do they differ?

What historic event occurred at Promontory in 1869?

What event ended the pony express? How was Utah involved in this event?

Why did the Mormons come to Utah? Who led them?

Where is the Sea Gull Monument? Why was it built?

What is Utah's most valuable mineral?

What two features of Utah's 1895 constitution helped the territory be admitted to the Union?

What is unusual about the drainage of the Great Basin and Range region of Utah?

Books to Read

ASHTON, WENDELL J. *Voice in the West.* Duell, 1950. A history of the *Deseret News,* a pioneer newspaper.

BURT, OLIVE. *Brigham Young.* Messner, 1956. A story for young people about the Utah colonizer.

CLARK, ANN N. *Blue Canyon Horse.* Viking, 1954. The story of an Indian boy and his horse.

HUNTER, MILTON R. *Utah Indian Stories.* 4th ed. Deseret Book Co., Salt Lake City, 1960.

KJELGAARD, JIM. *Coming of the Mormons.* Random House, 1953. (Landmark Books.) A narrative history for young people, which emphasizes the character and contributions of the Mormons.

MILLER, JOSEPH. *Monument Valley and the Navajo Country Arizona . . . Utah.* Hastings, 1951.

MULDER, WILLIAM, and MORTENSEN, RUSSELL A., Eds. *Among the Mormons: Historic Accounts by Contemporary Observers.* Knopf, 1958.

NELSON, ELROY. *Utah's Economic Patterns.* University of Utah Press, 1956. With Harline, O. L.: *Utah's Changing Economic Patterns.* 1964. Supplement to 1956 edition.

SORENSEN, VIRGINIA E. *The House Next Door: Utah 1896.* Scribner, 1954. How Utah struggled to achieve statehood, as seen through the eyes of a 16-year-old girl.

Utah: A Guide to the State. Hastings, 1954.

WEST, RAY B. *Kingdom of the Saints: The Story of Brigham Young and the Mormons.* Viking, 1957.

UTAH, UNIVERSITY OF, is a state-controlled coeducational school at Salt Lake City, Utah. It has schools of letters and science, education, mining and engineering, business, law, social work, medicine, fine arts, nursing, and pharmacy. Courses lead to bachelor's, master's, and doctor's degrees. Some classes are taught by television. The university was founded in 1850 as the University of Deseret. It received its present name in 1892. It is the oldest state university west of the Missouri River. For enrollment, see UNIVERSITIES AND COLLEGES (table).   A. RAY OLPIN

UTAH LAKE is the largest fresh-water lake in Utah. The lake lies in a valley between mountain ranges near the town of Provo, and is about 30 miles south of Great Salt Lake. Utah Lake is about 8 miles wide, and 23

miles long. It covers an area of about 150 square miles, and lies at a height of about 4,505 feet above sea level. The lake gets its water from streams which dash down the slopes of the Wasatch Range. Utah Lake empties into the Jordan River. The river flows on through Salt Lake City and empties into Great Salt Lake. For location, see UTAH (physical map).   A. R. MORTENSEN

UTAH STATE UNIVERSITY is a coeducational institution at Logan, Utah. It has a graduate school and colleges of agriculture; education; forest, range, and wildlife management; humanities and sciences; family life; business and social sciences; and engineering and technology. The university was founded in 1888. For the enrollment of Utah State University, see UNIVERSITIES AND COLLEGES (table).   DARYL CHASE

UTAMARO KITAGAWA, *oo tah mah roh kih tah gah woh* (1753-1806), was a leading Japanese printmaker. He turned public taste in the direction of bold drawing, striking poses, and unusual color contrasts. His beautiful women or pairs of lovers are tall and graceful. He often showed them only from the waist up, and drew faces and hands with great elegance under masses of jet-black hair. Toward the end of his life, he turned for novelty to exaggerations and distortions, which some of his followers carried even farther. Utamaro was born at Kawagoe, Japan. ALEXANDER C. SOPER

See also JAPANESE PRINT (picture).

UTE INDIANS, *yoot*, gave their name to the state of Utah. This western tribe lived in the mountains and plains along what is now the Colorado-Utah border and in northern New Mexico.

Before the coming of the white man, the Ute were hunters and seed-gatherers much like the Shoshoni (see INDIAN, AMERICAN [California-Intermountain Indians]). During the summer months, they moved in small family groups to the mountain valleys in search of berries, fish, and game. During the cold, snowy winters, they left the mountains and followed the antelope, deer, and buffalo into the warmer plateau regions to the south.

When the Ute acquired horses from the Spaniards in the 1700's, they changed their way of life. They became expert horsemen and ranged over a much wider area than before, hunting buffalo. Family groups joined together to form marauding bands. They obtained horses by raiding Spanish settlements or nearby Indian tribes. Sometimes they even bartered their own children for horses. Raiding and hunting led the Ute into warfare with powerful Plains tribes, including the Comanche, Kiowa, Cheyenne, and Arapaho. From them they copied such customs as the tepee, the sun dance, and the travois (see TRAVOIS). They also adopted the custom of using large defensive shields.

The government assigned reservations in Utah and Colorado to the Ute in the late 1800's. After several outbreaks, they settled down as farmers and cattlemen. The discovery of oil and minerals on their lands improved their economic condition. Many became skilled industrial workers. CHARLES E. DIBBLE

See also INDIAN WARS (Death on the Plains).

UTENSIL. See KITCHEN.

UTERUS. See MENSTRUATION; EMBRYO.

UTICA, *YOO tee kuh*, was an ancient city of North Africa. According to an ancient tradition, which archaeological evidence does not support, the Phoenicians built Utica about 1100 B.C. The city stood about 20 miles northwest of ancient Carthage, near the Gulf of Tunis. It lay about halfway between the modern African cities of Tunis and Bizerte.

In the days of its glory, Utica was almost as powerful as Carthage. When the Roman legions entered North Africa in the Third Punic War, Utica accepted Roman rule and became the capital of a Roman province in Africa.

Utica then became an important religious center. During the 600's, conquering Arab tribes invaded the city and destroyed it. Excavations by the French in the 1800's uncovered the huge amphitheater of ancient Utica. Other explorations brought to light buildings, quays, and sturdy fortifications. These findings proved the greatness of Utica. WILLIAM SCOTT FERGUSON

Shostal

Revolutionary War Memorial near Utica, N.Y., overlooks the Mohawk River and marks the Oriskany Battlefield.

UTICA, N.Y. (pop. 100,410; alt. 415 ft.), is an important commercial and industrial center in the Mohawk Valley along the New York State Barge Canal System. It lies about 90 miles northwest of Albany, halfway between Buffalo and New York City. The city lies in a rich agricultural and dairy region and is the gateway to the Adirondacks. Utica is also a port of entry.

The city covers an area of about 16 square miles. Utica has over 150 miles of streets, boulevards, and parkways, and more than 850 acres of public parks. With Rome, N.Y., it forms a metropolitan area of 330,771 persons.

Industry and Trade. During the late 1800's and early 1900's, Utica ranked first among the cities of New York in the production of cotton cloth. After World War II, when many textile companies began to move to southern states, Utica factories started to produce a variety of tools, machines, and manufactured articles. Important products include heating, ventilating, refrigerating, and air-conditioning equipment; electronic tools and products; pneumatic tools; paper products; sprayers; air compressors; fishing rods and tackle; and men's and boys' clothing. Two large insurance companies maintain headquarters in Utica. It is also a trading center for farmers of the Mohawk Valley.

Utica lies on the only water-level pass through the Appalachian Mountains, and has been on the direct route between the East and the West since the 1700's. The Governor Thomas E. Dewey Thruway, a superhighway linking Buffalo and New York City, passes through Utica. The city has an airport. Railroad, bus, and truck lines serve Utica. The city also is a major New York State Barge Canal System terminal.

History. A king's grant to William Cosby and his associates in 1734 included the site of Utica. Fort Schuy-

197

ler was built on the site during the French and Indian War (1754-1763). After the Revolutionary War, many persons from New England and the lower Mohawk Valley settled there. Utica was incorporated as a village in 1798. The name (from that of an ancient North African town) was drawn from suggestions placed in a hat. Utica was chartered as a city in 1832. It has a mayor-council form of government. WILLIAM E. YOUNG

UTILITARIANISM, *yoo* TIL *uh* TAIR *ih un iz'm,* is the doctrine that the goal of life is "the greatest happiness of the greatest number." Whatever brings about this happiness has "utility." Anything that obstructs such happiness is useless. Utilitarians hold that the most definite mark of happiness is pleasure. Jeremy Bentham, "the father of the Utilitarians," first developed this idea in England.

The name *Utilitarianism* was not used until John Stuart Mill, a disciple of Bentham, formed the Utilitarian Society in 1823. The society became a great center of liberal thought and helped to bring about many reforms. H. M. KALLEN

See also BENTHAM, JEREMY; MILL (family).

UTILITY, PUBLIC. See PUBLIC UTILITY.

UTOPIA, *yoo* TOH *pih uh,* is the name commonly given to an imaginary land where everything is supposed to be perfect. The name *utopia* comes from the Greek words *ou* and *topos,* meaning *no place.* The name refers particularly to a type of society with ideal economic and social conditions. People often apply the adjective *utopian* to plans of reform that they consider to be impractical and visionary.

The word *utopia* was used as the title of a famous book by Sir Thomas More. *Utopia* was first published in Latin in 1516 and was translated into English in 1551. It is partly in the form of a dialogue. The book gives More's views on the ideal government. But, like most writings on utopias, it also criticizes social and economic conditions of More's times.

More's *Utopia* is the report of a Portuguese sailor Raphael Hythlodaye. The sailor has made three voyages to America with the explorer Amerigo Vespucci, and tells More of his travels through wild and unexplored places. The greatest wonder he describes is the island of Utopia. This is the ideal commonwealth where all men are equal, prosperous, educated, and wise.

Several other books have presented an imaginary ideal state of society. One of the first books describing a utopia was Plato's *Republic,* written about 375 B.C. More recent utopias are described in Samuel Butler's *Erewhon,* which almost spells *nowhere* backwards (1872); Edward Bellamy's *Looking Backward* (1888); and H. G. Wells' *A Modern Utopia* (1905). GEORGE A. WICKES

See also BELLAMY, EDWARD; MORE, SIR THOMAS; PLATO; WELLS, "H. G.," HERBERT G.

UTRECHT, *YU trekt* (pop. 261,000; metropolitan area 405,000; alt. 3.5 ft.), a Dutch city, lies on the Rhine River, about 22 miles southeast of Amsterdam. For location, see NETHERLANDS (color map). Utrecht is called the city of spires and bridges because of its many churches and bridges. A triple avenue of trees, the *Maliebaan,* is one of the loveliest and most popular sights in Utrecht.

Industries include sawmills, machine shops, breweries, carpet works, and factories that make velvets, cottons, linens, and musical instruments.

Much Dutch history centers about this interesting old city. In 1579, the seven northern Protestant provinces united in Utrecht. The nation of The Netherlands grew out of this union. The treaty that ended the War of the Spanish Succession was signed at Utrecht in 1713 (see UTRECHT, PEACE OF). BENJAMIN HUNNINGHER

UTRECHT, *YU trekt,* **PEACE OF,** was one of the great international peace settlements of history. The conference opened in Utrecht, Holland, in 1712, at the end of the War of the Spanish Succession. In America, this was known as Queen Anne's War, one of the French and Indian Wars. Representatives from all major European nations met to discuss peace terms. They signed agreements at Utrecht in 1713.

The Peace of Utrecht made many changes in the map of Europe, and tried to establish a balance of power. It also helped to increase Great Britain's colonial and commercial power. The treaty recognized the French Duke of Anjou as King of Spain, but France agreed that Spain and France would never be united under one ruler. Great Britain acquired Gibraltar and the island of Minorca from Spain. Spain also gave Great Britain the *assiento* (contract) for supplying the Spanish colonies with African slaves. The Duke of Savoy took control of the Spanish island of Sicily. Austria received Milan, Naples, Sardinia, and the Catholic Netherlands from Spain. Holland, in the "barrier treaties," received the right to arm frontier towns against French aggression.

In America, France ceded Nova Scotia, Newfoundland, and the Hudson Bay Territory to Great Britain, but retained New France (Quebec). ROBERT G. L. WAITE

See also FRENCH AND INDIAN WARS (Queen Anne's War); SUCCESSION WARS (The War of the Spanish Succession).

UTRILLO, *oo* TREE *loh,* **MAURICE** (1883-1955), was a French painter. The streets and buildings of Paris furnished much of the subject matter for his best pictures. Montmartre was his particular favorite. He painted this subject many times with a deft brush, often using rather thin and usually light-colored pigment. In his most attractive work, he combines a fine ability to draw with the brush with a delicate color which suggests the atmosphere and picturesqueness of the subject. Utrillo was born in Paris. JOSEPH C. SLOANE

UVULA. See PALATE.

UZBEKISTAN, *ooz beck ih* STAN, or UZBEK SOVIET SOCIALIST REPUBLIC, is the most thickly populated Soviet state in central Asia. It lies in the foothills of the Tien Shan and Pamir mountains in Turkestan, and extends northwest to the Aral Sea. For location, see RUSSIA (political map).

The state covers 173,591 square miles and has a population of 9,997,000. The region produces large quantities of almonds, apricots, cotton, and raisins and other dried fruit. Stock and sheep raising and horse breeding are important activities. Mineral resources include natural gas, petroleum, and sulfur. The state also has electric-power stations and steel mills. Tashkent, the largest city in the Asian part of Russia, is the capital of Uzbekistan. GEORGE KISH

See also SAMARKAND; TASHKENT; TURKESTAN.

Vv is the 22nd letter of our alphabet. It came from a letter used by the Semites, who once lived in Syria and Palestine. They called the letter *waw*, their word for *hook*. They wrote the letter with a symbol borrowed from an Egyptian *hieroglyphic*, or picture symbol. The Greeks borrowed the letter from the Phoenicians and gave it a *Y*-shape. The Romans, when they adopted it, dropped the vertical stroke. They used it for the vowel sound, *u*, and the consonant sound, *v*. About A.D. 900, people began to write *v* at the beginning of a word and *u* in the middle. During the Renaissance, people began using *v* for the consonant and *u* for the vowel. But the change was not final for several hundred years. See ALPHABET.

Uses. *V* or *v* is about the 21st most frequently used letter in books, newspapers, and other material printed in English. *V* is the Roman numeral for five. As an abbreviation, *V* may stand for *veteran* or *volunteer*. It is the abbreviation for *verb* in grammars and dictionaries. In music, it stands for *violin* or *voice*. It may mean *various*, *volt*, *volume*, or *versus*. In chemistry, *V* is the symbol for the element *vanadium*.

Pronunciation. A person pronounces *v* by placing his lower lip on his upper teeth, closing his *velum*, or soft palate, and forcing his breath through his teeth and lips, vibrating his vocal cords. This sound may be spelled *ph*, as in *Stephen*. In German, it may have a sound like that of English *f*. In Spanish it may have a *b* sound. See PRONUNCIATION.   I. J. GELB and J. M. WELLS

The 22nd letter took its shape from an ancient Egyptian symbol for a supporting pole. The Romans gave it its present shape, but used it for both U and V sounds.

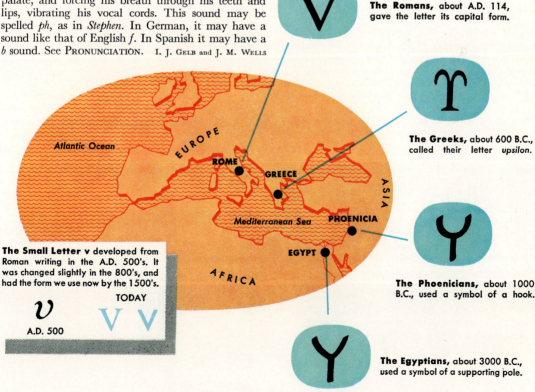

The Romans, about A.D. 114, gave the letter its capital form.

The Greeks, about 600 B.C., called their letter *upsilon*.

The Phoenicians, about 1000 B.C., used a symbol of a hook.

The Egyptians, about 3000 B.C., used a symbol of a supporting pole.

The Small Letter v developed from Roman writing in the A.D. 500's. It was changed slightly in the 800's, and had the form we use now by the 1500's.

v
A.D. 500

TODAY
V V

Atlantic Ocean
EUROPE
ROME
GREECE
ASIA
Mediterranean Sea
PHOENICIA
EGYPT
AFRICA

199

V-1, V-2. See GUIDED MISSILE (In World War II); ROCKET (Early Research; High-Altitude Experiments).

V-E DAY, or VICTORY IN EUROPE DAY, was officially proclaimed by President Harry S. Truman on Tuesday, May 8, 1945. It marked the surrender of the German armed forces and the end of the fighting against Germany.

The German surrender was signed at the headquarters of General Dwight D. Eisenhower in Reims, France, at 2:41 A.M. on May 7. Colonel General Alfred Jodl, chief of staff of the German armed forces, signed for Germany.   GEORGE E. MOWRY

See also WORLD WAR II (Victory in Europe).

V-J DAY, or VICTORY OVER JAPAN DAY, marked the end of World War II. At 7 P.M. on August 14, 1945, President Harry S. Truman announced that Japan had agreed to surrender unconditionally. Japan had been trying to end the war, and surrender rumors had raced through the United States for the four days before August 14. But President Truman's announcement made the surrender certain.

September 2, 1945, has since been declared the official V-J Day. On that day, the Japanese signed the terms of surrender aboard the battleship U.S.S. *Missouri* in Tokyo Bay.   GEORGE E. MOWRY

See also WORLD WAR II (Victory in the Pacific).

V-PARTICLE is a name that was originally given to nuclear particles that produced V-shaped tracks when they passed through a *cloud chamber* (see WILSON CLOUD CHAMBER). Scientists no longer use the term *V-particle*. They have found that V-shaped tracks are produced by *hyperons* and *K-mesons*. Scientists call any phenomenon that produces a V-shaped track a *V-event*. See also ATOM (Inside the Atom).

VAAL RIVER, *vahl,* is the largest branch of the Orange River in South Africa. It rises in the Drakensberg mountains in southeastern Transvaal. For 750 miles the Vaal is the boundary between Transvaal and the Orange Free State. It joins the Orange River in Cape Province. Dams on the Vaal supply water for Johannesburg. Only small boats can sail on it, because of rapids and periods of low water.   GEORGE H. T. KIMBLE

VACA, ÁLVAR NÚÑEZ CABEZA DE. See CABEZA DE VACA, ÁLVAR NÚÑEZ.

VACATION. The human body cannot operate at full efficiency without frequent rest. Doctors have long recognized that many illnesses of the body and nervous system can best be cured by a rest from normal, everyday activity. A change in routine helps restore people's bodies, minds, and spirits to full power. We call such a change a *vacation*.

To young persons, a vacation usually means the summer months when they do not have to attend school. For the average adult, a vacation is a definite period of time when he does not have to work at his regular job. The custom of giving employees a regular vacation with pay began fairly recently. It started with the development of factories, large stores, and large business offices. During the 1800's, employers began to discover that their employees worked more efficiently after a vacation. Many labor union contracts require that employees be given annual vacations.

Things to do on a vacation are almost countless. Present-day transportation has made it possible for vacationers to travel to almost any place they choose. This has given rise to the tourist industry.

There are many interesting places for the vacationist to go in the United States and Canada. For descriptions of these places, see the articles NATIONAL MONUMENT; NATIONAL PARK; and the Places to Visit section and Annual Events section of the articles on each of the states in the United States and each of the Canadian provinces.   BERNARD S. MASON

See also CAMPING; DUDE RANCH; HOBBY; SAFETY (Recreation); YOUTH HOSTEL.

VACCINATION. *VACK sih NAY shun,* means the injection of any dead or weakened viruses or germs into the body for the purpose of developing bodily resistance to diseases. The *vaccine* (material injected) works by causing the body to develop antibodies which act to prevent the disease (see ANTIBODY).

The word *vaccination* comes from the Latin word *vacca,* meaning *cow.* The term originally referred only to the injection of cowpox virus into the body to prevent smallpox.

Vaccines are carefully prepared to insure that they will not carry infection into the body. They are tested so that they will be strong enough to cause the body to develop resistance to the disease, but weak enough so that they will not cause serious symptoms of the disease

Wide World

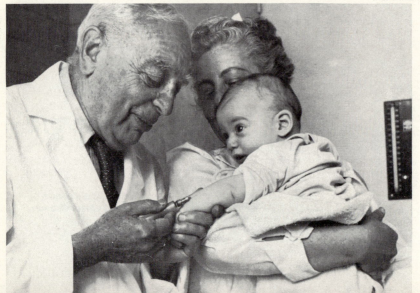

Doctors Vaccinate Babies against smallpox, polio, and other dread diseases. The vaccines, prepared from dead or weakened viruses, help the body build resistance.

before the body develops its resistance. Then they are injected into the body through a hollow needle inserted into a muscle or vein. See HYPODERMIC INJECTION.

The process of vaccination was developed by an English physician, Edward Jenner, in 1796, to combat smallpox. Its success against smallpox led to a search that still continues for vaccines that can be injected into the body to prevent other diseases.

The most dramatic development of a vaccine in modern times is the *Salk* vaccine, which prevents poliomyelitis. In 1958, a *four-in-one* vaccine was developed to immunize children against polio, whooping cough, diphtheria, and tetanus. Vaccination has also proved useful against typhoid fever, Rocky Mountain spotted fever, influenza, and tuberculosis. Measles vaccines with either dead or weakened germs were introduced in 1963 to immunize against the disease. AUSTIN EDWARD SMITH

Related Articles in WORLD BOOK include:

BCG
Inoculation

Jenner, Edward
Poliomyelitis

Salk, Jonas Edward
Smallpox

VACUUM, *VACK yoo um,* is a term taken from the Latin word *vacuus,* which means *empty.* A vacuum is a space which has no matter in it. Strictly speaking, there is no such thing as a vacuum, because all space as we know it contains some matter. In practice, we speak of a vacuum as a space from which most of the air or other gas has been taken, and in which the pressure is extremely low. But this is only a *partial vacuum.*

In the air we breathe, there are about four hundred billion times a billion molecules of gas to each cubic inch. Man can create partial vacuums in which there are only a few billion or even a few million molecules in each cubic inch. But no one has ever succeeded in creating an absolute vacuum—that is, in taking all the air out of an enclosed space. We cannot do this, even with the most powerful air pump or by chemical means. Among the most nearly complete vacuums that have

been attained is one in which the pressure of the gas is about one ten thousand-millionth of the normal pressure of the air. Scientists speak of *high* or *low partial vacuums,* depending upon how completely the air or any other gas has been taken out of an enclosed space. Any space in which the air pressure is about one thousandth of that of the atmosphere is usually called a vacuum.

The important thing about a vacuum is that it is usually a useful emptiness. For example, if we create a partial vacuum in any space, water or any other fluid may enter into it. We make use of this principle in drinking lemonade through a straw. We do not pull the liquid up through the straw. Instead, by sucking on one end of it, we take out some of the air that is in the straw. The air outside exerts pressure on the liquid and forces it up and out through the partial vacuum in the straw. The pump used to pump water into our homes, the air pumps which inflate automobile tires, and the gas intake of an automobile motor all make use of this principle. The vacuum cleaner is another example of the usefulness of a vacuum. In a vacuum bottle, a vacuum prevents heat from entering or leaving by conduction or convection. Most electronic tubes contain a high vacuum. This keeps the air or gas inside from being affected by the passage of electrons across the tube.

In the sugar-refining industry, a vacuum pan is used. This evaporates liquids at a temperature lower than the ordinary boiling point. The vacuum pan is made up of a closed vessel heated by a steam jacket. An air pump holds the steam in the air constantly from the surface of the liquid inside. The liquid boils and evaporates without danger of burning.

In some vacuum tubes in use today, as much air as possible is taken out of the tubes by means of an air pump. Then a chemical called a "getter" is placed in-

HOW WE USE A VACUUM

When a person sucks on a straw, a partial vacuum is created. Liquid from the drink rises to fill the space and reaches the mouth.

The pump creates a partial vacuum in a pipe. Water rises to fill the vacuum, then flows from the spout.

After water has been raised by steam pressure, a vacuum pulls it down out of the top of this glass coffee maker.

Airflow
Vacuum
Wing
Lower air pressure on top of the wing causes the airplane to rise.

Amplifying, X-ray, and photoelectric tubes all make use of a vacuum.

side the tube. This increases the vacuum by combining with a large part of the remaining air inside the tube. The chemical itself coats the inside surface of the tube.

One other important characteristic of a vacuum is the fact that sound cannot cross a high vacuum. This can be seen if we set an alarm clock ringing inside a bell jar in the laboratory. As the air inside the bell jar is pumped out, the sound of the clock's bell gradually grows less and less until such a high partial vacuum is reached that the ringing bell can be heard no more. MARCEL SCHEIN

See also PUMP; ELECTRONICS (Vacuum Tubes); VACUUM BOTTLE; VACUUM CLEANER.

VACUUM BOTTLE. We can keep liquids hot or cold for as long as 24 hours in vacuum bottles, sometimes called *Thermos* bottles. The vacuum bottle is designed to reduce greatly the exchange of heat between the inside of the bottle and the outside. The bottle is designed to limit the transfer of heat that may take place through (1) conduction, (2) convection, and (3) radiation. See HEAT.

The vacuum bottle has an inner container, which is made of glass. This inner container is a bottle within a bottle, sealed at the lips by melting the glass edges. Air is removed from the space between the two bottles to produce a near vacuum. Glass is a poor *conductor* of heat but a vacuum conducts heat even less. The vacuum between the bottles slows down the transfer of heat by *convection*. In order to reduce the transfer of heat by *radiation*, the facing surfaces of the glass bottles are coated with a silvery solution of aluminum which reflects heat. Cork is used for the stopper and for the

Cutaway View of a Vacuum Bottle

A BOTTLE INSIDE A BOTTLE

Glass bottle with silver surface

Vacuum space

Interior bottle

Outer container

Shock absorber

pads which hold the bottles in place in their outer container because cork is a poor *conductor* of heat. The outer container is made of metal or of molded plastic. The bottles are held in place within the container by a rubber collar at the top of the container. A spring at the bottom of the bottle acts as a shock absorber.

The first vacuum-insulated container was the Dewar flask. Sir James Dewar invented it in 1885 as a means of keeping heat away from liquid gases with which he was experimenting. He sold it under the trade name of *Thermos*, meaning *heat*.

Vacuum containers range in capacity from 2 ounces to 15 gallons. Vacuum containers have many uses. They are carried on exploring and scientific expeditions, and on transport planes. They are also used in the handling of certain chemicals and drugs, and for various scientific experimental purposes. JOHN T. R. NICKERSON

VACUUM CLEANER is a machine for removing dirt from floor coverings, upholstery, tapestries, and various other household furnishings. The first motor-driven cleaner of the vacuum type was invented by John S. Thurman of St. Louis, Mo. His first patent for a "pneumatic carpet renovator" was obtained in 1899. Vacuum cleaners became popular with housewives and are now a common piece of household equipment.

The vacuum cleaner does its work with a suction fan or an air exhausting fan. The fan or pump makes a partial *vacuum* (space where there is little air) within the cleaner. The cleaner gets its name from this. Outside air always tries to fill a vacuum. The outside air rushing into the vacuum picks up dirt and waste and carries it to the bag attached to the cleaner.

The two basic types of vacuum cleaners are rotating cylinder cleaners and straight suction cleaners. The *rotating cylinder cleaner* has either a stiff brush or a set of agitator bars that helps to loosen dirt in a rug. The vacuum in the cleaner then pulls the dirt into an upright bag that is attached to the handle of the cleaner. The *straight suction cleaner* removes dirt by suction only. It is also called a tank or cannister cleaner. The dirt is carried into the cleaner through a flexible tube that is attached to the cleaner's top or side. In some models, it is deposited in a tank of water to avoid raising dust.

The *hand* vacuum cleaner is a smaller machine. It is light enough to carry and is used for dusting and cleaning clothing, upholstered furniture, curtains, draperies, rugs, and carpets. This type of vacuum cleaner can also be used as a hair dryer. RAYMOND F. YATES

VACUUM PUMP. See PUMP.

VACUUM TUBE. See DE FOREST, LEE; ELECTRONICS (Vacuum Tubes).

VADUZ, *VAH doots* (pop. 3,398; alt. 1,499 ft.), is the capital of the principality of Liechtenstein. The city lies in an Alpine valley, in the shadow of high mountains. The major industry is cotton manufacturing. For location, see LIECHTENSTEIN (map). Vaduz was founded early in the Middle Ages, and many of the original buildings are still standing. The castle of the princes of Liechtenstein stands on a mountain high above the city. GEORGE KISH

VAGABOND POET. See LINDSAY, VACHEL.

VAGRANCY, *VAY gruhn sih*. A person who wanders from place to place, and who lives in idleness and without any settled home, is called a *vagrant*, or *vagabond*. Most states of the Union have laws against vagrancy,

The *Torres de Cuarte* in Valencia, Spain, built in the 1400's, once served as a main fortified entrance to the city.

Authenticated News

based on the idea that a vagrant has "no visible means of support" and may become a public charge. A person arrested for vagrancy may be sentenced to a term in jail. Law enforcement officers often arrest beggars and criminals as vagrants.   FRED E. INBAU

VAISYA. See CASTE.

VALDEMAR. See DENMARK (The Danish Empire).

VALDEZ GLACIER. See GLACIER (Famous Glaciers).

VALDIVIA, PEDRO DE. See CHILE (History).

VALDOSTA STATE COLLEGE. See UNIVERSITIES AND COLLEGES (table).

VALE OF KASHMIR. See KASHMIR.

VALEDICTORIAN. See GRADUATION.

VALENCE, *VAY lence*, is a number that indicates the ability of a chemical element to combine with other elements. In the past, valence had several slightly different meanings. The term is now gradually being replaced by more precise chemical descriptions.

Valence was first defined as the number of hydrogen atoms that can combine with each atom of an element. For example, each atom of oxygen can combine with two hydrogen atoms to form water (H_2O). Therefore, oxygen has a valence of two. A second definition of valence is based on the charges of ionized atoms. Sodium ions have one positive charge, so the valence of sodium is one. A third definition is based on the number of *bonds* (chemical links) that an atom forms with other atoms. Carbon atoms usually form four bonds, as in the compound *methane* (CH_4). As a result, carbon is said to have a valence of four.

Many elements can combine in so many ways that they have several valences. For example, sulfur has common valences of 2, 4, and 6.   JOHN P. FACKLER, JR.

See also CHEMISTRY (Valence); BOND (chemical); LEWIS, GILBERT N.

VALENCIA, *vuh LEN shuh* (pop. 161,413; alt. 1,509 ft.), lies in the fertile northern part of Venezuela, a short distance from the coast. For location, see VENEZUELA (color map). It is the country's largest manufacturing center. Industries include sugar mills, textile mills, and tanneries. Valencia was founded in 1555.

VALENCIA, *vuh LEN shuh* (pop. 503,358; alt. 49 ft.), is the third largest city in Spain. Only Madrid and Barcelona are larger than Valencia. Valencia lies on the Turia River, three miles from the Mediterranean coast and its port of Villanueva del Grao. For location, see SPAIN (color map). Hundreds of years ago, the Romans built walls around their settlement at Valencia. These walls were torn down in 1871. A gate called Torres de Serranos was built in 1238. Two towers were added in the late 1300's, and restored in 1930.

The city is one of the railroad centers of eastern Spain, and carries on a large export trade in oranges and other fruits. Valencia is noted for its silk, colored tiles, tobacco, textiles, and iron and bronze wares. The city's products also include cement, furniture, musical instruments, paper, toys, and perfumes and cosmetics.

Valencia was long occupied by the Moors. It has rows of white houses built in the Moorish style, and many famous public buildings dating from the 1200's, although today much of the city is modern. The University of Valencia is well known.   WALTER C. LANGSAM

VALENS, *VA lunz* (A.D. 328?-378), was an East Roman emperor. He was born in Pannonia, the younger brother of the Roman Emperor Valentinian I, who named him coruler in charge of the eastern provinces in A.D. 364. Valens had continual difficulties with the Goths. The Huns were pushing the Goths south toward the Roman frontier. Finally, Valens permitted them to live inside Roman territory on the south side of the Danube River. But the Romans treated the Goths so badly that they revolted. Valens at first put down the revolt. But in 378, the Goths, aided by the Alans and some Huns, fought him at Adrianople. Valens and about two-thirds of his men were killed in the battle. See also GOTH; VALENTINIAN (I).   ROBERT GEHLMANN BONE

VALENTINE, SAINT, is the name associated with two martyrs of the early Christian Church. Little is known about them. The Roman history of martyrs lists two Saint Valentines as having been martyred on February 14 by being beheaded. One supposedly died in Rome and the other at Interamna, now Terni, 60 miles from Rome. There is no conclusive evidence for doubting the existence of either of these two men.

The Saint Valentine who died in Rome seems to have been a priest who suffered death during the persecution of Claudius the Goth about A.D. 269. A basilica was built in his honor in Rome in A.D. 350, and a catacomb containing his remains was found on this location.

Another history of martyrs mentions a Saint Valentine who was bishop of Interamna and who may have been martyred in Rome. By being remembered both in Rome and in Interamna, he may have come to be considered as two persons, but this is not entirely certain.

The custom of exchanging valentines on February 14 can be traced to the English poet, Geoffrey Chaucer. He mentioned that birds began to pair off on that day (see VALENTINE'S DAY).   JAMES A. CORBETT and FULTON J. SHEEN

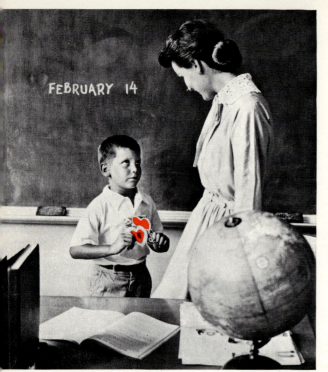

VALENTINE'S DAY

VALENTINE'S DAY is celebrated on February 14 as a festival of romance and affection. People send greeting cards called *valentines* to their sweethearts, their friends, and members of their families. Verses on many valentines contain tender thoughts. Other valentines may include humorous pictures and sayings. But almost all ask, "Be My Valentine."

Valentine's Day comes on the feast day of two different Christian martyrs named Valentine. But the customs connected with the day have nothing to do with the lives of the saints. They probably come from an ancient Roman festival called *Lupercalia* which took place every February 15. The festival honored Juno, the Roman goddess of women and marriage, and Pan, the god of nature.

Valentine's Day is not a business or bank holiday. Schools and businesses remain open as usual. But, during the weeks before the festival, merchants sell valen-

Hallmark Cards

Giving the Teacher a Valentine is an exciting moment for any young boy, especially if he hopes that it will make up for his mischief-making and uncompleted lessons in the past weeks.

Hallmark Cards

Popular Valentines of Today have fancy covers, decorated with flowers and paper lace. They open to reveal words of friendship, a sentimental verse, or a simple message of love.

Hallmark Historical Collection,
Courtesy Hallmark Cards

Elaborate German Mechanical Valentines were the most popular of all kinds from 1890 to 1910. Angelic figures adorned many of the cards. The ruffled paper folded flat for mailing.

tines and decorations for Valentine's Day parties and dances. School children decorate their classrooms with bright red paper hearts. On Valentine's Day, women and girls receive gifts, candy, or flowers from their favorite "valentines."

Valentine's Day Around the World

In the United States and Canada, children exchange valentines with their school friends. In some schools, the children hold a classroom party and place all the valentines in an attractive box that they have made. At the end of the day, the teacher or one child distributes the valentines. Some young persons send valentines through the mail without signing their names. They simply write, "Guess Who." Elementary-school children like to make their own valentines from paper doilies, red paper, wallpaper samples, and pictures cut from magazines. Sometimes they buy do-it-yourself valentine boxes that contain all the materials needed to make valentines. They often send their largest and most elaborate valentines to their mothers and teachers.

Older students enjoy Valentine's Day dances and parties. They may make candy baskets, favors, and place cards, all gaily trimmed with cupids and red hearts. Men often send their wives or sweethearts flowers or boxes of candy instead of valentine greeting cards. The candy boxes are usually shaped like hearts and tied with bright red ribbon.

In Great Britain, children sing special Valentine's Day songs and receive gifts of money, fruit, or candy. Housewives in the county of Rutland bake tasty Valentine's Day buns that contain caraway seeds and plums or currants. Years ago, children in Norfolk County played a game similar to tag on Valentine's Day. The person tagged had to pay a forfeit of some small valentine token. In the town of Norwich, a young suitor would secretly leave a basket of gifts on his loved one's doorstep. Then he would knock on the door and run away.

In Italy, people in some areas hold a Valentine's Day feast on February 14. In Sicily, some young unmarried women get up before sunrise on Valentine's Day. They stand by their windows, sometimes for hours, watching for a man to pass the house. Each girl believes that the first man she sees, or someone who looks like him, will become her bridegroom within the year.

In Denmark, some persons send pressed snowdrop flowers to special friends on Valentine's Day. The Danes call one type of valentine *gaekkebrev*, or joking letter. The sender writes an original rhyme but does not sign his name. He uses a code of dots, with one dot representing each letter of his name. If his young lady guesses his name and tells him, he rewards her with an Easter egg on the following Easter.

Beliefs and Customs

Years ago, people held many beliefs in connection with Valentine's Day. One of the oldest beliefs said that birds choose their mates on February 14. An old English superstition warned that it was bad luck to bring snowdrops into the house before Valentine's Day if unmarried girls in the home hoped to be married before the end of the year.

Most Valentine's Day customs were concerned with romance or the choice of a mate. Single girls had many ways of learning the identity of their future husbands. Sometimes a girl wrote her boy friends' names on bits of paper and rolled each name in a little piece of clay. She then dropped the clay into water. The first scrap of paper to rise to the top was supposed to contain the name of her true valentine. Some unmarried girls pinned five bay leaves to their pillows on the eve of Valentine's Day. They pinned one leaf to the center of the pillow and one to each corner, and believed they would see their future husbands in their dreams if the charm worked.

In Derbyshire, England, young women circled the church 12 times at midnight and repeated the words, "I sow hempseed, hempseed I sow, he that loves me best, come after me now." After that, their true valentine was supposed to appear. Some young ladies rose early on February 14, looked through their keyholes, and hoped to see two objects. If a girl saw only one object in her first peep through the keyhole, she supposedly had little chance of being married that year.

In some places, an unmarried girl would strike her forehead with a folded rose petal. If the petal cracked, the girl knew that her valentine loved her. When a girl finally married, she could no longer take part in romantic Valentine's Day customs. The poet Robert Herrick wrote of the bride:

> She must no more a-maying
> Or by rosebuds divine
> Who'll be her valentine.

History

The Romans celebrated their feast of Lupercalia as a lovers' festival for young people. Young men and women chose partners for the festival by drawing names by chance from a box. Then the partners exchanged gifts as a sign of affection. They usually continued to enjoy one another's company long after the festival. Many such courtships ended in marriage.

After the spread of Christianity, churchmen tried to give Christian meaning to the pagan festival. In 496, Pope Gelasius changed the Lupercalia festival of February 15 to Saint Valentine's Day on February 14. But the sentimental meaning of the old festival has remained to the present time.

Historians disagree about the identity of St. Valentine. One St. Valentine was a priest who lived in Rome during the 200's under Emperor Claudius II. The Romans jailed him for aiding persecuted Christians. People believe that he cured his jailkeeper's daughter of blindness. About A.D. 270, the Romans beheaded him on Palatine Hill at the site of an ancient altar to Juno. Many years later, Christians named a gate in Rome *Porto Valentini* after St. Valentine. The name was later

VALENTINES THROUGH

The Oldest Valentines in America are some small cards with German script, probably made by nuns and monks in the early 1700's.

An English Valentine from 1815, printed from a copperplate by James Kendrew, was highly colored by hand. It bears a sentimental verse.

The Comic Valentines of 1850 to 1870, printed on cheap paper and sometimes called "Penny Dreadfuls," probably began in America.

A Flowery Message of Love appeared on this lovely lithographic valentine, made by Louis Prang in Boston in 1884. Lithographs first became popular around 1840.

THE YEARS

A Decorated Satin Center framed by a raised design of English lace appeared on this 1850 valentine by Esther Howland, the first American manufacturer of valentines.

The "Unrequited Love," or "Despondent Lover" type of valentine was a favorite kind in the early 1800's. This card from the 1830's has a fancy, embossed border.

The Kate Greenaway Type of Valentine, which usually featured pictures of children and a lacy border, became popular in the late 1800's.

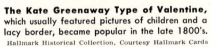

A Doily-like Greeting of the Kate Greenaway style has an elaborate border but little room devoted to verse. Drawings of "little women" type children highlight the card.

VALENTINE'S DAY

changed to *Porto del Popolo*. St. Valentine's remains are buried in the church of St. Praxedes in Rome.

Another St. Valentine was a bishop of Terni, about 60 miles from Rome. One source says that he was persecuted for converting a Roman family to Christianity. He was beheaded in Rome about A.D. 273.

Historians know little about early celebrations of Valentine's Day. According to *Popular Antiquities*, a book by John Brand published in 1877, people in England observed the holiday as early as 1446. In early days, young people chose their valentines by writing names on slips of paper, then drawing them by chance from a vase. An account of the celebration of the holiday in the 1700's describes how social groups met "in the homes of gentry" on the eve of Valentine's Day to carry out this custom. After drawing lots, each young man wore the paper with his lady's name on his sleeve for several days. The expression, "He wears his heart on his sleeve," probably came from this custom.

Young men often presented gifts to their valentines. In some places, the young man gave his lady a pair of gloves. Among wealthy families, men gave fancy-dress balls in honor of their valentines. The custom of sending sentimental messages gradually replaced that of giving fine gifts.

In the United States, Valentine's Day became popular in the 1800's, at the time of the Civil War. A writer in a magazine of 1863 wrote, "Indeed, with the exception of Christmas, there is no festival throughout the world which is invested with half the interest belonging to this cherished anniversary." Many valentines of that period were hand painted. They usually showed a fat cupid whose arrows pierced a heart. Some valentines had satin, ribbon, and lace trimmings. Feathers, mother-of-pearl, tassels, imitation gems, sea shells, and even dried flowers and seaweed decorated others. Some of the elaborate cards cost as much as $10 apiece. Young women proudly displayed their valentines and put them away with other keepsakes. Many old valentines, usually valued for their decorative qualities, have become collectors' items.

ELIZABETH HOUGH SECHRIST

Related Articles in WORLD BOOK include:

Cupid	Juno	Pan
Greeting Cards	Lupercalia	Valentine, Saint

Outline

I. **Valentine's Day Around the World**
   A. In the United States and Canada   C. In Italy
   B. In Great Britain   D. In Denmark
II. **Beliefs and Customs**
III. **History**

Questions

Who made Valentine's Day a holiday? When?

What symbols do people use for Valentine's Day?

What is a *gaekkebrev*?

What was the Lupercalia?

Who were the two St. Valentines? When did each die? How were they connected with our celebrations?

Why did unmarried girls pin bay leaves to their pillows on the eve of Valentine's Day?

When did Valentine's Day become popular in the United States?

Describe two beliefs connected with Valentine's Day. Where did they originate?

What custom probably led to the expression, "He wears his heart on his sleeve"?

How do school children celebrate Valentine's Day in the United States today?

To Make a Lace Doily Valentine, fold a rectangular sheet of paper in quarters. Snip off the corner with the double fold, and make cutouts along the folded edges for heart and diamond designs. Cut a fancy edge along the other two sides. Make two more folds in the paper and cut out designs. Open the doily, use a pin to prick designs around the cutouts, and paste it on a sheet of red paper. Then paste a fancy figure in the center.

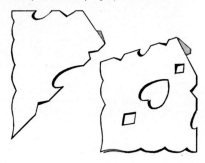

HOW TO MAKE A VALENTINE

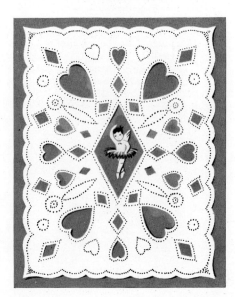

VALENTINIAN was the name of three western Roman emperors. Two of them were important.

Valentinian I (A.D. 321-375) became a soldier at an early age and won fame for his military deeds. In A.D. 364, he was chosen emperor after the death of Jovian. Valentinian appointed his brother Valens coruler, and gave him the eastern provinces to rule (see VALENS). Valentinian was a capable ruler and introduced many improvements. He provided free medical service for the poor, opened schools, and made all trials public. Valentinian was a Christian, but he allowed his people to have complete religious freedom. Throughout his reign, the Alamanni, the German tribes in the north, and the desert tribes in Africa, rebelled, and he fought many wars against them. He died during a campaign against the Quadi, a German tribe living in what is now called Moravia. He was born in Cibalis, Pannonia.

Valentinian III (A.D. 419-455) was the son of the Emperor Constantius and grandson of Theodosius I. He became emperor at the age of six. His mother, Placidia, governed for him during his childhood, and he became so dependent on her that after she died he was a weak and purposeless ruler. The barbarians attacked the Western Empire on all sides. Valentinian's general, Flavius Aëtius, won a great victory over Attila's Huns and defeated the Visigoths in southern Gaul, but the empire was too weak to resist fully, and was gradually broken up. The Vandals conquered Africa, the Scots and Picts won control of Britain, and the Visigoths and the Suevi took over much of Spain and Gaul. Valentinian began to levy high taxes to make up for the lost revenues from these provinces, and the people grew rebellious. In 454, Valentinian had Aëtius murdered, but a year later he was himself assassinated by Aëtius' followers. See also ATTILA. ROBERT GEHLMANN BONE

VALENTINO, RUDOLPH (1895-1926), known as "the great lover," became the most sensational romantic actor of the silent motion pictures. He made many films, including *The Sheik* and *Blood and Sand*. His Latin handsomeness made him a "matinee idol."

Valentino was born RODOLPHO D'ANTONGUOLLA in Castellaneta, Italy. He came to the United States when he was 18 to be a landscape gardener. When he failed at that, he became a window washer. He later became a professional dancer and went to Hollywood in 1919. He died suddenly after an operation, and thousands of women attended his funeral. NARDI REEDER CAMPION

See also MOTION PICTURE (picture, The Silent Era).

VALERA, EAMON DE. See DE VALERA, EAMON.

VALERIAN, *vuh LEER ih un* (? -A.D. 269?), was emperor of Rome from 253 to 259. He tried to stop the Persian invasion of Syria and Armenia, but was defeated and captured. He died a prisoner.

VALERIAN family includes more than 300 different kinds of perennial or annual herbs and some shrubs. These grow mostly in the Northern Hemisphere. Several members of this family are grown as garden or border flowers, and two as potherbs for flavoring food.

One group of valerians has strong-smelling underground parts. Its flowers are small and colored white or reddish. A well-known species is the *common valerian,* or *garden heliotrope.* It yields an oil used in medicine.

The two species grown as potherbs are called *corn salad,* or *lamb's-lettuce,* and *Italian corn salad.* Both grow about one foot high. They are native to southern Europe, but corn salad has been introduced in Central Europe and North America. Italian corn salad has five-inch leaves and pink flowers, whereas corn salad has three-inch leaves and blue flowers. Both are grown in spring and fall. Plants should be about 6 inches apart.

Scientific Classification. Valerians belong to the valerian family, *Valerianaceae.* Common valerian is genus *Valeriana,* species *V. officinalis;* corn salad is *Valerianella olitoria;* Italian corn-salad is *Valerianella eriocarpa.* THEODOR JUST

VALÉRY, *VAH lah REE,* **PAUL** (1871-1945), a French symbolist poet, became famous for poetry such as *Charmes* (1922), his dialogues, and his brief essays. He is the supreme example of a writer indifferent to his public. He was a fervent observer of humanity, and tried to express himself in the most meaningful way. He taught at the Collège de France and became a member of the French Academy. He was born in Sète, and moved to Paris when he was 20. WALLACE FOWLIE

VALET, *VAL et,* is a manservant who cares for his employer's clothing and other personal needs. In hotels, a valet is an employee who cleans and presses guests' clothes. During the Middle Ages, a young apprentice learning to become a knight was called a *valet.* See also HOTEL (picture); KNIGHTS AND KNIGHTHOOD.

VALHALLA, *val HAL uh,* was the great hall of the dead heroes in Norse mythology. The word means *Hall of the Slain.* It was the most magnificent palace in Asgard, and Odin feasted there with his heroes.

Valhalla had walls of gold and a roof of battle shields. Huge spears held up its ceiling. They were so highly polished that the gleam from them was the only light needed in the hall. Coats of mail and other armor hung on the walls. The 540 doors of the building were so wide that 800 men could enter side by side. The guests sat at long tables in the hall. They were the dead heroes who had been brought to Valhalla by the Valkyries, or battle maidens. The Valkyries waited on the tables and served luxurious food and drinks.

The heroes rode out to the battlefield to fight every morning. They often wounded each other terribly, but their hurts were healed before they returned to Valhalla for the noonday feast. PADRAIC COLUM

See also ASGARD; ODIN; VALKYRIE.

The Norse God Odin, in the great hall of Valhalla, receiving a visitor presented by Bragi, the god of poetry.

Historical Pictures

VALJEAN, JEAN. See Les Misérables.

VALKYRIE, *val KIR ih,* was one of the warlike goddess-maidens of Norse mythology. The Valkyries rode on swift horses and were armed with spears, shields, and helmets. Odin sent them to battlefields to choose dead heroes for Valhalla, where they served the warriors' feasts. The name means *those who choose the fallen.* Brunhild, the maiden Sigurd awakened from a magic sleep, was a Valkyrie. Richard Wagner built his opera *Die Walküre* around this theme. EINAR HAUGEN

See also MYTHOLOGY (pictures, In Battle, Arriving at Valhalla); BRUNHILD; ODIN; OPERA (Valkyrie); VALHALLA.

VALLE, *VAH yay,* JOSÉ CECILIO DEL (1780-1834), a Central American patriot and statesman, wrote the Central American Declaration of Independence from Spain of Sept. 15, 1821. He became a leader of Guatemala's independence movement in 1821. Mexico, after annexing Guatemala in 1822, imprisoned Valle for a time. He was elected vice-president of the Central American Confederation in 1823, but refused to serve. Valle was born in Honduras. HARVEY L. JOHNSON

VALLEJO, *vuh LAY oh,* Calif. (pop. 60,877; met. area 200,487; alt. 85 ft.), is the home of the California Maritime Academy, and of the Mare Island Naval Shipyard, the largest naval shipyard on the Pacific Coast. Vallejo lies about 30 miles northeast of San Francisco (see CALIFORNIA [political map]). Many of its residents work at the shipyard, but others live in Vallejo and work in other Bay Area communities. Founded in 1850, Vallejo was California's capital from 1851 to 1853. It has a council-manager form of government. GEORGE SHAFTEL

See also MARE ISLAND NAVAL SHIPYARD.

VALLETTA, *vuh LEH tuh* (pop. 18,300; met. area 208,000; alt. 145 ft.) is the capital and chief seaport of Malta. It lies on a narrow peninsula between the harbors on Malta's northeast coast. Valletta is the administrative, cultural, and commercial center of Malta. It serves as a naval base for both the British navy and the North Atlantic Treaty Organization (NATO). The Royal University of Malta, the island's only university, and the Royal Malta Library are both in Valletta. The Cathedral of Saint John and the Palace of the Grand Masters (now the governor's residence) are among the city's most beautiful buildings.

Valletta was founded in 1565 and named for Jean Parisot de la Vallette, Grand Master of the Knights of Malta. It became the capital of Malta in 1570.

See also MALTA (map; picture).

VALLEY is a natural trough in the earth's surface. It is the most important feature of the landscape. Systems of valleys extend through plains, hills, and mountains. Streams and rivers flowing through valleys drain interior land regions to the ocean. Many valleys have fertile soil and make excellent farmland.

All valleys are similar in shape. The bottom of a valley is called its *floor.* The floor usually slopes gradually in one general direction. Mountain valleys usually have narrow floors. But in low-lying plains, a valley floor may be several miles wide. The part of the valley floor along river banks is called the *flood plain.* The flood plain is part of the river channel, but it is used only during a flood. Buildings located on the flood plain are in danger

of damage when the river floods. The sides of a valley are called *valley walls* or *valley slopes.* The ridge formed where the walls of neighboring valleys meet is called a *divide.*

Kinds of Valleys. Various kinds of valleys are named according to their appearance. A deep valley with steep walls is called a *canyon.* One of the most famous canyons is Grand Canyon in Arizona. Along coastlines, valleys that are flooded by the ocean are called *drowned valleys.* Chesapeake Bay and Delaware Bay are drowned valleys. Where a valley joins a larger valley from the side, the two floors usually meet at the same level. But sometimes the floor of the side valley is higher than the floor of the main valley where they join. The side valley is then called a *hanging* valley. A river flowing through a hanging valley may form a waterfall where the water enters the main valley.

Not all valleys are on land. Many deep *submarine* canyons are found on the slopes leading up from the ocean floor to the edge of the continental shelf. Hudson Canyon is a submarine canyon. It extends south-eastward down the continental shelf to the Atlantic Ocean floor from a point near New York City.

How Valleys Are Formed. Most valleys on dry land are formed by the running water of streams and rivers, and by the erosion of slopes leading to them. Erosion moves material down the slopes to the valley floor where the stream carries it to a lake or to the ocean. In addition, the stream may erode its channel deeper.

A valley may also be formed when a long, narrow section of the earth's crust sinks below the surrounding area. A valley formed in this way is called a *rift valley.* One system of rift valleys extends about 4,000 miles from the Sea of Galilee south through the Red Sea, and into southeastern Africa.

Glaciated valleys are valleys that were enlarged by the action of glaciers. These valleys are often found high in mountains. They are U-shaped rather than V-shaped. SHELDON JUDSON

Related Articles in WORLD BOOK include:

Canyon	Imperial Valley
Death Valley	Khyber Pass
Delaware Bay	Matanuska Valley
Delaware Water Gap	Ocean (illustration,
Divide	Atlantic Ocean Floor)
Engadine	Shenandoah Valley
Erosion (pictures)	Trossachs
Gap	Valley of the Kings
Hanging Valley	Wyoming Valley

VALLEY CITY STATE COLLEGE. See UNIVERSITIES AND COLLEGES (table).

VALLEY FORGE, Pa. (pop. 450; alt. 100 ft.), is a village on the Schuylkill River, about 45 miles west of Philadelphia (see PENNSYLVANIA [political map]). General George Washington and his men camped

Ewing Galloway

National Memorial Arch in Valley Forge State Park honors the gallant American soldiers who camped there during the winter of 1777-1778.

Soldiers at Valley Forge, cold, hungry, and sick, endured what has been often called the "Winter of Despair" in 1777 and 1778.

there in the terrible winter of 1777 and 1778, during the Revolutionary War. These months were discouraging for the American cause. Washington's Continental Army had to endure several months of bitter suffering.

Conditions at Valley Forge. Washington led his troops to Valley Forge after his defeats at Philadelphia and Germantown, Pa. His soldiers had little food, and too little clothing to protect themselves from the cold. The Continental Congress could not provide additional supplies to fill the men's needs. The army of about 11,000 lived in crude log huts that they built themselves. On Dec. 23, 1777, Washington wrote: "We have this day no less than 2,873 men in camp unfit for duty because they are barefooted and otherwise naked."

More than 3,000 soldiers died during this period. Many others were either too weak or too sick to fight, because of a smallpox epidemic. At the same time, the people around Valley Forge were enjoying all the comforts of a rich countryside, because little fighting took place at this time. The British lived a gay life in Philadelphia. The American soldiers found the region about the camp unfriendly to them.

The winter at Valley Forge tested the loyalty of the American troops. Only dedicated patriots stayed with the Continental Army. Many persons criticized Washington, but he held his position at Valley Forge throughout the winter and spring. In spite of all the difficulties, he improved his troops with the help of Baron von Steuben. This remarkable Prussian general drilled the soldiers in a system of field formations. When spring came, Washington had a disciplined, well-trained army. The news of the alliance between France and the United States reached Valley Forge on May 6, 1778. It cheered Washington, and helped him to move successfully against the British in June.

Valley Forge State Park is located on about 2,000 acres of the camping ground. The park's buildings and monuments have been built in memory of Washington's Continental Army. The old stone house that he used as headquarters still stands there. Other buildings include the Washington Memorial Chapel, National Memorial Arch, Cloister of Colonies, and Valley Forge Museum of Natural History.　MARSHALL SMELSER

See also REVOLUTIONARY WAR IN AMERICA; WASHINGTON, GEORGE; STEUBEN, BARON VON.

VALLEY OF TEN THOUSAND SMOKES. See KATMAI NATIONAL MONUMENT.

VALLEY OF THE FALLEN. See SPAIN (Architecture).

VALLEY OF THE KINGS was the burial site of many Egyptian *pharaohs* (kings). It is often called the *Valley of the Tombs of the Kings.* This valley was a rocky wasteland on the western side of the Nile River across from the ancient capital of Thebes. For location, see EGYPT, ANCIENT (color map). The pharaohs decided to build secret graves to prevent grave robbing. They built the first tombs about 1500 B.C. Many great rulers of Egypt, including Ramses II, Amenhotep III, and Queen Tiy, were buried in the valley. When archaeologists entered the valley, they found that thieves had robbed most of the tombs. The tomb of King Tutankhamon, opened in 1922, was the first tomb archaeologists found that had not been robbed.　WILLIAM F. MCDONALD

VALLOMBROSA, *VAHL lohm BRO sah,* is the name of an Italian abbey founded about 1030 by Benedictine monks. It is located about 10 miles east of Florence, Italy.

VALMY, BATTLE OF. See ARMY (Famous Land Battles of History).

VALOIS, *VAH LWAH,* was the family name of a branch of the great Capetian line of French kings (see CAPETIAN DYNASTY). The House of Valois ruled France from 1328 to 1589. Philip VI, the first of the Valois kings, came to the throne after Charles IV died. Charles VIII died in 1498 without any sons, and the throne passed to Louis, Duke of Orléans. He died in 1515 without a male heir and the throne passed to Francis of Angoulême. Francis was crowned Francis I and became the first of the Angoulême branch of the House of Valois. Henry III, who died in 1589, was the last of the Angoulêmes, and Henry IV, who followed him, was the first Bourbon.　FRANKLIN D. SCOTT

See also CHARLES (VIII); FRANCIS (I) of France; HENRY (III) of France; LOUIS (XII); PHILIP (VI).

VALOIS-ORLÉANS, HOUSE OF. See ORLÉANS.

VALPARAÍSO, *VAHL pah rah EE soh* (pop. 252,900; met. area, 440,000; alt. 35 ft.), is the principal seaport and second largest city of Chile. Valparaíso lies on a wide inlet of the Pacific Ocean about 70 miles northwest of Santiago. For location, see CHILE (political map). *Valparaíso* is Spanish for *Valley of Paradise.*

Valparaíso is a modern and progressive city, and an

VALPARAISO UNIVERSITY

important manufacturing center. The chief products include cotton goods, machinery, tobacco, refined sugar, and liquor. The city has many fine public buildings and schools. An electric railroad joins Valparaíso with Santiago, and another line joins the city with the mining section of inland Chile. In 1906, a severe earthquake destroyed parts of the city.   ROBERT N. BURR

See also SOUTH AMERICA (picture, Steamships).

VALPARAISO UNIVERSITY. See UNIVERSITIES AND COLLEGES (table).

VALUE, in economics, means the power of a commodity to command other commodities in exchange. Value relates to the terms upon which one commodity exchanges for others. It must not be confused with price. A commodity's *price* means its exchange power in terms of money. Its *value* means its exchange power in terms of other commodities.

Value and Utility. In order to possess value, an article must have *utility*. That is, it must have the power to satisfy a want. For example, farm products always have value because everyone desires them. So farmers can usually find a market for their products. The desire for articles must be backed by purchasing power. No article will have any value if those who want it have no money or commodities to offer in exchange for it.

A thing may have great value and still be used in ways which harm mankind. For example, drugs and alcohol possess great utility. They are of benefit to man when used properly. But they become harmful when people misuse them or become addicted to them.

Value and Scarcity. In order to possess value, an article must be scarce. That is, it must be so limited in quantity that those who have it are able to get something else in exchange for it. Air, which has great utility, seldom has any value. There is so much of it that ordinarily everyone can have all he wants without having to pay anyone for it. But under certain conditions, air does have value. A good illustration is compressed air, which is bought and sold. HAROLD G. MOULTON

See also PRICE.

VALUE, in philosophy, is an aspect in our experience which goes beyond the sheer presence of facts. We not only see facts and events, but also judge their worth. Man seeks a standard for determining and relating values. Scholars have developed *axiology*, the study of the nature and kinds of value. Value theories bring out three important characteristics: interest, objectivity, and personal integration.

Objects which arouse our *interest* are recognized as carrying value. These objects include food, power, beauty, and moral integrity. Values are also determined by their *objectivity*, how well they are met by objects themselves. Valuable things have a structure of their own, which we must respect. These structures determine the range and order of our value responses. Our response to tool values like money differs from our response to terminal values like art and religion. Value exists in the *personal integration* of our interests with objective structures. We rank values according to their capacity to develop personal experience. JAMES COLLINS

See also MORAL AND SPIRITUAL VALUES.

VALUE, in color. See COLOR (Characteristics of Color).

VALUE ADDED BY MANUFACTURE is a statistic used to measure and compare manufacturing activity. For example, if a state had a total value added by manufacture of $10 billion in 1960 and $20 billion in 1967, its manufacturing activity has doubled. Value added by manufacture is one of the chief measures of economic activity used by the U.S. government.

Value added by manufacture is the increase in value of raw material after it has been turned into a finished product. It represents the effect of manufacturing in terms of money. To compute this value, economists subtract the cost of materials, supplies, containers, fuel, electricity, and contract work from the value of manufactured products as they leave the factory.

VALVE is a term used for various mechanical devices which open and close to control the flow of fluids in pipes and vessels. The term also is used in physiology for natural growths in the body which serve much the same purpose as mechanical valves. Among these are the valves of the heart, which open and close to control the flow of blood through the chambers of the heart.

There are several types of mechanical valves. Perhaps the best known are the *automatic*, the *nonautomatic*, and *slide* valves.

Automatic valves are opened and closed by the pressure and back pressure of the fluid. The valve proper is a

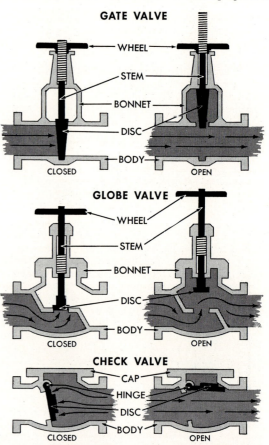

GATE VALVE
WHEEL — STEM — BONNET — DISC — BODY
CLOSED   OPEN

GLOBE VALVE
WHEEL — STEM — BONNET — DISC — BODY
CLOSED   OPEN

CHECK VALVE
CAP — HINGE — DISC — BODY
CLOSED   OPEN

Principal Types of Valves. The nonautomatic gate and globe valves are used to turn on or shut off the flow of liquids. The check, or automatic valve, allows a liquid to flow in one direction, but it closes shut to stop flow in the opposite direction.

little gate which swings open on one side of an opening. When the liquid pressure is behind the valve, the pressure forces the valve open, and pushes through. Then pressure on the other side forces the valve back against the opening, closing the valve. The valves in the heart operate in this way.

Nonautomatic valves are operated by an outside force. For example, the valve in a common water faucet is opened and shut by turning a handle.

A slide valve works like the valve on a steam-engine cylinder. The moving part of the valve slides back and forth across the openings made in the cylinder, opening and closing them by changing the direction of motion of the sliding part of the valve.   Otto A. Uyehara

See also Carburetor; Gasoline Engine; Safety Valve.

VAMPIRE, according to superstition, is a ghost that comes from the grave at night to suck the blood of living persons, especially young persons. It is supposed to take the blood from the neck while the victim is sleeping. The person is said to waste away and die, and then become a vampire himself. Wizards, witches, suicides, and those cursed by the church or their parents were believed to become vampires at death.

The vampire was said to renew its life from the blood of the living. To keep the body in the grave, it was thought that a stake must be driven through its heart. The book *Dracula* (1897), by Bram Stoker, tells the story of a family of vampires.   Wilson D. Wallis

See also Vampire Bat.

VAMPIRE BAT is the name given several different bats. The name is given particularly to certain bats in Central America and tropical America, which attack men, fowl, and other warm-blooded animals, and drink their blood. The best known is the *common vampire bat*, a small reddish-brown animal about 3 inches long. It has very sharp triangular-shaped front teeth, which cut like a razor. Its esophagus is short and narrow, and will permit nothing but fluids to pass.

Vampire bats sometimes attack persons who are sleeping. The bite itself is harmless and soon heals, but many such bats carry rabies. They have destroyed livestock in some localities, and have infected humans.

Weird stories have been told about the viciousness of these mammals. Their peculiar name comes from the superstitious legends about the vampire, an imaginary being which sucked the blood from humans and turned them into vampires.

Scientific Classification. True vampire bats make up the family *Desmodontidae*. They form three genera, *Desmodus*, *Diaemus*, and *Diphylla*. The common vampire bat is genus *Desmodus*, species *D. rotundus*. Frank B. Golley

See also Bat; Vampire.

VAN, LAKE. See Lake Van.

VANADIUM, *vuh NAY dih um* (chemical symbol, V), a silver-white metallic element, is one of the hardest of metals. Its atomic weight is 50.942; its atomic number is 23. The Swedish chemist Nils Sefström discovered it in 1830. Vanadium is rare and never occurs in its pure state. It is found in small quantities in the ores of copper, lead, and iron. Its chief ore mineral is patronite, a compound of vanadium and sulfur.

The usual heat methods of separating metals from their ores do not work on vanadium, because it has the high melting point of 1,735° C. First the sulfur is re-

William A. Wimsatt & David G. Allen
The Vampire Bat slashes its victim with its sharp upper teeth and drinks blood. Its bite may transmit rabies to the victim.

moved by roasting the patronite ore. Then the impure metal is combined with sodium carbonate to form sodium vanadate. A large amount of sulfuric acid is added. This causes the vanadium to combine with oxygen and form tiny masses of vanadium pentoxide, which go to the bottom of the mixture.

The vanadium pentoxide is heated in the presence of carbon or aluminum, which attracts the oxygen from the vanadium compound, leaving pure vanadium.

Vanadium has a wide range of uses in combination with other metals. Ferrovanadium—a combination of about 40 per cent vanadium with iron—is added to steel to make an alloy of great strength and elasticity. This vanadium steel is used to make automobile frames, gears, springs, and axles. Carbon-vanadium steels are used to make locomotive castings and forgings. Alloys of vanadium with aluminum and copper make excellent castings. A compound of vanadium and ammonium is used in making black aniline dye and in making vanadium ink. Other vanadium compounds are used in medicine.

Peru is one of the most important producers of vanadium. In the United States, Colorado, Utah, Arizona, and New Mexico are the largest producers of the metal. In Europe, vanadium comes from ores found largely in Germany and Finland. South West Africa and Zambia are important vanadium ore-producing regions in Africa.   Harrison Ashley Schmitt

See also Alloy.

VAN ALLEN RADIATION refers to a belt of radiation that surrounds such planets as Earth and Jupiter. Earth's belt seems to consist of electrons and protons trapped in Earth's magnetic field. Scientists once thought that two belts surround Earth. But discoveries in 1962 led scientists to believe that only one large belt exists. This belt begins about 500 miles above the equator, and extends outward about 40,000 miles. James A. Van Allen, an American physicist, discovered the belt in 1958 from information gathered by early United States space probes. See also Space Travel (picture, Radiation Belts).

MARTIN VAN BUREN

Painting by George P. A. Healy; The White
House, courtesy National Park Service.

The United States Flag had 25
stars when Van Buren took office.

J. Q. ADAMS
6th President
1825—1829

JACKSON
7th President
1829—1837

W. H. HARRISON
9th President
1841

TYLER
10th President
1841 — 1845

8TH PRESIDENT OF THE UNITED STATES 1837-1841

VAN BUREN, MARTIN (1782-1862), ran for President three times, but won only the first time. He served during the nation's first great depression, the Panic of 1837. The panic brought financial ruin and misery to millions. Many turned to the government for help, but Van Buren refused all public aid. He believed in Thomas Jefferson's theories that government should play the smallest possible role in American life. "The less government interferes," Van Buren explained, "the better for general prosperity."

Van Buren's erect bearing and high, broad forehead gave him a dignified appearance. He had served as Vice-President under Andrew Jackson, and, as President, Van Buren inherited much of Jackson's popularity. But during the three years of the panic, Van Buren bore the anger of a disappointed people. His enemies accused him of being a sly, scheming politician. They called him "The Little Magician" and "The Fox of Kinderhook." They ridiculed his courteous manners. When Van Buren continued to deal politely with his political rivals, they said this showed his lack of deep convictions.

By defending his Jeffersonian ideals, Van Buren demonstrated that actually he had both deep convictions and courage. Partly because he refused to compromise, Van Buren was defeated for re-election in 1840 by William Henry Harrison, whom he had beaten in 1836. Van Buren ran again for President in 1848, but finished a poor third.

In Van Buren's time, Washington, D.C., was still a city of muddy streets and few trees. One traveler said: "It looks as if it had rained naked buildings upon an open plain." But life in the capital reflected the excite-

ment of a growing country. The first railroad into Washington was completed in time to bring visitors from New York City and Philadelphia to Van Buren's inauguration. Frontiersmen such as Sam Houston mingled with courtly Southerners and proper New Englanders. Washington hostesses sought out the popular author, Washington Irving, for their dinner parties. Out West, the frontier town of Chicago became an incorporated city, and the Republic of Texas began its fight for statehood.

Early Life

Childhood and Education. Martin Van Buren was born in the Dutch community of Kinderhook, N.Y., on Dec. 5, 1782. He was the third of the five children of Abraham and Maria Hoes Van Buren. Martin had an older brother and sister, and two younger brothers. His mother was the widow of Johannes Van Alen, and had three other children by her first marriage. Abraham Van Buren ran a truck farm and a tavern. As a child, Martin enjoyed listening to the tavern patrons as they argued politics in the Dutch language.

IMPORTANT DATES IN VAN BUREN'S LIFE

1782 (Dec. 5) Born in Kinderhook, N.Y.
1807 (Feb. 21) Married Hannah Hoes.
1812 Elected to the New York Senate.
1819 (Feb. 5) Hannah Hoes Van Buren died.
1821 Elected to the United States Senate.
1828 Elected Governor of New York.
1829 Appointed Secretary of State.
1832 Elected Vice-President of the United States.
1836 Elected President of the United States.
1840 Defeated for re-election by William H. Harrison.
1848 Nominated for President by the Free Soil party.
1862 (July 24) Died in Kinderhook, N.Y.

214

Martin attended the village school. At the age of 14, he began to study law under Francis Sylvester, a local attorney. He showed great talent, and Sylvester soon let him work in court. Martin first took part in a court trial at the age of 15. Another lawyer from Sylvester's office had tried the case. As he was about to sum up his arguments, he turned to Martin and said: "Here, Mat, sum up. You may as well begin early." The boy was rewarded that day with a silver half dollar. He soon became a familiar sight in the village court.

In 1801, Van Buren moved to New York City to continue his studies. He was admitted to the bar in 1803, and opened a law office in Kinderhook with his half brother, James I. Van Alen.

Van Buren's Family. On Feb. 21, 1807, Martin Van Buren married his distant cousin and childhood sweetheart, Hannah Hoes (March 8, 1783-Feb. 5, 1819). Mrs. Van Buren died 18 years before her husband became President. The couple had four sons. Abraham, the eldest, was his father's White House secretary, and later

served on the staff of General Zachary Taylor during the Mexican War. John, the second son, became attorney general of New York.

Political and Public Career

Van Buren's enthusiasm for the ideas of Thomas Jefferson took him into politics as a Democratic-Republican (see DEMOCRATIC-REPUBLICAN PARTY). He was elected to the New York senate in 1812. Shortly after his re-election to the senate in 1816, Van Buren was appointed attorney general of New York.

U.S. Senator. In 1820, a split in the Democratic-Republican party of New York gave Van Buren a chance to show his ability as a political leader. Governor De Witt Clinton tried to get John C. Spencer into the U.S. Senate through a special election. Van Buren split with Clinton, and successfully managed the election of Rufus King, an independent Federalist. A year

THE WORLD OF PRESIDENT VAN BUREN

U.S. population was 17,700,000 in 1841. Iowa became a territory in 1838. No new states were formed during Van Buren's term.

Queen Victoria

WORLD EVENTS

1837 Queen Victoria succeeded to the British throne.
1837-1838 Rebellions broke out in Upper and Lower Canada.
1840 Britain issued the world's first postage stamp.
1840 Union Act joined Upper and Lower Canada.

IOWA TER.

World's First Postage Stamp

Charles Goodyear discovered how to vulcanize rubber in 1839.

The First Photograph made in the United States was taken by Samuel F. B. Morse in 1839.

First Great Depression paralyzed the U.S. economy in 1837.

The First Normal School organized in the United States opened in Massachusetts in 1839.

The Underground Railroad, organized to smuggle Negroes out of slavery in the South, had its beginnings in 1838.

From *A History of Old Kinderhook* by Edward A. Collier,
G. P. Putnam's Sons, 1914.

Van Buren's Birthplace was in the Dutch community of Kinderhook, N.Y. The house has been torn down, and the only record of what it looked like comes from drawings made during Van Buren's lifetime.

Painting by Henry Inman, Frick Art Reference Library

Angelica Singleton Van Buren, the President's daughter-in-law, served as hostess of the White House. Van Buren's wife, Hannah Hoes Van Buren, died 18 years before he became President.

later, when the other Senate seat was vacated, Van Buren's standing had so increased that the legislature elected him. Clinton and his followers were left with no voice in the national government, and soon lost their power in New York.

Van Buren took his seat in the Senate on Dec. 3, 1821. He became a leader in the fight against imprisonment for debt, a great social evil of the time. In 1828, Congress passed a law abolishing such imprisonment. Van Buren also tried to stop the extension of the slave trade. He introduced a bill forbidding the importation of slaves into Florida unless they were owned by settlers. This bill was defeated. Van Buren won re-election to the Senate in 1827. He soon became a supporter of Andrew Jackson for the presidency.

Secretary of State. Late in 1828, Van Buren resigned from the Senate after being elected governor of New York. He served as governor only two months, then resigned to become Secretary of State under President Jackson. Van Buren successfully pressed claims for damages to American shipping by French and Danish warships during the Napoleonic Wars. Under his leadership, the United States re-established trade with the British West Indies. The British had closed West Indian ports to American shipping in 1826 in retaliation for high American tariffs on British goods.

Vice-President. In 1831, Jackson appointed Van Buren U.S. Minister to Great Britain. But the Senate, by one vote, refused to confirm the appointment. By this act, Van Buren's enemies thought they had destroyed his career. Jackson took the Senate's action as a personal insult. In 1832, he supported Van Buren's nomination to the vice-presidency. He also made it clear that Van Buren was his choice to be the next President.

As Vice-President, Van Buren supported Jackson's decision to withdraw federal deposits from the Bank of the United States (see BANK OF THE UNITED STATES). Senate debates over the issue became increasingly bitter. At the height of the dispute, rumors sprang up of a plot to assassinate Van Buren. For a time, Van Buren carried loaded pistols as he presided over the Senate.

Election of 1836. With Jackson's support, Van Buren easily won the Democratic nomination for President in 1836. He defeated William Henry Harrison, the Whig candidate, by 97 electoral votes. In the vice-presidential race, no candidate won a majority of the electoral votes. The Senate then chose Van Buren's running mate, Representative Richard M. Johnson of

Kentucky. No other Vice-President has ever been elected by the Senate.

─────── **VAN BUREN'S ELECTION** ───────

Place of Nominating Convention...Baltimore

Ballot on Which Nominated.......1st

Whig Opponent..................William Henry Harrison

Electoral Vote....................170 (Van Buren) to
                                              73 (Harrison)

Popular Vote.....................765,483 (Van Buren) to
                                              739,795 (Harrison)

Age at Inauguration.............54

Van Buren's Administration (1837-1841)

The Panic of 1837. Van Buren owed the presidency to Andrew Jackson. But many of the problems that faced him as President had developed during Jackson's administration. Congress had failed to limit the sales of public lands to actual settlers, even though Jackson urged such action during his last year in office. Everyone was speculating in public lands, even clerks and shoeshine boys. State banks and branches of the Bank of the United States had joined the speculative splurge. They made vast loans without security in gold or silver. Unable to limit land sales, Jackson had issued his Specie Circular of July 1, 1836. It required the government to accept only gold and silver in payment for public lands. Banks could no longer make loans without security, and the speculation ended. A financial crash was inevitable. It came on May 10, 1837, just 36 days after Van Buren took office. Banks in Philadelphia and New York City

─────── **VAN BUREN'S CABINET** ───────

Secretary of State...............John Forsyth
Secretary of the Treasury.......Levi Woodbury
Secretary of War...............Joel R. Poinsett
Attorney General...............Benjamin F. Butler
	Felix Grundy (1838)
	Henry D. Gilpin (1840)
Postmaster General............*Amos Kendall
	John M. Niles (1840)
Secretary of the Navy...........Mahlon Dickerson
	James Paulding (1838)

*Has a separate biography in WORLD BOOK

closed, and soon every bank in the country did likewise. The first great depression in American history had begun.

The Independent Treasury. Van Buren felt no responsibility for the effects of the depression on the people. As President, he was worried only because federal funds on deposit in private banks were in danger. He therefore proposed that an independent treasury be created to hold government funds. A bill putting this plan gradually into effect passed Congress on July 4, 1840. Van Buren called it a "second Declaration of Independence." The independent treasury was abolished in 1841, after Van Buren left office. It was reestablished in 1846 under President James K. Polk.

Life in the White House. Van Buren avoided extravagant White House parties because of the depression. He limited his entertaining to simple dinners. Many visitors to the Executive Mansion found the atmosphere formal and austere, even with Van Buren's four sons present. The people of Washington admired the modesty and personal charm of the youths, all in their 20's. But many, especially Dolley Madison, regretted the lack of a woman in the household. She introduced the President's eldest son, Abraham, to Angelica Singleton of South Carolina. A romance soon developed, and the young people were married in late 1838. Angelica Van Buren assumed the role of White House hostess.

Growing Unpopularity. The depression was only one of many disturbances during Van Buren's administration. Border disputes developed with Canada. In 1839, a boundary dispute between Maine and neighboring New Brunswick nearly resulted in open warfare. Van Buren handled the problem with tact, and the dispute was settled peacefully. But he received little credit for his efforts. See NEW BRUNSWICK (Aroostook War).

Antislavery leaders blamed Van Buren for the expensive war to drive the Seminole Indians from Florida. They feared the region might become a new slave state. Proslavery leaders attacked the President for not working to annex Texas. They believed he did not want to admit a new slave state into the Union.

Election of 1840. The Democrats nominated Van Buren for re-election in 1840 in spite of his unpopularity. Vice-President Johnson had so many enemies that he failed to gain renomination. The Democrats could not agree on any vice-presidential candidate. As a result, Van Buren became the only presidential candidate in American history to seek election without a running mate. The Whigs again nominated William Henry Harrison for President, and chose former Senator John Tyler of Virginia as his running mate.

Harrison launched a boisterous campaign in which he attacked Van Buren as an aristocrat who had no interest in the unemployment caused by the depression. Using the slogan "Tippecanoe and Tyler too," Harrison campaigned on the basis of his colorful military career. Few persons were surprised when Van Buren lost by an electoral vote of 234 to 60. But many were amazed by the close popular vote. Of 2,400,000 votes cast, Van Buren lost by fewer than 150,000. See HARRISON, WILLIAM HENRY (Elections of 1836 and 1840).

Later Years

Van Buren retired to his country estate, Lindenwald, near his birthplace. He remained active in politics for

more than 20 years. In 1848, the antislavery Free Soil party nominated him for President (see FREE SOIL PARTY). He lost the election, but took so many New York votes from Democrat Lewis Cass that the Whig candidate, Zachary Taylor, was elected.

As the slavery disputes grew hotter, Van Buren made his antislavery position clear. But he remained a loyal Democrat, supporting Franklin Pierce in 1852 and James Buchanan in 1856. He opposed Abraham Lincoln at first in 1860, but gave him loyal support after the election. Van Buren died at Lindenwald on July 24, 1862, and was buried beside his wife in Kinderhook.

Authoritative books on Van Buren include *American Talleyrand* by H. M. Alexander and *Martin Van Buren* by E. M. Shepard. Van Buren wrote an autobiography, *An Inquiry into the Origin and Course of Political Parties in the United States.*   HUGH RUSSELL FRASER

Related Articles in WORLD BOOK include:

Depression	President of the United States
Harrison, William Henry	Vice-President of the United
Jackson, Andrew	States
Johnson, Richard Mentor	

Outline

I. Party Life
   A. Childhood and Education
   B. Van Buren's Family
II. Political and Public Career
   A. U.S. Senator   C. Vice-President
   B. Secretary of State   D. Election of 1836
III. Van Buren's Administration (1837-1841)
   A. The Panic of 1837
   B. The Independent Treasury
   C. Life in the White House
   D. Growing Unpopularity
   E. Election of 1840
IV. Later Years

Questions

Whose support assured Van Buren's nomination for President?

What events caused Van Buren to lose popularity?

How did Van Buren's candidacy in 1848 affect the presidential election?

What social evil did Van Buren oppose as Senator?

How did an attempt to ruin Van Buren in 1831 backfire?

Why did Van Buren refuse to give federal aid to the people during the Panic of 1837?

Why was Van Buren called "The Fox of Kinderhook"?

What was Van Buren's plan to protect federal funds from the effects of a depression?

Why did Vice-President Van Buren carry loaded pistols while presiding over the Senate?

Why was Van Buren the only man ever to run for President without a vice-presidential running mate?

VANCE, ZEBULON BAIRD (1830-1894), was a Confederate governor of North Carolina and a Democratic United States Senator. He opposed secession, but served in the Confederate Army. He became governor of North Carolina in 1862, and devoted himself to supplying North Carolina soldiers. He bought a steamship for the state, and brought food, arms, and medicines through the blockade. He was elected to the United States Senate in 1870, but was refused his seat. He became governor again in 1876 and served in the U.S. Senate from 1879 until his death. He was born in Buncombe County, North Carolina. Vance represents North Carolina in Statuary Hall.   W. B. HESSELTINE

Vancouver Is Canada's Leading Pacific Coast Port. Ships use its ice-free harbor, covering 48 square miles, all year. Many of the buildings of this busy commercial and industrial city face the Coast Mountains, north of Burrard Inlet. Stanley Park, *left background*, is a 1,000-acre peninsula that provides a playground for the people and a shelter for the harbor.

Coat of Arms

VANCOUVER, *van KOO vur,* British Columbia (pop. 384,522; met. area, 790,165; alt. 38 ft.), is Canada's leading Pacific Ocean port. It is also the industrial and commercial center of British Columbia. The city lies opposite Vancouver Island, about 15 miles north of the United States border. Young, bustling Vancouver was just another lumber town in 1886, when it received its city charter. By the early 1930's, it had become the third largest Canadian city, a position it still holds. About half the people of British Columbia live in Greater Vancouver.

Vancouver is called *Canada's Window on the Pacific.* The city's ice-free, landlocked harbor ranks as its

chief asset. Canada ships lumber, salmon, wheat, and many manufactured goods through this busy port the year round. Vancouver serves as the western terminal of Canada's two transcontinental railroads.

Evergreen forests grow almost to the city limits. They provide raw material for the city's chief manufacturing activity, the forest-products industry. The protective Coast Mountains, and warm winds blowing in from the Pacific, help give Vancouver a surprisingly mild climate for a city so far north. Residents enjoy golf and other outdoor activities throughout the year. For the monthly rainfall and temperature in Vancouver, see BRITISH COLUMBIA (Climate).

Location, Size, and Description

Vancouver lies in a magnificent setting near mountains and the Pacific Ocean. It covers about 44 square

218

WEST VANCOUVER

NORTH VANCOUVER

MARINE DR.

British Columbia

Alberta

PACIFIC OCEAN

● VANCOUVER

United States

VANCOUVER
Area of Large Map

Light gray shaded area shows Vancouver city limits

LIONS GATE BRIDGE

BURRARD INLET

BEAVER LAKE

STANLEY PARK

ZOO

LOST LAGOON

GEORGIA ST.

N

W E

S

ART GALLERY

HASTINGS

PUBLIC LIBRARY

CITY MUSEUM

ENGLISH BAY

BURRARD

FALSE CREEK

CORNWALL ST.

BLANCA ST.

4TH AVE.

8TH AVE.

BROADWAY

12TH AVE.

DUNBAR ST.

◄ UNIVERSITY OF BRITISH COLUMBIA

CITY HALL

KINGSWAY

KING EDWARD AVE. W.

LITTLE MOUNTAIN

University of British Columbia covers 1,000 acres on Point Grey. It has one of the largest enrollments of any school in Canada. Many of its buildings are of modern design.

National Film Board

33RD AVE.

WEST BOULEVARD

GRANVILLE ST.

OAK ST.

CAMBIE ST.

MAIN ST.

49TH AVE.

1 Inch = 0.8 Statute Miles

0   ¼   ½   ¾   1
Miles

S.W. MARINE D.

miles on the southern shore of Burrard Inlet. This harbor has a shore line 98 miles long. The flat, green, delta lands of the Fraser River basin spread south of the city. Two peaks of the Coast Mountains, the snow-capped Lions, rise in majestic grandeur north of Burrard Inlet, overlooking the suburbs of West and North Vancouver. Point Grey, a peninsula, juts three miles into the Strait of Georgia at the west end of Vancouver. The 1,000-acre campus of the University of British Columbia is on Point Grey. Another peninsula, Stanley Park, lies nearer the heart of the city. Its 1,000 acres of virgin evergreen forest form a protective shelter for the harbor.

Downtown Vancouver occupies slightly higher land just south and east of the park. Hastings Street, a busy commercial thoroughfare, crosses much of the city from east to west. The Marine Building, Vancouver's oldest skyscraper, rises 350 feet at its western end, near the busy docks. This building marks the heart of the city's financial district. Farther east along Hastings Street are department stores, and Victory Square with its monument to war heroes.

Granville Street, another main commercial street, runs into Hastings Street. It extends south from the water front to the North Arm of the Fraser River. Granville is a street of handsome banks, fine stores and shops, and several theaters.

Georgia Street, running parallel to Hastings Street, is known for its large hotels, the courthouse, the post office, and the Queen Elizabeth Theatre, where concerts and other cultural attractions are held. Many of Vancouver's tallest buildings stand along the street, including the Hotel Vancouver, the Vancouver Block, the Georgian Towers, and the Burrard Building.

Vancouver has had Chinese residents since its founding. The first Chinese came to help build the railroad. Today, most of the Chinese restaurants, food shops, and other buildings stand in a few blocks along Pender Street. Chinatown has several red-brick buildings decorated in Chinese style. Dried fish and goods from Hong Kong crowd the store windows.

The four-mile stretch of the harbor east of Stanley Park, between the First and Second Narrows, includes the Ballantyne and Lapointe piers, owned by the National Harbors Board. Here also are railroad docks, a fish dock, grain jetties, and storage plants. Oil docks, a sugar-refinery wharf, and seven grain elevators may be found farther east. Tugs and scows use the small, shallow inlet of False Creek southwest of the main harbor.

Vancouver boasts a number of fine beaches. In summer, bathers crowd the sands of Spanish Banks at Point Grey, and Kitsilano Beach and English Bay near Stanley Park. One of the world's longest suspension bridges, the 1,550-foot-long Lions Gate Bridge, spans Burrard Inlet at the First Narrows to connect Stanley Park with West Vancouver. A lift bridge crosses the Second Narrows (see BRIDGE [Movable Bridges]). Another bridge opened there in 1960. Other Vancouver bridges include Burrard, Granville, and Oak Street bridges.

The People and Their Work

The People. About 70 of every 100 Vancouver residents were born in Canada, and about 20 in Great Britain. During the depression years of the 1930's, people flocked to Vancouver from the Prairie Provinces in search of jobs and a mild climate. A number of European refugees came to the city just before World War II. Other Europeans and a number of Canadians arrived in the postwar years. Vancouver has about 250 churches. The largest denominations are the United Church of Canada and the Church of England.

Work of the People. Nearly half of Vancouver's factory workers are employed in sawmills, pulp and paper mills, veneer and plywood plants, and sash and door-planing mills. Vast stands of cedar, fir, hemlock, spruce, and other evergreen trees near the city furnish these sprawling mills and factories with their raw materials. Other leading industries include fish processing, food preparation, petroleum refining, printing and publishing, shipbuilding, and meat packing.

Vancouver's 1,300 factories make it Canada's most important manufacturing center west of Ontario. They produce more than $540,000,000 worth of goods annually. Hydroelectric power, crude oil piped in from Edmonton, Alta., and natural gas from the Peace River district provide the city's industries with fuel and power. Vancouver serves as the headquarters for almost every large business in British Columbia.

Transportation and Communication

The Port. Vancouver's harbor covers about 48 square miles, and has over 50 berths for ocean-going vessels. More than 50 steamship lines have offices in Vancouver, and about 30 countries maintain consular agencies to care for their commercial interests. Vancouver serves as the main Pacific transshipment point for eastern Canadian cities. Its longshoremen handle about $60,000,000 worth of overseas trade each year. The port is also the center for an important northern coastal trade. Ships can use the ice-free port all year.

The City Hall in Vancouver, British Columbia, has simple, modern design. It towers above the city on Mount Pleasant.

Black Star

In winter, Vancouver takes over some of the trade of the Great Lakes, which are closed by ice.

Railroads. Vancouver serves as the western terminal of the Canadian National Railways system and the Canadian Pacific Railway. It also is the terminus of the provincially owned Pacific Great Eastern Railway. The Great Northern Railway connects the city with Seattle, Wash., and other United States cities.

Aviation. Nearly 850,000 passengers pass through Vancouver International Airport every year. Trans-Canada Airlines, Canadian Pacific Air Lines, Pacific Western Airlines, and a few U.S. lines serve the city.

Local Transportation. Vancouver has more than 1,000 miles of streets. The provincial government operates the city's transportation facilities.

Communication. Seven radio stations and two television stations operate there. Two daily newspapers are published in the city, the morning *Vancouver Province* and the evening *Vancouver Sun*.

Schools and Libraries

Schools. About 78,000 students attend Vancouver's 120 public schools. The city has a School of Art and the Vancouver Vocational Institute. About 30 private schools, several privately supported language schools, and the provincial school for blind and deaf children are in Vancouver. The city is the home of the University of British Columbia. Simon Fraser University is located in nearby Burnaby.

Libraries. The central public library on Burrard Street, which opened in 1957, houses the city archives. The university library also owns several outstanding collections.

What to See and Do in Vancouver

Vancouver's mild climate makes it attractive the year round for sports enthusiasts. Golfers play in both winter and summer. Some swimmers brave the waters of English Bay even in winter. Fishermen test their skills every month of the year. The nearby Coast Mountains challenge hikers, mountain climbers, and skiers. Two chair lifts operate all year.

The City Museum displays many excellent Indian relics. Totem poles stand in Stanley Park, in Hadden Park, and in Totem Grove on the university grounds. The Maritime Museum preserves the famed arctic exploring vessel *St. Roch*. In 1940, it sailed from Vancouver to Halifax, N.S., by way of the Arctic. The voyage took two years. When the ship returned to Vancouver in 86 days in 1944, it became the first vessel to make the voyage through the Arctic in both directions. In 1950, it proceeded on from Vancouver, sailed through the Panama Canal, and returned to Halifax. The *St. Roch* thus was the first ship to sail around the North American continent.

The city and the university maintain art galleries. Vancouver sponsors an annual summer international festival of music, art, and motion pictures.

Vancouver has 120 public parks, covering almost 3,000 acres. Stanley Park is probably the best known, with its tall trees, Theatre Under the Stars, cricket ground, and zoo. Queen Elizabeth Park features an arboretum. Exhibition Park is a sports and recreation center. Its stadium was built for the British Empire Games of 1954. The annual Pacific National Exhibition, with agricultural and industrial displays, takes place nearby during the first week of September.

History and Government

Early Days. Captain George Vancouver, a British explorer, sailed into Burrard Inlet in 1792. He encountered Spanish explorers near Point Grey. But no one attempted settlement of the area for many years. In 1865, lumbermen discovered great timber stands in the region. They built Hastings Mill, and began large-scale lumbering operations. A townsite named Granville was laid out in 1870.

Railway Terminus. In 1884, the Canadian Pacific Railway chose a site on Burrard Inlet as the western terminus of the first transcontinental Canadian railroad. It named the site Vancouver, after the explorer. A fire destroyed most of the city shortly after its incorporation. But the first train had reached Vancouver from eastern Canada by 1887, and the city began its rapid growth. By 1891, the Canadian Pacific Steamship Company's ships were competing with ships from Seattle for the transpacific trade of northern North America. In 1904, the Great Northern Railway reached Vancouver from Seattle, linking it with transportation centers in the United States.

The Great Boom. Between 1900 and 1910, job opportunities made Vancouver the fastest-growing city in Canada. The salmon-canning and lumber-manufacturing industries created many of these jobs. Canadians, Americans, Englishmen, Chinese, Japanese, and East Indians poured into the city. Vancouver suffered a setback in 1913 with the collapse of a real-estate boom. But the opening of the Panama Canal, which lowered water-freight rates, helped restore prosperity. A great expansion took place in the 1920's as the lumber and fishing industries grew, and prairie wheat began to be shipped from the Pacific Coast to South America, Southeast Asia, and Europe. The city suffered severely during the depression of the 1930's, when it attracted unemployed persons from the Prairie Provinces, and experienced several violent demonstrations against the federal government. By the early 1930's, Vancouver was Canada's third largest city.

World War II brought great prosperity as shipbuilding and wartime industries expanded. Vancouver served as headquarters for the coastal defense staffs of the Canadian Army, Navy, and Air Force.

Recent Developments. Vancouver changed rapidly during the late 1940's and the 1950's. The city launched a great building program. Tall apartment buildings appeared, settlement stretched across Burrard Inlet, and new shopping centers sprang up. Old office buildings in the downtown area were replaced by modern ones, some decorated with murals or mosaics by local artists. The British Columbia Electric Company erected one of the most beautiful office buildings in Canada on Burrard Street. This 21-story, glass-walled building gleams like a beacon of light at night. Green and white glass mosaic tile covers some of the areas on the lower floors.

Vancouver has a mayor-council form of government. The people elect the mayor and 10 aldermen to two-year terms.

MARGARET A. ORMSBY

VANCOUVER

VANCOUVER, Wash. (pop. 32,464; alt. 75 ft.), is a port on the Columbia River, directly across from Portland, Ore. (see WASHINGTON [political map]). It is the state's seventh largest city and the seat of Clark County. Its mills produce lumber, veneer, plywood, wood pulp, and paper. Power from the nearby Bonneville Dam aids in the production of aluminum. The city also has food-processing plants. Vancouver is an important port. Its major exports include grain and lumber.

The oldest city in the state, Vancouver was founded by the Hudson's Bay Company in 1824. Captain George Vancouver, for whom the city is named, had entered the mouth of the Columbia River on an exploration trip in 1792. The old trading post site now lies in Vancouver Barracks, an army post established in 1849. Vancouver was incorporated as a city in 1857. It has a council-manager government.   HOWARD J. CRITCHFIELD

VANCOUVER, GEORGE (1758-1798), was a British explorer. Vancouver Island and cities in the state of Washington and in British Columbia, Canada, are named after him.

He was born at King's Lynn, Norfolk, England. He entered the navy as an able seaman at the age of 13. His early experiences were on Captain James Cook's two last voyages (see COOK, JAMES). Vancouver served as a midshipman on the last voyage.

An incident concerning Nootka Sound, off the west coast of Vancouver Island, threatened war between Great Britain and Spain, and it was felt that a naval force was needed on the spot. Vancouver was ordered there, and he sailed in April, 1791. He sailed by way of the Cape of Good Hope, Australia, and New Zealand, following Cook's example. He made valuable maps of the coasts of these areas. He reached the American continent in 1792. Vancouver participated in certain formalities involving Nootka Sound, and then sailed through Juan de Fuca Strait and around Vancouver Island, discovering the Gulf of Georgia on the way. He surveyed the Pacific Coast north of San Francisco for the first time. He returned

Brown Bros.
George Vancouver

to England via Cape Horn in 1795, and wrote his report on the voyage. His book, *A Voyage of Discovery to the North Pacific Ocean and Round the World in the Years 1790-1795,* was published in 1798.   WILLIAM P. BRANDON

VANCOUVER ISLAND is the largest island on the Pacific Coast of North America, and an important part of the Canadian province of British Columbia. Vancouver Island extends for 285 miles along the southwestern coast of Canada and is from 40 to 80 miles wide. Victoria, the largest city on Vancouver Island, is the capital of British Columbia. The chief towns on the island are Nanaimo and Port Alberni. The total population of Vancouver Island is 290,835.

Location, Size, and Surface Features. Vancouver Island is separated from the mainland of British Colum-

Vancouver Island shelters the southern coast of British Columbia. The island is about half the size of West Virginia.

bia by Queen Charlotte Strait, Johnstone Strait, and the Strait of Georgia. Juan de Fuca Strait lies south of the island. Vancouver Island covers an area of 13,049 square miles (see BRITISH COLUMBIA [physical map]). The island is the southern end of a partly sunken mountain chain, the Island, or Vancouver, Range. The tops of the range rise sharply from the Pacific Ocean to heights of 5,000 to 7,000 feet. Dangerous reefs and small, rocky islands are common along the western shore of the island. There are many winding, fiordlike bays, which are the valleys of the sunken range. Quatsino, Nootka, and Barkley sounds reach into the heart of the island. The eastern shore is less rugged and broken, and has a few level stretches.

Vancouver Island has the mildest climate in Canada because of the Japan Current. There is little winter in the southern part around Victoria, but in the northern and western mountains the winters are often severe.

The Island's Resources. The slopes of the mountains on Vancouver Island are covered with splendid fir, cedar, and hemlock forests. Lumbering is the island's chief industry. The island has several large pulp mills, sawmills, and plywood plants. Farms are cultivated in the valleys. The southeast coast produces many berries and flower bulbs. Excellent game fishing attracts many tourists to the island.

History. The Spanish explorer Juan Perez first visited Vancouver Island in about 1774. But it was not explored until 1792, when George Vancouver sailed around it. The island is named after him. Later the United States claimed the island, and the territory on the mainland north to 54°40'. But the United States surrendered its claims to Great Britain in 1846 by the terms of the Oregon Boundary Treaty. The first settlement on Vancouver Island was made in 1843, when the Hudson's Bay Company built Fort Victoria. In 1849 Vancouver Island became a British colony, and in 1866 it was united with mainland settlements to form British Columbia.   RODERICK HAIG-BROWN

See also JUAN DE FUCA, STRAIT OF; NANAIMO; NOOTKA INDIANS; VANCOUVER, GEORGE; VICTORIA (B.C.).

VANDAL. The Vandals were a warlike Germanic people who lived in northeastern Germany between the Oder and Vistula rivers in the early Christian Era. They moved south during the barbarian invasions of Europe and Africa. They were hardly more savage than the other invaders, but their name is still applied to people who destroy property recklessly or carelessly. In A.D. 406, the Vandals crossed the Rhine River and attacked the cities of Gaul. Later they fought the Goths and Romans in Spain.

The Vandals reached the peak of their power under their cruel king Genseric (or Gaiseric). In 429, Genseric and his people invaded North Africa. By 439, they had won all Roman North Africa, including Carthage. The Vandals were fanatical Arian Christians, and harshly persecuted the orthodox Christians there. Genseric, aided by a powerful pirate fleet which he had built, terrorized Rome and the Mediterranean area for 50 years. In 455, he captured Rome. The Vandals pillaged the city, but Genseric prevented his men from completely destroying it. See GENSERIC.

Genseric died in 477, but his son Huneric continued to raid and plunder the lands around the Mediterranean. Belisarius, a Byzantine general who served under the Emperor Justinian, overthrew the Vandal kingdom in the 530's. No trace remained.   WILLIAM C. BARK

VANDALIA COURT HOUSE. See ILLINOIS (Places to Visit).

VAN DE GRAAFF GENERATOR, also known as an *electrostatic generator,* is a device for building up a high

The First Van de Graaff Generator was built by Robert J. Van de Graaff at the Massachusetts Institute of Technology in 1931. Physicists use these atom smashers for atomic research.
Massachusetts Institute of Technology

electrical charge. It is a source of charged particles that may be used for atom smashing. In general, this generator is used to boost protons and other nuclear particles to energy of about 10 million electron volts (10 Mev.). The chief value of the machine is that narrow beams of protons of known energies can be produced. These beams are used to study nuclear forces.

Robert J. Van de Graaff made the first generator of this kind at the Massachusetts Institute of Technology. In the generator, a continuous belt of an insulating material moves past a source of negative electricity. This source sprays electrons on the belt. The belt then goes into a hollow metal dome where a fine metallic brush moves the electrons onto the dome surface. When the charge at the top of the dome is high enough, electrically charged particles are hurled at targets at the bottom of the generator.

Van de Graaff machines work at higher energy when they are enclosed in a pressure vessel. To prevent leakage of the electricity from the accelerator, a gas such as Freon, or air under pressure as high as 150 pounds per square inch, is put in the vessel. Electrostatic generators are widely used because they generate a constant supply of voltage.   RALPH E. LAPP

See also ATOM SMASHER.

VANDEGRIFT, ALEXANDER ARCHER (1887-   ), served as commandant of the United States Marine Corps from 1944 to 1947. In 1942, he took command of the First Marine Division and led it in the invasion of Guadalcanal (see WORLD WAR II [Guadalcanal]). He directed the landing on Bougainville in 1943, as commander of the First Marine Amphibious Corps. Named Marine Corps commandant on Jan. 1, 1944, Vandegrift became a permanent general, the first Marine officer to hold this rank.

He was born at Charlottesville, Va., and attended the University of Virginia. He received an appointment as a second lieutenant in the Marine Corps in 1909, and saw service in Haiti, Nicaragua, and Mexico. He retired in 1949.   DONALD W. MITCHELL

VANDENBERG, ARTHUR HENDRICK (1884-1951), was an American statesman and political leader. He was appointed United States Senator from Michigan in 1928. He was elected to the Senate a few months later and was re-elected in 1934, 1940, and 1946. He became a Republican leader in the Senate, and was active in molding United States foreign policy.

Vandenberg served as a United States representative at the United Nations conference in San Francisco in 1945. The next year he was a delegate to the Paris Peace conference. In 1947, Vandenberg became president pro tem of the Senate. He gave up his Senate duties in 1950 because of illness. Vandenberg was born in Grand Rapids, Mich., and was graduated from the University of Michigan.   F. JAY TAYLOR

VANDENBERG, HOYT SANFORD (1899-1954), served as chief of staff of the United States Air Force from 1948 to 1953. He was graduated from the United States Military Academy in 1923 and entered the Air Service. In 1942 and 1943, during World War II, he served as chief of staff of the Twelfth Air Force in North Africa. Vandenberg then became deputy commander in chief of the Allied Expeditionary Air Force, the great

VANDENBERG AIR FORCE BASE

American-British tactical air force which supported General Dwight D. Eisenhower in the 1944 European invasion. In August, 1944, Vandenberg took command of the United States Ninth Air Force, the largest of the American air forces in World War II. In 1947 he became vice-chief of staff of the United States Air Force. He was born in Milwaukee, Wis.   ALFRED GOLDBERG

VANDENBERG AIR FORCE BASE, Calif., is the training center for U.S. Air Force ballistic missile crews. Space satellites are launched from the base and from nearby Point Arguello. The base covers over 64,000 acres and lies about 10 miles northwest of Lompoc. It was established as Camp Cooke, an army post, in 1941. It became an air force base in 1956 and was renamed for General Hoyt S. Vandenberg.   RICHARD M. SKINNER

VANDERBILT is the name of an American family prominent in business and finance.

Cornelius Vanderbilt (1794-1877) founded the family fortune. At 16 he owned a small vessel that sailed between Staten Island and New York City. By 1850 he became the leading steamboat owner in the country, breaking down rivalry and securing a monopoly. Called the "Commodore," he started steamship lines to Europe and a line to San Francisco with an overland route through Nicaragua. Shipping interests netted him more than $1 million when he sold out. He began to invest in railroads when he was 70, and owned through lines as far west as Chicago by 1873. He became president of the New York Central Railroad. When he died, Vanderbilt left a fortune of about $100 million. He was born on May 27, 1794, at Staten Island, N.Y.

William Henry Vanderbilt (1821-1885) was the son of Cornelius Vanderbilt. His father bought him a small farm because he had poor health. It was successful, and his father made him manager of the Staten Island Railroad. He became president of the New York Central at his father's death. He acquired other railroads and extended the Vanderbilt system. He was born on May 8, 1821, at Brunswick, N.J.

Cornelius Vanderbilt II (1843-1899), son of William Henry Vanderbilt, served as first vice-president of the New York Central and later as chairman of the board. He was born on Nov. 27, 1843, at Staten Island, N.Y.

William Kissam Vanderbilt (1849-1920), another son of William Henry Vanderbilt, became a second vice-president of the New York Central, and helped found Vanderbilt Clinic in New York City. He was born on Dec. 12, 1849, at Staten Island, N.Y.

Cornelius Vanderbilt

Cornelius Vanderbilt III (1873-1942), son of Cornelius Vanderbilt II, developed several devices used in railroading. He was a colonel in World War II and a director of railroad and banking companies. He was born on Sept. 5, 1873, in New York City.

Harold Stirling Vanderbilt (1884-   ), son of William Kissam Vanderbilt, became a director of the New York Central. He also became a well-known contract bridge expert and a prominent yachtsman. He was born on July 6, 1884, at Oakdale, N.Y.

Cornelius Vanderbilt, Jr. (1898-   ), son of Cornelius Vanderbilt III, became a well-known reporter, columnist, and author. He was born on April 30, 1898, in New York City.   HAROLD F. WILLIAMSON

VANDERBILT CUP RACE. See AUTOMOBILE RACING.

VANDERBILT MANSION. See NEW YORK (Places to Visit).

VANDERBILT UNIVERSITY is a coeducational, privately controlled school in Nashville, Tenn. It has a college of arts and science, a graduate school, and schools of divinity, engineering, law, medicine, and nursing. The university cooperates with the George Peabody College and Scarritt College so that students may receive credit for work taken in the other institutions. Vanderbilt was chartered as Central University in 1872. Its name was changed to Vanderbilt University in 1873 in honor of Cornelius Vanderbilt, benefactor of the school. For enrollment, see UNIVERSITIES AND COLLEGES (table).   ROBERT A. McGAW

Uffizi Gallery

Hugo van der Goes combined vivid realism with brilliant colors in his famous *Adoration of the Shepherds*.

VAN DER GOES, *vahn dur KOOS,* **HUGO** (1440?-1482), was the leading Flemish painter of his generation. He was influenced by Jan van Eyck and Roger van der Weyden, earlier Flemish artists. But he surpassed them in the earthy solidity of his figures and in his greater understanding of human psychology.

A few of van der Goes' pictures prove him one of the best portrait artists of his time, but his main contribution to Flemish art consists of several large altarpieces. Among them is the *Adoration of the Shepherds*, painted for an Italian merchant who lived in Bruges, Belgium. It is famous for the vivid portrayal of three adoring shepherds and the charming heads of the merchant's children. His last work is the *Death of the Virgin*, an unforgettable study of human pathos.

Little is known about van der Goes' youth. In 1467, he was accepted as a master in the artists' guild at Ghent. About 1478, he entered a monastery near Brussels as a lay brother.   JULIUS S. HELD

VAN DER WAALS, JOHANNES DIDERIK (1837-1923), a Dutch theoretical physicist, became famous for his work on the behavior of liquids and gases. He won the 1910 Nobel prize in physics for developing the famous equation of state which bears his name. The equation takes into account the forces between the molecules of the gas. Van der Waals was born at Leiden, The Netherlands, on Nov. 23, 1837. He served as professor of physics at Leiden from 1877 until his retirement in 1907. R. T. ELLICKSON

VAN DER WEYDEN, *vahn der VIE dun*, **ROGER** (1399?-1464), was a Flemish painter, and a founder of the Flemish movement in painting. He is celebrated for the courtly dignity of his figures, his skillful manner of composition, and his subtle observation of human emotion. He was also a keen student of nature, and painted everything down to the smallest detail in his panels. With an unfailing sense for the beauty of line and the gracefulness of motion, he created masterpieces which influenced Flemish, German, and French art for

Museo del Prado

Descent from the Cross by Roger van der Weyden shows the tragic pathos which marked the works of the Flemish painter.

many years. Some of Van der Weyden's works are lost, but many of his paintings are still preserved. These include *The Madonna with St. Luke*, *The Last Judgment*, and the *Adoration of the Magi*, a *triptych*, or a picture in three panels.

Van der Weyden was born in Tournai, Belgium. He moved to Brussels in the 1430's, where he was appointed "painter of the town." In 1450 he made a trip to Italy. He received commissions from Duke Philip the Good of Burgundy and members of his court. Van der Weyden's portraits preserved the haughty manners and proud bearing of the nobles who were in the court of Duke Philip. JULIUS S. HELD

VAN DEVANTER, WILLIS (1859-1941), served as an associate justice of the Supreme Court of the United States from 1911 to 1937. His opinions as a Supreme Court justice were consistently conservative. He also served between 1903 and 1910 as a federal circuit judge. Van Devanter was born in Marion, Ind., and was

graduated from DePauw University and the Cincinnati Law School. He practiced law in Indiana and Wyoming, and served as chief justice of the supreme court of Wyoming in 1889 and 1890. H. G. REUSCHLEIN

VAN DIEMEN'S LAND. See TASMANIA (History).

VAN DINE, S. S. (1888-1939), is the pen name of an American author and critic known for his detective stories. They include *The Canary Murder Case* (1927), *The Bishop Murder Case* (1929), and *The Powwow Murder Case* (1932), featuring his detective hero, Philo Vance. He was also an art and literary critic for newspapers and magazines. He was born WILLARD HUNTINGTON WRIGHT in Charlottesville, Va., and wrote several books under this name. He was educated at Pomona College in California, at Harvard University, and also in Europe. FREDERICK J. HOFFMAN

VAN DOREN is the family name of two American writers, brothers.

Carl Clinton Van Doren (1885-1950) won the 1939 Pulitzer prize in biography for *Benjamin Franklin*. It is a biography from which one can learn how to write biographies. He wrote *The Great Rehearsal* (1948), an account of the drafting and ratification of the Constitution of the United States. He edited letters of Benjamin Franklin and his sister, Jane Mecom, and published *Jane Mecom* (1950). Van Doren was editor of The Literary Guild from 1926 to 1934, and of The Living Library from 1946 until his death. He was born in Hope, Ill., and was graduated from the University of Illinois. He taught at Columbia University. EDWIN H. CADY

Mark Van Doren (1894-   ) is a distinguished poet, critic, biographer, and fiction writer. He won the 1940 Pulitzer prize in poetry for *Collected Poems*. His other poetry includes *Collected and New Poetry, 1924-1963* (1963) and *Narrative Poems* (1964). Van Doren's *Shakespeare* (1939) was widely praised. He edited *Anthology of World Poetry* (1928) and *The Oxford Book of American Prose* (1932). His fiction works include *Nobody Say a Word and Other Stories* (1953), *Home with Hazel and Other Stories* (1957), and *Collected Stories* (1962).

He was born in Hope, Ill., and was graduated from the University of Illinois in 1914. He received his Ph.D. from Columbia University, where he began teaching in 1920. He served as literary editor of the *Nation* magazine from 1924 to 1928. Van Doren defended humanistic studies and helped found the Great Books movement. WILLIAM VAN O'CONNOR

Carl Van Doren
Vorst

Mark Van Doren
Champaign-Urbana Courier

Vandyke's Painting, The Children of Charles I, shows the rich, warm style of this Flemish painter's work. He also created an atmosphere of elegance around his subjects from high court society. This is one of the many paintings Vandyke did after Charles I of England appointed him painter of the court.

William II, Prince of Orange, is one of the many Vandyke portraits which are prized museum pieces. His use of color shows the influence of another great Flemish painter, Peter Paul Rubens. Vandyke set the style for later portrait painters with his flattering portraits of aristocratic people.

VAN DRUTEN, *DROO t'n,* **JOHN** (1901-1957), an American dramatist, became well known for his comedies and his sensitive, sympathetic development of character, particularly of women. His important plays include *There's Always Juliet* (1931), *The Distaff Side* (1933), *Old Acquaintance* (1940), *The Damask Cheek* (1942), *The Voice of the Turtle* (1943), *Bell, Book, and Candle* (1950), and *I Am a Camera* (1951). He wrote several novels and an autobiography, *The Widening Circle* (1957). He also directed several plays. Van Druten was born in London, England.   GEORGE FREEDLEY

VANDYKE, or **VAN DYCK, SIR ANTHONY** (1599-1641), a Flemish painter, gained fame for the many portraits he painted of the Flemish, Italian, and English society of his time. No other artist equaled him in combining a good likeness with subtle flattery. One of his famous portraits, *Charles I,* appears in color in the PAINTING article. Vandyke also painted many religious and some mythological pictures noted for their muted but softly glowing colors. His paintings include *The Taking of Christ, Rinaldo and Armida, Portrait of Isabella Brant,* and *The Children of Charles I.*

Anthony Vandyke

Vandyke was born in Antwerp, Belgium, the son of a rich silk dealer. He studied with Hendrik van Balen, a prominent painter, but became an independent artist when he was 16. He assisted Peter Paul Rubens with some large commissions until about 1620. Rubens strongly influenced Vandyke (see RUBENS, PETER PAUL).

In 1620 Vandyke went to England. He traveled to Italy in 1621, and became active in many cities, including Palermo and Genoa. The portraits he painted of members of the Genoese nobility belong to his finest works. His best religious pictures were done after his return to Antwerp in 1627.

In 1632 Vandyke went to London, where King Charles I appointed him painter of the court. Vandyke's English portraits form a valuable record of the elegant costumes worn in the court of Charles I. Vandyke was so much in demand that he gave clients hourly appointments and hired assistants to prepare his canvases. He was buried in St. Paul's Cathedral in London.

See also CHARLES (I) of England (picture).

VAN DYKE, HENRY (1852-1933), was an American Presbyterian clergyman, educator, novelist, essayist, poet, and religious writer. His writing is delicate, vivid, and full of idealism, as in his *Companionable Books* (1922). He wrote *The Poetry of Tennyson* (1889), *The Story of the Other Wise Man* (1896), *Fisherman's Luck* (1899), *The Blue Flower* (1902), and *Collected Poems* (1911). Van Dyke was born at Germantown, Pa. From 1913 to 1916, he served as United States Minister to The Netherlands and Luxembourg.   HARRY H. CLARK

VÄNERN. See LAKE VÄNERN.

VAN EYCK, *ike,* **JAN** (1380?-1440), is considered the founder of the early Flemish movement in painting. The great *Ghent Altarpiece* (1432) is largely his work, though it may have been begun by his brother Hubert van Eyck (1366?-1426). It is a *triptych* (picture in three panels), painted two stories high. It contains hundreds of figures, some sparkling in rich costumes

222

Van Eyck's Ghent Altarpiece contains a detailed allegory called *The Adoration of the Lamb, below*. The Virgin Mary, Christ enthroned, and John the Baptist appear in the upper panels.

and armor and others dressed in the plain colors of hermits and pilgrims. The figures of Adam and Eve are especially famous because they show keen observation of the human body. In one panel, *top left*, Van Eyck painted the Madonna as the Queen of Heaven, wearing a crown and jeweled costume.

In all his work, Van Eyck was a master of detail. He did not invent oil painting, but he greatly perfected its technique. His colors have greater delicacy and shine with more subtle light effects than those used by previous artists. He painted some striking portraits, among them the wedding portrait, *The Marriage of Giovanni Arnolfini and Giovanna Cenami*, which appears in color in the PAINTING article.

Van Eyck was born at Maaseyck, The Netherlands. He later lived at The Hague and at Bruges, Belgium.

VAN FLEET, JAMES ALWARD (1892-   ), an American military leader, trained the armed forces which checked Communist aggression in Greece and Korea. In 1948, President Harry S. Truman sent General Van Fleet to Greece to train and equip the Greek forces. From 1951 to 1953, Van Fleet served in Korea. He commanded the United States Eighth Army, which included ground units contributed by other United Nations members. He helped train 10 South Korean divisions to fight beside other UN troops in Korea.

Van Fleet was born in Coytesville, N.J. He was graduated from the U.S. Military Academy in 1915. He commanded a machine gun battalion in France during

World War I. During World War II, he led the Eighth Infantry Regiment of the Fourth Infantry Division in the Normandy landing in 1944. He later commanded the Fourth and Ninetieth Infantry Divisions and the U.S. Third Corps. He retired in 1953 with the rank of general, but was recalled to active duty in 1961 to help train army guerrilla fighters.   MAURICE MATLOFF

VAN GOGH, *van GO*, **VINCENT** (1853-1890), was a Dutch painter whose tragic life and brilliant canvases have made him almost a legend. Intense, difficult, and unhappy, he spent his life searching for an emotional relief he never really found. From his deeply religious family, he inherited a desire to serve his fellow man. After disappointments in both love and religious ministry, he turned to art. His early work is dark and thickly painted, but has a massive solidity. *The Potato Eaters* (1885) is the masterpiece of this early period.

Van Gogh was born on Mar. 30, 1853, in Zundert, The Netherlands. He was supported for most of his life by his devoted brother Theo, an art dealer. Under the influence of the brilliant coloring of Impressionism, Van Gogh's palette soon grew light and even gay. His brush began to form thick linear strokes, which give an unusual animation to the surfaces of his pictures. Van Gogh moved to Arles in southern France. He had severe mental disturbances, however, and after a few months he entered the sanitarium at St. Remy. His art, now expressionistic, expressed his inner reactions to the world through turning, swirling brush strokes, thick paint, and brilliant color. *The Starry Night* (1889) appears in color in the PAINTING article.

In 1890 Van Gogh was placed in the care of Dr. Gachet, a friend of many leading painters. Van Gogh committed suicide in July.   JOSEPH C. SLOANE

See also EXPRESSIONISM; FLOWER (color picture, Flowers in Art); LETTER WRITING (picture, Some Famous Letters).

Van Gogh Painted This Self-Portrait in the 1880's.

VANGUARD

VANGUARD. See SOLAR ENERGY (picture); SPACE TRAVEL (Artificial Satellites).

VAN HISE, CHARLES RICHARD (1857-1918), was an American geologist and educator. He was a member of the United States Geological Survey from 1883 to 1900, specializing on ancient rocks of the Lake Superior region. From 1903 to 1918 he served as president of the University of Wisconsin. His book, *Conservation of Natural Resources in the United States* (1910), was important in this field. Van Hise was born in Fulton, Wis. He taught geology at the University of Wisconsin and at the University of Chicago.   CARROLL LANE FENTON

VAN HORNE, SIR WILLIAM CORNELIUS (1843-1915), was a railroad executive of great ability. He became, in turn, general manager, vice-president, and president of the Canadian Pacific Railway. It was mainly his driving force that made possible the prompt construction of that railroad. His executive skill enabled the company to pull through its difficult early years. Van Horne was born near Joliet, Ill.   W. R. WILLOUGHBY

VANIER, GEORGES PHILIAS (1888-   ), became Governor-General of Canada in 1959. He was the first French-Canadian and the first Roman Catholic to hold the office. Vanier won fame as a soldier and diplomat. He lost a leg while fighting in France in World War I. Later he became a major general. Vanier served as Canadian ambassador to France from 1945 until he retired from the foreign service in 1953. He was born in Montreal.

VANILLA is the name of a group of climbing orchids. The vanilla extract which is used to flavor chocolate, ice cream, pastry, and candy comes from these plants. The vanilla vine has been cultivated in Mexico for hundreds of years. This type of vanilla has been introduced into other tropical areas. Madagascar, together with the Comoro and Réunion Islands, now produces over three-fourths of the world's supply. Another variety grows on the island of Tahiti in the South Pacific Ocean.

The vanilla vine has little rootlets by which the plant attaches itself to trees. The cultivated plant lives for about 10 years. It produces its first crop at the end of three years.

The plant produces a fruit in the shape of a cylindrical pod or *bean*, from 5 to 10 inches long. The fruit has an oily black pulp that contains a large number of tiny black seeds. The pods are gathered when they are a yellow-green in color. Then the curing, or drying, process takes place. This process shrinks the bean, turns it a rich, chocolate-brown color, and gives it the flavor and aroma of vanilla as we know it.

Vanilla extract is prepared by a complicated and expensive process. The beans are chopped into small pieces and then percolated with alcohol and water. Scientists have developed many substitutes for vanilla flavor because of its high cost. But no imitation product can reproduce the many natural components that give pure vanilla its delicate flavor.

Scientific Classification. Vanilla is in the orchid family, *Orchidaceae*. The vine of Mexico and Madagascar is genus *Vanilla*, species *V. fragrans*.   G. W. TAYLOR

A Wild Vanilla Vine in Mexico Is Inspected by a Workman.

Beans of the Wild Vanilla Vine
Visual Education Service; New York Botanical Garden

VANITY FAIR, "a Novel Without a Hero," was written by William Makepeace Thackeray in 1847 and 1848. Instead of a hero, it has two heroines, Becky Sharp and Amelia Sedley. The two are friends but different in character. Becky, an orphan, is clever and scheming, and determined to get ahead in the world. Amelia, whose parents are rich, is gentle and good, but rather dull. Thackeray contrasts their lives and shows how both illustrate the vanity of social pretense. Part of the action takes place in Brussels during the Battle of Waterloo, and gives a vivid impression of the excitement and confusion.   GEORGE A. WICKES

See also THACKERAY, WILLIAM MAKEPEACE.

VAN LEEUWENHOEK, ANTON. See LEEUWENHOEK, ANTON VAN.

VAN LEYDEN, *LIE dun,* **LUCAS** (1494?-1533), a Dutch engraver, was also a painter, draftsman, and designer of woodcuts. He produced an astonishingly large number of works. Born in The Netherlands, he was influenced by the German, Albrecht Dürer, and the Italian, Marcantonio Raimondi. Most of Van Leyden's engravings have Biblical subjects, but some show the life of his time. Among his paintings are *The Last Judgment* and *Moses Striking the Rock.*   JULIUS S. HELD

VAN LOON, *van LOHN,* **HENDRIK WILLEM** (1882-1944), an American historian, biographer, journalist, and lecturer, won a 1922 Newbery medal for his history of the world, *The Story of Mankind* (1921). He wrote and illustrated many other works for children, and they were equally popular with grownups. They include *Ships* (1935); *Ancient Man* (1920); *The Story of the Bible* (1923); *Tolerance* (1925); *America* (1927); *Van Loon's Geography* (1932); *The Arts* (1937); *Van Loon's Lives* (1942); and *Thomas Jefferson* (1943).

Van Loon served as a newspaper correspondent in Russia during the Revolution of 1905, in various European countries in 1906 and during World War I. During World War II he wrote material and broadcasted for the United States and for The Netherlands.

Harris & Ewing
Hendrik Van Loon

Van Loon was born in Rotterdam, The Netherlands, and came to the United States at the age of twenty. He was graduated from Cornell University and from the University of Munich.   MERLE CURTI

VAN RENSSELAER, *van REHN suh ler,* was the name of a family of Dutch landowners in New York state.

Kiliaen Van Rensselaer (1595-1644) was one of the leading colonizers of New Netherland, later the English colony of New York. In 1629, the Dutch West India Company authorized large grants of land in New Netherland to company members who promised to colonize their lands. As a result, a class of great landowners, called *patroons,* developed. Kiliaen Van Rensselaer was the greatest of them. He established the huge manor of Rensselaerswyck, which included two counties and part of a third on both banks of the Hudson River south of Albany. Van Rensselaer, a wealthy diamond merchant of Amsterdam, where he was born, was suc-

cessful because he invested much money and supplied his farmers with cattle, horses, tools, and mills. But he never visited his colony on the Hudson.

Stephen Van Rensselaer (1764-1839), an American army officer and politician, was the eighth and last of the Dutch patroons of Rensselaerswyck. He was lieutenant governor of New York and a U.S. Representative. He helped bring about construction of the Erie and Champlain canals. He served as a major general in the War of 1812, and was chancellor of New York University from 1835 to 1839. He was born in New York City.   IAN C. C. GRAHAM

VAN'T HOFF, *vahnt HAHF,* **JACOBUS HENDRICUS** (1852-1911), was a Dutch chemist who received the first Nobel prize for chemistry in 1901. He discovered the laws of chemical dynamics and osmosis. He was the first to note that the properties of solutions depend upon the number, not the kind, of dissolved particles. He also showed that the simple gas laws apply to dilute solutions.

Van't Hoff also did fundamental work in stereochemistry. This branch of chemistry is concerned with the arrangement of atoms in the spaces of the molecules. Van't Hoff was born in Rotterdam. While teaching at the Prussian Academy of Sciences in Berlin, he did important research on the formation and decomposition of double salts.   K. L. KAUFMAN

VAN WIE, VIRGINIA. See GOLF (Golf Immortals).

VAN WINKLE, RIP. See RIP VAN WINKLE.

VANZETTI, BARTOLOMEO. See SACCO-VANZETTI CASE.

VAPOR, *VAY pur,* in physics, is the term applied to the gaseous state into which solids and liquids pass when they are heated. In a technical sense, both steam and oxygen are vapors. It is customary, however, to make a distinction between gases and vapors. Gases retain the form of air at all pressures at ordinary temperatures. Vapors resume their liquid or solid state under high pressure at ordinary temperatures. The process of converting a substance from solid or liquid form into a vapor is called *vaporization. Evaporation* and *boiling* of liquids are forms of vaporization. In evaporation, the change to a vaporous condition takes place slowly. In boiling, it occurs very rapidly. The formation of vapor directly from a solid state is called *sublimation.* Vaporization in connection with atmospheric conditions bears an important relation to climate. Water vapor is always present in the air. When condensed under varying conditions, water vapor forms clouds, dew, rain, and snow. See also BOILING POINT; EVAPORATION; GAS.   LOUIS MARICK

VAPOR LAMP is a source of electric light that uses a vapor or gas, rather than a wire, to produce light. The first vapor lamp consisted of a tube filled with vapor and a small pool of mercury at one end. When the tube was tipped, the mercury rolled through the gas, causing it to glow. Modern vapor lamps are rather short and stocky. They are used outdoors for street and highway lighting. A short quartz tube inside a larger glass tube causes the gas between them to glow. Different gases give various colors. For example, sodium gives yellow or orange light. Fluorescent lights are a form of vapor lamp.   KARL A. STALEY

See also ELECTRIC LIGHT.

VAPOR LOCK occurs in a gasoline engine when some of the gasoline boils in the fuel-supply system. Excessive heating of the engine may cause boiling, or *vaporization*, of the fuel. This reduces the amount of fuel pumped to the engine, because vapor takes up more space than liquid. The engine then runs erratically or stops until the vaporized gasoline cools and turns to liquid. Vapor locks occur most frequently during long, steep climbs on hot days, or when slowing suddenly after a hard drive. See also FUEL INJECTION. WILLARD L. ROGERS

VARA. See WEIGHTS AND MEASURES (Miscellaneous Weights and Measures).

VARANGIAN. See VIKING (The Swedish Vikings).

VARDAMAN, JAMES KIMBLE (1861-1930), a Mississippi Democrat, served as governor from 1904 to 1908 and as a United States Senator from 1913 to 1919. As governor, Vardaman stopped the practice of leasing state convicts to work for corporations and individuals. As a senator, he opposed the United States' entry into World War I, and was one of six senators who voted against the declaration of war on Germany in 1917. Vardaman was born near Edna, Tex., and moved to Mississippi in 1868. CHARLOTTE CAPERS

VARDON, HARRY. See GOLF (Golf Immortals).

VARE, GLENNA C. See GOLF (Golf Immortals).

VARGAS, *VAHR gus,* **GETÚLIO DORNELLAS** (1883-1954), served as president of Brazil from 1930 to 1945 and from 1950 to 1954. He was the governor of Rio Grande do Sul for two years before he seized the presidency in 1930 with a group of reforming army officers. Vargas was forced out by an army ultimatum in 1945, but he was elected president again in 1950. He was born in São Borja on April 19, 1883. He committed suicide when the army demanded his resignation again in 1954. HAROLD E. DAVIS

See also BRAZIL (History; picture).

VARIABLE STAR. See STAR (The Changing, or Variable, Stars).

VARIATION. See EVOLUTION (Variation and Change; The Cause of Variations); COMPASS (Variation).

VARIATIONS, in music, consist of repeating some elements of a musical idea while altering others. This technique is the principle behind the development of musical ideas, and gives variety while retaining coherence.

Composers of all periods have freely used the variation technique. Early variations used by classic composers usually repeated the melody clearly, changing the accompaniment and sometimes the harmonies. Variations became more complicated in the romantic music of the 1800's. In this and later music, it is often difficult to see any resemblance between variations and the original theme. GRANT FLETCHER

See also MUSIC (Variation Form).

VARICELLA. See CHICKEN POX.

VARICOSE VEIN, *VAR ih kohs,* is a swollen vein caused by some body condition that interferes with the flow of blood toward the heart. Veins in the legs often become varicose, especially when a person stands a great deal. Heart and liver diseases, gout, pregnancy, abdominal tumors, and tight garters are among the various other causes of varicose veins.

In advanced cases of varicose veins, bluish knotty lumps form along the vein. The patient feels consider-able pain in the leg. The chief danger is that the vein will burst, and cause hemorrhage. The diseased veins can also keep the tissues from getting enough nourishment. Water may collect under the skin and cause dropsy. Then the leg is likely to develop ulcers.

Physicians recommend wearing an elastic stocking or bandage, which will support the varicose vein with steady pressure. Physicians often inject the veins with drugs that tend to shrink them or they may remove the veins by surgery. A disorder known as *piles* is varicose veins of the rectum. HYMAN S. RUBINSTEIN

See also HEMORRHOID.

VARIETY. See CLASSIFICATION (Groups).

VARIETY MEATS. See MEAT AND MEAT CARVING.

VARIOMETER. See GLIDER.

VARISCITE. See MINERAL (color picture).

VARNA, *VAHR nah* (pop. 119,769; alt. 10 ft.), formerly STALIN, is a Black Sea port in Bulgaria. It lies about 120 miles southeast of Bucharest. For location, see BULGARIA (color map). The city manufactures metal, textile, leather, and tobacco products. It is a commercial fishing center, the home of a university and a naval academy, and a summer-resort area. IRWIN T. SANDERS

VARNISH is a transparent liquid used to protect wood, metal, and other materials from air and moisture, and to improve their appearance. A varnish leaves a hard, glossy film when it dries.

Clear varnishes protect the surface of wood while allowing the natural grain of the wood to show through. *Varnish stains* contain dyes that change the color of the wood but still bring out the grain. Varnishes used on metal are sometimes called lacquers. Lacquers help prevent corrosion without dulling the metallic appearance. Varnishes are also used to protect insulating wires, masonry, and paper from moisture.

Varnishes can be baked on by heating the varnished articles in ovens at temperatures of 150° F. to 400° F. Baking improves the wearing quality of the object.

Types of Varnish. There are two main classes of varnishes, spirit and oleoresinous. *Spirit varnishes* are made of chemicals called *resins.* The resins are dissolved in a quickly-evaporating solvent such as alcohol. These varnishes dry when the solvent evaporates. Shellac is a common spirit varnish. Other examples are Japan, dammar, and pyroxylin lacquers.

Oleoresinous varnishes are mixtures of resins and drying oils that are heated and dissolved in turpentine or petroleum products. These varnishes dry in two ways, by evaporation of the solvent, and by the hardening of the resin-oil mixture when it combines with oxygen. Oleoresinous varnishes withstand outdoor conditions well. Spar varnish, used on the wood exterior of boats, is an oleoresinous varnish.

Making Varnish. Both natural resins and synthetic resins are used in making varnish. *Natural resins* are extracted from living plants and from fossil plants. Shellac, dammar, and rosin are common natural resins. *Synthetic resins* include such chemical compounds as phenol-formaldehyde, urea-formaldehyde, alkyd (glyceryl phthalate), and cumar.

In making spirit varnishes, the resin is dissolved by churning it with the solvent. Small amounts of heat are sometimes used to speed the dissolving process. After the resin is dissolved, the varnish is refined by filtering and is then ready for use.

In making oleoresinous varnishes, the oil and resin are cooked in closed kettles that hold 5,000 gallons or more. The mixture is kept at a temperature between 450° F. and 700° F. until it reaches the desired *body* (thickness). Then the mixture is cooled and thinners are added. Some natural resins will not dissolve easily in oils. These resins are *run* (heated at about 600° F. until 15 to 30 per cent evaporates).

Drying oils are added to the varnish to hasten the drying time. Linseed oil was probably the first oil to be used in varnishes. Many other drying oils are used to-day, such as, perilla, tung, dehydrated castor, soybean, and fish oils. Compounds of lead, cobalt, or manganese are often added to quicken drying.

Varnishes are named by giving the number of gallons of oil that have been mixed with 100 pounds of resin. For example, a 30-gallon tung-oil kauri varnish is made with 30 gallons of tung oil and 100 pounds of kauri resin. Varnishes used on surfaces exposed to weather contain more oil than those used indoors. JOHN R. KOCH

See also LACQUER; SHELLAC; RESIN; AIRBRUSH.

VARRO, MARCUS TERENTIUS (116-27 B.C.), was a Roman writer. He wrote 74 separate works in 620 books, on a wide variety of subjects, but only fragments of them remain. They include writings on oratory, history, literature, philosophy, grammar, law, geography, and agriculture. His treatise *On Farming* and part of his treatise *On the Latin Language* are his only surviving works. His only creative work was *Menippean Satires*, a mixture of prose and verse. Varro was born in a Sabine village in Italy. He fought for Pompey against Julius Caesar at the battle of Pharsalus in 48 B.C., but Caesar later forgave him. Varro held various offices and rose to the praetorship. MOSES HADAS

See also ENCYCLOPEDIA (The First Reference Works).

VARVE. See ARCHAEOLOGY (Absolute Chronology).

VASA, HOUSE OF. See GUSTAVUS.

VASCO DA GAMA. See DA GAMA, VASCO.

VASCULAR SYSTEM is the complete circulation system of the body which carries all the fluids, including the blood, the lymph, and chyle. It is made up of the heart, arteries, veins, capillaries, and lymphatics.

See also BLOOD; CIRCULATION; also the Trans-Vision three-dimensional color picture with HUMAN BODY.

VASE, *vays*, or *vayz*; in Great Britain, often *vahs*, or *vahz*. A vase is a hollow vessel of pottery, stone, metal, glass, or other material. It is usually rounded and deeper than it is wide. A vase is generally decorative, or ornamental, and designed to please the eye by its graceful shape, color, or patterns applied on its surface. Vases are now used chiefly for ornament or to hold flowers. Sometimes they are used for other household purposes. Vases also hold the ashes of the cremated dead.

Pottery or earthenware vases have been made in almost every age of the world's history. Many relics have been preserved and new ones are constantly being discovered. Pictures on these relics often reveal the artistry of the people and sometimes something of their life. One of the most famous ancient vases is the Portland vase, found near Rome in the 1600's. It was found in a tomb believed to be that of Alexander Severus. The Portland vase is of transparent dark blue, coated with milky-white glass cut in cameo style. It is located in the British Museum. EUGENE F. BUNKER, JR.

See also GLASSWARE (pictures).

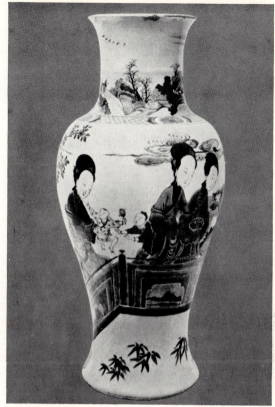

Metropolitan Museum of Art
This Chinese Vase Was Made in the Early 1700's.

VASELINE. See PETROLATUM.

VASHTI. See ESTHER.

VASODILATOR NERVES. See BLUSHING.

VÁSQUEZ DE CORONADO, FRANCISCO. See CORONADO, FRANCISCO VÁSQUEZ DE.

VASSAL. See FEUDALISM.

VASSAR, MATTHEW (1792-1868), was an American brewer who founded Vassar College. He was born in East Tuddingham, England, and was brought to the United States in 1796. He established a successful brewery in Poughkeepsie, N.Y., and made a large fortune. He also owned a whaling dock in Poughkeepsie, and was part owner of a whaling fleet. Vassar became interested in higher education for women, and in 1861 gave a large sum of money to found Vassar College. The wide publicity given to the venture created interest in college education for women throughout the world. Gifts by Vassar to the college during his life totaled over $800,000. ROBERT H. BREMNER

VASSAR COLLEGE is a liberal arts school for women at Poughkeepsie, N.Y. It is privately controlled and offers courses in languages and literature, arts, physical sciences, and social sciences. Vassar students live in 10 campus residence houses on a 950-acre campus. Vassar was founded in 1861. It was the first women's college to have the equipment and resources equal to those of men's colleges. The Vassar school colors are rose and gray. For enrollment, see UNIVERSITIES AND COLLEGES (table). SARAH GIBSON BLANDING

See also VASSAR, MATTHEW.

227

VATICAN CITY, *VAT ih kuhn* (pop. 1,000; alt. 98 ft.), is the smallest independent state in the world. It serves as the spiritual and governmental center of the Roman Catholic Church, the largest Christian church in the world. Vatican City covers only 108.7 acres. But it exercises spiritual sway over about 572 million Roman Catholics. Its ruler is the pope. Vatican City lies entirely within the city of Rome, Italy. But it is foreign soil to Italian citizens. Vatican City has been an independent sovereign state since the signing of the Treaty of the Lateran in 1929. For location, see ITALY (color map); ROME (map, Modern Rome).

The official name of Vatican City in Italian is STATO DELLA CITTÀ DEL VATICANO (The State of Vatican City). *The Vatican* is a short name for the state as a whole, and also for the city that makes up the state. People often use the term *Vatican* to refer to the pope and the government of Vatican City, in much the same way as they use the term *Washington* to refer to the U.S. President and his administration.

Description

Vatican City is about as large as an average city park. It lies on Vatican Hill in northwestern Rome, just west of the Tiber River. High stone walls surround most of the city. The irregularly-shaped area within these walls contains picturesque buildings in several architectural styles. It also contains many courtyards, landscaped gardens, and quiet streets. The huge St. Peter's Church, with its stately dome, dominates the entire city.

St. Peter's Church is the largest Christian church in the world. Contrary to popular belief, it is a basilica, not a cathedral. St. John Lateran, in Rome, is the cathedral church of the pope (see BASILICA; CATHEDRAL; LATERAN). For a history and description of St. Peter's Church and St. Peter's Square, see SAINT PETER'S CHURCH.

The Boundaries of Vatican City, marked by a white line in this picture, enclose an area of about one-sixth of a square mile in northwestern Rome. The dome of the famous Saint Peter's Church dominates the skyline of the Papal State.

Vatican Palace is a group of connected buildings with well over 1,000 rooms. The various chapels, apartments, museums, and other rooms cluster around several open courts. The pope's apartment, the offices of the Secretariate of State, and reception rooms and halls occupy one part of the palace. The remainder is devoted largely to the Vatican Museum, the Vatican Archive, and the Vatican Library.

Vatican Museum has a priceless collection of statuary, including the famous *Apollo Belvedere* and the *Laocoön* (see the pictures in the articles on APOLLO and LAOCOÖN). The museum also has large sections devoted to pagan and Christian inscriptions, and to Egyptian and Etruscan antiquities. The many rooms and chapels within the museum are decorated by the works of such master artists as Fra Angelico, Pinturiccio, Raphael, Titian, and Leonardo da Vinci. Some of Michelangelo's greatest paintings decorate the ceiling and one large wall of the Sistine Chapel (see MICHELANGELO; SISTINE CHAPEL).

Vatican Archive contains important religious and historical documents. Pope Paul V organized the archive in 1612. It houses such important documents as the original report on the trial of Galileo (1633), the request of the English Parliament for the annulment of the marriage of Henry VIII to Catherine of Aragon (1530), and the concordat of Napoleon (1801). Pope Leo XIII opened the archive to scholars in 1881. Since then, many European nations have created historical institutes to search the archives for information on their particular countries.

Vatican Library has one of the world's largest and most valuable collections of early manuscripts and books. See VATICAN LIBRARY.

Other Buildings belonging to Vatican City but located outside the city walls include the basilicas of St. John Lateran, St. Paul's-outside-the-Walls, and St. Mary Major, all in Rome; and the pope's summer villa and the Vatican observatory at Castel Gandolfo.

Administration

The pope, as absolute ruler of Vatican City, heads all branches of the government. But, since he devotes his time primarily to spiritual and ecclesiastical matters, he delegates most of his temporal authority to other officials.

The internal domestic affairs of Vatican City are directed by a Governor, whose duties resemble those of the mayor of a city. Foreign affairs are handled by the Cardinal Secretary of State, who also coordinates ecclesiastical and political affairs. The Vatican has civil law courts in addition to the Tribunal of the Sacred Roman Rota, which handles religious cases. But most civil criminal cases are prosecuted by the Italian government. The Congregation of the Ceremonial directs papal ceremonies and audiences, and also handles matters of protocol and etiquette. Vatican

finances are controlled by a number of administrations, or departments. Each administration handles a different set of funds.

Vatican City issues its own postage stamps, coins, and automobile license plates. The pope's yellow-and-white banner is the official state flag (see FLAG [color picture, Flags of Europe]).

Public Works. The Vatican maintains its own mail system, telephone and telegraph systems, water supply, and lighting and street-cleaning services. It also has its own bank, a large printing plant, and a rarely occupied jail. Although the state has its own railroad station, no one has ever bought a ticket to Vatican City. The 300 yards of track that connect the station with an Italian railroad carries only freight.

Armed Forces. Vatican City does not have an army or navy capable of fighting a war. But it does have its own "armed forces." The most famous of these are the Swiss Guards, who protect the pope and serve as sentries. Their yellow, orange, and blue uniforms are said to have been designed by Michelangelo or Raphael

The Assembly Hall of Cardinals, in the Vatican Palace, Is Richly Decorated with Paintings and Carvings.

W. Bosshard, Black Star

VATICAN CITY

(see Swiss Guards). Other armed forces include the Noble Guards (bodyguards and escorts of the pope); the Palatine Guards (the pope's militia); and the Pontifical Gendarmery (the pope's police force).

Diplomatic Corps of Vatican City includes about 60 *legates* (ambassadors), as well as other diplomatic personnel. The highest ranking legates are the *nuncios*. Legates of lesser rank are called *internuncios*. Nuncios and internuncios head the Vatican's delegations to other countries. They also look after the welfare of the Roman Catholic Church in those countries. Most European and Latin-American countries receive nuncios or internuncios from the Vatican. Papal representatives in countries that have no formal diplomatic relations with the Vatican are called *apostolic delegates*. Such delegates have no diplomatic status and hold authority only in ecclesiastical matters. Apostolic delegates serve in the U.S., Canada, Great Britain, Mexico, and several other countries. See Legate; Nuncio.

Communications. The Vatican publishes *L'Osservatore Romano*, one of the most influential daily newspapers in the world. Other Vatican publications include *Osservatore della Domenica*, a weekly publication; and the *Acta Apostolicae Sedis*, which prints official church documents. The Vatican's powerful radio transmitter broadcasts news and papal messages in 30 languages, including Latin.

History

Vatican Hill was once the site of Roman emperor Nero's public gardens and circus. Many early Christians suffered martyrdom there. According to tradition, St. Peter was crucified on the hill and buried nearby. The early popes believed that a shrine built in the A.D. 100's marked the site of Peter's tomb. Because of this belief, they erected Vatican City on that spot.

In the A.D. 300's, the Christian emperor Constantine the Great built a basilica over the tomb in which St. Peter was believed to be buried. The Vatican Palace and other structures were gradually built around the basilica. But the main residence of the popes during the Middle Ages was the Lateran Palace in Rome, not the Vatican. From 1309 to 1377, the popes lived at Avignon, France. On their return to Rome, they found the Lateran Palace badly burned, so they moved to the Vatican Palace. Beginning in the 1500's, St. Peter's Church was built on the site of the Old Basilica of Constantine.

Through the years, the popes gained control over an area in central Italy called the Papal States. In 1870, after a series of political defeats, Pope Pius IX lost his power over the Papal States. In protest, he and his successors withdrew inside the Vatican and refused to deal with the Italian government. Finally, in 1929, the Treaty of the Lateran was signed. By this treaty, the pope gave up all claim to the Papal States, and Italy agreed to the establishment of the independent State of Vatican City. For the provisions of the Treaty of the Lateran, see Papal States.

In 1939, Pope Pius XII initiated a series of excavations beneath St. Peter's Church. These excavations unearthed, among other things, a tomb thought to be the original tomb of St. Peter.   Joachim Smet

See also Pope; Roman Catholic Church.

The Square of Saint Peter's Church, Which Is the Largest and Most Famous Church in the Christian World.
United Press Int.

VATICAN COUNCIL is the name of two *ecumenical* (general) councils of the Roman Catholic Church that were held in Vatican City in Rome. An ecumenical council is a meeting of church leaders called by a pope for a special purpose. There have been 21 ecumenical councils.

The first Christian council, the Council of Nicaea, took place in 325. The 20th and 21st councils are called *Vatican Councils* I and II. Vatican I was held in 1869 and 1870. Vatican II was held from 1962 to 1965. This article describes the Vatican councils. For background information on these councils see ROMAN CATHOLIC CHURCH. For information on earlier councils, see NICENE COUNCILS; TRENT, COUNCIL OF.

Vatican I

Vatican I was called by Pope Pius IX. It opened Dec. 8, 1869, and is remembered primarily for approving the doctrine of *papal infallibility*. This doctrine states that the pope can commit no error when he speaks as head of the church to proclaim, in matters of faith and morals, what is to be accepted by all Roman Catholics as the teaching laid down by Jesus Christ and His apostles. At the outbreak of the Franco-Prussian War in 1870, the council was suspended. It never reconvened.

Vatican II

Pope John XXIII announced his intention of calling a worldwide church council on Jan. 25, 1959. He said the council would provide an *aggiornamento* (renewal or updating) of Catholic religious life and doctrine.

Pope John opened the first session Oct. 11, 1962, and closed it Dec. 8, 1962. He died on June 3, 1963, and the remaining three sessions were held under his successor Pope Paul VI. The second session ran from Sept. 29 to Dec. 4, 1963; the third session from Sept. 14 to Nov. 21, 1964; and the final session from Sept. 14 to Dec. 8, 1965.

Vatican II was one of the most widely-discussed religious events of the century. Religious officials, journalists, and other observers—both Catholic and non-Catholic—from all over the world reported and interpreted the actions of the council.

The Documents. The council *promulgated* (officially announced) 16 documents. The documents defined the nature of the church, gave the bishops greater influence in church affairs, and gave laymen a more active part in the liturgy. The documents also proclaimed a historic church position on religious liberty, and expressed new and liberalized positions on the church's relations with non-Catholic and non-Christian faiths.

The council approved these documents in the form of four *constitutions*, three *declarations*, and nine *decrees*. Constitutions were the council's most solemn documents. They dealt generally with the internal workings of the church.

The Constitution on the Church was the most important of the documents. It set the theological basis for all other council documents, and described the nature of the church. It described the laity and hierarchy as "members of the people of God," and forbade any separation between them. The constitution portrayed the bishops and the pope as a "college," with the pope as leader. It implied a greater sharing by the bishops in the exercise of the authority of the church and gave the bishops a larger role in church government.

The Constitution on the Sacred Liturgy permitted the use of the *vernacular* (local language) in place of Latin in parts of the Mass. The Mass liturgy was revised to allow greater participation by the congregation. The vernacular was also approved for other sacraments, such as baptism, eucharist, and marriage.

The Constitution on Divine Revelation emphasized the vital part sacred scriptures (the Bible) play in the church's life and liturgy. By stressing the importance of the Bible, this constitution narrowed the differences between Roman Catholics and Protestants on the issue of divine revelation.

The Pastoral Constitution on the Church in the Modern World was the first ecumenical document to be addressed to all men, not just Roman Catholics. The first part discussed man's relationship to the world, to the church, and to God. The church rejected atheism, but said that atheists should be respected and loved because they are God's creatures.

The second part took up urgent problems facing mankind. One chapter dealt with family life, and others dealt with social, economic, and political problems of today. The council condemned all forms of war as a means of settling international disputes, but it said countries had the right to self-defense. It called for the community of nations to organize and work to relieve the suffering of poor and starving peoples.

The Declaration on Christian Education endorsed the right of parents to choose freely the type of education they wish for their children.

The Declaration on the Relationship of the Church to Non-Christian Religions emphasized the respect owed to all men as sons of a common Creator. The document said the church rejects nothing that is "true and holy" in religions such as Hinduism, Buddhism, Islam, and Judaism. The declaration condemned any form of discrimination, particularly anti-Semitism. It stated the Jews had no collective responsibility for the death of Christ.

The Declaration on Religious Freedom stated that all men have the right to religious freedom. This was a dramatic change in the church's historical position. The declaration, however, repeated the church's claim to be the one true faith.

The Decree on the Instruments of Social Communication declared that means of communication such as the press and motion pictures should be used for moral purposes.

The Decree on Ecumenism pledged the church to work for the unity of all Christianity, and encouraged Roman Catholics to participate in the ecumenical movement. The decree permits Catholics to join non-Catholics in common prayer, with the permission of local bishops.

The Decree on Eastern Catholic Churches reasserted the equality of Eastern Rite Catholic churches with the Western Latin rite. The decree set forth circumstances under which Catholics and Eastern Orthodox Church members could participate together in the sacraments and liturgy.

The Decree on the Bishops' Pastoral Office in the Church discussed in detail the collegiality of bishops described in the *Constitution on the Church*. It directed the bishops to form national and regional conferences to meet local conditions and problems. The document called for a synod of bishops to meet with the pope periodically in Rome as an international senate or advisory board.

The Decree on the Appropriate Renewal of the Religious Life gave directions for modernizing the religious life of monks, priests, brothers, and nuns.

The Decree on Priestly Formation urged reforms in both the intellectual and spiritual training of candidates for the priesthood. It granted national church leaders more authority to regulate seminaries.

The Decree on the Ministry and Life of Priests reaffirmed the laws of *celibacy* (unmarried state) for Roman Catholic priests, without modifying the Eastern Rite discipline allowing married or celibate clergy.

The Decree on the Apostolate of the Laity expanded the examination of the role of Catholic laymen in church affairs described in the *Constitution on the Church*. The decree urged the laity to use its initiative in both religious and temporal affairs.

The Decree on the Church's Missionary Activity called for greater cooperation and support between well established churches and missionary churches.

Other Events. On Oct. 4, 1965, Pope Paul made a historic journey to speak before the United Nations in New York City. The pope made the trip in the name of the entire council "for the cause of peace in the world." He pleaded for the support of all nations in promoting peace and outlawing war.

The final days of the council witnessed two other historically significant events. On December 6, Pope Paul met with Protestant observers of the council and more than 1,000 bishops in a joint prayer service.

On December 7, the pope read a declaration removing a sentence of excommunication on the Patriarch of Constantinople which dated back to 1054. A similar declaration read in Istanbul by the Patriarch of Constantinople removed a sentence of excommunication passed against a group of papal legates in 1054. The declarations were a step toward ending the division between the Roman Catholic and Eastern Orthodox churches. Mark J. Hurley

VATICAN LIBRARY is the library of the Roman Catholic Church in Vatican City. It has one of the world's most important collections of early manuscripts and books. The Vatican Library was founded by Nicholas V, pope from 1447 to 1455, as a library for handwritten manuscripts. It is still chiefly a manuscript library, although it now also has about 350,000 printed books in its collection. The library's manuscripts number more than 50,000, over 31,000 of which are valuable old Latin works. There are also nearly 4,000 Greek and Oriental manuscripts in the library.

Many of the manuscripts are kept in closed rooms and may be seen only with the permission of the librarian. But the current practice of the Vatican Library is to make such materials available to all competent scholars. Fulton J. Sheen

See also LIBRARY (picture, Vatican Library).

VÄTTERN, LAKE. See SWEDEN (Location).

VAUBAN, SEBASTIEN LE PRESTRE (1633-1707), MARQUIS DE VAUBAN, best known as a French military engineer, was equally brilliant as a statesman and economist. He was an outstanding military and state adviser of Louis XIV. He contributed to the sciences of fortification and siegecraft. Vauban courageously advised against the renewed persecution of Protestants and proposed badly needed economic reforms, but Louis XIV lacked the wisdom to take his advice. Vauban was born at Saint Léger de Fourgeret. William Bark

VAUDEVILLE, *VAW duh vil,* is a form of entertainment made up of music, singing, dancing, and other performances, which are given in a series of short, independent acts. The term originated in France. It is believed to have been applied to drinking songs written by a man in Vire in the Vaux de Vire, a valley of Normandy.

At first, vaudeville served simply as a separate entertainment added to the regular drama. It was usually music and dancing between acts of the play. In England and in the United States, a similar form of entertainment known as the *Varieties* developed. It was given in theaters called *variety halls.*

In 1883, Benjamin Keith opened in Boston the first American vaudeville house, the Gaiety Museum. Another important early vaudeville house was Tony Pastor's in New York City. Around 1900, several large *chains* (circuits) of vaudeville theaters came into existence and achieved great popularity. The principal chains of theaters were the Keith-Albee and the Orpheum circuits. With the arrival of sound motion pictures in 1927, vaudeville began to decline. But vaudeville performers became popular in night clubs, and also on radio and television variety shows. Glenn Hughes

VAUGHAN WILLIAMS, *VAWN WIL yumz,* **RALPH** (1872-1958), was one of Great Britain's foremost composers. His music mingles the flavors of English folk songs and Tudor church music, both of which he studied intensively. He produced such distinguished music as the *Sixth Symphony* (1947); an opera, *The Pilgrim's Progress* (1951); *Seventh Symphony,* or *Sinfonia Antarctica* (1952); and *Eighth Symphony* (1956). He composed music for the coronation of Queen Elizabeth II in 1953.

In 1904 Vaughan Williams became active in the Folk Song Society, and edited *The English Hymnal* in 1905. By 1914, he had written *A Sea Symphony* (1910), *A London Symphony* (1914), and several other choral and orchestral works. Some of his other popular works include *The Lark Ascending* (1921), *Sir John in Love* (1929), and *Flourish for a Coronation* (1937).

Vaughan Williams was born in the parish of Down Ampney, Gloucestershire. Halsey Stevens

See also EPSTEIN, SIR JACOB (picture).

VAULT, *vawlt,* in architecture, is a roof or ceiling in the form of an arch. The four main kinds of vaults are the barrel vault, the dome, the groined vault, and the ribbed, or Gothic, vault. The simplest form is the *barrel vault,* which is a continuous arch. Each part is held in place by the part next to it. The *dome* is a vault in the form of a hemisphere built upon a circular base. Some domes are oval or slightly pointed. The *groined vault* is formed by joining together two or more barrel vaults at right angles. The lines at which the vaults join are called *groins.* In a *ribbed vault,* arched ribs are built in the places where groins would otherwise be. The ribs rest on pillars and make massive walls unnecessary. In Gothic architecture, ribs were both structural and decorative.

The word *vault* also applies to rooms designed for the safekeeping of valuables. Such a vault is usually made of steel, with heavy walls and ceiling, and it is entered through a steel door. In bank vaults, such a door gener-

Northern Trust Co.

The Door of a Bank Vault weighs many tons, and has hundreds of delicate locking and alarm mechanisms.

ally has complicated locking and burglar alarm systems.

In cemeteries, certain enclosures or buildings of stone or metal are called vaults. They are used as temporary or permanent places of burial. TALBOT HAMLIN

VEAL is the flesh of cattle that are too young and small to be marketed as beef. These cattle are divided into vealers and calves. *Vealers* are milk-fed animals under 12 weeks old. *Calves* are older than vealers, and although they eat grass or grain, their flesh is still not mature enough to sell as beef.

Vealers and calves sell by weight and grades. The grades are prime, choice, good, medium, common, and cull. The best grades of veal are plump, and light pink to light gray in color. The flesh of lower grades of veal is thin and watery.

Calf flesh is darker in color and has a more pronounced grain than vealer flesh. Calves have much more fat covering than vealers. Both types of animals have little trimming waste when marketed.

The physical make-up and chemical composition of veal is about the same as beef. Veal contains more water than beef does. But it contains less connective tissue and little fat.

Many persons prefer vealers and calves to beef, because the meat is tender. But veal lacks the aging which contributes to the delicious flavor of beef. Veal is more popular among the people of Europe than it is in North America. JAMES A. BEALL

See also BEEF; CATTLE (Beef Cattle); MEAT AND MEAT CARVING.

VEBLEN, *VEB lun,* **THORSTEIN BUNDE** (1857-1929), an American economist, was one of the most original and creative thinkers in the history of American economic thought. His first book, *The Theory of the Leisure Class* (1899), is a scholarly and satirical protest against the false values and social waste of the upper classes. *The Theory of Business Enterprise* (1904) criticizes the capitalist system, and predicts that it will drift into either fascism or socialism.

In *The Engineers and the Price System* (1921), Veblen assigned to scientists and engineers an important position in building a new planned economic society. Veblen was born at Cato, Wis. He was graduated from Carleton College and received his Ph.D. in 1884 from Yale University. DUDLEY DILLARD

VECELLI, TIZIANO. See TITIAN.

VECTOR, in mathematics. See MOTION (Newton's Laws of Motion).

VEDA, *VAY duh.* Vedas are the oldest sacred books of India. The word *veda* means *knowledge.* The Vedas were probably composed between 1000 and 600 B.C. They describe the religion and popular superstitions of early Aryan peoples in India, and are written in Old Sanskrit. They contain hymns to the nature gods, and *Brahmanas* (discussions on religion and sacrifices). Sometimes the *Upanishads* are added to the Vedas. These are essays on philosophy and the one God. The Upanishads are a literature by themselves, and are the chief documents of ancient Hinduism.

The Vedas appear in four collections. The Rig-Veda is the oldest and most beautiful. It pictures a strong people singing at the world's beginning. The Rig-Veda is followed by the Yajur-Veda, containing prayers and litanies; the Sama-Veda, a hymn book; and the Atharva-Veda. The Atharva-Veda shows a tired and fearful people who, in despair, have resorted to magic charms to obtain their goals. GEORGE NOEL MAYHEW

See also HINDUS; SANSKRIT LANGUAGE AND LITERATURE.

VEERY, *VEER ih,* is a bird that belongs to the thrush family. It lives in the northeastern parts of the United States and Canada. The veery is also known as Wilson's thrush or as the nightingale. It has brownish upper parts, a whitish, faintly spotted breast, and is about 7 inches long. The veery builds its nest of leaves in the lower branches of bushes or small trees. The female lays from three to five eggs, which are greenish blue in color.

Scientific Classification. The veery belongs to the thrush family, *Turdidae.* It is classified as genus *Hylocichla,* species *H. fuscescens.* LEON A. HAUSMAN

VEGA, *VEE guh,* is the third brightest star in the northern celestial hemisphere. It is on the western triangle of the constellation Lyra, and is often called the *arc light of the sky.* Its light resembles the bluish-white color of a diamond. In 12,000 years, Vega will become the earth's polestar. See also ASTRONOMY (How to Use a Star Map); LYRA.

VEGA, *VAY gah,* **LOPE DE** (1562-1635), LOPE FÉLIX DE VEGA CARPIO, the creator of Spain's national classical theater, won fame for his lyric poetry and dramas. He has been credited with writing as many as 1,800 plays. The titles of about 800 are known, and about 500 of the plays are preserved. He also wrote novels, poems, and dialogues. His powerful imagination, his adventurous life, and his interest in all sorts of people and places made him a typical Renaissance figure.

Lope de Vega subordinated ideas and character to plot, producing comedies of intrigue. He developed several types of dramas. His representative plays are *Peribáñez and the Commander of Ocaña, Sheep Fountain,* and *The Knight of Olmedo.* He also wrote *Punishment Without Vengeance* and *The New Art of Writing Plays.*

Lope de Vega was born in Madrid, and studied at the University of Alcalá de Henares. He began his career as a playwright while still a youth. In 1588, he joined the Spanish Armada. Late in life, he became a priest. HARVEY L. JOHNSON

See also SPANISH LITERATURE (Drama).

VEGETABLE

Vegetables Supply Important Food Needs to Our Diet.

VEGETABLE. We eat vegetables every day, yet it is very difficult to say exactly what we mean by the word *vegetable*. Sometimes the word is used in the phrase "the vegetable kingdom," which means very much the same thing as the entire world of plants. According to another meaning, vegetables are foods that we obtain from the leaves, stems, flower clusters, roots, tubers, seeds, or fruits of plants. Vegetables are usually eaten without first being processed and milled as cereal grains such as wheat and oats are. Vegetables are also considered different from fruits. Fruits generally may be eaten raw just as they come from the plant, while vegetables are more often cooked. But even this rule is not absolutely sure. The tomato, for example, is a fruit that is used as a vegetable. Such common vegetables as lettuce and celery are usually not cooked.

There is one entire group of vegetables in which the part of the plant that botanists call the *fruit* is commonly eaten. These vegetables are tomatoes, peppers, eggplants, cucumbers, melons, and squashes.

S. H. Wittwer, the contributor of this article, is Professor of Horticulture at Michigan State University.

Some vegetables are important because of their leaves or stems. They include cabbage, lettuce, spinach, mustard, kale, endive, cress, parsley, asparagus, and rhubarb. Still others are important because of their roots or their underground stems and leaves. These include white potatoes, sweet potatoes, carrots, beets, turnips, rutabaga, parsnips, salsify, and onions. The seeds of other vegetables are an important part of our diet. These include vegetables such as peas, beans, soybeans, and sweet corn.

Vegetables are a great deal more important in supplying our food needs today than they have ever been before. This is because we understand what kinds of foods the human body needs much better than our grandfathers did. Vegetables are important to us because of the vitamins and minerals they contain. They are especially rich in such vitamins as vitamin A, thiamin, niacin, and vitamin C. They are also important sources of necessary minerals, including calcium, phosphorus, and iron. Doctors recommend that in addition to potatoes we eat one green, leafy vegetable and one yellow vegetable every day. Vegetables also give bulk to the diet, which helps the digestive processes. Together with the animal foods, which provide much protein, and the starchy foods, which provide carbohydrates, vegetables are among the three important types of food we should eat every day. Most vegetables, however, do not have great caloric or energy-giving value. With few exceptions, such as peas and beans, they do not contain proteins of much value to our diet.

The production of vegetables is an important part of American agriculture. Market gardeners live near centers of population. Truck farmers live farther away. They grow vegetables and ship them by refrigerator car or truck to all parts of the country. Some vegetables, such as tomatoes and lettuces, are grown indoors in greenhouses during the winter in the northern parts of the United States. Most vegetable farmers sell their products to the canning industry. Quick-freezing processes are used to preserve many kinds of vegetables.

Growing vegetables in home gardens is a cheap way of providing food for the table. Furthermore, it ensures getting the most nourishment from vegetables that rapidly lose part of their food value after they have been harvested.

Each year plant diseases and insects destroy millions of dollars worth of vegetables. There is no single remedy to protect against such destruction, because different diseases and insects attack different plants. Anyone intending to plant his own garden should become familiar with the various plant destroyers.

In order to grow vegetables properly, the gardener must know the special requirements of each vegetable. He must know how to prepare the soil and how to plant or transplant the crops. He must know how to cultivate and care for each separate crop of vegetables. He must know what fertilizers are needed and in what kinds of soil and in what climate each vegetable grows best. Many vegetables are ready to eat long before the fruits and seeds ripen. The gardener must know just when each kind of vegetable has reached its most edible stage, and must then harvest it at once.

Kinds of Vegetables

There are many different ways of classifying vegetables. Botanists may group them by the botanical families to which they belong. The cook may group them most conveniently by the ways in which they are used and prepared for the table. But the gardener is chiefly interested in a classification of vegetables which is based upon the kind of climate the vegetables require and the way in which they are grown. The following are the most important kinds of vegetables based upon this classification:

(1) Rapidly growing hardy crops which cannot endure the heat of summer. These crops are grown in the winter in the Southern States. In the North, they are planted as soon as the soil can be worked in the spring, usually three or four weeks before the last frost. Important vegetables in this group are leaf lettuce, radishes, spinach, mustard, cress, turnips, and peas.

(2) Moderately hardy but slowly developing crops

LEADING VEGETABLE GROWING STATES AND PROVINCES

Tons of vegetables grown each year

State/Province	Tons
California	8,208,000 tons
Idaho	2,305,000 tons
Maine	2,022,000 tons
Florida	2,006,000 tons
New York	1,908,000 tons
Ontario	1,438,000 tons
Texas	1,418,000 tons
Michigan	1,354,000 tons
Wisconsin	1,321,000 tons
Washington	1,130,000 tons

Based on the latest government statistics.

LEADING VEGETABLE GROWING COUNTRIES

Tons of vegetables grown each year

Country	Tons
Russia	83,000,000 tons
China (Mainland)	70,000,000 tons
Poland	54,000,000 tons
Brazil	31,000,000 tons
Germany (West)	23,000,000 tons
United States	21,000,000 tons
Indonesia	16,000,000 tons
France	14,000,000 tons
India	14,000,000 tons
Germany (East)	13,000,000 tons

Based on the latest government statistics.

that must be well advanced in growth before the heat of summer comes. These include early potatoes and onions grown from seed. They should be planted with the vegetables of Group 1.

(3) Perennial crops to be planted at the same time as those in Group 1. These include asparagus, chives, garlic, and rhubarb.

(4) Moderately hardy crops that grow slowly and that endure summer heat well. Some of these are grown as winter and late spring crops in the southern states. In the North, they may be planted one to two weeks before the last frost. Carrots, beets, parsnips, salsify, and parsley are usually planted in a row as seeds. Early cabbage, early cauliflower, Italian broccoli, and head lettuce are usually started indoors, and the young plants are transplanted outside.

(5) Moderately tender crops. These crops cannot endure freezing temperatures and must be planted so that the seedlings emerge after the last frost. They include snap beans, sweet corn, and popcorn.

(6) Very tender crops that are extremely sensitive to cold. The wise gardener will not plant them until two to three weeks after the last frost. Lima beans, soybeans, cucumbers, muskmelons, summer squash, winter squash, pumpkins, okra, and watermelon are usually planted in rows. Tomatoes, peppers, eggplant, and sweet potatoes are usually started indoors, and the young plants are transplanted outdoors.

(7) This group includes the fall garden vegetables. They are usually not successful if planted early in the spring garden. They are planted during the summer months, and the crop matures in time for harvesting in the fall of the year. Among these leafy fall garden vegetables are endive, kale, collards, and Chinese cabbage. S. H. WITTWER

Related Articles. See the Agriculture section of the various state, province, and country articles for a discussion of vegetables grown there, such as ARKANSAS (Agriculture). Additional related articles in WORLD BOOK include:

VEGETABLES

Artichoke	Eggplant	Pepper
Asparagus	Endive	Potato
Bean	Garlic	Pumpkin
Beet	Horse-	Radish
Broccoli	Radish	Rhubarb
Brussels	Kale	Rutabaga
Sprouts	Kohlrabi	Salsify
Cabbage	Leek	Shallot
Carrot	Lentil	Sorrel
Cauliflower	Lettuce	Soybean
Celery	Lima	Spinach
Celtuce	Bean	Squash
Chayote	Muskmelon	Sweet Potato
Chinese	Mustard	Swiss Chard
Cabbage	Okra	Taro
Chive	Onion	Tomato
Collards	Parsley	Turnip
Corn	Parsnip	Watermelon
Cowpea	Pea	Yam
Cress	Peanut	
Cucumber		

OTHER RELATED ARTICLES

Agriculture	Horticulture
Canning	Nutrition (The Basic Seven)
Farm and Farming	Plant (color picture,
Food (color picture,	Vegetables Unknown to
Weekly Food	Our Forefathers)
Requirements)	Truck Farming
Food, Frozen	Vegetable Oil
Food Preservation	Vegetarianism
Gardening	

VEGETABLE IVORY. See IVORY PALM.

VEGETABLE OIL is any oil that comes from seeds, flowers, or fruits. Vegetable oils contain almost 100 per cent fat. They digest slowly, but have an energy value of more than 4,000 Calories a pound. See FAT.

Vegetable oil is used chiefly for cooking, medicine, lubrication, and paints. Processors obtain edible oil by cleaning the fruits, flowers, or seeds, then pressing out all the oil possible. No heat is used in this process. Oil obtained in this way is known as *cold-pressed* oil. Sometimes processors refine such oil after it is pressed. After the edible oil has been extracted, oil for industrial use is removed from the seeds, flowers, or fruits by combining pressure with either heat or chemicals, or both.

The best-known kinds of vegetable oil are olive oil, cottonseed oil, coconut oil, peanut oil, corn oil, linseed oil, soybean oil, castor oil, and safflower oil. Hydrogenated oils are made from vegetable oils.

Olive Oil comes from pressed ripe olives. It is excellent for sautéing, and is much used in salad dressings. Spain and Italy rank as the chief producers of olive oil. California produces almost all the olive oil made in the United States. See OLIVE OIL.

Cottonseed Oil is sold pure, or mixed with olive oil for use in salads. It is also a base for some cooking fats. When taken from the cotton seed, it is red, but it is bleached to a milk-white oil before it is sold. See COTTON (Cottonseed Products).

Coconut Oil is a nut oil used mainly in confections and fillings for baked goods. It does not spoil easily. See COCONUT PALM.

Peanut Oil more closely resembles olive oil than any of the other vegetable oils. As an edible product, it is mainly a salad oil. But cooks can use it for frying. It also has important uses in cosmetics and medicines. See PEANUT.

Corn Oil comes from the part of the corn kernel called the germ. It is used for salad dressings, and in margarines. It is combined with other fats for frying. See CORN OIL.

Linseed Oil is extracted from flaxseed and is used as the principal source of drying oil for paint and varnish. It is also used in making linoleum, oilcloth, and printer's ink. See LINSEED OIL.

Soybean Oil plays an important part in the manufacture of margarine, shortenings, and salad oil. It is also an ingredient in paints. See SOYBEAN.

Castor Oil comes from the seeds of the castor-oil plant. Castor oil has important uses in industry. It is a valuable *lubricant* (oil) for machinery. Doctors may recommend castor oil to patients suffering from constipation. See CASTOR OIL.

Safflower Oil comes from the flowers of a thistle-like plant (see SAFFLOWER). Some doctors prescribe it to replace animal fats in the diet. They believe it helps keep down the cholesterol level in the blood.

Hydrogenated Vegetable Oils result when vegetable oils are combined chemically with hydrogen to harden them. Hydrogenated vegetable oils are generally white. They have no particular taste or smell and are often used in cooking for this reason. They keep well without refrigeration.   LEONE RUTLEDGE CARROLL

See also OIL; SHORTENING.

VEGETARIANISM, *VEJ uh TAI rih un ism,* is the practice of living on a meatless diet. Vegetarians consider all animal flesh as meat—including the flesh of fish and fowl. Most vegetarians exclude meat from their diet, but eat butter, cheese, eggs, and milk. However, some vegetarians eat only food from plants. They exclude from their diet both meat and animal products such as butter, cheese, eggs, and milk. The term *vegetarianism* came into use in the late 1840's, but the idea of such a diet is hundreds of years old.

Vegetarians have several reasons for their beliefs. Health is an important reason. Vegetarians point out that animals raised for meat are subject to diseases, and eating the meat of diseased animals can make men ill. They also claim that vegetables, cereal grains, and fruits contain all the elements that the body needs to stay healthy. Vegetarians argue that meat is expensive, and that it is more economical to use land for growing plants than for raising animals. Some persons are vegetarians because of religious beliefs or personal moral codes. They believe it is wrong to kill any animal for food.

Vegetarians must plan their diets carefully in order to stay healthy. Vegetables are sources of essential minerals and vitamins, and cereals are among man's cheapest and most readily available sources of energy. But diets that include no animal products may not have enough proteins. Proteins are especially important to growth and the repair of body tissues. Corn is a healthful food, but its proteins lack two kinds of amino acids that the body must have. As a result, persons who base their diet on corn may develop a disease called *kwashiorkor.* Kwashiorkor causes swelling and stunted physical and mental development. The disease results from a low-protein diet based on corn. It is common in parts of Africa and Central and South America.

Most vegetarians try to get the proteins they need by eating the seeds of legumes such as beans, peas, and peanuts. These foods are rich in proteins. Vegetarians can also buy specially prepared food supplements to add essential nutrients to their diets.   WILLARD J. JACOBSON

See also NUTRITION.

VEGETATION. See GRASSLAND; PLANT.

VEIN, *vayn,* is a crack or seam in a rock, filled with mineral matter. Water carrying the mineral in solution deposits the mineral matter in the rock openings. The solution may be ground water which seeps down through the rocks and deposits the mineral in the cracks. The minerals may also be deposited by heated water which rises from some depth below the rocks, or by some vapor given off from nearby rocks.

Veins are of different depths and thicknesses. Some veins range in thickness from a thin sheet to a layer many feet thick. They vary in length from a few inches to several miles. Granite or pegmatite *dikes,* or rock layers in cracks of other rocks, are often called veins. There is no sharp distinction between veins and dikes. In general, however, the material of veins was deposited gradually or in successive stages, whereas the material of dikes is usually accumulated all at once.

Some veins stand out like low ridges that cross each other in strange patterns. The material of such veins resists weather conditions more than the rock of which they are a part. The material of other veins offers poorer resistance to weather conditions. These veins seem to be etched out like grooves below the surface of the rock.

Some veins contain the ores of one or more metals and are known as *metalliferous veins*. Many mines of metallic ores are dug along such veins.   ELDRED D. WILSON

See also GEOLOGY (Terms [Dike]).

VEIN is a blood vessel which carries blood toward the heart. The blood circulates in the body through a system of tubes called blood vessels. The three kinds of vessels are arteries, capillaries, and veins. Veins return blood to the heart after it has given out nourishment to the tissues and taken up waste products and poisons. Blood in veins is called *venous* blood. See the Trans-Vision three-dimensional color picture with HUMAN BODY.

The blood returning from the body cells has lost much of its oxygen, and is brownish in color. It circulates through the right side of the heart and then goes to the lungs. Here it gives off its waste carbon dioxide and takes on a new supply of oxygen. Red blood from the lungs returns to the heart through the pulmonary veins. Then it begins its trip through the body.

The veins begin at the capillaries. At first they are very tiny, and are called *venules*. Small veins join to form larger ones. Finally all the venous blood of the body pours into two very large veins which open into the heart. One of these, the *superior vena cava*, carries blood from the head and arms. The other, the *inferior vena cava*, carries it from the trunk and legs.

Veins, like arteries, have walls made of three layers. But the vein walls are thinner, less elastic, and less muscular than those of the arteries. The lining membrane of

Gaspar Cardinal de Borja Velasco, by Velázquez, shows how well the painter portrayed the personality of his subjects.
The Metropolitan Museum of Art

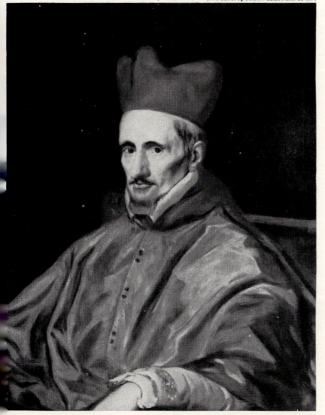

the veins is the *intima*. In many of the larger veins, the intima has folds which serve as valves. These folds lie against the wall when the blood is flowing freely. Several things can cause the blood to slow down or stop—the weight of blood above the vessel, effects of gravity, pressure on a vein, or low fluid pressure. Then the valves open out, and stop the blood from flowing backward. The valves are usually just above the place where two veins join. There are no valves in the veins of the abdomen, brain, and lungs, or in the smaller veins.

Veins that are swollen, stretched, or coiled on themselves are *varicose* veins. *Phlebitis* is inflammation of a vein. In this disease a blood clot forms, and causes pain and stiffness.   JOHN B. MIALE

Related Articles in WORLD BOOK include:

Aneurysm	Heart	Phlebitis
Artery	Jugular Vein	Varicose Vein
Bloodletting		

VELÁZQUEZ, *vuh LAS kez* (1599-1660), was a Spanish painter. No other artist has matched him in expressing the characteristics of his homeland. His genius lay in his ability to grasp the personality of his subject and fix it on canvas.

When he was only 26, Velázquez became the official court painter to King Philip IV of Spain. At the court, he began the brilliant series of portraits which immortalized him. He did many portraits of the king and his court, especially the court dwarfs and jesters. Velázquez also painted historical events of his time, scenes of everyday life, and still-lifes, with outstanding results. His religious paintings were less successful.

The Metropolitan Museum of Art
Velázquez painted this well-known portrait of himself.

Two of Velázquez' most outstanding works are *The Maids of Honor* (*Las Meninas*) and *The Surrender of Breda*. *The Maids of Honor* appears in color in the PAINTING article.

Velázquez was born DIEGO RODRÍGUEZ DE SILVA Y VELÁZQUEZ in Seville, then the center of Spanish culture and business. His wealthy family recognized that the boy had rare talent, and sent him to study with Francisco Herrera, a noted painter of the time. Herrera also recognized Velázquez' talent and encouraged him.

In 1613, Velázquez left the temperamental Herrera and entered the studio of Francisco Pacheco, a kinder and more academic painter. Velázquez studied under Pacheco until 1618, and was married to his daughter. He did a famous portrait of her, which is sometimes called *The Sybil*. In 1622 Velázquez visited Madrid and the famous palace of Escorial, where he first painted King Philip IV.   EDWARD S. SHORTER

VELCRO. See CLOTHING (Interesting Facts).

VELD. See SOUTH AFRICA (Land Regions).

VELLUM is fine animal skin used for paper. See BOOK (Early Forms of Books); BOOKBINDING (History); PARCHMENT (Fine Parchment).

237

VELOCIPEDE, *vuh LAHS uh peed*, is a name for any relatively light vehicle propelled by the rider or riders. The name was applied especially to early forms of bicycles and tricycles. See also BICYCLE.

VELOCITY, *vuh LAHS uh tih*, is the rate at which a body moves in space in a given direction. Velocity is expressed in distance and time, such as miles an hour or feet a second. There is an important difference between speed and velocity. *Speed* indicates the rate of motion in any direction. When a body is said to have a speed of 40 miles per hour, it indicates that that is the rate in any direction. But *velocity* indicates the rate of motion in one fixed direction. This means that a body may have a velocity of 40 miles per hour north of one particular point. Mathematically, velocity is a *vector* quantity, because it has both speed and direction.

Types of Velocity. Velocity may be *uniform*, which means the spaces traveled during a given unit of time are the same throughout the motion. To find the uniform velocity of a body we need only divide the distance traveled by the time. This could be stated in the formula $V = \frac{d}{t}$ where V is equal to velocity, d is equal to distance, and t is equal to time.

Velocity may be *variable*. This means that the spaces passed in a given unit of time are not equal throughout the motion. For example, a moving object could have a velocity of 100 feet per second at a certain instant and then change to 200 feet per second by speeding up. If the object gained speed uniformly, its average velocity would be equal to its initial velocity plus its final velocity divided by two. This could be written

Av. $V = \frac{V_1 + V_2}{2}$ where Av. V represents the average velocity, V_1 is equal to the initial velocity and V_2 is equal to the final velocity.

Accelerated Velocity. Variable velocity may be positively or negatively accelerated. A *positively accelerated* velocity means that, during each portion of time, the body passes through a greater space than during the preceding portion of time. A falling body has a positively accelerated velocity. In *negative acceleration*, such as a train stopping, a smaller space is traveled in each successive unit of time. ROBERT F. PATON

See also ACCELERATION; MOTION; FALLING BODIES, LAW OF; CALCULUS.

VELON. See FIBER (Synthetic Fibers); SARAN.

VELOUR, *vuh LOOR*, is a soft, velvety cloth made of wool, or of rayon and wool blends. Velour has a pile surface on one side and a plain or satin weave on the other. Velour is used for making women's coats, draperies, and upholstery material.

VELVET is a cloth with a soft, deep *nap* (surface). Clothmakers call this nap the *pile*. Velvet is made of silk, rayon, nylon, cotton, or a mixture of two or more of these yarns.

To make the pile, manufacturers of velvet weave two pieces of material at the same time, using three *warp* (lengthwise) yarns and two *weft* (crosswise) yarns. In each piece of material, they weave one set of weft yarns with one set of warp yarns in a plain or twill weave. Then they weave the extra warp yarn into the two pieces of material, first into one and then into the other. Finally, the two pieces of velvet are cut apart. Manufacturers also produce velvet in a single layer fabric. They insert wires as weft yarns and then withdraw the wires. As the wires are withdrawn, a small knife on the end of them cuts the warp yarns to produce a soft pile.

Velvet is usually made with silk yarn in the pile and cotton in the background. Silk velvet has only silk yarn. Velvet cloth comes in 36- to 39-inch widths.

Sometimes a pile fabric is woven by using extra weft yarn. Such cloth is called *velveteen*. When the pile is woven in ridges and cut, the cloth is *corduroy*. If thicker than $\frac{1}{8}$ inch, the cloth is *plush*. KENNETH R. FOX

See also CORDUROY; VELVETEEN.

VELVET LEAF. See INDIAN MALLOW.

VELVETEEN is a short-pile cotton fabric that resembles velvet but is woven singly with the weft forming the piles. It comes in widths of 18, 20, and 36 inches. It is used in clothing, heavy curtains, and draperies.

VENA CAVA. See HEART (How the Heart Works).

VENATION. See BOTANY (Terms).

VENDETTA, *ven DET uh*, is a family feud once common in Italy, especially in Corsica and Sicily. One family fought another, often savagely, to avenge a personal injury or murder. The victim's nearest relative had to take revenge on the offender. If the offender could not be punished, vengeance had to be taken on his next of kin. Vendettas were similar to the family feuds that have taken place in the hills of Kentucky and Tennessee. See also FEUD. WILLIAM H. MAEHL

VENDING MACHINE is a device that dispenses a product or service when money is put into it. Vending machines dispense many types of merchandise, including candy, cigarettes, chewing gum, and soft drinks. In some areas, drive-in vending machine centers are open 24 hours a day. They sell prepared foods, grocery items, and beverages.

Many businesses, schools, and hospitals use special types of vending machines in their lunchrooms. These machines dispense soup, sandwiches, complete hot meals, and a variety of beverages and desserts. Most airports in the United States have vending machines that sell air travel insurance. Coin-operated washing machines and dry-cleaning machines are familiar types of service vending machines.

How Vending Machines Work. Most vending machines accept coins only. With some types, the user must insert the exact change before the machine will operate. With others, the user can insert a coin larger than the purchase price. The machine will refund the proper amount of change along with the item. Some vending machines, known as *currency-changers*, will even accept paper money and make change. Some vending machines can distinguish between bills of different denominations. They return the proper amount of change for each denomination that they can accept.

The Vending Machine Industry is composed of manufacturing companies, operating companies, and companies that supply the products sold in the machines. The manufacturers produce the machines. The operating companies place them in suitable locations, and keep them stocked and in proper working order. Operating companies usually pay a fee to the owner of the location where a machine is placed for the use of his space. The fee paid to the owner of the location is based on the amount of sales the vending machine makes.

History. A device that dispensed holy water in a Greek temple in the 200's B.C. is the earliest known vending machine. The first machines in the U.S., chewing gum dispensers, appeared on New York City train platforms in the late 1880's. Cigarette vending machines first appeared in the 1920's. Since that time, vending machines have developed into a major industry in the U.S. Sales reached nearly $3 billion a year in the 1960's. THOMAS B. HUNGERFORD

See also COIN MACHINE; AUTOMAT.

VENEER, *vuh NEER,* is a thin sheet of wood of uniform thickness cut by peeling, slicing, or sawing logs. It is used primarily in making plywood panels. These panels are made from sheets of veneer glued together. Single sheets of veneer are used to make fruit baskets, crates, and packing boxes.

Most veneer is cut from the Douglas fir, but many other varieties of wood are also used. There are several ways of cutting veneer, but the most popular is the *rotary-cut* method. In this method, the log is placed in a lathe and then revolved against a knife extending across the length of the log. The veneer is unwound in a long ribbon, much like unrolling a bolt of wrapping paper or cloth. Veneers are cut in a wide range of thicknesses, varying from $\frac{1}{110}$ inch to $\frac{3}{8}$ inch. Most rotary veneers are cut in thicknesses from $\frac{1}{7}$ inch to $\frac{1}{20}$ inch.

In the mid-1960's, the United States produced about 950 million cubic feet of veneer logs a year. Canada produced over $1\frac{1}{2}$ billion square feet of veneer yearly. HARRY E. TROXELL

See also MAHOGANY; PLYWOOD.

VENER. See LAKE VÄNERN.

VENERABLE BEDE, THE. See BEDE.

VENEREAL DISEASE, *vuh NEER ee ul,* is a general term for several serious diseases. The chief venereal diseases are syphilis and gonorrhea. They get their name from Venus, the Roman goddess of love, because they are most often caught through sexual contact with an infected person. The disease is rarely transmitted by infected objects because the germs die quickly outside of the human body. It is important that persons who have venereal diseases see a doctor for treatment.

Syphilis is an infection by a tiny spiral germ, or spirochete, known as *Treponema pallidum.* This germ usually enters the body through a break in the skin or mucous membrane. Once in the body, it may attack any kind of tissue.

Syphilis is highly contagious in its early stages, but usually it does not make the person extremely ill at this time. The germs may cause a sore at the place where they entered, and later infect the lymph glands or cause sores of the mouth or skin. Other symptoms are nervousness, fever, anemia, and loss of weight. These symptoms may disappear by themselves, but meanwhile the germ spreads through the blood to other parts of the body. In its final stages it may attack the brain, spinal cord, valves of the heart, and blood vessels. Some of the diseases it brings are syphilitic meningitis, general paralysis, and locomotor ataxia. The final stage may occur many years after infection.

Infected mothers can give syphilis to their unborn children, because the tissues between mother and child do not filter out the spirochetes. It is important for a

woman to be examined for this disease before she has a baby. If she is infected, proper treatment will prevent infection of the child. Many states do not issue marriage licenses until a medical test has shown that the persons are free from venereal disease. The Wassermann and Kahn blood tests are widely used to discover syphilis, even when the symptoms have disappeared.

Persons who have syphilis can be cured, especially if they go to a physician for treatment in the early stages. The German doctor Paul Ehrlich was the first to discover a drug that kills the germ. Treatment with chemicals of arsenic, bismuth, and mercury cure the disease, but the treatment takes a long time. Treatment with penicillin is quicker. A single injection, given several weeks after exposure but before symptoms develop, has been effective in many cases.

Gonorrhea usually affects the mucous membrane, especially of the sex organs and the eyes. It is caused by a bacterium known as the *gonococcus.* Symptoms are irritation and a discharge of pus. They may begin three days to three weeks after infection. Sometimes the disease clears up by itself, but it may spread on the mucous membrane and is highly contagious. Gonorrhea is more serious, especially in women, than many persons believe. It does great damage when it spreads through the reproductive organs. It often destroys the eyes, especially of babies. Infected mothers do not give the disease to their unborn children, but the infant may pick up the germ while being born. It is now common practice to drop silver nitrate solution in the eyes of infants immediately after birth. This prevents the possibility of blindness from gonorrhea.

Gonorrhea can be cured with sulfa drugs or penicillin. In some cases the treatment has taken only a few days. The sulfa drugs have also been taken to prevent catching the disease. Often a single penicillin pill taken a few hours after exposure stops the infection. Syphilis and gonorrhea are important social problems.

Other Venereal Diseases include chancroid, Vincent's infection, and venereal lymphogranuloma. The last is an infection which attacks the lymph glands of the groin. PAUL R. CANNON

See also DISEASE (table, Main Contagious Diseases in the U.S.); EHRLICH, PAUL; TABES; WASSERMANN TEST.

VENESECTION. See BLOODLETTING.

VENETIA, *vee NE shih ah,* is the general name given to a district in northeastern Italy. In ancient times, the region was the Roman province of Venetia. Later it was divided into the three *compartimenti* (states) of Venezia Tridentina, Venezia Euganea, and Venezia Giulia. For location, see ITALY (political map).

VENETIAN BLIND is a window blind made of slats. Venetian blinds are given this name because they were widely used in Venice during the 1600's. Similar curtains had been developed earlier by the Japanese, who used bamboo rods. Today, Venetian blinds have slats made of metal, wood, or some other sturdy material. They are hung on tapes in such a way that each slat slightly overlaps the next one when they are closed. The slats are operated by cords and pulleys which can be adjusted to keep out sunlight but still admit breezes.

VENEZIA TRIDENTINA. See TRENTINO-ALTO ADIGE; TYROL.

VENEZUELA

Oil Drilling Rigs dot Venezuela's Lake Maracaibo. The lake has more than 2,000 oil wells.

Spirited Folk Dances are a popular form of Venezuelan entertainment.

Wide World; Gendreau

VENEZUELA, VEN ee ZWEE luh, is a republic on the northern coast of South America. The name *Venezuela* is Spanish for *little Venice*. When Spanish explorers reached the country, they found an Indian village built on wooden poles above the shallow waters of Lake Maracaibo. The village reminded them of Venice, Italy, and they named it Venezuela. The official name of the country is REPÚBLICA DE VENEZUELA (REPUBLIC OF VENEZUELA). Caracas is the capital and largest city.

Venezuela covers an area a little larger than Texas and Oklahoma. The country has rich deposits of petroleum, iron ore, diamonds, gold, copper, bauxite, man-

------------ FACTS IN BRIEF ------------

Form of Government: Republic.

Capital: Caracas.

Official Language: Spanish.

Divisions: One Federal District, two territories, 20 states, and 72 islands which are federal dependencies.

Head of State: President (five-year term).

Congress: Senate, 51 members (five-year terms); Chamber of Deputies, 133 members (five-year terms).

Area: 352,143 sq. mi. *Greatest distances:* (east-west) 928 mi.; (north-south) 790 mi. *Coastline,* 1,750 mi.

Elevation: *Highest,* 16,411 feet above sea level, Pico Bolívar; *Lowest,* sea level, along the coast.

Population: *1961 census*—7,285,799 (including 31,800 Indian rainforest inhabitants); distribution, 51 per cent rural; 49 per cent urban. *1967 estimate*—9,228,000; density, 26 persons to the square mile. *1972 estimate*—11,004,000.

Chief Products: *Agriculture,* cacao, cattle, coffee, corn, cotton, rice, sugar cane, tobacco. *Mining,* diamonds, gold, iron ore, natural gas, petroleum. *Manufacturing and Processing,* petroleum products, textiles.

Flag: Seven white stars (for the original seven provinces) are centered on three stripes of yellow (for Venezuela), blue (for the Atlantic), and red (for Spain, Venezuela's former ruler). See FLAG (color picture, Flags of the Americas).

National Holiday: Independence Day, July 5.

National Anthem: "Gloria al Bravo Pueblo" ("Glory to the Brave People").

Money: *Basic unit,* bolívar. For its value in dollars see MONEY (table, Values). See also BOLÍVAR.

W. Donald Beatty, the contributor of this article, is Assistant Chairman, Department of History, at the University of Minnesota, and coauthor of Introduction to Hispanic American History.

ganese, salt, marble, and other minerals. Petroleum pours over $1 million a day into the treasury. It also pays for the great building expansion that is making Venezuela one of the most modern countries in Latin America.

Christopher Columbus discovered Venezuela on Aug. 1, 1498. He went ashore on the peninsula of Paria. Thus, Venezuela became the first part of the mainland of the Western Hemisphere on which Columbus actually landed. Cumaná in northeastern Venezuela

Venezuela (in black) is slightly larger than Texas and Oklahoma together.

240

VENEZUELA

is the oldest continuously occupied settlement in South America founded by Europeans. It dates back to 1512.

The Land and Its Resources

Location, Size, and Surface Features. Venezuela covers 352,143 square miles. It faces the Caribbean Sea along the northern coast of South America. The *Color Map* shows that Colombia borders Venezuela on the west, Brazil on the south, and Guyana on the east.

The country has four geographic regions. They are (1) the Maracaibo lowlands, (2) the northern highlands, (3) the Orinoco plains, and (4) the Guiana highlands.

The low, flat *Maracaibo Lowlands* of northwestern Venezuela are almost surrounded by mountains. Lake Maracaibo dominates the region, and is the largest lake in South America. It covers 6,300 square miles. Swamps dot the shores of the lake.

The *Northern Highlands* region consists of four sections. The *Sierra Nevada de Mérida* forms the southwestern part of the highlands and includes the highest mountains in Venezuela. The range starts on the Colombia border south of Lake Maracaibo and extends in a northeastern direction toward the Caribbean Sea. The *Segovia highlands*, an area of low mountains, lie north of the Sierra Nevada de Mérida.

Two parallel ranges border the Caribbean coast between the city of Puerto Cabello and Cape Codera. The coastal range rises abruptly out of the sea, and is the higher of the two ranges. Fertile valleys lie between the mountains. This region is the *central highlands*, and is the social, economic, and political center of Venezuela. The fourth section of the northern highlands is the *northeastern highlands*. It consists of low-lying mountains in the Araya and Paria peninsulas.

The *Orinoco Plains* cover about 120,000 square miles. This vast, flat area lies between the northern highlands and the Orinoco River. The mighty Orinoco rises in southern Venezuela. It flows 1,700 miles and empties into the Atlantic Ocean through a series of channels on Venezuela's northeastern coast. A number of branches of the Orinoco, including the Caroní and Caura rivers, run through the plains.

About half of Venezuela lies south of the Orinoco plains in the *Guiana Highlands*. The region consists of a high plateau, out of which rise many higher *mesas* (flat-topped land masses with steep sides). Angel Falls in the northeastern part of the Guiana highlands is the highest waterfall in the world. The height of the falls is 3,212 feet, about twenty times as high as Niagara Falls in the United States.

The Guiana highlands furnished the settings for two famous novels, Sir Arthur Conan Doyle's *Lost World* and W. H. Hudson's *Green Mansions*.

A number of small islands lie off the northern coast. The largest is Margarita, which is famous for its pearl fisheries.

VENEZUELA MAP INDEX

States

AMAZONAS (TER.)	11,757	C 2
ANZOÁTEGUI	382,002	B 3
APURE	117,577	B 1
ARAGUA	313,274	A 2
BARINAS	139,271	B 1
BOLÍVAR	213,543	B 3
CARABOBO	381,636	A 2
COJEDES	72,652	B 2
DELTA AMACURO (TER.)	33,979	B 3
DEPENDENCIAS FEDERALES (LOS ROQUES) (DEPENDENCY)*	861	A 2
DISTRITO FEDERAL (FEDERAL DISTRICT)	1,257,515	A 2
FALCÓN	340,450	A 1
GUÁRICO	244,966	B 2
LARA	489,140	A 1
MÉRIDA	270,668	B 1
MIRANDA	492,349	A 2
MONAGAS	246,217	B 3
NUEVA ESPARTA	89,492	A 3
PORTUGUESA	203,707	B 2
SUCRE	401,992	A 3
TÁCHIRA	399,163	B 1
TRUJILLO	326,634	B 1
YARACUY	175,291	A 2
ZULIA	919,863	B 1

Cities and Towns

Acarigua	31,737	B 2	Caicara	3,082	B 2
Altagracia	14,000	A 1	Calabozo	15,286	B 2
Altagracia de Orituca	13,860	B 2	Cantaura	14,096	B 3
Aragua de Barcelona	6,830	B 3	Capatárida	1,277	A 1
Aroa	3,930	A 2	Caracas	786,710	
Barcelona	40,773	A 3		*1,550,000	A 2
Barinas	25,707	B 1	Caripe	3,651	A 3
Barquisi-			Caripito	19,003	A 3
meto	196,557	A 2	Carora	22,251	A 1
Barrancas	4,034	B 3	Carúpano	38,210	A 3
Bobures	9,397	B 1	Churuguara	4,446	A 2
Cabimas	93,347	A 1	Ciudad		
Cagua	14,241	A 2	Bolívar	56,032	B 3
			Ciudad		
			Bolivia	1,719	B 1

Coro	44,757	A 2	San Carlos [del		
Cuicas	963	B 1	Zulia]	14,478	B 1
Cumaná	71,563	A 3	San		
El Callao	3,270	B 3	Cristóbal	96,102	B 1
El Mene	3,332	A 1	San Felipe	27,774	A 2
El Pao	2,663	B 3	San Fernando		
El Samán	1,154	B 2	de Apure	21,544	B 2
El Sombrero	5,592	B 2	San José de		
El Tigre	41,550	B 3	Guanipa	19,658	B 3
El Tocuyo	14,803	B 2	San Juan de		
El Vigía	8,515	B 1	Colón	9,210	B 1
Encontrados	9,565	B 1	San Juan de		
Guanare	16,935	B 2	los Morros	25,821	B 2
Guasdualito	4,549	B 1	San Lorenzo	4,760	B 1
Guasipati	3,382	B 3	San Mateo	1,829	B 3
Güiria	10,724	A 3	San Rafael	7,110	A 1
Irapa	3,657	A 3	Santa Ana	3,584	B 3
La Asunción	5,541	A 3			
La Guaira	20,275	A 2			
Lagunillas	67,869	A 1			
La Vela	4,567	A 2			
La Victoria	23,126	A 2			
Libertad	1,171	B 2			
Los Taques	8,505	A 1			
Los Teques	34,874	A 2			
Machiques	13,685	A 1			
Maiquetía	73,015	A 2			
Maracaibo	432,902	A 1			
Maracay	134,123	A 2			
Maturín	53,445	B 3			
Mérida	40,404	B 1			
Motatán	4,358	B 1			
Ocumare del Tuy	14,019	A 2			
Pariaguán	6,094	B 3			
Pedregal	1,166	A 1			
Porlamar	20,807	A 3			
Pueblo Nuevo	2,837	A 2			
Puerto Ayacucho	5,418	B 2			
Puerto Cabello	50,973	A 2			
Puerto Cumarebo	7,951	A 2			
Puerto La Cruz	54,694	A 3			
Punda de Piedras	2,257	A 3			
Punto Fijo	41,750	A 1			
Quiriquire*	7,520	A 3			
Río Caribe	7,188	A 3			
Río Chico	2,584	A 2			
Rubio	11,813	B 1			
San Antonio	14,697	B 1			
San Carlos	11,656	B 2			

Santa Rita	11,623	A 1
Siquisique	2,354	A 2
Soledad	5,259	B 3
Timaquillo	8,305	B 2
Tovar	8,827	B 1
Trujillo	19,358	B 1
Tucacas	3,783	A 2
Tucupita	9,575	B 3
Tumeremo	3,121	B 3
Upata	12,421	B 3
Valencia	161,413	A 2
Valera	44,566	B 1
Valle de la Pascua	24,051	B 2
Villa de Cura	19,644	A 2
Yaritagua	6,036	A 2
Zaraza	9,624	B 2

Physical Features

Angel Falls		B 3	Los Hermanos (Is.)	A 3
Apure R.		B 2	Los Monges (Is.)	A 1
Arauca R.		B 2	Los Roques (Is.)	A 2
Aves, Islas (Is.)		A 2	Los Testigos (Is.)	A 3
Blanquilla, Isla (Isl.)		A 3	Manapire R.	B 2
Boca Araguao (River Mouth)		B 3	Maracaibo, Lago de (Lake)	B 1
Boca Grande (River Mouth)		B 3	Margarita, Isla (Isl.)	A 3
Cabo Codera (Cape)		A 2	Meta R.	B 2
Canal R.		C 2	Mt. Roraima	B 3
Capanaparo R.		B 2	Negro R.	C 2
Caroní R.		B 3	Orchila, Isla (Isl.)	A 2
Casiquiare R.		C 2	Orinoco R.	B 2
Caura R.		B 3	Paragua R.	B 3
Cerro Bolívar (Mtn.)		B 3	Paraguaná, Penín de (Peninsula)	A 1
Cerro Yumari (Peak)		C 2	Paria, Penín de (Peninsula)	A 3
Coche, Isla (Isl.)		A 3	Portuguesa R.	B 2
Cuchivero R.		B 2	Punta Escarceo	
Cuquenam R.		C 3	(Pt.)	A 3
Golfo de Paria (Gulf)		A 3	Punta Peñas (Pt.)	A 3
Golfo de Venezuela (Gulf)		A 1	Serra do Curupira (Mts.)	C 3
Golfo Triste (Gulf)		A 2	Serra Parima (Mts.)	C 3
Guárico R.		B 2	Sierra de Perijá (Mts.)	B 1
Kukenaam Falls		B 3	Sierra Maigualide (Mts.)	B 2
Lago de Maracaibo (Lake)		B 1	Sierra Pacaraima (Mts.)	C 3
La Columna (Pico Bolívar), Highest Point in Venezuela		B 1	Tocuyo R.	A 2
La Gran Sabana (Plateau)		B 3	Tortuga, Isla (Isl.)	A 2
			Ventuari R.	C 2

*Population of metropolitan area, including suburbs.
*Does not appear on the map; key shows general location.

Source: Latest available official figures.

Rich Petroleum Deposits in Venezuela make it one of the most wealthy countries in Latin America. But many Indian families still trudge to market with pack mules just as their ancestors did hundreds of years ago.

Climate varies according to altitude, from the humid heat of the coastlands to the biting cold of the mountains. The Maracaibo region has the highest average temperature in Latin America. Its temperature seldom falls below 82° F. Caracas and other Venezuelan cities have a springlike climate all year, with the temperature averaging about 70° F. The Orinoco plains have a dry season from December through April, and a wet season from May to November. During the dry season, vast stretches of ground become as hard and dry as cement. But, during the rainy season, rivers overflow and flood thousands of square miles of plains.

Natural Resources. Venezuela has valuable deposits of petroleum, gold, iron ore, manganese, copper, coal, asphalt, diamonds, and salt. Petroleum is the country's greatest mineral resource.

Forests cover a large part of the country. More than 600 kinds of trees grow in Venezuela. They yield rare woods, wild rubber, chicle for chewing gum, and balata, a gum used for wire insulation. Much of this forest wealth remains untouched because the rugged countryside makes it hard to reach.

The People and Their Work

The People. About seven out of ten Venezuelans are *mestizos* (mixed white and Indian). Most mestizos are farmers who live in the northern highlands. About one out of five persons is white. These people live chiefly in Caracas, and dominate the political and economic life of the country. About one out of ten persons is a Negro. The Negroes live along the Caribbean coast, and work as farmers and general laborers. Only a

Public Housing Projects provide low-cost housing for thousands of persons in Caracas. The Government tore down shacks, leveled hills, and filled ravines to make room for the city's attractive apartment buildings and parks.

Workers with Machetes cut away the jungle to make space for growing industries. The iron-ore port of Puerto de Hierro on the Paria Gulf was built as an export center for much of Venezuela's rich iron ore. Trains and river barges carry the ore from the mines to the port. Ocean-going ships then take the ore to the United States to be processed in mills.

Bethlehem Steel Corporation

few pure-blooded Indians inhabit Venezuela. They live west of Lake Maracaibo and south of the Orinoco River. During the 1950's, Venezuela encouraged immigration of skilled workers to aid its economic expansion. By 1956, more than 340,000 immigrants had come from Italy, Spain, Portugal, France, and Austria. Only Canada received more immigrants during this period.

Way of Life. Huge housing projects have changed the living habits of thousands of people in the northern highlands. Many people have moved from tiny shacks into comfortable, government-built apartments. But many still live in shacks made of scrap lumber.

Perhaps the most distinctive Venezuelan is the *llanero*. Llaneros are the herdsmen of the Orinoco plains. They are famous for their horsemanship, strength, and love of freedom. Their life often is rugged and lonely. Indians in the Guiana highlands lead a primitive life that has changed little during hundreds of years of history.

Corn is the basis for many Venezuelan dishes. *Hallaca* is the local version of the Mexican tamale. It is a corn-meal cake stuffed with meat. The people also enjoy *sancochos* (meat and vegetable stews). Mérida candies, shaped and colored like fruits, are famous. Hot chocolate is almost as popular a drink as coffee in Venezuela.

Beach resorts offer excellent swimming and deep-sea fishing. Big-game hunting is good near Lake Maracaibo and in the Guiana highlands. Most Venezuelan towns have pits for cockfights. Bullfighting also is popular, as are baseball, soccer, tennis, and golf.

Cities. Most of Venezuela's cities have grown up in the northern highlands, on or near the Caribbean Sea coast. A number of the chief cities have port facilities. La Guaira, which lies next to Caracas, serves as the seaport for the capital. Maracaibo, on the shores of Lake Maracaibo, leads in coffee exports. It is the country's second largest city and the center of the petroleum industry. Other leading seaports include Puerto Cabello and Cumaná. Ciudad Bolívar, the leading southern city, stands on the banks of the great Orinoco River.

See the separate articles on Venezuelan cities listed in the *Related Articles* at the end of this article.

Mining. Venezuela ranks among the world's leading petroleum-producing countries. Venezuela's wells yield about 3 million barrels of oil a day. Over 70 per cent of the petroleum comes from the Lake Maracaibo area, which supplies about one-tenth of the world's supply of oil.

Foreign companies, mostly from the United States, operate the wells. Venezuelan law provides that 60 per cent of the net oil profits be paid into the national treasury. These profits amount to more than $1 million a day. The law also requires that at least one-tenth of the oil be refined within Venezuela.

The famous pitch lake of Gúanoco lies near the Gulf of Paria. The lake covers about 1,000 acres and is the world's largest deposit of natural asphalt.

The Guiana highlands contain some of the richest deposits of iron ore in the world. The Bethlehem Steel Corporation began to develop El Pao mountain in 1941. El Pao is believed to contain 70 million tons of high-grade iron ore. In 1947, the United States Steel Corporation discovered another rich iron-ore deposit in the same area. This deposit is Cerro Bolívar, a 2,018 foot-high mountain. Experts believe that Cerro Bolívar is the largest iron-ore deposit in the world. It holds more than a billion tons of high-grade ore.

Venezuela is rich in natural gas, gold, and diamond deposits. Other minerals include manganese, copper, coal, salt, asbestos, bauxite, and sulfur.

Agriculture. More than half the people of Venezuela are agricultural workers. The northern highlands are the major farming region. Venezuela devotes more acreage to corn than to any other crop. But coffee is the most valuable commercial crop. Other crops raised in the country include sugar cane, rice, cotton, sisal, sesame, tobacco, vegetables, fruits, and cacao. Cattle graze on the grass-covered Orinoco plains.

Manufacturing has grown slowly in Venezuela. But now the government helps manufacturers with high taxes on foreign manufactures, and with money grants. Venezuela produces cotton materials and other textiles, cement, beer, cigarettes, shoes, drugs, refined oil, building materials, fats and oils, and tires and tubes. Modern packing plants prepare beef for local use and for shipment to other countries throughout the world.

Trade. Venezuela trades mostly with the United States. Canada and other members of the British Commonwealth rank next in Venezuelan trade. Venezuela is the world's leading petroleum-exporting country. Petroleum accounts for 90 per cent of the country's total exports. Iron ore is another leading export item. Coffee and cacao lead the agricultural exports. Major imports include machinery, iron and steel products, textiles, vehicles, chemicals, wheat, and flour.

Transportation and Communication. Venezuela has about 15,000 miles of roads, more than half of which are hard-surfaced highways. The 583-mile Simón Bolívar Highway runs between Caracas and the Colombian border south of Lake Maracaibo. It is the Venezuelan part of the Pan American Highway.

Venezuela has about 775 miles of railroads, mostly along the Caribbean coast. The longest cable railway in the Western Hemisphere was completed in Venezuela in 1955. It is more than 11,000 feet long, and connects Caracas with the top of nearby Mt. Avila.

The Orinoco River and its branches provide about 10,000 miles of navigable rivers. Coastal shipping also is important. A 5½-mile-long concrete bridge spans Lake Maracaibo. Several domestic and international airlines serve the country.

Telephone and telegraph lines join most of the cities. Venezuela also has radio and television stations.

Social and Cultural Achievements

Education. The law requires all children to attend primary school from the age of seven until they receive a Primary Education Certificate. Primary schools have six grades. Secondary education is offered in two stages, four-year and one-year. The four-year course resembles a high-school course in the United States. The one-year course offers pre-university training.

Venezuela has five state universities, Central University, in Caracas; Los Andes University, in Mérida; Zulia University, in Maracaibo; Carabobo University,

in Valencia; and Oriente University, in eastern Venezuela. Central University dates from the 1700's. The country also has two private universities.

Religion. At least nine out of ten Venezuelans belong to the Roman Catholic Church. But people of all religions are free to worship as they please.

The Arts. Venezuela has two types of arts, the popular and the more formal. In the first type, the Indian, Spanish, and Negro groups have formed a local culture. These local arts include pottery making, weaving, and local dances such as the gay *joropo*. There also are typically Venezuelan musical instruments such as the *cuatro*, which resembles the old-fashioned guitar, and the *maracas*, made of gourd shells.

Literature, painting, and architecture belong to the more formal arts. Andrés Bello is one of the better-known poets. Others include José Antonio Maitín and José Antonio Pérez Bonalde. Novelists include José Gil Fortoul, Manuel Romero Garcia, Gonzalo Picón Febres, and Rufino Blanco Fombona. Former President Rómulo Gallegos not only was a politician, but also is a well-known novelist.

Venezuela has produced several noted artists. Among them are Arturo Michelena and Martín Tovar y Tovar. Modern architecture reveals a talent for using brilliant colors as part of the design.

Government

National Government. Venezuela calls itself a republic, but it has spent many of the years since gaining its independence under dictatorship. The constitution, which is not always followed, calls for a president to be elected by direct popular vote every five years.

The Venezuelan Senate has 51 members. The federal district and each of the 20 states sends two representatives to the Senate. If more than 27,000 votes are polled in the federal district, or in one of the states, one extra representative goes to the senate.

The Chamber of Deputies has 133 members. One deputy is elected for every 50,000 persons. States or territories having less than 50,000, elect only one deputy. All senators and deputies are elected by the people for five-year terms. All citizens over 18 years may vote.

Dave Forbert, F.P.G.

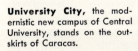

University City, the modernistic new campus of Central University, stands on the outskirts of Caracas.

Hamilton Wright

Angel Falls, the world's highest waterfall, drops 3,212 feet. The falls are over twice as high as the world's tallest building, the 1,472-foot Empire State Building in New York.

The Autopista, or Caracas-La Guaira Expressway, cuts through rocky mountain terrain as it climbs from the seaport of La Guaira to Caracas. The 10½-mile freeway required two twin-tube tunnels and three superbridges to master the steep mountain roadbed.

Local Government. The President appoints the governors of the states, Federal District, and two territories. Locally-elected councils administer the affairs of the districts and municipalities.

History

Early Days. Alonso de Ojeda (1466?-1515), a Spaniard, led an expedition to Venezuela in 1499, the year after Columbus discovered Venezuela. Amerigo Vespucci, for whom America was named, may have been a member of Ojeda's exploring party. Spaniards settled in the country soon after it was first explored.

The settlers fought a long struggle with the warlike Carib Indians of the coastal region. Diego de Losada (c.1520-1569) and other Spanish conquerors pushed inland and waged war with the Teques and other Indian tribes.

In the 1500's, Emperor Charles V of Spain leased the right to settle in Venezuela to the Welser merchant family of Augsburg, Germany. Venezuela thus became the first German colony in the Western Hemisphere. The emperor cancelled the Welser contract in 1546 because the Spaniards protested against letting non-Spaniards settle in the Western Hemisphere. The German colony then returned to Spanish rule.

In the 1600's, English, Dutch, and French pirates attacked Venezuela from the sea. Caracas was attacked and nearly destroyed twice. English pirates referred to the Venezuelan coast as the Spanish Main (see SPANISH MAIN). Venezuela became a Spanish captaincy-general (an administrative unit) in the 1700's.

Struggle for Independence. Francisco de Miranda (1750?-1816), a native of Caracas, failed in the first important Venezuelan movement for independence in 1806. Napoleon forced the king of Spain to abdicate in 1808, and replaced him with Joseph Bonaparte. But Venezuela remained loyal to the Spanish throne. In 1810, Venezuela ousted its captain-general, or governor, and replaced him with a *junta* (council) in the name of the king. In 1811, the junta withdrew in favor of a representative congress. The congress declared Venezuelan independence on July 5, 1811. This was the first formal declaration of independence by one of Spain's colonies in the Americas.

Hamilton Wright

Miranda became dictator in 1812, but Spanish forces soon captured him. Simón Bolívar, the *Great Liberator*, was left to carry on the struggle for Venezuelan freedom (see BOLÍVAR, SIMÓN). Bolívar suffered defeat and exile, but in 1819 he led his troops over the icy Andes into New Granada (now Colombia). At the battle of Boyacá in New Granada, Bolívar defeated the Spaniards. He set up the Republic of Great Colombia, including Venezuela, New Granada, and Quito (now Ecuador). Bolívar became president of Great Colombia.

Spanish royalists began a fight against Bolívar in Venezuela in 1821. In the battle of Carabobo, fought near Caracas in June, Bolívar crushed Spanish power in the area. Venezuela separated from Great Colombia in 1829, and in the following year, set up its own government under President José Antonio Páez (1790-1873).

Strife and Dictatorship. A long period of internal strife followed Bolívar's death in 1830. Páez controlled the country about twenty years. At least five major rebellions broke out against his government. Presidents in the 1850's included José Tadeo Monagas (1784-1868) and his brother José Gregorio Monagas (1795-1858). In 1870, General Antonio Guzmán Blanco (1829-1899) seized power. He ruled Venezuela for almost 20 years.

Venezuela's history has been marked by boundary disputes with every one of its neighbors, but all the controversies have been settled peacefully. In the late 1800's, Venezuela and Great Britain disagreed over the boundary between Venezuela and British Guiana (now Guyana). In 1895, this dispute caused U.S. President Grover Cleveland to send a warning message to the British that created tension between the United States and Great Britain. But Britain and Venezuela reached a settlement in 1899. General Cipriano Castro (1858?-1924) seized the presidency in the same year.

Early 1900's. Castro plunged Venezuela deeply into debt. Germany, Italy, and Great Britain blockaded Venezuelan ports to force the country to pay its debts.

In 1908, Castro went to Europe for surgical treatment. He no sooner had left the country than his right-hand man, General Juan Vicente Gómez (1857?-1935), took over the presidency. Gómez ruled as a dictator until his death in 1935.

Venezuela remained neutral during World War I. Eleazar Lopez Contreras followed Gómez as president in 1935. He served as provisional and then constitutional president until 1941.

Struggle for Power. In 1941, General Isaias Medina Angarita (1897-1952) followed Lopez Contreras as president. Venezuela broke diplomatic relations with Germany, Italy, and Japan in 1941, and opened its ports to the Allies for the duration of World War II. A revolution broke out in 1945, and a liberal government headed by President Rómulo Betancourt (1908-) took power. Betancourt expanded the constitutional rights of the people. Venezuela became a charter member of the United Nations in 1945.

In December, 1946, a military group made an unsuccessful effort to seize the government. In 1947, the people chose Rómulo Gallegos (1884-) as president. But, in 1948, a military group ousted Gallegos. Lieutenant General Carlos Delgado Chalbaud (1909-1950) took over the duties of president. After Delgado Chalbaud's assassination, Germán Suarez Flámerich (1907-) succeeded to the presidency in 1950.

The 1950's. In 1953, Venezuela adopted its 24th constitution since independence. It gave Marcos Pérez Jiménez (1914-), elected president that year, complete governmental power. During his regime, Venezuela invested millions of dollars of petroleum profits in a vast public works program. Industrial expansion, financed the same way, included enlarged iron-ore mining along the Orinoco River, and a new hydroelectric power plant on the Caroni River.

Venezuela's political parties formed the *Patriotic Junta* and rebelled in January, 1958. They forced Pérez Jiménez to resign. He was later charged with taking millions in public funds for his personal use. In December, Rómulo Betancourt was elected president with a coalition government.

The 1960's. Venezuela adopted a new constitution in 1961. It limited the president to a five-year term. The country broke diplomatic relations with Cuba in 1961. Communists then launched a terror campaign aimed at ousting Betancourt, in which hundreds died. But despite terrorist threats to harm voters, a record 90 per cent of the population voted in the 1963 election. Raúl Leoni (1906-) was elected to succeed Betancourt.   W. DONALD BEATTY

Related Articles in WORLD BOOK include:

Outline

I. **The Land and Its Resources**
II. **The People and Their Work**
III. **Social and Cultural Achievements**
IV. **Government**
V. **History**

Questions

What has petroleum done for Venezuela? How does the country rank as a petroleum producer?

What are the leading crops? Where do most of them grow?

What are the country's four geographic regions? How do they differ from each other?

What are the following: *Llaneros? Mestizos?*

Why is Simón Bolívar important in Venezuelan history?

Who can vote in Venezuelan elections? How does Venezuela help illiterates to vote?

What are Venezuela's leading imports and exports?

Why is July 5 an important Venezuelan holiday?

How does the system of Venezuelan government compare with that of the United States?

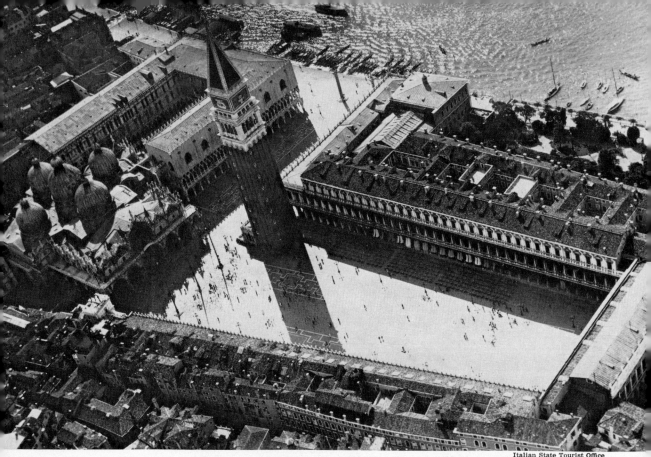

The Piazza of Saint Mark is in the center of Venice. The Cathedral of Saint Mark and the Doge's Palace stand behind the Campanile of Saint Mark, a high bell tower overlooking the Piazza,

VENICE, *VEN is* (pop. 360,241; alt. 5 ft.), is often called the *Queen City of the Adriatic.* Its name in Italian is VENEZIA. No other city is quite like this port of northern Italy. Venice is not built on solid ground. Instead, it lies on a cluster of small mud islands at the head of the Adriatic Sea. Venice has canals for streets, and has gondolas, or flat-bottomed boats, for taxicabs. Picturesque stone bridges cross the canals, and splendid palaces stand along the banks. These beautiful buildings recall the days when Venice was a great city-state, the mistress of the Mediterranean Sea (see CITY-STATE). Today, Venice is the third largest port in Italy. It is the capital of Veneto (Venetia), one of Italy's 20 political regions.

Location and Description. About 120 small islands make up the city of Venice in a sheltered lagoon off the northeastern coast of Italy. The lagoon is between the mouths of the Piave and Po rivers. A sand bar called the Lido borders the lagoon on the east. This sandy island makes a beach resort for Venetians. A causeway, or road raised above the water, connects the western end of Venice with the mainland. For location, see ITALY (political map).

The islands fall into two main groups. These groups are separated by the Grand Canal, which winds through the length of the city in an S-shaped curve. There are also more than 150 smaller canals. The buildings of the city stand on the islands. Narrow lanes and streets pass between the buildings, and the islands are connected by four hundred bridges, chiefly built of stone. These bridges arch above the canals to let the high-prowed gondolas pass beneath. The Rialto Bridge is in the heart of the city. It crosses the Grand Canal with a single arch thirty-two feet high. Shops are built along each side of the bridge. Another famous bridge is the Bridge of Sighs, which crosses from the Doge's Palace to an old prison. Under the bridges and through the canals sail hundreds of boats—motor launches as well as long, flat-bottomed, black gondolas with their graceful, curved ends.

Famous Buildings. The buildings which line the curving canals of Venice are built on piles, or posts, sunk deep in the mud. Venice, like all cities, has many humble homes. But it also has hundreds of splendid palaces which were built as homes for the rich merchant princes of the Renaissance. Venetian architects followed the styles of the long period between the Byzantine Empire and the Renaissance. Their buildings are Byzantine, Gothic, and Renaissance. The early Venetian architects also developed their own distinct style.

Most Venetian buildings and palaces are rich, and highly decorated. The façades, or fronts, of many of the buildings have colonnades (rows of pillars) and loggias (open galleries), and are colorful with mosaics. These are pictures set in small, colored, inlaid pieces of tile and stone. Inside, many of the palaces are rich with mural paintings and collections of the works of great artists.

The Piazza of Saint Mark. Some of the most famous buildings of Venice are on a square called the Piazza of Saint Mark (San Marco), in the heart of the city. This square was named for the patron saint of Venice, who was buried in Venice in A.D. 829.

The Cathedral of Saint Mark and the Doge's Palace are on the eastern side of the Piazza. The cathedral is second only to Saint Sophia, in Istanbul, as a fine example of Byzantine architecture. The Doge's Palace is an example of the Italian Gothic style of architecture. It contains a priceless collection of paintings. The south side of the Piazza is occupied by the New Procuratie, and the north side by the Old Procuratie. These buildings were put up in 1496 and 1584 as residences for Venetian officials called *procurators*. The Procuraties are splendid examples of Renaissance architecture. Near the New Procuratie is the famous Campanile, or bell tower, of Saint Mark. The Piazza also has an old clock tower built in 1496.

The Piazza of Saint Mark is a busy place both night and day. Many tourists have come to the Piazza to see the famous mosaics and winged lions of the cathedral, and to feed the flocks of pigeons which make their home in the square. Shops and cafes stand on each side of the two Procuraties. Often there are band concerts in the square on moonlight nights.

Along the Grand Canal. Many very interesting buildings stand along the Grand Canal from the Piazza to the Rialto Bridge. These buildings include the Church of Santa Maria della Salute, the Academy of Fine Arts, the Palazzo Rezzonico where Robert Browning died, and the Palazzo Macenigo, which was once the home of Lord Byron. The Rialto Bridge with its many shops, is a scene of great activity. Beyond the Rialto are the markets, the Municipal Museum, which has fine collections of gems, carvings, and other works of art, and many beautiful palaces. The chief shopping street, the Merceria district, lies between the Piazza and the Rialto. Southwest of the Merceria are the famous theaters of

Venice—the Fenice, the Rossini, and the Goldoni.

Churches. Venice has many churches besides the Cathedral of Saint Mark which are known throughout the world for their architecture and their paintings. San Salvatore, built in 1534, is famous for its beautiful dome; and the Gothic Church of the Frari, built in 1330, is noted for its beautiful altarpieces. The Church of San Cassiano has a masterpiece by Il Tintoretto called "The Crucifixion." The Jesuit Church is beautifully inlaid with marble. The church of San Sebastiano has altarpieces by Paul Veronese. The imposing church of Santa Maria della Salute, which dates from the 1600's, also has famous paintings by Titian. The church of San Giorgio Maggiore is noted for its bell tower.

Industry and Trade. Venice is no longer the greatest trading center of the Mediterranean, but the city still handles a great amount of trade. A new port, called Marghera, has good facilities for freight. Venice is third among Italian ports in the volume of freight handled. Goods of all kinds are received at Venice.

The most important manufacturing industries of Venice are those for which the city has been famous for hundreds of years. Fragile, beautiful glass comes from the islands of Murano. The women of Burano make exquisite handmade lace. Venice is also known for its brocades, tapestries, wood carvings, bronze statues and art objects, jewelry, and mosaics. The Venetians learned the art of making mosaics from the Byzantines, and have made beautiful mosaics ever since. Venice became a shipbuilding center in the 1900's.

Venetian retail shops rival those of Paris in the amount of trade they do and the beauty of their wares. Tourists who come to Venice are the main customers for these shops. The tourist trade is an important source of income to Venetians.

History. Venice was founded in A.D. 452. People from the mainland of Italy fled to the mud islands in the

Mondadori Press

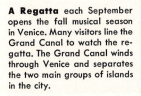

A Regatta each September opens the fall musical season in Venice. Many visitors line the Grand Canal to watch the regatta. The Grand Canal winds through Venice and separates the two main groups of islands in the city.

Karl Gullers

Gondolas Provide Taxi Service on Venice's Canals. In addition, many of these flat-bottomed boats carry merchandise.

Adriatic to escape from invading barbarians who came down from northern Europe. The new settlement was at first only a cluster of huts, but the city grew rapidly. By the 600's, Venice was almost independent of the Eastern Roman Empire. In 697 a ruler called the *Doge* was appointed to govern all the islands.

The Crusaders stopped at Venice on their way to the Holy Land, and helped the Venetians extend their conquests. By the middle of the 1400's, Venice had become the strongest sea power of the Christian world. The city was the center of an empire which extended to other islands, including Crete, and to parts of Italy (see CRETE).

Venice had a great merchant fleet, defended by many warships. The Venetian merchant princes built magnificent palaces and encouraged Venetian artists. Venice was one of the great cultural centers of the Renaissance. Discovery of a new sea route to India by the Cape of Good Hope, in the late 1400's, weakened Venetian trade. Gradually, Venice lost most of its empire. In 1797 Napoleon divided what was left of the Venetian empire between Austria and France. Most of the Venetian lands went to Austria. In 1866, Venice became part of the new unified Italy.

Venice suffered little damage during World Wars I and II. The city was taken over by the Germans in 1943, and was attacked by Allied planes. But Allied bombers raided only the port of Marghera, and were careful to spare Venice itself. The city remained in German hands until 1945.   BENJAMIN WEBB WHEELER

Related Articles in WORLD BOOK include:

Architecture (color picture, Ca' D'Oro Palace)
Bridge of Sighs
Campanile
Doge
Flag (color picture, Historical Flags of the World)

Glass (The Middle Ages)
Gondola
Lace
Saint Mark, Cathedral of
Venetian Blind

VENICE OF THE EAST. See BANGKOK.

VENICE OF THE NORTH. See STOCKHOLM.

VENIRE, *vee NI ree,* is the name of a writ that a judge issues in preparation for a trial by jury. *A writ of venire* orders the sheriff to summon a certain number of properly qualified citizens to serve as jurors. After the sheriff receives such a writ, he brings a body of qualified citizens into court on a particular day. Then a jury may be chosen from the number. The full name for the writ is *venire facias juratores.*   THOMAS A. COWAN

VENISON. See DEER (White-Tailed Deer).

VENIZELOS, *ven uh ZEL us,* **ELEUTHERIOS** (1864-1936), was the dominant figure in Greek politics from 1910 to 1935. He helped Greece acquire many Aegean islands, Crete, and other territories. He brought Greece into World War I in 1917 on the side of the Allies. He prepared for the unsuccessful Greek invasion of Turkey from 1920 to 1922. Venizelos served as prime minister three times, and persuaded the Greeks to establish a republic. He was born on Crete. See also GREECE (History).   R. V. BURKS

VENN DIAGRAM. See SET THEORY (Diagraming Sets).

VENOM is the poison of some snakes and spiders. See SNAKE (Poisonous Snakes); SPIDER.

VENOUS BLOOD. See VEIN.

VENTILATION. Many years ago, long before there was knowledge of the make-up of the air, man had experiences which indicated that there was "bad air" and "good air." Bad air seemed to have a bad effect on health and life. Good air appeared to be beneficial to life and health. It was noted on many occasions that when many persons were crowded together in small spaces, such as jails or the holds of ships, the air became foul and smelly. Persons often became ill, and sometimes died.

The study of ventilation did not really make much progress until the chemistry of air became known. This occurred at about the time of the American Revolutionary War. Several chemists discovered the chemical properties of air. It was found that the oxygen in the air that human beings breathed was needed for life (see OXYGEN). It was also found that human beings breathed out another gas called *carbon dioxide.* As a result of this new knowledge, it was generally believed that carbon dioxide was poisonous when it was breathed again.

These old ideas about ventilation have now been discarded. They have been replaced by new knowledge based on information chiefly obtained since 1900.

The use of buildings for shelter brings about the grouping of a large number of persons in a somewhat unnatural way. Outdoor air coming into a room changes in its chemical nature. The amount of oxygen is perhaps very slightly decreased. The amount of carbon dioxide is increased. But these small changes are of little or no importance for our comfort or health.

There are important changes which take place in the air of rooms where persons are active. One is the change in the temperature of the air. The temperature is increased because of the heat given off by the human bodies. The amount of water vapor of the air is increased because of the moisture given off by the human bodies. In addition, the air of the room becomes "smelly," because of perspiration and oily matter given off from the skins, noses, throats, and clothing of the persons in the room. These odors are usually called *body odors.*

HOW TO VENTILATE A ROOM

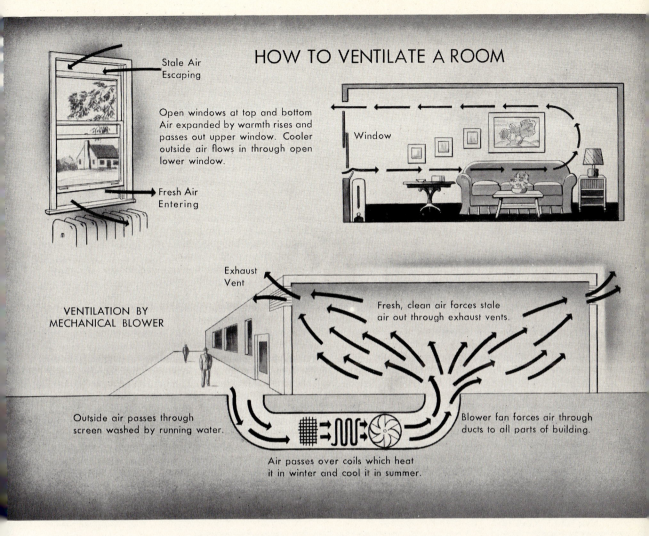

Stale Air Escaping

Open windows at top and bottom Air expanded by warmth rises and passes out upper window. Cooler outside air flows in through open lower window.

Fresh Air Entering

Window

VENTILATION BY MECHANICAL BLOWER

Exhaust Vent

Fresh, clean air forces stale air out through exhaust vents.

Outside air passes through screen washed by running water.

Blower fan forces air through ducts to all parts of building.

Air passes over coils which heat it in winter and cool it in summer.

Requirements of Ventilation. When many persons are crowded into a room, and when the temperature is high, we need ventilation in order to remove the excess heat and the body odors. Ventilation may be defined as the air which must be supplied to enclosed space to remove the heat and body odors of the occupants.

The correct temperature of a room depends on the age of the people in it. For school children, the temperature should be about 70° F. For average older persons it should be about 75° F. For elderly persons it should be about 80° F.

The quantity of air required for proper ventilation will vary depending on the heat sources in the particular room and the number of persons in it. Under ordinary conditions, the amount of air required will be between 10 and 30 cubic feet per minute for each person. On the other hand, if a man is at work in a confined boiler room where a large amount of heat comes from the boiler, it may be necessary to supply as much as 500 or 1,000 cubic feet of cool air per minute.

If the room cannot be supplied with sufficient cool air to keep its temperature at a comfortable level, then the person or persons in such a room will feel uncomfortably warm or hot, and will begin to perspire. Perspiration is the body's effort to lose additional heat by means of evaporation. Overheating of the body makes physical work more difficult. The heart begins to pump the blood faster in an effort to aid the body in keeping cool. This extra work that the heart is called upon to do results in fatigue or a tired feeling. Under these conditions, mental work such as study or homework becomes increasingly difficult.

The Kind of Air Needed by Man. Good air is air that is free from dust, soot, and odors. It is neither uncomfortably warm, nor so cool that people will feel chilly because of a rapid loss of body heat.

All air contains a certain amount of moisture. Outdoors, this moisture comes from the evaporation of water from rivers, lakes, and the oceans, and from rain which falls from the clouds. The amount of moisture outdoors varies very widely according to the season of the year and the geographical location. Indoors, the amount of moisture in the air depends on three things. One is the moisture content of the air brought in from the outside. Another is the changes produced by the heat added indoors (from radiators and the bodies of the

VENTILATION

people). The third is the moisture added by the breath of the persons indoors.

Indoors, in the wintertime, where no special sources of moisture are present other than people, the humidity (moisture) will be between 12 per cent and 25 per cent. This humidity count is relatively low because of the infiltration of dry outside air.

If the temperature of the air indoors is comfortable, then the amount of moisture present under ordinary conditions does not influence comfort. Only as the temperature gets high (over 75° F.) does too much moisture produce an additional factor of discomfort and make a person perspire very rapidly.

Kinds of Ventilation. The air for ventilation purposes may all be obtained from outdoors, passed over heating or cooling coils to bring it to the correct temperature, and then blown into the room. In the wintertime, this may require the addition of a considerable amount of heat, for the temperature outdoors may be very low. It may be costly to produce this large amount of heat.

Usually, in good ventilating systems, the air is cleaned by passing it through filters where odors are removed or the air is washed by a stream of water. Outside air may be mixed with recirculated inside air to provide a greater heating or cooling capacity.

How Air Is Circulated. In all ventilating systems the air is conducted in circular pipes or rectangular ducts. The air is moved in such ducts by means of a fan or fans.

In most air-conditioning systems, a certain amount of outdoor air is mixed with a certain amount of air taken from the room. The combined volume is passed through a washing and filtering device and then heated or cooled to the proper temperature before being blown into the room. Air is withdrawn from the room by means of a duct which brings it back to the conditioning apparatus. Most air-conditioning systems also remove excess moisture from the air.

The walls and window frames of all buildings are not airtight—even brick and stone are porous. Even if no provisions are made for forced ventilation, air is entering a building from outdoors at all times. The heat exchange between indoors and outdoors is greatly increased by windows, for windows are relatively thin barriers to the transfer of heat.

Special Problems of Ventilation. In certain cases, such as in the boiler rooms of ships in the tropics, man's activity has produced situations which require ventilation *not* for the control of limited amounts of heat but for the control of tremendous amounts of heat. In still other cases, such as mines, tunnels, and garages, poisonous gases may be given off which must be removed or reduced to a safe level if men are to be expected to work. Such problems are often difficult to solve and very frequently the solution is expensive. Temperatures of 125° F., which is very close to the limit of endurance of human beings, have been observed in the boiler rooms of steamships in the tropics.   MERL BAKER

See also AIR CONDITIONING; BLOWING MACHINE; ELECTRIC FAN; HUMIDITY; AIR CLEANER.

VENTRICLE. See HEART.

VENTRILOQUISM, *ven TRIL oh kwiz'm*, is the art of projecting, or "throwing," the voice so that it seems to come from a different source. It takes long and steady practice to develop this ability. The sounds are produced in the usual method adopted in talking, but the lips are held as nearly motionless as possible. The tongue is drawn well back and only the tip is moved. A deep breath is taken in and exhaled very slowly. Sounds are modified, or changed, by the muscles of the throat and the palate. Consonants are often changed to avoid lip-moving syllables. For instance, the letter *p* becomes a *k*. *B* is treated in the same way, and is quickly slurred into a *g* or *k*. Lack of facial expression on the part of the performer helps to fool his audience. The performer also constantly directs the attention of his audience to the place from which the sound is supposed to come. The-

Birth of Venus, by Sandro Botticelli, is one of the most famous paintings of the Italian Renaissance. Botticelli gave the beautiful goddess of love a graceful, smooth elegance in a classical landscape.

atrical ventriloquists often use a puppet with whom they pretend to carry on a conversation (see PUPPET).

Ventriloquism is an ancient art. The Greeks thought it was the work of demons. They believed the voice came from the abdominal region. The word ventriloquism comes from the Latin *venter*, meaning *belly*, and *loqui*, meaning *to speak*.   GLENN HUGHES

VENTRIS, MICHAEL GEORGE FRANCIS (1922-1956), a British architect, solved one of the great mysteries of archaeology. He deciphered *Linear B*, a language used by the ancient Greeks about 3,500 years ago. Inscriptions in Linear B were first found on clay tablets discovered at Knossos, Crete, about 1900. But all efforts to decipher them failed until Ventris, an amateur cryptographer, succeeded in 1953. He proved that Linear B was Greek written in the alphabet used by the Minoans, the people of ancient Crete. As a result, scholars changed their views about the early history of ancient Greece. Ventris was born at Wheathampstead, England.

See also GREECE, ANCIENT (Helladic Civilization); AEGEAN CIVILIZATION.

VENTURI. See CARBURETOR.

VENUS, *VE nus*, was the goddess of love and beauty in Roman mythology. The Greeks called her *Aphrodite*. Most stories say that she was born from the foam of the sea near the island of Cythera. In spite of her beauty, Venus married the ugly, lame god Vulcan (see VULCAN). But Venus fell in love with the god of war, Mars (Ares). Their son Cupid (Eros) was the god of love (see CUPID).

Venus also loved two mortals, Adonis and Anchises. Adonis was a handsome young hunter who was killed by a boar (see ADONIS). Venus and Anchises were the parents of Aeneas, the great Trojan hero who survived the fall of Troy and lived to found a new nation in Italy. Aeneas was thought to be an ancestor of Romulus, so the Romans worshiped Venus as the mother of their race (see AENEAS).

Venus helped start the Trojan War by giving Helen of Sparta to Paris, the prince of Troy. In return for this gift, Paris judged Venus to be the most beautiful of the goddesses (see TROY).

Venus was a great friend of lovers, and helped them with their problems. She even lent them her magic girdle, or sash, at times. It had the power to make its wearer loved.   VAN JOHNSON

See also ASTARTE; TANNHÄUSER; VENUS DE MILO.

VENUS is the most brilliant planet in our solar system. It was named for Venus, the goddess of beauty and love in ancient mythology. Venus is closer to the sun than any other planet except Mercury. It is both a morning and an evening star. For this reason, the Greeks gave the planet two names. They called Venus *Phosphorus*, or *Lucifer* (Light Bearer), when it was a morning star. When it appeared as an evening star, they called it *Hesperus*.

The average distance of Venus from the earth is 92,-957,000 miles. Its path brings it about 24,564,000 miles from the earth, which is nearer than any other heavenly body except the moon, the asteroids *Geographos* and *Eros*, and an occasional comet. Its greatest distance is 161,350,000 miles. Venus makes its revolution around the sun in 224.7 days. Some astronomers think it turns once in its 224.7-day revolution around the sun. But certain observations point to a faster rotation.

Venus is about the same size as the earth. Its diameter is 7,700 miles, and its surface is more than nine-tenths as great as that of the earth. Its density is only a little less than the earth's density. Venus has great power to reflect light, eight times as much power as the moon. It reflects more than half the light which falls on it.

Astronomers know that Venus has an atmosphere. Actually we do not see the planet, but a layer of clouds floating in the atmosphere around it. Most scientists agree that the planet is surrounded by an unbroken layer of clouds. Rocks could not reflect so much light.

Scientists discovered in 1956 that Venus gives off a continuous radio signal caused by heat energy. On Dec. 14, 1962, the spacecraft Mariner II passed within 22,000 miles of Venus. Mariner II sent back information that the surface of Venus is dry, sandy, and very hot—about 800° F. Scientists have concluded that life, as we know it, could not exist on Venus.

Venus appears in different shapes, like the moon. It varies from crescent to full circle, and then decreases again. In its travel around the sun, Venus sometimes crosses between the earth and the sun. To the naked eye it then appears as a black spot on the sun. The track is seldom across the center of the sun, but when it is, Venus takes about eight hours to pass across the face of the sun. These transits of Venus were once studied by astronomers with great interest, in order to determine the parallax and distance of the sun. Now astronomers can calculate the dates of the transits years in advance. Transits of Venus were observed in 1631, 1639, 1761, 1769, 1874, and 1882. The next transits will occur on June 8, 2004, and June 6, 2012.   E. C. SLIPHER

See also EVENING STAR; PLANET; SPACE TRAVEL.

The Phases of the Planet Venus. The orbit of Venus around the sun is inside the earth's orbit. Because Venus circles the sun faster than the earth does, there are times when it is on one side of the sun and the earth is on the other. Then Venus appears small, but very bright because of the light reflected from the sun. The two upper left photographs show this phase. When the planet is between the sun and the earth, it appears very large. But its dark side faces the earth and only sections of its sunlighted edges can be seen. The three moonlike photographs show Venus in this phase.

E. C. Slipher, Lowell Observatory

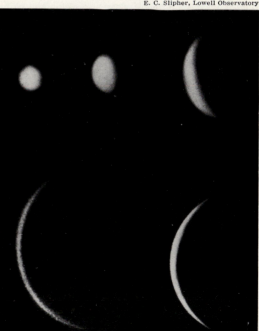

VENUS DE MILO

VENUS DE MILO, *ME loh,* is a magnificent Greek statue. It is made of marble and represents Venus, or Aphrodite. It is one of the great treasures of the Louvre museum, in Paris. It received the name *Venus de Milo,* or *Venus of Melos,* because a peasant found it on the Greek island of Melos in 1820. For hundreds of years, the statue had remained hidden in an underground cave near the ruins of an ancient theater. During these centuries, it had suffered considerable damage. It was in two parts when found. Pieces of the arms were found with it, as well as a pedestal with an inscription. These later disappeared, and no one has ever found them. The Marquis de Rivière, French ambassador to Turkey, bought the statue. After it was repaired, he gave it to Louis XVIII of France, who presented it to the Louvre. No one knows who made the Venus de Milo, or exactly when. It was probably made during the first or second century B.C., under the influence of some master whose work belonged to an earlier and greater period of Greek art. See also SCULPTURE (picture, Ancient Greek Sculpture); EUROPE (color picture).   FLORENCE HOPE

VENUS'S-FLYTRAP, or DIONAEA, *DI oh NE uh,* is a plant found in North Carolina and northern South Carolina which traps insects in its leaves and digests them. Because of this habit it is called a carnivorous, or meat-eating, plant. Venus's-flytrap grows in bogs in which the soils lack available nitrogen, and thus the insects take the place of nitrogen in the plant's diet. This plant is sometimes grown in greenhouses as a curiosity. It does best in a damp atmosphere but needs sunshine.

Venus's-flytrap grows about a foot high. It bears a cluster of small, white blossoms at the top of the flower stalk. The blossoms rise from a tuft of oddly shaped leaves. The leaves have two parts—a lower bladelike portion and an upper part with two lobes hinged to a rib. The surface of each lobe has three sensitive hairs, and the edges are fringed with sharp bristles.

When an insect lights on one of these hairs, the two lobes of the leaves close like a trap and hold the insect inside. The soft parts of the insect are digested by a fluid secreted by special glands of the leaf. After the plant has taken in the food, the trap opens, and the leaf is in position for another victim. When a leaf has caught several insects, it withers and dies.

Scientific Classification. Venus's-flytrap belongs to the sundew family, *Droseraceae.* It is classified as genus *Dionaea,* species *D. muscipula.*   THEODOR JUST

Hugh Spencer, NAS

The Venus's-Flytrap snares insects in its leaves. A fluid secreted by glands in the leaves enables the plant to digest its victims.

VENUS'S-GIRDLE is a transparent sea animal that belongs to a group of animals called *ctenophores* (comb jellies). It has a slim, flat body that resembles a long ribbon. Its mouth is in the middle of the lower edge. Bands of tiny hairlike structures called *cilia* are on the upper edge of the body. These cilia beat back and forth to move the animal through the water.

Scientific Classification. Venus's-girdles belong to the phylum *Ctenophora.*   ROBERT D. BARNES

VERACRUZ, *VAIR uh KROOZ,* or BAY rah KROOS, has the largest population of any Mexican state, 3,348,-844 persons. It covers an area of 28,114 square miles, and has a 430-mile coastline on the Gulf of Mexico (see MEXICO [color map]). Oil wells throughout Veracruz produce about two-thirds of the country's petroleum. The largest city, Veracruz, is Mexico's chief port. Other large cities in the state include Orizaba and Jalapa, the capital. Veracruz was one of the original states of Mexico.   CHARLES C. CUMBERLAND

See also OLMEC INDIANS; ORIZABA.

VERACRUZ (pop. 167,260; alt. 10 ft.), officially VERACRUZ LLAVE, *YAH vay,* is the chief port of Mexico. The city overlooks a fine harbor on the Gulf of Mexico, 200 miles east of Mexico City. For location, see MEXICO (color map). The city's products include cement, chocolate, cigars, flour, seafood, shoes, and textiles.

Hernando Cortes founded Veracruz in 1519 (see CORTES, HERNANDO). The city was the first Spanish settlement in Mexico. The United States Army captured the city in 1847 during the Mexican War. The French occupied it during their invasion of Mexico in the 1860's. United States Marines occupied Veracruz for a short time in 1914, after a dispute with Mexico over the arrest of a group of American sailors. JOHN A. CROW

VERB is a word, such as *go, think, send, resist,* or *exasperate,* that occurs in constructions like "Let's *go*"; "I *think* so"; "They *sent* me a letter"; "They will *resist* it"; or "That might *exasperate* him." Verbs have a general meaning of action or state of being, but other words that are not verbs may also have these meanings. Nouns like *theft, onslaught, resistance,* and *exasperation* indicate action and state of being.

Verbs as a group do have a set of *characteristics of form* in common. They also have the possibility of occurring in certain positions in sentences.

Form Characteristics of verbs can be illustrated by the different forms of the verb *fall.* These forms are *fall, falls, fell, fallen,* and *falling. Fall* is the base form, or infinitive, with or without the preceding particle *to. Fall* is also the form of the first and second person singular and plural, as in *I fall, we fall. Falls* is the form of the third person singular, used with a subject such as *he, she, it,* another pronoun, or a noun. *Fell* is the past tense form. *Fallen* is the past participle. It is used after an auxiliary verb, such as *be* and its forms (*am, is, are, was,* and *were*) or *have* and its forms (*has, have* and *had*). It is also used alone, when the verb is used as a modifier, as in "*Fallen* leaves covered it." *Falling* is the present participle, used as a modifier and after *be,* as in "The *falling* snow blinded him" and "He was *falling.*" All verbs have these forms. English verbs have only one form in the past tense.

The past tense and past participle of many verbs are identical, as in "I *thought* so" (past tense) and "I had always *thought* so" (past participle). The base form, past tense, and past participle of a few verbs are identical, as in "I *put* it there every day" (base form); "I *put* it there yesterday" (past tense); and "I have *put* it there often" (past participle).

Auxiliary verbs do not have the characteristics of the other verbs. *Can, may, go, should, might,* and *must* are auxiliary verbs. In sentences, these verbs are followed by the base form of a verb, as in *can go* or *may think.* The verbs *do, be,* and *have* are also used as auxiliaries, as in *did help, was watching,* and *has tried.*

Regular and Irregular Verbs are distinguished according to the way in which they form the past tense and past participle. The majority of English verbs are *regular.*

They form the past tense and past participle by adding to the base form either a *d* sound, as in *rubbed, hugged, flowed,* and *raised;* a *t* sound, as in *walked, hoped, laughed,* and *missed;* or an *ed* sound as in *ended, hated, rotted,* and *exasperated.* These endings are written as *d* or *ed.* All regular verbs have a past participle identical with the past tense.

Irregular verbs form the past tense and past participle in various ways. Some change the vowel, as in *come, came; drive, drove;* and *fall, fell.* Some make other changes as well, as in *think, thought; teach, taught,* and *stand, stood.* Some change a final *d* to *t,* as in *build, built; bend, bent;* and *spend, spent.* Some have a past tense identical with the base form, as in *put, put; cost, cost;* and *set, set.* Many irregular verbs, like regular ones, have a past participle identical with the past tense, as in *think, thought, thought* and *build, built, built.* Some irregular verbs have a distinct form for the past participle, as in *fall, fell, fallen; drive, drove, driven; go, went, gone;* and *lie, lay, lain.*

Incorrect usage of irregular verbs often indicates carelessness or lack of knowledge. "I *seen* it"; "He *come* home yesterday"; "He *done* it"; and "He must have *fell* in" show incorrect usage.

Careful speakers would say instead, "I *saw* it"; "He *came* home yesterday"; "He *did* it"; and "He must have *fallen* in."

Transitive and Intransitive Verbs. Verbs may be classified as either transitive or intransitive. A *transitive* verb takes an object. A sentence using a transitive verb is not complete with only a subject and a verb.

Find, send, and *encourage* are ordinarily transitive verbs. An *intransitive* verb does not take an object. A sentence using an intransitive verb can be complete with only a subject and a verb, as in "He is *speaking.*" *Walk, speak,* and *swim* are ordinarily intransitive. Many verbs are transitive in some sentences and intransitive in others.

Linking, or Copulative, Verbs occur in two general structures. In one, the verb is followed by an adjective, as in "He *is* good" or "It *smelled* good." Verbs such as *seemed, looked, tasted, smelled, became, sounded, turned,* and various others could be used as linking verbs. Some occur only in limited contexts, as in "The text *ran* short." In the other linking-verb structure, a noun following the verb refers to the person or thing in the subject, as in "He is *my father*"; "He became *mayor*"; and "He seemed an *interesting person.*" In American English, *be, become, remain,* and *seem* are the only verbs commonly used in this construction. British English uses a few others.

Finite and Nonfinite Verbs. A finite verb is used with a subject, and agrees with it. It changes form according to the number or person of the subject, as in "He drives" and "They drive."

Nonfinite verbs, or verbals, are those which have no subject. There are three kinds of nonfinite verbs in English: the present participle, such as *driving* and *seeing;* the past participle, such as *driven* and *seen;* and the infinitive, *to drive* and *to see.* They are used after auxiliary verbs. The present and past participles are frequently used as modifiers, and the infinitive may also be used as a modifier.

Substantive, or Gerund. The present participle may be used as a substantive, or gerund, as in "*Driving* is fun."

PAUL ROBERTS

Related Articles in WORLD BOOK include:

Conjugation	Mood	Person	Tense
Infinitive	Number	Sentence	Voice
Inflection	Participle		

VERBENA, *ver BE nuh,* is the name of a group of plants in the vervain family which grow both wild and in the garden. Various kinds of verbena grow in many parts of the world, from the tropics to the North Temperate Zone. The wild plants, usually called *vervains,* grow in moist meadows. They bloom from June to September.

In tropical countries some species grow as tall as trees, but those in the temperate climates range from a few inches to 3 to 4 feet in height. Almost all of them have four-sided stems, and opposite or alternate leaves. Several wild European species have been introduced into America and are troublesome weeds in many parts of the United States.

Many cultivated verbena have flower clusters of pink, red, white, purple, or any other color except yellow. They are grown as annuals in the northern states. The seeds are planted in pots under glass in the winter. They can also be grown from cuttings.

They may be grown in the open in the deep South, and will bloom early in the spring. *Moss verbena* is used for hanging baskets.

Scientific Classification. Verbenas belong to the vervain family, *Verbenaceae.* The common garden plant is genus *Verbena,* species *V. hybrida.* The moss verbena is *V. tenuisecta.*

See also SAND VERBENA.

VERDANDI. See NORNS.

VERDE, CAPE. See CAPE VERDE.

VERDE ISLANDS, CAPE. See CAPE VERDE ISLANDS.

The Verbena is a colorful annual much used in flower-garden borders. It blooms continuously throughout the summer in many parts of the world.

J. Horace McFarland

253

VERDI, GIUSEPPE

VERDI, *VAIR dee,* **GIUSEPPE** (1813-1901), an Italian opera composer, was one of the musical giants of his time. He began his career as a composer in Milan in 1836. His first operas were only moderately successful, and the tragic loss of his wife and two children between 1838 and 1840 brought his work to a stop. But the Biblical story, *Nabucco,* revived his interest. It was a major success in 1842, and was soon followed by *I Lombardi* (1843) and *Ernani* (1844).

His Famous Operas. By 1845, Verdi enjoyed international fame. The demands from managers were so great that the music he composed in this period is uneven. Even so, *Macbeth* (1847) and *Luisa Miller* (1849) are important as marking stages in his approaching maturity. Between 1851 and 1853, Verdi produced *Rigoletto* (1851), *Il Trovatore* (1853), and *La Traviata* (1853). These three operas, with *Aïda* (1871), have come to represent Italian opera to much of the world.

In the next few years, Verdi relaxed by studying and farming on his estate near Le Roncole. He became involved in the political difficulties of Italian unification. He composed operas and supervised their production in St. Petersburg, London, and Paris. *Un Ballo in Maschera* (1859), *La Forza del Destino* (1862), and *Don Carlos* (1867) represent this period.

Ewing Galloway
Giuseppe Verdi

The completion of the Suez Canal in 1869 brought a request for an opera from Verdi for the new Cairo opera house. At first he refused, but the attractive libretto and financial arrangements persuaded him. *Aïda* was performed in 1871. This opera, with its vivid use of local color, its beautiful melodies, its restrained but poignant sense of tragedy, its vital characterizations, and its spectacular setting, is a masterpiece.

His Last Works. Verdi's final compositions were an amazing climax to his career. The *Requiem Mass,* for soloists, chorus, and orchestra, came in 1874. Then Arrigo Boito provided Verdi with his two final librettos, both Shakespearean: *Otello* (1887) and *Falstaff* (1893). These works of Verdi's old age supremely justify his basically Italian approach to opera, which grows out of the conviction that the human voice has an inexhaustible capacity for expression.

Verdi was born at Le Roncole (now Roncole Verdi), the son of a poor innkeeper. He studied at the nearby market town of Busseto, and tried to enter the Milan Conservatory, but was refused admission. Undismayed, he composed and studied privately with the conductor of the La Scala opera. He returned to Busseto in 1833 as director of the town's music. In 1860, Verdi became a member of the Italian Parliament from Busseto for a short period of time. THEODORE M. FINNEY

See also OPERA (Some of the Famous Operas).

VERDIGRIS, *VUR dih grees,* or *VUR dih gris,* is a poisonous pigment produced by the action of acetic acid on copper. The color of this pigment varies from blue to green. Verdigris is used commercially in dyeing, calico printing, the manufacture of Paris green, and the manufacture of paint. Because the pigment is likely to fade and react chemically with other substances, it is used less often than in the past. Verdigris is sometimes used in the making of liniments and salves. It must never be taken internally because it is highly poisonous. In case of poison from verdigris, the antidote is milk and white of egg. GEORGE L. BUSH

See also ACETIC ACID.

VERDIN, or GOLDTIT, is a small, yellow-headed bird of the titmouse family. It is about $4\frac{1}{2}$ inches long and lives in the arid portions of Texas and the southwestern United States and in Mexico. Its body is ash-colored and the breast is lighter. The nest of the verdin is often quite large, and is shaped like a ball. It is made of twigs and built in a thorny tree. The female verdin lays from four to six eggs, which are pale blue with brown specks. The birds are too small to fight to protect their young, but their thorny nests give ample protection against most enemies, especially since they leave only a small opening on the bottom as an entrance. Sometimes they build a "porch" around the opening to hide it. They eat caterpillars and other small insects.

Scientific Classification. The verdin is a member of the titmouse family, *Paridae.* It is classified as genus *Auriparus,* species *A. flaviceps.* LEONARD W. WING

The Verdin builds its nest of twigs in a thorny tree. The scratchy thorns protect the eggs and young birds from enemies.

Cruickshank, National Audubon Society

VERDUN, *ver DUN,* Quebec (pop. 78,317; alt. 45 ft.), a suburb of Montreal, lies on the Island of Montreal on the north bank of the St. Lawrence River. Verdun adjoins the southeast section of Montreal.

For Verdun's location, see QUEBEC (political map).

Parks, gardens, and recreational areas line the city's river front. Verdun has about 20 public schools. It was incorporated as a village in 1875. Verdun became a town in 1907, and a city in 1912. The city has a council-manager government. M. G. BALLANTYNE

VERDUN, BATTLES OF. Verdun, one of the oldest cities of France, has been a battleground ever since Attila the Hun ravaged it in A.D. 450. This fortified city on the Meuse River in northern France is about 50 miles from the German border. It has often played an important part in resisting enemy invasion.

The most famous battle took place during World War I. On Feb. 21, 1916, German troops launched a surprise attack, expecting to crush Verdun in a few days. The Germans hoped that, by capturing a key to the French line, they would damage French morale, and could easily defeat other French armies. They also hoped that the victory would impress German allies and neutral nations. The French, led by General Henri Pétain, defended the area stubbornly. After 11 months, the Germans withdrew. Many of the best French and German troops were slaughtered because of inept generalship, but the French hailed Pétain as a hero. During World War II, German forces easily captured Verdun in 1940, and American forces recaptured it in 1944. STEFAN T. POSSONY

See also PÉTAIN, HENRI P.

VERDUN, TREATY OF, divided Charlemagne's empire into three parts. Charlemagne's grandsons fought over control of the empire after their father died in 840, and finally signed the treaty in 843. Charles the Bald received most of what is now France. Louis the German took almost all the land east of the Rhine, which became modern Germany. Lothair kept the title of emperor, and ruled a strip of land in the middle, from the North Sea to central Italy. As a result of the treaty, the lands that were to become France and Germany were effectively divided. The section in between remained a battleground for a thousand years. Italy soon fell away from Lothair's kingdom. In later years part of his kingdom became known as *Lotharingia*, or, later, Lorraine. The partition agreed upon at Verdun marked the end of the political unity of the Christian countries of western Europe. EDWIN J. WESTERMANN

VEREENIGING, TREATY OF. See BOER WAR.

VÉRENDRYE, SIEUR DE LA. See MANITOBA (Exploration).

VERLAINE, *vur LAYN,* **PAUL** (1844-1896), was a famous symbolist French poet. A subtle, tender melancholy pervades his early poems, such as *Les Fêtes Galantes* (1869). Other volumes, including *Romances sans Paroles* (1874), show a delicate musical quality. Many of his poems have been set to music by Gabriel Fauré and Claude Debussy. Verlaine was born at Metz. His personal life was unhappy and disorganized. He was imprisoned for two years for shooting the poet Arthur Rimbaud after a serious quarrel. WALLACE FOWLIE

See also FRENCH LITERATURE (The 1800's).

VERMEER, *vur MAYR,* **JAN** (1632-1675), was a Dutch painter. He was often called Vermeer van Delft to distinguish him from the landscape painter Jan Vermeer van Haarlem. Most of Vermeer's paintings show young, middle-class people, alone or in small groups, in simply furnished rooms. They sit or stand before light

© The Frick Collection, New York

Jan Vermeer's *Officer and Laughing Girl* **shows the dramatic effect of light and dark contrasts that appear in the works of this famous Dutch painter of the 1600's.**

walls, illuminated from a window generally placed at the left. His painting *The Artist in His Studio* appears in color in the PAINTING article.

There is always an air of quiet and timeless happiness in Vermeer's canvases. The light is clear and soft, and the outlines of all forms seem slightly blurred. His favorite colors, blue and yellow, make a lovely, cool harmony. His two outdoor scenes are among the finest landscapes of the 1600's.

Vermeer's works include *Girl with a Water Jug, The Milk Maid, The Studio,* and *View of Delft.* He was born in Delft, and spent his entire life there. Vermeer was a painstaking worker and he painted only about 40 known pictures. JULIUS S. HELD

VERMES. See WORM.

VERMICELLI. See MACARONI.

VERMICULITE, *vur MIK yu lite,* is a mineral of the mica family. It is found as laminated flakes. In the United States it is mined chiefly in Montana and South Carolina. When expanded by heat, vermiculite can be used industrially in building materials for insulation and soundproofing.

VERMIFORM APPENDIX. See APPENDIX, VERMIFORM.

VERMILION, *ver MIL yun,* is a pigment or coloring matter used in making paint. Its color varies from crimson to a brilliant yellow-red. Formerly made from the mineral cinnabar, it is now made from mercury and sulfur ground together and treated with caustic-potash solution. This may be heated and stirred to form a black sulfide which yields the pigment, after long steaming. The name *vermilion* comes from a Latin word meaning *little worm,* and refers to the dried bodies of insects from which carmine, another red dye, is obtained. See also CARMINE; CINNABAR. THOMAS MUNRO

VERMILION RANGE. See MINNESOTA (Natural Resources).

Grant Heilman
Vermont Village in Winter

VERMONT

THE GREEN MOUNTAIN STATE

VERMONT, a New England state, is famous for its Green Mountains. These tree-covered peaks run the entire length of central Vermont. They divide the state into eastern and western sections. The beauty of the Green Mountains helps make Vermont one of the most scenic states. Every year, the mountains attract thousands of skiers and other tourists. Montpelier is the capital of Vermont, and Burlington is the largest city.

Manufacturing is the chief economic activity in Vermont, as it is in all the other New England states. But farming is also important in Vermont—much more so than in the rest of New England. Vermont is the only New England state in which farm products account for more than a fourth of the value of all goods produced. It is also the only New England state in which more than half the people live in farm areas. Only five Vermont cities and towns have more than 10,000 persons. They are Burlington, Rutland, Bennington, Brattleboro, and Barre. Vermont has the smallest population of any state east of the Mississippi River. It ranks

47th among all the states in population. Only Wyoming, Nevada, and Alaska have fewer persons.

Forests cover more than three-fifths of Vermont, and a variety of mineral deposits lie under the ground. These natural resources provide the raw materials for two of the state's main manufacturing industries—wood processing and stone processing. Trees from Vermont's forests supply wood for making paper, furniture, and many other products. Vermont granite and marble are used in buildings, memorials, and tombs. Slate is used for roofing and for other purposes.

Vermont is the only New England state without a coastline on the Atlantic Ocean. However, water borders more than half the state. The Connecticut River forms Vermont's entire eastern border. Lake Champlain extends along the northern half of the western border. In addition to the Green Mountains, Vermont has many other mountains and hills. These include the White Mountains, the Granite Hills, and the Taconic Mountains.

256

Maple Sugar Season in Groton

Vermont (blue) ranks 43rd in size among all the states, and 2nd in size among the New England States (gray).

Photos, Dick Smith
Autumn near Peacham

The contributors of this article are T. D. Seymour Bassett, Curator of the Wilbur Collection of the Guy W. Bailey Library, and University Archivist of the University of Vermont; J. Rowland Illick, Chairman of the Department of Geology and Geography at Middlebury College; and Seargent P. Wild, Associate Editor of the Rutland Herald.

Early in the Revolutionary War, Vermont's Green Mountain Boys, led by Ethan Allen, gained fame for their capture of Fort Ticonderoga from the British. But Vermont did not join the newly formed United States after the war. It remained an independent republic until about 10 years after the last battle. Then, on March 4, 1791, Vermont entered the Union as the 14th state. It was the first state admitted to the Union after the 13 original colonies.

During the 1850's, Vermont began a voting record unequaled by any other state. From then until the 1960's, Vermont voters chose only Republicans in elections for President and governor. They also chose Republicans in all elections for the U.S. Senate and House of Representatives between the mid-1800's and the mid-1900's. No state has voted so many times in a row for major candidates of the same party. Two Vermont Republicans, Chester A. Arthur and Calvin Coolidge, became President of the United States.

The word *Vermont* comes from *Vert Mont,* the French words for *Green Mountain.* Vermont's nickname is the *Green Mountain State.* For the relationship of Vermont to other states in its region, see NEW ENGLAND.

——————— FACTS IN BRIEF ———————

Capital: Montpelier.

Government: *Congress*—U.S. Senators, 2; U.S. Representatives, 1. *Electoral Votes,* 3. *State Legislature*—senators, 30; representatives, 150. *Counties,* 14. *Voting Age,* 21 years.

Area: 9,609 square miles (including 333 square miles of inland water), 43rd in size among the states. *Greatest Distances:* (north-south) 155 miles; (east-west) 90 miles.

Elevation: *Highest,* Mount Mansfield, 4,393 feet above sea level. *Lowest,* Lake Champlain in Franklin County, 95 feet above sea level.

Population: *1960 census*—389,881; rank, 47th among the states; distribution, 61 per cent rural, 39 per cent urban; density, 41 persons to the square mile. *1965 estimate*—410,000.

Chief Products: *Manufacturing,* machinery (including machine tools), processed food, stone products, wood products (including paper). *Agriculture,* apples, hay, maple sugar and maple syrup, milk, potatoes, poultry and eggs. *Mining,* asbestos, granite, marble, slate, talc.

Statehood: March 4, 1791, the 14th state.

State Motto: *Freedom and Unity.*

State Song: "Hail Vermont," by Josephine Hovey Perry.

Constitution of Vermont was adopted in 1793. Vermont had two earlier constitutions, adopted in 1777 and 1786. The constitution of 1777 was the most liberal of its time. It gave all adult male citizens the right to vote, without regard to their race or religion, or whether or not they owned property. It also forbade slavery.

Amendments (changes) to the constitution may be proposed every 10 years by a two-thirds vote of the state senate. The proposed amendments must be approved by a majority vote in the house of representatives. At the next legislative session two years later, the amendments require approval by a majority of both the house and the senate. Finally, to become law, amendments need the approval of a majority of the people who vote on the proposals in an election.

Executive. The governor of Vermont is elected to a two-year term. He receives a $13,750 yearly salary. The governor may be re-elected any number of times. For a list of all the governors of Vermont, see the *History* section of this article. Vermont voters also elect the lieutenant governor, attorney general, auditor, secretary of state, and treasurer to two-year terms. The governor appoints most other top executive officials, with senate approval.

Legislature of Vermont is called the *general assembly*. It consists of a 30-member senate and a 150-member house of representatives. The voters in each of Vermont's 12 senatorial districts elect from one to six senators, depending on total population. Voters in each of 106 representative districts and subdistricts elect one or two representatives, depending on voter population. Senators and representatives serve two-year terms. The general assembly meets in odd-numbered years.

Courts. The supreme court, Vermont's highest court, has a chief justice and four associate justices. Supreme court justices and Vermont's six superior court judges are elected by the legislature to two-year terms. The legislature usually re-elects the men until their death or retirement. Each county has one or two probate courts, whose judges are elected to two-year terms. The governor, with the senate's approval, appoints the judges of Vermont's district and municipal courts.

Local Government in Vermont is centered in towns. Vermont towns are similar to townships in other states. That is, they are geographic areas that may include several communities and large rural districts under one government. In Vermont, there are 238 towns with local governments. Five towns—Averill, Ferdinand, Glastenbury, Lewis, and Somerset—have too few inhabitants to have governments. They range in population from no persons in Glastenbury and Lewis to 16 persons in Averill and Ferdinand. Each of Vermont's eight cities also has a local government.

Vermont towns use the *town meeting* form of government, the purest type of democracy. A town meeting allows citizens to take a direct part in government business. Each March, town voters assemble to elect officials, approve budgets, pass laws, and decide other local business. Vermont cities operate under council-manager or mayor-council governments. The cities must submit changes in their charters to the legislature for approval. The powers of Vermont county governments are limited mainly to judicial affairs.

Town Meetings allow Vermont citizens to take a direct part in governing their communities. A town meeting is the purest form of democracy, because it is government by the people rather than by elected representatives. Each year, residents assemble to elect officials, approve budgets, pass laws, and decide other local business. All town voters may attend.

Hanson Carroll

The State Seal

Symbols of Vermont. On the state seal, the 14 branches on the pine tree represent the 13 original states and Vermont. The wavy lines at the top symbolize the sky and the wavy lines on the bottom stand for the sea. The cow and the sheaves of wheat represent dairying and agriculture. The seal, designed in 1779, was modified and adopted in 1937. The state flag, adopted in 1923, carries the Vermont coat of arms. It shows a view of the Green Mountains.

Flag, flower, and bird illustrations, courtesy of Eli Lilly and Company

Taxation provides about 60 per cent of the state government's income. Almost all the rest comes from federal grants and other U.S. government programs. An individual income tax brings in more than a fourth of the state's tax income. Motor fuel taxes and drivers' license and vehicle registration fees also bring in more than a fourth of the income. Other Vermont taxes, in order of importance, include those on alcoholic beverages, tobacco products, and corporation net income.

Politics. Vermont has voted for more Republican presidential candidates than any other state. Vermont gave its electoral votes to the Republican candidate in all 27 presidential elections from 1856 through 1960. In 1964, the state supported Democrat Lyndon B. Johnson in his landslide victory over Republican Barry M. Goldwater. Vermont has never had a Democratic U.S. Senator. All Vermont U.S. Representatives between 1853 and 1959, and all Vermont governors between 1853 and 1963, were Republicans. The people also vote strongly Republican in local elections. For Vermont's electoral votes and voting record in presidential elections, see ELECTORAL COLLEGE (table).

State Capitol in Montpelier has a dome covered with gold leaf. At the top of the dome is a statue of Ceres, the Roman goddess of agriculture. The beautiful Doric columns are made of native Vermont granite. Montpelier has been the state capital since 1808. Many towns served as temporary capitals between 1777 and 1808.

Arthur Griffin

The State Flag

The State Bird
Hermit Thrush

The State Flower
Red Clover

The State Tree
Sugar Maple

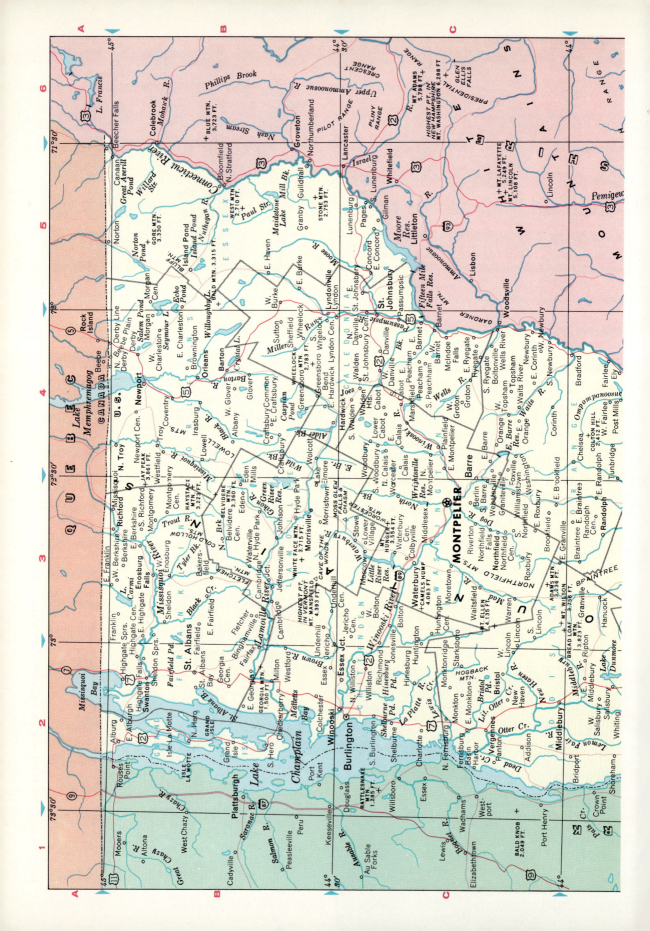

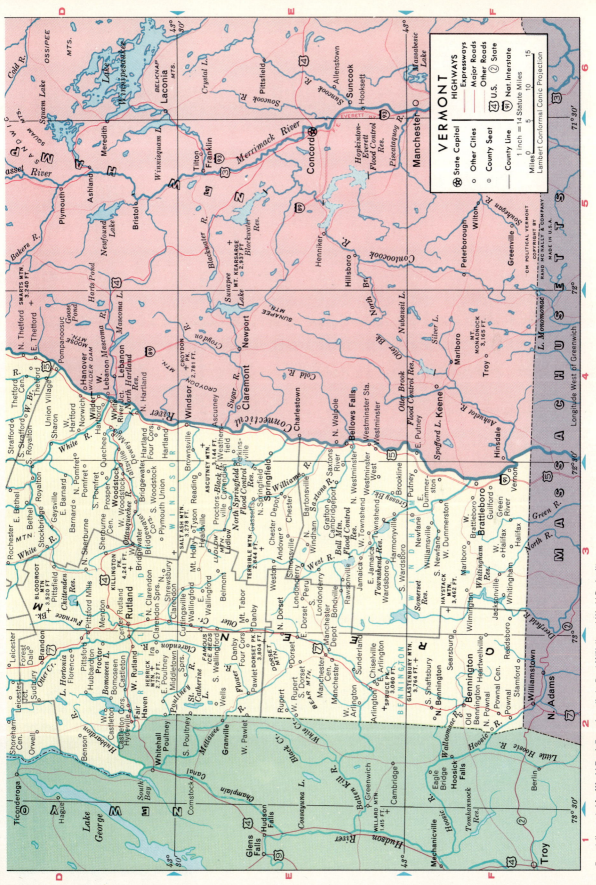

VERMONT

HIGHWAYS

Expressways
Major Roads
Other Roads
⓲ U.S. ② State
⑧ Nat. Interstate

✪ State Capital
⊙ Other Cities
○ County Seat
County Line

1 inch = 14 Statute Miles

Miles   0   5   10   15

Lambert Conformal Conic Projection

CM POLITICAL VERMONT
COPYRIGHT BY
RAND MCNALLY & COMPANY
MADE IN U.S.A.

Especially created for **World Book Encyclopedia** by Rand McNally and World Book editors

VERMONT MAP INDEX

Population

410,000 ..... Estimate 1965
389,881 1960
377,747 1950
359,231 1940
359,611 1930
352,428 1920
355,956 1910
343,641 1900
332,422 1890
332,286 1880
330,551 1870
315,098 1860
314,120 1850
291,948 1840
280,652 1830
235,981 1820
217,895 1810
154,465 1800
85,425 1790

Counties

Addison, 20,076 ..... C 2
Bennington, 25,088 ..... E 2
Caledonia, 22,786 ..... C 4
Chittenden, 74,425 ..... C 2
Essex, 6,083 ..... B 5
Franklin, 29,474 ..... B 3
Grand Isle, 2,927 ..... B 2
Lamoille, 11,027 ..... B 3
Orange, 16,014 ..... D 4
Orleans, 20,143 ..... B 4
Rutland, 46,719 ..... D 2
Washington, 42,860 ..... C 3
Windham, 29,776 ..... F 3
Windsor, 42,483 ..... D 3

Cities, Towns, and Villages

Addison, 60 (645▲) ... C 2
Albany, 169 (560▲) .. B 4
Alburg, 426 (1,123▲) . B 2
Andover, (215▲) ..... E 3
Arlington, 1,111 (1,605▲) ..... E 2
Averill,* 16 ..... B 5
Bakersfield, 225 (664▲) ..... B 3
Barnard, 75 (435▲) ... D 3
Barnet, 250 (1,445▲) . C 4
Barre, 10,387 ..... C 4
Barton, 1,169 (3,066▲) ..... B 4
Beebe Plain, 140 ..... A 4
Beecher Falls, 350 ... A 5
Bellows Falls, 3,831 .. E 4
Belvidere Center (Belvidere), 75 (155▲) ..... B 3
Bennington, 8,023 (13,002▲) ..... °F 2
Benson, 60 (549▲) .... D 2
Berlin, 100 (1,306▲) .. C 3
Bethel, 100 (1,356▲) .. D 3
Binghamville, 115 .... B 3
Bloomfield, 120 (212▲) B 5
Boltonville, 105 ..... C 4
Bradford, 760 (1,619▲) D 4
Braintree, 100 (536▲) . D 3
Brandon, 1,675 (3,329▲) ..... D 2
Brattleboro, 11,734 ... F 3
Bridgewater, 175 (776▲) ..... D 3
Bridgewater Corners, 100 ..... D 3
Bridport, 100 (653▲) .. D 2
Bristol, 1,421 (2,159▲) ..... C 2
Brookline, 89 (127▲) .. E 3
Burlington, 35,531 .. °C 2
Cabot, 244 (763▲) .... C 4
Calais, 150 (684▲) .... C 4
Cambridge, 217 (1,295▲) ..... B 3
Cambridgeport, 100 ... E 3
Canaan, 275 (1,094▲) . B 5
Castleton, 375 (1,902▲) D 2
Castleton Corners, 140 ..... D 2
Cavendish, 250 (1,223▲) ..... E 3
Center Rutland, 225 .. D 2
Charlotte, 160 (1,271▲) C 2
Chelsea, 500 (957▲) . °D 4
Chester, 923 (2,318▲) . E 3
Chester Depot, 350 ... E 3
Clarendon, 75 (1,091▲) ..... D 3
Colbyville, 120 ..... C 3
Colchester, 225 (4,718▲) ..... B 2
Concord, 389 (956▲) .. C 5
Coventry, 130 (458▲) .. B 4
Craftsbury, 175 (674▲) B 4
Craftsbury Common, 90 ..... B 4
Cuttingsville, 100 ..... E 3
Danby, 250 (891▲) .... E 3
Danville, 300 (1,368▲) C 4
Derby, 433 (2,506▲) .. B 4
Derby Line, 849 ..... A 4
Dewey Mills, 100 .... D 4
Dorset, 300 (1,150▲) .. E 2
Duxbury, 150 (546▲) . C 3
East Alburgh, 75 ..... B 2
East Arlington, 500 .. E 2
East Barnet, 100 ..... C 4
East Barre, 550 ..... C 4
East Berkshire, 200 .. B 3
East Burke, 110 ..... B 5
East Calais, 110 ..... C 4
East Concord, 250 .... C 5
East Corinth, 200 .... C 4
East Dorset, 140 ..... E 2
East Dummerston, 85 . F 3
East Fairfield, 150 ... B 3
East Granville, 75 .... C 3
East Hardwick, 195 ... B 4
East Highgate, 110 ... B 3
East Middlebury, 320 D 2
East Montpelier, 200 (1,200▲) ..... C 4
East Poultney, 300 ... D 2
East Randolph, 130 .. D 3
East Richford, 100 ... A 3
East Ryegate, 170 .... C 4
East St. Johnsbury, 150 ..... C 5
East Thetford, 100 ... D 4
East Wallingford, 150 E 3
Eden, 65 (430▲) ..... B 3
Enosburg Falls (Enosburg), 1,321 (1,966▲) ..... B 3
Essex, 300 (7,090▲) .. B 2
Essex Junction, 5,340 . C 2
Fair Haven, 2,378 .... D 2
Fairfax, 350 (1,244▲) . B 2
Fairfield, 100 (1,225▲) B 3
Fairlee, 400 (569▲) ... D 4
Ferrisburg, 170 (1,426▲) ..... C 2
Fletcher, 125 (399▲) .. B 3
Florence, 80 ..... D 2
Forest Dale, 450 ..... D 2
Foxville, 100 ..... C 4
Franklin, 185 (796▲) . B 3
Gaysville, 100 ..... D 3
Georgia Center (Georgia) 100 (1,079▲) ..... B 2
Gilman, 600 ..... C 5
Glastenbury* ..... F 2
Glover, 230 (683▲) ... B 4
Grafton, 150 (426▲) .. E 3
Grand Isle, 100 (624▲) ..... B 2
Graniteville, 860 ..... C 4
Granville, 110 (215▲) . D 3
Green River, 60 ..... F 3
Greensboro, 115 (600▲) ..... B 4
Greensboro Bend, 100 ..... B 4
Groton, 387 (631▲) ... C 4
Guildhall, 100 (248▲) °B 5
Guilford, 100 (823▲) . F 3
Halifax, 100 (268▲) .. F 3
Hancock, 160 (323▲) . D 3
Hardwick, 1,521 (2,349▲) ..... B 4
Hartford, 450 (6,355▲) ..... D 4
Hartland, 200 (1,592▲) ..... D 4
Hartland Four Corners, 116 ..... D 4
Healdville, 150 ..... E 3
Highgate Center (Highgate), 300 (1,608▲) ..... B 2
Highgate Falls, 125 .. B 2
Highgate Springs, 125 B 2
Hinesburg, 200 (1,180▲) ..... C 2
Huntington, 118 (518▲) ..... C 3
Huntington Center, 100 ..... C 3
Hyde Park, 474 (1,219▲) ..... °B 3
Hydeville, 300 ..... D 2
Irasburg, 200 (711▲) .. B 4
Island Pond, 1,319 ... B 5
Isle La Motte, 125 (238▲) ..... B 2
Jacksonville, 240 ..... F 3
Jamaica, 250 (496▲) .. E 3
Jeffersonville, 346 ... B 3
Jericho, 275 (1,425▲) . B 3
Jericho Center, 120 .. C 3
Johnson, 941 (1,478▲) B 3
Lake Elmore, 75 ..... B 3
Leicester, 50 (551▲) .. D 2
Leicester Junction, 100 ..... D 2
Lincoln, 250 (481▲) .. C 3
Londonderry, 200 (898▲) ..... E 3
Lowell, 135 (617▲) ... B 4
Lower Cabot, 150 ..... C 4
Lower Village, 75 .... C 3
Ludlow, 1,658 (2,386▲) E 3
Lunenburg, 250 (1,237▲) ..... C 5
Lyndon, 250 (3,425▲) . B 4
Lyndon Center, 274 .. B 4
Lyndonville, 1,477 ... B 4
Manchester, 403 (2,470▲) ..... °E 2
Manchester Center, 600 ..... E 2
Manchester Depot, 800 ..... E 2
Marshfield, 313 (891▲) ..... C 4
McIndoe Falls, 155 ... C 4
Middlebury, 3,688 (5,305▲) ..... °C 2
Middlesex, 80 (770▲) . C 3
Middletown Springs, 275 (381▲) ..... E 2
Milton, 817 (2,022▲) .. B 2
Missisquoi, 100 ..... B 3
Monkton, 130 (551▲) . C 2
Monktonridge, 75 .... C 2
Montgomery, 250 (876▲) ..... B 3
Montgomery Center, 375 ..... B 3
Montpelier, 8,782 ... °C 3
Moretown, 150 (788▲) . C 3
Morgan Center, 80 ... B 5
Morristown, 65 (3,347▲) ..... B 3
Morrisville, 2,047 .... B 3
Moscow, 100 ..... C 3
Mount Holly, 70 (517▲) ..... E 3
New Haven, 150 (922▲) ..... C 2
Newbury, 391 (1,452▲) C 4
Newfane, 146 (714▲) . °F 3
Newport, 5,019 ..... °B 4
Newport Center, 288 .. B 4
North Bennington, 1,437 ..... F 2
North Clarendon, 200 . D 3
North Danville, 80 ... C 4
North Derby, 81 ..... A 4
North Ferrisburg, 200 ..... C 2
North Hartland, 150 . D 4
North Hero, 50 (328▲) ..... °B 2
North Hyde Park, 230 ..... B 3
North Montpelier, 140 C 4
North Pownal, 275 ... F 2
North Springfield, 600 ..... E 3
North Thetford, 100 .. D 4
North Troy, 961 ..... D 4
North Westminster, 368 ..... E 4
Northfield, 2,159 (4,511▲) ..... C 3
Northfield Center, 100 C 3
Northfield Falls, 325 C 3
Norton, 100 (241▲) ... A 5
Norwich, 500 (1,790▲) D 4
Old Bennington, 205 .. F 2
Orleans, 1,240 ..... B 4
Orwell, 250 (826▲) .... D 2
Passumpsic, 180 ..... C 4
Pawlet, 165 (1,112▲) .. E 2
Peacham, 75 (433▲) .. C 4
Perkinsville, 167 ..... E 3
Pittsfield, 100 (254▲) . D 3
Pittsford, 671 (2,225▲) D 2
Pittsford Mills, 200 .. D 2
Plainfield, 507 (966▲) C 4
Plymouth Union, 75 .. D 3
Pomfret, 20 (600▲) ... D 3
Post Mills, 200 ..... D 4
Poultney, 1,810 (3,009▲) ..... D 2
Pownal, 325 (1,509▲) . F 2
Pownal Center, 75 .... F 2
Proctor, 1,978 (2,102▲) ..... D 2
Proctorsville, 476 ..... E 3
Putney, 250 (1,177▲) .. F 3
Quechee, 300 ..... D 4
Randolph, 2,122 (3,414▲) ..... D 3
Randolph Center, 140 D 3
Reading, 165 (472▲) .. E 3
Readsboro, 577 (783▲) F 3
Richford, 1,663 (2,316▲) ..... B 3
Richmond, 765 (1,303▲) C 3
Ripton, 70 (1,310▲) .. D 2
Riverton, 100 ..... C 3
Rochester, 350 (879▲) D 3
Roxbury, 225 (364▲) .. C 3
Royalton, 150 (1,388▲) ..... D 3
Rupert, 150 (603▲) ... E 2
Rutland, 18,325 ..... °D 3
St. Albans, 8,806 .... °B 2
St. Albans (Town of)* (2,303▲) ..... B 2
St. Albans Bay, 350 .. B 2
St. Johnsbury, 6,809 (8,869▲) ..... °C 4
St. Johnsbury Center, 300 ..... C 4
Salisbury, 130 (575▲) . D 2
Saxtons River 725 .... E 3
Sharon, 155 (485▲) ... D 4
Sheffield, 225 (342▲) . B 4
Shelburne, 250 (1,805▲) ..... C 2
Sheldon, 300 (1,281▲) B 3
Sheldon Springs, 250 . B 3
Sherburne Center (Sherburne) 60 (266▲) ..... D 3
Shoreham, 130 (786▲) . D 2
South Barre, 300 .... C 3
South Burlington, 6,903 ..... C 2
South Dorset, 160 .... E 2
South Hero, 70 (614▲) ..... B 2
South Londonderry, 250 ..... E 3
South Lunenburg, 100 C 5
South Newfane, 100 .. F 3
South Northfield, 65 . C 3
South Pomfret, 150 ... D 3
South Poultney, 100 .. E 2
South Royalton, 450 .. D 3
South Ryegate, 346 ... C 4
South Shaftsbury, 600 ..... F 2
South Strafford, 75 .. D 4
South Wallingford, 120 ..... E 3
South Woodstock, 85 . D 3
Springfield, 6,600 (9,934▲) ..... E 4
Stamford, 150 (600▲) . F 2
Starksboro, 150 (502▲) ..... C 2
Stowe, 534 (1,901▲) .. C 3
Strafford, 100 (548▲) . D 4
Sunderland, 40 (566▲) E 2
Sutton, 125 (476▲) .... B 4
Swanton, 2,390 (3,946▲) ..... B 2
Taftsville, 100 ..... D 4
Thetford, 100 (1,049▲) ..... D 4
Thetford Center, 150 .. D 4
Topsham, 150 (638▲) . C 4
Townshend, 170 (643▲) ..... E 3
Troy, 150 (1,613▲) .... B 4
Tunbridge, 125 (743▲) D 4
Tyson, 75 ..... E 3
Underhill, 225 (730▲) B 3
Underhill Center, 150 . B 3
Vergennes, 1,921 ..... C 2
Vernon, 130 (865▲) .. F 3
Waits River, 75 ..... C 4
Waitsfield, 175 (658▲) ..... C 3
Wallingford, 900 (1,439▲) ..... E 3
Wardsboro, 125 (322▲) E 3
Warren, 200 (469▲) .. C 3
Washington, 200 (565▲) ..... C 4
Waterbury, 2,984 (4,303▲) ..... C 3
Waterbury Center, 400 C 3
Waterville, 250 (332▲) B 3
Weathersfield, 30 (1,254▲) ..... E 4
Websterville, 750 ..... C 4
Wells, 200 (419▲) .... E 2
Wells River, 472 ..... C 4
West Barnet, 113 ..... C 4
West Berkshire, 95 ... B 3
West Bridgewater, 95 D 3
West Burke, 369 ..... B 5
West Charleston, 150 . B 4
West Dummerston, 90 F 3
West Enosburg, 75 .... B 3
West Fairlee, 185 (333▲) ..... D 4
West Halifax, 100 .... F 3
West Hartford, 100 ... D 4
West Pawlet, 280 ..... E 2
West Rupert, 160 ..... E 2
West Rutland, 2,302 . D 2
West Topsham, 100 ... C 4
West Townshend, 95 .. E 3
Westfield, 90 (347▲) .. B 4
Westford, 90 (680▲) .. B 2
Westminster, 333 (1,602▲) ..... E 4
Weston, 200 (442▲) ... E 3
Wheelock, 70 (246▲) .. B 4
White River Junction, 2,546 ..... D 4
Whiting, 70 (304▲) ... D 2
Whitingham, 100 (838▲) ..... F 3
Wilder, 1,322 ..... D 4
Williamstown, 400 (1,553▲) ..... C 3
Williamsville, 125 .... F 3
Williston, 250 (1,484▲) C 2
Wilmington, 591 (1,245▲) ..... F 3
Windsor, 3,256 (4,468▲) ..... E 4
Winooski, 7,420 ..... C 2
Wolcott, 150 (633▲) .. B 4
Woodbury, 250 (317▲) C 4
Woodstock, 1,415 (2,786▲) ..... °D 3
Worcester, 140 (417▲) C 3

▲Population of entire town (township), including rural area.

*Does not appear on map; key shows general location.

°County Seat.

Source: Latest census figures.

Rural Children Take a Bus to School.
Clemens Kalischer

Veteran Farmers Discuss Their Crops.
Bullaty-Lomeo

The 1960 United States census reported that Vermont had 389,881 persons. The population had increased 3 per cent over the 1950 figure, 377,747. The U.S. Bureau of the Census estimated that by 1965 the state's population had reached 410,000.

Fewer persons live in Vermont than in any other state east of the Mississippi River. West of the river, only Wyoming, Nevada, and Alaska have smaller populations. About 61 per cent of Vermont's people live in rural areas. Vermont is the only New England state with a larger rural than urban population.

Burlington is Vermont's largest city. It has almost twice as many people as Rutland, the second largest city. Vermont's other cities, in order of size, are Barre, St. Albans, Montpelier, Winooski, Newport, and Vergennes. Bennington and Brattleboro have the largest populations among Vermont's 243 towns. See the separate articles on Vermont cities, towns, and villages listed in the *Related Articles* at the end of this article.

Most Vermonters were born in the United States. More than half the people born in other countries came from Canada. More Vermonters belong to the Roman Catholic Church than to any other religious group. Other large religious groups, in order of size, include members of the United Church of Christ, Methodists, Baptists, and Episcopalians.

Like other New Englanders, the people of Vermont have long been called *Yankees*. This word is used to mean such traits as thrift, conservative manners, reserved speech, and respect for individual rights.

Schools. The town of Guilford voted funds for a free public school in 1761. Bennington set up a school fund shortly afterward. Vermont's constitution of 1777 required each town to have a public school. In 1780, Bennington established the state's first secondary school. Vermont's first state-wide school fund was approved by the legislature in 1825. Samuel Read Hall, a pioneer educator, established the first U.S. teacher-training school at Concord in 1823.

A state commissioner of education and a seven-member board of education supervise Vermont's public-school system. The governor, with the senate's approval, appoints the board members to six-year terms. The board members, with the governor's approval, appoint the commissioner for an indefinite term.

Vermont's city and town school districts are administered by local boards of directors. The largest local districts also have a superintendent of schools. The smaller districts are grouped into *supervisory unions*, each with about 50 teachers and a superintendent. The supervisory unions work with the local boards of directors in managing school affairs.

Vermont law requires children between the ages of 7 and 16 to attend school. For the number of students and teachers in Vermont, see EDUCATION (table).

Libraries. Vermont's first library opened in Brookfield in 1791. It is one of the oldest libraries still operating in the United States. Today, Vermont has more than 200 public libraries. The largest public library is the State Library in Montpelier. It specializes in legal reference works, and has the state's best collection of early Vermont newspapers. The Bailey Library of the University of Vermont is the state's largest.

Museums. The Vermont Historical Society Museum in Montpelier features collections of Vermont town histories; animal, bird, and rock specimens; and old coins, manuscripts, tools, and weapons. The museum owns the first globes made in the United States. The globes were made by James Wilson during the early 1800's. The museum also houses a printing press that may be the first one used in the United States. This press may be the one set up by Stephen Daye in Cambridge, Mass., in 1639. The Bennington Museum has collections of early American glassware, pottery, Vermont art, and historic flags. The University of Vermont's Robert Hull Fleming Museum in Burlington displays works of art from many periods. The Saint Johnsbury Athenaeum has fine paintings. The Sheldon Museum in Middlebury houses early Vermont documents, household furnishings, portraits, and tools. The Tom Daniels Museum in Orwell has many items used by Indians. The famous Shelburne Museum is described in the *Places to Visit* section of this article.

UNIVERSITIES AND COLLEGES

Vermont has eleven regionally accredited four-year universities and colleges. For enrollments and other information, see UNIVERSITIES AND COLLEGES (table).

Name	Location	Founded
Bennington College	Bennington	1932
Castleton State College	Castleton	1867
Goddard College	Plainfield	1938
Johnson State College	Johnson	1828
Lyndon State College	Lyndonville	1944
Marlboro College	Marlboro	1947
Middlebury College	Middlebury	1800
Norwich University	Northfield	1819
St. Michael's College	Winooski	1904
Trinity College	Burlington	1925
Vermont, University of	Burlington	1791

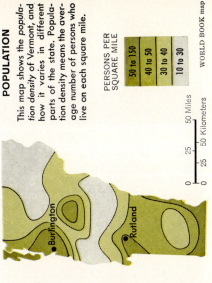

POPULATION

This map shows the population density of Vermont, and how it varies in different parts of the state. Population density means the average number of persons who live on each square mile.

PERSONS PER SQUARE MILE
- 50 to 150
- 40 to 50
- 30 to 40
- 10 to 30

WORLD BOOK map

Paddlewheeler *S.S. Ticonderoga* in Shelburne Museum

Arthur Griffin

Marble Quarry in Proctor

Arthur Griffin

Hanson Carroll

Fishing on the West River

VERMONT / *A Visitor's Guide*

Vermont's mountains, lakes, and streams offer a variety of recreational activities. Visitors to the Green Mountains can hike on the Long Trail. This footpath in the wilderness winds through the mountains from Massachusetts to Canada. Overnight camps lie along the trail every six to eight miles. In winter, tourists flock to 40 ski resorts in the Green Mountains and other ranges. The largest ski resorts are near Manchester, Rutland, Stowe, Waitsfield, and Wilmington. The skiing season usually lasts from mid-December to mid-April. Visitors also enjoy summer boating on Vermont's larger lakes and fishing in the state's many streams.

Many vacationers go to Vermont just for the beautiful scenery. In the fall, much of the state is ablaze with the orange, purple, red, and yellow colors of turning leaves. Vermont's quiet towns and villages are other favorite scenes. They are noted for their white churches.

PLACES TO VISIT

Following are brief descriptions of some of Vermont's many interesting places to visit.

Bennington Battle Monument, in Bennington, is a 306-foot-high granite tower. It honors the colonists who defeated the British in the Battle of Bennington in 1777. The tower is the world's second highest battle monument. Only the 570-foot San Jacinto Battle Monument near Houston, Tex., is higher.

Coolidge Birthplace, in Plymouth, is now a combination store and post office. A nearby museum houses many possessions of President Calvin Coolidge. A sim- ple gravestone marks his grave in the town cemetery.

Granite Quarries cut deeply into Millstone Hill in Barre. Visitors can watch large granite blocks being quarried. They can also see granite being sawed, pol- ished, and carved in the world's largest stone-finishing plant.

Marble Quarries and Marble Exhibit are Proctor's chief attractions. The quarries are among the world's largest. The exhibit, in the display rooms of the Ver- mont Marble Company, features the world's largest collection of various kinds of marble.

Arthur Griffin

Bennington Battle Monument

Robert H. Perry

Skiing on Killington Peak near Rutland

Old Constitution House, in Windsor, is the building in which Vermont's first constitution was written. This two-story frame house was built as a tavern in 1772.

Shelburne Museum, in Shelburne, is a reconstruction of an early American village. The museum buildings house one of the world's most complete collections of items used by early Vermont settlers. The items include carriages, china, dolls, furniture, glass, hunting decoys, paintings, pewter, rugs, and toys. The paddle-wheel steamship *Ticonderoga,* which once sailed Lake Champlain, is part of the museum.

Smuggler's Notch, near Stowe, is a wide gap between Mount Mansfield and the Sterling Mountains. The notch got its name during the War of 1812, when smugglers brought goods through the notch from Canada to Boston.

National Forest. Green Mountains National Forest, established in 1911, is located in south-central Vermont. For the forest's chief features, see NATIONAL FOREST (table).

State Parks and Forests. Vermont has 29 state parks and 20 state forests. For information on them, write to Commissioner of Forests and Parks, State Office Building, State Street, Montpelier, Vt. 05602.

ANNUAL EVENTS

Skiing contests rank among Vermont's most popular annual events. Ski jumping and racing contests are held in many parts of the state throughout the winter. Vermont's maple-sugar season begins when the winter snows start melting, usually in March. People gather at maple-sugar houses to watch maple syrup being made from maple sap. October is the best month to see the brilliant colors of Vermont's autumn leaves. Other annual events in Vermont include the following.

March-July: Town Meeting Day, state-wide (first Tuesday in March); County Dairy Festivals, state-wide (June); Cracker Barrel Bazaar in Newbury (late July); Maple-Sugar Parties in Barton and Morgan (late July).

August-November: Lumberjack Roundup at Lake Dunmore (mid-August); Trail Rides in South Woodstock (late August); Fairs in Barton, Bondville, Bradford, Essex, Lyndonville, Rutland, Tunbridge, and Wilmington (mid-August to mid-September); Summer Theater Festivals in Dorset, Weston, Winooski, and other communities (no fixed dates). Forest Festival, state-wide (no fixed date); Deer Hunting Season (sixteen days, starting on the second Saturday in November).

265

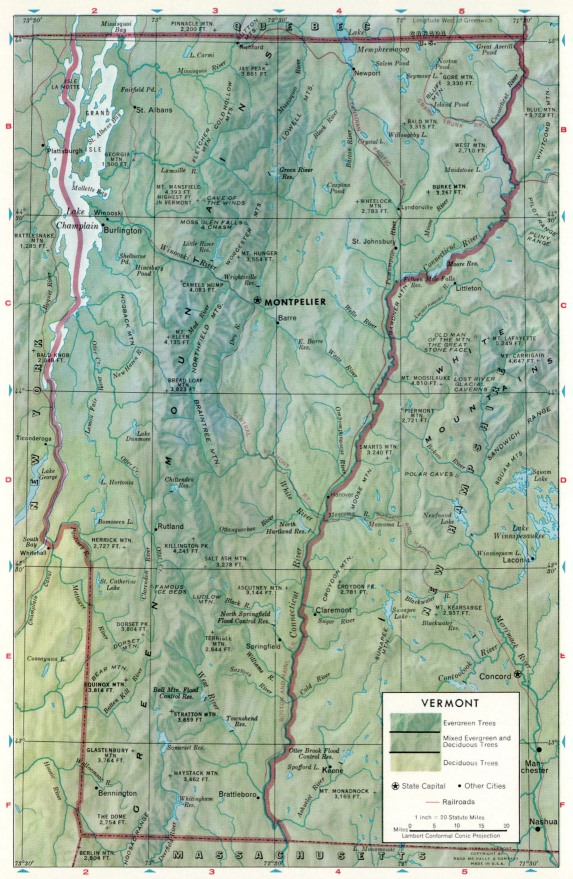

VERMONT

Evergreen Trees

Mixed Evergreen and
Deciduous Trees

Deciduous Trees

✪ State Capital   • Other Cities

⎯⎯ Railroads

1 inch = 20 Statute Miles

Miles 0   5   10   15   20

Lambert Conformal Conic Projection

RAND M^cNALLY & COMPANY
MADE IN U.S.A.

VERMONT / The Land

Land Regions. Vermont has six main land regions: (1) the White Mountains, (2) the Western New England Upland, (3) the Green Mountains, (4) the Vermont Valley, (5) the Taconic Mountains, and (6) the Champlain Valley.

The White Mountains region covers the northeastern corner of Vermont and parts of New Hampshire and Maine. In Vermont, the region includes a series of *monadnocks*. A monadnock is a mountain composed of rock that did not wear down when the land around it was leveled by erosion. The monadnocks have rounded slopes and rise between about 2,700 and 3,300 feet above sea level. The highest ones are Gore Mountain (3,330 feet), Burke Mountain (3,267 feet), and Mount Monadnock (3,140 feet). Swift-running streams cut between the monadnocks and flow into the Connecticut and other rivers.

The Western New England Upland covers most of eastern Vermont. It also extends into Massachusetts and Connecticut. This region is sometimes called the *Vermont Piedmont*. In the east, it consists of the broad, fertile lowlands of the Connecticut River Valley. Farmers in the valley raise dairy cattle and grow apples and strawberries. The lowlands rise gradually to hills in the west. The Granite Hills, located near Barre, include 1,700-foot Millstone Hill. Many lakes lie among hills in the northern part of the Western New England Upland.

The Green Mountains region covers central Vermont. The famous Green Mountains make up all but the northeastern corner of the region. In the northeast, the Green Mountains taper off into the Northfield, Worcester, and several other low mountain ranges.

Mount Mansfield, one of the Green Mountains, is the highest peak in Vermont. It rises 4,393 feet above sea level. Killington Peak (4,241 feet), Mount Ellen (4,135 feet), and Camel's Hump (4,083 feet)—all in the Green Mountains—are Vermont's next tallest peaks. The Green Mountains region is the center of Vermont's tourist industry, and an important source of minerals.

The Vermont Valley is a narrow region that stretches about halfway up western Vermont from the Massachusetts border. The region includes the valleys of several small rivers, including the Batten Kill and the Walloomsac.

The Taconic Mountains region covers a narrow strip in southwestern Vermont. The region also extends into Massachusetts. In Vermont, it includes many moun-

**Land Regions
of Vermont**

tains. The highest ones are Equinox Mountain (3,816 feet), Dorset Peak (3,804 feet), Little Equinox Mountain (3,320 feet), Mother Myrick Mountain (3,290 feet), and Bear Mountain (3,260 feet). Swift-running streams cut through the mountains, and the mountains surround many scenic lakes.

The Champlain Valley, also called the *Vermont Lowland*, borders Lake Champlain. This region includes Burlington, the state's largest city; and some of Vermont's best farmland. The valley has many dairy farms and apple orchards. Farmers in the region also raise corn, hay, oats, and wheat on rolling hills and broad fertile lowlands. Lake Champlain has a series of islands, including Grand Isle and Isle La Motte. These islands are part of Vermont.

Rivers and Lakes. The Connecticut River forms Vermont's entire eastern border. But New Hampshire controls the river as the result of a ruling by the Supreme Court of the United States. In 1937, the Court established New Hampshire's western border as the low water mark on the Vermont side of the Connecticut River. Slow-running Otter Creek is the longest river within Vermont. It rises near East Dorset, flows 90 miles north, and empties into Lake Champlain. The Batten Kill River also rises near East Dorset. It flows south into New York. Most other Vermont rivers run

267

VERMONT

down the slopes of the Green Mountains. Some flow down the eastern slopes and empty into the Connecticut River. Others wind down the western slopes and empty into Lake Champlain. Three large rivers—the Missisquoi, the Lamoille, and the Winooski—rise east of the Green Mountains and pass through the mountains. Then the rivers empty into Lake Champlain.

Vermont has about 430 lakes and ponds. Most of them are in the northeast. Lake Champlain, in the northwest, is the largest lake in New England. It covers 490 square miles, and is shared by Vermont, New York, and Quebec. Of this total, 268 square miles are in Vermont. Lake Memphremagog is the second largest lake in Vermont. It covers about 10 square miles in the state, and about 20 square miles in Quebec. Bomoseen Lake, west of Rutland, is the largest lake entirely within Vermont. It covers about 4 square miles.

Dick Smith

A Farm Field adds a golden tint to the countryside surrounding Waterbury Center in Vermont's Green Mountains. The scenic Green Mountains region, which covers central Vermont, attracts many tourists to the state.

Mount Mansfield, *below,* is the highest peak in Vermont. It rises 4,393 feet in the Green Mountains region.

Grant Heilman

Pleasure Boats ride at anchor on the calm waters of Lake Champlain near South Hero. The lake is the largest in New England.

Hanson Carroll

Arthur Griffin

Dairy Cattle Graze along the Connecticut River, *right.* The river forms Vermont's eastern boundary.

VERMONT / Climate

Summers in Vermont are short, with few hot days. Summer nights are cool and crisp, especially in the mountains. Vermont has an average July temperature of 68° F. The state's highest temperature, 105° F., was recorded in Vernon on July 4, 1911.

Vermont winters are long and cold, with an average January temperature of 19° F. Bloomfield had the state's record low temperature, −50° F., on Dec. 30, 1933. Snowfall in the Connecticut River Valley and the Champlain Valley ranges from 60 to 80 inches yearly. Vermont's mountains receive from 80 to 120 inches of snow a year. Snow plays an important part in Vermont's economy. The deep snows on mountains attract thousands of skiers to the state. Yearly *precipitation* (rain, melted snow, and other forms of moisture) in Vermont averages about 40 inches.

John H. Harris

The West River winds through the snowy hills in southern Vermont. Snowfall is heavy throughout the state.

SEASONAL TEMPERATURES

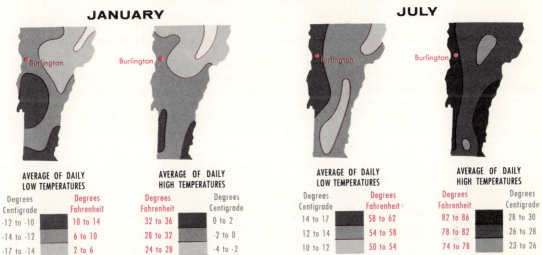

JANUARY

AVERAGE OF DAILY LOW TEMPERATURES

Degrees Centigrade	Degrees Fahrenheit
-12 to -10	10 to 14
-14 to -12	6 to 10
-17 to -14	2 to 6
-19 to -17	-2 to 2

AVERAGE OF DAILY HIGH TEMPERATURES

Degrees Fahrenheit	Degrees Centigrade
32 to 36	0 to 2
28 to 32	-2 to 0
24 to 28	-4 to -2
20 to 24	-7 to -4

JULY

AVERAGE OF DAILY LOW TEMPERATURES

Degrees Centigrade	Degrees Fahrenheit
14 to 17	58 to 62
12 to 14	54 to 58
10 to 12	50 to 54

AVERAGE OF DAILY HIGH TEMPERATURES

Degrees Fahrenheit	Degrees Centigrade
82 to 86	28 to 30
78 to 82	26 to 28
74 to 78	23 to 26

AVERAGE YEARLY PRECIPITATION
(Rain, Melted Snow, and Other Moisture)

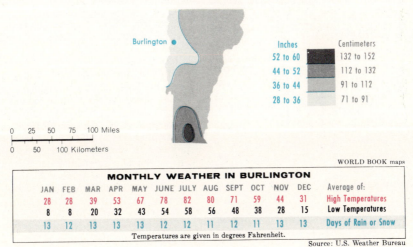

Inches	Centimeters
52 to 60	132 to 152
44 to 52	112 to 132
36 to 44	91 to 112
28 to 36	71 to 91

0 25 50 75 100 Miles
0 50 100 Kilometers

WORLD BOOK maps

MONTHLY WEATHER IN BURLINGTON

	JAN	FEB	MAR	APR	MAY	JUNE	JULY	AUG	SEPT	OCT	NOV	DEC	Average of:
	28	28	39	53	67	78	82	80	71	59	44	31	High Temperatures
	8	8	20	32	43	54	58	56	48	38	28	15	Low Temperatures
	13	12	13	13	13	12	12	11	12	11	13	13	Days of Rain or Snow

Temperatures are given in degrees Fahrenheit.

Source: U.S. Weather Bureau

268a

Manufacturing is Vermont's most important economic activity. The tourist industry ranks second, followed by agriculture and mining. The Burlington area and Windsor County are Vermont's chief manufacturing regions. The tourist industry, centered in the Green Mountains, adds about $1½ million a year to Vermont's economy. Farms and mines are in many parts of the state.

Natural Resources of Vermont include valuable mineral deposits, thick forests, abundant wildlife, and some fertile soil.

Soil. Vermont's most fertile areas are its river valleys, where flooding streams have deposited rich soils. Many parts of the state are rocky, and have only a thin covering of soil or none at all.

Forests cover more than three-fifths of Vermont. The state's hardwood trees include, in order of value, maples, birches, beeches, ashes, poplars, and basswoods. Softwood trees, also in order of value, include spruces, red and white pines, hemlocks, and cedars.

Minerals. Large asbestos, marble, and talc deposits make the Green Mountains region Vermont's chief mineral area. Valuable marble deposits are also found in the Vermont Valley and the Taconic Mountains. Most of Vermont's slate comes from the Taconic Mountains. The Granite Hills have granite deposits.

Plant Life. Many kinds of ferns grow in the mountain regions of Vermont. A variety of grasses and sedges grows in the forests and lowlands. Anemones, arbutuses, buttercups, daisies, gentians, goldenrods, lilacs, pussy willows, and violets grow throughout the state.

Animal Life. The white-tailed deer is Vermont's most common game animal. Fur-bearing animals found in the state include bears, bobcats, foxes, minks, muskrats, raccoons, and skunks. Many hedgehogs, rabbits, squirrels, and woodchucks live in the forests.

Manufacturing accounts for about two-thirds of the value of goods produced in Vermont. Goods manufactured there have a *value added by manufacture* of about $326,598,000 yearly. This figure represents the value created in products by Vermont industries, not counting such costs as materials, supplies, and fuel.

Machinery has a value added of about $76,627,000 annually. This figure includes the manufacture of electrical and nonelectrical machinery, and machine tools. Machine tools, such as drills, grinders, and lathes, come chiefly from Springfield and Windsor. Burlington produces business machines. Scales are made in Rutland and St. Johnsbury, and electrical aircraft instruments in Bellows Falls and Vergennes.

Food Processing has a value added of about $35 million yearly. Many Vermont cities and towns have factories that process food. The state's processed foods include beverages, candy, canned and frozen foods, dairy products, and meat products.

Wood Processing. About 500 Vermont factories depend on trees from the state's forests for raw materials. The manufacture of paper and paper products is Vermont's leading wood processing industry. These products have a yearly value added of about $32,642,000. Paper and paper products are made throughout the state. Vermont's wood-processing industry also includes production of baskets, boxes, building supplies, door and window frames, furniture, lumber, and toys.

Stone Products. Factories in many parts of Vermont make building stone, and markers, memorials, and tombs from granite. Granite polishing is another important Vermont activity. Barre is the center of the state's granite industry. The manufacture of marble products, including memorials and tile, is also important. Proctor and Rutland are the state's chief marble centers. Other stone products made in Vermont include bricks, cement blocks, chimney blocks, and concrete.

Other Products. Textile mills operate in Hartford, Northfield, and several other Vermont towns. Brattleboro, Burlington, and Rutland have printing and publishing plants. Other Vermont manufactured products include chemicals, clothing, and plastics.

Agriculture accounts for 29 per cent of the value of goods produced in Vermont. This percentage of farm products in relation to total products is the highest among the New England states. Vermont farmers earn about $141,400,000 yearly. The state's 12,100 farms cover almost half of Vermont's land area. Vermont farms average 300 acres in size. Much of the farmland is covered by trees.

Milk accounts for 65 per cent of Vermont's farm income. Vermont has almost as many cattle as people.

PRODUCTION IN VERMONT

Total yearly value of goods produced—$493,128,000

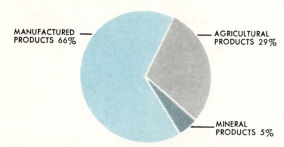

MANUFACTURED PRODUCTS 66%

AGRICULTURAL PRODUCTS 29%

MINERAL PRODUCTS 5%

Note: Manufacturing percentage based on value added by manufacture. Other percentages based on value of production.

Source: Latest available U.S. Government statistics

EMPLOYMENT IN VERMONT

Average yearly number of persons employed—143,250

		Number of Employees
Manufacturing	𝍖	35,100
Agriculture	𝍖	24,000
Services	𝍖	23,400
Wholesale & Retail Trade	𝍖	21,800
Government	𝍖	17,300
Transportation & Public Utilities	𝍖	7,100
Construction	𝍖	7,000
Finance, Insurance & Real Estate	𝍖	4,400
Forestry	𝍖	1,950
Mining	𝍖	1,200

Source: Employment statistics supplied by employers to government agencies

The cattle produce about 230 million gallons of milk yearly. About half the milk is used to make cheddar cheese, chiefly in the Boston, Mass., area.

The sale of meat animals, especially calves, earns almost 10 per cent of Vermont's farm income. Poultry and egg sales bring in another 5 per cent.

Crops account for about 10 per cent of the state's farm income. Potatoes rank as the leading vegetable, and apples as the leading fruit. Hay, oats, and corn grown in Vermont are used as animal feed.

Vermont is one of the leading states in producing maple sugar and maple syrup. Between 300,000 and 500,000 gallons of maple syrup yearly come from the state's maple trees. Some of the syrup is made into sugar.

Mining in Vermont accounts for about $25,130,000 yearly. This figure represents about 5 per cent of the value of Vermont products. The percentage of mining products in relation to total products is the highest among the New England states. Vermont leads all the states in asbestos production, and is among the leaders in granite, marble, and slate.

The largest U.S. granite quarries are near Barre. Fine-grained white marble is mined throughout western Vermont. Red and green marble occur in a few deposits. Fair Haven is Vermont's slate-mining center. The country's largest asbestos mines are near Hyde Park. About nine-tenths of the asbestos mined in the United States comes from this region. Sand and gravel are mined in every Vermont county. Limestone is mined in Addison and Chittenden counties. Talc comes from many parts of the state.

Electric Power. Hydroelectric dams on many Vermont rivers provide power for the state's industries. The three largest power dams are on the Connecticut River. They are the Comerford Dam near Barnet, the Samuel C. Moore Dam near Passumpsic, and the Wilder Dam near Wilder. Vermont and New Hampshire share the power generated by these dams. Vermont also gets electric power from two sources in New York—the St. Lawrence Seaway Power Project and the Niagara Falls Power Project. The power is transmitted overland and by underwater cable through Lake Champlain. For Vermont's kilowatt-hour production, see ELECTRIC POWER (table).

Transportation. Vermont has about 14,000 miles of roads and highways, most of which are paved. Interstate 89 and Interstate 91 are the chief highways. When completed, Interstate 89 will extend northwest from White River Junction to the Canadian border near

FARM, MINERAL, AND FOREST PRODUCTS

This map shows where the state's leading farm, mineral, and forest products are produced. The urban areas (shown on the map in red) are the state's important manufacturing centers.

Franklin. Interstate 91 will run north and south from Guilford to Derby Line. These highways were scheduled to be completed during the late 1960's. Airlines serve Burlington, Montpelier-Barre, Newport, Rutland, and White River Junction. About 600 miles of railroad track cross Vermont.

Communication. Eight daily newspapers and 24 weekly newspapers are published in Vermont. *The Vermont Gazette* was published in Westminster for a brief period, beginning in 1780. *The Rutland Herald* is Vermont's oldest continuously published newspaper. It was begun as a weekly in 1794, and is now a daily. Other important newspapers include the *Burlington Free Press* and the *Brattleboro Reformer*.

Vermont's first radio station, WSYB, opened in Rutland in 1930. The first television station, WCAX-TV, began broadcasting from Burlington in 1954. Vermont now has 17 radio stations and 1 television station.

Factories in Proctor make memorials, tile, and other products from marble. The manufacture of stone products is one of Vermont's leading industries. Factories throughout Vermont use granite, building stone, and marble from the state's quarries.

Carlos H. Elmer

Confederate Soldiers robbed banks in St. Albans in 1864, and fled into Canada. This was the northernmost action of the Civil War.

St. Albans
● Fairfield

Samuel de Champlain, probably the first white man to reach Vermont, claimed the eastern shores of Lake Champlain for France in 1609.

Gathering Maple Sap became important in Vermont during the late 1700's. The state is famous for sugar and syrup made from maple sap.

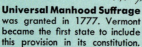

★ MONTPELIER

Universal Manhood Suffrage was granted in 1777. Vermont became the first state to include this provision in its constitution.

Vermont Joined the Union in 1791. It was the first territory after the original 13 colonies to become part of the United States.

The Green Mountain Boys, led by Ethan Allen, captured Fort Ticonderoga from the British in 1775.

● Plymouth

HISTORIC VERMONT

Fort Dummer became Vermont's first permanent white settlement in 1724. Colonists built it to warn villages in western Massachusetts of Indian attacks.

Chester A. Arthur
born in Fairfield

Calvin Coolidge
born in Plymouth

Indian Days. Vermont was chiefly an Indian hunting ground before the white man came. The Abnaki, Mahican, and Penacook tribes of the Algonkian Indian family first claimed the region. Powerful New York Iroquois Indians drove the Algonkian out. The Algonkian returned during the early 1600's. With help from the French, they defeated the Iroquois.

Exploration and Settlement. Samuel de Champlain of France was probably the first white man to explore what is now Vermont. He discovered Lake Champlain in 1609, and claimed the Vermont region for France. In 1666, the French built a fort dedicated to Saint Anne on Isle La Motte in Lake Champlain. In 1690, Jacobus de Warm led British soldiers from Albany, N.Y., to a point near the site of present-day Middlebury, Vt. De Warm founded a fort at Chimney Point, west of Middlebury. Vermont's first permanent white settlement was made at Fort Dummer, in what is now Brattleboro. Fort Dummer was built by Massachusetts settlers in 1724 to protect that colony's western settlements from raids by the French and Indians.

The Lake Champlain region became a major battleground during the French and Indian War (1754-1763). In this war, England gained from France the control of Vermont and much of the rest of North America. See FRENCH AND INDIAN WARS.

Land Disputes. Benning Wentworth, the royal governor of New Hampshire, made 131 grants of Vermont land between 1749 and 1763. This land was called the *New Hampshire Grants.* But New York claimed the same land and granted it to other settlers. In 1764, England recognized the grants made by New York. England ordered settlers who held New Hampshire Grants to surrender their land or pay New York for it. In 1770, these settlers organized a military force called the *Green Mountain Boys* to defend their land. The Green Mountain Boys attacked many New York settlers and drove them from Vermont. See GREEN MOUNTAIN BOYS.

The Revolutionary War began in Massachusetts in 1775, before the Vermont land disputes were settled. Vermonters united to fight the British. Ethan Allen, Benedict Arnold, and more than 80 Green Mountain Boys captured Fort Ticonderoga from the British in May, 1775. Colonial troops held the fort until 1777, when the British drove them out. The troops retreated south from Fort Ticonderoga, with the British in pursuit. At Hubbardton, a rear guard led by Seth Warner stopped the retreat and fought the British. The rear guard was defeated. But the fighting delayed the British long enough to allow the rest of the colonists to escape.

The Battle of Bennington, on Aug. 16, 1777, was a major Revolutionary War conflict. It is often thought of as a Vermont battle. But it was actually fought just west of Vermont, in New York. The battles of Bennington and Saratoga (also in New York) marked the end of British land operations in the northern colonies.

Independent Republic. On Jan. 15, 1777, Vermont settlers declared their territory an independent republic. They named it *New Connecticut.* In July, 1777, Vermont adopted its first constitution and its present name.

New Hampshire and New York still claimed parts of Vermont. But Vermont ignored the claims. In 1783,

George Washington wrote that he believed it would be necessary to send troops to overthrow the Vermont government. But this never happened, and Vermont remained an independent republic for 14 years. In 1790, Vermont settled its dispute with New York by paying that state $30,000. New Hampshire also gave up its claim to Vermont. Such improved relations with neighboring states helped clear the way for Vermont's admission to the Union. On March 4, 1791, Vermont became the 14th state.

The 1800's. During the War of 1812, Vermont volunteers fought the British in the battles of Chippewa, Lundy's Lane, and Plattsburg. But the war was unpopular in Vermont, because trade with British-controlled Canada had become important to the state's economy. Hard times came to Vermont after the war. During a prosperous period from 1823 to 1836, many persons moved from Vermont to the growing Midwest. They feared future economic hardships in Vermont.

The Champlain Canal, which opened in 1823, connected Lake Champlain and New York's Hudson River. The canal allowed Vermont farmers to ship their goods by water all the way to New York City, a major market. Farmers in the Champlain Valley prospered, especially those who raised Spanish Merino sheep for wool. By 1840, Vermont had six times as many sheep as persons. Many small, water-powered mills were built in Vermont to process the wool from the sheep. During the mid-1800's, competition from western states and other countries made wool prices drop. By 1860, Vermont farmers had sold half their sheep to be used as meat. This crisis caused Vermont to change from a sheep-raising state to a dairy-farming state.

During the Civil War (1861-1865), about 34,000 Vermonters served with the Union forces. The northern-

As an Independent Republic

	Name	Party	Term
1.	Thomas Chittenden	None	1778-1789
2.	Moses Robinson	None	1789-1790
3.	Thomas Chittenden	None	1790-1791

As a State

	Name	Party	Term
1.	Thomas Chittenden	None	1791-1797
2.	Paul Brigham	None	1797
3.	Isaac Tichenor	Federalist	1797-1807
4.	Israel Smith	*Dem.-Rep.	1807-1808
5.	Isaac Tichenor	Federalist	1808-1809
6.	Jonas Galusha	Dem.-Rep.	1809-1813
7.	Martin Chittenden	Federalist	1813-1815
8.	Jonas Galusha	Dem.-Rep.	1815-1820
9.	Richard Skinner	Dem.-Rep.	1820-1823
10.	Cornelius P. Van Ness	Dem.-Rep.	1823-1826
11.	Ezra Butler	†Nat. Rep.	1826-1828
12.	Samuel C. Crafts	Nat. Rep.	1828-1831
13.	William A. Palmer	Anti-Masonic	1831-1835
14.	Silas H. Jennison	Whig	1835-1841
15.	Charles Paine	Whig	1841-1843
16.	John Mattocks	Whig	1843-1844
17.	William Slade	Whig	1844-1846
18.	Horace Eaton	Whig	1846-1848
19.	Carlos Coolidge	Whig	1848-1850
20.	Charles K. Williams	Whig	1850-1852
21.	Erastus Fairbanks	Whig	1852-1853
22.	John S. Robinson	Democratic	1853-1854
23.	Stephen Royce	Republican	1854-1856
24.	Ryland Fletcher	Republican	1856-1858
25.	Hiland Hall	Republican	1858-1860
26.	Erastus Fairbanks	Republican	1860-1861
27.	Frederick Holbrook	Republican	1861-1863
28.	J. Gregory Smith	Republican	1863-1865
29.	Paul Dillingham	Republican	1865-1867
30.	John B. Page	Republican	1867-1869
31.	Peter T. Washburn	Republican	1869-1870
32.	George W. Hendee	Republican	1870
33.	John W. Stewart	Republican	1870-1872
34.	Julius Converse	Republican	1872-1874
35.	Asahel Peck	Republican	1874-1876
36.	Horace Fairbanks	Republican	1876-1878
37.	Redfield Proctor	Republican	1878-1880
38.	Roswell Farnham	Republican	1880-1882
39.	John L. Barstow	Republican	1882-1884
40.	Samuel E. Pingree	Republican	1884-1886
41.	Ebenezer J. Ormsbee	Republican	1886-1888
42.	William P. Dillingham	Republican	1888-1890
43.	Carroll S. Page	Republican	1890-1892
44.	Levi K. Fuller	Republican	1892-1894
45.	Urban A. Woodbury	Republican	1894-1896
46.	Josiah Grout	Republican	1896-1898
47.	Edward C. Smith	Republican	1898-1900
48.	William W. Stickney	Republican	1900-1902
49.	John G. McCullough	Republican	1902-1904
50.	Charles J. Bell	Republican	1904-1906
51.	Fletcher D. Proctor	Republican	1906-1908
52.	George H. Prouty	Republican	1908-1910
53.	John A. Mead	Republican	1910-1912
54.	Allen M. Fletcher	Republican	1912-1915
55.	Charles W. Gates	Republican	1915-1917
56.	Horace F. Graham	Republican	1917-1919
57.	Percival W. Clement	Republican	1919-1921
58.	James Hartness	Republican	1921-1923
59.	Redfield Proctor	Republican	1923-1925
60.	Franklin S. Billings	Republican	1925-1927
61.	John E. Weeks	Republican	1927-1931
62.	Stanley C. Wilson	Republican	1931-1935
63.	Charles M. Smith	Republican	1935-1937
64.	George D. Aiken	Republican	1937-1941
65.	William H. Wills	Republican	1941-1945
66.	Mortimer R. Proctor	Republican	1945-1947
67.	Ernest W. Gibson	Republican	1947-1950
68.	Harold J. Arthur	Republican	1950-1951
69.	Lee E. Emerson	Republican	1951-1955
70.	Joseph B. Johnson	Republican	1955-1959
71.	Robert T. Stafford	Republican	1959-1961
72.	F. Ray Keyser, Jr.	Republican	1961-1963
73.	Philip H. Hoff	Democratic	1963-

*Democratic-Republican   †National Republican

most land action of the war took place in Vermont in 1864. A group of 22 Confederate soldiers raided banks in St. Albans, and escaped to Canada with more than $20,000.

Agriculture declined in Vermont after the war. More and more Vermont farmers left the state for cities, or for better farmland in the Midwest and elsewhere. Most of the French Canadians and Europeans who moved to Vermont settled in cities to work in factories. The late 1800's brought great growth to Vermont's wood-processing and cheese-making industries. Burlington grew rapidly as a port city that processed lumber from Canada and shipped it to U.S. cities. The granite industry boomed in Barre. Vermont's once important textile industry declined during the late 1800's. Many textile mills moved to the South, where labor costs were lower.

The 1900's. Manufacturing replaced agriculture as Vermont's most important economic activity during the early 1900's. The value of Vermont's manufactured products more than tripled between 1900 and 1920. Vermont factories supplied lumber, machinery, and other products for the armed forces after the United States entered World War I in 1917.

Vermont's tourist industry also grew rapidly during the early 1900's. Many large resort hotels and vacation camps were built. In 1911, Vermont became the first state with an official publicity bureau to attract tourists.

In 1923, Calvin Coolidge, born in Vermont, became the 30th President of the United States. He had been elected Vice-President under President Warren G. Harding, who died in office. Coolidge was a shy man who was quiet in public. To many persons, he seemed to be a "typical Vermont conservative."

The nationwide Great Depression of the 1930's brought severe hardship to Vermont. Many small factories and lumber mills closed. Some textile mills that closed never reopened. Vermont farmers were hurt by falling prices and reduced sales. Vermont's economy improved during the late 1930's.

The worst flood in Vermont history occurred in November, 1927. Waters from the Winooski River and branches of the Connecticut River swept away entire sections of towns. The flood caused 60 deaths and millions of dollars in damage.

During World War II (1939-1945), the state's factories again produced war materials for the United States and the other Allies. After the war, Vermont increased its efforts to attract new industries. The Vermont Development Department was established in 1949, and promoted industrial development. The Municipal Bond Act of 1955 gave Vermont communities permission to issue revenue bonds. The money from the bonds was used to finance industrial building programs.

Vermont Today continues its industrial growth. Some of the nation's biggest corporations, including General Electric Company and International Business Ma-

268f

chines Corporation, have built factories in the state. Most of the industry that Vermont attracts would be considered "small" in many other states. Vermont lacks the natural resources and nearness to large and deep waterways that are needed to handle "heavy" industry. But even small firms with a dozen or so workers are a great economic help to Vermont's small towns.

Vermont's tourist industry is also growing. The amount of money spent yearly by tourists in Vermont more than doubled between the mid-1940's and the early 1960's. At the same time, spending by skiers increased by almost 10 times. Skiers now spend about $40 million annually in the state.

Vermont's population growth has been relatively slow. Among the northeastern states, Vermont had the lowest rate of population increase between 1950 and 1960. About half of Vermont's towns now have fewer persons than they had a hundred years ago. Even so, the population of the state has increased since then because of the growth of cities and larger towns.

Since the mid-1950's, the number of Vermont farms has decreased at a rate of about 3 or 4 per cent annually. However, the average farm size has increased.

Politically, Vermont remains a Republican stronghold. The Republicans hold such control of Vermont politics that the election of a few Democrats in the 1950's and 1960's was reported in newspapers throughout the United States. William H. Meyer, elected to the U.S. House of Representatives in 1958, was the state's first Democratic Congressman since 1853. In 1962, Philip H. Hoff won election as Vermont's first Democratic governor since 1853. In 1964, Lyndon B. Johnson became the first Democrat ever to win Vermont's presidential electoral votes.

T. D. Seymour Bassett, J. Rowland Illick, and Seargent P. Wild

VERMONT / Study Aids

Related Articles in World Book include:

BIOGRAPHIES

Aiken, George D.	Collamer, Jacob
Allen, Ethan	Coolidge, Calvin
Arthur, Chester A.	Flanders, Ralph E.
Champlain, Samuel de	Morrill, Justin S.
Chittenden, Thomas	Warner, Seth

CITIES, TOWNS, and VILLAGES

Barre	Proctor	Saint Albans
Burlington	Rutland	Saint Johnsbury
Montpelier		

PHYSICAL FEATURES

Connecticut River	Lake Champlain
Green Mountains	Lake Memphremagog

OTHER RELATED ARTICLES

Green Mountain Boys   New England

Outline

I. **Government**
  A. Constitution
  B. Executive
  C. Legislature
  D. Courts
  E. Local Government
  F. Taxation
  G. Politics
II. **People**
III. **Education**
  A. Schools B. Libraries C. Museums
IV. **A Visitor's Guide**
  A. Places to Visit B. Annual Events
V. **The Land**
  A. Land Regions B. Rivers and Lakes
VI. **Climate**
VII. **Economy**
  A. Natural Resources
  B. Manufacturing
  C. Agriculture
  D. Mining
  E. Electric Power
  F. Transportation
  G. Communication
VIII. **History**

Questions

How long was Vermont an independent republic?
How did Vermont's population growth between 1950 and 1960 compare with that of other northeastern states?
What is Vermont's chief economic activity?
When did Vermont lose its claim to the Connecticut River? What state won this dispute?
How many Vermont towns have no local government? Why do they not have their own government?
What voting record did Vermont set from the 1850's until the 1960's?
Where did the northernmost land action of the Civil War take place?
Who were the Green Mountain Boys?
Where was the first U.S. teacher-training school established? When?
Why was the War of 1812 unpopular in Vermont?

Books for Young Readers

Allen, Merritt P. *Green Cockade*. McKay, 1942. The *Flicker's Feather*. 1953. Revolutionary War stories.
Coblentz, Catherine C. *The Blue Cat of Castle Town*. Longmans, 1949. A Vermont town during the Revolution.
Dean, Leon W. *Stark of the North Country*. Rinehart, 1941. *Border Bullets*. Farrar, 1953. *The White Ox*. 1953.
Felton, Harold W. *Horse Named Justin Morgan*. Dodd, 1962. A history of Vermont and the Morgan horse.
Frost, Frances M. *Windy Foot at the Country Fair*. McGraw, 1947. *Sleigh Bells for Windy Foot*. 1948. *Maple Sugar for Windy Foot*. 1950.
Jackson, Edgar N. *Green Mountain Hero*. Lantern, 1961 A story about famed Ann Story's son.
Meigs, Cornelia L. *Covered Bridge*. Macmillan, 1936. *Call of the Mountain*. Little, Brown, 1940.
Ripley, Sheldon N. *Ethan Allen: Green Mountain Hero*. Houghton, 1961.
Viereck, Phillip. *Independence Must Be Won*. Day, 1964. Vermont during the Revolutionary War.

Books for Older Readers

Crockett, Walter H. *History of Lake Champlain, 1909-1936*. McAuliffe's Paper Co., Burlington, Vt., 1960.
Duffus, Robert L. *Williamstown Branch: Impersonal Memories of a Vermont Boyhood*. Norton, 1958. *Waterbury Record: More Vermont Memories*. 1959.
Fisher, Dorothy Canfield. *Vermont Tradition: The Biography of an Outlook on Life*. Little, Brown, 1953.
Hill, Ralph N. *The Winooski: Heartway of Vermont*. Rinehart, 1949. *Contrary Country: A Chronicle of Vermont*. 1950. *Yankee Kingdom: Vermont and New Hampshire*. Harper, 1960.
Lee, W. Storrs. *The Green Mountains of Vermont*. Holt, 1955.
Nuquist, Andrew E. *Town Government in Vermont*. Univ. of Vermont, 1964.

VERMONT, UNIVERSITY OF

VERMONT, UNIVERSITY OF, is a state-controlled co-educational school in Burlington, Vt. It has colleges of agriculture and home economics, arts and sciences, education and nursing, technology, and medicine; a graduate college; and a school of dental hygiene. The university confers bachelor's, master's, M.D., and Ph.D. degrees. It was the first university in the United States to admit women to Phi Beta Kappa.

The University of Vermont was chartered in 1791. The Vermont Agricultural College was chartered in 1864, and joined with the University in 1865 to form the University of Vermont and State Agricultural College. For its enrollment, see UNIVERSITIES AND COLLEGES (table). L. E. VAN BENTHUYSEN

VERMOUTH. See ALCOHOLIC DRINK (Fermented Liquors).

VERNAL EQUINOX. See EQUINOX.

VERNAL FALLS. See YOSEMITE NATIONAL PARK (Waterfalls).

VERNE, JULES (1828-1905), a French writer beloved by the youth of all continents, extraordinarily anticipated the discoveries of the 1900's. Books written by Jules Verne will long survive as the earliest and most amazing models of science fiction. His most famous novels include *From the Earth to the Moon* (1865), *Twenty Thousand Leagues Under the Sea* (1870), *The Mysterious Island* (1870), *Around the World in Eighty Days* (1872), and *Michael Strogoff* (1876).

Verne's novels carry the reader all over the earth, under it, and above it. They build up breathless tales around balloons, submarines, and the already anticipated rockets and interplanetary travel. They have the quality of robust health, and never resort to morbid thrills for excitement.

Brown Bros.
Jules Verne

Verne is never condescending or falsely childish in tone. He wrote for adults and for serious readers, as did Mark Twain and Alexandre Dumas. His books are still widely read by adults, and delight the youths who thirst for adventure. Yuri A. Gagarin of Russia, the first man to orbit the earth in a space ship (1961), greatly admired Verne's writing. Verne was born and educated at Nantes. He led an uneventful life after studying law in Paris, and traveled little himself. HENRI PEYRE

See also SPACE TRAVEL (picture, Man's Dream of Space Travel).

VERNIER, *VUR nih er*, is an instrument used in measuring lengths and angles. It is named for Pierre Vernier, a French mathematician who invented it in the 1600's.

The most common vernier has a short graduated scale, or "ruler," which slides along a longer scale. The subdivisions on the short rule are nine-tenths as long as the subdivisions on the long scale. Nine small divisions on the large scale are equal to 10 on the small scale.

In using the vernier, the large scale is laid along the material to be measured, a small pipe, for example. The small scale is slid until it reaches the end of the pipe.

Now we check to see which of its divisions lines up with one of the divisions on the large scale. Suppose the 5, or fifth division from the zero end of the small scale, lines up with 25 on the large scale. Since each division on the small scale is one-tenth smaller than the large divisions, five divisions are equal to only four and one-half on the large scale. Therefore, the end of the small scale rests at $25-4.5$, or 20.5 on the large scale.

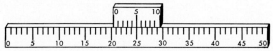

The Vernier Scale Measures Lengths and Angles.

Engineers often use calipers with a vernier attachment (see CALIPER). Some of them read to $\frac{1}{1000}$ inch without a magnifier. The beam of the caliper is divided into inches and tenths, and each tenth is divided into fourths. The vernier is divided into 25 parts. The beam may be divided into fiftieths of an inch, and the vernier has 20 divisions to each of its 19. HERMAN J. SHEA

VERNON, MOUNT. See MOUNT VERNON (Va.).

VERONA, *vuh RO nuh* (pop. 230,907; alt. 194 ft.), is an Italian city on the Adige River. It lies near the Tirolese Alps, 71 miles west of Venice. For location, see ITALY (color map). Shakespeare used Verona as the scene of his play *Romeo and Juliet*. The house in which Juliet is said to have lived still stands.

Verona presents a fascinating combination of ancient, medieval, and modern civilizations. The city was a prosperous Roman colony before the time of Christ, and there are still many interesting Roman ruins, including a magnificent amphitheater built by the Emperor Diocletian. During the Middle Ages, Verona was an important art center. The great painter, Paolo Veronese, was born there. Verona has an active trade in wine, fruits, and marble. SHEPARD B. CLOUGH

VERONA, CONGRESS OF. See SPAIN (Dissatisfaction and Revolt).

VERONAL. See BARBITURATE.

VERONESE, *VAY roh NAY say*, **PAOLO** (1528-1588), painted in and around Venice at the end of the Italian Renaissance. His real name was PAOLO CAGLIARI, but he was called Veronese because he was born in Verona. He became most popular for his paintings of historical subjects and myths, and for representations of the life of Venetian aristocrats. He also painted religious subjects and portraits. His figures are robust and handsome, splendidly costumed, and theatrically posed in rich settings. His major works include *Marriage at Cana* in the Louvre in Paris; *Mars and Venus* in the Metropolitan Museum of Art, New York City; and frescoes in the Villa Maser, near Venice. ROBERT O. PARKS

See also OLD TESTAMENT (picture).

VERONICA, *vuh RON ih kuh*, **SAINT,** is traditionally supposed to have been one of the women of Jerusalem who followed Christ on His way to Calvary. She is said to have offered Christ her linen veil, to wipe the sweat from His face. Tradition has it that the imprint of His features remained on the cloth, and the miraculous relic is said to have been preserved in Rome since the year 700. It was exhibited in Saint Peter's in 1854. But other cities also claim to possess this relic. Saint Veronica's feast day is July 12. FULTON J. SHEEN

VERRAZANO, *VAIR rah TSAH noh,* **GIOVANNI DA** (1485?-1527?), an Italian navigator and pirate, is believed to have sailed to America in 1524. Little is known about his early life. But about 1521, he is thought to have served France as a privateer, attacking Spanish ships. In 1524, King Francis I of France supposedly commissioned him to explore the shores of America. Historians believe Verrazano may have touched the shores of North Carolina and then sailed north along the Atlantic Coast. They believe he entered New York harbor, discovered the Hudson River, and explored the New England coast. He may also have sighted Nova Scotia and Newfoundland. Verrazano was born near Florence, Italy. It is believed that the Spaniards hanged him as a pirate.　　　　　FRANKLIN L. FORD

VERRAZANO-NARROWS BRIDGE is one of the longest suspension bridges in the world. It spans the Narrows channel between Brooklyn and Staten Island in New York City. The center span of the $325 million bridge is 4,260 feet, the world's longest. WILLIAM E. YOUNG

VERRES, GAIUS. See CICERO, MARCUS TULLIUS.

VERROCCHIO, *vuh RAWK ih oh,* or *vair RAWK kyoh,* **ANDREA DEL** (1435-1488), was an Italian sculptor, painter, and goldsmith. Donatello was his master, and Verrocchio, in turn, taught Leonardo da Vinci. Verrocchio made the statue of David for the Palazzo Vecchio in Florence. A study for *Boy with a Dolphin* is in the National Gallery in Washington, D.C.

Verrocchio's portrait busts have great subtlety of characterization. He also designed and made tombs for several members of the Medici family. His most famous work is the equestrian statue in bronze of Bartolommeo Colleoni in Venice, but he did not live to cast it himself. Verrocchio was born in Florence.　MARVIN C. ROSS

See also SCULPTURE (Italy; picture, Italian Renaissance Sculpture); JOHN THE BAPTIST (picture).

VERSAILLES, *ver SY,* or *ver SAYLZ* (pop. 86,759; alt. 445 ft.), is a city in northern France. It lies 12 miles southwest of Paris (see FRANCE [political map]). It is famous as the site of the historic palace of Versailles, built by King Louis XIV. Versailles is also the capital of the Seine-et-Oise department, and a center of education.

The Versailles Palace is more than a half mile long and has enormous wings. It contains hundreds of rooms, including the famous Hall of Mirrors. The reception rooms of Louis XIV show the splendor of his time. Other rooms show the ornate style of the Louis XV period and the delicate work of the reign of Louis XVI.

The park of Versailles was laid out by the famous garden designer André Le Nôtre in a formal pattern of lawns, walks, and fountains. In its center, a broad walk called the *tapis vert* (green carpet) leads to the mile-long Grand Canal. One branch of the canal leads toward the Grand Trianon and Petit Trianon, two small palaces which Louis XIV and Louis XV built for their favorite court ladies.

History. Originally, Versailles was the site of a modest hunting lodge built by Louis XIII. In 1661, Louis XIV began building a palace on the same location. He hired the best architects, sculptors, and landscape gardeners. Historians estimate he spent more than $100 million on the palace. Later kings added more rooms.

The luxury and wastefulness of court life at Versailles helped bring about the French Revolution. In 1789, the States-General met at Versailles. This meeting signaled the beginning of the Revolution.

The German army made Versailles its headquarters during the siege of Paris in 1870-1871. At the end of the Franco-Prussian War, Versailles was the capital of France for a time. The Treaty of Versailles was signed in the Hall of Mirrors after World War I.

In the 1920's, John D. Rockefeller, Jr., gave France $2,850,000, part of which was used to restore the Versailles palace and park to their original appearance. The palace is now a national museum.　ROBERT E. DICKINSON

The Magnificent Palace at Versailles, Built by Louis XIV, Now Contains Fine Painting and Sculpture Exhibits.

The Treaty of Versailles marked the official end of World War I. Thirty-two Allied countries took part in drawing up the document. The most important work of negotiation was in the hands of the four statesmen shown above. They are, *left to right,* Premier Vittorio Orlando of Italy, Prime Minister David Lloyd George of Great Britain, Premier Georges Clemenceau of France, and President Woodrow Wilson of the United States. The treaty was signed in 1919 by all the Allies except the United States.

VERSAILLES, TREATY OF, officially ended World War I. Fighting ended when Germany accepted the Armistice of Nov. 11, 1918. But the war did not officially end until the Treaty of Versailles went into effect on Jan. 10, 1920. The treaty was signed on June 28, 1919, in the Hall of Mirrors of the Palace of Versailles, near Paris.

Thirty-two allied countries took part in negotiating the treaty. The United States played an important part in drawing it up. President Woodrow Wilson and Premiers David Lloyd George of Great Britain and Georges Clemenceau of France were known as the "Big Three" because they almost completely controlled the course of negotiations. But the United States never ratified the Versailles Treaty. The Senate refused to give its consent. Instead, the United States made a separate treaty of peace with Germany in 1921. This treaty reserved for the U.S. all the advantages it might have had under the Versailles Treaty, but accepted none of the obligations.

Making the Treaty. The people of the defeated countries, and most other people, expected that the treaty of peace would be based upon the famous Fourteen Points set forth by President Wilson in his speech of Jan. 8, 1918 (see WILSON, WOODROW [The Fourteen Points]). They soon learned that this was impossible, for several of the Allies had entered into secret agreements during the war which affected boundaries, the distribution of territory, and many other matters.

From the beginning, it was clear that no one would have much to say about the terms of the treaty except the five "great powers," the United States, Great Britain, France, Italy, and Japan. President Wilson was so eager to see a League of Nations established that he yielded many of the other points in order to protect this one. As a result, most of the provisions of the treaty were compromises that came nearer the desires of France and Great Britain than those of Wilson.

Provisions of the Treaty. The four outstanding provisions of the treaty revised boundaries, set reparations, disarmed Germany, and established the League of Nations (see LEAGUE OF NATIONS). Germany lost the provinces of Alsace and Lorraine, much of Schleswig, the districts of Eupen and Malmédy, southeastern Silesia, Posen, and a strip of West Prussia, which was granted to Poland as a corridor to the sea. The mouth of the Memel River and the surrounding territory was ceded to the Allies and later transferred to Lithuania. The city of Danzig, taken from Germany, became a free city under the jurisdiction of the League of Nations. Germany lost all its overseas colonies, and its rights in Turkey and China. The Saar Valley, with its valuable coal fields, was placed under control of the League of Nations for 15 years. The Rhineland was to be demilitarized. It was to be occupied for 15 years in order to assure Germany's good behavior.

Reparations. Germany had to turn over to the Allies livestock for the farms the German armies had laid waste, ships, railroad cars, locomotives, and other materials to replace those destroyed during the war, and large quantities of coal to repay France for the losses in its own mines. Germany was also required to pay large yearly sums in cash.

The treaty did not decide on the total amount of these cash payments. Instead, it provided for a reparations commission which was to determine the actual sum and to arrange the details of payment. In 1921 the figure was finally set at 132 billion gold marks, or about $33 billion.

Efforts to collect the reparations failed. The Dawes

Plan in 1924 and the Young Plan in 1929 also failed to solve this problem. In 1932 the Lausanne Agreement brought reparations payments to an end.

Ratification. The first German representatives sent to sign the peace treaty resigned when they found out what was in it. A few slight changes, such as the provision for a *plebiscite* (popular vote) in Silesia, were made in response to their objections. The Allies also threatened to take over more German territory if the German government refused to sign. A second German delegation signed the treaty, and after hot debate the German Reichstag approved it. The Allied Powers, except for the United States, ratified it.   DWIGHT E. LEE

See also TRIANON, TREATY OF; WORLD WAR II (Problems Left by World War I).

VERSE, BLANK. See BLANK VERSE.

VERSE, FREE. See FREE VERSE.

VERSO. See BOOK (Parts of a Book).

VERST is a measure of distance used in Russia. It equals .66288 of a land mile.

VERTEBRA, *VER tuh bruh,* is any one of the bones that make up the spinal column. A child has 33 vertebrae. But an adult has a total of 26, because several of them unite in later life (see SPINE). Some long-tailed vertebrate animals have many more vertebrae.

A vertebra has a central body with a *pedicle* (bony extension) on each side. The pedicles join bilateral *laminae* to form an *arch* enclosing an opening called the *vertebral foramen.* The spinal cord passes through this opening. A *spinous process* and two *transverse processes* extend from the arch. The transverse processes bear *articular processes* that connect with the articular processes of adjoining vertebra.   GORDON FARRELL

See also SKELETON; VERTEBRATE.

VERTEBRATE, *VUR tuh brayt,* is an animal that has a bony spinal column, or backbone, and a brain case, or cranium. The backbone is made up of separate bones called *vertebrae.* The ribs and the bones which support the jointed limbs of the animal are attached to the backbone. The ribs form a cage which can expand and which protects the heart, lungs, and other internal organs. The bodies of vertebrate animals are symmetrical. This means they have two sides which are alike or nearly so. Vertebrate animals never have more than two pairs of limbs. The spinal cord of the nervous system runs through the column of vertebrae.

The vertebrates make up a subdivision of the major phylum *Chordata,* one of the basic large groups in the animal kingdom. *Chordata* means *having a chord,* and refers to the segmented or solid column which characterizes all members of the phylum. There are seven classes of vertebrate animals. They are the lampreys and their relatives *(Agnatha),* the cartilaginous fishes, the sharks and skates with jaws but with no bones *(Chondrichthyes),* the bony fishes *(Osteichthyes),* the frogs and their relatives *(Amphibia),* the reptiles *(Reptilia),* the birds *(Aves),* and the mammals *(Mammalia).* Primitive chordates have a rod called a *notochord* that supports their bodies, rather than a vertebral column.   WILLIAM C. BEAVER

Related Articles in WORLD BOOK include:

Amphibian	Invertebrate	Salamander
Amphioxus	Lamprey	Shark
Bird	Mammal	Skate
Fish	Newt	Tail
Hagfish	Reptile	

VERTEX. See ANGLE.

VERTICAL-SPEED INDICATOR. See AIRCRAFT INSTRUMENTS (The Rate-of-Climb Indicator).

VERTICAL TAKE-OFF AIRCRAFT. See CONVERTIPLANE; HELICOPTER.

VERTIGO. See DIZZINESS.

VERTUMNUS. See POMONA.

VERUS, LUCIUS. See MARCUS AURELIUS.

VERVAIN. See VERBENA.

VERWOERD, HENDRIK F. See SOUTH AFRICA (Nationalism; The Republic).

VERY HIGH FREQUENCY WAVE (VHF) refers to the band of electromagnetic waves that range in frequency from 30 megacycles (30 million cycles) a second to 300 megacycles (300 million cycles) a second. VHF wave lengths range from 1 to 10 meters. The Federal Communications Commission has assigned portions of the VHF band to TV and FM stations and to "ham" radio operators. The VHF band assigned to TV ranges from 54 to 216 megacycles. The VHF band assigned to FM ranges from 88 to 108 megacycles. VHF waves travel in straight lines, like light waves. For this reason, their transmission is ordinarily limited to line-of-sight paths. Otherwise, obstructions, such as buildings, reflect them. See also FREQUENCY MODULATION; SHORT WAVE; TELEVISION (How TV Travels).   SAMUEL SEELY

VERY PISTOL. See PISTOL; FIREWORKS.

VESALIUS, *vee SAY lih us,* **ANDREAS** (1514-1564), was one of the foremost anatomists of all time. His book, *Concerning the Fabric of the Human Body,* or *Fabrica* (1543), contained the first complete description of the human body. For this, he is called the *father of anatomy.*

Vesalius became a professor at the University of Padua at the age of 23. Because he dared to correct many of Claudius Galen's errors based on animal dissection, followers of Galen bitterly attacked him. Discouraged, he burned most of his writings and resigned from Padua in 1544. He later became physician to Charles V and Philip II of Spain. Vesalius was born in Brussels, Belgium. He started his anatomical studies by dissecting the bodies of dead criminals.   CAROLINE A. CHANDLER

See also MEDICINE (picture, Human Anatomy).

VESPA. See WASP (Social Wasps).

VESPASIAN, *ves PAY zhun* (A.D. 9-79), was a Roman emperor. He was born TITUS FLAVIUS VESPASIANUS near Reate. He rose rapidly in the army and won fame in Britain and Germany as commander of a legion. In A.D. 51, he was elected consul, and in 63, he became governor of Africa. While fighting in the Near East in 70, he was proclaimed emperor. He left his son, Titus, in command of the troops and started for Rome. After defeating some rivals, he ruled the Roman Empire.

Vespasian was an able administrator. He introduced many governmental improvements, and the country again became prosperous. In Rome, he began the Arch of Titus and the Colosseum. His son, Titus, succeeded him as emperor.   ROBERT GEHLMANN BONE

See also COLOSSEUM; TITUS.

VESPER. See EVENING STAR.

VESPERS is the principal evening service of the breviary (see BREVIARY). Scholars believe that this hour may correspond to the evening sacrifice described in the Old Testament. Some scholars believe that it commemorates the descent from the cross.

273

Vespucci Explored the Coast of South America (the area shown in black) in 1497. It was first called the New World.

VESPUCCI, *ves POO chee,* **AMERIGO** (1451-1512), an Italian merchant-explorer, claimed to have discovered the continent of America in 1497. In 1492 Christopher Columbus had no idea that he discovered the Western Hemisphere. He thought that the islands he explored were part of the Indies. He first set foot on the mainland of America on his third voyage in 1498.

When Vespucci claimed that he had discovered the new continent, or the New World, as it was called, Columbus did not dispute his claim. Vespucci's letters describing his discovery were published, and in 1507 someone suggested that the new continent, which was actually South America, be named *America* "because Amerigo discovered it." Scholars no longer believe he was the actual discoverer, but his name was accepted for South America, and gradually came into use for North America as well.

Vespucci was born in Florence and was educated by his uncle, a Dominican priest. He became interested in astronomy and learned all that he could about the subject. For a time he was a merchant in Florence, and later in Seville and Cadiz, Spain. In 1495 he became connected with a firm which fitted out ships for long voyages. He claimed he made voyages in 1497, 1499,

Young Vestal Virgins in the Temple of Vesta are shown how the sacred fire is tended, to keep it burning always.

Joseph Boggs Beale, Modern Enterprises

Brown Bros.

Amerigo Vespucci Gave His Name to America.

1501, and 1503. The first two were for Spain, and the last two for Portugal. Vespucci did not take a leading part in these expeditions. He was only a pilot, or *astronomer,* as pilots were then called. In 1505 Vespucci became a Spanish subject and from 1508 until his death he was chief pilot of Spain. FRANKLIN L. FORD

See also AMERICA; COLUMBUS, CHRISTOPHER.

VESTA was the goddess of fire on the hearths of home and state in Roman mythology. The Greeks called her Hestia. She was the oldest daughter of Saturn, the god of the harvest, and Rhea, the goddess of the growth of natural things (see RHEA; SATURN). Vesta was also the sister of Jupiter, the king of the gods (see JUPITER). Vesta never married, but watched over the life of the home, and each house had a shrine to her. She was the symbol of the home, and every meal began and ended with an offering to her.

Every city had a public hearth where a fire burned to Vesta. Persons who left the city took some of the old fire with them to start the new fire in their homes. A circular temple to Vesta stood in the center of Rome. A sacred fire, guarded by six young *vestal virgins,* burned there constantly. The Romans believed the fire was a safeguard against national disaster.

Living conditions in primitive times partly explain the worship of Vesta. Fires were hard to make, and for that reason, one was always kept burning. People obtained fire from the chief or ruler, whose daughters kept it burning. After fire-making became simple, these customs remained as symbols.

The festivals of Vesta, called *Vestalia,* were held on June 9. The worship of Vesta in homes was closely associated with that of the *Lares,* or the spirits of ancestors, and *Penates,* the gods of the hearth (see LARES AND PENATES). NATHAN DANE II

VESTIBULE, or **VESTIBULAR CANAL.** See EAR (The Inner Ear; picture).

VESUVIUS, *veh SOO vih us*, is the only active volcano on the mainland of Europe. It is probably the most famous volcano in the world. It rises on the Bay of Naples, about 7 miles southeast of the city of Naples. Vesuvius has been studied by scientists more than any other volcano because it erupts frequently and is easy to reach.

Vesuvius is a cone within the rim of Mount Somma, a big crater formed when the top of the mountain collapsed in the eruption of A.D. 79. The height of Vesuvius changes with each eruption. In June, 1900, the cone was 4,275 feet high. But after the eruption of 1906, it was only 3,842 feet high. The top of the active cone is a cup-shaped crater, ranging from 50 to 400 feet across. Vesuvius spouts columns of steam, cinders, and sometimes small amounts of lava into the air.

Many people live on the lower slopes of the mountain and on the plains at its foot, in spite of Vesuvius' history of disastrous eruptions. The soil is extremely fertile and the area is famous for its vineyards of wine grapes.

Early Eruptions. Early man probably saw Vesuvius in eruption. Roman legends say that the gods had once used the mountain as a battleground, but at the time of Christ it had been dormant for hundreds of years. A series of earthquakes alarmed the people in the neighborhood of Vesuvius for 16 years following A.D. 63. The first recorded eruption occurred on Aug. 24, A.D. 79, when the cities of Herculaneum, Pompeii, and Stabiae were covered by ashes and lava. An eyewitness account of the disaster has come down to us from the Roman author, Pliny the Younger. His uncle, Pliny the Elder, was killed during the eruption.

In 472, ashes poured from the crater in such great amounts that they were carried by the wind as far as Constantinople (now Istanbul). Streams of lava and boiling water fell on the villages at the foot of the mountain in 1631. About 18,000 persons were said to have been killed. There were other destructive eruptions in 1794, 1822, 1855, 1872, 1880, 1895, 1906, 1929, and 1944.

Recent Eruptions. The greatest destruction in recent years occurred in April, 1906, when several towns were destroyed. In the eruption of March, 1944, which destroyed the village of San Sebastiano, soldiers of the Allied armies helped the people of nearby towns escape the lava and volcanic dust.

A Plume of White Smoke Drifts from Vesuvius and over the farms and vineyards that nestle on its slopes. Despite the danger of eruptions, farmers make their homes there.

Vesuvius in Eruption is a sight that arouses awe and wonder. Great clouds of volcanic dust are blown from the crater and lava pours over its edges. This is the great eruption of 1944.

VETCH

Before the eruption of 1944, thousands of visitors came to Vesuvius every year. They could go down into the crater for some distance and see a crimson stream of lava flow from the cone and turn into a bed of cold stone. A cable railway which took visitors to within 450 feet of the edge of the crater was destroyed in this eruption. Many people still visit the area.

A Royal Observatory was established on the slopes of the mountain in 1844. Since that time scientists have kept a constant watch over the volcano during and between eruptions. One observer lost his life standing by his post, and another probably had his life shortened by the effects of poison gases. GORDON A. MACDONALD

See also HERCULANEUM; MOUNTAIN (table; picture chart); NAPLES; POMPEII; VOLCANO.

VETCH is the common name of a group of leguminous plants. Vetches are used for hay, for green manure, as pasture crops, for silage, and as a cover crop for orchards. There are many different kinds of vetch. *Common vetch*, or *tare*, is the most common in the United States, and hairy vetch also grows widely. Purple vetch is becoming important in the Pacific Coast States. Certain flowering vetches are grown for ornamental purposes. Some Europeans eat vetch beans.

Vetches have weak stems which trail across the ground. Farmers often sow oats and rye with vetches because the stiff stems of these plants help to keep the vetch plants off the ground. Vetches require a cool growing season. They grow most successfully in well-drained loam or sandy loam soil. Only hairy vetch can survive a very cold winter. The *vetch bruchid*, a small weevil, destroys the green seed of some vetches.

Scientific Classification. Vetches are of the pea family, *Leguminosae*. Common vetches are genus *Vicia*, species *V. sativa*. Hairy vetches are *V. villosa*. Purple vetches are *V. atropurpurea*. ROY G. WIGGANS

Leaves and Blossoms of Vetch. The plant is highly valuable as a cattle food, and for renewing soil fertility.

N.Y. Botanical Garden

VETERANS ADMINISTRATION administers all laws covering the relief of, and benefits for, former members of the armed forces. The problem of providing for the needs of war veterans of the United States has become a greater one with each succeeding war. With the passage of the Servicemen's Readjustment Act of 1944, the veterans' assistance program became one of the largest activities of the federal government. The agency has charge of pensions, vocational rehabilitation for disabled veterans, veterans' hospitals, soldiers' homes, government insurance, loans for homes and businesses, and education and training.

About 180,000 employees throughout the United States handle the various services and funds of the Veterans Administration. They distribute billions of dollars each year to carry out the promises written into law for veterans. There are over 22 million war veterans in the United States. Pensions costing more than $2,600,000,000 a year are paid to 3,500,000 veterans or their surviving dependents. On any given day, an average of 106,000 patients receive care in Veterans Administration hospitals. The Veterans Administration

Veterans Administration

The Veterans Administration Hospital in Nashville, Tenn., is one of the largest VA hospitals in the United States.

operates a large life-insurance business, with more than 6,400,000 veterans still carrying their wartime term insurance or converted policies.

Other Services. The agency also guarantees loans. Under the law it must guarantee a part of private loans to veterans who request them for buying homes, businesses, and farms. By the end of 1955, 10 years after World War II, veterans had borrowed $33,834,000,000, of which $18,296,000,000 was guaranteed by the government.

The government provided payments to meet part of the expenses of a college education for veterans of World War II and the Korean War. The payments to World War II veterans covered all fees up to a certain maximum, and a monthly allowance which differed for single veterans and those with dependents. Veterans of the Korean War received only a monthly allowance, based on the number of dependents, to meet all their expenses. By the end of 1956, more than 10,000,000 veterans had received education and training, and about 656,000 disabled veterans had received vocational rehabilitation. Education and training benefits for World War II veterans ended in July, 1956.

History. Veterans of the Revolutionary War and the War of 1812 received pensions under laws adopted in 1792 and 1818. Temporary help had already been given veterans in the form of cash bonuses and land grants. The office of the Commissioner of Pensions was set up on March 3, 1849, to administer all military pension laws under the direction of the Secretary of the Interior. The first home for invalid and disabled soldiers was established in Washington, D.C., on March 3, 1851. Today the Veterans Administration has 18 such homes. It operates more than 160 hospitals.

During World War I the Bureau of War Risk Insurance was created to administer insurance against death or disability of members of the military and naval forces. Another part of this law set up the Federal Board for Vocational Education to provide for vocational rehabilitation of disabled veterans of the armed forces. With these new agencies, there were five different bureaus to administer the needs of veterans, including the United States Public Health Service. To eliminate the duplication, Congress created the Veterans Bureau in 1921. In July, 1930, the Veterans Administration was created by consolidating the Veterans Bureau with the National Home for Disabled Volunteer Soldiers and the Bureau of Pensions. GLENN W. MILLER

Related Articles in WORLD BOOK include:

Bonus	Pension (Military Pension)
Bradley, Omar N.	Soldiers' Homes
GI Bill of Rights	War Risk Insurance

VETERANS' BONUS. See BONUS (Other Bonuses).

VETERANS DAY commemorates the courage and patriotism of all the men and women who have served in the United States armed services. It is celebrated on November 11. Other countries, such as Great Britain and France, celebrate November 11 as Armistice Day to commemorate the end of fighting in World War I on Nov. 11, 1918. Canada observes Remembrance Day on November 11 (see REMEMBRANCE DAY).

Veterans Day celebrations in the United States include parades and speeches. Special services are held at the Tomb of the Unknown Soldier in Arlington National Cemetery, Arlington, Va. In 1919, President Woodrow Wilson proclaimed November 11 as Armistice Day to remind Americans of the tragedies of war. A law adopted in 1938 made the day a federal holiday. In 1954, Congress changed the name to Veterans Day to honor all United States veterans. RAYMOND HOYT JAHN

VETERANS' EMPLOYMENT SERVICE. See EMPLOYMENT SECURITY, BUREAU OF.

VETERANS OF FOREIGN WARS OF THE UNITED STATES (VFW) is one of the largest veterans' organizations in the United States. It seeks to develop comradeship among its members, assist needy veterans and their widows and children, organize memorial services for deceased veterans, and promote patriotism. It has about $1\frac{1}{4}$ million members in the United States and its territories, and in other countries.

Any officer or enlisted man, either on active duty in the armed services or honorably discharged, who fought in any foreign military campaign of the United States, may join the VFW. The membership includes veterans of the Spanish American War, the Boxer Rebellion, the Philippine Insurrection, campaigns on the Mexican

border, Nicaraguan expeditions, World Wars I and II, and the Korean War.

The annual national *encampment* (convention) governs the VFW. Encampment delegates determine the organization's policies. They also elect a commander in chief to head the VFW. A national council of administration represents the national encampment between sessions. It has 15 regional representatives.

National Headquarters, VFW

VFW Emblem

The VFW National Home for Veterans' Orphans at Eaton Rapids, Mich., provides care for the children of deceased veterans. It has family-size houses, a hospital, a swimming pool, a gymnasium, a nursery, and a community social center. VFW posts in the United States sponsor Buddy Poppy sales each year. Part of the money from these sales helps support the home.

The Military Order of the Cooties is the honor branch of the VFW. Only those members who have made outstanding contributions toward furthering the objectives of the VFW may qualify for the order. Its members devote their time to helping veterans in hospitals.

Bob Dewey, *The Cootie Courier*

The VFW's Military Order of the Cooties is an honor branch. Members devote their time to helping hospitalized veterans.

The first attempts to form organizations of veterans of foreign wars began in the late 1890's. Three of these organizations combined in 1913 to form the VFW. The organization's headquarters are located at 34th Street and Broadway, Kansas City, Mo. 64102. E. L. JENKINS

VETERANS' ORGANIZATIONS include former members of a nation's armed services. They limit membership to veterans who served during a particular war or military campaign. Or they may accept only veterans who fought overseas, or were disabled. Large veterans' organizations have developed in such countries as France, Great Britain, Germany, and the United States.

VETERANS' ORGANIZATIONS

Veterans' organizations have been chiefly patriotic and social in purpose. They try to develop the comradeships formed during war, and to support the laws and government of the nation. They also provide care for the widows and children of deceased veterans. Veterans' organizations conduct memorial services, and take care of the graves of deceased veterans.

These groups usually have great political influence because of their large membership. They use this power to obtain legislation that will benefit veterans, such as pensions, education, and care for disabled veterans.

In the United States, the Society of the Cincinnati was the first veterans' organization. Major General Henry Knox suggested that officers of the continental army should organize a society of veterans who fought in the Revolutionary War. The Society of the Cincinnati began operating in 1783, with George Washington as its first president.

The veterans' organizations formed after the War of 1812 and the Mexican War were not large. After the Civil War, with its large armies, powerful veterans organizations came into existence. The Grand Army of the Republic (GAR), an organization of veterans of the Union Army, began its work in 1866. It had enough influence to control the Republican party for almost 40 years. It reached its highest membership in 1890. The support of the GAR often meant the difference between victory and defeat for candidates in the North. The United Confederate Veterans held a similar position in the South.

Attempts to organize the veterans of foreign military campaigns began in the late 1890's. The United Spanish War Veterans, founded in 1898, included men who fought in the Spanish-American War. Three groups of veterans of foreign wars joined together in 1913 to form the Veterans of Foreign Wars. In 1919, following World War I, men who fought in France formed a veterans' organization called the *American Legion*. The Disabled American Veterans was established in 1920.

After World War II, veterans formed new organizations. The American Veterans of World War II and Korea (AMVETS) was founded in 1944. It has a membership of about 125,000. The American Veterans Committee (AVC) began in 1944. Its membership is about 25,000.

In Canada, the 240,000-member Canadian Legion is the country's largest veterans' organization. It was founded in 1925, and has about 2,000 branches in Canada. The Army, Navy, and Air Force Veterans in Canada is the country's oldest veterans' group. It was founded in 1837, and ranks second in size. Other Canadian veterans' organizations include the Canadian Corps Association, Canadian Paraplegic Association, Canadian Pensioners Association of the Great War, and the War Amputations of Canada.   H. J. GUINIVAN, JR.

278

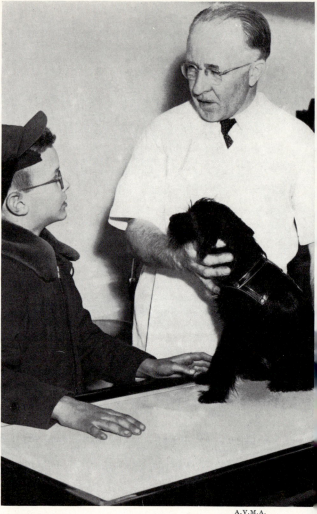

A.V.M.A.

VETERINARY MEDICINE, *VEHT ur uh NEHR ih,* is the branch of medicine that deals with the diseases of animals. An animal doctor is called a *veterinarian.* His work is especially valuable because many animal diseases can be transmitted to human beings. Such diseases are called *zoonoses.* Examples of these are rabies, brucellosis, tuberculosis, parrot fever (psittacosis), and rabbit fever (tularemia).

Treating pets is one of the most profitable fields in veterinary medicine. The veterinarian plays an important role in the control of rabies. The proper vaccination of dogs against rabies and the diagnosis of the disease are part of his duties.

In Cities, most veterinarians are associated with pet hospitals. Many animal hospitals contain equipment much like that used in hospitals for human beings. There, animals may be cared for during illnesses, and surgery may be performed if necessary.

Many veterinarians also are associated with the public health services of cities, states, or the federal government. In this service, their special skills and knowledge are helpful in controlling animal-borne diseases. They

A Veterinarian, *left,* treats animals to keep them healthy, just as a physician treats human beings. Dogs and other animals live longer, happier lives with good medical care.

A Tilting Table, *right,* helps veterinarians take care of large animals such as horses and cows. Here, two veterinarians prepare to take X-ray pictures of a horse's head.

Twin Calves, *below,* are used in a veterinary research project. Veterinarians make openings into the calves' stomachs to study how the calves digest various kinds of food.

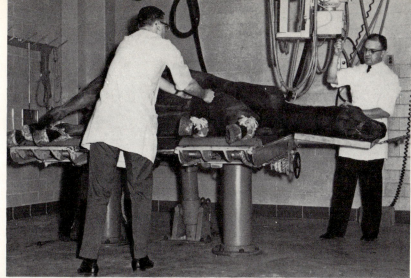

Dept. of Veterinary Clinics, School of Veterinary Science and Medicine, Purdue University

Kansas State University

may inspect meat and meat products, or direct some of the operations in slaughtering and packing houses. They may work in laboratories testing milk or other dairy products, or preparing serums and vaccines.

On Farms. Perhaps the most important activity of the veterinarian is the care and treatment of livestock. Veterinarians keep farm animals in good condition, to prevent outbreaks of animal diseases. Epidemics of animal diseases, called *epizootics,* may be very dangerous, not only to the animals but to human beings as well.

Veterinarians have played an important part in controlling bovine tuberculosis, a form of tuberculosis that can be passed from cows to human beings. In 1917, the federal government began a program to wipe out this disease. A cooperative plan set up by the federal and state government allows veterinarians to test dairy cattle for tuberculosis. Another plan has been established for the control and eradication of bovine brucellosis. This disease also can be transferred to human beings (see BANG'S DISEASE).

Veterinarians give many kinds of inoculations to protect farm animals against disease. For example, they inoculate young pigs against hog cholera. At one time, this dread disease often swept from farm to farm, killing all the hogs in an entire farming community.

Other Services. Circuses and zoos constantly require the services of veterinarians to keep their animals healthy. Veterinarians may also be employed in government service, where they often specialize in the study and treatment of wildlife.

Careers in Veterinary Medicine. Persons who want to become veterinarians usually have two years of training in a college of liberal arts. They then spend three or four years in specialized study. During this time they study anatomy, surgery, chemistry, physiology, breeding and feeding of animals, and many other professional subjects.

Nineteen colleges and universities in North America are recognized by the American Veterinary Medical Association as meeting the minimum requirements established by its Council on Education. These schools offer courses of study that lead to the degree of Doctor of Veterinary Medicine (D.V.M.). After earning a diploma, the graduate must comply with the license laws of his state before he is allowed to practice his profession.

After he is licensed, the veterinarian may go into private practice. He may join the veterinary services of the government or the armed forces. If he is interested in research, he may want to work with the U.S. Department of Agriculture, an agricultural experiment station, or a veterinary college. Veterinarians often work in commercial laboratories that produce serums and vaccines.

The American Veterinary Medical Association serves to maintain the professional standards of veterinary medicine. It holds annual meetings to which local and state groups send representatives. Headquarters of the Association are located at 600 S. Michigan Ave., Chicago, Ill.   D. W. BRUNER

VETO, *VEE toh,* is a Latin word which means *I forbid.* In American government, the word *veto* usually refers to the President's power to kill a law that the legislative branch has already passed.

The President of the United States has a *limited* veto power. It is not absolute. A vote of a two-thirds majority of the members present in both houses of Congress can override it. The sovereign of Great Britain still holds the power of *absolute* veto. But no British king or queen has used this power since 1707.

When the two houses of Congress pass a bill or joint resolution, it is presented to the President of the United States. Then one of the following four things must happen:

The President may approve the bill. If so, he signs it and it becomes law.

The President may allow the bill to become law without his signature. This can take place under the clause in the Constitution which provides that "if any bill shall not be returned by the President within 10 days (Sundays excepted) after it shall have been presented to him, the same shall be a law in like manner as if he had signed it, unless the Congress by their adjournment prevent its return, in which case it shall not be a law."

The President may retain the bill, in the expectation that Congress will adjourn within 10 days and thus the bill will be defeated. This method is called the *pocket veto.* It is used by Presidents who find certain bills unsatisfactory but do not want to veto them openly.

The President may veto the bill. If he does, he must send a message to Congress stating his reasons.

Presidents' Use of the Veto. When the Constitution was adopted, Alexander Hamilton declared that Presidents would use the veto power with great caution. But when a President has vetoed a bill, Congress has rarely overridden him to make the bill a law. Congress passed six bills over Woodrow Wilson's veto. It defeated Grover Cleveland's veto five times. It reversed Calvin Coolidge's veto four times, Herbert Hoover's three times, and Theodore Roosevelt's and William Howard Taft's, only once each. Congress defeated none of the vetoes of William McKinley and Warren G. Harding. It reversed nine of Roosevelt's vetoes and eleven of Truman's.

Vetoing a bill defeats all parts of it. All provisions and "riders" attached to the bill are vetoed with it and cannot be saved.

Governors' Veto Power. State governors also have a veto power. In some states, however, the governor's veto

may be overridden by a simple majority of the members present in the houses of the legislature, rather than by a required two-thirds majority. Most governors can veto parts of appropriation bills.   PAYSON S. WILD, JR.

See also UNITED NATIONS (The Veto Power); UNITED STATES, GOVERNMENT OF (color diagram).

VETTISFOSS, *VET is FAWS,* is a waterfall in western Norway. It ranks as one of the country's highest waterfalls. Vettisfoss measures 850 feet in height. Many tourists visit the area. See also NORWAY (Rivers, Waterfalls, and Lakes).

VEVAY, *VEE vay,* Ind. (pop. 1,503; alt. 525 ft.), lies on the Ohio River across from Kentucky. Vevay is the county seat of Switzerland County and the center of a fertile farming region. Its most important products are tobacco and milk. The city is about 90 miles southeast of Indianapolis (see INDIANA [political map]). Some Swiss colonists settled on the site of Vevay in 1801. In the early years, the Swiss settlers planted vineyards and produced a wine which became famous throughout the Middle West.   PAUL E. MILLION, JR.

VFW. See VETERANS OF FOREIGN WARS OF THE UNITED STATES.

VHF WAVE. See VERY HIGH FREQUENCY WAVE.

VIA APPIA or **APPIAN WAY.** See APPIAN WAY.

VIA FLAMINIA. See FLAMINIAN WAY.

VIA SACRA. See ROME (Forums).

VIA SALARIA. See SALT (History).

VIADUCT, *VI uh dukt,* is like a bridge, except that it crosses over dry land instead of water. Some viaducts do cross water, but they also cross dry land instead of merely extending from bank to bank as a bridge does. Most viaducts are made up of a series of supports under beam-and-slab or arch construction. Viaducts are used to carry railroad tracks over valleys and gorges. Some viaducts are built higher than the general level of the land to carry railroads over highways, or to make a safe crossing for highways over railroads.

The ancient Romans built the first viaducts. The aqueducts they built to carry water to cities often were designed to serve also as roadways.

Viaducts Help Make the Flow of Traffic Safe and Easy.
International Harvester Co.

One of the longest viaducts ever built was a portion of the 110-mile Key West extension of the Florida East Coast Railway. Viaducts that extended over the open sea formed 30 miles of this extension. Parts were destroyed by a hurricane in 1935, but these were rebuilt as a highway a few years later. The main part of the pier viaduct over the mouth of the River Tay in Scotland has 84 steel spans and is over 2 miles long. The Tunkhannock viaduct on the Lackawanna Railway is one of the largest steel and concrete viaducts in the world. It is 2,375 feet long and includes 10 spans of 180 feet each. Another famous viaduct is the 3½-mile Pulaski Skyway between Newark and Jersey City. Other well-known viaducts are the Pecos River viaduct in Texas and the Landwasser viaduct across the Albula Pass, in the canton of Graubünden, Switzerland.   R. G. HENNES

See also BRIDGE (pictures); PULASKI SKYWAY.

VIATICUM, *vy AT ih kum,* in the Catholic Church, is the last communion, or Holy Eucharist, administered to the dying or those in danger of death. During a long illness it may be given several times. It is given before Anointing of the Sick. In Latin, the word means *provision for a journey.* In the early Christian Church, it was applied to anything that gave spiritual comfort to the dying. See also ANOINTING OF THE SICK.   FULTON J. SHEEN

VIBRATION, in mechanics, indicates to-and-fro motion, or *oscillation,* of a particle. The two types of vibration are *natural* and *artificial.* An earthquake causes a natural vibration. But most vibrations are artificial, because some man-made device causes them. For example, engineers design special devices called *vibrators* that cause vibration or shaking. Foundries use a special vibrator to loosen a mold that has been placed in sand. Vibrators are also used in medicine to stimulate the circulation and the muscles. If objects did not vibrate, it would be impossible to speak to anyone, because all sound begins with a vibrating object. When a person speaks, his vocal cords begin the vibrations.

Aside from a relatively few valuable uses, vibration is undesirable in industry and in most daily living. It may cause weakening of structures and produce wear and inefficiency. In cities, trucks, subways, elevated trains, and other traffic cause much vibration. These vibrations sometimes enter the steel structure of a large building, and can be felt throughout the building. Engineers deal with this problem by using special materials that absorb vibration. Pneumatic tires are used in an effort to reduce the vibrations on moving automobiles. Automobile engines are mounted on rubber supports to reduce vibration as much as possible. Vibration dampers have also been designed in crankshafts. More cylinders have been added to engines in order to decrease the effect of vibration and provide a smoother flow of power.

Many industries must deal with the problem of vibration and its effect on machinery. Rotating parts of machines give trouble from vibration unless they are accurately balanced, especially at high speeds. The supports of such rotating parts were once bolted to the machine frame or its foundation. To reduce the effect of vibration in machines, the supports for high-speed rotating parts are now sometimes mounted on springs, rubber, or some other kind of flexible connection.

Mechanical vibrations have various frequencies and amplitudes. *Frequency* is the number of complete vibrations during a certain time. *Amplitude* is the maximum distance the particle travels from its normal position of *equilibrium,* or rest.   ROBERT L. WEBER

See also SOUND; WAVES.

VIBURNUM is the name for a group of shrubs and small trees of the honeysuckle family. These plants grow in large numbers throughout North America, Europe, and Asia. They have white or pink flowers, and leaves which sometimes turn various colors in the autumn. Gardeners like viburnum shrubs for borders.

Scientific Classification. The viburnum belongs to the honeysuckle family, *Caprifoliaceae.* Some of the common American kinds are genus *Viburnum,* species *V. acerifolium, V. alnifolium,* and *V. trilobum.*   ALFRED C. HOTTES

See also HONEYSUCKLE.

Flowers of the Viburnum make it one of the most attractive shrubs used to ornament gardens. The plant produces berries that are coral red, later purple. Bees are likely to be seen hovering about them.

J. Horace McFarland

VICAR, *VICK ur,* is a person who represents and performs duties for a higher official in a church. The term comes from the Latin word *vicarius,* meaning a *substitute.* The pope of the Roman Catholic Church is called the Vicar of Christ on earth. *Vicars apostolic* are bishops who serve as personal representatives of the pope in mission areas. A *vicar general* acts as the deputy of a bishop, and a *vicar capitular* administers a diocese in the absence of a bishop. The Church of England uses the title of vicar for the head of a parish who, for some reason, may not be called the rector. In the Episcopal Church of the United States, the term usually refers to the priest in charge of a parish chapel.   R. PIERCE BEAVER and FULTON J. SHEEN

VICE-ADMIRAL. See RANK IN ARMED SERVICES.

VICE-PRESIDENT is the second highest executive in the government of some countries. In Brazil, under the constitution, he is popularly elected for a five-year term, serves as president of the senate, and cannot serve two terms in a row. In Bolivia, the vice-president assumes the presidency in the event of the president's death or failure to assume the office. The vice-president of Argentina presides over the senate, but has no other political power. In Chile, there is no permanent vice-president. But when the president is ill or leaves the country, he can appoint a temporary vice-president. In some Communist nations of eastern Europe, vice-presidents are heads of ministries or hold honorary titles without administrative duties.   IRVING G. WILLIAMS

See also VICE-PRESIDENT OF THE UNITED STATES.

John Adams
1789-1797
Washington

Thomas Jefferson
1797-1801
J. Adams

Aaron Burr
1801-1805
Jefferson

George Clinton
1805-1812
Jefferson-Madison

Elbridge Gerry
1813-1814
Madison

Daniel D. Tompkins
1817-1825
Monroe

John C. Calhoun
1825-1832
J. Q. Adams-Jackson

Martin Van Buren
1833-1837
Jackson

Richard M. Johnson
1837-1841
Van Buren

John Tyler
1841
W. H. Harrison

George M. Dallas
1845-1849
Polk

Millard Fillmore
1849-1850
Taylor

William R. D. King
1853
Pierce

John C. Breckinridge
1857-1861
Buchanan

Hannibal Hamlin
1861-1865
Lincoln

Andrew Johnson
1865
Lincoln

Schuyler Colfax
1869-1873
Grant

Henry Wilson
1873-1875
Grant

THE VICE-PRESIDENTS
OF THE UNITED STATES

Eleven of the 38 Vice-Presidents have become Presidents. Under the picture of each Vice-President is listed his term of office and the President under whom he served.

William A. Wheeler
1877-1881
Hayes

Chester A. Arthur
1881
Garfield

Thomas A. Hendricks
1885
Cleveland

Levi P. Morton
1889-1893
B. Harrison

Adlai E. Stevenson
1893-1897
Cleveland

Garret A. Hobart
1897-1899
McKinley

Theodore Roosevelt
1901
McKinley

Charles W. Fairbanks
1905-1909
T. Roosevelt

James S. Sherman
1909-1912
Taft

Thomas R. Marshall
1913-1921
Wilson

Calvin Coolidge
1921-1923
Harding

Charles G. Dawes
1925-1929
Coolidge

Charles Curtis
1929-1933
Hoover

John N. Garner
1933-1941
F. Roosevelt

Henry A. Wallace
1941-1945
F. Roosevelt

Harry S. Truman
1945
F. Roosevelt

Alben W. Barkley
1949-1953
Truman

Richard M. Nixon
1953-1961
Eisenhower

Lyndon B. Johnson
1961-1963
Kennedy

An asterisk indicates the Vice-Presidents who later became Presidents.

VICE-PRESIDENT OF THE UNITED STATES is only a heartbeat away from the most powerful elective office in the world. He must be ready to assume the presidency at a moment's notice if the President dies.

Eleven Vice-Presidents have become President, eight because of the death of a President. These eight so-called "accidental Presidents" were John Tyler, Millard Fillmore, Andrew Johnson, Chester A. Arthur, Theodore Roosevelt, Calvin Coolidge, Harry S. Truman, and Lyndon B. Johnson. The only men to win the presidency by election while holding office as Vice-President have been John Adams, Thomas Jefferson, and Martin Van Buren.

The United States Constitution also provides that the Vice-President shall take over the presidency as the result of a President's being disabled. But no one has ever decided how seriously a President must be disabled so that the Vice-President should take over. Presidents James A. Garfield, Woodrow Wilson, and Dwight D. Eisenhower all suffered serious illnesses. But their Vice-Presidents carefully avoided assuming the role of President. In 1965, Congress proposed an amendment to the Constitution, spelling out procedures in case of presidential disability.

The Vice-President serves as the presiding officer of the United States Senate, and has the title of *President of the Senate*. The Constitution gives him no other official duty. For more than a hundred years the absence of political importance of the job caused it to be treated as somewhat of a joke. Some persons have humorously suggested that the Vice-President be addressed as "His Superfluous Excellency."

Yet the Founding Fathers had high hopes for the vice-presidency. James Iredell of North Carolina, a delegate to the Constitutional Convention of 1787, explained that there would be "two men . . . in office at the same time; the President, who will possess, in the highest degree, the confidence of the country, and the

VICE-PRESIDENT OF THE UNITED STATES

Vice-President, who is thought to be the next person in the Union most fit to perform this trust."

The prestige of the vice-presidency has gradually increased since the early 1920's. Beginning in 1933 with the presidency of Franklin D. Roosevelt, Vice-Presidents have regularly attended meetings of the Presi-

Irving G. Williams, the contributor of this article, is Director of the Social Sciences Area at St. John's University, and author of The American Vice-Presidency: New Look.

dent's Cabinet. Dwight D. Eisenhower and John F. Kennedy did more than any other Presidents to establish the importance of the office of Vice-President. Eisenhower's Vice-President, Richard M. Nixon, and Kennedy's Vice-President, Lyndon B. Johnson, had important duties and responsibilities. When Kennedy was assassinated in 1963, many experts believed that Johnson was the best-prepared "accidental President."

The Vice-President has an office in the Capitol in Washington, D.C. There is no official residence for the Vice-President. But in 1966, Congress provided funds to build such a residence. Secret service agents guard the Vice-President and his family.

Choosing a Vice-President

Nomination of the vice-presidential candidate usually comes as an anticlimax to a political convention. The excitement of selecting the presidential nominee is over, but the delegates must still choose his *running mate*. Often there is no real contest. The presidential nominee frequently indicates his preference for Vice-President, in which case the delegates usually nominate him. A contest develops only if the presidential nominee makes no choice.

Many factors may influence the selection of a vice-presidential nominee. After a bitter convention, the

---

FACTS IN BRIEF ABOUT THE VICE-PRESIDENT

Qualifications: The United States Constitution provides that a candidate must be a "natural-born" U.S. citizen and must have lived in the United States for at least 14 years. He must be at least 35 years old. No law or court decision has yet defined the exact meaning of the term *natural-born*. Authorities assume that the term applies to all citizens born in the United States and its territories. But they are not certain if the term also includes children born to United States citizens in other countries.

How Nominated: By a national political convention.

How Elected: By a majority vote of the Electoral College, held in December following the general election

held on the first Tuesday after the first Monday in November of every fourth year.

Inauguration: Held at noon, January 20, after election by the Electoral College. If the date falls on Sunday, the ceremony is held on Monday, January 21.

Term: The Vice-President is elected for four years, and can serve any number of terms.

Income: $43,000 annual salary, $10,000 expense allowance, and about $135,000 allowance for clerical assistance.

Removal from Office: Impeachment by a majority vote of the House of Representatives, and trial and conviction by a two-thirds vote of those present in the Senate. No Vice-President has ever been impeached.

Hubert H. Humphrey
1965-
Johnson

The Coat of Arms of the Vice-President of the United States displays the American eagle. It is similar to the President's coat of arms and to the *Great Seal* of the United States. ▶

Library of Congress

VICE-PRESIDENT OF THE UNITED STATES

winning presidential nominee may support a candidate who can help restore party harmony. His choice for Vice-President may be one of the losing candidates for the presidency, or a supporter of one of the losers. In 1844, the Democrats nominated Senator Silas Wright of New York for Vice-President. They did this to appease former President Martin Van Buren, who had failed to win the Democratic presidential nomination. But Wright, a close friend of Van Buren, declined the selection. He was the only man actually nominated for Vice-President by a convention who refused to run.

Often the Vice-President comes from one of the states considered to be especially important in the election. This may be a state in which the election outcome is expected to be very close, or it may simply be a state with a large electoral vote. By appealing to local loyalties, the vice-presidential candidate may strengthen his party's vote in his "home" state.

Sometimes the vice-presidency has been "traded" by a presidential candidate for help in winning the nomination. For example, an influential governor or U.S. Senator may be promised the vice-presidential nomination in return for swinging his state's delegates to a certain presidential candidate.

The vice-presidential choice often is made to *balance the ticket*. If an older man is nominated for President, a younger man may be chosen for Vice-President. A presidential nominee from the East may be balanced with a vice-presidential nominee from the West. If the presidential nominee is known as a conservative, the vice-presidential nominee may be a liberal. By balancing the ticket, party leaders hope to appeal to the largest possible number of voters.

The system of selecting a Vice-President helps the party win the election. It does not necessarily produce the man best qualified to serve as Vice-President. The custom of balancing the ticket with men of conflicting political beliefs has often been criticized. Theodore Roosevelt said early in his political career: "It is an unhealthy thing to have a Vice-President and President represented by principles so far apart that the succession of one to the place of the other means a change as radical as any party overturn." This occurred when John Tyler succeeded William Henry Harrison. And, ironically, it also happened when Roosevelt later succeeded William McKinley.

The Campaign. The vice-presidential candidate plays an active role in the election campaign. He travels widely, makes speeches, shakes hands with thousands of persons, appears on radio and television, and does everything possible to help his party win.

The presidential and vice-presidential candidates usually map out separate campaign routes for maximum coverage of the country. They may later change places to cover all strategic areas with repeated campaigning. The vice-presidential campaigner may also visit smaller cities that the presidential nominee bypassed.

Election. Voters select the same electors for the Vice-President when they choose presidential electors. They cannot split the ticket. That is, a person cannot vote for electors of the presidential candidate of the Republican party and for electors of the vice-presidential candidate of the Democratic party. He must vote for one slate of electors pledged to the two candidates of one party.

The Electoral College elects the President and Vice-President on separate ballots (see ELECTORAL COLLEGE). If the Electoral College fails to choose the Vice-President by a majority vote, the U.S. Senate elects him from among the two leading candidates. At least two thirds of the Senate must be present at the voting, and the winner must receive a majority vote of the entire membership. Such an election has occurred only once. In 1837, the Senate elected Richard M. Johnson, a Democrat, by a vote of 33 to 16 over Francis Granger, a Whig. Johnson had fallen one vote short in the Electoral College. He became such a politically controversial figure that the Democrats refused to renominate him in 1840. In fact, they failed to nominate any vice-presidential candidate—the only time any convention has done so.

Inauguration. Until 1933, the President and Vice-President were normally inaugurated in separate cere-

The Vice-President of the United States takes his oath of office immediately before the President is sworn in on the January 20 following the election. Inauguration ceremonies usually take place on the east steps of the Capitol in Washington, D.C.

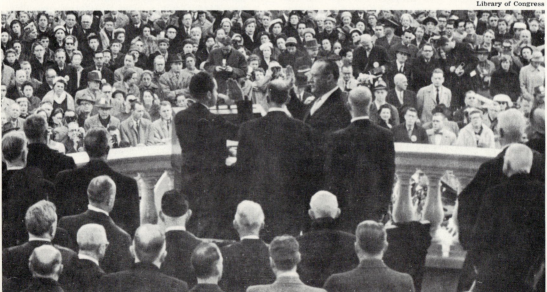

THE VICE-PRESIDENTS OF THE UNITED STATES

Name	Birthplace	Occupation or Profession	Political Party	Age at Inauguration	Term	President
1. Adams, John (a)	Braintree, Mass.	Lawyer	Federalist	53	1789-1797	Washington
2. Jefferson, Thomas (a)	Shadwell, Va.	Planter	Democratic-Republican	53	1797-1801	J. Adams
3. Burr, Aaron	Newark, N.J.	Lawyer	Democratic-Republican	45	1801-1805	Jefferson
4. Clinton, George (c)	Little Britain, N.Y.	Soldier	Democratic-Republican	65	1805-1809	Jefferson
				69	1809-1812	Madison
5. Gerry, Elbridge (c)	Marblehead, Mass.	Businessman	Democratic-Republican	68	1813-1814	Madison
6. Tompkins, Daniel D.	Fox Meadows, N.Y.	Lawyer	Democratic-Republican	42	1817-1825	Monroe
7. Calhoun, John C. (d)	Abbeville District, S.C.	Lawyer	Democratic-Republican	42	1825-1829	J. Q. Adams
			Democrat	46	1829-1832	Jackson
8. Van Buren, Martin (a)	Kinderhook, N.Y.	Lawyer	Democrat	50	1833-1837	Jackson
9. Johnson, Richard M.	Beargrass, Ky.	Lawyer	Democrat	56	1837-1841	Van Buren
10. Tyler, John (b)	Charles City County, Va.	Lawyer	Whig	50	1841	W. H. Harrison
11. Dallas, George M.	Philadelphia, Pa.	Lawyer	Democrat	52	1845-1849	Polk
12. Fillmore, Millard (b)	Locke, N.Y.	Lawyer	Whig	49	1849-1850	Taylor
13. King, William R. D. (c)	Sampson County, N.C.	Lawyer	Democrat	66	1853	Pierce
14. Breckinridge, John C.	Lexington, Ky.	Lawyer	Democrat	36	1857-1861	Buchanan
15. Hamlin, Hannibal	Paris, Me.	Lawyer	Republican	51	1861-1865	Lincoln
16. Johnson, Andrew (b)	Raleigh, N.C.	Tailor	National Union (e)	56	1865	Lincoln
17. Colfax, Schuyler	New York, N.Y.	Auditor	Republican	45	1869-1873	Grant
18. Wilson, Henry (c)	Farmington, N.H.	Businessman	Republican	61	1873-1875	Grant
19. Wheeler, William A.	Malone, N.Y.	Lawyer	Republican	57	1877-1881	Hayes
20. Arthur, Chester A. (b)	Fairfield, Vt.	Lawyer	Republican	50	1881	Garfield
21. Hendricks, Thomas A. (c)	Muskingum County, O.	Lawyer	Democrat	65	1885	Cleveland
22. Morton, Levi P.	Shoreham, Vt.	Banker	Republican	64	1889-1893	B. Harrison
23. Stevenson, Adlai E.	Christian County, Ky.	Lawyer	Democrat	57	1893-1897	Cleveland
24. Hobart, Garret A. (c)	Long Branch, N.J.	Lawyer	Republican	52	1897-1899	McKinley
25. Roosevelt, Theodore (b) (a)	New York, N.Y.	Author	Republican	42	1901	McKinley
26. Fairbanks, Charles W.	Unionville Center, O.	Lawyer	Republican	52	1905-1909	T. Roosevelt
27. Sherman, James S. (c)	Utica, N.Y.	Lawyer	Republican	53	1909-1912	Taft
28. Marshall, Thomas R.	North Manchester, Ind.	Lawyer	Democrat	58	1913-1921	Wilson
29. Coolidge, Calvin (b) (a)	Plymouth, Vt.	Lawyer	Republican	48	1921-1923	Harding
30. Dawes, Charles G.	Marietta, O.	Lawyer	Republican	59	1925-1929	Coolidge
31. Curtis, Charles	Topeka, Kans.	Lawyer	Republican	69	1929-1933	Hoover
32. Garner, John N.	Red River County, Tex.	Lawyer	Democrat	64	1933-1941	F. Roosevelt
33. Wallace, Henry A.	Adair County, Ia.	Farmer	Democrat	52	1941-1945	F. Roosevelt
34. Truman, Harry S. (b) (a)	Lamar, Mo.	Businessman	Democrat	60	1945	F. Roosevelt
35. Barkley, Alben W.	Graves County, Ky.	Lawyer	Democrat	71	1949-1953	Truman
36. Nixon, Richard M.	Yorba Linda, Calif.	Lawyer	Republican	40	1953-1961	Eisenhower
37. Johnson, Lyndon B. (b) (a)	near Stonewall, Tex.	Teacher	Democrat	52	1961-1963	Kennedy
38. Humphrey, Hubert H.	Wallace, S.Dak.	Pharmacist	Democrat	53	1965-	Johnson

(a) Elected to the presidency.
(b) Succeeded to the presidency upon the death of the President.
(c) Died in office.
(d) Resigned.
(e) The National Union party consisted of Republicans and War Democrats. Johnson was a Democrat.

Each Vice-President has a separate biography in WORLD BOOK.

monies. The Vice-President took his oath of office in the Senate. Today, both officials are inaugurated in the same ceremony in January following their election. The Vice-President is sworn into office immediately before the President is inaugurated. The retiring Vice-President usually administers the oath of office to his successor. If no Vice-President is in office, the president *pro tempore*, or temporary president, of the Senate administers the oath.

In the early days, the Vice-President made an inaugural address. This custom has disappeared with the adoption of the combined ceremony in which the President gives the inaugural address.

Roles of the Vice-President

The Vice-President can be only as important as the President chooses to let him be. Regardless of his personal ability and prestige, the Vice-President can do little on his own. He has almost no political power, unless the President chooses to consult him on matters of party policy and patronage, or appointments to political offices. Even the Vice-President's role as a Cabinet member depends on the wishes of the President.

With the active support of the President, the Vice-President can exert tremendous influence. His presence at Cabinet meetings gives him working contact with the heads of all the executive departments of the government. His attendance at conferences between the President and Congressional leaders strengthens his own power with the legislative branch. If the President gives him important diplomatic missions, the Vice-President can play a leading role in the shaping of foreign policy.

A Typical Day for the Vice-President might begin with a breakfast conference called by the President. Perhaps a legislative meeting follows. The two men confer with their party's Congressional leaders about legislation being debated by the Senate and the House of Representatives. The Vice-President may then go to his office in the Senate wing of the Capitol. He reads and answers his mail, and sees callers who have appointments. Tourists or unexpected visitors on emergency matters also may arrive. If the Senate is meeting that day, the Vice-President enters about noon to preside at the opening of the session. He may remain in the chair of the Senate, depending on the nature of the day's business and his own schedule. If he leaves, the president *pro tempore* or another senator takes over his duties.

The Vice-President spends many evenings away from his home. He must make various kinds of public appearances, many of which require him to make speeches. He may go to the airport to greet dignitaries from other nations. His ceremonial duties may require the Vice-President to dedicate a public-works project, open an athletic tournament, or present an award to a contest-winner.

President of the Senate. When presiding over the Senate, the Vice-President performs the duties of chairman. He cannot take part in any Senate debates. Nor can he vote, except in the rare case of a tie. John Adams cast a deciding vote 29 times, more than did any other Vice-President.

The Vice-President enforces the rules established by the Senate for its own guidance. Senators can speak only after being recognized by the Vice-President or the president *pro tempore*. By using this power of recognition, the Vice-President can either aid or hold back legislation by permitting only certain Senators to speak. He also has the power to make rulings in disputes over procedure by interpreting the rules of the Senate. But the Senate can overrule his decisions by a majority vote. In 1919, Vice-President Thomas R. Marshall ruled three times in one day on a certain point. He was fighting to save the controversial Versailles Treaty and United States membership in the League of Nations. The Senate overruled Marshall three times and finally defeated the treaty.

The president of the Senate also directs the counting of electoral votes for President and Vice-President. Early Vice-Presidents could decide whether to count or disallow disputed votes. Congress has since assumed this power, leaving the Vice-President only formally in charge of counting electoral votes.

If the Vice-President succeeds to the presidency upon the President's death or resignation, the vice-presidency remains vacant until the next inauguration. But in 1965, Congress proposed a constitutional amendment whereby the new President would appoint a Vice-President with the approval of Congress.

Administration and Policy-Making. The Vice-President attends meetings of the President's Cabinet. He serves as chairman of the National Aeronautics and Space Council. He also is a member of the National Security Council, the highest advisory body to the President on matters of foreign and defense policies. See CABINET; NATIONAL SECURITY COUNCIL.

The President may assign the Vice-President general counseling and liaison activities. Such duties may involve trips abroad to spread good will, exchange information, and learn about the attitudes of various nations toward the United States. The Vice-President may also act as an intermediary between the President and his political party, both in Congress and in the party. He explains, persuades, and threatens, if he must, to build party support for the President's program.

Social Duties. One of the oldest functions of the Vice-President is to serve as ceremonial assistant to the President. He attends many events at which the President cannot be present. The President is the formal leader of Washington society, but the Vice-President is the actual leader. The Chief Executive makes few social appearances except at the receptions that he himself gives. The Vice-President often plays host to dignitaries from other countries.

Some Vice-Presidents have enjoyed their ceremonial and social duties, but others have not. Calvin Coolidge took a typically characteristic and philosophic approach. When his hostess at a dinner once remarked to him how annoying it must be to have to dine out so often, Coolidge replied: "Have to eat somewhere." John N. Garner drew the line on social life. He usually

---

INTERESTING FACTS ABOUT THE VICE-PRESIDENTS

Who was the youngest Vice-President to be inaugurated? Breckinridge, 36. **The oldest?** Barkley, 71.

Who was the only Vice-President who ever resigned? Calhoun.

What Vice-President was accused of taking bribes and left the office under a scandal? Colfax.

Who was the first Vice-President to attend meetings of the Cabinet regularly? Coolidge.

Who was the first Vice-President to become a regular member of the National Security Council? Barkley.

What Vice-President presided over the Senate with a brace of pistols beside him? Van Buren.

Who was the only Vice-President, since 1804, to be elected President while holding office as Vice-President? Van Buren.

What Vice-President-elect was so ill that he died without ever performing the duties of his office? King.

Who was the first Vice-President to succeed to the presidency, then win the office by election? T. Roosevelt.

Who was the first Vice-President to be assigned administrative duties by the President? Wallace.

Who was the only Vice-President who had to be selected by the Senate because the Electoral College failed to agree? R. Johnson.

Who was the first Vice-President nominated at a national political convention? Van Buren.

What state has had the most Vice-Presidents? New York.

What Vice-Presidents died in office? Clinton, Gerry, King, Wilson, Hendricks, Hobart, Sherman.

Who was the youngest Vice-President to succeed to the presidency upon the death of the President? T. Roosevelt, 42. **The oldest?** Truman, 60.

What teams of President and Vice-President were re-elected to second terms? Washington and Adams, Monroe and Tompkins, Wilson and Marshall, F. Roosevelt and Garner, Eisenhower and Nixon.

What was the only team of President and Vice-President defeated for a second term? Hoover and Curtis.

What Vice-Presidents served under two different Presidents? Clinton, Calhoun.

What Vice-President took his oath of office in another country? King, in Havana, Cuba.

went to bed early, and refused to receive calls from 6 P.M. to 7 A.M., saying these hours "are my own."

History of the Vice-Presidency

Early Days. Most historians believe that Alexander Hamilton first proposed the office of Vice-President. Not all the delegates to the Constitutional Convention supported the idea. But on Sept. 6, 1787, the convention approved his proposal. The Founding Fathers originally provided that the man who received the second highest electoral vote for President should become Vice-President. Each elector had two votes, which he cast for the two men he considered best qualified for the presidency. Under this system, John Adams became the first Vice-President and Thomas Jefferson the second.

Adams and Jefferson developed different views of the vice-presidency. Adams, after becoming the first Vice-President, wrote his wife: "My country has in its wisdom contrived for me the most insignificant office that ever the invention of man contrived or his imagination conceived." Jefferson declared that "the second office in the government is honorable and easy; the first is but a splendid misery."

The rise of political parties caused the breakdown of this election system. In 1796, the Electoral College gave the greatest number of votes to Adams, a Federalist. Jefferson, a Democratic-Republican, received the next largest number of votes, and became Vice-President. The conflicting party loyalties of President Adams and Vice-President Jefferson created discord in the administration.

In the election of 1800, Jefferson and Aaron Burr both ran on the Republican ticket. The two men tied with 73 electoral votes each, and the election was given to the House of Representatives, where each state has one vote in a presidential election. Burr hoped for Federalist support, and made a bid to be elected President instead of Vice-President. But he failed. After 36 ballots, Jefferson won a majority of the House votes, and Burr became Vice-President. The weakness of the system became apparent during this election. In 1804, Congress adopted Amendment 12 to the Constitution, which provided for separate ballots for President and Vice-President. This amendment solved the immediate problem, but it also lessened the prestige of the vice-presidency. The Vice-President was no longer elected as the second choice for the presidency.

Tyler Takes Over. The Constitution provides that in case of the death or disability of the President, "the powers and duties" of the office shall devolve on the Vice-President. Just how this would work remained uncertain until 1841, when William Henry Harrison died in office, the first President to do so. His Vice-President was John Tyler. Former President John Quincy Adams and some other political leaders believed that Tyler should be called merely *Acting President*, not President. They opposed Tyler's receiving the full presidential salary and even his occupying the White House. Tyler ignored the opposition. He took the oath and title of *President*, moved into the White House, and asserted the full presidential powers. His action was not challenged legally, and he thereby established the right of the Vice-President to full succession.

Vice-Presidents have responded in various ways when

a President has become disabled. Vice-President Chester A. Arthur never saw James A. Garfield during the President's 80-day illness. Arthur remained in Washington, D.C., most of the time and received reports of the President's condition from Secretary of State James G. Blaine. He refused to assume the Chief Executive's duties for fear that he would be doing wrong. Vice-President Thomas R. Marshall also declined to take up the President's duties during Woodrow Wilson's six-month illness. During Dwight D. Eisenhower's illnesses in 1955 and 1956, Vice-President Richard M. Nixon presided at meetings of the Cabinet and the National Security Council. He kept in close touch with the President. These experiences, and the 1963 assassination of President John F. Kennedy, led Congress, in 1965, to propose a constitutional amendment setting procedures for presidential succession.

Growth of the Vice-Presidency. In 1791, Vice-President John Adams attended a Cabinet meeting. No other Vice-President did so until after World War I. In 1918, President Wilson asked Vice-President Marshall to preside over the Cabinet while Wilson was attending the Paris Peace Conference. After Wilson returned home, Marshall was again excluded from Cabinet meetings.

President Warren G. Harding invited Vice-President Calvin Coolidge to attend all Cabinet meetings. Coolidge did so until he became President after Harding's death. Vice-President Charles G. Dawes publicly declared that he would not attend Cabinet sessions, because if he did so "the precedent might prove injurious to the country." Knowing Dawes' views, Coolidge did not invite him to participate. Nor did President Herbert Hoover invite Vice-President Charles Curtis to attend.

Since the first term of President Franklin D. Roosevelt, all Vice-Presidents have regularly attended Cabinet meetings. President Eisenhower strengthened the vice-presidency further by directing that Vice-President Nixon should preside at Cabinet meetings in the President's absence. Previously, the Secretary of State had presided at such times. Congress made the Vice-President a member of the National Security Council in 1949. Eisenhower directed in 1954 that the Vice-President, rather than the Secretary of State, should preside over the council when the President was absent.

President John F. Kennedy further extended the duties of the Vice-President. As Vice-President, Lyndon B. Johnson served as Chairman of the National Aeronautics and Space Council and headed the President's Committee on Equal Employment Opportunity. Johnson traveled on many diplomatic and goodwill missions for the President. Kennedy regarded Johnson as a close adviser and kept him informed of domestic and international events. As President, Johnson continued to upgrade the vice-presidency. Hubert H. Humphrey was Johnson's Vice-President.   IRVING G. WILLIAMS

Related Articles. See the separate biography of each Vice-President listed in the *table* in this article. Other related articles in WORLD BOOK include:

Cabinet	Franking and Penalty
Electoral College	Privileges
Flag (color picture, Flags	National Security Council
of the United States	President of the United
Government)	States

VICEROY

Questions

What is meant by "balancing a ticket"?

What are the legal qualifications for a vice-presidential candidate?

What official duties does the Constitution give the Vice-President?

In what various ways have Vice-Presidents responded when a President has become disabled?

What happened in 1800 to bring about a change in the method of electing the Vice-President?

How did the vice-presidency change after 1804?

How has the vice-presidency grown in importance since World War I?

How can a Vice-President be removed from office?

Who proposed the office of Vice-President?

How is the Vice-President elected if the Electoral College fails to select one by majority vote?

What is the annual salary of the Vice-President?

VICEROY. See BUTTERFLY (color picture).

VICEROY is an official who rules a province or colony in the name of a king. The term *viceroy* means *in place of the king*. The British governor-general of India was a viceroy. Before 1920, the lord lieutenant of Ireland was often called a viceroy.

VICHY, *VISH ih* (pop. 30,614; alt. 870 ft.), is a resort town on the Allier River in south-central France. For location, see FRANCE (political map). During World War II, Vichy was the capital of unoccupied France from July, 1940, until November, 1942. Marshal Henri Philippe Pétain headed the Vichy government. In November, 1942, German troops occupied all France. Vichy remained the seat of the German-controlled French government until 1944. Then Allied troops invaded France and freed it.

During the months that France was under German occupation, the name *Vichy* came to stand for *collaboration* with the Germans. The name took on this meaning because French government officials at Vichy made compromises and concessions to meet German demands. For many years before World War II, health-giving waters had made Vichy famous as a health resort.   ROBERT E. DICKINSON

VICKSBURG, Miss. (pop. 29,143; alt. 200 ft.), is a major Mississippi River port. It is on the west border of the state (see MISSISSIPPI [political map]). Products include chemicals, fabricated metals, and machinery.

The Spaniards established an outpost in the area about 1790. In 1825, the settlement was incorporated as Vicksburg. During the Civil War, Vicksburg fell to the Union Army on July 4, 1863, after a 47-day siege (see CIVIL WAR [Vicksburg]). Vicksburg is the seat of Warren County and has a commission form of government.   CHARLOTTE CAPERS

VICKSBURG NATIONAL MILITARY PARK. See NATIONAL PARK (National Military Parks).

VICTOR was the name of three popes of the Roman Catholic Church. They served as follows:

Victor I, Saint   (189-199)
Victor II   (1055-1057)
Victor III   (1086-1087)

Victor I (?-199), SAINT VICTOR, took a vigorous stand against Eastern bishops who celebrated Easter on the 14th day of Nisan in the Jewish calendar instead of Sunday. He enforced the Roman practice of Easter celebration on Asiatic bishops. He was born in Africa.

Victor II (1018?-1057) was the fourth and last of the German popes chosen by the Holy Roman Emperor. He accepted the papacy on condition that Emperor Henry III return to the Holy See its lawful possessions. He also fought clerical marriage and *simony* (the buying or selling of sacred offices).

Victor III (1027?-1087) followed the reform and political policies of Pope Gregory VII, and excommunicated the antipope, Clement III (see GREGORY [VII]). He did his greatest work as abbot of Monte Cassino and negotiator for the papacy with the Normans in southern Italy.   THOMAS P. NEILL and FULTON J. SHEEN

VICTOR EMMANUEL was the name of a king of Sardinia and two kings of Italy.

Victor Emmanuel I (1759-1824) ruled as king of Sardinia from 1814 to 1821. Faced with a revolution in 1821, he abdicated his throne in favor of his brother, Charles Felix, rather than grant his people a constitution and declare war on Austria.

Ewing Galloway
Victor Emmanuel III

Victor Emmanuel II (1820-1878) was king of Sardinia from 1849 to 1861 and the first king of Italy from 1861 to 1878. He took the leadership in uniting Italy. His first step was to get the Austrians out of Italy. He made an alliance with France, and in 1859 the two countries defeated Austria. Victor Emmanuel gained Lombardy. Revolutions began in central Italy shortly after. In 1860, Giuseppe Garibaldi conquered the Kingdom of the Two Sicilies. As a result, central Italy (except for Rome) and the Kingdom of the Two Sicilies joined Sardinia in 1861 to form a united kingdom of Italy. Victor Emmanuel became king. Venetia joined the kingdom in 1866, and Rome joined in 1870.

Victor Emmanuel II was born in Turin, Italy. He received military and religious training.

Victor Emmanuel III (1869-1947) became king of Italy after the assassination of his father, Humbert I, in 1900. The people honored and respected him during the early years of his reign, but later they came to despise him. Victor Emmanuel refused to proclaim martial law to stop Benito Mussolini's march on Rome in 1922. The king made no protest when Italy became a fascist dictatorship. Victor Emmanuel tried to save the monarchy in 1946 by abdicating in favor of his son, Crown Prince Humbert. But the gesture proved futile, because the Italian people voted to abolish the mon-

archy in a 1946 election. Victor Emmanuel III was
born in Naples. R. JOHN RATH

Related Articles in WORLD BOOK include:

Cavour, Count di
Fascism
Garibaldi, Giuseppe
Italy (History)
Mussolini, Benito

Papal States
Sardinia, Kingdom of
Savoy
Sicilies, Kingdom of
the Two

VICTORIA (1819-1901) was one of the greatest rulers
in English history. She was queen of the United Kingdom of Great Britain and
Ireland, and empress of
India. *The Victorian Era*,
named for her, included
most of the 1800's. In this
era, Great Britain reached
the height of its power.
The Victorian Age fea-
tured great industrial expansion at home and im-
perial expansion abroad. A
period of sentiment and
self-indulgence ended as
Victoria came to the
throne. The English peo-
ple became high-minded,
modest, self-righteous, and enterprising.

Historical Pictures Service
Queen Victoria

Victoria ruled for 63 years, from 1837 to 1901, the
longest reign of any British monarch. She became queen
at a time when the people neither liked nor respected
the throne. But by being above reproach she raised the
throne to a position of respect and veneration. In later
years she became the symbol of Great Britain's greatness. Victoria was a wise and capable monarch, but the
greatness of her country was due more to such ministers
as Sir Robert Peel, Lord Palmerston, Benjamin Disraeli, William Gladstone, and Lord Salisbury than it
was to her. Great Britain was a constitutional monarchy, and Victoria could only warn, advise, or encourage the prime minister.

Events of Her Reign. Many great events took place
during Victoria's reign. In 1837 small rebellions broke
out in Canada. Upper and Lower Canada were united
in 1840 and given self-government. Britain fought the
Opium War in China (1839-1842), the Crimean War
(1854), the South African War (1899), and small wars
with the Chinese, Abyssinians, and Afghans.

A mutiny broke out in India in 1857, and the following year India was transferred from the East India
Company to government control. Victoria was proclaimed empress of India in 1877. The British seized
control of Egypt and many other areas. The colonies in
British North America and Australia were federated
and became powerful, self-governing states. Britain became a free-trade country. The franchise was extended,
and local government democratized. In Ireland the
Anglican Church was disestablished and the land system reformed. Parliament passed acts improving labor
conditions, making education compulsory, and reforming the civil service.

Early Years. Victoria was born at Kensington Palace
on May 24, 1819. She was the only child of Edward,
Duke of Kent, fourth son of George III, and of Victoria Maria Louisa, daughter of Francis, Duke of Saxe-
Coburg-Gotha. Victoria's father died before she was

a year old, and she was reared by her mother.

Her uncle William IV died on June 20, 1837, and
she immediately followed him on the throne. She was
crowned at Westminster Abbey on June 28, 1838.
When she came to the throne, the union between Britain and the Electorate of Hanover (in Germany) ended,
because a woman could not occupy the Hanoverian
throne. Victoria had been carefully reared and had had
little contact with the outside world. Lord Melbourne,
her first prime minister, educated her in politics and
government, and in the art of living.

In February, 1840, the queen married her cousin,
Prince Albert of Saxe-Coburg-Gotha. It was a happy
marriage. The Prince Consort had a difficult position,
but he carried out his duties well. He was a student,
philanthropist, and businessman, and the people respected him. Victoria and Albert had four sons and five
daughters. The eldest child, Princess Victoria, married
the Crown Prince of Germany.

In 1861 Prince Albert died. Victoria never recovered
from her grief. She withdrew from social activities and
dressed in mourning for many years. Avoiding London,
she lived for the most part at Osborne on the Isle of
Wight, and at Balmoral in Scotland. After the death of
her husband, the only adviser to whom she showed
affection was Benjamin Disraeli, whom she called
"Dizzy." In 1887 the people of the empire celebrated
the golden jubilee of her reign with great rejoicing. Ten
years later her diamond jubilee was celebrated as a
great "festival of empire." Immense crowds greeted
the queen as the royal procession made its way to Saint
Paul's Cathedral to give thanks.

Victoria died at her winter home on the Isle of
Wight on Jan. 22, 1901. Her eldest son then became
Edward VII. JAMES L. GODFREY

Related Articles in WORLD BOOK include:

Albert, Prince
Connaught,
Duke of
Doll (Famous Collectors)
Edward (VII) of England

English Literature
(The Victorian Age)
Great Britain (The
Reign of Victoria)
Windsor

VICTORIA is the smallest state on the Australian
mainland. Only the island of Tasmania covers a smaller area among the Australian states. Victoria, one of
Australia's chief farming regions, was also the first area
in Australia to develop a large-scale manufacturing
industry. This activity began in the 1860's. Melbourne,
on Port Phillip Bay, is the capital (see MELBOURNE).

Location, Size, and Description. Victoria lies at the
southeastern tip of Australia. It covers 87,884 square
miles. See AUSTRALIA
(political map).

Low hills border the
coast line of Victoria.
The Dandenong Ranges
stand east of Melbourne.
The Great Dividing
Range and several other
mountain ranges cover
much of eastern and
central Victoria. In the
northeast, these moun-
tains are called the Aus-

Victoria Is Shown In Black.

tralian Alps. Gum and eucalyptus trees grow in the mountains of Victoria. Mount Bogong, the highest peak in Victoria, rises 6,508 feet in the eastern part of the state.

Rivers and Bays. The Murray River is Victoria's chief waterway. The Hume Dam on this river irrigates the northern river valley (see HUME DAM). Other rivers include the Goulburn, Loddon, Campaspe, and Mitta Mitta (all tributaries of the Murray), and the Glenelg, Snowy, and Yarra. See MURRAY RIVER.

Port Phillip Bay, one of the largest and deepest bays in the world, covers 875 square miles.

Natural Resources. The discovery of gold in 1851 brought the first large population wave to Victoria. Lignite (brown coal) is now the chief mineral produced. In 1957, the state began developing a lignite deposit in the Gippsland district. This is believed to be the largest single lignite deposit in the world. Other mineral resources include antimony, silver, and tin. Victoria also has fertile soil and gum and eucalyptus forests.

Climate. Victoria has a cooler climate than most of Australia, because it lies farther south than the rest of the mainland. January temperatures average 70°F., and July temperatures average 50°F. From 10 to 20 inches of rain falls in the northwestern section of the state. Most of the southern part has an annual rainfall of 20 to 40 inches. A small area in the east has from 40 to 60 inches of rain a year.

The People and Their Work. Victoria has a population of about 3,195,261. About two-thirds of the people live in the Melbourne metropolitan area. Most of them are of British descent.

Chief crops include barley, hay, oats, potatoes, and wheat. Many kinds of fruit grow in Victoria. Stock raising and dairy farming are also important industries. The state has iron foundries, textile factories, and woolen mills. Products include agricultural implements, chemicals, dyes, foods, leather, paints, paper, rubber products, tobacco, and wines.

Transportation. The state owns about 4,000 miles of railroads. Several airlines serve Victoria, and it has about 101,500 miles of roads.

Education. Children between the ages of 6 and 14 must attend school. Elementary and high school education is free. The University of Melbourne was founded in 1853. Monash University was founded in 1958.

Government. The British Crown appoints a governor for Victoria, on the advice of the Victorian parliament. But a premier actually heads the government, assisted by a cabinet of ministers. The legislature consists of a 34-member upper house that serves six years, and a 66-member lower house that serves three years. Victoria sends 10 senators and 33 representatives to the federal parliament at Canberra.

History. George Bass, a British navigator, sighted the eastern coast of Victoria in 1797. But colonists did not settle permanently until 1835. The territory formed part of New South Wales until 1851, when it became a separate colony. It was named for Queen Victoria.

In 1851, discoveries of gold in Ballarat and Bendigo brought thousands of settlers to Victoria. After the gold rush, many miners became farmers. The settlers won self-government in 1855. Victoria joined the Commonwealth of Australia in 1901. C. M. H. CLARK

British Columbia Govt. Travel Bureau

The Legislative Buildings of Victoria, B.C., form an imposing group overlooking the head of Victoria harbor.

VICTORIA, British Columbia (pop. 54,941; met. area 154,152; alt. 56 ft.), is the capital and second largest city of British Columbia. The city stands on a rolling, rocky peninsula at the southern tip of Vancouver Island. The Gulf of Georgia separates it from the mainland. Victoria is 80 miles northwest of Seattle, Wash., and 80 miles southwest of the city of Vancouver. For location, see BRITISH COLUMBIA (political map).

Victoria is one of the most interesting cities in Canada, and is often called the Dominion's most "English" city. It has neat flower gardens and narrow, winding streets. Its buildings include the stone legislature buildings, the Empress Hotel, the Victoria University buildings, and the Canadian United Services College. The Dominion Government Astrophysical Observatory and the Dominion Meteorological Observatory are in the city (see DOMINION OBSERVATORY).

Victoria has mild winters and cool summers, and flowers bloom during most of the year. Average temperatures are 39°F. in January and 60°F. in July and August. The city serves as a winter sanctuary for birds migrating from colder regions of the continent. Victoria's annual rainfall of 27 inches is less than that of any other city on the North Pacific Coast, because it is on the sheltered east side of the island's mountains. Nearby Esquimalt has one of the world's largest dry docks.

Industry and Trade. Victoria, an important fishing and lumbering center, serves as a port for ships from the Orient and Australia. It has shipyards, and roofing and furniture plants. It is a favorite tourist attraction.

History. The Hudson's Bay Company established Victoria in 1843 as its Pacific Coast fur-trading headquarters. James Douglas, who later became governor of the colony, named it in honor of Queen Victoria. Victoria became the capital of the colony of Vancouver Island in 1858, and of the colony of British Columbia in

1868. It was made the capital of the province when British Columbia became a part of Canada in 1871. The city grew rapidly during the Fraser River gold rush of 1858, and again when the first railroad reached the Pacific Coast in 1885. It served as a key Canadian naval base during World War II. Many retired people move to Victoria to enjoy its mild climate. The city has a mayor-council government.   RODERICK HAIG-BROWN

See also BRITISH COLUMBIA (color pictures).

VICTORIA, Hong Kong (pop. 674,962; met. area 2,800,000; alt. 50 ft.), serves as the capital of that British crown colony. Large offices and government buildings stand along the waterfront in the central part of the city. The crowded Chinese section surrounds the downtown area of the bustling city. See also HONG KONG.

VICTORIA, LAKE. See LAKE VICTORIA.

VICTORIA, UNIVERSITY OF, is a coeducational institution at Victoria, B.C. It is supported by the province. Formerly affiliated with the University of British Columbia, it became a separate university in 1963. The university offers courses in arts, science, and education. For enrollment, see CANADA (table, Universities and Colleges).   JOSEPH B. CLEARIHUE

VICTORIA CROSS. See DECORATIONS AND MEDALS (Decorations and Medals of Other Countries).

VICTORIA DAY commemorates the birthday of Queen Victoria on May 24, 1819. The people of the British Commonwealth have always celebrated the birthday of the ruling monarch as a patriotic holiday. During the long lifetime of Queen Victoria, her birthday came to have a special meaning. After her death, people continued to celebrate her birthday as a day on which to express their loyalty to the British Empire.

In the early 1900's, the people of Canada celebrated Queen Victoria's birthday as Empire Day. The name was changed to Commonwealth Day in 1947. Canadians now celebrate Victoria Day and the official birthday of the reigning monarch as a legal holiday on the Monday before May 25.   RAYMOND HOYT JAHN

VICTORIA DESERT. See GREAT VICTORIA DESERT.

VICTORIA FALLS is a waterfall that David Livingstone discovered in South Africa in 1855. The explorer named it in honor of Queen Victoria of England. Victoria Falls lies between Rhodesia and Zambia, about halfway between the mouth and source of the Zambezi River. The Zambezi is about a mile wide at this point and drops suddenly into a deep, narrow chasm. A canyon about 40 miles long permits the water to flow out. The height of the falls varies from 256 feet at the right bank to 355 feet in the center.

The mist and spray created by Victoria Falls can be seen for several miles. This cloud and the constant roar caused the people of the area to name the falls *Mosiloatunya*, which means the *smoke that thunders*. A public park is near the falls. Since 1938, a hydroelectric plant has produced a small amount of power at the falls. A railway bridge crosses the river just below the point where the waters rush out of the chasm.   HARRY R. RUDIN

See also AFRICA (color picture); RHODESIA; SEVEN WONDERS OF THE WORLD; WATERFALL.

VICTORIA LAND is part of the Antarctic subcontinent. It lies on the shore of the Ross Sea almost due south of New Zealand. Sir James Ross claimed the region for Great Britain during his 1839-1843 expedition. Victoria Land is also called South Victoria Land.

VICTORIAN AGE. See ENGLISH LITERATURE (The Victorian Age); GREAT BRITAIN (History).

VICTORY, WINGED. See WINGED VICTORY.

VICTORY, WINGLESS. See ACROPOLIS.

VICTORY LOAN. See LIBERTY LOAN.

VICUÑA, *vih KOON yuh,* is the smallest member of the camel family. It lives in the Andes Mountains of Ecuador, Peru, and Bolivia, in areas from 12,000 to 18,000 feet above sea level. Its home is generally above the snow line and hard to reach. The vicuña and guanaco are the two wild members of the camel family in South America. The other two, the alpaca and llama, are domesticated. None of the four has a hump.

The vicuña is about 3 feet high at the shoulder and weighs 75 to 100 pounds. It has a long, slender neck. Vicuñas eat grass. They usually live in herds which contain one male and 6 to 10 females. They have remarkable sight, speed, and endurance.

Vicuñas have finer fleece than any other wool-bearing animal. The hairs are less than two thousandths of an inch thick—less than half as thick as the finest

New York Zoological Society
The Vicuña Is a Humpless Member of the Camel Family.

sheep's wool. The color of the upper body is reddish yellow to deep tan or reddish brown. The belly and lower legs are white. The fleece grows until it hangs below the flanks and knees. Only the inner fleece is used. It is especially good for high-grade worsted. The Peruvian government controls the slaughter of the animals and the sale of the fleece in that country.

The ancient Inca Indians protected vicuñas and hunted them only once in four years. Only royalty could use the fleece.

Scientific Classification. The vicuña belongs to the camel family, *Camelidae.* It is classified as genus *Lama,* species *L. vicugna.*   DONALD F. HOFFMEISTER

See also GUANACO; ANIMAL (color picture, Animals of the Mountains).

VIDEO. See TELEVISION.

The Danube Canal winds through the heart of Vienna. Beautiful public buildings, art centers, parks, and churches make the city of Vienna one of the most popular tourist centers in the world.

Authenticated News

VIENNA, *vih EN uh,* or WIEN (pop. 1,627,566; met. area, 1,990,000; alt. 550 ft.), is the capital of Austria. It is sometimes called the *Queen of the Danube.* Vienna lies on the Danube River, at a point where trade routes cross. It is a great port, trading center, and manufacturing city. Vienna became the capital of the Austrian Empire under the Hapsburgs, a European royal family which ruled in central Europe from 1273 to 1918. During the 1700's and 1800's, Vienna gained fame as a world center for literature, music, science, and learning. It became known as the *Paris of the South.* The city had a great university, a splendid library, and many beautiful buildings. The Viennese people were known for their gaiety and charm, their wit and ability to enjoy life. Vienna was the home of the waltz, the operetta, and the coffeehouse where men gathered to discuss the arts and politics. The hardships of World Wars I and II caused Vienna to lose much of its gaiety. Since 1945, the Viennese, helped by donations from throughout the country, have done much to restore their city to its prewar importance.

Location, Size, and Description. Vienna is built on the south bank of the Danube River, about 330 miles southeast of Berlin. The city stands at the head of a narrow, fertile plain between the Carpathian Mountains and the Alps. Vienna lies just west of a mountain gap which leads into the broad Hungarian plain. Its location is important because many roads from western to eastern Europe and from northern Europe to the

Balkan Peninsula lead through the city. See AUSTRIA (color map).

Vienna covered an area of 106½ square miles until the Nazi occupation, when its boundaries were extended to include a total of 469 square miles. Before World War II, nearly two million persons, or over one-third of the people of Austria, lived in Vienna. During the war, the population decreased by about 500,000, but it grew again after the war. Also after the war, the city changed its boundaries to make it nearer to its prewar size. Vienna now covers about 160 square miles.

A branch of the Danube River called the Danube Canal runs through Vienna from northwest to southeast. Many beautiful bridges have been built across the canal. A small stream, called the Wien, flows into it.

The center of Vienna is called the Inner City. Vienna has several wide boulevards, which were built where ancient city walls once stood. The inner boulevard, or *Ringstrasse,* is the city's most famous street. A circle of splendid parks edges this boulevard. The Ringstrasse surrounds the Inner City, where most of the government buildings and other famous buildings are located. The Inner City still has many narrow, irregular streets, but some old sections have been replaced by modern avenues and apartment houses. In 1893 a boulevard called the *Gürtelstrasse* was built outside the circle made by the Ringstrasse.

Famous Buildings. Saint Stephen's Cathedral is probably the most famous building in Vienna. The church stands near the central part of the Inner City. Its graceful Gothic spire rises 450 feet above the city. Saint Stephen's was badly damaged during World War II, but was repaired after the war.

The buildings of the imperial palace, called the Hofburg, lie southwest of Saint Stephen's Cathedral. From the 1200's until 1918 the Hofburg was the residence of the Hapsburg rulers of Austria. The Imperial Library is one of the Hofburg's finest buildings.

Just opposite the palace are two beautifully domed buildings in Italian Renaissance style. These are the museums of art and of natural history. The modern Greek-style parliament building stands northeast of the museums. The *Rathaus*, or Town Hall, is a Gothic building in the center of a small park. The clock tower on the Rathaus is 320 feet high. The building has in it the city library, the Historical Museum, and a famous historical collection of weapons.

North of the Rathaus Park is the University of Vienna, built in Renaissance style. The Court, or Hofburg, Theater, another Renaissance building, faces the Rathaus on the inner side of the Ringstrasse. Other fine buildings on this boulevard include the Academy of Art, the Stock Exchange, and the Austrian Museum of Art and Industries. The Opera House, also located here, was partially destroyed during World War II. Renovation of the building was completed in 1955.

Vienna has many gardens, parks, squares, and beautiful monuments. The city is famous for its workers' apartment buildings, which were put up after World War I for families with low incomes. These were modern housing developments with libraries, swimming pools, and playgrounds. Outside the city, other housing developments were built in the form of garden suburbs.

The People. The people of Vienna speak the German language and are descended from the same stock as the Germans of southern Bavaria. But the Viennese culture has always been different from that of Germany. Even the language has had a softer sound than German ordinarily has. The Viennese were Austrians, but they were also citizens of the world. Their character is expressed in the famous Viennese word *Gemütlichkeit*. This word expresses the Viennese enjoyment of the good things of life, including friendship, music, and dancing.

Most of the people of Vienna are Roman Catholics. The city once had about 200,000 Jews, but they were almost all killed or driven away in World War II.

Education and Culture. Vienna has been the home of many famous composers, writers, and scientists. Great composers, such as Joseph Haydn, Wolfgang Amadeus Mozart, Ludwig van Beethoven, Franz Peter Schubert, Johannes Brahms, and Johann Strauss, all made their homes in Vienna. Arnold Schönberg, the modern composer, was also a Viennese. Sigmund Freud, who developed psychoanalysis, lived in Vienna until the time of the Nazi occupation.

The University of Vienna has for many years been a famous center of learning. It has been especially well known for its medical college. The city also had many special schools, including the Conservatory of Music, the Polytechnic Institute, and an academy of Oriental languages. Vienna has long been famous for its many fine museums and art galleries.

Industry and Trade. At various times, the chief products manufactured in Vienna have included machinery, clothing, textiles, chemicals, optical instruments, metalware, furniture, paper, musical instruments, and malt liquors. The city has also produced many skillfully made and beautiful objects of art including jewelry, paintings, and statues. Viennese shops have been famous for their women's clothes and accessories.

Railroad and water routes lead from Vienna to all parts of Europe. The city has a fine harbor, which was made by building a lock at the entrance of the Danube Canal. But Viennese industry and trade suffered severely after World War I. Vienna, once the trading center of a huge empire, became only the big capital of a small country, and has never regained its importance.

History. Vienna was once a Celtic settlement on the shore of the Danube River. Early in Christian times the Romans seized the settlement and built there a fortified town which they called Vindobona. Vindobona became one of the chief shipping points on the Danube. In the 400's, the last Roman legion withdrew. Vindobona came under the control of the Franks in the late 700's. The present Austrian name *Wien*, or Vienna, first appeared by about 1000.

The Hapsburg family made Vienna their capital when they gained the imperial throne of Germany in the 1200's. The city grew rapidly in wealth and importance. In 1529 and again in 1683, the Turks attacked Vienna, but they failed to capture the city. Napoleon marched triumphantly into the city in 1805. But in 1814, his victorious enemies met in the Congress of Vienna, and took away all his conquests. In 1848,

De Cou, Ewing Galloway

Belvedere Palace, completed in 1723, is one of the many imposing buildings to be seen in and near historic Vienna.

the people of Vienna fought in the streets, but government troops suppressed the rebellion.

The Hapsburgs continued to rule in their capital until after World War I. In 1914, Vienna became the first war capital of Europe, when Austria declared war on Serbia, and World War I began. The city was made the capital of the Austrian Republic at the end of the war.

Vienna had one of the most modern and efficient city governments in the world during the 1920's. Socialists (Social Democrats) remained in office in Vienna even after Engelbert Dollfuss became dictator of Austria in 1933. But in 1934 the national government declared the Socialist party illegal, and arrested the city's officials. Workers fought in the streets for four days.

In 1938 German forces seized Austria. Vienna became the capital of a German province. It ceased to be a center of European culture and learning. During World War II, Vienna was badly damaged. Soviet forces took the city in 1945. Allied troops occupied Vienna until 1955, when Austria regained its independence. During this period, much of the city was rebuilt, including the famed Vienna Opera House.   R. JOHN RATH

VIENNA, CONGRESS OF, was a meeting of European political leaders in 1814 and 1815. The men met after the defeat of Napoleon to restore royal rulers to power and to change the boundaries of European countries. They hoped to return the European political system to the system that existed before 1789. The French Revolution of 1789 had ended royal rule in France. Napoleon had conquered many European countries and had overthrown their rulers in the early 1800's. See FRENCH REVOLUTION; NAPOLEON I.

Prince von Metternich of Austria, William von Humboldt of Prussia, Lord Castlereagh of Great Britain, and Czar Alexander I of Russia plotted to control the Congress. But they could not agree on how to divide Poland and Saxony, a Germanic province. French diplomat Talleyrand took advantage of their disagreements to give defeated France a voice at the Congress.

The Congress of Vienna changed the borders of countries without considering the wishes of people living in the countries. For example, Belgium and The Netherlands were united in spite of their different languages and customs. Austria took some Italian provinces. Sweden got Norway from Denmark. Austria, Prussia, and Russia took parts of Poland. A Germanic Confederation replaced the Holy Roman Empire. Russia got Finland from Sweden and Bessarabia, in southeastern Europe, from Turkey. The Congress of Vienna also restored to power royal rulers in France, The Netherlands, and several German and Italian states.   ROBERT G. L. WAITE

See also AIX-LA-CHAPELLE, CONGRESS OF.

VIENTIANE, *VYAN TYAHN* (pop. 162,300; alt. 557 ft.), is the administrative capital and largest city of Laos. The city stands beside the Mekong River near the border between Thailand and Laos. Vientiane is an important trading center. It has an airport, and is linked by ferryboat with a railroad that runs south to Bangkok, Thailand. River transportation connects the city with other towns along the Mekong.

Vientiane was part of the Kingdom of Lan Xang in the 1300's. During the 1700's, it became an independent kingdom. Siam (now Thailand) annexed the Kingdom of Vientiane in the early 1800's. The French made it part of Laos in 1893, and governed it as part of French Indochina until 1947.   FRANK M. LeBAR

See also LAOS (map); LUANG PRABANG.

VIEQUES ISLAND. See PUERTO RICO (The Land).

VIERECK, PETER (1916-   ), an American poet and political writer, won the 1949 Pulitzer prize in poetry for *Terror and Decorum* (1948). His political books include *Shame and Glory of the Intellectuals* (1953). He was born in New York City.

by Rand McNally for WORLD BOOK

VIETNAM, *veeEHTnahm,* is a hot, humid, tropical land that borders the South China Sea in Southeast Asia. Long and narrow, it is somewhat smaller than California. But Vietnam has about twice as many people as California, the most heavily populated state in the United States.

Much of the land in Vietnam is fertile, especially the land near the Red River in the north and the Mekong River in the south. Most of the people live in small villages near the rivers. They raise rice on small farms. Vietnam has few big cities and little industry.

Since 1954, Vietnam has been divided into two countries, North Vietnam and South Vietnam. During the 1960's, the divided land became the site of a fierce war involving not only North Vietnam and South Vietnam, but also the United States and several other countries.

This article contains general information on Vietnam. For detailed information on the war, see the separate article, VIETNAM WAR.

Government

The official name of South Vietnam is REPUBLIC OF VIETNAM. The capital is Saigon. The DEMOCRATIC REPUBLIC OF VIETNAM is the official name of Communist North Vietnam. Its capital is Hanoi.

South Vietnam became a republic in 1955. The constitution provides for a president and a one-house legislature, both elected by the people. But in 1963, a military *junta* (council) seized control of the government and suspended the constitution. Since then, several governments, most of them military juntas, have ruled the nation. In September, 1966, the people elected a new assembly. The assembly is charged with writing a new constitution.

The national government has difficulties governing the villages far from Saigon. The Vietnamese have traditionally dealt with local, rather than national, government officials. Also, the *Viet Cong* (Communist guerrillas) have controlled many South Vietnamese villages during the war. They tried to convince the village people that the national government could not help them. In order to destroy the remaining ties between the villages and the national government, the Communists mined roads, destroyed railroads, and killed local officials.

North Vietnam. A Communist dictatorship has ruled North Vietnam since 1954. The Lao Dong (Communist) party controls the government. Communist party members control the national government and the local governments.

Wesley R. Fishel, the contributor of this article, is Professor of Political Science at Michigan State University, and the author of Problems of Freedom: South Vietnam Since Independence. *The photographs throughout this article were taken by Henry Gill.*

The Vietnamese People are of Mongolian and Indonesian descent. The small girl, *left*, and the village elder, *above*, live on the Mekong delta. Their village has often been attacked by Viet Cong.

Forms of Government: *South Vietnam*, Republic; 44 provinces, 6 cities with the status of provinces. *Head of State:* President. *North Vietnam*, Communist dictatorship; 27 provinces. *Head of State:* President.

Capitals: *South Vietnam*, Saigon; *North Vietnam*, Hanoi.

Official Language. Vietnamese.

Area: 127,242 square miles: *South Vietnam*, 65,948 square miles; *North Vietnam*, 61,294 square miles. *Greatest distances:* (north-south), 1,000 miles; (east-west), 300 miles. *Coastline*, about 1,250 miles.

Population: *1967 estimate*—35,600,000 (*South Vietnam*, 16,376,000; *North Vietnam*, 19,224,000). *Density*, 280 persons to the square mile (*South Vietnam*, 248; North Vietnam, 314). *Distribution*, 90 per cent rural, 10 per cent urban. *1972 estimate*—39,600,000 (*South Vietnam*, 18,216,000; *North Vietnam*, 21,384,000).

Chief Products: *Agriculture*, rice and rubber. *Manufacturing and Processing*, sugar refining and rice milling. *Mining*, coal.

Flag: *South Vietnam*. Three red stripes lie on a field of yellow. Red stands for success, yellow for independence. The stripes represent South Vietnam's three original states. *North Vietnam*. A gold star (for Communism) appears on a field of red (for revolution). See FLAG (color pictures, Flags of Asia).

National Anthem: *South Vietnam*, "Tieng Goi Thanh Nien" ("Call to Youth"); North Vietnam, "Tien Quan Ca" ("Forward Soldiers").

Money: *Basic unit, South Vietnam*, Piaster; *North Vietnam*, Dong. For the piaster's value, see MONEY (table).

People

Vietnam has a total population of over 35 million. More than 19 million persons live in North Vietnam, and more than 16 million persons live in South Vietnam. Almost 90 per cent of the people are Vietnamese, a mixture of Mongolian and Indonesian peoples.

Most Vietnamese are rice farmers who live in small lowland villages near river deltas. They work their rice paddies with simple wood plows pulled by water buffaloes. The rice they grow is their main food. The farmers and their families usually live in houses made of wood. The houses have dirt floors, and no electric lights or running water. Wood planks serve as beds. Vietnamese farmers cling to this way of life. Most of them would rather live in the overcrowded deltas than move to the forest and mountain regions of the west, where there is more unused land available. The farmers consider the forests and mountains suitable only for savages and wild animals.

About a million Montagnards and about 850,000 Chinese live in Vietnam. Montagnards are mountain people who live by hunting, fishing, and farming. They use tools and methods much like those of their forefathers. Most of the Chinese live in cities in the south. They are businessmen, merchants, and shopkeepers. Other peoples of Vietnam include Chams, Indians, Khmers, Malays, and Pakistanis.

Cities. Only about 10 per cent of the people of Vietnam live in cities and towns. Saigon, the largest city

VIETNAM

in all of Vietnam, is a major port, and a transportation and industrial center in South Vietnam. Other large cities in South Vietnam include Da Lat, Da Nang, and Hue. Hanoi, the largest city in North Vietnam, is also a transportation and industrial center. Haiphong is the chief port and the only other large city in the north.

Religion does not play a major role in Vietnamese life. About 35 per cent of the people are Buddhists, about 10 per cent are Roman Catholics, and about 15 per cent practice local religions called Cao Dai and Hoa Hao. The largest group of people practice a religious faith that combines Taoism and Confucianism with Buddhism and ancestor worship.

Education has always been prized in Vietnam. Almost two-thirds of the people in both North Vietnam and South Vietnam can read and write. But since 1954, both nations have tried to teach more people to read and write. They have also tried to train more skilled industrial workers and to increase the number of persons attending universities.

Land

Vietnam is about 1,000 miles long, extending from China south to the Gulf of Siam. It occupies the eastern coast of the Indochinese Peninsula.

Vietnam is often described as a farmer's carrying pole with a rice basket hanging from each end. In the north, the fertile delta of the Red River is one of the "baskets." The Mekong River delta in the south is the other. At its widest point, in the deltas, Vietnam extends as much as 300 miles from the borders of Cambodia and Laos to the South China Sea. At its narrowest point, in the central region, Vietnam is only about 40 miles wide.

Vietnam is a tropical land. Winds from India and Southeast Asia give it a monsoon climate (see MONSOON). Vietnam can be divided into three natural regions.

Northern Vietnam is bordered by China on the north and Laos on the west. High mountains rise along the borders, and the highest peak in Vietnam, Fan Si Pan, towers 10,308 feet near the town of Lao Cai. The land slopes down from the mountains to the lowlands of the Red River delta.

Northern Vietnam has two seasons. From November to April, the weather is damp and cool. The average January temperature in Hanoi, in the northern region, is 63° F. From May to October, the area has typhoons, high temperatures, and heavy rains. Its average temperature in June is 82° F. Hanoi receives about 68 inches of rainfall a year.

Central Vietnam is a narrow coastal plain crowded with people. The land rises to a plateau in the west, then to forested mountains. Central Vietnam receives less rain and is cooler than both the northern and southern regions.

Southern Vietnam is a low, flat, marshy region around the Mekong River delta and the city of Saigon. The fertile soils of the delta make this region the most productive agricultural area in Vietnam. Large rubber, tea, and coffee plantations lie north and northeast of Saigon.

Southern Vietnam also has a dry season and a wet season. Humidity is high throughout the year, but almost all of the rain falls in the summer. The Saigon area receives about 80 inches of rain between April and October. From November through May, the weather is dry and cool. The temperature in Saigon ranges from 64° F. to 92° F.

Natural Resources. Nearly half of Vietnam is covered with forests. The most important forest products are bamboo, cinnamon, and quinine. Coal, iron ore, manganese, phosphate, tin, and zinc deposits are found in North Vietnam. Coal, lead, limestone, molybdenum, peat, and zinc are the major mineral deposits in South Vietnam.

Economy

The economies of both North and South Vietnam depend on farming. Each nation ranks among the world's leading rice producers. The war has hurt rice

---

VIETNAM MAP INDEX

Cities and Towns

An Loc ....10,240..G 4	Chau Phu ....G 3	Ham Tan ....G 4	Nam Dinh .86,132..B 4	Song Cau ....F 5
An Nhon ....F 5	Cheo Reo ....F 5	Hanoi ...414,620	Nha Trang 52,660..F 5	Tam Ky ....E 5
Bac Can ....A 3	Con Son ...2,200..H 4	*643,576..B 3	Ninh Binh ....B 3	Tan An ...14,870..G 4
Bac Giang .15,738..B 4	Da Lat ...56,000..G 5	Ha Tien ....G 3	Phan Rang 22,550..G 5	Tay Ninh ..18,260..G 4
Bac Ninh ..22,520..B 4	Da Nang .126,000..D 5	Ha Tinh ....C 3	Phan Thiet 77,770..G 5	Thai Binh ....B 4
Bac Quang ....A 3	Dien Bien Phu .....B 2	Hoa Binh ....B 3	Phu Cuong .46,800..G 4	Thai
Ba Don ....D 4	Di Linh ....7,110..G 5	Hoai Nhon ....E 5	Phuoc Binh 1,970..G 4	Nguyen ..21,846..B 3
Ban Me	Dinh Lap ....B 4	Hoi An ....17,420..E 5	Phuoc Le ..13,750..G 4	Thanh Hoa 31,211..C 3
Thuot ...30,050..F 5	Dong Hoi ....D 4	Hon Gai ..35,412..B 4	Phuoc Vinh .3,000..G 4	Tien Yen ....B 4
Bao Ha ....A 3	Duong Dong ....G 2	Hue .....105,500..D 4	Phu Tho ..10,888..B 3	To Bong ....F 5
Ben Cat ....G 4	Gia Dinh .27,400..G 4	Khanh An ....H 3	Phu Vinh .31,450..H 4	Truc Giang 15,530..G 4
Bien Hoa ..27,310..G 4	Gia Nghia ..1,420..G 4	Khanh	Pleiku ....16,920..F 4	Tuyen Quang ....B 3
Cam Pha ....B 4	Ha Dong ..25,001..B 3	Hung ....34,610..H 3	Quang Ngai .9,640..E 5	Tuy Hoa ..21,220..F 5
Cam Ranh ....G 5	Ha Giang ....A 3	Kontum ...23,610..E 5	Quang Tri .10,890..D 4	Viet Tri ..21,501..B 3
Can Tho ...71,100..G 3	Hai Duong .24,752..B 4	Lang Son .15,071..B 4	Quang Yen ....B 4	Vinh ......43,945..C 3
Cao Bang ....A 4	Haiphong .182,496	Lao Cai ....A 3	Quan Long 32,520..H 3	Vinh Loi ....H 3
Cao Lanh ..5,260..G 3	*369,248..B 4	Loc Ninh ....G 4	Qui Nhon ..36,880..F 5	Vinh Long .30,210..G 3
		Long Xuyen 24,830..G 3	Rach Gia ..44,690..G 3	Vinh Yen ....B 3
		Moc Hoa ...6,030..G 3	Saigon ..1,400,000..G 4	Vung Tau ....G 4
		My Tho ...58,100..G 4	Son La ....B 2	Xuan Loc ..8,620..G 4
		Na Cham ....A 4	Son Tay ...19,213..B 3	Yen Bai ....B 3

Physical Features

Ben Goi (Bay) ....F 5	Dao Bach Long	Hon Chuoi (Isl.) ..H 3	Mouths of the	Red R. ....B 3
Black R. ....B 2	Vi (Isl.) ....B 4	Hon Gio (Isl.) .....D 4	Mekong R. ....E 5	Siam, Gulf of .....G 1
Ca R. ....C 3	Dao Phu Quoc (Isl.) G 3	Hon Khoai (Isl.) ..H 3	Mui Bai Bung (Pt.) H 3	South China Sea ..D 5
Cam Ranh Bay ....G 5	Deo Hai Van (Pass) D 4	Hon Me (Isl.) .....C 4	Mui Ron (Cape) ...C 4	Tonkin, Gulf of ...C 4
Cap Lay (Cape) ...D 4	Deux Frères (Is.) ..H 4	Hon Panjang (Isl.) H 2	Mui Vung Tau	Varella, Cap
Cap Varella (Cape) F 5	Fan Si Pan (Mtn.) A 2	Îles de Poulo	(Cape) ....G 4	(Cape) ....F 5
Con Son (Is.) .....H 4	Grande Catwick	Dama (Is.) ......H 3	Nui Vong Phu	Vung Ha Long
Cu Lao Cham (Isl.) E 5	(Isl.) ....G 5	Kao Tao (Isl.) .....B 4	(Mtn.) ....H 4	(Bay) ....B 4
Cu Lao Hon (Isl.) .G 5	Gulf of Siam ......G 1	Lay, Cap (Cape) ...D 4	Plain of Reeds ....G 3	Xuy Nong Chao
Cu Lao Re (Isl.) ..E 5	Gulf of Tonkin ....C 4	Lo R. ....B 3	Poulo Sapate (Isl.) H 5	(Is.) ....B 4

*Population of metropolitan area, including suburbs.
Source: Latest official figures.

292

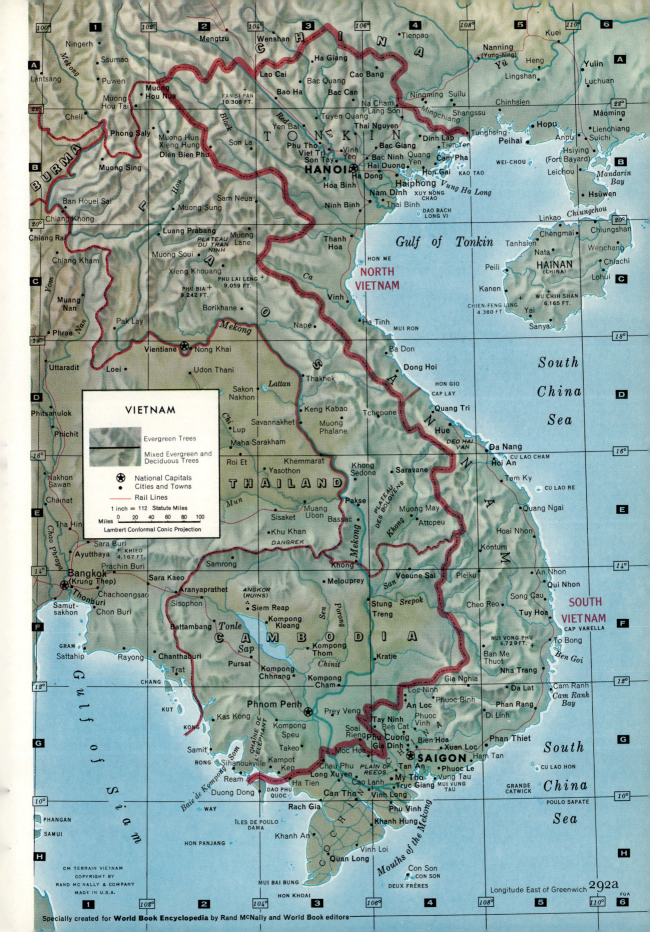

VIETNAM

Evergreen Trees

Mixed Evergreen and
Deciduous Trees

★ National Capitals
• Cities and Towns
—— Rail Lines

1 inch = 112 Statute Miles

Miles 0 20 40 60 80 100

Lambert Conformal Conic Projection

Gulf of Tonkin

NORTH VIETNAM

South China Sea

SOUTH VIETNAM

THAILAND

CAMBODIA

BURMA

HAINAN (CHINA)

Gulf of Siam

Mouths of the Mekong

CM TERRAIN VIETNAM
COPYRIGHT BY
RAND MC NALLY & COMPANY
MADE IN U.S.A.

292a

Longitude East of Greenwich

FGA

Specially created for **World Book Encyclopedia** by Rand McNally and World Book editors

Downtown Saigon Streets are crowded with automobiles, bicycles, motorscooters, and pedi-cabs. The street vendor, *above left*, carries dishes and eating utensils to serve the food that she sells to passersby.

East Central Vietnam gradually rises from sand dunes along the coast, *foreground*, to mountain peaks. Farmers cultivate the fertile land near the river, *center*. Thick tropical forests cover the mountain sides, *background*.

production and other parts of the economy. Goods have become scarce, and prices have risen.

In South Vietnam, rice is grown on 85 per cent of the farmland. Rice is the main food and cash crop, but rubber is the chief export. Other major crops include coconut, coffee, corn, *kenaf* (a fiber), manioc, peanuts, sugar cane, tea, and tobacco.

South Vietnam has relatively little industry. Most factories are near Saigon. Manufactured products include batteries, bicycle tires, cigarettes, glass, kitchen utensils, matches, paper, plastics, soap, soft drinks, and textiles. The nation also has rice mills and sugar refineries.

Many railroads and highways in South Vietnam have been destroyed during the war. As a result, the nation depends heavily on air and water transportation. Saigon and Da Nang have been the chief ports in South Vietnam, but U.S. Army Engineers began building a new port and industrial area at Cam Ranh Bay in 1965.

In North Vietnam, rice is also the major crop. Other important crops include corn, sweet potatoes, and sugar cane. But North Vietnam has serious farm problems, and sometimes rice, vegetables, and meat must be imported.

Industry has developed more rapidly in North Vietnam than in South Vietnam. Before Vietnam was divided into two nations in 1954, most of the industries were located in the north. They included coal mines, a cement plant, textile mills, tanneries, and soap and tile factories.

Since 1954, Russia, Communist China, and other Communist nations have given North Vietnam money and have helped the nation build an engineering works, and cigarette, fertilizer, glass, match, plastics, and rubber factories.

History

Groups of Vietnamese settled in the Red River delta about 400 B.C. Chinese invaders conquered them in 111 B.C., and ruled them for almost a thousand years. The Vietnamese revolted in A.D. 939 and created their own empire. They moved south, and had conquered most of central Vietnam by the late 1400's. They controlled most of southern Vietnam by the late 1700's.

French Rule. Roman Catholic missionaries from France came to Vietnam in the 1600's. The Vietnamese rulers tried to keep the French from founding missions. Persecution of the missionaries led French emperor Napoleon III to send a fleet to Vietnam. French forces seized Saigon and *Cochin China* (southern Vietnam) in the early 1860's, and made them a colony in 1864. During the next 20 years, the French gained control of *Annam* (central Vietnam) and *Tonkin* (northern Vietnam). The three divisions of Vietnam, along with Laos and Cambodia were combined to form French Indochina.

France ruled the area until 1940, when Japanese invaders seized Indochina during World War II. Vietnam declared its independence in 1945 at the end of the war. France recognized the new government, but withdrew its recognition in 1946 when the Indochina War broke

WORLD BOOK photos by Henry Gill

Vietnamese Farmers Still Use Ancient Tools. A farmer stands on his crude wooden rake to weight it down as the team of water buffalo pull it through a rice paddy.

out between the French and the *Vietminh* (a Communist-supported group). Most Vietnamese were more opposed to the French than to the Vietminh, and they refused to help the French. The fighting ended in 1954 with the defeat of French forces at Dien Bien Phu, in northern Vietnam.

South Vietnamese Independence. An international agreement, signed at Geneva, Switzerland, on July 21, 1954, divided Vietnam into two parts. The Communists took over the northern half of the country, and a non-Communist government took control in the south. The people of South Vietnam chose Ngo Dinh Diem as chief of state in 1955. Diem declared Vietnam a republic and made himself its president.

In 1957, the Viet Cong began raids in South Vietnam. The *Viet Cong* are Communist-supported guerrilla forces from both North Vietnam and South Vietnam. As a result of the Indochina War, most of the southern provinces had no local government. So, the government in Saigon could not control or protect many of the villages. The Viet Cong mined roads, destroyed railroads, and killed local officials, teachers, and other leaders. For a discussion of military events in Vietnam since 1957, see VIETNAM WAR.

The 1960's. In March, 1962, South Vietnam began to move thousands of persons into *fortified* (guarded) villages to protect them from the Viet Cong guerrillas. But the program failed. The Viet Cong easily defeated the village men, who had no military training. They killed the village men and carried off food and weap-

ons. The South Vietnamese began to criticize the government. Ngo Dinh Nhu, Diem's brother, organized secret police to enforce Diem's rule. An attempt to kill Nhu and his wife, Madam Nhu, failed early in 1962. To tighten his control, Diem declared *martial law* (military government), a curfew, and *censorship* (news control).

In 1963, criticism of the government's policies increased. Rioting broke out in Saigon and Hue. Several Buddhist monks and nuns burned themselves to death in protest against Diem. The United States urged Diem to change his policies, but he refused. On Nov. 1, 1963, a military junta led by Duong Van Minh seized control of the government. The rebels killed Diem and his brother.

A Revolutionary Military Council set up a government with Minh as chief of state. Several groups in succession held power for brief periods until June, 1965. Another military group took control then, and named Nguyen Cao Ky premier. Ky's government put down a Buddhist-led uprising in 1966. In September, 1966, South Vietnamese voters elected a new assembly, which was to write a new constitution. WESLEY R. FISHEL

Related Articles in WORLD BOOK include:

Cholon	Mekong River
Colombo Plan	Mongol Empire
Haiphong	Ngo Dinh Diem
Hanoi	Rubber
Ho Chi Minh	Saigon
Indochina	Vietnam War

292c

VIETNAM WAR is the struggle to keep South Vietnam free from Communist control. Since 1957, forces supported by Communist North Vietnam have attempted to take over South Vietnam. These forces included guerrillas and terrorists of the South Vietnam National Liberation Front, commonly called the *Viet Cong* or *VC;* and units of the North Vietnam People's Army (PAVN). Fighting the Communist forces were the South Vietnamese army (ARVN); units of the United States Army, Navy, Marines, Air Force, and Coast Guard; and smaller units from South Korea, Australia, and a few other nations.

The fighting in South Vietnam started on a small scale when the guerrillas began to attack government officials in South Vietnam. It soon grew into a savage, full-scale war that threatened world peace. The war became a test of strength between the Communist nations, which supplied the Viet Cong, and the U.S. and other non-Communist nations which aided South Vietnam.

The United States believed that a non-Communist South Vietnam was necessary for the defense of Southeast Asia. The Communists called the struggle in Vietnam a *war of national liberation*. They accused the South Vietnamese government of being a "puppet" of the U.S. They pledged to overthrow the government. They wanted to unite Vietnam under one rule, as stated in the Geneva Accords of 1954, which had ended the Indochina War and divided Vietnam. But the United States and South Vietnam did not sign the Accords.

In 1960, the guerrillas began to gain ground. Their methods varied from propaganda and persuasion to military force and terror. They conquered many villages and sometimes defeated South Vietnamese army units in battle. They tried to turn the villagers against the Saigon government through speeches, radio broadcasts, pamphlets, posters, and meetings. The Communists hoped to cause the collapse of the government by a revolution. They almost succeeded in doing so before U.S. troops arrived. By 1964, about 4 million of the 15 million South Vietnamese were under VC control.

War was never officially declared. However, in 1966, about 700,000 South Vietnamese, more than 300,000 Americans, and 60,000 other Free World forces were fighting against an estimated 200,000 Communist guerrillas and regular troops backed by about 300,000 soldiers of the PAVN. There was no fixed *front* (battle line). The Communists used *guerrilla war* tactics, including ambushes, hit-and-run raids, and hand-laid bombs and mines. Free World forces conducted big air raids and "search-and-destroy" operations in which troops were transported by large helicopters. The ground and air forces were supported by the navy.

Causes of the War

Before World War II, Vietnam was a part of French Indochina, which also included Cambodia and Laos. During World War II, Japan occupied Indochina, but much of the area came under French control again after the war. Ho Chi Minh, Communist leader of the League for the Independence of Vietnam (Vietminh), became head of an independent government in north Indochina.

Disagreements soon arose between France and Ho Chi Minh. Fighting broke out on Dec. 19, 1946, and

continued for eight years. The French were defeated in May, 1954, at Dien Bien Phu and a peace agreement was arranged. A nine-nation conference meeting in Geneva, Switzerland, ended the war in Laos and Cambodia and divided Vietnam. The area in Vietnam north of the 17th parallel was controlled by Communists led by Ho Chi Minh. It became known as the Democratic Republic of Vietnam. The territory south of the parallel became the Republic of Vietnam after Emperor Bao Dai was deposed in 1955. It was then ruled by President Ngo Dinh Diem, who had U.S. backing.

The Geneva conference also said the country must be unified in 1956 through an election supervised by an international commission. But Diem refused to hold the election. He and the United States feared that the popu-

VIETNAM WAR

This map shows the military situation in Vietnam in the summer of 1966. A South Vietnamese commander governs each of the four Corps Areas. The map also locates the main bases or camps occupied by United States personnel.

⊛ National Capital
• Other City or Town
☐ U.S. Military Base or Camp

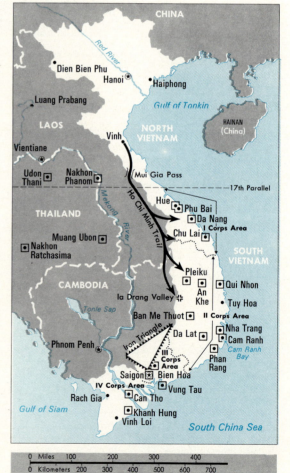

Source: Data for map from *Air Force and Space Digest*   WORLD BOOK map-FGA

The Fighting Men in South Vietnam, including Americans, *above,* and South Vietnamese, *right,* battled in the air and on the ground to keep the country free of Communist control.

lar Ho Chi Minh would win the election and the Communists would gain control of the united Vietnam.

In 1950, the United States and France had begun to aid the South Vietnamese with equipment and military advisers. American economic aid did much to rehabilitate the war-torn country, but Diem's government did not give enough aid to the peasants. Diem gave increasing power to his own family, particularly to his brother, Ngo Dinh Nhu. In 1956, Diem ended local elections and appointed his own village officials to be certain of their support. This increased the feeling against his government. See also VIETNAM (History).

First Stages of the War

The Viet Cong Raids began in early 1957. Guerrillas began to attack farm villages, particularly in the Mekong Delta. The guerrillas were called Viet Cong (Vietnamese Communists) by the South Vietnamese government. The Viet Cong were under Communist control, but many of them were not Communist party members. They fought against the South Vietnamese government because they resented its lack of freedom and its failure to provide the people with the necessities of life. Some of the toughest Viet Cong had been fighting for about 20 years, first against Japan, then France, and finally against the South Vietnamese government and the U.S.

By 1960, the Viet Cong had about 20,000 men. They

The contributor of this article, Keyes Beech, is a Pulitzer Prize winning reporter and Far Eastern correspondent for the Chicago Daily News. *The critical reviewer, Bernard B. Fall, is Professor of International Relations at Howard University and the author of several books on Vietnam. The photographs throughout this article were taken by Henry Gill.*

were outnumbered by the South Vietnamese army ten to one, but were strong enough to attack South Vietnamese forts and army units. They used guerrilla tactics, striking here and there unexpectedly. South Vietnamese troops tried to protect the entire country, and failed.

The National Liberation Front (NLF), a political group, was organized in December, 1960, to support the Viet Cong. The Front set up local councils to govern areas of South Vietnam controlled by the Viet Cong, built factories to manufacture weapons, and supplied ammunition, medical supplies, and money to the Viet Cong. Many of the VC's supplies and troop reinforcements came from North Vietnam, chiefly over a system of roads and trails known as the *Ho Chi Minh Trail.*

In 1961, the South Vietnamese government built barbed wire fences and *moats* (ditches) around many villages to protect them from Viet Cong raiders. These villages were known as *strategic hamlets.* The villagers were given weapons but they were no match for the VC. When the VC captured a fortified village, they killed the leaders and took supplies and weapons.

From Guerrilla Terror to War. By 1961, the Viet Cong had become so successful in South Vietnam that the U.S. was forced to choose between allowing the collapse of the South Vietnamese government and supplying larger military forces. Late in 1961, U.S. General Maxwell D. Taylor recommended greater military support. By February, 1962, 4,000 U.S. military advisers had arrived.

In January, 1963, at Ap-Bac in the Mekong Delta, a well-armed Viet Cong force stood off 2,000 Vietnamese soldiers, shot down five helicopters, and killed three American advisers. This marked the beginning of large-scale VC offensive operations.

A War-Torn Village in South Vietnam is surrounded by a barbed wire fence and a moat. The defenses were built in 1961 as part of a project to keep out the Viet Cong. Anyone outside the fence after a curfew was assumed to be a VC. The project failed, however, because the villagers had no military training and the VC easily overcame them.

Viet Cong Prisoners are taken to a camp for questioning. Tags around their necks tell where they were found, the weapons they carried, and what they were doing when captured. The VC are hard to identify because they usually wear no special uniform.

Helicopters Speed the Wounded to Hospitals and greatly reduce the death rate in the Vietnam war. Helicopters are also used in "search-and-destroy" operations against the Viet Cong, and to bring food, ammunition, and medical supplies to troops in the field.

The Street Riots of 1966 protested against the South Vietnamese government of Premier Nguyen Cao Ky. After Buddhist monks urged the people to riot, children began to throw bricks and rocks at government troops. The children wore or carried plastic bags which they pulled down over their faces like gas masks when troops tried to stop the riot with tear gas.

WORLD BOOK photos by Henry Gill

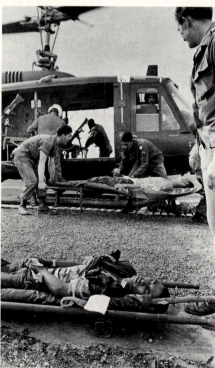

At the same time, South Vietnam's internal situation grew worse. The Buddhists claimed that Diem, a Catholic, was treating them unjustly because of their religious beliefs. Some Buddhist monks committed suicide by fire as a sign of protest. When South Vietnamese troops raided and wrecked some Buddhist *pagodas* (temples) in August, 1963, the U.S. criticized the Diem government and suspended economic aid. This encouraged South Vietnamese generals to overthrow the Diem government on Nov. 1, 1963. Diem and his brother Nhu were killed the next day. A series of short-lived regimes governed South Vietnam until a *junta* (committee) headed by Nguyen Cao Ky came to power in June, 1965.

The Gulf of Tonkin Incident. On July 30, 1964, South Vietnamese naval craft raided islands in the Gulf of Tonkin north of the 17th parallel. Two U.S. destroyers were patrolling nearby. North Vietnamese PT boats, probably while pursuing the South Vietnamese, attacked the destroyers. Two PT boats were sunk. U.S. planes then bombed the PT boat bases. This was the first U.S. attack on North Vietnamese territory.

After the Tonkin Gulf incident, President Johnson asked Congress for powers "to take all necessary measures to repel any armed attack against the forces of the United States and to prevent further aggression." The Congress granted these powers by an overwhelming vote. The Tonkin Gulf resolution became a key legal basis for U.S. support of South Vietnam in the war.

Escalation of the War

By 1964, the Vietnam war had become a major issue in the Cold War (see COLD WAR). Communist countries, particularly China, considered the war an important test of "national liberation war" tactics. The United States and its allies felt that defeat of the Viet Cong would be a defeat for Communists everywhere. They believed that the loss of South Vietnam would mean Southeast Asia would fall to Communism "like a set of dominoes." This was called the *Domino Theory*.

As more men and weapons reached the battle zone, the war expanded. Battles were bigger, and more men were killed. When one side grew stronger, the other side made greater efforts to increase its power. This step-by-step rise in tempo was called *escalation*.

The Viet Cong strength continued to grow. On Feb. 7, 1965, the Viet Cong attacked two U.S. camps at Pleiku. Eight Americans were killed and about 125 were wounded. That same day, U.S. and South Vietnamese planes began to bomb arms factories, barracks, roads, and bridges in North Vietnam. But the raids failed to stop the flow of supplies and reinforcements to the Viet Cong. So in June, 1966, the United States began to bomb oil depots in the suburbs of Hanoi and Haiphong in North Vietnam. In return, whole North Vietnamese army divisions (10,000-man units) slipped into South Vietnam to fight U.S. troops.

American Combat Forces. In March, 1965, President Johnson ordered U.S. Marines to South Vietnam. On June 8, the U.S. announced that American troops would be used in offensive operations if the South Vietnamese government requested it. In July, Johnson ordered a major buildup of U.S. forces in South Vietnam. All U.S. troops were placed under the command of General William C. Westmoreland. Within a year, more than 300,000 U.S. troops were operating there, and 90,000 men served at sea with the U.S. Seventh Fleet. Other nations also sent troops to South Vietnam. South Korea sent almost 50,000 men, Australia 4,500, the Philippines 2,000, New Zealand 250, and Thailand 200.

Recent Developments. In December, 1965, President Johnson began a *peace offensive*. The United States stopped bombing North Vietnam and sent diplomats to many foreign capitals to gain support for a peace conference. But the Communists refused to consider U.S. peace offers, and on Jan. 31, 1966, U.S. bombers again began to attack North Vietnam. The U.S. asked the United Nations to help end the war. But the Communist countries called the peace offers a trick to mask new fighting. President Johnson replied that, despite the bombing, his offer to discuss peace terms was open.

In February, 1966, President Johnson and Premier Ky met in Honolulu to review the war and discuss economic and social development programs for South Vietnam. However, Ky's popularity in South Vietnam was not high, and many Vietnamese thought he was a puppet of the United States. Buddhist leaders, noting his lack of popularity, demanded a new, more representative government. Ky removed the popular Gen. Nguyen Chanh Thi from command in March, 1966, and Buddhist uprisings broke out in the cities of Da Nang and Hue. Ky's troops crushed the rebels. In September, 1966, the people elected an assembly which was to write a new constitution for South Vietnam. KEYES BEECH

Critically reviewed by BERNARD B. FALL

See also COLD WAR; HO CHI MINH; INDOCHINA; NGO DINH DIEM.

VIEUX CARRÉ. See NEW ORLEANS (French Quarter).

VIGELAND, GUSTAV. See NORWAY (The Arts; picture, Oslo's Frogner Park).

VIGIL. See KNIGHTS AND KNIGHTHOOD (picture).

VIGILANTE, *vij uh LAN tee*, is a member of a self-appointed citizen group or vigilance committee. *Vigilante* comes from the Latin verb *vigilare* (to watch).

During pioneer days of United States history, the authorities often found themselves unable to enforce the laws. Sometimes the only law officer for many miles around was the United States marshal, and it was impossible for him to police all his territory. In these situations, the citizens frequently formed vigilance committees. These committees took the law into their own hands and dealt out swift punishment to persons that they considered to be offenders. Sometimes innocent persons were punished. But often the vigilantes were the only force to preserve order in the half-settled frontier territories. One of the early vigilance groups was the San Francisco Vigilance Committee, formed in 1851. See PIONEER LIFE (Law and Order). JOHN R. ALDEN

VIGNY, *vee NYEE,* **ALFRED DE** (1797-1863), COMTE DE VIGNY, was a leading French romantic poet. He was one of the most thoughtful and philosophical French romantic writers. His best poems were published in a volume called *Poèmes Antiques et Modernes* (1882). His play *Chatterton* (1835) was considered a major triumph for the Romantic movement. He also wrote *Les Destinées* (1864); and a diary, *Journal d'un Poète* (1867). He was born in Touraine. WALLACE FOWLIE

J.DNNARD

Culver

VIKING was a member of the Scandinavian bands of sea rovers who launched a series of devastating and successful raids on England, France, Germany, Ireland, Italy, and Spain between the 700's and the 1100's. The vikings also explored and settled Greenland and Iceland. They tried to establish settlements in America, but did not succeed.

Vikings were also called Northmen, Norsemen, or Danes. They were a Nordic people, and were the ancestors of the Norwegians, Swedes, and Danes of today.

They spoke a German dialect that resembled the language spoken in England at the time. The vikings used the Runic alphabet (see RUNE).

The vikings were an adventurous people who loved war and fighting. They were skillful and daring seamen. They were also the most efficient shipbuilders in Europe. Their swift, high-prowed ships carried raiding parties to most of the known world at that time and across the Atlantic to the unknown. The vikings killed, stole, and burned wherever they landed. The churches

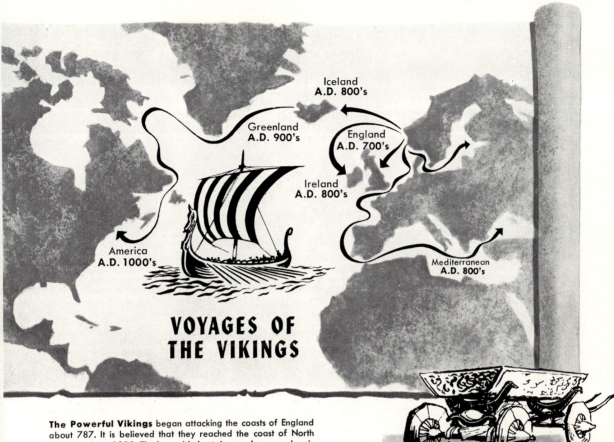

Iceland
A.D. 800's

Greenland
A.D. 900's

England
A.D. 700's

Ireland
A.D. 800's

America
A.D. 1000's

Mediterranean
A.D. 800's

VOYAGES OF
THE VIKINGS

The Powerful Vikings began attacking the coasts of England about 787. It is believed that they reached the coast of North America about 1000. The horned helmet, bronze lance, and curious curved trumpet, *left*, show the skill of viking craftsmen. The finely carved chariot, *right*, dates from about the 850's.

of Europe offered a special prayer for help against the vikings. It was "God, deliver us from the fury of the Northmen."

One of the major causes for the viking invasions was the growth of population in their own countries, which increased the need for land and for other sources of income. Political conditions at home may have added to this restlessness. In addition, the vikings were always a seafaring people, who lived near or on the shores of the sea. The term *viking* may have come from the old Norse word *vik*, meaning *bay* or *inlet*. It was easy for these people to take to their ships and seek fortunes elsewhere when the situation became serious at home.

Viking invasions were at first simply acts of piracy and plunder. But, in many cases, they led to important settlements. The vikings strongly influenced the development of Europe for many years. The daring and imagination with which they roamed the seas gave rise to many colorful stories and poems, called *sagas*, about their deeds. But fiction can hardly surpass the amazing reality of viking deeds.

Life of the Vikings

The Work of the People. The vikings did not spend all their time at sea or in raiding. They planted crops in the spring before they set out on raids, and returned in the middle of summer to harvest them. After the harvest, the raiders left home again, and did not return until winter.

During the winter, the vikings spent their time at home preparing for next year's raids. They also enjoyed playing various games during the long, cold evenings. They played a game similar to chess, and various dice games. The king and the nobles often had special entertainment such as horse fights, performing dogs, music, or jugglers, for their guests.

Some of the vikings worked in the cod, herring, and seal fisheries. Others made salt or tar. Two important occupations were the making of metal tools and weapons, and shipbuilding. The vikings were amazingly skillful shipbuilders and navigators. They usually built small, shallow ships, about 70 feet long and 16 feet wide. But they did construct some ships that measured as long as 300 feet. The ships were propelled by oars, with sometimes a single sail to help in maneuvering. The ships usually carried small crews of about 30 or 40 men. But they were so skillfully made and so daringly handled that the vikings could go anywhere in them.

Characteristics. The ferocity of the viking raiders terrified the people of Europe. Not only were they cruel, but also they carried on their raids with zest and efficiency. The viking raiders struck swiftly and secretly.

The Vikings Were Daring Explorers as well as fierce fighters. Although they did not know of the compass, the sextant, and other instruments of navigation, viking raiders fearlessly sailed their small boats across great expanses of ocean.

After hiding their boats, they pounced on their unsuspecting victims. The raiders had the upper hand before the invaded people knew what had happened. They killed, robbed, burned, and then escaped with such thorough preparation and with such speed that their victims had no opportunity even to try to punish them.

The vikings seemed to go mad during the heat of battle. *Berserker*, their name for a warrior, has come to be associated with insanity (see BERSERKER). These warriors seemed to enjoy destroying their victim's property, and went about it with horrible thoroughness. Fire was one of their favorite weapons. The vikings were equally merciless in killing the defeated, slaying not only men but also women and children. They often raided religious centers, because these were good sources of booty, and were poorly defended.

Although the vikings fought with savage cruelty, they had great courage. They enjoyed fighting, but they also loved adventure, as their amazing voyages show.

The qualities of intelligence and imagination that made the vikings such good navigators helped them in other ways. They soon learned to find and steal the horses when they invaded a village or town. As they began to settle in the invaded areas, they became skillful horsemen. Some of the invaded people learned to protect themselves against the swift raids of the vikings by surrounding their cities and towns with stout walls. But the vikings quickly learned how to besiege and subdue walled towns. They also became masters in fortifying the places that they captured.

The vikings learned rapidly from the more civilized people they attacked. For example, they quickly adopted the Christian religion. The vikings originally worshiped the Norse gods, such as Odin and Thor (see MYTHOLOGY). In the 800's, Christian missionaries began to travel among them to preach their religion. Before long, many vikings in Ireland, England, Normandy, and the Scandinavian countries became devout Christians.

As the vikings became more civilized, they gave up their cruelty and their savage love of destruction. Another impressive sign of the viking's intelligence was their ability to shift from piracy to peaceful and productive commerce. It is true that the viking pirates destroyed much. They disturbed the old way of life in medieval Europe. But this often permitted experimentation and the growth of new ideas. By quickly changing from pirates to traders, the vikings helped develop commerce. The viking invasions helped create a new Europe.

Viking Invasions

The viking voyages and conquests include the searoving activities of the Swedes, Danes, and Norwegians. Medieval writers did not always distinguish carefully from what country their attackers came. They often used such terms as *viking*, *Northman*, or *Dane* in a general way. But it is possible to discover what areas each of the different Scandinavian peoples invaded.

The Swedish Vikings raided along the rivers of Germany, and conquered the area that is now western Russia. Small bands of Swedish sailors, called *Varangians*, established themselves on the shores of the Baltic Sea, the Gulf of Finland, and Lake Ladoga in the 800's. From there, they sailed up the Volkhov River and crossed the Dnepr River.

The Varangians built forts that soon became towns and trading centers. Kiev was the capital of the Varangian state. The word *Russia* may come from the name of a Varangian tribe, called *Rus*, or *Rhos*.

The Varangians soon pushed south from their strongholds on the Dnepr River to the Black Sea, and from there to the Bosporus. They raided and pillaged the entire area. In the early 900's, they attacked Constantinople (now Istanbul). The Byzantine emperor had to pay a large sum of gold in order to save the city. The courage, daring, and skill of these raiders impressed the Byzantines, and the emperor set up a special Varangian guard for his personal protection. The Varangians were too few in number to maintain their identity over so great a stretch of land. By the year 1000, they had merged completely with the surrounding Slavic peoples.

The Danish Vikings raided England, France, Spain, and areas along the coast of the Mediterranean Sea. Their travels covered most of western Europe. They sailed up such great rivers as the Elbe, Garonne, Loire, Rhine, Rhône, Schelde, Seine, and Somme. Few of the larger towns in this area escaped their destructive raids. Many of them suffered repeated attacks. For example, the Danes destroyed Paris in 845 and 856. They besieged the city again in 885. This time, the Frankish emperor Charles the Fat paid the Danes to keep them from destroying it again. Many cities of Spain, including Seville, suffered from the attacks of the Danes.

These tireless raiders sailed through the Strait of Gibraltar into the Mediterranean Sea. They attacked Provence in southern France, the Balearic Islands, and Italy. The Danes also defeated the Moors in Morocco.

The Danes in England. The Danish raids on England began late in the 700's, and continued for more than 300 years. In the late 800's, a powerful Danish force established a base on English soil at York. The Danes marched from this base to conquer wherever they could. They were particularly successful in Northumbria, East Anglia, and the northern half of Mercia. The territory they controlled was called *the Danelaw,* and they forced the English to pay a tax, the *Danegeld* (see DANEGELD). The invaders met strong opposition from Alfred, King of Wessex. Alfred checked the forward progress of the invaders in 878. His success against the Danes is one reason for his title of "Great" (see ALFRED THE GREAT).

For a time, Alfred's successors continued to hold back the Danes. They even recaptured some territory. But new raiding parties attacked England in 980. Both Danes and Norwegians took part in these raids. Olaf Trygvasson, also called King Olaf I of Norway, joined King Sweyn Forkbeard of Denmark in the early 990's. These two viking leaders had one success after another. They returned home in 995, but Sweyn resumed the attacks in 1003. His raiders swept through England.

In 1013, Ethelred, King of Wessex, fled the country and Sweyn became King of England. His son Canute, or Knut, succeeded him. Canute later became king of Denmark and Norway also. Under Canute, the vikings held a huge empire and completely controlled the North Sea. After he died, they lost control of England.

The Danes in France. The vikings who occupied and gave their name to Normandy in northern France were mostly Danes. Rollo, or Hrolf, led the vikings in a long and bitter struggle with Charles the Simple, King of the West Franks. King Charles could not drive the invaders out, and they could not gain ground against the Franks. In 911, the invaders and the invaded reached an agreement. King Charles recognized Rollo as duke of Normandy. Rollo became a Christian, and pledged his loyalty to the king. He also agreed to defend Normandy and help repel future invaders. The Danes of Normandy kept in touch with their homeland for a long time. Scandinavian influences still remain, particularly in the names of places and even in the clothes and customs of the Norman people. See NORMAN.

The Norwegian Vikings traveled to such areas as the Faeroe Islands, Greenland, the Hebrides, Iceland, Ireland, the Orkney Islands, Scotland, and *Vinland* (the mainland of North America). The influence of the Norwegians in Scotland and Ireland lasted throughout the Middle Ages. They founded the city of Dublin in about 840. It was the center of viking power in Ireland for many years.

The exploration and settlement of Iceland and Greenland were more daring and colorful than any other Norwegian exploits during the viking period. The literature of Iceland tells the story of these fearless Norwegian sailors.

Some of the Icelandic sagas tell of Norwegian voyages to America. According to the sagas, Bjarni Herjulfsson was the first viking to see North America, when a storm blew his ship off course. Herjulfsson did not land on this new territory. But Leif Ericson supposedly visited the land (see ERICSON, LEIF). He named it *Vinland* (see VINLAND). The sagas tell of trips from Greenland and Iceland to Vinland for about 12 years.

For many years, scientists tried to discover exactly where the vikings established settlements in North America. In 1961, Norwegian archaeologists discovered the remains of a viking settlement near Flower's Cove in northern Newfoundland. Many scientists accept the ruins as proof that vikings lived there about A.D. 1000. Some believe the ruins may be the remains of Ericson's settlement in Vinland.   WILLIAM BARK

Related Articles in WORLD BOOK include:

Alfred the Great	Kensington	Rune
Danegeld	Rune Stone	Saga
Eric the Red	Mythology	Ship and Shipping
Ericson, Leif	Norman	(The Vikings)

VIKING. See ROCKET (High-Altitude Experiments).

The Viking Chieftain Rollo sailed up the Seine River and attacked Paris in A.D. 845. Many vikings settled in Normandy.
Culver

VILLA, "PANCHO," FRANCISCO

VILLA, *VEE yah,* **"PANCHO," FRANCISCO** (1877-1923), was a Mexican bandit chieftain. He sought to control Mexico after the fall of President Porfírio Díaz in 1910. After the murder of President Francisco Madero in 1913, Victoriano Huerta became president. Villa supported him briefly. When Venustiano Carranza moved to gain control of Mexico in 1914, Villa attacked him. Álvaro Obregón defeated Villa and helped Carranza become acting chief of Mexico (see MEXICO [A New Constitution]; OBREGÓN, ÁLVARO).

Brown Bros.
Francisco Villa

The United States encouraged Villa at first, but President Woodrow Wilson turned to Carranza because of reports of Villa's brutalities. Villa retaliated against Americans in Mexico, stopping trains and shooting those on board. In 1916 he raided Columbus, N.Mex. His cavalry attacked the town, killing 16 people. President Wilson sent General John J. Pershing into Mexico in pursuit of Villa. Hampered by orders not to use Mexican railroads, General Pershing failed to capture Villa. All Mexicans, including President Carranza, bitterly resented Pershing's expedition. The expedition was withdrawn in 1917 (see WILSON, WOODROW [Crisis in Mexico]).

Obregón drove Carranza from power in 1920 and pacified Villa by a grant of land. Villa was shot from ambush by enemies in 1923. He was born in Río Grande, Mexico. His real name was DOROTEO ARANGO, but he changed it to Villa during the revolutionary upheavals. DONALD E. WORCESTER

VILLA DE GUADALUPE HIDALGO, *VEE yah day GWAD 'l oop ee DAL goh* (pop. 127,368; alt. 7,322 ft.), is a suburb of Mexico City (see MEXICO [color map]). Factories in this industrial center make chemicals, electrical appliances, paper, shoes, textiles, and other products. The basilica of Our Lady of Guadalupe, Mexico's patron saint, is the city's most famous landmark. Villa de Guadalupe Hidalgo became a village in 1751, and was incorporated as a city in 1828. ROBERT C. WEST

VILLA-LOBOS, *VEE lah LOH boos,* **HEITOR** (1887-1959), was a Brazilian composer, conductor, and educator. His works were among the first serious music to use Brazilian folk and popular melodies, rhythms, and musical instruments. He composed symphonies, ballets, operas, and chamber music. Some of his most popular works are written in forms he invented called the *Bachiana Brasiliera* and *Chôros*.

Villa-Lobos was born in Rio de Janeiro, Brazil. In 1932, he became superintendent of musical education in Rio de Janeiro. DAVID EWEN

VILLA MADONNA COLLEGE. See UNIVERSITIES AND COLLEGES (table).

VILLA MARIA COLLEGE. See UNIVERSITIES AND COLLEGES (table).

VILLAGE is any small group or community of houses and dwellings. In local government, the term *village* has a more specific meaning. It refers to a community which the state has chartered as a municipality. Such a village is governed by a village president and a board of trustees. The village usually has its own clerk, treasurer, and police official. H. F. ALDERFER

See also CHARTER; CITY AND LOCAL GOVERNMENTS.

VILLANELLE. See POETRY (table, Terms).

VILLANOVA UNIVERSITY is in Villanova, Pa., near Philadelphia. It is controlled by the Augustinian Fathers of the Roman Catholic Church. It is chiefly a school for men, but women may attend the colleges of engineering and nursing, the graduate school, and the summer and evening sessions. The university also has colleges of commerce and finance, education, law, and liberal arts and sciences. Courses lead to B.A., B.S., M.A., M.S., and Ph.D. degrees. Villanova was founded in 1842. For enrollment, see UNIVERSITIES AND COLLEGES (table). JOSEPH A. FLAHERTY

VILLARD, OSWALD GARRISON (1872-1949), a staunch liberal, was editor of the New York *Evening Post* and then the *Nation*. In 1897 he joined the *Evening Post*, which his father had bought, together with the *Nation*, in 1881. He remained with the *Evening Post* until 1918, when financial difficulties, resulting in part from his pacifist policies during World War I, forced him to sell the newspaper. He edited the *Nation*, a weekly journal of opinion, from 1918 to 1933, and continued to support liberal causes. He helped found the National Association for the Advancement of Colored People in 1909.

Born in Wiesbaden, Germany, he graduated from Harvard University in 1893. He was the grandson of the famous abolitionist William Lloyd Garrison. I. W. COLE

VILLEDA MORALES, RAMÓN. See HONDURAS (Recent Developments).

VILLEIN, *VIL in,* was an agricultural worker whose status was midway between that of freeman and slave during the Middle Ages in England. The villein was different from the slave because the villein's person was not the property of his master. He was different from the freeman because he was bound to a plot of land which was not his. In return for the use of this land and protection on it, the villein was required to render certain manual and other services to the lord of the manor. The children of villeins were born into the same bondage as their parents.

Lands held in villeinage often were handed down from father to son until the family acquired a right to them by *prescription* (long use). But the villein still had to serve his master. The villein's sole title to his land was a copy of the entries on the court roll. For this reason, villeins came to be called *tenants by copy of court roll*. Tenure of this type was called *copyhold*. This tenure existed until it was practically abolished by the Copyhold Act of 1894. The Property Act of 1925 ended all tenure by copyhold.

Villeinage began to decline in the 1100's when the villein began to exchange his labor services for money payments. In the end, the villein became a free tenant who paid a rent for his land. By the early 1500's, few villeins were left in England. The contempt in which the villeins were commonly held may be responsible for the fact that we get the word *villain* from the earlier word *villein*. BRYCE LYON

See also FEUDALISM; SERF.

VILLI, plural of villus. See INTESTINE.

VILLON, *VEE YAWN,* **FRANÇOIS** (1431?-1463?), a vagabond poet of France, lived among the outcasts of Paris. He was jailed frequently and once was even condemned to death, but was later pardoned. Living at the end of the Middle Ages, he echoed the earthiness and ribaldry of his time. But he mingled it with the restless individualism of the coming Renaissance.

In his *Testaments* of 1456 and 1461 and in other poems, he showed his satirical vein, his religious crises, and his constant preoccupation with death. Though not one of the greatest of his time, Villon was the poet of the Middle Ages most strikingly similar to present-day poets. He was born in Paris. WERNER P. FRIEDERICH

VILNIUS (pop. 287,000; alt. 500 ft.) is the capital of Lithuania, now a state of Russia. It is called VILNA in the Russian language and WILNO in the Polish language. Vilnius lies in southeastern Lithuania (see RUSSIA [political map]). It was the old capital of Lithuania, and became the capital again when the country declared its independence from Russia after World War I. It was the capital of independent Lithuania from 1918 to 1940.

Many Poles lived in the Vilnius area, and Polish forces seized and held it from 1920 to 1939. Russia restored the city to Lithuania when it seized eastern Poland in 1939. But Soviet troops again seized Vilnius in 1940. Germany captured Vilnius in 1941, but lost it three years later. The communists made Vilnius a railroad and manufacturing city. From 1600 onward, it had been a center for Lithuanian, Jewish, and Polish culture. But the communists have tried to introduce Russian culture to the city. FRANCIS J. BOWMAN

VIMINAL HILL. See ROME (The City Today).

VIÑA DEL MAR, *VEE nyah thel MAHR* (pop. 115,-500; alt. 40 ft.), is a city on the Pacific coast of Chile (see CHILE [political map]). Its fine climate, wide beaches, luxurious villas, and hotels and clubs make Viña del Mar one of the most popular resorts in South America. The city also has several food-processing plants and oil refineries. See also CHILE (color picture, Well-to-Do Chileans). ROBERT N. BURR

VINCENNES, Ind. (pop. 18,046; alt. 430 ft.), a manufacturing and trading center in southwestern Indiana, is the oldest town in the state. It lies on the Wabash River, which forms the Indiana-Illinois boundary in the region. The town is about 100 miles southwest of Indianapolis (see INDIANA [political map]). Hundreds of interested persons visit Vincennes every year to see its historical buildings and memorials. These include the building in which the legislature of the Indiana Territory held its first sessions; the mansion called *Grouseland*, built by William Henry Harrison while he was territorial governor; and the George Rogers Clark Memorial, which stands on the site of old Fort Sackville. The nearby Lincoln Memorial Bridge crosses the Wabash River at the place where the Thomas Lincoln family crossed when they went from Indiana to Illinois in 1830.

Industry and Trade. Vincennes is well situated for a manufacturing and trading center. Railroads, major highways, and the Wabash River provide good transportation. The city lies in a region which contains coal, and oil and natural-gas fields. The chief industries of Vincennes produce batteries, containers, electronic instruments, fiberboard, fiberglass products, shoes,

L. B. Read

The Saint Francis Xavier Church, or Old Cathedral, was completed in 1841. It stands on the site of a log church which was built about the time Vincennes was founded by the French.

structural steel products, and window glass. Vincennes University has its campus in the city.

History. Historians disagree as to the date of the first settlement on the site of Vincennes. Some say settlers came shortly after 1700, which would make Vincennes one of the oldest settlements outside the original 13 colonies. All historians agree that a French fur-trading village stood there by 1727. The French community that grew up there devoted itself mainly to farming.

In 1732, a fort was established at the village and placed under the command of the Sieur de Vincennes. His name was given to the town soon after Indians captured and put him to death about 1736. The fort at Vincennes became Fort Sackville after France gave up the eastern part of the Mississippi Valley to the British in 1763.

During the Revolutionary War, George Rogers Clark occupied the fort. The British seized Fort Sackville in December, 1778, but, later that winter, Clark recaptured it for the Americans. This victory helped win the old Northwest for the new United States. Maurice Thompson's *Alice of Old Vincennes* features the Revolutionary period in Vincennes history.

Vincennes was the capital of Indiana Territory from 1800 to 1813. The town became the county seat of Knox County early in the territorial period. It was incorporated as a city in 1856. Vincennes has a mayor-council form of government. PAUL E. MILLION, JR.

VINCENT DE PAUL, SAINT. See SISTER OF CHARITY.

VINCENT OF BEAUVAIS. See ENCYCLOPEDIA (The First Reference Works).

VINCENTIANS. See RELIGIOUS ORDERS.

VINCENT'S ANGINA. See TRENCH MOUTH.

VINCI, LEONARDO DA. See DA VINCI, LEONARDO.

VINE usually means a plant that has a weak and flexible stem requiring some kind of support. Some vines can climb walls, trellises, or other plants. Other vines creep along the ground. Some vines have tendrils which wind around their support. Other vines have disks which cling to the object which they are climbing. There are two important kinds of vines—*woody* vines and *herbaceous* vines. Grapes are woody vines. Sometimes the woody vine is fairly short, and can support itself. Then it is somewhat like a shrub. It is often difficult to tell the difference between such a vine and a shrub. Common kinds of herbaceous vines include cucumbers, garden peas, and beans.   WILLIAM C. BEAVER

Related Articles in WORLD BOOK include:

Bean	Cranberry	Morning-Glory
Betel	Gourd	Pea
Bignonia	Grape	Pelican Flower
Bittersweet	Greenbrier	Philodendron
Bramble	Honeysuckle	Smilax
Clematis	Hop	Virginia Creeper
Cowpea	Ivy	Wisteria

VINEGAR is a sour liquid for seasoning foods. It also is used in pickling and processing fruits, vegetables, and meats. The name *vinegar* is from the French word *vinaigre*, which means *sour wine*. But many kinds of vinegar are not made from wine.

Vinegar is a result of the chemical change known as *fermentation*. A *dilute* (weak) alcohol is the raw material from which all vinegar is made. The alcohol may be produced from the fermentation of the juice of any fruits, berries, or even melons. Malt vinegar is made from cereals. Vinegar is also made from sugar solutions, such as molasses, sugar sirup, or honey.

Making Vinegar. Cider vinegar is a popular type made in the United States. It is made from the juice of apples, or *cider*. Fermentation changes the fruit sugar in the apple juice into alcohol and carbonic gas. The carbonic gas evaporates, or passes off, leaving only the alcohol and fruit flavors, or *esters*. Oxidation changes cider into vinegar. The oxygen in the air comes in contact with the alcohol in the cider, and with the aid of the vinegar bacteria (*mycoderma aceti*) the alcohol changes into vinegar.

The two general methods of making vinegar are the slow, natural process and the quick process. The *slow* process may take from one to two years, depending on temperature and access to air. The fermented liquid may be kept in a special oak barrel, or cask, with holes to permit air circulation. It should be only about four-fifths full, so as to allow ample air space. The alcohol in the cider, being lighter than the other part of the liquid, tends to rise to the top. As the alcohol comes in contact with air, acetic acid is formed. As the top layer changes into acetic acid, it increases in weight and gradually sinks to the bottom of the barrel. This continues until almost all the alcohol becomes vinegar.

In the *quick* method, the fermented cider is circulated continuously through vats called *generators*. The generators are filled with such porous material as corncobs, rattan shavings, or coke. Lukewarm, strong cider vinegar is circulated through the porous material for 24 to 48 hours. Then the fermented cider is fed into the top of the generator through a revolving spray, or *sparger*. The cider is split into drops, and each drop is brought

into contact with currents of air that enter through holes near the bottom of the generator. An efficiently operated generator will convert 1,000 to 2,000 gallons of cider into vinegar in 48 to 72 hours.

During the process of converting fermented fruit juices into vinegar, particularly cider vinegar, a slimy scum called *mother of vinegar* (*bacterium xylinum*) forms. This actually retards the process, because it slows down the circulation of air. Manufacturers try to prevent the formation of vinegar mother. It clogs the generators.

Kinds of Vinegar. The special flavors, colors, and odors of the different kinds of vinegar come from the substances from which they are made. Cider vinegar has an applelike odor, and is brown or yellow. Distilled vinegar is water-white in color and has no flavor, other than acidity. Molasses is the most abundant source of this type of vinegar. But some distilled vinegar is made from *whey* (liquid part of milk) which contains sugar. Four per cent is the legal minimum acid strength for commercial vinegar.   WALTER H. HILDICK

See also ACETIC ACID; CIDER; FERMENTATION.

VINEGAR BIBLE. See BIBLE (Some Famous Bibles).

VINEGAR EEL is the name of a tiny worm that lives in vinegar. It belongs to the roundworm phylum, or group. It is closely related to the roundworms that live in beer and in the intestines of man and animals. The vinegar eel is about $\frac{1}{16}$ inch long and must be seen through a microscope to be observed clearly. The vinegar eel is slender and threadlike. People often find it swimming in a barrel of cider vinegar or in a bottle of unpasteurized vinegar. Vinegar eels are entirely harmless when eaten by man. The mother vinegar eel gives birth to tiny worms that are no longer than $\frac{1}{100}$ inch.

Scientific Classification. Vinegar eels are in the order *Nematoidea* and the family *Anguillulidae*.   J. A. McLEOD

See also ROUNDWORM.

VINEGAR JOE. See STILWELL, JOSEPH WARREN.

VINER, CHARLES. See BLACKSTONE, SIR WILLIAM.

VINEYARD. See GRAPE.

VINLAND is the name early Scandinavian explorers gave to a region on the east coast of North America. Many historians believe that Norwegian vikings visited this coastal area almost 500 years before Christopher Columbus discovered America in 1492. Some historians believe Vinland was probably in the region of Cape Cod, Mass. Others believe it was in Newfoundland. In the early 1960's, archaeologists found the remains of a viking settlement near Flower's Cove, Newfoundland.

Early Norse *sagas* (stories of heroic deeds) tell of the explorers' voyages. Many historians do not consider these stories as completely reliable. These dramatic tales describe a land that was rich, fertile, and had a mild climate. The Norsemen called the region *Vinland* (also spelled *Vineland* or *Wineland*) because of the grapes they found growing there. The sagas tell that Leif Ericson, son of Eric the Red, visited Vinland about A.D. 1000. Historians believe the Norsemen had to abandon Vinland because they could not defend their settlements against hostile Indians.   WILLIAM BARK

VINSON, *VIN s'n,* **FREDERICK MOORE** (1890-1953), became Chief Justice of the United States in 1946. He served as a Democratic member of the United States House of Representatives from Kentucky from 1923 to 1929, and again from 1931 to 1938. He then served until 1943 as associate justice of the United States

Frederick M. Vinson

Court of Appeals for the District of Columbia.

Vinson became director of the Office of Economic Stabilization in 1943, and then director of the Office of War Mobilization and Reconversion. President Harry S. Truman named him Secretary of the Treasury in 1945. Vinson served about a year, and had an important part in arranging financial settlements at the close of World War II. He was born in Louisa, Ky., and studied at Centre College.　MERLO J. PUSEY

VINYL, *VY nil,* is a chemical substance used in manufacturing several kinds of plastics. It is used in phonograph records, playing cards, raincoats, fabrics, and other products. Vinyl, written CH_2CH-, is a hydrocarbon radical. Vinyl plastics are *polymers* (large molecules) of compounds such as vinyl chloride CH_2CHCl.

Vinylite, which takes its name from vinyl, is a widely used plastics molding compound. It is manufactured by Union Carbide Corporation.　J. HARRY DuBois

See also PLASTICS (Types of Plastics).

VINYON. See FIBER (Synthetic Fibers).

VIOL is the name of a class of stringed instruments played with a bow. Instruments of the violin type developed from the viols. Viols were the chief bowed string instruments in use from about 1500 to 1700.

Viols had a flat back, sloping shoulders, a broad, thin neck, and angular corners. These instruments were usually larger and more awkward than today's violins. Early viols had from five to seven strings. Some of the fingerboards had frets, while others did not. Today's violin comes from the treble viol, the viola from the tenor viol, and the cello from the larger viola da gamba, or *knee fiddle.* The double bass has many features of the *basso da camera,* or contrabass viol.　CHARLES B. RIGHTER

See also BASS; CELLO; VIOLA; VIOLIN.

VIOLA, *vee O luh,* is a stringed instrument played with a bow. It is similar to a violin in shape and the way it is played. It is a little larger than the violin and ranges from 14 inches to 17 inches in length. The viola is the tenor voice in the string quartet and in the string section of the orchestra. It is sometimes used as a solo instrument.　CHARLES B. RIGHTER

See also VIOLIN.

VIOLA DA GAMBA. See CELLO.

VIOLET is the common name of a group of flowering plants. Their blossoms are among the most attractive of all cultivated or wild flowers. Violets grow throughout most of the world. They bloom in groups in early spring. Heart-shaped leaves partly conceal the five-petaled flowers. Each flower grows on a slender flower stalk. There are more than 300 species of violets in the world. About 100 of these grow in the United States. Certain varieties bear white and yellow flowers, but the blue and purple violets are world favorites.

Among the purple violets are the common purple *meadow,* or *hooded, violet,* and the *bird's-foot violet,* whose blue and purple, golden-hearted flowers often bloom twice a year, in the spring and in the summer.

The Bird's-Foot Violet Often Blooms Twice a Year.

The *dog violet* is so called by the English because it lacks fragrance. The word *dog* is a term of contempt. It is quite different from *dogtooth violet,* a member of the lily family. The pansy is a cultivated kind of violet.

The blue violet was adopted as state flower by Illinois, New Jersey, Rhode Island, and Wisconsin. The violet is also the flower for the month of March.

Scientific Classification. Violets belong to the violet family, *Violaceae.* They are in the genus *Viola.* The blue violet is classified as *V. papilionacea;* the bird's-foot, *V. pedata;* the dog, *V. canina.* The wild form of the cultivated pansy is *V. tricolor.*　THEODOR JUST

See also FLOWER (color picture, Flowers of the Woodland); PANSY.

The Viola looks like a large violin. It has a rich, full tone that is pitched between that of the violin and the cello.

VIOLIN

Yehudi Menuhin, *left,* won acclaim as one of the world's greatest violinists before he reached the age of 20. He gave his first recital at the age of seven.

United Press Int.; St. John's Lutheran School

VIOLIN is the best-known and most widely used of all stringed instruments. The first violins were built around the year 1500, but the early instruments did not produce the clear-sounding, full-bodied tone we hear today. The noble "queen of all instruments" achieved its present excellence as a result of the efforts of countless violinmakers, of properly selected woods and varnishes, and of minute adjustments of proportions.

Violins are made with great care. The wood used in them has an important influence on the tone they produce. The wood must be carefully seasoned so that no part of the violin will warp. Many different kinds of woods are used for the 70 different pieces in each violin. The pieces are shaped to fit together exactly. All the parts are glued together, and the varnishing is as important as the work of shaping the pieces.

Parts. The largest part of a violin is a hollow wooden box called the *chest*. It is made of thin, curved pieces of wood. The bottom part of the chest is called the *back*, and the top part, the *belly*. The back and the belly are joined by sidepieces called *ribs*. Around the back and the belly is an inlay called *purfling*. The purfling prevents cracks that form on the edges of the violin from going farther into its body. The thin, narrow part of a violin is the *neck*.

A violin has four strings. These extend almost the length of the instrument, from the *tailpiece* on the belly to the *head,* or *pegbox,* at the end of the neck. The pegbox contains *pegs* (pins) which are used to tighten or loosen the strings. The *fine tuner,* attached to the tailpiece, enables a violinist to achieve fine shades of tun-

PARTS OF A VIOLIN

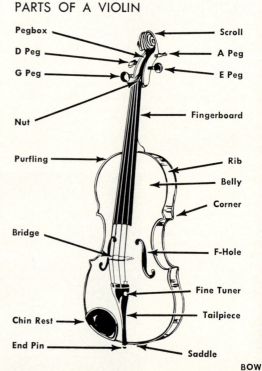

Pegbox — Scroll
D Peg — A Peg
G Peg — E Peg
Nut — Fingerboard
Purfling — Rib
— Belly
— Corner
Bridge — F-Hole
— Fine Tuner
Chin Rest — Tailpiece
End Pin — Saddle

BOW

302

ing without using the pegs. Joined to the neck and extending over the belly is the *fingerboard*. The strings are raised above the upper end of the fingerboard by a tiny ridge called the *nut* and above the lower end by a small *bridge*. Two *f*-shaped sound holes are cut in the belly at the sides of the bridge. The tailpiece is attached to the *button*, or *end pin*, at the bottom of a violin. The *saddle* at the lower end of the instrument protects the belly's edge from the pressure of the heavy string holding the tailpiece.

The *bass-bar*, *soundpost*, *linings*, and *blocks* inside the violin are also important in the construction of the instrument. Each part must be carefully made and adjusted to ensure the delicate musical qualities of the instrument.

The tone depends much upon the strings for its quality. Strings in early violins were made of catgut from the intestines of sheep and other animals. In modern violins, the top string, tuned in E, is made of metal, and the lowest string, in G, is usually of catgut overwound with silver, copper, or aluminum wire. Various materials are used for the two middle strings, in D and A.

Violinists play the instrument with the *bow*. It is a curved stick about 27 inches long. About 150 horsehair threads are stretched from the *tip* to an adjustable *frog*. The modern bow was developed by a Frenchman, François Tourte, in the late 1700's. He made the bow longer, lighter, and more willowy than earlier types of bows, and reversed the curve used in them.

Playing the Violin. The musical tones of the violin are made by guiding the bow back and forth over the strings. This movement causes the strings to vibrate and to give off sound. While the violinist moves the bow with one hand, he *stops* the strings with the other, pressing them against the fingerboard to determine the pitch of the tone.

There are many different ways to bow a violin, including *sustained* (long, smooth strokes), *staccato* (short, sharp strokes), *détaché* (broad, separate strokes), *spiccato* (bouncing strokes with the bow), and *bow tremolo* (rapidly repeated short strokes). The violinist can also play *pizzicato*, plucking the strings with his fingers.

The violin section is the largest and one of the most important in the orchestra. The *concertmaster* (principal violin player) is often the assistant conductor of the orchestra. The violin is also popular with players of folk music, who often call the instrument a *fiddle*. It is less commonly used in modern dance orchestras.

History. From the 1500's to the 1700's, Cremona, in northern Italy, was the most important center of violinmaking. During the 1600's, Nicolo Amati, the son and grandson of violinmakers, produced instruments of astonishing sweetness and inimitable tone. For a long time, the beauty of Amati violins was regarded as unsurpassable. Then, in the 1800's, some persons began to prefer the instruments of Amati's greatest pupil, Antonio Stradivari. His larger, flatter model equaled the Amati violins in tenderness, but exceeded them in volume and roundness of tone. Stradivari violins became the unrivaled ideals of tonal perfection and beauty of workmanship. Stradivari is considered the greatest violinmaker of all time.

Many of the outstanding violin performers of earlier times were also active composers for the instrument. They include Arcangelo Corelli, Antonio Vivaldi,

HISTORIC VIOLINS

The first reference to stringed instruments appears in Persian and Chinese writings from the 800's. Developments over the next 800 years led to the superb violins of Stradivari.

From *Harvard Dictionary of Music* by Willi Apel, © 1950, Harvard University Press; Lyon & Healy

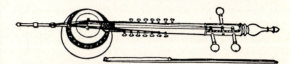

The Kemantche, an ancient Persian stringed instrument, consisted of a long stick extending through half of a coconut.

The European Rebec, popular in medieval times, resembled a long slender pear. It probably originated in the Orient.

The Vielle ranked as the most important stringed instrument in the 1100's and 1200's. This European fiddle had five strings.

The Tenor Viol, a forerunner of the present-day violin, lacks the tone brilliance and versatility that the violin possesses.

The Viola d'Amore was held and played like the violin of today. It was used in Europe in the 1500's and 1600's.

Violins Made by Antonio Stradivari in the late 1600's and early 1700's have never been surpassed in tone, power, and form.

VIOLONCELLO

Giuseppe Tartini, and especially Niccolò Paganini, who was acclaimed for his technical feats. Some of the most significant concertos for the violin were written by Ludwig van Beethoven, Felix Mendelssohn, Johannes Brahms, and Peter Tchaikovsky, who did not play the violin at all. String quartets, made up of two violins, a viola, and a cello, play some of the noblest pieces in all musical literature.   KARL GEIRINGER

Related Articles in WORLD BOOK include:

VIOLINISTS

Auer, Leopold	Sarasate y Navascues,
Elman, Mischa	Pablo de
Francescatti, Zino	Ševčík, Otakar
Heifetz, Jascha	Spalding, Albert
Kreisler, Fritz	Spohr, Louis
Kreutzer, Rodolphe	Stern, Isaac
Kubelik (Jan)	Szigeti, Joseph
Menuhin, Yehudi	Tartini, Giuseppe
Milstein, Nathan	Thibaud, Jacques
Nikisch, Arthur	Vivaldi, Antonio
Oistrakh, David	Wieniawski, Henri
Paganini, Niccolò	Zimbalist, Efrem
Primrose, William	

OTHER RELATED ARTICLES

Amati	Cello	Stradivari, Antonio	Viola
Bow	Guarneri	Viol	

VIOLONCELLO. See CELLO.

VIPER is any one of a group of poisonous snakes. Vipers have a pair of long, hollow fangs in the upper jaw. Many of them have a deep hollow in the side of the head, a little lower than the eye and in front of it. Snakes with this hollow, or pit, are *pit vipers*. Those without it are *true vipers*.

True vipers live in Africa, Europe, Asia, and the East Indies. Pit vipers live in the Americas, the East Indies, Asia, and Europe east of the lower Volga River. Of every 100 snakes, about eight are vipers. Over half of the vipers have the pit.

A viper's poison is formed in special glands. The hollow fangs then carry it into the victim's body the way a hypodermic needle injects serum. All vipers can be dangerous to man, but many of the small kinds rarely, if ever, kill anyone with their bite. Certain kinds of large vipers are so harmless that they will not bite unless someone teases or annoys them.

Vipers have a head much broader than the neck, and eyes with catlike pupils, but so do many other snakes.

Vipers, therefore, cannot be recognized with any degree of certainty by the shape of the head and pupils. Most vipers have thick bodies and rather short tails.

The facial pit of the pit viper is connected with the brain by a well-developed nerve. The nerve, a sense organ, is highly sensitive to heat. It helps the pit viper to locate and secure its warm-blooded prey.

The most familiar American vipers are the *rattlesnakes, water moccasin, copperhead, bushmaster,* and *fer-de-lance.* The last two live in many parts of tropical America, but not in the United States. Only the bushmaster lays eggs. The others bear their young alive.

The *common viper,* or *adder,* is the only poisonous reptile of Great Britain. Other familiar true vipers include the *Gaboon viper* and *puff adder* of Africa, and *Russell's viper* of Asia and the East Indies. Most true vipers bear their young alive.

Scientific Classification. True vipers make up the viper family, *Viperidae.* The common European viper, or adder, is genus *Vipera,* species *V. berus.* Others include the Gaboon viper, *Bitis gabonica;* the puff adder, *B. arietans;* and Russell's viper, *Vipera russelli.* Pit vipers make up the pit viper family, *Crotalidae.* They include: the rattlesnakes, which are genera *Crotalus* and *Sistrurus;* the bushmaster, *Lachesis muta;* the copperhead, *Agkistrodon mokasen;* the water moccasin, *A. piscivorus;* and the fer-de-lance, *Bothrops atrox.*   CLIFFORD H. POPE

Related Articles in WORLD BOOK include:

Adder	Fer-de-Lance	Snake
Bushmaster	Rattlesnake	Water Moccasin
Copperhead		

VIPER'S BUGLOSS, *BYOO glahs,* is a plant that is also known as blue thistle. It has a spotted stem and showy blue flowers. It is a biennial, and seeds planted one year will not produce flowers until the next year. The flowers are reddish when they are budding, but turn blue when they open fully. The viper's bugloss grows widely in the dry pastures of the eastern United States. People once thought viper's bugloss cured viper bites.

Scientific Classification. Viper's bugloss belongs to the borage family, *Boraginaceae.* It is classified as genus *Echium,* species *E. vulgare.*   WALTER C. MUENSCHER

VIRACOCHA. See INCA (Religion).

VIRCHOW, *FIHR koh,* **RUDOLF** (1821-1902), a German scientist and political leader, is considered the father of *pathology* (the study of diseased body tissue). He did important research in leukemia, tuberculosis, rickets, tumors, and trichinosis. His hygienic reforms in Berlin were important advances in public health.

Virchow entered politics in 1862, and was elected to

The Rhinoceros Viper Lives in Swamp Areas in the Rain Forests of Central Africa.
New York Zoological Society

The Yellow-Throated Vireo builds its nest high in the tree-tops. It has a weak but musical song.

A. A. Allen

the Prussian Assembly. After Germany was united, he served in the Reichstag (parliament) until 1893. He became a leader of the Liberal party and a bitter opponent of Chancellor Otto von Bismarck. Virchow was born in Pomerania.　　ROBERT G. L. WAITE

VIREO, *VIR ee oh,* is the name of a family of small birds. They stay close to the foliage in the forests, and feed on insects. People also call the birds *greenlets* because of their greenish color. Vireos live only in North America, chiefly in the tropics. A few species migrate as far north as the United States and Canada.

The best-known vireo is the red-eyed vireo. People can recognize this bird by its red eyes, which have a white line with a black border above them. The note it sings sounds rather conversational, as if the bird were talking to any listener. Since it repeats this note continually, the vireo is often called the *preacher bird.*

Vireos build cup-shaped nests which hang from forked branches in the trees. The female lays three or four white eggs marked with a few dark specks near the large end. Vireos help man by eating harmful insects.

Scientific Classification. Vireos make up the family *Vireonidae.* The red-eyed vireo is genus *Vireo,* species *V. olivaceus.*　　LEONARD W. WING

See also BIRD (color picture, Favorite Songbirds).

VIRGIL, or VERGIL (70-19 B.C.), was the greatest Roman poet. His *Aeneid,* the national epic of Rome, is a masterpiece of world literature (see AENEID; EPIC). It was read all through the centuries when other pagan writings were ignored.

His Works. The *Aeneid* is almost a Roman Bible. Its object was to show that Rome was founded and became great in accordance with a divine plan, that Augustus, like Aeneas before him, was a divinely appointed leader, and that Rome's mission was to bring peace and civiliza-

tion to the world. The first six of its 12 books are modeled on Homer's *Odyssey* and the rest on Homer's *Iliad* (see ILIAD; ODYSSEY). There are also touches from other Greek poems, especially the *Argonautica* of Apollonius of Rhodes. But Virgil fused his literary borrowings and influences into a new creation that is as original and powerful as it is profound.

The *Aeneid,* Virgil's last work, was started about 30 B.C. In his youth, Virgil wrote the *Eclogues,* or *Bucolics,* poems about shepherds, in imitation of Theocritus' idyls. He then wrote four books of *Georgics,* didactic poems on types of agriculture. Other pieces, collected under the title *Virgilian Appendix,* were probably written by others.

His Life. Virgil was born near Mantua, in northern Italy. His full name in Latin was PUBLIUS VERGILIUS MARO. He attended schools at Cremona, Milan, and Naples, and then studied rhetoric and philosophy at Rome. In 42 B.C. his farm was taken to provide bonuses for victorious veterans of Philippi. His youthful poetry had won him powerful friends who introduced him to Octavian, the future Emperor Augustus (see AUGUSTUS). Octavian made good his losses.

From this time on, Virgil lived at Rome or Naples. He was one of the literary men gathered in the circle of Maecenas, who was a great patron of literature and a kind of secretary of public relations to the emperor Augustus. Because of his earlier Epicurean leanings, Virgil probably disapproved of strongly centralized government, but he now realized that only an Augustus could bring peace and security. So he willingly accepted Maecenas' suggestion that he write patriotic poems, first the *Georgics* and then the *Aeneid.* Virgil became ill while visiting Greece, and died soon after landing at Brindisi, before the *Aeneid* was finished. He had left word that the poem, which he considered imperfect, should be burned. But Augustus prevented this, and Virgil's friends Varius and Tucca prepared it for publication. See also ACHATES.　　MOSES HADAS

From a painting by Jalabert

Virgil, the great epic poet, is shown reciting his poetry, in this painting by the French artist Charles François Jalabert. Horace, another famous Roman poet, wears a laurel wreath. Virgil's writings are considered among the best in Latin.

VIRGIN ISLANDS

The Territorial Flag

Fritz Henle

Virgin Islands Fishermen catch bonito, red snapper, kingfish, and Spanish mackerel to add variety to their menu. Nets are hung on poles on the beach when not being used or mended.

The Territorial Seal

VIRGIN ISLANDS is the name of two groups of small islands east of Puerto Rico. They lie between the Caribbean Sea and the Atlantic Ocean. One of the groups consists of St. Croix, St. John, and St. Thomas islands, together with many nearby islets. This group is called THE VIRGIN ISLANDS OF THE UNITED STATES. It is the easternmost United States possession. The other group includes Anegada, Jost van Dyke, Tortola, and Virgin Gorda islands, with their own surrounding islets. It is called the BRITISH VIRGIN ISLANDS.

Christopher Columbus discovered the Virgin Islands on his second voyage to the Americas in 1493. The fresh beauty and untouched appearance of their hills rising from the sea charmed him. He named the group the Virgin Islands, in memory of St. Ursula and her 11,000 maidens (see URSULA, SAINT).

Columbus claimed all the islands for Spain, but the Spaniards did not settle there. The British Virgin Islands have been under the British flag since 1672. About that same time, Denmark established a permanent settlement on St. Thomas. The Danes took possession of St. John in 1717, and bought St. Croix from France in 1733. In 1917, Denmark sold its West Indian possessions to the United States for $25 million, or about $295 an acre.

All the Virgin Islands except Anegada and St. Croix are rugged and hilly. A few good harbors in the group make it an important trade center. The soil is fertile, but the land has not been intensively cultivated. The Virgin Islands produce limited amounts of beef cattle, some fruits and vegetables, and sugar cane, used to make sugar and rum. Watch movements and textiles are among the major exports of the American islands.

The Virgin Islands of the United States proved to have great military importance during World War II, especially as an outpost to protect the Panama Canal. Today, the island group is a popular tourist and resort area. Congress created the Virgin Islands National Park on Aug. 2, 1956, adding greater interest in the group as a tourist center.

The rest of this article deals with the Virgin Islands of the United States. For information on the British-owned islands, see VIRGIN ISLANDS, BRITISH.

The Land and Its Resources

Location and Size. The Virgin Islands of the United States lie about 40 miles east of Puerto Rico, just west of the British Virgin Islands. The group forms the westernmost part of a great chain of West Indian islands called the Lesser Antilles (see ANTILLES; WEST INDIES). Miami, Fla., lies about 1,100 miles to the northwest, and Panama is about 1,200 miles to the southwest. The Virgin Islands cover 132 square miles. Rhode Island, the smallest state in the Union is over nine times as large. The islands have a general coastline of 117 miles, and a *tidal shoreline*, including offshore islands, sounds, bays, rivers, and creeks, of 175 miles.

Islands. All the American islands, except St. Croix, are rugged and hilly. Only three of the islands are inhabited. Hills on the three major islands reach heights of 1,000 to over 1,550 feet above sea level. Countless bays and inlets cut into the coasts of the islands. Fossils of ancient animals indicate that the sea once covered the Virgin Islands. The composition of the rocks that form much of the land suggests that volcanoes pushed the islands up from the ocean floor. Some of the tiny islets that make up the Virgin Islands are mere rocks jutting from the water. Plant life grows on other islets.

St. Croix (kroy) (pop. 17,000), the largest of the Virgin

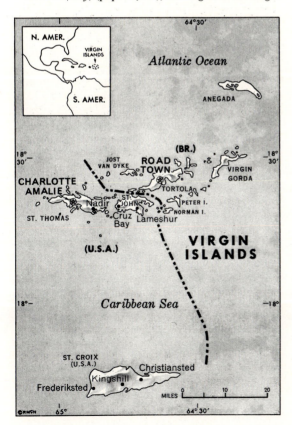

Islands, lies about 40 miles south of St. Thomas. It covers 84 square miles. St. Croix makes up about two-thirds of the island group's total area. Tourism is the island's chief industry. Christiansted and Frederiksted are the only two cities on the island. Spanish-speaking people still call St. Croix *Santa Cruz*, the name Christopher Columbus gave it.

St. John (pop. 1,000) lies two miles east of St. Thomas, and less than a mile from British Tortola. It covers 20 square miles. The Virgin Islands National Park spreads over about three-fourths of the island (see VIRGIN ISLANDS NATIONAL PARK). Villages are at Cruz Bay and Coral Bay, and tourist developments operate along Caneel Bay. Most of the people live on small plots of land, and raise just enough fruits and vegetables to feed themselves. The islanders make charcoal and pick bay leaves which are made into bay rum (see BAY RUM).

St. Thomas (pop. 18,000) covers 28 square miles. Its central range of hills offers lovely views of the ocean. Crown Mountain, the highest point in the entire group, rises 1,556 feet above sea level. The only large town on the island is Charlotte Amalie, the capital of the Virgin Islands. The harbor at Charlotte Amalie provides safe anchorage for even the largest ships. Most of the people depend on tourists for their income.

Natural Resources of the Virgin Islands cannot support the people, who must depend on the United States for most of their products. But the excellent climate, attractive beaches, and lovely scenery make the islands a favorite with vacationers. Tropical flowers and trees flourish, including the bougainvillea, canaria, flame tree, and hibiscus. The seas abound with fish, but most of them are not suitable for commercial fishing. The islands have no minerals of commercial value.

Climate. The Virgin Islands have a delightful tropical climate the year around. The growing season never ends. Trade winds blow over the islands most of the year, and there are no extremes of heat or cold. The

--- FACTS IN BRIEF ---

Capital: Charlotte Amalie (since 1917).

Government: *Territorial Legislature*—a one-house legislature of 11 senators.

Area: 132 square miles. *Coastline,* 117 miles.

Elevation: *Highest,* Crown Mt. on St. Thomas island, 1,556 feet above sea level; *Lowest,* sea level along the coasts.

Population: 32,099 (1960 census); 36,000 (1966 estimate). *Density,* 243 persons to the square mile. *Distribution,* urban, 56 per cent; rural, 44 per cent.

Chief Products: *Agriculture,* fruits and vegetables, livestock, nuts, sugar cane. *Manufacturing and Processing,* clothing, jewelry, rum, sugar, watch movements, wool yarn.

Territorial Seal: The coat of arms of the United States, with the American eagle and the shield of the United States, lies in the center of the seal. The words "Government of the Virgin Islands of the United States" encircle the coat of arms. Adopted in 1917.

Territorial Flag: A golden American eagle with the shield of the United States on its breast appears on a white field. The eagle holds a sprig of green laurel in its right talon, and a bundle of blue arrows in its left talon. The blue letters *V* and *I* are to the left and right of the eagle. Adopted in 1917. See FLAG (color picture, Flags of the States and Territories).

Fritz Henle

Scenic Ruins of Princess Plantation, an old sugar-cane farm, are a landmark on Saint Croix, the largest island.

Fritz Henle

Workmen Cut Sugar Cane with long-bladed machetes on Saint Croix Island. Cane sugar is an important export crop.

temperature ranges between 70° F. and 90° F., and averages 78° F. The islands receive from 40 to 60 inches of rainfall a year. The amount of rainfall varies widely from island to island, and higher elevations may get from 50 to 60 inches of rainfall during a year. The heaviest rains generally occur during spring and autumn.

The People

The 1960 United States Census reported that the Virgin Islands had a population of 32,099. By 1966, the population had increased to about 36,000. Of every 100 islanders, 64 are Negro and 17 Caucasian. The rest of the people are of mixed race or belong to other races. Of every 100 islanders, 63 were born in the Virgin Islands, 12 in Puerto Rico, and 8 in the continental U.S. The rest moved to the islands from other countries. The largest religious groups there include Episcopalians, Lutherans, Methodists, Moravians, and Roman Catholics.

Virgin Islanders speak and read English. They speak in a soft drawl, and tend to simplify English grammar. For example, an islander says "we' en ga" for "we haven't got."

Charlotte Amalie, the capital and largest city in the Virgin Islands, serves as the tourist center of St. Thomas. The city's excellent harbor makes it the chief trade center of the entire group. Frederiksted (pop. 2,177), is a St. Croix trade center. Christiansted (pop. 5,137), serves as the local government center on St. Croix. There are also a number of very small villages in the Virgin Islands.

Work of the People

The Tourist Industry is the Virgin Islands' major industry. About 500,000 tourists visit the islands each year, and they add about $50 million to the economy of the islands each year. Visitors enjoy excellent bathing beaches, fishing, hotels, restaurants, and shops. Ruins of castles and forts built by pirates during the 1700's are also popular. A popular event is the carnival held on St. Thomas at the end of April.

Most Virgin Islanders work in the tourist industry. The rest are employed in agriculture, manufacturing, construction, and other industries. Virgin Islanders earn an average of about $1,750 per person each year.

Agriculture. Cane sugar was once the only farm crop exported. Now, however, some vegetables are being exported to the U.S. mainland. Most of the sugar grows on St. Croix. Annual production totals about 15,000 tons. Dairy herds and beef cattle provide the second largest source of farm income. There are slaughterhouses on St. Croix and St. Thomas. Most of the food the Virgin Islanders eat must be imported.

Manufacturing. Five distilleries on the islands produce rum, the chief industrial product. Excise taxes collected on exported rum provide more than $8,000,-000 for the U.S. Treasury annually. These taxes have paid for the original cost of the islands and more than pay for their maintenance.

Many new industries have been started on the islands. These include an aluminum plant, a knitting mill, watch assembly plants, and clothing factories. Watch movements, jewelry, clothing, and wool yarn are the major exports. Most exports are shipped to the United States.

Transportation. Three scheduled airlines fly to the Virgin Islands, and several steamship lines serve Charlotte Amalie, Frederiksted, and Christiansted. About 1,800 freighters and liners dock at island ports each year.

Resort Cabins Edge Many Beaches of the Virgin Islands. Thousands of Americans visit the islands every year, attracted by the warm climate, picturesque scenery, and fine fishing.

St. Croix and St. Thomas have paved roads. The Virgin Islands are the only U.S. possession where motorists drive on the left-hand side of the road, as they do in Great Britain.

Communication. The six newspapers published in the Virgin Islands are the *Daily News* and the *Home Journal* on St. Thomas and the *St. Croix Avis*, the *West End News*, the *News Current*, and the *Virgin Island Times* on St. Croix. The islands have daily airmail service and a local telephone system. Two telephone cables and a radiotelephone network connect the group with Puerto Rico and the United States mainland. St. Croix and St. Thomas have radio stations.

Education

The public-school system of the Virgin Islands provides education from kindergarten through high school. A seven-man Insular Board of Education supervises the system, which includes about 40 schools and more than 8,600 students. About 98 of every 100 persons can read and write. Children must attend school between the ages of $5\frac{1}{2}$ and 16. The College of the Virgin Islands, a two year college, admitted its first class in 1963.

Four public libraries operate in the islands, at Charlotte Amalie, Christiansted, Cruz Bay, and Frediksted. The islands also have two museums. The Virgin Islands

Museum is at Charlotte Amalie and the St. Croix Museum stands in Christiansted.

Government

The Virgin Islands are administered by the United States Department of the Interior. The Revised Organic Act of the Virgin Islands, passed by Congress in 1954, serves as the constitution. The Department of the Interior administers the group through a governor, appointed by the President. He serves until replaced.

The territorial legislature consists of a *unicameral* (one-house) body of 11 members called *senators*. The people elect the senators to two-year terms. St. Croix and St. Thomas each elect two senators, St. John elects one, and six are elected at large. The governor may veto any bills, but his veto may be overridden by a two-thirds majority of the legislature. If the governor vetoes a bill twice, it is sent to the President of the United States for final action. The legislature meets at Charlotte Amalie on the second Monday in January for a 60-day session. The governor may call special sessions.

A federal district court known as the District Court of the Virgin Islands heads the judicial system of the islands. This court has jurisdiction over certain local affairs as well as in federal cases. The President appoints the court's single judge with the advice and con-

Government House at Charlotte Amalie on Saint Thomas Island serves as the Capitol of the Virgin Islands. The legislature meets here.

sent of the U.S. Senate. The judge of the federal district court and all municipal court judges serve eight-year terms. All residents of the Virgin Islands who are 21 years of age or older may vote in local elections. The islanders do not send representatives to the U.S. Congress, and cannot vote in national elections of any kind.

History

Exploration. Christopher Columbus sighted the Virgin Islands in 1493, during his second voyage to the Americas. Warlike, cannibalistic Carib Indians lived on the islands at that time. They fought with members of Columbus' crew at Sugar Bay on St. Croix. The Caribs continued to attack Europeans throughout the 1500's and most of the 1600's. In the mid-1500's, Emperor Charles V of Spain ordered his soldiers to kill the Indians and take their lands. All the Indians had died or left the Virgin Islands by the time the British and Danes began settlement of the group in the 1600's. See INDIAN, AMERICAN (table, Indian Tribes [Latin America]).

Early Settlement. A group of English settlers visited the Virgin Islands in 1607 on their way to establish a colony at Jamestown, Va. The Spaniards used the islands as a place to hide their treasure ships from pirates, but never settled there. No Europeans attempted settlement until 1625, when Dutch and English settlers landed on St. Croix. They lived there until the mid-1600's, when Spaniards from Puerto Rico drove them out. Within 20 years the Spaniards were driven out by the French. The French controlled the island until 1733, when they sold it to the Danes for $150,000.

The Danes formally claimed St. Thomas in 1666 by establishing a settlement on the island. Eric Smidt was named the first governor, but his colony failed. The Danes made no new settlement on St. Thomas until 1672. In 1717, the Danes settled on St. John.

The Danish West Indies, which included St. Croix, St. John, and St. Thomas, remained under Danish control during most of the years until 1917. They surrendered twice to the British during the Napoleonic Wars. The British quartered thousands of English-speaking soldiers and sailors on the islands during the second British occupation, from 1807 to 1815. They established English as the common language of the people.

Commercial Development. The Danish West India Company controlled the development of the Virgin Islands for the first hundred years of Danish rule. The Danes made St. Thomas a free port in an effort to develop the islands into an important trade center (see FREE PORT). In the early 1700's, landowners used slave labor in developing sugar and cotton plantations.

A bloody slave uprising in 1733 destroyed St. John's economic prospects, because other countries feared using the island's trade facilities. This revolt caused the Danes to increase military authority in the group. An uprising on St. Croix in 1848 caused immediate abolition of slavery on July 3, 1848. Continued efforts by the Danes to develop the islands proved unsuccessful.

On Aug. 4, 1916, Denmark and the United States signed a treaty transferring control of the Virgin Islands to the United States. The treaty was formally ratified on Jan. 17, 1917. Actual control of the islands was transferred on March 31, 1917. The United States paid Denmark $25,000,000 for the islands. James H. Oliver served as the territory's first governor.

Progress Under the United States. In 1927, Congress passed a law making the people of the Virgin Islands citizens of the United States. In 1936, persons who could read and write English were granted the right to vote in local elections. At the close of World War II, the United States set aside $10 million for the further development of the islands. Projects included schools, hospitals, roads, and sewage and water systems.

Congress passed the Revised Organic Act of the Virgin Islands in 1954. It provided for a regular legislature to replace the old legislative assembly. In 1955, Congress created the Virgin Islands National Park on St. John. Buck Island Reef National Monument was established near St. John in 1962. John D. Merwin became the first native-born governor, in 1958. Ralph M. Paiewonsky, also native-born, succeeded him in 1961. Paiewonsky helped attract new industries to the islands. During the mid-1960's, the government built health centers, housing projects, and schools.   RALPH M. PAIEWONSKY

Related Articles in WORLD BOOK include:

Outline

C. Tourist Industry E. Communication
D. Transportation

IV. Education
V. Government
VI. History

Questions

Of what important military value were the Virgin Islands to the United States during World War II?

How does automobile driving in the Virgin Islands differ from that in the United States?

Who was the first white man to see the Virgin Islands?

How do the Virgin Islands compare in size with the smallest American state?

How did the Virgin Islands receive their name?

For what is each major island important?

What happens if the governor twice vetoes a bill passed by the legislature?

What industry provides the largest source of income?

When did Denmark establish its first permanent colony in the Virgin Islands? Where?

Taxes on what product paid for the original cost of the Virgin Islands?

VIRGIN ISLANDS, BRITISH, are a territory of Great Britain in the West Indies. They lie near the western end of the Lesser Antilles (see ANTILLES). A channel called *the Narrows* separates the group from The Virgin Islands of the United States. For location, see VIRGIN ISLANDS (map). The British Virgin Islands cover 59 square miles and have a population of 8,000. The group consists of 32 small islands, the largest of which are Anegada, Jost van Dyke, Tortola, and Virgin Gorda islands. Road Town (pop. 891) is the capital and only urban area. Important products include beef cattle, fish, fruits and vegetables, and rum.   J. ANTONIO JARVIS

See also BRITISH WEST INDIES; WEST INDIES.

VIRGIN ISLANDS NATIONAL PARK lies chiefly on St. John, the smallest of the three chief American-owned Virgin Islands in the Caribbean Sea. The park was dedicated on Dec. 1, 1956. Laurance S. Rockefeller donated more than 5,000 acres for the park.

The park covers an area of 15,150 acres. It occupies two-thirds of St. John, 15 acres on St. Thomas Island, and 5,650 acres of waters and smaller islands. Lush tropical vegetation grows throughout the park. The rugged land rises to 1,277 feet at Bordeaux Peak.

Mules and jeeps provide the chief methods of transportation. The park is reached by a 2½-mile ferry trip from eastern St. Thomas Island across Pillsbury Sound to Cruz Bay, the main village on St. John. Tourist accommodations remain limited, but plans have been made for camp grounds, hotels, and cottage colonies.

Virgin Islands National Park has many reminders of the Danish occupation of St. John, which lasted from the 1700's to 1917. Remains of Danish sugar mills and lavish plantations can be found.   OTIS P. STARKEY

VIRGIN MARY was the mother of Jesus. Her family lived quietly and humbly in Nazareth. She gave birth to Jesus in a stable at Bethlehem. She had gone there with her husband, Joseph, to have their names put down as members of the House of David. This was the way the census was taken at that time.

The sufferings of Jesus brought great sorrow into Mary's life. At the Crucifixion, He asked His beloved disciple, John, to take care of her. Little is known about her later life. It is believed that she died in Jerusalem about A.D. 63. She is venerated by the Roman Catholic, Anglican, and Eastern Orthodox churches as the Mother of God.

National Gallery of Art, Washington, D.C., Widener Collection
The Virgin with Saint Inez and Saint Tecla, painted by El Greco, shows a contrast between the Virgin Mary's flowing dark robe and the faintly flushed skin of the Child Jesus.

The story of Mary has always been a favorite subject of artists and musicians. Many great paintings and songs have been based on the incidents and traditions of her life.   FREDERICK C. GRANT and FULTON J. SHEEN

Related Articles in WORLD BOOK include:

Anne, Saint	Christmas	Joseph
Annunciation	Immaculate	Madonna and Child
Assumption	Conception	Magnificat
Ave Maria	Jesus Christ	Our Lady of Fatima

VIRGIN OF GUADALUPE. See MEXICO (Way of Life [Religion]).

VIRGINAL is an ancient keyboard instrument in which small pieces of quill or leather pluck a set of strings. It usually has a rectangular case, with the keyboard on the longer side. The virginal has a light, clear, and somewhat tinkling tone. It was particularly popular as a solo instrument in Elizabethan England. Leading composers of the times wrote for it. The *Fitzwilliam Virginal Book*, assembled around 1625 and containing nearly 300 numbers, is the most important collection of music for virginals.   KARL GEIRINGER

311

George Washington's Home at Mount Vernon

VIRGINIA

The Mother of Presidents

VIRGINIA is perhaps the most historic of all the 50 states. Some of the most important events in American history took place there. The first permanent English settlement in America was made at Jamestown in 1607. In 1619, the Jamestown colonists established the first representative legislature in America. Some of the greatest battles of the Revolutionary War and Civil War were fought in Virginia. American independence from Great Britain was assured when George Washington forced Lord Cornwallis to surrender at Yorktown in 1781. The Civil War ended when the Confederate forces surrendered at Appomattox in 1865.

Virginia was named for Queen Elizabeth I of England, the *Virgin Queen.* Historians think the English adventurer Sir Walter Raleigh suggested the name about 1584. That year, Elizabeth gave Raleigh permission to colonize the Virginia region. Virginia is also known as the *Old Dominion.* King Charles II gave it this name because it remained loyal to the crown during the English Civil War of the mid-1600's. Virginia is one of four states officially called *commonwealths.* The others are Kentucky, Massachusetts, and Pennsylvania.

Virginia has the nickname *Mother of Presidents* because eight U.S. Presidents were born there. They include four of the first five Presidents—George Washington, Thomas Jefferson, James Madison, and James Monroe. Other Presidents born in Virginia were William Henry Harrison, John Tyler, Zachary Taylor, and Woodrow Wilson. Virginia also has the nickname *Mother of States.* All or part of eight other states were formed from western territory once claimed by Virginia. These states are Illinois, Indiana, Kentucky, Michigan, Minnesota, Ohio, West Virginia, and Wisconsin.

Tourists from all parts of the United States come to Virginia to see its battlefields, famous old churches, colonial homes, and other historic sites. Famous homes include George Washington's Mount Vernon, Thomas Jefferson's Monticello, and George Mason's Gunston Hall. The Tomb of the Unknown Soldier and the grave of President John F. Kennedy are in Arlington National Cemetery. The cemetery surrounds the mansion of Robert E. Lee and his wife, Mary Custis Lee. Williamsburg, Virginia's second colonial capital, has been restored to look as it did in the 1700's. Antique furnishings, horse-drawn carriages, and guides in colonial costumes add to the historic atmosphere.

Many tourists also come to see Virginia's beautiful scenery. The Skyline Drive along the top of the Blue Ridge offers spectacular views of the Shenandoah Valley. In this fertile valley, General Thomas J. "Stonewall" Jackson won victories over Union armies during the Civil War. Virginia's natural wonders include the Natural Bridge, Natural Chimneys, Natural Tunnel, and many large caves and caverns.

Tobacco has been a leading crop in Virginia since John Rolfe first planted it in early colonial days. Virginia also ranks high among the states in raising apples, broiler chickens, peanuts, and turkeys. Virginia's famous Smithfield hams come from peanut-fed hogs.

Virginia is an outstanding example of the industrialization of the South in modern times. Virginia factories produce chemicals, synthetic fibers, textiles, and tobacco products. Shipyards in the Hampton Roads area build ships for the U.S. Navy and for commercial use.

Richmond, the capital of the Confederacy from May, 1861, to April, 1865, is Virginia's capital. Norfolk is the largest city. For the relationship of Virginia to other states in its region, see SOUTHERN STATES.

Jack Zehrt, FPG
Springtime in the Blue Ridge Mountains

The contributors of this article are Raymond C. Dingledine, Jr., Professor of History at Madison College; John E. Leard, Managing Editor of the Richmond Times-Dispatch; *and Anthony Sas, Associate Professor of Geography at Madison College.*

Virginia (blue) ranks 36th in size among all the states, and 9th in size among the Southern States (gray).

Fox Hunting in Southern Virginia
John Freeman, Publix

FACTS IN BRIEF

Capital: Richmond.

Government: Congress—U.S. Senators, 2; U.S. Representatives, 10. *Electoral Votes*, 12. *State Legislature*—senators, 40; delegates, 100. Counties, 96. *Voting Age*, 21 years.

Area: 40,815 square miles (including 977 square miles of inland water), 36th in size among the states. *Greatest Distances:* (east-west) 452 miles; (north-south) 209 miles. *Coastline*, 112 miles.

Elevation: *Highest*, Mount Rogers in Grayson and Smyth counties, 5,729 feet above sea level. *Lowest*, sea level.

Population: *1960 census*—3,966,949; rank, 14th among the states; distribution, 56 per cent urban, 44 per cent rural; density, 97 persons to the square mile.

1965 estimate—4,416,000.

Chief Products: *Manufacturing and Processing*, chemicals, clothing, electrical machinery, food products, furniture, textiles, tobacco products, transportation equipment. *Agriculture*, corn, cattle, fruits (especially apples), hay, hogs, peanuts, poultry, soybeans, tobacco, vegetables. *Mining*, coal, clay, gypsum, kyanite, salt, sand and gravel, stone, zinc. *Fishing Industry*, crabs, drumfish, mackerel, menhaden, oysters, shad.

Statehood: June 25, 1788, the 10th state.

State Motto: *Sic Semper Tyrannis* (Thus ever to tyrants). Adopted in 1776.

State Song: "Carry Me Back to Old Virginia." Words and music by James A. Bland.

Constitution. Virginia's present constitution was adopted in 1902. The state had four earlier constitutions, adopted in 1776, 1830, 1851, and 1869. The present constitution has nearly a hundred *amendments* (changes). Amendments may be proposed in either house of the state legislature. To become law, they must be approved by a majority of both houses in two successive sessions. Then they must be approved by a majority of persons who vote on the issue in an election. The constitution may also be amended by a constitutional convention. Such a convention is called by a majority of the legislature with the approval of a majority of the voters.

Executive. The governor is elected to a four-year term. He cannot serve two terms in a row. He receives a yearly salary of $30,000. For a list of all the governors of Virginia, see the *History* section of this article.

The lieutenant governor also is elected to a four-year term. The governor appoints almost all the top state officials, including the secretary of state, adjutant general, treasurer, and controller. These officials serve varying terms. The people elect the attorney general to a four-year term. The legislature elects the auditor, who serves a four-year term.

Legislature of Virginia is called the *general assembly*. It is the oldest representative legislature in America. It traces its history to the House of Burgesses, formed in 1619 (see HOUSE OF BURGESSES).

The general assembly consists of a 40-member senate and a 100-member house of delegates. Voters in each of the 33 senatorial districts elect from one to three senators, depending on population. Voters in each of the 63 delegate districts elect from one to eight delegates, also depending on population. Senators serve four-year terms, and delegates serve two-year terms.

The general assembly holds regular sessions in even-numbered years. Sessions begin on the second Wednesday in January. They last 60 days, but may be extended 30 days by a three-fifths vote of the legislators. The governor may call special sessions.

By law, the legislature must *reapportion* (redivide) itself within two years after each U.S. census to provide equal representation based on population. In 1962, the legislature reapportioned both houses, but the Supreme Court of the United States ruled the reapportionment unconstitutional. In 1964, the legislature reapportioned itself again. The Supreme Court of the United States approved the 1964 reapportionment.

Courts. The highest state court in Virginia is the supreme court of appeals. It has 7 justices, who are elected by the general assembly to 12-year terms. The justice who has served longest becomes chief justice for the rest of his term.

Virginia *courts of record* include circuit courts in counties, and circuit, corporation, or hustings courts in cities. The judges of these courts are elected by the general assembly to eight-year terms. Lower courts in Virginia include county, municipal, juvenile, and domestic relations courts. The judges of most of these courts are appointed by the circuit or corporation courts to four-year terms. In some cities and towns, the judges are elected to four-year terms.

Local Government. Virginia has 96 counties. Each county except Arlington is governed by a board of supervisors. Arlington has a county board. In most counties, voters elect other officials, including a commissioner of revenue, treasurer, sheriff, commonwealth's attorney, and county clerk. The clerk has an eight-year term. Other officials serve four-year terms. A few counties have a county-manager or county-executive government. In these counties, a county manager or the board of supervisors appoints executive officials.

Any Virginia town with 5,000 or more persons may become an independent city if the people so wish. Virginia has 34 independent cities. Unlike the cities of most other states, these 34 cities are legally separate from the counties in which they are located. The first council-manager government in a U.S. city was established in Staunton in 1908. Today, all Virginia cities have council-manager governments. Some towns have council-manager governments, and the others have mayor-council governments.

Taxation. Taxes and license fees bring in about three-fifths of the state government's income. Virginia collects taxes on motor fuels, and on individual and corporation incomes. It also receives money from the sale of alcoholic beverages in state-owned stores. A general sales tax went into effect in 1966. The federal government provides about 28 per cent of the state's revenue, in the form of grants and other assistance programs.

Virginia State Chamber of Commerce

Governor's Mansion in Richmond stands northeast of the Capitol. The Federal-style brick home was built in 1813. It replaced an earlier governor's residence built on the same site.

The State Seal

Symbols of Virginia. On the state seal, the standing figure represents Virtue dressed as a woman warrior. She stands triumphant over Tyranny. The Latin motto means "Thus ever to tyrants." The seal was designed by George Wythe, a signer of the Declaration of Independence. It was first adopted in 1776. The present version was adopted in 1930. The state flag was probably first used during the mid-1800's, but it was not adopted until 1930.

Flag and flower illustrations, courtesy of Eli Lilly and Company

Politics. The Democratic party has controlled Virginia politics throughout most of the state's history. Virginia's only elected Republican governor was Gilbert C. Walker, who served from 1870 to 1874. In 1881, William E. Cameron was elected governor on the Readjuster ticket. He later declared himself a Republican.

Virginia Democrats are split into two groups. The larger, more conservative group was headed by Harry F. Byrd, former governor and U.S. Senator, until he retired in 1965. Its members have been called "Byrd Democrats" (see BYRD, HARRY FLOOD). Members of the other group, often called "liberal Democrats," have their greatest strength in the urban areas of the north and the east. The conservative Democrats sometimes support Republican candidates in presidential elections. For this reason, Virginia has voted Republican in several national elections. For the state's electoral votes and voting record in presidential elections, see ELECTORAL COLLEGE (table).

State Capitol in Richmond was designed by Thomas Jefferson. The original building was completed in 1792. The Capitol was modeled after a Roman temple in Nimes, France. The Confederate Congress met in the Capitol during the Civil War. Richmond has been the state capital since 1780. Earlier capitals were Jamestown (1607-1699) and Williamsburg (1699-1780).

Virginia Dept. of Conservation and Economic Development

The State Flag

The State Bird
Cardinal

The State Flower
Flowering Dogwood

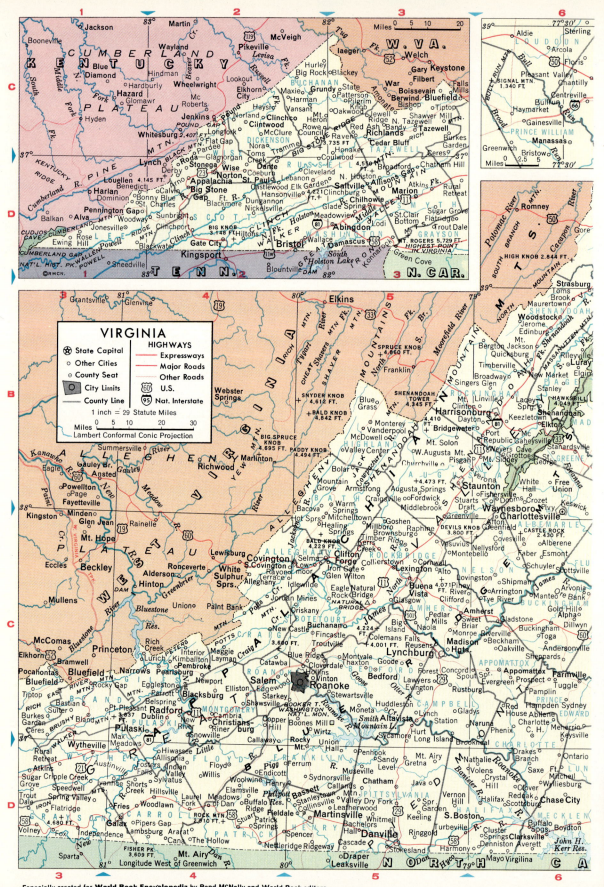

VIRGINIA

HIGHWAYS

⊛ State Capital
○ Other Cities
● County Seat
City Limits
County Line

Expressways
Major Roads
Other Roads
60 U.S.
95 Nat. Interstate

1 inch = 29 Statute Miles

Miles 0 5 10 20 30

Lambert Conformal Conic Projection

WASHINGTON D.C. (inset map)

Dranesville · Bethesda · Silver Spr. · 77° · 39°
Herndon · Sunset Hills · Langley · McLean · 518 FT. · 495 · Lewinsville · WASHINGTON D.C.
Vienna · Falls Church · FORT MYER · 50
Oakton · Merrifield · 50 · Arlington · BOLLING A.F.B. · Silver Hill
Fairfax · Annandale · Alexandria · Camp Springs
Fairfax Station · Burke · Springfield · M.D. · Clinton
Clifton · 495 · Groveton · 11
Newington · Lorton · Mt. Vernon · Wellington · Ft. Washington
©RMCN.

Chesapeake Bay area (inset)

Jamestown · Grove · Yorktown · York R. · COLONIAL NAT'L. · NORTHAMPTON
Harris Grove · Dandy · HIST. PARK · Capeville · Cheapside
COLONIAL NAT'L. HIST. PARK · James River · Seaford · Hornsbyville · Grafton · Chesapeake · Kiptopeke
Surry Hill · Poquoson · Messick · C. CHARLES · FISHERMAN I.
Bacons Castle · Rushmere · Bay
Pons · 64 · Hampton · Buckroe Beach · CHESAPEAKE BAY BRIDGE-TUNNEL
Smithfield · Rescue · Battery Park · Phoebus · Fort Monroe · OLD PT. COMFORT · HAMPTON ROADS BRIDGE-TUNNEL · 37°
Raynor · Benns Church · Newport News · Hampton Roads · Norfolk · Lynnhaven Roads · CAPE HENRY
ISLE OF WIGHT · Longview · Crittenden · Eclipse · Elizabeth Park · 58
Isle of Wight · Hobson · 17 · Virginia Beach
Zuni · Everets · L. Prince · Portsmouth
Chuckatuck · River · Driver · Chesapeake · 58
Windsor · 460 · Nansemond R. · 17
Myrtle · Nansemond · 158 460
Buckhorn · Suffolk · Magnolia · 17 · 76°
76°30'Dismal Swamp · ©RMCN.

RICHMOND (inset)
77°30' · Chickahominy · HANOVER · ©RMCN.
Bon Air · Highland Sprs. · James R.
37° · 60 · Sandston · 60 · 37°
30' · Midlothian · HENRICO · Varina
CHESTERFIELD · Falling Creek Cr. · Richmond Heights · Varina Grove
Falling Cr. · Swift Cr. · 95
Chesterfield · Drewrys Bluff
Beach · Chester · Bermuda Hundred
Walthall · Hopewell
Matoaca · Ettrick · Colonial Hts. · PRINCE GEORGE
Sutherland · Colonial Hts. · Prince George
DINWIDDIE · Petersburg · 460 · 301 · 2.5 5 · 10
77°30' · 11 · Miles

Main map — Virginia

W. VA. · 78° · Frederick
Back Creek · HARPERS FY. NAT'L. MON. · Brunswick · 40
Brucetown · Charles Town · Lovettsville · M.D. · 240 · 70
Hayfield · Winchester · Berryville · Waterford
Stephens City · Wht. Post · Millwood · Bluemont · Ashburn · Leesburg · Darnestown
Middletown · Paris · Upperville · Sterling · Herndon · McLean · 495 · WASHINGTON D.C. · Annapolis
Riverton · Boyce · Aldie · BULL RUN MTS. · Vienna · Capitol Hgts. · 50
Front Royal · Middleburg · Rectortown · 1,340 FT. · Arlington · Fairfax · Alexandria · Upper Marlboro
Limeton · Markham · The Plains · Clifton · Wellington · Mt. Vernon
Bentonville · Hume · Haymarket · Manassas · Occoquan · FORT BELVOIR · MARYLAND
Washington · FAUQUIER · Cresthill · Nokesville · Woodbridge · Indian Head
Sperryville · Warrenton · Jeffersonton · Casanova · Dumfries · Triangle · QUANTICO M.C.A.S. · La Plata · Prince Frederick
SHENANDOAH · Brandy · Midland · Garrisonville · Mathias Point
Eggbornsville · Culpeper · Remington · Roseville · Stafford · Brooke · Dahlgren · Colonial Beach · GEO. WASHINGTON BIRTHPLACE NAT'L. MON. · Leonardtown
Criglersville · Morrisville · Stafford · Falmouth · King George · Oak Grove · WESTMORELAND
Etlan · Lignum · Fredericksburg · Parker · Port Royal
Madison · Achsah · Rapidan · Burr Hill · CLARK MTN. · Sealston · Gera · POTOMAC RIVER
NAT. PK. · Aroda · Unionville · Orange · Spotsylvania · Rappahannock · Guinea
Montpelier Station · Barboursville · Thornhill · SPOTSYLVANIA · Po R. · Bowling Green · Montross · New Kinsale · Callao
Gordonsville · Holladay · Jones · Brokenburg · Partlow · Milford · Warsaw · Heathsville · Burgess
1,814 FT. · Louisa · Ladysmith · Hustle · Centralia · Tidewater · NORTHUMBERLAND · SMITH PT. · TANGIER I.
Campbell · Mineral · Penola · Point · Newtown · Dunnsville · Sharps · Farnham · Fair Port · Reedville · Tangier
Poindexter · Frederics Hall · Beaverdam · Tappahannock · Lorne · Biscoe · Morattico · Mila · Lively · Lancaster
Troy · Kents Store · Apple Grove · Hewlett · Mangohick · Center Cross · Water View · Lancaster · Fleeton
Palmyra · Caledonia · Montpelier · Aylett · King · Mollusk · Kilmarnock · White Stone
Fk. Union · Dabneys · Gum Spring · Ashland · Hanover · KING AND QUEEN · Truhart · Weems · Irvington · WINDMILL PT.
Bremo Bluff · Columbia · Goochland · Glenallen · Laurel · Peake · King and Queen · Saluda · Urbanna · Deltaville · CHERRY PT.
New Canton · Crozier · Manakin · Lakeside · Mechanicsville · Highland Sprs. · Sweet Hall · W. Point · Hartfield · Gwynn
Cartersville · POWHATAN · RICHMOND · Bon Air · Elko · Providence Forge · Plum Point · New Upton · Gressitt
Cumberland · Liburn · Midlothian · Sandston · NEW KENT · York R. · Toano · Naxera · New Point
Powhatan · Moseley · Drewrys Bluff · James R. · CHARLES CITY · Gloucester · Schley
Appomattox R. · Chula · CHESTERFIELD · Chesterfield · Elko · Ruthville · Gloucester Point · MATHEWS · Mathews
Amelia C. H. · Mattoax · Chester · CHARLES CITY · Williamsburg · COLONIAL NAT'L HIST. PARK · Susan · NEW PT. COMFORT
Rice · Jetersville · Winterpock · Colonial Hts. · FORT LEE · Claremont · Yorktown · Severn · Maryus · Cape Charles
Burke- ville · Jennings · Ordinary · Mannboro · Ettrick · Hopewell · Savedge · Surry · Seaford · Perrin · Cheriton
Crewe · AMELIA · Sutherland · Hebron · Church Road · PRINCE GEORGE · Brandon · Claremont · Poquoson · Wicomico · Oyster
Green Bay · Nottoway · Wilsons · Dinwiddie · Prince George · Disputanta · Carsley · Bacons Castle · Messick · Townsend · SMITH I.
NOTTOWAY · Blackstone · Petersburg · Stony Cr. · Carson · Dendron · 64 · Fox Hill · C. CHARLES · 37°
Nutbush · Victoria · Waverly · Newport News · Hampton · FALSE CAPE
Kenbridge · McKenney · Wakefield · Smithfield · Rescue · Norfolk · CAPE HENRY
Lunenburg · Rawlings · Stony Creek · SUSSEX · Ivor · Isle of Wight · Eclipse · Atlantic Ocean
Dundas · Danieltown · Alberta · Warfield · Littleton · Dory · Windsor · Portsmouth · Virginia Beach
Bagleys Mills · Meredithville · Purdy · Jarratt · Yale · Sedley · Walters · Chesapeake
Meherrin · Wightman · BRUNSWICK · 301 · Gray · Grizzard · Courtland · Carrsville · Holland · Suffolk · Dismal Swamp
S. Hill · La Crosse · Merchant · Ante · SOUTHAMPTON · Franklin · FALSE CAPE
Redlawn · 58 · Lawrenceville · Drewryville · Capron · Newsoms · Handsom · Dismal Swamp L.
Norvell · White Plains · Gasburg · Triplett · GREENSVILLE · Boykins · Somerton · Whaleyville · Drummond
DAM · Lake Gaston · Barley · Branchville
R O L I N A · 77° · 13 · 76°

Miles · 0 · 2.5 · 5 · 10
Chesapeake Bay

PT. LOOKOUT · 76° · M.D. · Greenbackville · 38°
SMITH I. · Crisfield · New Church
Saxis · Chincoteague · ASSATEAGUE I.
SMITH PT. · Hallwood · WALLOPS I.
Reedville · Accomac · Parksley
Harborton · Onancock · Keller · Melfa · Wachapreague
Jamesville · Painter · Exmore · PARRAMORE I.
Nassawadox · Willis Wharf · Wachapreague · Quinby
HOG I. · Eastville · CEDAR I.
CM POLITICAL VIRGINIA
COPYRIGHT BY
RAND McNALLY & COMPANY
MADE IN U.S.A.
FEA

Population

4,416,000	.Estimate 1965
3,966,949	1960
3,318,680	1950
2,677,773	1940
2,421,851	1930
2,309,187	1920
2,061,612	1910
1,854,184	1900
1,655,980	1890
1,512,565	1880
1,225,163	1870
1,219,630	1860
1,119,348	1850
1,025,227	1840
1,044,054	1830
938,261	1820
877,683	1810
807,557	1800
691,737	1790

Metropolitan Areas

Lynchburg 110,701
Newport News-Hampton 224,503
Norfolk-Portsmouth 578,507
Richmond 436,044
Roanoke 158,803

Counties

Accomack ..30,635..C 9
Albemarle .30,969..C 6
Alleghany ..12,128..C 4
Amelia ......7,815..C 7
Amherst ...22,953..C 5
Appomattox .9,148..C 6
Arlington .163,401..A 7
Augusta ...37,363..B 5
Bath ....5,335..C 5
Bedford ...31,028..C 5
Bland ....5,982..C 3
Botetourt ..16,715..C 5
Brunswick .17,779..D 7
Buchanan ..36,724..C 2
Buckingham ...10,877..C 6
Campbell ..32,958..C 5
Caroline ..12,725..B 7
Carroll ...23,178..D 4
Charles City .5,492..C 7
Charlotte .13,368..C 6
Chesterfield 71,197..C 7
Clarke .....7,942..A 6
Craig ......3,356..C 4
Culpeper ..15,000..D 7
Cumberland .6,360..C 6
Dickenson .20,211..C 2
Dinwiddie .22,183..C 7
Essex ......6,690..C 8
Fairfax .261,417..B 7
Fauquier ..24,066..B 7
Floyd .....10,462..D 4
Fluvanna ...7,227..C 6
Franklin ..25,925..D 5
Frederick .21,941..A 6
Giles .....17,219..C 4
Gloucester .11,919..C 8
Goochland ..9,206..C 7
Grayson ...17,390..D 3
Greene .....4,715..B 6
Greensville 16,155..D 7
Halifax ...33,637..D 6
Hanover ...27,550..C 7
Henrico ..117,339..C 7
Henry .....40,335..D 5
Highland ...3,221..B 5
Isle of Wight ..17,164..D 8
James City .11,539..C 8
King and Queen ....5,889..C 8
King George .7,243..B 7
King William .7,563..C 7
Lancaster ..9,174..C 8
Lee ....25,824..D 1
Loudoun ...24,549..A 7
Louisa ....12,959..C 7
Lunenburg .12,523..D 6
Madison ....8,187..B 6
Mathews ....7,121..C 8
Mecklenburg 31,428..D 6
Middlesex ..6,319..C 8
Montgomery 32,923..C 4
Nansemond 31,366..D 8
Nelson ....12,752..C 6
New Kent ...4,504..C 8
Northampton ..16,966..C 9
Northumberland ..10,185..C 8
Nottoway ..15,141..C 6
Orange ....12,900..B 6

Page ....15,572..B 6
Patrick ...15,282..D 4
Pittsylvania 58,296..D 5
Powhatan ...6,747..C 7
Prince Edward ..14,121..C 6
Prince George ..20,270..C 7
Prince William ..50,164..B 7
Pulaski ...27,258..C 4
Rappahannock ..5,368..B 6
Richmond ...6,375..C 8
Roanoke ...61,693..C 4
Rockbridge .24,039..C 5
Rockingham 40,485..B 6
Russell ...26,290..D 2
Scott .....25,813..D 2
Shenandoah 21,825..B 6
Smyth .....31,066..D 3
Southampton ..19,931..D 7
Spotsylvania ..13,819..B 7
Stafford ..16,876..B 7
Surry ......6,220..C 8
Sussex ....12,411..D 7
Tazewell ..44,791..C 3
Warren ....14,655..B 6
Washington 38,076..D 3
Westmoreland ..11,042..B 8
Wise ......43,579..C 2
Wythe .....21,975..D 3
York ......21,583..C 8

Cities and Towns

Abilene ......60..C 6
Abingdon ..4,758.°D 3
Accomac ....414.°C 9
Achsah ....35..B 4
Acredale* ..1,022..D 8
Afton ....75..B 6
Alberene ....300..C 6
Alberta .....430..D 7
Aldie ....75..B 7
Alexandria ..91,023††B 7
Alleghany ...150..C 4
Alisonia ....160..D 4
Allisons Gap ...600..D 3
Altavista ..3,299..C 5
Amelia Court House ....800.°C 7
Amherst ...1,200.°C 5
Amonate .....875..C 3
Andersonville ..65..C 6
Annalee Heights* ..2,000..B 7
Annandale .5,000..A 7
Appalachia .2,456..D 2
Apple Grove ..25..C 7
Appomattox .1,184.°C 6
Ararat ......300..D 4
Arcadia* .....25..C 5
Arcola ....40..A 6
Arcturus* ....40..B 7
Ark* ....75..C 8
Arlington .163,401..B 7
Aroda ....80..B 6
Arrington ...250..C 6
Arvonia .....700..C 6
Ashburn .....200..A 7
Ashland ...2,773..C 7
Atkins ......400..D 3
Augusta Springs ..300..B 5
Austinville .750..D 4
Averett ......25..C 5
Aylett ....60..C 7
Bachelors Hall ....50..D 5
Bacons Castle ...C 8
Bacova .....175..B 5
Bagleys Mills .10..D 6
Bandy ....800..C 3
Barboursville .150..B 6
Barley ....50..D 5
Bassett ...3,148..D 5
Bastian .....700..C 3
Battery Park .240..A 8
Bay Colony* .850..D 8
Bayside* ..6,000..D 8
Beach ....70..B 9
Beaverdam ...50..C 7
Bedford ...5,921.°C 5
Belle Haven .371..C 9
Belle View* 3,500..B 7
Belspring ...400..C 4
Belvedere* .1,100..B 7
Benedict .....30..D 1
Bentonville .350..B 6
Bergton .....100..B 6
Bermuda Hundred ..30..B 9
Berryville .1,645.°A 7

Big Island ...500..C 5
Big Rock ....300..C 2
Big Stone Gap ..4,688..D 2
Birdsnest* ..125..C 9
Biscoe ....75..C 7
Bishop ......900..C 3
Blackey .....200..C 3
Blacksburg .7,070..C 4
Blackstone .3,659..C 6
Blackwater ...50..D 1
Blaineville* ..40..B 6
Bland ....500.°C 3
Bloomfield* ..25..A 7
Bloxom .....349..C 9
Blue Grass ...75..B 5
Blue Ridge ..900..C 5
Bluefield .4,235..C 3
Bluemont ....225..A 7
Bocock* ......65..C 5
Boissevain ..600..C 3
Bolar ....45..B 5
Bomar* ....50..D 1
Bon Air ...1,500..C 7
Bonny Blue ..504..D 1
Boones Mill .371..C 5
Boston ....40..B 6
Bowling Green 528.°B 7
Boyce ....384..A 6
Boydton ....449.°D 6
Boykins ....710..D 7
Branchville .158..D 7
Brandy Station 200..B 7
Bremo Bluff .100..C 6
Bridgewater .1,815..B 6
Bristol ...17,144††D 2
Bristow ......50..A 7
Broadford ...600..D 3
Broadway ...646..B 6
Brodnax .....561..D 6
Brokenburg* .100..B 7
Brooke ......100..B 7
Brookneal .1,070..C 6
Brownsburg .300..C 5
Brucetown ...200..A 6
Brunswick ....D 7
Buchanan .1,349..C 5
Buckingham .218.°C 6
Bucknell Manor* .2,000..B 7
Buckroe Beach (part of Hampton) ....A 9
Buena Vista .6,300††C 5
Buffalo Ridge ...D 4
Buffalo Springs ..50..D 6
Bullrun ......A 6
Burgess ....570..C 8
Burke ......150..A 6
Burkes Garden ..100..C 3
Burkeville ..705..C 6
Burr Hill ...100..B 7
Caledonia .....C 6
Callands ....20..D 5
Callao ......150..C 8
Callaway ....130..C 4
Calverton ...200..B 7
Calvin ....25..D 2
Cambria ....722..C 4
Campbell .....40..B 6
Cana ....65..D 4
Cape Charles 2,041..C 8
Capeville ....200..A 9
Capron .....327..D 7
Carrsville ...200..D 8
Carsley ......75..C 7
Carson ......160..C 7
Cartersville ..85..C 6
Casanova ....100..B 7
Cascade .....500..D 5
Castlewood ..500..D 2
Catawba ......25..C 4
Cedar Bluff .995..C 3
Center Cross .200..C 8
Central Point .200..B 7
Centreville ..600..A 6
Ceres ....75..C 3
Chamberlayne Heights* ..1,000..C 7
Chantilly ...400..A 6
Charles City .20.°C 7
Charlotte Court House ..555.°C 6
Charlottesville ..29,427††.°B 6
Chase City .3,207..D 6
Chatham ...1,822.°D 5
Chatham Hill .75..D 3
Cheapside ...150..A 9
Cheriton ....761..C 8
Chesapeake ..73,647††A 9
Chesconessex* ..60..C 9
Chester ...2,000..C 7
Chesterfield .135.°C 7
Chilesburg* ..85..B 7
Chilhowie .1,169..D 3
Chincoteague 2,131..C 9

Christiansburg ..3,653.°C 4
Chuckatuck ..250..A 8
Chula ....125..C 7
Church Road ..65..C 7
Church View* .100..C 8
Churchville ..400..B 5
Claremont ...377..C 8
Clarksville .1,530..D 6
Cleveland ...415..C 2
Clifford ....135..C 5
Cliffview* ..150..D 4
Clifton .....230..B 7
Clifton Forge .5,268††C 5
Clinchburg ..450..D 3
Clincho .....975..C 2
Clinchport ..302..D 2
Clintwood .1,400.°C 2
Clover ......261..D 6
Cloverdale ..500..C 5
Cluster Springs 150..D 6
Coeburn ...2,471..D 2
Colemans Falls ..180..C 5
Collierstown .150..C 5
Collinsville .3,586..D 5
Colonial Beach ..1,769..B 8
Colonial Heights .9,587††C 7
Columbia .....86..C 6
Concord .....400..C 6
Conicville* ..45..B 6
Copper Hill ..40..C 4
Cornwall ....100..C 5
Coulwood ....125..D 2
Council ......50..C 2
Courtland ...855.°D 7
Covesville ..150..C 6
Covington 11,062††.°C 5
Craigsville .978..B 5
Cresthill ....50..B 6
Crewe .....2,012..C 6
Criglersville ..45..B 6
Cripple Creek .300..D 3
Crittenden ..250..A 8
Crozet .....900..B 6
Crozier .....100..C 7
Crystal Hill .150..D 6
Culmore* ..1,700..B 7
Culpeper ..2,412.°B 6
Cumberland ..250.°C 6
Dabneys ......15..C 7
Dahlgren ....475..B 7
Damascus ..1,485..D 3
Dandy ....400..A 8
Danieltown ...40..D 7
Dante ......436..D 2
Danville ..46,577††D 5
Dayton .....930..B 6
Deltaville ..500..C 8
Dendron .....403..C 8
Denniston ....50..D 6
Derby ....800..D 2
Dewitt ......100..C 7
Diamond Springs* .1,500..D 8
Dillwyn .....515..C 6
Dinwiddie ...200.°C 7
Disputanta ..350..C 7
Dominion .....D 1
Dooms ....200..B 6
Dorchester* .150..D 2
Dory ....D 7
Drakes Branch 759..D 6
Dranesville ..A 6
Draper* .....233..D 4
Drewrys Bluff ...250..C 7
Drewryville ..200..D 7
Driver ......160..A 8
Dry Fork ....250..D 5
Dublin ....1,427..C 4
Duffield* ....97..D 2
Dumfries ..1,368..B 7
Dundas ......200..D 6
Dungannon ...444..D 2
Dunn Loring* .1,500..B 7
Dunnsville ...50..C 8
Eagle Rock ..450..C 5
Eastville ...261.°C 9
Eclipse .....290..D 8
Edgewood ....500..C 4
Edinburg ....517..B 6
Edwardsville* .60..C 8
Eggbornsville ..B 6
Eggleston ...300..C 4
Elamsville ....D 4
Elgin ....B 6
Elizabeth Park (part of Norfolk) ....A 9
Elk Garden ..200..D 3
Elko ....20..C 7
Elkrun* ......35..B 7
Elkton ....1,506..B 6
Elliston ....600..C 4

Elmont ......150..C 7
Emporia ...5,535.°D 7
Endicott ....300..D 4
Esmont ......100..C 6
Etlan ....100..B 6
Ettrick ...2,998..C 7
Everets ......25..A 8
Evergreen ...150..C 6
Evington ....200..C 5
Ewing ....500..D 1
Exmore ....1,566..C 9
Faber ....80..C 6
Fair Port ...650..C 8
Fairfax ..13,585††.°A 6
Fairfax Station ..175..A 6
Fairlawn* .1,325..C 4
Falling Creek ....B 9
Falls Church ..10,192††A 7
Falls Mills .500..C 3
Falmouth ..1,478..B 7
Farmville .4,293.°C 6
Farnham .....300..C 8
Ferrum ......400..D 4
Fieldale ..1,499..D 5
Fincastle ...403.°C 5
Fishersville .700..B 6
Flat Gap ......C 2
Flatridge ....50..D 3
Fleeton ......C 8
Flint Hill ...200..B 6
Floris ....75..A 6
Floyd ......487.°D 4
Fordwick ....150..B 5
Forest ......250..C 5
Fork Union ..200..C 6
Fort Blackmore ....250..D 2
Fort Mitchell .150..D 6
Fort Monroe (part of Hampton) ......A 9
Fosters Falls .200..D 4
Fox ....30..D 3
Fox Hill (part of Hampton) ....C 8
Franconia* .3,000..B 7
Franklin ..7,264††D 8
Franklin Park* .1,300..B 7
Fredericks Hall ....60..C 7
Fredericksburg ..13,639††B 7
Free Union ...60..B 6
Fries ......1,039..D 4
Front Royal .7,949.°B 6
Gainesville ..150..A 6
Galax .....5,254††D 4
Garrisonville .200..B 7
Gasburg .....100..D 7
Gate City ..2,142.°D 2
Glade Spring 1,407..D 3
Gladstone ...150..C 5
Gladys ......180..C 5
Glamorgan ....D 2
Glasgow ...1,091..C 5
Glass ....40..D 5
Glen Lyn* ...222..C 4
Glen Wilton .300..C 5
Glenallen ...500..C 7
Glenwood* .1,857..D 5
Gloucester ..500.°C 8
Gold Hill .....C 5
Goochland ...200.°C 7
Goode ....250..C 5
Gordonsville 1,109..B 6
Gore ....200..A 6
Goshen .....99..C 5
Grafton .....200..A 8
Gray ....40..D 2
Green Bay ...100..C 6
Green Cove ..200..D 3
Greenbackville 300..B 9
Greenfield ..140..C 6
Greenville ..400..B 5
Greenwich ...100..A 6
Gressitt .....300..C 8
Gretna .....900..D 5
Grottoes ....969..B 6
Grove ....A 8
Groveton ....400..A 7
Grundy ....2,287.°C 2
Guinea ....75..B 7
Gum Spring ...40..C 7
Gwynn ....400..C 8
Halifax .....792.°D 6
Hallwood ....269..C 9
Hamilton ....403..A 7
Hampden .....200..C 6
Hampton ..89,258††C 8
Handsom ......90..D 7
Hanover .....250.°C 7
Hansonville ..80..D 2
Harborton ...350..C 9
Harman .....700..C 2
Harmony ......40..D 5
Harris Grove .100..A 8

††Independent City, not part of any county.
*Does not appear on the map; key shows general location.

°County Seat.
Source: Latest census figures.

Harrison-
burg ....11,916††.°B 6
Hartfield ....200..C 8
Hayfield ....150..A 6
Haymarket .257 B 7
Haysi ....485..C 2
Healing
Springs ....200..C 8
Heathsville ..225.°C 8
Hebron ....20..C 7
Henry ....125..D 5
Herndon ..1,960..B 7
Hewlett ....200..C 7
Highland
Park* ..2,500..D 8
Highland
Springs ..5,000..C 7
Hillsboro* ..124..C 6
Hillsville ..905.°D 4
Hiltons ....250..D 2
Hiwassee ....400..D 4
Hobson ....250..A 8
Holland ....338..D 8
Hollins ..1,000..C 5
Holmes Run
Acres* ..1,000..B 7
Holmes Run
Park* ..1,000..B 7
Honaker ....851..C 3
Hopewell ..17,895††C 7
Hornsbyville ..525..A 8
Hot Springs ..200..C 5
Huddleston ....85..C 5
Hume ....130..B 7
Huntly ....25..B 6
Hurley ....400..C 2
Hurt ....800..C 5
Hustle ....65..B 7
Hybla
Valley* ..1,500..B 7
Idlewilde
(part of
Covington) ....C 4
Independence .679.°D 3
Indian Valley .75..D 4
Inman* ....650..D 2
Interior ....40..C 4
Iron Gate ....716..C 5
Irvington ....570..C 8
Isle of Wight ..60.°D 8
Ivanhoe ....800..D 4
Ivor ....398..D 8
Ivy ....250..B 6
Jamestown ....5..A 8
Jamesville ....300..C 9
Jarratt ....608..D 7
Java ....25..D 5
Jefferson
Village* ..2,000..B 7
Jeffersonton ..300..B 7
Jennings
Ordinary ....50..C 6
Jericho* ..2,300..D 8
Jerome ....75..B 6
Jetersville ....175..C 6
Jewell Ridge ..500..C 3
Jones ....B 7
Jonesville ....711.°D 1
Jordan Mines ..30..C 4
Keeling ....30..D 5
Keezletown ....175..B 6
Keller ....263..C 9
Kenbridge ..1,188..D 6
Kents Store ....20..C 6
Kerrs Creek ....C 5
Keswick ....300..C 6
Keysville ....733..C 6
Kilmarnock ..927..C 8
Kimballton ..350..C 4
King and Queen
Court House .65.°C 8
King George ..240.°B 7
King William ..40.°C 7
Kinsale ....250..B 8
Kiptopeke ....A 9
Konnarock ....400..D 3
Laburnum
Manor* ..2,500..C 7
Lacey Spring ..170..B 6
LaCrosse ....726..D 6
Ladysmith ....100..B 7
Lake Bar-
croft* ..1,800..B 7
Lakeside ..19,000..C 7
Lambsburg ....250..D 4
Lancaster ....100.°C 8
Langley ....500..A 7
Laurel ....500..C 7
Laurel Fork ....25..D 4
Lawrenceville 1,941.°D 7
Lawyers ....15..C 6
Layman ....C 4
Leatherwood ....D 5
Lebanon ..2,085.°D 2
Leesburg ..2,869.°A 7
Lenox* ..1,520..D 8
Lewinsville ....60..A 7
Lewis
Gardens* ..1,380..C 7

Lexington ...7,537.°C 5
Lightfoot ....300..C 8
Lignum ....120..B 7
Lilburn ....C 7
Limeton ....100..B 6
Lincoln ....150..A 7
Linville ....180..B 6
Littleton ....40..D 7
Lively ....350..C 8
Lloyd Place* 2,282..B 7
Lodi ....35..D 3
Long Island ..75..C 5
Longfork ....C 2
Longview ....A 8
Lorne ....100..C 7
Lorton ....25..A 7
Louisa ....576.°B 7
Lovettsville ..217..A 7
Lovingston ..375.°C 6
Lowmoor ....900..C 5
Lunenburg ....40.°D 6
Luray ....3,014.°B 6
Lurich ....50..C 4
Lynch Station 400..C 5
Lynch-
burg ...54,790††C 5
Madison ....301.°B 6
Madison
Heights ..3,000..C 5
Maggie ....25..C 4
Magnolia ....160..A 8
Mallow* ....300..C 5
Manakin ....330..C 7
Manassas ..3,555.°B 8
Manassas
Park* ..5,342..B 7
Mangohick ....50..C 7
Mannboro ....25..C 7
Manteo ....25.°C 6
Mappsville ..150..C 9
Marion ....8,385.°D 3
Markham ....100..B 7
Marshall ....500..B 7
Martins-
ville ..18,798††.°D 5
Maryus ....200..C 8
Mathews ....500.°C 8
Matoaca ....2,000..C 7
Maurertown ..225..B 7
Max Meadows .900..D 4
Maxie ....370..C 2
Mayo ....50..D 5
McClure ....500..C 2
McDowell ....127..B 5
McGaheysville ..250..B 6
McKenney ....519..D 7
McLean ..2,000..B 7
Meadows of
Dan ....30..D 4
Meadowview ..750..D 3
Mechanicsville ..C 7
Meherrin ....300..C 6
Melfa* ....409..C 9
Meredithville ..60..D 7
Merrifield ..1,000..A 7
Messick
(part of
Poquoson) ....C 8
Middlebrook ..140..B 5
Middleburg ..761..B 7
Middletown ..378..A 6
Midland ....100..B 7
Midlothian ..400..C 7
Midway Island ..B 7
Mila ....25..C 8
Milford ....250..B 7
Millboro ....300..C 5
Millwood ....400..A 6
Mineral ....366..B 7
Mitchelltown ..400..B 5
Mollusk ....325..C 8
Moneta ....170..C 5
Monroe ....800..C 5
Montebello ....50..C 5
Monterey ....270.°B 5
Montpelier ....125..C 7
Montpelier
Station ....150..B 6
Montross ....394.°B 8
Montvale ....500..C 5
Morattico ....250..C 8
Morrisville ....100..B 7
Moseley ....100..C 7
Mount Airy ....45..D 5
Mount Clinton 170..B 6
Mount Heron ..100..C 2
Mount Jackson 722..B 6
Mount Sidney .500..B 6
Mount Solon ..140..B 6
Mount Vernon 101..B 7
Mountain Grove 25..B 5
Mountain Valley .D 5
Nansemond ..120..A 8
Naola ....50..C 5
Narrows ..2,508..C 4
Naruna ....250..C 5
Nassawadox ..650..C 9
Nathalie ....125..D 6
Natural Bridge 600..C 5

Naxera ....250..C 8
Nellysford ...140..C 6
New Alex-
andria* ..1,500..B 7
New Canton ..350..C 6
New Castle ..200.°C 4
New Church ..250..C 9
New Kent ....25.°C 8
New Market ..783..B 6
New Point ....100..C 8
New River ....600..C 4
Newington ...180..A 7
Newland ....90..B 8
Newport ....100..C 4
Newport
News ...113,662††D 8
Newsoms ....423..D 7
Newtown ....65..C 7
Nickelsville ...291..D 2
Nokesville ....100..B 7
Nora ....200..C 3
Norfolk ...304,869††D 8
Norfolk
Highlands* 1,000..D 8
North ....150..C 8
North Holston 200..D 3
North Linkhorn
Park* ....300..D 8
North
Pulaski* ..1,156..C 4
North Spring-
field* ....5,000..B 7
North Taze-
well ....713..C 3
Norton ....5,013††D 2
Norvello ....75..D 6
Nottoway ....100.°C 6
Oak Grove ....400..B 8
Oakton ....350..A 6
Oakwood ....250..C 3
Occoquan ....301..B 7
Olive* ....7,000..D 8
Onancock ..1,759..C 9
Onley ....415..C 9
Ontario ....100..D 6
Orange ....2,955.°B 6
Ore Bank
(part of
Arvonia) ....C 6
Oriskany ....110..C 5
Oyster ....250..C 9
Paint Bank ..100..C 4
Painter ....349..C 9
Palmyra ....350.°C 6
Pamplin ....312..C 6
Pardee ....200..C 2
Paris ....100..A 7
Parker ....100..C 8
Parklawn* ..1,000..B 7
Parksley ....850..C 9
Parrott ....650..C 4
Partlow ....30..B 7
Patrick
Springs ....500..D 4
Patterson ....400..C 3
Pearisburg ..2,268.°C 4
Pedlar Mills ....35..C 5
Pembroke ..1,038..C 4
Penhook ....45..D 5
Pennington
Gap ....1,799..D 1
Penola ....25..C 7
Perrin ....300..C 8
Peters-
burg ...36,750††C 7
Phoebus
(part of
Hampton) ....A 8
Phenix ....259..C 6
Pilgrim Knob .100..C 3
Pimmet
Hill* ....1,000..B 7
Piney River ...300..C 5
Pipers Gap ...25..D 4
Pleasant
Hill* ....2,636..D 8
Plum Point ....200..C 8
Pocahontas ..1,313..C 3
Poindexter ....B 7
Point Pleasant ....C 3
Poplar
Heights* ..1,000..B 7
Poquoson ..4,278..C 8
Port
Republic ....500..B 6
Port Royal ...128..B 7
Ports-
mouth 114,773††.°D 8
Pound ....1,135..C 2
Powhatan ....300.°C 7
Prince George ..80.°C 7
Prospect ....125..C 6
Providence
Forge ....130..C 7
Pulaski ...10,469.°C 4
Purcellville ..1,419..A 7
Purdy ....100..D 7
Quicksby ....150..B 6
Quimby ....200..C 9

Radford ...9,371††C 4
Raphine ....300..C 5
Rapidan ....220..B 6
Raven ....900..C 3
Rawlings ....50..D 7
Rectortown ...250..B 7
Red Ash ....500..C 3
Red House ....50..C 6
Redlawn ....40..D 8
Redoak ....50..D 6
Reedville ....400..C 8
Remington ...288..B 7
Rescue ....325..D 8
Reusens (part of
Lynchburg) ....C 5
Rice ....300..C 6
Rich Creek ...748..C 4
Richlands ..4,963..C 3
Rich-
mond ..219,958††.°C 7
Richmond
Heights ....100..B 9
Ridge* ...20,000..C 7
Ridgeway ....524..D 5
Rileyville ....250..B 6
Riner ....125..C 4
Ringgold ....150..D 5
Riverton ....250..B 6
Riverville ....50..C 6
Roanoke ...97,110††C 5
Rocky Gap ...250..C 3
Rocky Mount 1,412.°C 5
Roda ....300..D 2
Rose Hill ....600..D 1
Roseville ....30..B 7
Round Hill ...430..A 7
Rowe ....125..C 2
Rural Retreat .413..D 3
Rushmere ....125..A 8
Rustburg ....350.°C 5
Ruthville ....150..C 7
St. Charles ...368..D 1
St. Clair
Bottom ....200..D 3
St. Paul ....1,156..D 2
Salem ...16,058.°C 4
Saltville ....2,844..D 3
Saluda ....300.°C 8
Sandston ....4,500..C 7
Sandy Level ...20..D 5
Saratoga
Place* ..1,478..B 7
Savedge ....60..C 7
Saxe ....125..D 6
Saxis ....577..C 9
Schley ....175..C 8
Schuyler ....450..C 6
Scottsburg ....188..D 6
Scottsville ....353..C 6
Seaford ....900..C 8
Sealston ....150..B 7
Sebrell ....200..D 7
Sedley ....500..D 8
Selma ....850..C 5
Severn ....300..C 8
Sharps ....100..C 8
Shawsville ....300..C 4
Shenandoah .1,839..B 6
Shipman ....500..C 6
Shorts Creek ...50..D 4
Singers Glen .102..B 6
Skippers ....75..D 7
Sleepy
Hollow* ..1,200..B 7
Smithfield ....917..D 8
Snowville ....100..C 4
Somerton ....35..D 8
South
Boston ....5,974††D 6
South Hill ..2,569..D 6
Speedwell ....200..D 3
Spencer ....200..D 4
Sperryville ....300..B 6
Spotsylvania ..150.°B 7
Spout Spring ..100..C 5
Spring
Garden ....100..D 5
Spring Valley ..25..D 3
Springfield ..10,783..A 7
Stafford ....500.°B 7
Stanardsville ..283.°B 6
Stanley ....1,039..B 6
Stanleytown ..500..D 5
Starkey ....400..C 4
Staunton ..22,232††.°B 5
Stephens City .876..A 6
Sterling ....300..A 7
Stewartsville ..150..C 5
Stonega ....800..D 2
Stony Creek ...437..D 7
Strasburg ..2,428..B 6
Stratford
Hills* ..1,200..C 7
Stuart ....974.°D 4
Stuarts Draft .600..C 5
Suffolk ..12,609††.°D 8
Sugar Grove ...800..D 3
Sunset Hills ...100..A 6
Surry ....288.°C 8

Susan ....350..C 8
Sussex ....75.°D 7
Sutherland ....65..C 7
Sweet Briar ...850..C 5
Sweet Hall ....50..C 8
Sylvatus ....100..D 4
Tangier ....876..C 9
Tappahan-
nock ...1,086.°C 8
Tazewell ..3,000.°C 3
Temperance-
ville ....400..C 9
Thaxton ....150..C 5
The Hollow ...25..D 4
The Plains ...484..B 7
Tidewater ....170..C 8
Timber Ridge ...C 5
Timberlake* .2,400..C 5
Timberville ...412..B 6
Tiptop ....100..C 3
Toano ....250..C 8
Toga ....100..C 8
Toms Brook ...244..B 6
Toms Creek ...250..D 2
Townsend ....120..C 9
Trammel ....900..C 2
Triangle ....2,948..B 7
Triplet ....250..D 7
Trout Dale ....273..D 3
Troutville ....524..C 5
Troy ....40..C 6
Truhart ....55..C 8
Turbeville ....75..D 5
Tye River ....130..C 6
Tyler Park* .1,000..B 7
Union Hall ....50..D 5
Unionville ....250..B 7
Upperville ....250..B 7
Urbanna ....512..C 8
Valley Center ..30..B 5
Vanderpool ....25..B 5
Vansant ....850..C 2
Varina ....100..B 9
Verona ....500..B 6
Vesuvius ....400..C 5
Victoria ....1,737..D 6
Vienna ...11,440..B 7
Village ....140..C 3
Vinton ....3,432..C 5
Virgilina ....286..D 6
Virginia
Beach ...85,218††D 9
Volens ....50..D 6
Volney ....40..D 3
Wachapreague 507..C 9
Wakefield ..1,015..D 8
Wallace ....200..D 2
Walters ....135..D 8
Warfield ....80..D 7
Warm
Springs ....300.°B 5
Warrenton ..3,522.°B 7
Warsaw ....549.°C 8
Washington ....255.°B 6
Water View ...150..C 8
Waterford ....247..A 7
Waverly ....1,601..C 7
Waynes-
boro ...15,694††B 6
Weber City* .1,274..D 2
Weems ....250..C 8
Wellington ..8,000..B 7
West Augusta ...B 5
West Lawn* 1,400..B 7
West Point ..1,678..C 8
Weyers Cave ..300..B 6
Whaleyville ....402..D 8
White Hall ....55..B 6
White Plains ...50..D 7
White Post ...200..A 6
White Stone ...395..C 8
Whitmell ....35..D 5
Wicomico ....300..C 8
Willis ....70..D 4
Willis Wharf ..528..C 9
Willow
Lawn* ..2,500..C 7
Wilsons ....150..C 7
Win-
chester 15,110††.°A 6
Windsor ....579..D 8
Winterpock ...130..C 7
Wirtz ....75..C 5
Wise ....2,154.°D 2
Woodbridge .1,100..B 7
Woodlawn ....30..D 4
Woodley
Hills* ..2,000..B 7
Woodstock ..2,083.°B 6
Woodway ....400..D 2
Woolwine ....100..D 4
Wylliesburg ...150..D 6
Wytheville ..5,634.°D 3
Yale ....150..D 7
Yorkshire* .1,500..B 7
Yorktown ....311.°C 8
Zuni ....155..A 7

††Independent City, not part of any county.
*Does not appear on the map; key shows general location.

°County Seat.
Source: Latest census figures.

VIRGINIA /People

The 1960 United States census reported that Virginia had 3,966,949 persons. The population had increased 20 per cent over the 1950 figure, 3,318,680. The U.S. Bureau of the Census estimated that by 1965 the state's population had reached about 4,416,000.

Nearly two-fifths of Virginia's people live in the metropolitan areas of Lynchburg, Newport News-Hampton, Norfolk-Portsmouth, Richmond, and Roanoke. These five areas are Standard Metropolitan Statistical Areas as defined by the U.S. Bureau of the Budget (see METROPOLITAN AREA). For their populations, see the *Index* to the political map of Virginia. About 14 per cent of Virginia's people live in Alexandria, Arlington County, Fairfax, Fairfax County, and

POPULATION

This map shows the *population density* of Virginia, and how it varies in different parts of the state. Population density means the average number of persons who live on each square mile.

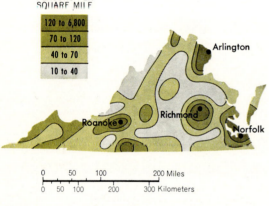

PERSONS PER SQUARE MILE

120 to 6,800	
70 to 120	
40 to 70	
10 to 40	

0   50   100   200 Miles
0 50 100   200   300 Kilometers

WORLD BOOK map

Virginia Dept. of Conservation and Economic Development

Sunbathers Relax on the sandy beaches of the Potomac River in Westmoreland State Park. Residents of Richmond and of the Washington, D.C., area often spend summer weekends in the park.

Falls Church. These cities and counties form part of the Washington, D.C.-Maryland-Virginia metropolitan area.

Almost all Virginians were born in the United States. Many are of English, German, or Scotch-Irish ancestry. About 21 per cent of the people are Negroes.

Southern Baptists and Methodists make up the largest religious groups in Virginia. Other religious groups, in order of size, include National Baptists, Roman Catholics, Presbyterians, and Episcopalians.

Virginia Dept. of Conservation and Economic Development

Social Life in small Virginia towns often centers around informal luncheons. Townspeople also meet at club picnics and church socials. These businessmen in Exmore are discussing their town's commercial affairs.

Schools. The Syms Free School was founded at Hampton in 1634, and the Eaton Free School began there about 1640. These were the first free schools in what is now the United States. Some Virginia planters and merchants established private schools called *oldfield schools*. They built these schools in open fields. Beginning in the mid-1700's, many *academies* were founded. The academies were combined elementary schools and high schools. In 1810, the general assembly created a Literary Fund to help poor children receive an education.

Virginia's state-wide public-school system began in 1870. Like most other southern states, Virginia had separate schools for Negroes and whites. State law required children between the ages of 7 and 16 to attend school. In 1954, the Supreme Court of the United States ruled that racial segregation in public schools is unconstitutional. Five years later, in 1959, some Virginia schools began to desegregate. The state's school attendance law was repealed in 1959. That same year, Prince Edward County closed its public schools to avoid integration. The county reopened the schools in 1964. Many school districts have passed local school attendance laws.

A seven-member board of education administers Virginia's school system. The governor appoints a superintendent of public instruction to serve during the governor's term of office. For the number of students and teachers in Virginia, see EDUCATION (table).

The College of William and Mary, founded in Williamsburg in 1693, is the second oldest institution of higher learning in the United States. Harvard University is the oldest. Phi Beta Kappa, the honorary scholastic society, was founded at William and Mary in 1776 (see PHI BETA KAPPA).

Libraries and Museums. Virginia's first public library was established in Alexandria in 1794. Today, the state has more than 70 public libraries and 25 bookmobiles. The State Library in Richmond, founded in 1828, is the largest library in Virginia that is not connected with a college or university.

The White House of the Confederacy, now known also as the Confederate Museum, was Jefferson Davis' Richmond home. It has more than 16,000 Civil War relics, including the original provisional constitution of the Confederacy. The Battle Abbey in Richmond has pictures of Civil War battles and southern heroes.

The Virginia Museum of Fine Arts in Richmond is the oldest state-supported art museum in the United States. The Valentine Museum, also in Richmond, has exhibits on Richmond and Virginia history. The Mariners Museum in Newport News displays models and paintings of ships, and other items that show the development of shipping. The Edgar Allan Poe Shrine in Richmond has exhibits connected with the poet's years in that city.

University of Virginia in Charlottesville was founded in 1819 through the efforts of Thomas Jefferson. The school held its first classes in 1825. Jefferson became the institution's first rector, and held this position until his death in 1826. He designed the Rotunda, which was modeled after the Pantheon in Rome.

Ewing Galloway

Washington and Lee University in Lexington became a degree-granting institution in 1782. It was named for George Washington and Robert E. Lee. Washington gave the school its first large endowment. Lee was a president of the school.

———— UNIVERSITIES AND COLLEGES ————

Virginia has 28 regionally accredited universities and colleges. For enrollments and further information, see UNIVERSITIES AND COLLEGES (table).

Name	Location	Founded
Bridgewater College	Bridgewater	1880
Eastern Mennonite College	Harrisonburg	1917
Emory and Henry College	Emory	1836
Hampden-Sydney College	Hampden-Sydney	1776
Hampton Institute	Hampton	1868
Hollins College	Hollins College	1842
Longwood College	Farmville	1884
Lynchburg College	Lynchburg	1903
Madison College	Harrisonburg	1908
Mary Baldwin College	Staunton	1842
Medical College of Virginia	Richmond	1838
Old Dominion College	Norfolk	1930
Presbyterian School of Christian Education	Richmond	1914
Radford College	Radford	1910
Randolph-Macon College	Ashland	1830
Randolph-Macon Woman's College	Lynchburg	1891
Richmond, University of	Richmond	1830
Richmond Professional Institute	Richmond	1917
Roanoke College	Salem	1842
St. Paul's College	Lawrenceville	1888
Sweet Briar College	Sweet Briar	1901
Virginia, University of	Charlottesville	1819
Virginia Military Institute	Lexington	1839
Virginia Polytechnic Institute	Blacksburg	1872
Virginia State College	Petersburg	1882
Virginia Union University	Richmond	1899
Washington and Lee University	Lexington	1782
William and Mary, College of	Williamsburg	1693

University of Virginia

Boys' Fife and Drum Corps Parade in Williamsburg

VIRGINIA / *A Visitor's Guide*

Virginia is known for its stately old homes and other historic sites. The most popular homes include George Washington's Mount Vernon near Alexandria, and Thomas Jefferson's Monticello near Charlottesville. Williamsburg, the second colonial capital, has been restored to look as it did in colonial days. See MONTICELLO; MOUNT VERNON; WILLIAMSBURG.

Many visitors drive along the crest of the Blue Ridge. They travel on the Skyline Drive in the north, and on the Blue Ridge Parkway in the south. In spring, azaleas, dogwoods, and laurels bloom on the mountain slopes. In autumn, the leaves of hardwood trees and shrubs turn bright red, orange, and yellow.

The Atlantic Ocean, Chesapeake Bay, and tidal rivers offer beach sports, fishing, and sailing. Virginia Beach, southeast of Norfolk, is an especially popular ocean resort. Hunters seek game in Dismal Swamp and in the forested highlands of western Virginia.

PLACES TO VISIT

Following are brief descriptions of some of Virginia's many interesting places to visit.

Caverns are common in western Virginia. Many of them feature colorful limestone formations.

Churches. *Bruton Parish Church* (built from 1710 to 1715) in Williamsburg is one of the nation's oldest Episcopal churches. George Washington and Robert E. Lee worshiped at *Christ Church* (1767-1773) in Alexandria. The Second Virginia Convention met in 1775 at *St. John's Church* (1741) in Richmond. There, Patrick Henry gave his famous call for liberty or death. *St. Luke's Church* (1632) near Smithfield is thought to be the oldest brick church in the original 13 states that is still standing. *St. Paul's Church* (1739) in Norfolk was the only building left after Virginia troops burned the town in 1776. Robert E. Lee and Jefferson Davis worshiped in Richmond's *St. Paul's Episcopal Church* (1844), the "Church of the Confederacy."

Homes. *Berkeley* (1726), near Richmond, was the family home of President Benjamin Harrison and the birthplace of President William Henry Harrison. *Carter's Grove* (1751) is among the most beautiful of the old plantations along the James River. *Gunston Hall* (1755), near Lorton, was the home of George Mason, the author of the Virginia Bill of Rights. The *John Marshall House* (about 1790) in Richmond was long the home of the great Chief Justice of the United States. *Stratford Hall* (about 1730), near Montross, was the birthplace of Robert E. Lee.

Jamestown Festival Park, on the James River, has reproductions of old James Fort and of the three ships that brought the first settlers to Jamestown in 1607.

Mineral Springs are visited to promote health. They include Craig Healing Springs, Healing Springs, Hot Springs, and Warm Springs.

Natural Bridge is a famous landmark south of Lexington. Water carved away softer rock and left the hard rock that forms the bridge. See NATURAL BRIDGE.

Natural Chimneys are seven colorful rock towers. They rise more than a hundred feet near Mount Solon.

Natural Tunnel, near Gate City, is a giant passageway cut through the Purcell Ridge by the waters of Stock Creek. A railroad runs through the tunnel.

National Parks, Monuments, and Forests. The National Park Service administers many areas in Virginia. Shenandoah National Park in the Blue Ridge, George Washington Birthplace National Monument in Westmoreland County, and Booker T. Washington National Monument near Roanoke are described under their own names in WORLD BOOK. See the NATIONAL PARK article for a description of Virginia's three national historical parks. They are (1) Appomattox Court House near Appomattox; (2) Colonial, which includes Yorktown and most of Jamestown Island; and (3) Cumberland Gap, which extends into Kentucky and Tennessee.

Manassas National Battlefield Park is the site of the Battles of Manassas, or Bull Run, in 1861 and 1862. Richmond National Battlefield Park includes the sites of several battles in which Confederate forces successfully defended Richmond in 1862 and 1864. Petersburg National Battlefield is the site of the last major fighting of the Civil War. The Fredericksburg and Spotsylvania

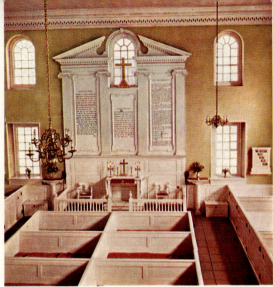

Pohick Church near Alexandria

Natural Bridge near Lexington

County Battlefields Memorial includes parts of the battlefields of Fredericksburg, Chancellorsville, the Wilderness, and Spotsylvania Court House.

State Forests and Parks. Virginia has six state forests, nine state parks, and several other historical, natural, and recreational areas. For information on Virginia's state parks, write to Director, Department of Conservation and Economic Development, Division of Parks, State Office Building, Richmond, Va. 23219.

ANNUAL EVENTS

Many of Virginia's most beautiful homes and gardens are open to the public during Historic Garden Week. This event takes place the last week in April.

Another popular event is Pony Penning on Chincoteague Island, held on the last Wednesday and Thursday in July. The ponies live on nearby Assateague Island. But at Pony Penning time they are driven across the shallow channel to Chincoteague, where some of them are sold.

Other annual events in Virginia include the following.

January-May: Robert E. Lee Birthday Celebration at Stratford Hall near Montross (January 19); International Azalea Festival in the Norfolk area (April); Founders Day Celebration at the University of Virginia in Charlottesville, on Thomas Jefferson's birthday (April 13); Shenandoah Apple Blossom Festival in Winchester (late in April); Jamestown Day in Jamestown (May 13); Horse Shows in Blacksburg, Fort Myer, and Richmond (May).

June-December: Virginia Beach Music Festival (mid-June); Highlands Arts and Crafts Festival in Abingdon (first two weeks in August); Jousting Tournament at Natural Chimneys near Mount Solon (August); Horse Shows in Hot Springs, Staunton, and Warrenton (August); Labor Day Regatta in Norfolk (first Monday in September); State Fair in Richmond (last week in September); Yorktown Day in Yorktown (October 19); Tobacco Festival in Richmond (October); Annual Autumn Pilgrimage, with tours of churches, homes, and plantations, in Tidewater region (October).

Models of Sailing Ships in Jamestown Festival Park
McLean House near Appomattox

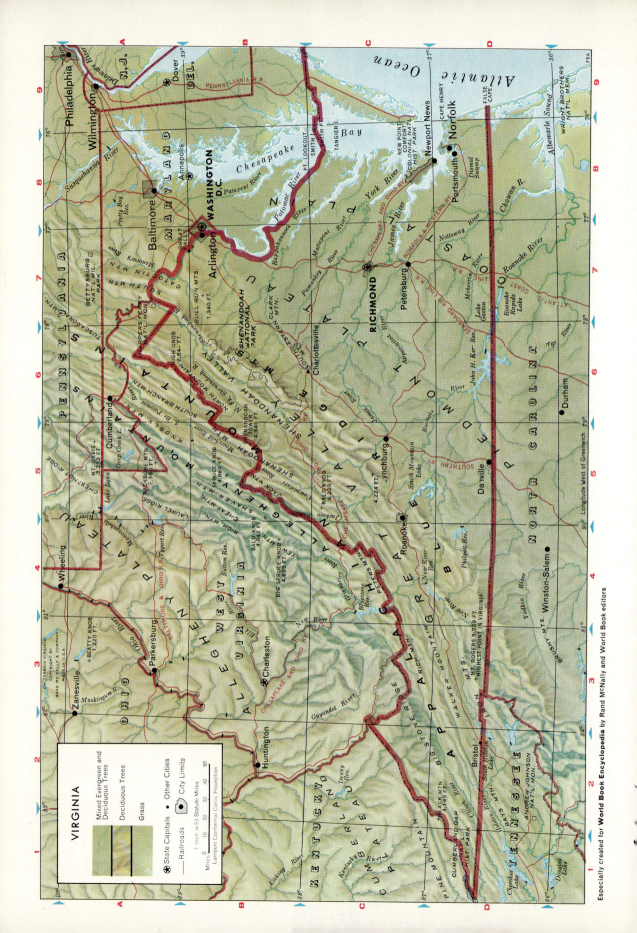

VIRGINIA

Mixed Evergreen and
Deciduous Trees

Deciduous Trees

Grass

✪ State Capitals   • Other Cities

—— Railroads   City Limits

Miles 0 10 20 30 40 50

1 inch = 53 Statute Miles

Lambert Conformal Conic Projection

Especially created for **World Book Encyclopedia** by Rand McNally and World Book editors

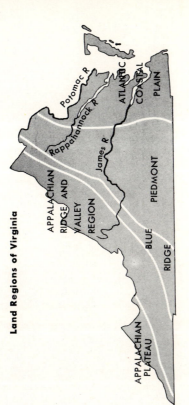

Land Regions of Virginia

Pinnacle Overlook provides a breath-taking view of Cumberland Gap National Historic Park in southwestern Virginia. From this spot, visitors can see parts of Kentucky and Tennessee.

Virginia Dept. of Conservation and Economic Development

VIRGINIA / The Land

Land Regions. Virginia has five main land regions: (1) the Appalachian Plateau, (2) the Appalachian Ridge and Valley Region, (3) the Blue Ridge, (4) the Piedmont, and (5) the Atlantic Coastal Plain.

The Appalachian Plateau is a rugged region in the southwestern part of the state. It has an average elevation of 2,000 feet. Many streams flow westward through the region. In some places, they have cut deep gorges. The plateau is covered with forests and has valuable coal fields.

The Appalachian Ridge and Valley Region consists of a series of parallel mountain ridges that extend northeast and southwest along most of the state's western border. The Great Valley, or Valley of Virginia, lies in the eastern part of this region. The Great Valley is actually a series of separate river valleys. The largest of these is the Shenandoah Valley in the north. A prominent mountain ridge, the Massanutten, divides the Shenandoah Valley into two parts for much of its length. The Appalachian Ridge and Valley Region has many caves and other rock formations created by the action of water on limestone.

The Blue Ridge borders the Appalachian Ridge and Valley Region on the east. It is the main eastern range of the Appalachian Mountain System, and an outstanding feature of Virginia. Northeast of Roanoke, the ridge is narrow and rises sharply from the lower land east and west of it. South of Roanoke, the Blue Ridge broadens into a plateau with mountain peaks, valleys, and deep ravines. The highest peaks in Virginia—Mount Rogers (5,729 feet) and Whitetop Mountain (5,520 feet)—are in the southern part of the Blue Ridge.

The Piedmont, in central Virginia, is the state's largest land region. It is an elevated, gently rolling plain, about 40 miles wide in the northeast and widening to about 140 miles wide at the North Carolina border. The Piedmont has an average elevation of 800 to 900 feet in the west. It slopes gradually to an average elevation of 200 to 300 feet in the east. Many rivers and streams flow southeastward across the Piedmont. They break into low waterfalls at the eastern edge of the region, known as the *fall line* (see FALL LINE).

The Atlantic Coastal Plain is a lowland region about a hundred miles wide that extends north and south along the Atlantic Ocean. It is sometimes called the *Tide-*

325

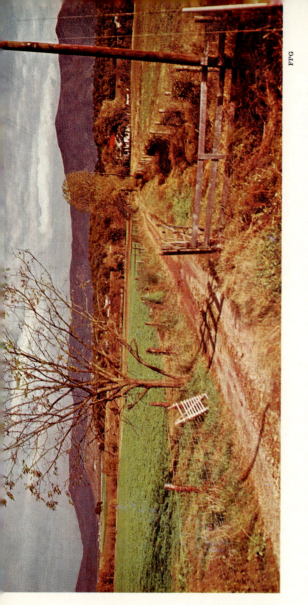

FPG

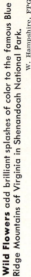

Wild Flowers add brilliant splashes of color to the famous Blue Ridge Mountains of Virginia in Shenandoah National Park.

W. Hampshire, FPG

Gently Rolling Farmland surrounds the town of Appomattox in the Piedmont, the largest land region in Virginia.

Herbert Lanks, FPG

VIRGINIA

Shenandoah Valley is a beautiful rolling area in the Appalachian Ridge and Valley Region of northwest Virginia. Many springs and caverns are scattered through the valley.

water, because tidal water flows up its bays, inlets, and rivers. Chesapeake Bay divides the region into a western mainland section and a large peninsula called the *Eastern Shore*. The region has many salt marshes and swamps. The largest of these is Dismal Swamp, in the southeast.

Coastline. Virginia has a general coastline of 112 miles. The *tidal shoreline* (including small bays and inlets) is 3,315 miles. Sand bars and islands along the coast have created several lagoons. A long, sandy beach stretches southward from the Norfolk area.

Rivers and Lakes. Several rivers flow from the western mountains and the Piedmont into Chesapeake Bay. These rivers include the Rappahannock, James, and York. They divide the Tidewater area into a series of peninsulas. The Potomac River forms Virginia's northeastern border. It is an important transportation route between Alexandria and Chesapeake Bay. The Shenandoah River flows northward through the Great Valley and empties into the Potomac.

The Roanoke River flows southeastward across the Piedmont into North Carolina. The New River begins in North Carolina and flows north and west through southwestern Virginia into West Virginia. Several rivers in the southwestern corner of the state, including the Clinch, Holston, and Powell, flow southwestward toward the Tennessee Valley.

Virginia's largest natural lake is Lake Drummond (3,200 acres) in Dismal Swamp. Many artificial lakes have been formed in the state by damming rivers for hydroelectric power, recreation, or other purposes. The largest of these man-made lakes is Buggs Island Lake on the North Carolina border. About 36,140 acres of this lake are in Virginia.

SEASONAL TEMPERATURES

JANUARY

AVERAGE OF DAILY LOW TEMPERATURES

Degrees Fahrenheit	Degrees Centigrade
32 to 36	0 to 2
28 to 32	-2 to 0
24 to 28	-4 to -2
20 to 24	-7 to -4

AVERAGE OF DAILY HIGH TEMPERATURES

Degrees Fahrenheit	Degrees Centigrade
52 to 56	11 to 13
48 to 52	9 to 11
44 to 48	7 to 9
40 to 44	4 to 7

JULY

AVERAGE OF DAILY LOW TEMPERATURES

Degrees Fahrenheit	Degrees Centigrade
70 to 74	21 to 23
66 to 70	19 to 21
62 to 66	17 to 19
58 to 62	14 to 17
54 to 58	12 to 14

AVERAGE OF DAILY HIGH TEMPERATURES

Degrees Fahrenheit	Degrees Centigrade
88 to 92	31 to 33
84 to 88	29 to 31
80 to 84	27 to 29
76 to 80	24 to 27

AVERAGE YEARLY PRECIPITATION
(Rain, Melted Snow, and Other Moisture)

Inches	Centimeters
48 to 56	122 to 142
40 to 48	102 to 122
32 to 40	81 to 102

0 50 100 200 Miles
0 100 200 300 Kilometers

MONTHLY WEATHER IN NORFOLK AND ROANOKE

	JAN	FEB	MAR	APR	MAY	JUNE	JULY	AUG	SEPT	OCT	NOV	DEC	Average of:
NORFOLK	50	51	59	66	75	84	86	85	80	70	60	57	High Temperatures
	33	33	46	56	65	69	68	64	52	43	34	34	Low Temperatures
	11	11	12	10	11	11	12	12	8	8	8	10	Days of Rain or Snow
ROANOKE	11	11	12	10	11	11	11	11	8	8	10	9	Days of Rain or Snow
	47	49	57	67	77	84	87	85	80	70	57	48	High Temperatures
	29	30	36	44	53	61	65	64	58	46	37	30	Low Temperatures

Temperatures are given in degrees Fahrenheit.

Source: U.S. Weather Bureau

FPG

Cool Sea Breezes refresh bathers at Virginia Beach. This popular resort area lies on the Atlantic Coastal Plain.

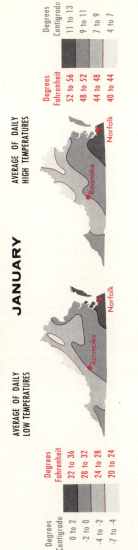

VIRGINIA/Climate

The climate of Virginia is mild and generally free of extreme heat and cold. Temperatures vary from east to west as the elevation of the land and the distance from the ocean increase. In January, temperatures average 41° F. in the Tidewater area, and about 32° F. in parts of the Blue Ridge. July temperatures average 78° F. in the Tidewater and about 68° F. in the mountains. The highest temperature recorded in the state, 110° F., occurred at Columbia on July 5, 1900, and at Balcony Falls on July 15, 1954. The record low, −29° F., occurred at Monterey on Feb. 10, 1899.

Virginia's *precipitation* (rain, melted snow, and other forms of moisture) is highest in the Shenandoah Valley, where it averages about 36 inches a year. Yearly precipitation in the south averages about 44 inches. Snowfall ranges from 5 to 10 inches in the Tidewater to 25 to 30 inches in the western mountains.

Throughout most of its history, Virginia had an agricultural economy based on tobacco and other plantation crops. Manufacturing industries grew rapidly after about 1930. Today, the economy is based largely on manufacturing. Virginia's location near highly populated areas in the northeastern United States is favorable for industry. Deposits of coal and other natural resources, good transportation by land and water, and a growing population also favor industry.

The tourist industry greatly aids the Virginia economy. About 40 million persons visit the state yearly and spend about $750 million. Virginia also benefits from the Norfolk Naval Base and from other U.S. government installations in the state. About 265,000 persons who live in Virginia are members of the U.S. armed forces or are civilian employees of the federal government. Most of them live in the Hampton Roads area or in counties and cities near Washington, D.C.

Natural Resources of Virginia include varied soils, many mineral deposits, valuable forest land, and much marine life, especially in Chesapeake Bay.

Soil. Most of the western, mountainous part of Virginia has shallow, rocky soils. The valley soils are stony and not very fertile, except in parts of the Shenandoah Valley and other areas where the soil contains much lime. Soils are stony and shallow in the northern part of the Blue Ridge, but deeper and darker in the southwest. Piedmont soils are generally light in color and have a loamy texture. Most soils in the Atlantic Coastal Plain are sandier than those in other parts of Virginia. The sandy soils are generally deep and easily cultivated.

Minerals. Coal is Virginia's most important mineral resource. Most of the coal is in the southwestern part of the state. Virginia's coal reserves are estimated at 12 billion tons. *Bituminous* (soft) coal makes up most of these reserves. The famous Pocahontas coal of Tazewell County is among the bituminous deposits. Virginia has deposits of *semianthracite* (fairly hard) coal in Montgomery and Pulaski counties.

Virginia stones include basalt, granite, limestone, marble, sandstone, shale, slate, and soapstone. Most of the limestone is found in the western valleys. The Atlantic Coastal Plain has large deposits of clay, and sand and gravel. Lead and zinc occur in Wythe County.

PRODUCTION IN VIRGINIA

Total yearly value of goods produced—$3,728,193,000

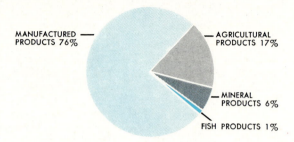

MANUFACTURED PRODUCTS 76%

AGRICULTURAL PRODUCTS 17%

MINERAL PRODUCTS 6%

FISH PRODUCTS 1%

Note: Manufacturing percentage based on value added by manufacture. Other percentages based on value of production.

Source: Latest available U.S. Government statistics

EMPLOYMENT IN VIRGINIA

Average yearly number of persons employed—1,310,194

	Number of Employees
Manufacturing	290,700
Wholesale & Retail Trade	228,800
Government	202,600
Agriculture	177,000
Services	146,500
Construction	89,200
Transportation & Public Utilities	83,600
Finance, Insurance & Real Estate	50,700
Forestry	17,250
Mining	15,900
Fishing	7,944

Source: Employment statistics supplied by employers to government agencies

Some manganese is found along the western slopes of the Blue Ridge. Other Virginia minerals include feldspar, gypsum, kyanite, mica, pyrite, salt, and titanium.

Plant Life. Commercially valuable forests cover about 60 per cent of Virginia's land area. These forests consist mainly of second- and third-growth trees. Hardwoods are the most common trees in the western part of the

Dan River Mills

Experts Classify Cotton in Danville. These *classers* inspect cotton samples cut from the bales. They judge the cotton fiber on its quality, length, and strength. After the cotton has been classified, it is sent to textile mills to be woven into cloth. Textiles are among the most valuable products manufactured in Virginia.

Shipyards operated by the Newport News Shipbuilding and Dry Dock Company are among the largest in the nation. Many famous ships come to the shipyards for repairs. This picture shows the aircraft carrier USS *Enterprise*, the world's largest ship, foreground. The *United States*, the world's fastest ocean liner, steams into a nearby berth.

Newport News Shipbuilding Photo

state. Oak is the most important hardwood for lumber production. Other hardwoods include ash, beech, birch, gum, hickory, locust, maple, and poplar. Evergreen trees are most extensive in the east. Pines, including loblolly, eastern white, pitch, and shortleaf, have the greatest value. Other evergreens in Virginia include hemlock, red cedar, and spruce.

The flowering dogwood, the state flower, blooms throughout Virginia in early spring. Wild azaleas, mountain laurels, redbuds, rhododendrons, and other flowering plants grow in the mountain areas. Wild flowers in Virginia fields and forests include blue lobelias, lowland laurels, morning-glories, and violets.

Animal Life. Deer and some elk roam the wooded areas of Virginia. Black bears and wildcats live in the western mountains and in Dismal Swamp. Small animals include foxes, muskrats, opossums, rabbits, and raccoons. Virginia has many game birds, including ducks, geese, quails, ruffed grouse, and turkeys.

Fresh-water fishes include bass, carp, perch, pickerel, pike, and trout. Drumfish, flounder, mackerel, menhaden, and shad are found in the Atlantic Ocean, in Chesapeake Bay, and in the state's many inlets. Clams, crabs, oysters, and scallops also live in Chesapeake Bay and in shallow coastal waters.

Manufacturing accounts for about 76 per cent of the value of goods produced in Virginia. Goods manufactured there have a *value added by manufacture* of about $2,851,000,000 yearly. This figure represents the value created in products by Virginia industries, not counting such costs as materials, supplies, and fuels. Virginia's chief manufactured products, in order of importance, are (1) chemicals and related products, (2) processed foods, (3) tobacco products, and (4) textiles.

Chemical Products manufactured and processed in Virginia have a value added of about $590 million yearly. The leading chemical products are synthetic fibers, such as nylon. They are made in Bridgewater, Covington, Front Royal, Martinsville, Narrows, and Waynesboro, and in Chesterfield County. Bristol, Lynchburg, and Richmond have drug factories. The largest fertilizer plants are in Danville, Hampton, Norfolk, and Portsmouth. Factories along Chesapeake Bay process fertilizer and oil from menhaden, a kind of fish.

Processed Foods account for about $296 million yearly in value added. Virginia factories produce bakery products, candy, cooking oil, dairy products, and frozen foods. Factories along Chesapeake Bay process crabs and oysters. Winchester is the center of the apple-products industry. Many Virginia factories make feed for livestock and poultry.

Tobacco Products have an annual value added of about $290 million. These products include mainly cigarettes and pipe tobacco. The largest factories are in Richmond and Petersburg.

Textiles have a value added of about $252 million yearly. Mills produce fabrics made of cotton, wool, nylon, and rayon. Among the chief textile centers are Danville, Charlottesville, Galax, Lynchburg, and Richmond.

Other Important Industries produce clothing, electrical machinery, electronics and communications equipment, furniture, lumber and wood products, metal products, transportation equipment, and products of clay, glass, pulp, and stone. The Newport News Shipbuilding and Dry Dock Company is one of the largest shipbuilding and ship-repairing centers in the United States. Portsmouth and Norfolk also have shipyards.

Agriculture. Virginia has a farm income of about 633\frac{1}{2}$ million a year. This figure represents about 17 per cent of the value of all goods produced in the state. Virginia has about 97,600 farms. They average 135 acres in size.

Livestock, dairying, and poultry raising provide more than half of Virginia's farm income. Farmers raise beef and dairy cattle in all parts of the state. They also raise hogs, horses, and sheep. The state is known for its Smithfield hams, which come from peanut-fed hogs. Virginia is a leading producer of broiler chickens and turkeys. Rockingham County is one of the leading counties in the United States in turkey production.

Virginia is a major tobacco-producing state. Farmers grow tobacco on only a small part of Virginia's cropland. But tobacco provides more farm income than any other crop. Most of the tobacco is grown in the Piedmont region south of the James River. Other leading field crops include corn, hay, and soybeans. Peanuts are grown in the southeast, especially around Suffolk. Winter wheat is raised in the Shenandoah Valley.

Most commercial production of vegetables takes place near Chesapeake Bay. The state's leading vegetable crops include asparagus, beans, cucumbers, lettuce, potatoes, and spinach. Apple orchards cover many

328a

FARM, MINERAL, AND FOREST PRODUCTS

This map shows where the state's leading farm, mineral, and forest products are produced. The major urban areas (shown on the map in red) are the state's important manufacturing centers.

WORLD BOOK map

Millions of Apples cover the ground in Winchester in the Shenandoah Valley. These apples will later be processed into vinegar or applesauce. Virginia ranks among the leading states in the production of apples.

Tom Hollyman, Photo Researchers

E. L. Korb, Alpha

A Worker Cuts Tobacco Leaves on a farm in the Piedmont region of southern Virginia. Farmers raise tobacco on only a small part of Virginia's land. But tobacco provides more farm income than any other crop grown in the state.

A Flock of White Turkeys gathers around the feeding trough on a farm in Rockingham County in northwestern Virginia. This county is one of the leading counties in the United States in the production of turkeys. Virginia is also known for its Smithfield hams, which come from hogs raised on peanuts.

Bradley Smith, Photo Researchers

328b

acres in Virginia, especially in the western valleys. The state also has peach and pear orchards. Strawberries are a leading crop on the Eastern Shore.

Mining accounts for about 6 per cent of the value of goods produced in Virginia, or about $222,494,000 a year. Coal is the most important mining product. The state produces about 31,654,000 tons of coal yearly. Bituminous coal comes from Buchanan, Dickenson, Russell, Tazewell, and Wise counties. Most of the state's semianthracite coal is mined in Montgomery County.

Stone production in Virginia totals about 22,934,000 tons a year. Limestone from the western valleys is used in making cement and lime. Albemarle and Nelson counties have the largest soapstone quarries in the United States. Basalt, granite, marble, and sandstone are also quarried in the state. Sand and gravel production takes place on the Atlantic Coastal Plain.

Zinc is mined in Wythe County. Virginia also produces brick clay, gypsum, kyanite, salt, and yellow ocher.

Fishing Industry. Virginia ranks among the leading fishing states. Its yearly fish catch has a value of about $21,701,000. Virginia leads the nation in crab and oyster production. Other seafoods include clams, drumfish, flounder, mackerel, scallops, and shad. Menhaden are processed into fertilizer and oil.

Electric Power. Most of Virginia's electric power comes from steam plants that burn coal. The main steam plants are near the large cities in the eastern part of the state. Hydroelectric power plants operate at Philpott Dam on the Smith River and at John H. Kerr and Smith Mountain dams on the Roanoke River. For Virginia's kilowatt-hour production, see ELECTRIC POWER (table).

Transportation. The Little River Turnpike was the first U.S. toll road. It was built in the late 1780's from Alexandria to Snicker's Gap in the Blue Ridge. Today, almost all of Virginia's 50,800 miles of roads and highways are paved. Long bridges cross the Tidewater rivers. The 23-mile-long Chesapeake Bay Bridge-Tunnel connects the Tidewater mainland at Norfolk with the Eastern Shore at Cape Charles.

The first Virginia railroad began operating in 1831. It carried coal on flatcars pulled by mules. The 12-mile-long wooden track went from the mines of Chesterfield County to Richmond. Today, Virginia has about 3,730 miles of railroad track.

About 95 airports serve Virginia. Dulles International Airport, the largest airport in the United States, lies near Chantilly. Washington National Airport is near Alexandria. Charlottesville, Lynchburg, Newport News, Norfolk, Richmond, and Roanoke also have major airports.

Large ships can travel on Chesapeake Bay and up the James and Potomac rivers for many miles. Hampton Roads, at the junction of the James, Nansemond, and Elizabeth rivers, is an important harbor area. Norfolk, on Hampton Roads, is one of the leading ports in the United States. Other important ports include Newport News on Hampton Roads, Alexandria on the Potomac, and Hopewell and Richmond on the James. The Dismal Swamp Canal and the Albemarle and Chesapeake Canal form part of the Atlantic Intracoastal Waterway (see ATLANTIC INTRACOASTAL WATERWAY).

Communication. In 1736, William Parks, Virginia's public printer, founded the *Virginia Gazette*, the first newspaper in the colony. The *Alexandria Gazette* began in 1784 as a weekly, and became a daily in 1800. It is one of the oldest continuously published dailies in the United States. The *Richmond Times-Dispatch*, the *Richmond News Leader*, and the *Virginian-Pilot* of Norfolk are among the most widely read newspapers in the South.

Virginia's first commercial radio station, WTAR, began operating in Norfolk in 1923. The state's first television station, WTVR, was established in Richmond in 1948. Today, Virginia has 143 radio stations and 11 television stations.

VIRGINIA / History

Indian Days. When the first English colonists arrived in the Virginia region, Indian tribes of three major language groups lived there. The Powhatan, members of the Algonkian language group, lived in the coastal area. The Monacan and Manahoac, who spoke the Siouan language, occupied the Piedmont region. Other Siouan tribes in the Virginia region included the Nahyssan along the James River, and the Occaneechi on the Roanoke River. Other major tribes in the region spoke the Iroquoian language. They included the Susquehanna near the upper Chesapeake Bay, the Cherokee in the southwest, and the Nottoway in the southeast.

Early Settlement. The first Europeans who settled in Virginia were a group of Spanish Jesuits. In 1570, they established a mission, perhaps on the York River. Indians wiped out the settlement a few months later.

In 1584, Queen Elizabeth I of England gave the English adventurer Sir Walter Raleigh permission to establish colonies in America. Raleigh and others soon sent expeditions there. These expeditions failed because they did not have enough supplies. Raleigh and Queen Elizabeth gave the name *Virginia* to what is now the eastern part of the United States.

The Jamestown Settlement. In 1606, King James I chartered the Virginia Company of London (often called the London Company) for colonization purposes. In May, 1607, colonists sent by the company established the first permanent English settlement in America, at Jamestown. The colony, led by Captain John Smith, survived many hardships. In 1609, Smith was injured and had to return to England. The following winter, so many settlers died from lack of food that the period became known as the *starving time*. In the spring, the discouraged colonists started to leave Jamestown. But they returned after they met the ships of Governor Thomas West, Lord de la Warr, at Hampton Roads. The ships brought supplies and new colonists. After Lord de la Warr returned to England, Thomas Gates and Thomas Dale served as deputy governors.

Progress of the Colony. John Rolfe, one of the colonists, began to raise tobacco in 1612. Rolfe developed a method of curing tobacco. He proved that tobacco

VIRGINIA

could be successfully exported. Tobacco exporting helped save the colony by giving the people a way to support themselves. In 1614, Rolfe married Pocahontas, a daughter of Powhatan, chief of the Indian confederation around Jamestown. Their marriage brought a period of peace between the Indians and the colonists.

By 1619, each free colonist had been granted land of his own. That year, the Virginia Company made plans to send a boatload of young women to the colony to become wives of the lonely settlers. Also in 1619, Dutch traders brought Negroes to Virginia for the first time.

The first representative legislature in America, the House of Burgesses, was formed in 1619. Its first meeting was called by Governor George Yeardley, who acted on instructions from the Virginia Company. The House of Burgesses met with the governor and his council to make laws for the colony. This combined lawmaking body was called the General Assembly of Virginia.

Powhatan, the friendly Indian chief, died in 1618. In 1622, his successor, Chief Opechancanough, led an attack on the colonists and massacred 347 of them.

Royal Governors and Cromwell. In 1624, King James I revoked the Virginia Company's charter and made Virginia a royal colony. The colonists often quarreled with the royal governors sent by England. Sir William Berkeley, governor from 1642 to 1652, had

IMPORTANT DATES IN VIRGINIA

1607 The Virginia Company of London established Jamestown.

1612 John Rolfe helped save the colony by introducing tobacco growing and exporting.

1619 America's first representative legislature, the House of Burgesses, met in Jamestown. Dutch traders brought the first Negroes to Jamestown.

1624 Virginia became a royal colony.

1676 Nathaniel Bacon led a rebellion against the government.

1693 The College of William and Mary was founded.

1775 George Washington became commander in chief of the Continental Army.

1776 Virginia declared its independence and adopted its first constitution. Thomas Jefferson of Virginia wrote the Declaration of Independence.

1781 Lord Cornwallis surrendered at Yorktown in the final battle of the American Revolutionary War.

1784 Virginia gave up its western land claims to the United States.

1788 Virginia became the 10th state on June 25.

1789 George Washington, a Virginian, became the first President of the United States.

1792 Kentucky was formed from three of Virginia's western counties.

1801-1825 Three Virginians served as President: Thomas Jefferson (1801-1809), James Madison (1809-1817), and James Monroe (1817-1825).

1801-1835 John Marshall of Virginia served as Chief Justice of the United States.

1841 William Henry Harrison, born in Virginia, became President. Harrison died a month later. Vice-President John Tyler, also a Virginian, became President.

1849 Zachary Taylor, another Virginian, became President.

1861-1865 Virginia seceded from the Union and became the major battleground of the Civil War.

1863 West Virginia was formed from the northwestern part of Virginia.

1870 Virginia was readmitted to the Union.

1902 The state adopted its present constitution.

1912 Woodrow Wilson became the eighth Virginian to be elected President.

1927 Governor Harry F. Byrd sponsored a reorganization of the state government.

1940-1945 New industries opened during World War II, adding to the state's industrial growth.

1959 The first public school integration in Virginia took place in Arlington County and Norfolk.

1964 The Chesapeake Bay Bridge-Tunnel connecting Norfolk and the Eastern Shore was opened.

HISTORIC VIRGINIA
The Mother of Presidents

Walnut Grove

Cyrus McCormick invented the reaper near Walnut Grove in 1831.

GEORGE WASHINGTON

THOMAS JEFFERSON

JAMES MADISON

JAMES MONROE

WILLIAM HENRY HARRISON

JOHN TYLER

ZACHARY TAYLOR

WOODROW WILSON

Cumberland Gap

Cumberland Gap was the "Gateway to the West" for many early pioneers. This high pass cuts through the Appalachian Mountains.

good relations with the colonists. But in 1652, Berkeley was forced to surrender Virginia to the rule of Oliver Cromwell, who had overthrown King Charles I.

From 1652 until Charles II became king in 1660, the Virginia colonists were allowed to take almost complete charge of their own government. In spite of the political freedom they enjoyed under Cromwell, most of the colonists remained loyal to the English royalists. Some British supporters of the future King Charles II, called *Cavaliers*, sought refuge in Virginia.

In 1660, after Berkeley had been elected by the royalist Virginia assembly, Charles II reappointed him governor. Berkeley's new term brought widespread discontent. The governor kept the same members of the House of Burgesses in office for 14 years. He also allowed a *Tidewater aristocracy* to rule the colony. This group included the heads of the wealthy eastern families.

Westward Expansion By the mid-1600's, many small farmers had pushed westward to the eastern edge of the Piedmont. This area is known as the *fall line* (see FALL LINE). The interests of the western farmers differed from those of the Tidewater aristocracy. The westerners

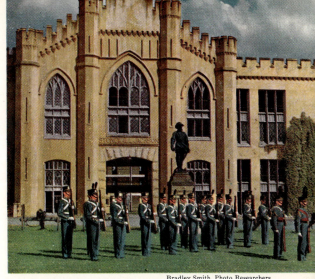

Virginia Military Institute's cadet barracks serve as a backdrop for the parade area. The Lexington college is sometimes called the *West Point of the South*. Its graduates have played an active part in every U.S. war since VMI was founded in 1839.

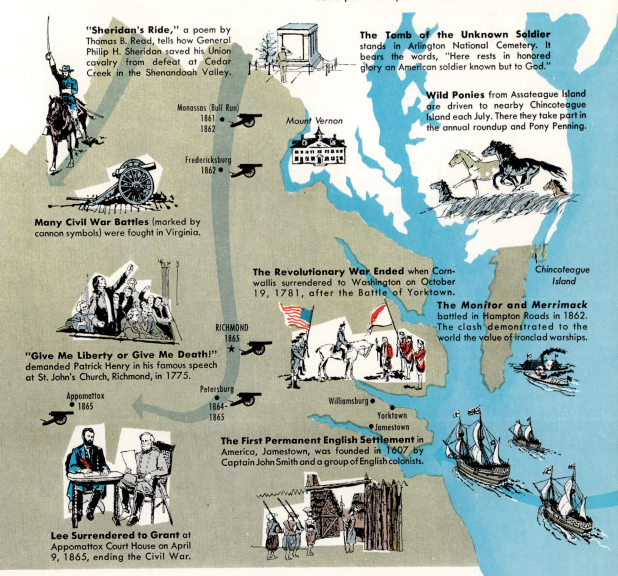

"Sheridan's Ride," a poem by Thomas B. Read, tells how General Philip H. Sheridan saved his Union cavalry from defeat at Cedar Creek in the Shenandoah Valley.

The Tomb of the Unknown Soldier stands in Arlington National Cemetery. It bears the words, "Here rests in honored glory an American soldier known but to God."

Manassas (Bull Run)
1861
1862

Mount Vernon

Wild Ponies from Assateague Island are driven to nearby Chincoteague Island each July. There they take part in the annual roundup and Pony Penning.

Fredericksburg
1862

Many Civil War Battles (marked by cannon symbols) were fought in Virginia.

The Revolutionary War Ended when Cornwallis surrendered to Washington on October 19, 1781, after the Battle of Yorktown.

Chincoteague Island

The Monitor and Merrimack battled in Hampton Roads in 1862. The clash demonstrated to the world the value of ironclad warships.

RICHMOND
1865

"Give Me Liberty or Give Me Death!" demanded Patrick Henry in his famous speech at St. John's Church, Richmond, in 1775.

Appomattox
1865

Petersburg
1864-
1865

Williamsburg

Yorktown
Jamestown

The First Permanent English Settlement in America, Jamestown, was founded in 1607 by Captain John Smith and a group of English colonists.

Lee Surrendered to Grant at Appomattox Court House on April 9, 1865, ending the Civil War.

wanted protection from the Indians, and fewer political and economic regulations. They resented the British Navigation Acts, which greatly restricted colonial trade (see NAVIGATION ACT). A group of discontented colonists rebelled in 1676. They were led by Nathaniel Bacon, a young planter (see BACON'S REBELLION). In 1699, the capital was moved from Jamestown to Williamsburg.

By 1700, Virginia had a population of about 58,000 and was the largest North American colony. The growing population took up all the land along the tidal rivers and creeks. So, many pioneers moved westward into the Piedmont, the Great Valley, and the mountains. Germans and Scotch-Irish from Pennsylvania also settled in the Great Valley. The westward expansion of the English colonists conflicted with the interests of the French, and led to the French and Indian War of 1754-1763 (see FRENCH AND INDIAN WARS).

During the early 1770's, frequent Indian raids spread terror along the western frontier. In 1774, these attacks led to a campaign against the Indians called Lord Dunmore's War, after Virginia's governor, John Murray, Earl of Dunmore. A group of Virginia soldiers led by Andrew Lewis defeated the Shawnee Indians at Point Pleasant (now in West Virginia) on Oct. 10, 1774. Indian attacks then decreased in western Virginia.

The Course Toward Independence. Like many other colonists, Virginia's leaders were disturbed by the laws passed by the English Parliament without the consent of the colonies (see REVOLUTIONARY WAR IN AMERICA [Causes of the War]). Although most Virginians were loyal to the king, they favored liberty and wanted to govern their own affairs. Virginia's western leaders, including Patrick Henry and Thomas Jefferson, led the way in voicing the complaints of the colonists. Patrick Henry's resolutions, called the Virginia Resolves, helped arouse the colonists against the Stamp Act in 1765 (see STAMP ACT).

In 1774, the English Parliament ordered the port of Boston closed, following the Boston Tea Party in 1773 (see BOSTON TEA PARTY). The House of Burgesses, in sympathy with the Boston colonists, made the day of the port closing a day of fasting and prayer. This action angered Lord Dunmore, and he dissolved the House of Burgesses. Its members then met without official permission on Aug. 1, 1774, in Williamsburg. They called themselves the First Virginia Convention. The members elected delegates to the First Continental Congress (see CONTINENTAL CONGRESS). A Virginia delegate, Peyton Randolph, was chosen president of the congress.

At the Second Virginia Convention, on March 23, 1775, at St. John's Church in Richmond, Patrick Henry made his famous plea for the colonial cause: "Is life so dear or peace so sweet as to be purchased by the chains of slavery? Forbid it, Almighty God! I know not what course others may take, but as for me, give me liberty or give me death!"

Independence and Statehood. In 1775, the Second Continental Congress elected George Washington, a Virginian, as commander in chief of the Continental Army. Virginia became an independent commonwealth in June, 1776, when it adopted its first constitution. The constitution included a declaration of rights written by George Mason. This declaration was the first bill of rights in an American constitution. Patrick Henry was elected as the commonwealth's first governor. The capital of the commonwealth was moved from Williamsburg to Richmond in 1780.

Virginia militiamen drove Lord Dunmore from the colony after several skirmishes early in July, 1776. Also in 1776, the colony submitted to the Continental Congress a resolution calling for American independence (see DECLARATION OF INDEPENDENCE).

During the Revolutionary War (1775-1783), a larger proportion of persons in Virginia opposed the English than in any other southern colony. The Declaration of Independence was written by Thomas Jefferson, who later served as the state's second governor. Virginia also contributed the great cavalry leader "Light-Horse Harry" Lee, and Daniel Morgan, the hero of the battles of Saratoga and Cowpens. In 1778, George Rogers Clark won victories in the Northwest Territory. He took from the British Kaskaskia and Cahokia in what is now Illinois, and Vincennes in present-day Indiana. This territory had long been claimed by Virginia. In 1781, American forces won the final victory of the war on Virginia soil when Lord Cornwallis surrendered to George Washington at Yorktown.

Until 1789, the 13 former colonies were loosely joined under the Articles of Confederation (see ARTICLES OF CONFEDERATION). Virginia had *ratified* (approved) the Articles on July 9, 1778. In order to persuade Maryland to accept the Articles, Virginia promised in 1781 to give up its claim to the Northwest Territory. Virginia did so in 1784 (see NORTHWEST TERRITORY).

The Articles of Confederation soon proved ineffective. James Madison and other Virginians led in creating the Constitution of the United States to replace the Articles. Virginia ratified the Constitution on June 25, 1788, and became the 10th state of the Union. See UNITED STATES CONSTITUTION.

The Mother of Presidents. Virginia furnished the United States with four of its first five presidents— George Washington, Thomas Jefferson, James Madison, and James Monroe. Washington was elected as the first President in 1789. He appointed Jefferson as the first secretary of state, and Edmund Randolph as the first attorney general. In 1792, the westernmost counties of Virginia became the state of Kentucky.

Thomas Jefferson, James Madison, and James Monroe were often called the *Virginia Dynasty*. During their presidential terms, they strengthened the new nation and added new territory to it. Another Virginian, John Marshall, served as Chief Justice of the United States from 1801 to 1835.

In 1830, Virginia adopted a new constitution, chiefly as a result of growing discontent in the western counties. The new constitution gave the westerners more representation in the general assembly. But eastern leaders kept control of the government.

In 1841, two more Virginians became President. William Henry Harrison and John Tyler had been born in the same Virginia county. Harrison died a month after his inauguration, and Tyler became President. During the Mexican War (1846-1848), Virginia furnished many of the chief military leaders. These men included Thomas J. Jackson, Joseph E. Johnston, Robert E. Lee, and Winfield Scott. General Zachary

Taylor, known as *Old Rough and Ready*, was also born in Virginia. Largely because of his military fame, Taylor was elected President in 1848.

The western counties continued to press for reforms in government. Their demands were incorporated into the constitution of 1851. This constitution gave all white men the right to vote. It also provided for the election of the governor and other officials by popular vote. Until that time, only landowners could vote, and the general assembly had elected the governor.

The Civil War and Reconstruction. South Carolina and six other southern states withdrew from the Union during the winter of 1860-1861. But Virginia remained in the Union. Most Virginians hoped that compromise could save the Union and prevent war. President Abraham Lincoln called for troops on April 15, 1861. Two days later, a Virginia convention voted to *secede* (withdraw) from the Union. Many westerners in Virginia would not agree to secede. They set up an independent government in northwestern Virginia that stayed loyal to the Union. On June 20, 1863, 48 counties of northwestern Virginia became the state of West Virginia. Two other counties joined them in November, 1863.

Richmond was the capital of the Confederacy from May, 1861, to April, 1865, when it surrendered to Union troops. Danville served briefly as the last headquarters of the Confederacy. Virginia's Robert E. Lee gained lasting fame as the South's outstanding military leader. The state contributed other leading Confederate generals, including Stonewall Jackson, Joseph E. Johnston, George E. Pickett, and Jeb Stuart.

The South won its greatest victories on Virginia battlefields—the first and second battles of Manassas (Bull Run), Jackson's Valley Campaign, and the battles of Fredericksburg and Chancellorsville. More battles were fought in Virginia than in any other state. Union armies repeatedly tried to seize Richmond and the Shenandoah Valley. This fertile valley was called the *Granary of the Confederacy*. The 1862 battle between the *Monitor* and the *Merrimack* (renamed the *Virginia* by the Confederate navy) at Hampton Roads was the first fight between ironclad warships. This battle marked a turning point in naval warfare. The Civil War, like the Revolutionary War, ended in Virginia. Lee surrendered to General Ulysses S. Grant at Appomattox on April 9, 1865. See CIVIL WAR.

After the war, the federal government passed the Reconstruction Act of 1867, which placed Virginia under army rule as Military District No. 1. This act also provided for a state constitutional convention to draw up a new constitution for Virginia. The constitutional convention, headed by Judge John C. Underwood, met in December, 1867. It was controlled by Radical Republicans, and nearly a third of its members were Negroes. A constitution was adopted in 1869. It gave Negroes

---

THE GOVERNORS OF VIRGINIA

	Party	Term		Party	Term
Under Articles of Confederation			28. James McDowell	Democratic	1843-1846
1. Patrick Henry	None	1776-1779	29. William Smith	Democratic	1846-1849
2. Thomas Jefferson	None	1779-1781	30. John Buchanan Floyd	Democratic	1849-1852
3. William Fleming	None	1781	31. Joseph Johnson	Democratic	1852-1856
4. Thomas Nelson, Jr.	None	1781	32. Henry A. Wise	Democratic	1856-1860
5. Benjamin Harrison	None	1781-1784	33. John Letcher	Democratic	1860-1864
6. Patrick Henry	None	1784-1786	34. William Smith	Democratic	1864-1865
7. Edmund Randolph	None	1786-1788	35. Francis H. Pierpont	Republican	1865-1868
			36. Henry H. Wells	Republican	1868-1869
Under United States Constitution			37. Gilbert C. Walker	Republican	1869-1870
1. Edmund Randolph	None	1788	38. Gilbert C. Walker	Republican	1870-1874
2. Beverly Randolph	None	1788-1791	39. James L. Kemper	Democratic	1874-1878
3. Henry Lee	Federalist	1791-1794	40. Frederick W. M. Holliday	Democratic	1878-1882
4. Robert Brooke	*Dem.-Rep.	1794-1796	41. William E. Cameron	†Readjuster-Rep.	1882-1886
5. James Wood	Dem.-Rep.	1796-1799			
6. James Monroe	Dem.-Rep.	1799-1802	42. Fitzhugh Lee	Democratic	1886-1890
7. John Page	Dem.-Rep.	1802-1805	43. Philip W. McKinney	Democratic	1890-1894
8. William H. Cabell	Dem.-Rep.	1805-1808	44. Charles T. O'Ferrall	Democratic	1894-1898
9. John Tyler	Dem.-Rep.	1808-1811	45. James Hoge Tyler	Democratic	1898-1902
10. James Monroe	Dem.-Rep.	1811	46. Andrew Jackson Montague	Democratic	1902-1906
11. George William Smith	Dem.-Rep.	1811			
12. Peyton Randolph	Dem.-Rep.	1811-1812	47. Claude A. Swanson	Democratic	1906-1910
13. James Barbour	Dem.-Rep.	1812-1814	48. William Hodges Mann	Democratic	1910-1914
14. Wilson Cary Nicholas	Dem.-Rep.	1814-1816	49. Henry Carter Stuart	Democratic	1914-1918
15. James Patton Preston	Dem.-Rep.	1816-1819	50. Westmoreland Davis	Democratic	1918-1922
16. Thomas Mann Randolph	Dem.-Rep.	1819-1822	51. Elbert Lee Trinkle	Democratic	1922-1926
17. James Pleasants, Jr.	Dem.-Rep.	1822-1825	52. Harry Flood Byrd	Democratic	1926-1930
18. John Tyler, Jr.	Dem.-Rep.	1825-1827	53. John Garland Pollard	Democratic	1930-1934
19. William Branch Giles	Democratic	1827-1830	54. George C. Perry	Democratic	1934-1938
20. John Floyd	Democratic	1830-1834	55. James H. Price	Democratic	1938-1942
21. Littleton Waller Tazewell	Whig	1834-1836	56. Colgate W. Darden, Jr.	Democratic	1942-1946
22. Wyndham Robertson	Whig	1836-1837	57. William M. Tuck	Democratic	1946-1950
23. David Campbell	Democratic	1837-1840	58. John S. Battle	Democratic	1950-1954
24. Thomas Walker Gilmer	Whig	1840-1841	59. Thomas B. Stanley	Democratic	1954-1958
25. John Mercer Patton	Whig	1841	60. J. Lindsay Almond, Jr.	Democratic	1958-1962
26. John Rutherfoord	Whig	1841-1842	61. Albertis S. Harrison, Jr.	Democratic	1962-1966
27. John Munford Gregory	Whig	1842-1843	62. Mills E. Godwin, Jr.	Democratic	1966-

*Democratic-Republican   †Readjuster-Republican

the right to vote, and provided for a state-wide system of public schools. Virginia was readmitted to the Union on Jan. 26, 1870. See RECONSTRUCTION.

A major problem facing Virginia after the war was its debt of more than $45 million. The legislature finally provided that this debt should be reduced according to the state's ability to pay. An agreement was reached with the state's creditors in 1892. This agreement reduced the debt to about $25 million. It also assigned part of the debt to West Virginia. That state had been a part of Virginia when the debt was acquired (see WEST VIRGINIA [Civil War and Statehood]).

Progress in Government and Industry. Modern industry in Virginia began during the early 1880's, when cigarette factories, cotton textile plants, and shipbuilding plants were built. In 1902, the state adopted its present constitution. In 1912, another man born in Virginia, Woodrow Wilson, was elected President. Carter Glass of Lynchburg, then a congressman, became the "father" of the Federal Reserve banking system.

During the early 1900's, many Virginians moved to other states in search of better job opportunities. This movement reached a peak in the 1920's, when more than 400,000 persons left the state.

Harry F. Byrd served as governor from 1926 to 1930. He used the recommendations of a study commission to reorganize the state government and make it more efficient. In 1933, Byrd was appointed to the U.S. Senate, where he served over 30 years. Throughout this period, Byrd played a leading role in Virginia politics.

The 1930's were an important period of change in Virginia. Federal government activities in the state during the Great Depression created jobs and helped stop the flow of population from the state. Synthetic textile industries were established in many parts of Virginia and helped boost the state's economy.

The 1940's and 1950's. During World War II (1939-1945), new industries in Virginia helped meet the needs of the armed forces. Shipyards at Hampton Roads built many of the navy's ships. The war also brought thousands of servicemen and servicewomen to the Virginia suburbs of Washington, D.C., and to the Norfolk area. After the war, many federal civilian employees settled in Virginia, and military employment stayed at fairly high levels.

In 1950, the general assembly established a fund to help Virginia's cities and counties build new school buildings. In 1952, the legislature established a state-wide minimum salary schedule for teachers. At each session after that, teachers' salaries were raised.

The issue of school integration raged during the late 1950's. In 1954, the Supreme Court of the United States ruled that racial segregation in public schools is unconstitutional. Two years later, in 1956, the Virginia legislature passed laws to close any public school that the federal courts ordered integrated. In 1959, these so-called "massive resistance" laws were declared invalid by federal and state courts. On Feb. 2, 1959, public schools in Arlington County and Norfolk became the first in Virginia to integrate. Prince Edward County stopped operating public schools in 1959, after a federal court had ordered its schools integrated.

Virginia Today is making progress in education, highway construction, and industrial growth. In 1962, the legislature created the Virginia public school authority. This agency borrows money and lends it to cities and counties for building schools. The legislature also continued to raise teachers' salaries. Prince Edward County reopened some public schools in 1964. Almost all the children who attended were Negroes.

In 1963, the number of Virginia counties dropped from 98 to 96. The city of Virginia Beach annexed all of Princess Anne County. The city of South Norfolk and the county of Norfolk combined as the city of Chesapeake. In 1964, Virginia's $200 million Chesapeake Bay Bridge-Tunnel was opened. This project is a 23-mile-long series of bridges, tunnels, and causeways. It is the largest structure of its kind in the United States. The bridge-tunnel connects the Norfolk area with the Eastern Shore, and is used by motorists traveling along the Atlantic Coast. Also in 1964, Smith Mountain Dam was completed on the Roanoke River. It is the largest concrete arch dam east of the Mississippi River.

Virginia's industrial growth continued during the 1960's. The greatest growth occurred in the clothing, metals, and electrical and nonelectrical machinery industries. New factories opened in the manufacturing areas along the James River. But the greatest growth took place in the Piedmont region and in the western valleys. In 1964, the general assembly passed legislation to reduce certain taxes in order to make the state more attractive to industry.

RAYMOND C. DINGLEDINE, JR.; JOHN E. LEARD; and ANTHONY SAS

VIRGINIA /Study Aids

Related Articles in WORLD BOOK include:

BIOGRAPHIES

Bacon, Nathaniel
Berkeley, Sir William
Blair, John
Boyd, Belle
Braxton, Carter
Byrd (family)
Byrd, Harry F.
Dinwiddie, Robert
Glass, Carter
Harrison, Benjamin
 (1726?-1791)
Harrison, William H.

Henry, Patrick
Jefferson, Thomas
Johnston, Joseph E.
Lee, Francis L.
Lee, Henry
Lee, Richard H.
Lee, Robert E.
Madison, James
Marshall, John
Mason, George
Monroe, James
Nelson, Thomas

Pickett, George E.
Powhatan
Randolph (family)
Rolfe, John
Seddon, James A.
Smith, John
Spotswood, Alexander

Stuart, James E. B.
Taylor, Zachary
Tyler, John
Washington, George
Washington, Martha Custis
Wilson, Woodrow
Wythe, George

CITIES

Alexandria
Charlottesville
Fredericksburg
Hampton
Lexington

Lynchburg
Newport News
Norfolk
Petersburg
Portsmouth

Richmond
Roanoke
Williamsburg
Yorktown

Annapolis Convention
Civil War
Colonial Life in America
Harpers Ferry
House of Burgesses
Jamestown

Kentucky and Virginia
Resolutions
London Company
Revolutionary War in
America

MILITARY INSTALLATIONS

Fort Belvoir
Fort Eustis
Fort Lee

Fort Monroe
Langley Air Force
Base

Norfolk Naval Base
Quantico Marine
Corps Schools

PHYSICAL FEATURES

Allegheny Mountains
Appalachian Mountains
Blue Ridge Mountains
Chesapeake Bay
Cumberland Gap
Delmarva Peninsula
Hampton Roads
James River

Luray Caverns
Piedmont Region
Potomac River
Rappahannock River
Roanoke River
Shenandoah River
Shenandoah Valley

PRODUCTS

For Virginia's rank among the states in production, see the following articles:

Apple
Coal
Nut

Oyster
Peanut

Sweet Potato
Textile

Tobacco
Turkey

OTHER RELATED ARTICLES

Arlington County
Arlington National Cemetery
Chesapeake Bay Bridge-
Tunnel
George Washington
Birthplace National
Monument

Monticello
Morris Plan Bank
Mount Vernon
Shenandoah National
Park
Southern States

Outline

I. Government
  A. Constitution
  B. Executive
  C. Legislature
  D. Courts
  E. Local Government
  F. Taxation
  G. Politics

II. People

III. Education
  A. Schools
  B. Libraries and Museums

IV. A Visitor's Guide
  A. Places to Visit
  B. Annual Events

V. The Land
  A. Land Regions
  B. Coastline
  C. Rivers and Lakes

VI. Climate

VII. Economy
  A. Natural Resources
  B. Manufacturing
  C. Agriculture
  D. Mining
  E. Fishing Industry
  F. Electric Power
  G. Transportation
  H. Communication

VIII. History

Questions

Why is Virginia called the *Old Dominion?* The *Mother of Presidents?* The *Mother of States?*

What conditions favor industry in Virginia?

Why did the population increase in the Virginia suburbs of Washington, D.C., and in the Norfolk area during the 1940's and 1950's?

What are Virginia's four chief manufactured products?

What was the *Virginia Dynasty?*

Where was the first council-manager government in a U.S. city established?

What was the *Granary of the Confederacy?*

Where is the longest bridge-tunnel in the United States?

What is Virginia's most important mineral resource?

What points were connected by the first U.S. toll road? When was this road built?

Books for Young Readers

AMERICAN HERITAGE. *Thomas Jefferson and His World.* Meredith, 1960.

BARKSDALE, LENA. *That Country Called Virginia.* Knopf, 1945. History of the state.

DANIELS, JONATHAN. *Robert E. Lee.* Houghton, 1960.

DINGLEDINE, RAYMOND C., JR., and others. *Virginia's History.* Rev. ed. Scribner, 1964.

HENRY, MARGUERITE. *Misty of Chincoteague.* Rand McNally, 1947. *Sea Star, Orphan of Chincoteague.* 1949.

JONES, WILLIAM P. *Patrick Henry.* Houghton, 1961.

JUDSON, CLARA I. *George Washington.* Follett, 1961.

LATHAM, JEAN L. *This Dear-Bought Land.* Harper, 1957.

LAWSON, MARIE. *Pocahontas and Captain John Smith: The Story of the Virginia Colony.* Random House, 1950.

MONSELL, HELEN A. *John Marshall: Boy of Young America.* Bobbs, 1949. *Dolly Madison, Quaker Girl.* 1953. *Woodrow Wilson, Boy President.* 1959.

NESBITT, MARION. *Captain John Smith's Page.* Lippincott, 1957. The founding of Jamestown as seen by a teen-age boy who landed with Captain John Smith.

PETERSHAM, MAUD. *The Silver Mace: A Story of Williamsburg.* Macmillan, 1956.

RINK, PAUL. *Conquering Antarctica: Richard E. Byrd.* Britannica Books, 1961.

SIMKINS, FRANCIS B., and others. *Virginia: History, Government, Geography.* Scribner, 1957.

VANCE, MARGUERITE. *Martha, Daughter of Virginia: The Story of Martha Washington.* Dutton, 1947. *Patsy Jefferson of Monticello.* 1948. *Lees of Arlington: The Story of Mary and Robert E. Lee.* 1949.

Books for Older Readers

DOWDEY, CLIFFORD. *The Seven Days: The Emergence of Lee.* Little, Brown, 1964.

FINNEY, GERTRUDE E. *Muskets Along the Chickahominy.* McKay, 1953. An adventure story of colonial Virginia in the late 1600's.

FREEMAN, DOUGLAS S. *Lee of Virginia.* Scribner, 1958. A biography written for teen-agers.

GOTTMAN, JEAN. *Virginia at Mid-Century.* Holt, 1955.

HASSLER, WILLIAM W. *Colonel John Pelham: Lee's Boy Artillerist.* Garrett and Massie, Inc., Richmond, Va., 1960.

HEMPHILL, W. EDWIN, and others. *Cavalier Commonwealth: History and Government of Virginia.* 2nd ed. McGraw, 1963.

KANE, HARNETT T. *Lady of Arlington.* Doubleday, 1953. A biographical novel of Mrs. Robert E. Lee.

KOCHER, ALFRED L., and DEARSTYNE, HOWARD. *Colonial Williamsburg.* Revised. Colonial Williamsburg, 1961.

MAPP, ALF J., JR. *Virginia Experiment: The Old Dominion's Role in the Making of America, 1607-1781.* Dietz, 1957.

MORTON, RICHARD L. *Colonial Virginia.* 2 vols. Univ. of North Carolina Press, 1960.

ROSENBERGER, FRANCIS C., ed. *Virginia Reader: A Treasury of Writings from the First Voyages to the Present.* Dutton, 1948.

THANE, ELSWYTH. *Potomac Squire.* Duell, 1963. Biography of George Washington as a family man and a country gentleman.

Virginia: A Guide to the Old Dominion. Oxford, 1940.

VIRGINIA, UNIVERSITY OF

VIRGINIA, UNIVERSITY OF, is a state-controlled co-educational school at Charlottesville, Va. The women's college of the university is Mary Washington College at Fredericksburg. At Charlottesville, women are permitted to enter only the graduate and professional courses.

The University of Virginia has a college of arts and sciences; departments of law, medicine, engineering, education, and graduate studies; and a graduate school of education. Thomas Jefferson founded the university in 1819.

The school colors are orange and blue. Its athletic teams are called the Cavaliers. For enrollment, see UNIVERSITIES AND COLLEGES (table).

See also JEFFERSON, THOMAS (picture, The University of Virginia); VIRGINIA (color picture).

VIRGINIA CITY, Nev. (pop. 600; alt. 6,340 ft.), is perhaps the most celebrated and best-preserved ghost town in the West. Mark Twain wrote about the turbulent early days of this former mining center in his book *Roughing It.* The town lies in the Virginia Range, 23 miles southeast of Reno. For location, see NEVADA (political map).

Virginia City serves as a tourist center. As many as 40,000 persons visit the town each week during the summer. The town was founded in 1859, just two years after the discovery of gold and silver in the surrounding mountains. Virginia City's population swelled to 23,000 residents in 1876, at the peak of the Comstock Lode's producing power. LUCIUS BEEBE

See also COMSTOCK LODE; WESTERN FRONTIER LIFE (Frontier Towns); NEVADA (color picture).

VIRGINIA CREEPER is a rambling, creeping plant of the vine family. It grows in almost all parts of America, and is often called *woodbine,* and *American,* or *five-leaved,* ivy.

The Virginia creeper's strong but slender tendrils have long branches ending in tiny disks. The disks stick to surfaces on which the plant grows. A single tendril with five branches bearing these disks would, even after

J. Horace McFarland

Virginia Creeper adds brilliant color to stone fences and bare walls in autumn when its leaves turn a flaming red.

10 years' exposure to all sorts of weather, hold up a weight of 10 pounds.

The Virginia creeper looks somewhat like poison ivy, but the leaves of the poison ivy are made up of three leaflets, and those of the Virginia creeper of five. In the autumn the Virginia creeper has flaming foliage and bunches of dark blue berries.

Scientific Classification. The Virginia creeper belongs to the vine family, *Vitaceae.* It is genus *Parthenocissus,* species *P. quinquefolia.* J. J. LEVISON

See also IVY; POISON IVY (picture).

VIRGINIA MILITARY INSTITUTE is a state-controlled military college of engineering, arts, and sciences at Lexington, Va. Qualified graduates receive the B.S. or B.A. degree and either reserve or regular commissions in the armed forces. The institute offers majors in biology (premedical); chemistry; civil and electric engineering; English; history; mathematics; and physics.

All students are cadets. They wear uniforms, live in

Cadet Barracks at Virginia Military Institute face the spacious parade ground area. Located in Lexington, Va., the school has often been called "The West Point of the South." The Institute opened in 1839. It was burned during the Civil War.

Virginia Military Institute

barracks, eat in the same mess hall, and generally lead the lives of soldiers in an atmosphere incorporating a high degree of discipline. V.M.I. graduates have entered practically every field of civic endeavor, and have played an active part in every United States war since the Institute was founded in 1839.

For 10 years before the Civil War, Thomas J. "Stonewall" Jackson was a professor of artillery tactics and natural philosophy at V.M.I. (see JACKSON, "STONEWALL," THOMAS JONATHAN). General of the Army George C. Marshall, a V.M.I. graduate, became Army Chief of Staff during World War II (see MARSHALL, GEORGE CATLETT).

On May 23, 1964, President Lyndon B. Johnson dedicated the George C. Marshall Research Library at the Virginia Military Institute. Among the other dignitaries taking part in the ceremony were former President Dwight D. Eisenhower and General Omar N. Bradley, both of whom served under General Marshall in World War II. LLOYD J. DAVIDSON

For enrollment, see UNIVERSITIES AND COLLEGES (table).

VIRGINIA PLAN. See RANDOLPH (Edmund); UNITED STATES CONSTITUTION (The Compromises).

VIRGINIA POLYTECHNIC INSTITUTE is a coeducational land-grant university in Blacksburg, Va. The university has two-year branch colleges at Clifton Forge-Covington, Danville, Roanoke, and Wytheville. It offers an engineering program cooperatively with Richmond Professional Institute in Richmond. The Blacksburg campus has colleges of agriculture, architecture, arts and sciences, business, engineering, and home economics. It also has a graduate school. Both college work and technical study programs are offered at the branch colleges. The university was founded in 1872 as a land-grant college (see LAND-GRANT COLLEGE OR UNIVERSITY). For the enrollment of Virginia Polytechnic Institute, see UNIVERSITIES AND COLLEGES (table). T. MARSHALL HAHN

VIRGINIA REEL. See FOLK DANCING.

VIRGINIA RESOLUTIONS. See KENTUCKY AND VIRGINIA RESOLUTIONS.

VIRGINIA STATE COLLEGE is a state-supported coeducational college at Petersburg, Va. It has a branch at Norfolk, Va. A land-grant college, it has schools of agriculture, arts and sciences, education, home economics, industries, and commerce; and divisions of general education, field services, and graduate studies. It offers bachelor's and master's degrees.

The state of Virginia founded the school as the Virginia Normal and Collegiate Institute in 1882. Its present name was adopted in 1946. For the enrollment of Virginia State College, see UNIVERSITIES AND COLLEGES (table). ROBERT P. DANIEL

VIRGINIA UNION UNIVERSITY. See UNIVERSITIES AND COLLEGES (table).

VIRGINIUM is a name formerly given to chemical element number 87. The element is now known as francium. See FRANCIUM.

VIRGINIUS MASSACRE was an event in 1873 that almost involved the United States in a war with Spain. During a Cuban revolt against Spain, the Spanish gunboat *Tornado* captured a merchant ship called the *Virginius* on the high seas off Jamaica. A United States citizen, Captain John Fry, commanded the *Virginius*, and flew the American flag. The Spanish authorities

executed Captain Fry, 36 of the crew, and 16 passengers. The Spanish claimed the vessel was taking men and arms to aid the Cuban rebels.

The affair caused great excitement in the United States. But Spain agreed to surrender the ship and survivors, and denied any hostile intent. Later, authorities discovered that the *Virginius* was owned by Cubans, was illegally registered, and had no right to fly the American flag. The vessel was wrecked and left off Cape Fear on its way to the United States. JOHN D. HICKS

VIRGIN'S-BOWER. See CLEMATIS.

VIRGO is the sixth sign of the zodiac. It is also the name of a constellation of stars from which the sign Virgo (meaning the *Virgin*) received its name. But the position of the stars in relation to the sun is not what it was when the zodiac was first named, and the constellation Virgo is now chiefly in the sign Libra. The sun enters the sign of Virgo about August 23. The astronomical symbol for the sign is ♍. The star Spica is near Virgo's left hand. There is a great concentration of spiral galaxies in and near Virgo. See also SPICA; ZODIAC. I. M. LEVITT

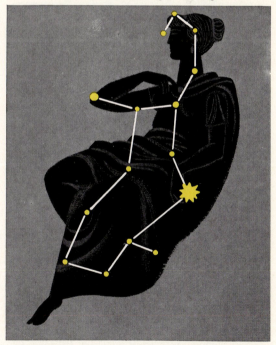

The Constellation Virgo, the Virgin

VIRTANEN, *VIR tah nen,* **ARTTURI ILMARI** (1895-), a Finnish biochemist, won the 1945 Nobel prize in chemistry for his researches and inventions in agricultural and nutritive chemistry. He discovered the AIV method, named from his initials, of preserving green fodder in storage by adding acids which prevent the deteriorating process. He showed that artificially acidified fodder has no harmful effect on cattle or milk. He also studied the utilization of nitrogen by plants. Virtanen was born in Helsinki. GERALD HOLTON

VIRTUAL IMAGE. See LENS.

VIRUS

VIRUS, *VYE rus,* is a microorganism, or tiny germ. Viruses are smaller than bacteria. The largest virus can be seen through the highest power lenses of the ordinary laboratory microscope, but most viruses can be seen only with an electron microscope. All except the largest viruses pass through porcelain filters whose openings are so tiny that bacteria cannot pass through. Because of their ability to pass through filters, the smallest viruses are often called *filtrable* viruses.

Viruses are made up of a central core of nucleic acid surrounded by a protein coat. They are such incomplete organisms that they must live like parasites on larger living cells. A virus particle attaches itself to a cell. The core of the virus penetrates and directs the life processes of the cell so that many more virus particles are formed. These new particles are then set free to attack other cells. The host cell may be injured or even destroyed by the infecting virus.

In 1898, Martinus Willem Beijerinck (1851-1931), a Dutch botanist, first recognized that something smaller than bacteria could cause disease. He isolated what he thought was a living fluid that caused disease in tobacco plants. He called his discovery *virus,* a Latin word meaning *poison.* In 1935, Wendell M. Stanley, an American biochemist, showed that viruses really are solid particles that contain protein.

Virus Diseases in Man. Doctors believe that more than 50 diseases of man are caused by viruses. These diseases include poliomyelitis, measles, chickenpox, mumps, and influenza. Viruses also cause *hepatitis* (a liver disease), *herpes simplex* (cold sores or fever blisters), and *herpes zoster* (shingles). Although scientists know that viruses cause many diseases of the respiratory tract, they have not isolated the virus that causes the common cold. Viruses cause many tumors in small animals. Some researchers believe a virus may cause cancer in human beings. However, this has not been proved.

Treatment. Viruses are not susceptible to the antibiotics or similar drugs that are so effective against bacteria. Because viruses are associated with the life processes of the cells of the ill person, it would be difficult to destroy the virus without hurting the cells. Therefore, doctors prescribe treatments designed primarily to make the patient comfortable, and, if possible, to prevent the development of complications.

Prevention. An attack of a virus disease often makes a person immune for life. Because of this, doctors try to make people immune before they get the disease. They make vaccines from the living virus. The strength of the virus is weakened by chemicals. Doctors use such vaccines as protection against influenza, yellow fever, smallpox, and poliomyelitis. See VACCINATION.

Virus Diseases in Animals. Some viruses that cause diseases in animals apparently cannot cause disease in human beings. For example, fowl pox, swine fever, and dog distemper are limited to animals. But animals can give human beings many other serious virus diseases. For example, dogs can give people rabies. Parrots, parakeets, and pigeons can transmit psittacosis to humans.

Virus Diseases in Plants. Many plants are susceptible to virus diseases. These diseases include the various plant *mosaics,* which destroy plants important to man.

Some of these plant viruses can be duplicated in a laboratory. FREDERICK C. ROBBINS

Related Articles in WORLD BOOK include:

SOME VIRUS DISEASES

Chicken Pox	Influenza	Shingles
Cold, Common	Measles	Sleeping Sickness
Dengue	Mosaic Disease	(Encephalitis
Distemper	Mumps	Lethargica)
Foot-and-Mouth	Poliomyelitis	Smallpox
Disease	Psittacosis	Virus Pneumonia
Hepatitis	Rabies	Yellow Fever

UNCLASSIFIED

Bacteria	Disease	Interferon
Bacteriology	(Virus Diseases)	

VIRUS PNEUMONIA is an infection of the lungs caused by viruses. These germs are so tiny that only the largest can be seen even under a powerful microscope (see VIRUS). Virus pneumonia has been recognized as a distinct disease only since the early 1900's.

This type of pneumonia is very contagious. Doctors believe it is spread by breathing air containing these germs. Persons with the disease may cough or sneeze, spraying into the air fine droplets with the tiny germs. If another person breathes the air with these germs he may contract the disease. X-ray pictures of persons with virus pneumonia show shadows on the lungs. Very sick patients find breathing difficult. They develop *cyanosis,* a blue condition of the skin caused by lack of oxygen. It may take seven days to several months for a person to recover from virus pneumonia. MARK D. ALTSCHULE

See also PNEUMONIA.

VISA, *VEE zuh,* is an endorsement that government officials place on a passport to show that the passport is valid (see PASSPORT). Officials of the country which a traveler is entering grant the visa. It certifies that the passport has been examined and approved. Immigration officers then permit the bearer to enter the country and proceed on his journey. A government that does not want a certain person to enter the country can refuse to grant him a visa, and thus prevent him from coming into the country.

VISCOSE PROCESS. See RAYON.

VISCOSITY, *vis KAHS uh tih,* is the property of a fluid that causes it to resist flowing. Fluids with *high viscosity,* such as molasses, flow more slowly than those with *low viscosity,* such as water. All fluids, which includes both liquids and gases, have viscosity of some degree.

A fluid resists flowing because of frictional forces acting within it. As the fluid flows, its molecules must work against these internal forces. Temperature is one factor that influences viscosity. Hot liquids have a lower viscosity than cold liquids. But hot gases have a higher viscosity than cold gases.

Manufacturers make lubricating oils with various viscosities to meet many operating requirements. The viscosity of air is important in aerodynamics. It causes a portion of the drag on airplanes (see AERODYNAMICS [Skin Friction]). CLARENCE E. BENNETT

VISCOUNT, *VI kownt,* is a title which is held by certain British noblemen. A viscount ranks below an earl and above a baron. John Beaumont, an officer and deputy to an earl, was the first to receive the title in 1440. Today it is usually given to men whom the ruler wishes to honor. See also NOBILITY.

VISHINSKY, *vee SHIN skih,* **ANDREI YANUARIEVICH** (1883-1954), was a Russian prosecutor and diplomat. He became a revolutionary in 1902 and participated actively in an uprising in 1905.

Vishinsky joined the Communist party in 1920. From 1933 to 1938, he was a ruthless prosecutor in the Communist party purge trials. Vishinsky became a deputy commissar of foreign affairs in 1940. He served as foreign minister from 1949 to 1953. As the chief Russian delegate in the United Nations, he became notorious for speeches against the Western world. He was born in Odessa.   ALBERT PARRY

VISHNU is the world-preserver in Indian religion. In India there are three great names for God: Brahma, Vishnu, and Siva. The creator of the world is Brahma. The preserver of the world is Vishnu. The destroyer is Siva.

Followers of Vishnu are called Vishnavites. Vishnu is believed to have sent his will to the world through mighty heroes. Three of the greatest hero-teachers are Rama of old India; Krishna, the chariot driver of Prince Arjuna; and Buddha, the prophet of eastern Asia.

Many Vishnavites believe that Buddha, the last of the prophet-heroes, will be followed by another teacher. Thoughtful followers of Vishnu use the *Bhagavad-Gita* as their holy book.   GEORGE NOEL MAYHEW

See also BUDDHA; RAMAYANA; SIVA; ANGKOR.

VISIBILITY, DISTANCES OF. Because the earth's surface curves, we can see only a small section of its surface at one time. The higher we are, the more of the earth's surface we can see.

The U.S. Coast Guard gives the distances a person can see at various heights above sea level in clear

The High Viscosity of Cold Molasses causes it to flow from the bottle in a slow and sluggish stream. If molasses is heated, the viscosity is lowered and the molasses flows much more freely.
Press Syndicate

weather. These distances, given in nautical miles, are as follows:

Height (Feet)	Distance (Miles)	Height (Feet)	Distance (Miles)
5	2.5	100	11.5
10	3.6	200	16.2
15	4.4	300	19.9
20	5.1	400	22.9
25	5.7	500	25.6
30	6.3	600	28.0
35	6.8	700	30.3
40	7.2	800	32.4
45	7.7	900	34.4
50	8.1	1,000	36.2
75	9.9		

VISIGOTH. See GOTH.

VISION. See EYE.

VISITATION ORDER. See FRANCIS DE SALES, SAINT.

VISOR. See ARMOR (During the Middle Ages; picture, Armor Parts).

VISTA. See ECONOMIC OPPORTUNITY, OFFICE OF.

VISTAVISION. See MOTION PICTURE (Wide-Screen Processes).

VISTULA RIVER, *VIS tyoo luh,* is an important waterway of East Central Europe. It carries much of the river traffic in Poland. The Vistula rises in the Carpathian Mountains in southern Poland, and then takes a circular course northward. It empties by several branches into the Baltic Sea. Danzig lies at the mouth of the Nogat, the easternmost branch. See POLAND (color map).

Light boats sail up the river as far as Kraków. Warsaw is on the east bank. The Vistula is frozen two to three months of the year.

Canals connect the Vistula River with the Oder, the Dnepr, and the Nemen, all navigable rivers. The Vistula is 678 miles long and drains an area of about 74,000 square miles.   M. KAMIL DZIEWANOWSKI

VISUAL ACUITY. See EYE (Vision Tests).

VISUAL EDUCATION. See AUDIO-VISUAL MATERIALS.

VITAL STATISTICS are a record of the most basic human events—birth, marriage, divorce, sickness, and death. They indicate what is happening or what has happened to the population of a country, state, or other community. Vital statistics can also show what is likely to occur in the future. They come from birth and death certificates, marriage licenses, disease and divorce reports, and other official records. Government officials collect, tabulate, analyze, and publish these records.

Kinds of Vital Statistics. The total number of births, marriages, divorces, sicknesses, and deaths are useful statistics, but the *rate* at which they are happening is often more significant. The rate is the number of human events measured in proportion to part or all of the population. The importance of the rate can be seen in comparing births in the United States and Canada. In 1960, many more births occurred in the U.S. than in Canada. The U.S. had 4,258,000 births, and Canada, 478,551. But Canada had a higher birth rate—26.9 for every 1,000 persons as against 23.7 in the U.S. (see BIRTH AND DEATH RATES).

The *crude rate* is the number of events in a given year

VITAMIN

divided by the total population. The crude rate is most often stated as so many occurrences per 1,000 persons. It disregards age, sex, and other characteristics of the population. Thus a country that has a large number of young adults has a higher birth rate and a lower death rate than a country that has a large number of older adults.

Sometimes statisticians combine several factors to study vital statistics. For example, they may relate cause of death, place of residence, color, sex, and age. They may determine the specific rate for lung cancer deaths among urban white males 20 to 44 years old per 1,000 such males in the population.

Interpreting Vital Statistics. Government workers, scientists, educators, businessmen, and others use vital statistics for many purposes. Legislators study population trends when they draft housing, employment, and other legislation. Health authorities need statistics to administer public health. Sociologists study them to learn what causes divorces. School administrators use vital statistics in planning facilities for the future. Insurance statisticians use death records to prepare life expectancy tables and life insurance rates. Market research workers study statistics to make marketing plans.

Collecting and Publishing Vital Statistics. In the United States, state laws regulate registration of vital records. Physicians, funeral directors, clergymen, and attorneys most commonly register such records. Doctors or hospital attendants file birth certificates with local registrars. Doctors or coroners return death certificates to funeral directors who file them with local registrars to obtain burial permits. The local registrars send birth and death certificates to their county health department or to the state registrar of vital statistics. Doctors also report cases of disease to local or state health departments.

Town or county clerks issue marriage licenses. After the ceremony has been performed, the minister or other marriage officer sends the record certifying the marriage to the license clerk. The licensing office sends the marriage record or a copy to the state registrar. Attorneys file divorce records with the clerk of the court that granted the decree. The court clerk reports the divorce to the state registrar.

State bureaus of vital statistics and state health departments maintain files of vital records and compile statistics. The state governments send reports of births, deaths, *fetal deaths* (stillbirths), diseases, marriages, and divorces to the National Vital Statistics Division of the National Center for Health Statistics. The center is a Public Health Service agency in the United States Department of Health, Education, and Welfare. The division tabulates, analyzes, and publishes national data. The Public Health Service publishes the annual *Vital Statistics of the United States*, the *Monthly Vital Statistics Report*, and other statistical data.

The United States and other countries report vital statistics to the Statistical Office of the United Nations. The UN issues the annual *Demographic Yearbook* and other statistical publications.

See also CENSUS; DIVORCE; MARRIAGE; POPULATION.

Scientists have discovered more than 25 vitamins that are necessary for good health. They believe that there are many more.

VITAMIN, *VYE tuh min*, is a complex substance that is essential to the human body for health and growth. But human beings do not need vitamins for fuel. Fuel is supplied by fats and carbohydrates. The human body makes some vitamins itself, but often in amounts too small to meet its needs. Others are not made in the body at all, and must be supplied. All the functions of many of the vitamins are not completely known. But doctors do know that vitamins have such specific uses that one cannot replace, or act for, another. The continued lack of one vitamin in an otherwise complete diet results in a *deficiency* disease, such as rickets, scurvy, and pellagra. See DISEASE (Nutritional Diseases).

The best way to obtain vitamins is to eat foods in which they occur naturally. There are also preparations of pure vitamins that contain a single vitamin, or a combination of several vitamins. Vitamin preparations should be used only if prescribed by a doctor.

Scientists have discovered about 25 different vitamins that are important to the nutritional needs of human beings, animals, and microorganisms. Investigators believe that further study will show there actually are many more vitamins.

Kinds of Vitamins

Scientists divide vitamins into two general classes. One group, the *fat-soluble* vitamins, dissolves in fats. Among these are vitamins A, D, E, and K. The other group, the *water-soluble* vitamins, dissolves in water. Vitamin C and the B-complex vitamins are among these. Many vitamins have two or more names. As the vitamins were discovered, researchers often named them for the letters of the alphabet. But when investigation allowed scientists to break them down chemically, the more descriptive chemical names were given.

Vitamin A was the first fat-soluble vitamin to be discovered. It occurs only in animals. However, several substances that occur in plants are converted into vitamin A by the body. These plant substances are called *carotenes*, or *provitamins* A. An abundance of vitamin A is supplied by carrots, spinach, sweet potatoes, milk, liver, egg yolk, and green and yellow vegetables.

Vitamin A aids in the building and growth of body cells. Because of this, it is essential for the growth of children and for normal development of babies before birth. It is especially needed for bone growth and for normal tooth structure. Vitamin A helps build resistance to infection, and keeps the skin healthy. It also helps the eyes to function normally in light that varies in intensity. For example, when a person enters a

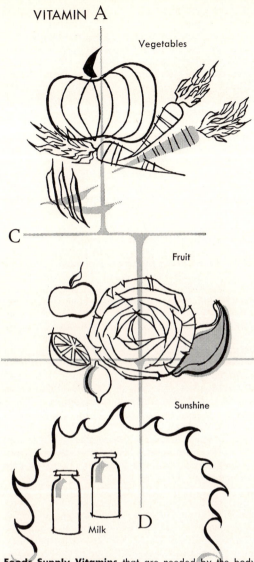

VITAMIN A

Vegetables

C

Fruit

Sunshine

Milk

D

Foods Supply Vitamins that are needed by the body. If children do not get enough vitamins, they will not grow properly. When older persons lack certain vitamins, they often develop various diseases. Each vitamin has a specific duty to perform. One of them cannot take the place of another. Although each kind of food may have more than one vitamin, no one food contains all that are needed to keep the body healthy. Usually people can get all the vitamins necessary for health by following a diet containing a variety of foods.

THIAMINE

RIBOFLAVIN   NIACIN

Meats

Cheese   Poultry

darkened room from the sunlight, his eyes must adjust to the limited indoor light so that he can see. Persons without enough vitamin A may develop an eye disease.

Vitamin B Complex is a group of more than 15 known water-soluble vitamins. The vitamins that make up this group were first believed to be only one vitamin. Researchers later found that several different vitamins make up the vitamin B complex.

Vitamin B_1, also called *thiamine*, prevents and cures beriberi, a disease of the nervous system (see BERIBERI). It contains sulfur and nitrogen. Good sources of vitamin B_1 are yeast, meats (especially pork), whole-grain and enriched cereals, soybeans, nuts, peas, and green vegetables. Like vitamin A, this vitamin is needed for growth. The body also needs vitamin B_1 so that it can change carbohydrates into energy (see CARBOHYDRATE). People need vitamin B_1 to have a good appetite and to prevent fatigue.

Riboflavin was originally called *vitamin G* and *B_2*. It is most abundant in such foods as yeast, milk, liver, eggs, poultry, fish, and green and leafy vegetables. People need this vitamin for growth, for healthy skin, and for the proper functioning of the eyes. In addition, riboflavin promotes the body's use of oxygen. When a person does not get enough of this vitamin, cracks may develop in the skin at the corners of his mouth. He may also have inflamed lips and a sore tongue, and scaliness of the skin around his nose and ears. His eyes may become very sensitive to light.

Niacin, also called *nicotinic acid*, helps prevent pellagra (see PELLAGRA). The best sources of niacin are lean meat, whole-grain and enriched cereal and bread, and green vegetables. Milk and eggs, even though they have little niacin, are good pellagra-preventive foods because they contain *tryptophane*, an amino acid (see AMINO ACID). Tryptophane substitutes for some of the body's niacin needs.

Niacin is essential to growth and to the proper use of oxygen. Without it, thiamine and riboflavin cannot function properly in the body. Persons without enough niacin may develop disorders of the alimentary canal, the skin, and the nervous system.

Vitamin B_{12}, or *cyanocobalamin*, contains *cobalt*, a mineral known to be important in the nutrition of plants. Scientists do not know all the things vitamin B_{12} does for the body. But investigators have found that injections of tiny amounts of this vitamin help in treating persons with pernicious anemia (see ANEMIA). Eggs, milk, meat, liver, and other animal proteins supply vitamin B_{12} in the diet. Researchers have found that persons who eat only vegetables sometimes lack vitamin B_{12}. But even a small amount of animal protein seems to be able to supply enough of this vitamin.

Other B-Complex Vitamins have been discovered, including *pyridoxine* (B_6); *pantothenic acid; biotin* (vitamin H); *folic acid; para-aminobenzoic acid;* and *inositol*. Scientists have studied many of these vitamins extensively, but most of them are still under investigation. Doctors know that several are essential to human nutrition. They have found that a varied diet that contains thiamine, riboflavin, and niacin seems also to supply the other vitamins of the B-complex group.

Vitamin C, or *ascorbic acid*, is a water-soluble vitamin.

335

Doctors sometimes call it the *antiscorbutic* vitamin because it prevents and cures scurvy (see Scurvy). The body does not store vitamin C. Therefore it must be supplied daily in the diet. Good sources are citrus fruits, tomatoes, raw cabbage, strawberries, and cantaloupe. The fruit of the acerola, or Puerto Rican cherry, has the highest concentration of vitamin C known. Vitamin C is essential for healthy blood vessels and sound bones and teeth. Persons who lack this vitamin may have sore gums, hemorrhages under the skin, and general fatigue.

Vitamin D is a group of about 10 fat-soluble vitamins that prevent rickets (see Rickets). The vitamins in this group are produced from certain *sterols* found in plants and animals by exposure to ultraviolet light. Only two of these vitamins are important in nutrition. One is vitamin D_2, formed by irradiating *ergosterol*. The other, vitamin D_3, occurs in fish-liver oils, irradiated milk, and all irradiated animal foodstuffs (see Cod-Liver Oil; Halibut-Liver Oil). Scientists believe that vitamin D_3 forms in the skin when the body is exposed to sunlight. Because of this, it has been called the "sunshine vitamin." Doctors have found that lack of vitamin D leads to serious bone changes. However, they have found that excessive amounts also cause serious bone changes. They call this condition *hypervitaminosis D*.

Vitamin E, or *tocopherol*, is a fat-soluble substance that scientists believe may be necessary for reproduction. All the functions of this vitamin are not known. The best sources of vitamin E are wheat-germ oil and lettuce. Whole-grain cereals, meat, milk, eggs, liver, and most vegetables also contain it.

Vitamin K includes a group of fat-soluble vitamins that are essential for making the blood clot. These vitamins are rather abundant in food. They are found particularly in the green leafy vegetables such as spinach, cabbage, kale, and cauliflower. Pork liver is also an excellent source. Intestinal bacteria manufacture vitamin K in the body. Therefore, deficiencies of this vitamin are rarely the result of poor diet. But deficiencies can result when something interferes with the normal function of the intestines. Doctors sometimes give mothers vitamin K before childbirth as a precaution against hemorrhages in the newborn baby.

History

Diseases such as scurvy, rickets, and beriberi have been known for centuries. But the idea that they might be due to a *deficiency* (lack) in diet is comparatively new. One of the earliest men to realize this was Kanehiro Takaki (1849-1915), surgeon-general of the Japanese navy. In 1882, he greatly reduced the number of beriberi cases among naval crews by adding meat and vegetables to their diet of rice. Christiaan Eijkman (1858-1930), a Dutch medical officer in the East Indies, studied beriberi in prison camps. About 1900, he and a co-worker showed that people who ate *polished* rice (with the hulls removed) developed the disease. Those who ate whole rice, hull and all, did not. They stated that rice hulls contain a factor necessary to health.

Casimir Funk (1884-   ), a Polish biochemist working in London, tried to isolate this anti-beriberi factor from rice hulls in 1912. He did not manage to get it pure. From his studies, he thought it belonged to a class of chemical compounds called *amines*, and named it *vitamine* (amine essential to life). Meanwhile, Frederick G. Hopkins (1861-1947), of Cambridge University in England, had published his work in 1906 showing the effect of diet on the growth of rats. He stated that substances called "accessory food factors," found in certain foods, were essential for growth and normal development. The word *vitamin* (with the "e" dropped) came to be used to cover all substances of this type. At first scientists thought only two existed, water-soluble vitamin and fat-soluble vitamin. Elmer J. McCollum (1879-   ), an American biochemist, showed that the fat-soluble vitamin actually consisted of a mixture of vitamins. Joseph Goldberger (1874-1929), an American physician, showed that the water-soluble vitamin was also a mixture. Since then, many vitamins of both types have been isolated and identified. But scientists believe still others may be discovered.   Lord Todd

Related Articles in World Book include:

Ascorbic	Diet	McCollum, Elmer V.
Acid	Food (How Our	Nutrition (with
Biotin	Bodies Use Food)	Science Project)
Citrin	Goldberger, Joseph	

VITASCOPE. See Motion Picture (The First Motion Pictures).

VITERBO COLLEGE. See Universities and Colleges (table).

VITREOUS HUMOR. See Eye (The Eyeball; color diagram, Parts of the Eye).

VITRIOL, OIL OF. See Sulfuric Acid.

VIVALDI, *vee VAHL dee,* **ANTONIO** (1677?-1741), was a famous Italian violinist and composer. He is reported to have written nearly 50 operas. But he is probably best known for his instrumental compositions, including sonatas for one or two violins, and concertos for various instruments. Some of these concertos express a poetic program, such as the Concerto for Five Instruments, called *La Pastorella*, and *Le Quattro Stagioni*, (*The Four Seasons*). Johann Sebastian Bach, who deeply admired Vivaldi's works, took over some of the features of formal construction from Vivaldi's concertos. Bach also arranged several of Vivaldi's compositions for the harpsichord and the organ. Vivaldi was born in Venice. He spent most of his life there, and served as violinist at the cathedral of Saint Mark. Vivaldi also directed the Ospedale della Pietà, a charitable institution where orphaned girls were trained in various fields of music.   Karl Geiringer

VIVARIUM, *vih VAIR ih um,* is the name of a small indoor inclosure used for keeping pet animals or plants, or both. It usually has glass sides and may hold earth and water for such land and water animals as small turtles or frogs. See also Terrarium.

VIVIPAROUS ANIMAL, *vy VIP uh rus,* is an animal whose young are born alive. This, in general, is true only of the higher animals. Most fish hatch from eggs, but a few, such as the guppy, are born alive. Some snakes bear live young, but others lay eggs.

VIVISECTION, *viv ih SEK shun,* is the practice of operating on live animals in order to study facts used in the advance of medical science. The literal meaning of the word is *cutting of the living*. The strict meaning takes in only cutting operations, but in practice the word also covers many other types of operations in which animals are used for experiments. Examples include experiments with new medicines, with disease germs, and the use of animals in nutrition and diet studies. Another term for vivisection is *animal experimentation*.

People often object to vivisection because they feel it is cruel. But enormous benefits result from vivisection. Few of the great discoveries of medical science would have been possible without it. Through animal experiments, scientists discovered the antitoxin which prevents and cures diphtheria, and the anesthetic properties of ether and chloroform. They learned how to prevent death from diabetes by the manufacture and injection of insulin; how to develop and test out such antibacterial agents as sulfonamides, penicillin, tetracycline, and many others; and how mosquitoes spread yellow fever. There is hardly any field of medical practice that has not been advanced by vivisection.

Scientists do everything they can to carry out animal experiments in a humane way. When they operate, they use an anesthetic to make the animal unconscious. As far as possible, the scientists make their investigations while the animal is unconscious. If the animal is seriously mutilated, they kill it before it becomes conscious again. WARREN H. COLE

See also ANTIVIVISECTION; GUINEA PIG.

VIZCAÍNO DESERT is a vast, sparsely inhabited wasteland in central Baja (Lower) California, Mexico's long peninsula. It covers about 6,000 square miles, from about Rosario in the north to La Paz in the south. The desert has an average annual rainfall of less than 5 inches. In some years no rain falls. JOHN A. CROW

VIZIER, *vih ZEER*, or *VIZ yer*, is the title some Moslem countries give to certain high officials, such as ministers of state. The word *vizier* comes from the Arabic word *wazir*, which means a *bearer of burdens*. The viziers headed the departments of government in the Ottoman Empire. During the 1800's, the highest officer of the realm was the Grand Vizier, who was somewhat like a prime minister. SYDNEY N. FISHER

VIZSLA, *VEEZ lah*, is a short-haired hunting dog also known as the *Hungarian pointer*. Vizslas resemble other short-haired pointing breeds except that they have deep, rusty-gold coats. The dog weighs about 50 pounds and has a *docked* (shortened) tail. Dog experts believe the breed is descended from dogs brought into central Europe by the Magyars about 1,000 years ago (see MAGYAR). Central Europeans first used the dogs to hunt with falcons and later to point and retrieve game birds on the Hungarian plains. JOSEPHINE Z. RINE

VLADIMIR I (?-1015), a Russian grand duke, won fame for establishing Christianity as Russia's official religion. In 972, he became ruler of Novgorod in Russia, but had to flee for his life to Scandinavia. Later he returned, defeated and killed his brother, who was ruling in Kiev, and became grand duke in Kiev.

Vladimir was born a pagan of viking origin. In 988, he was converted to Christianity. He married Anna, the sister of the Byzantine emperor Basil II. Vladimir I founded cities and built churches, schools, and libraries. He promoted trade, established relations with the pope and European rulers, and ably defended Russia against its eastern neighbors. Vladimir I died in 1015, and later was declared a saint. WALTHER KIRCHNER

VLADIVOSTOK, *VLAH dih vahs TAWK* (pop. 353,-000; alt. 100 ft.), is the most important Russian port on the Pacific Ocean. It lies in southeastern Siberia, near the Korean border. For the location of Vladivostok, see RUSSIA (color map).

Vladivostok's fine harbor, formed by the Bay of the Golden Horn, has an area of about two square miles. The harbor is usually frozen between January and March, but icebreakers keep it open. Vladivostok is a base for fishing fleets. Most goods coming to Russia from Pacific ports pass through Vladivostok. The city has shipyards and fish canneries. It also produces mining equipment. The city lies near the east end of the Trans-Siberian Railroad, the longest railroad in the world (see TRANS-SIBERIAN RAILROAD). The Russians founded Vladivostok in 1860. It became a naval base after Russia lost Port Arthur to Japan in 1905. Today, most of Vladivostok's merchant fleet uses the new port of Nakhodka, 50 miles to the east. THEODORE SHABAD

VLAMINCK, *VLAH MANK*, **MAURICE DE** (1876-1958), a French painter, used gloomy, dark, and almost streaky colors. His effects were extremely powerful in a stormy, expressionistic manner. Unlike many contemporary artists, Vlaminck used deep spaces and strong perspectives to add intensity to his scenes. He was originally a *fauve* but later developed a personal landscape style, influenced by primitive art and Paul Cézanne's work. He was born in Paris. JOSEPH C. SLOANE

VOCABULARY is the total number of words in a language. It is also the collection of words a person knows and uses in speaking or writing.

The vocabulary of a language is always changing and growing. As life becomes more complex, people devise or borrow new words to describe man's activities. The total vocabulary of the Anglo-Saxon language, from which English stems, included roughly 50,000 words. No one knows the exact number of words in the English vocabulary today, but it contains at least 600,000 words.

A person has two kinds of vocabulary. His *active* or *use* vocabulary consists of words he uses in speaking or writing. His *passive* or *recognition* vocabulary consists of words he understands when listening or reading. A person's recognition vocabulary is often many times larger than his use vocabulary. This means he understands words he hears or reads which he does not habitually use in speaking or writing. For Americans, the average use vocabulary is 10,000 words, but the average recognition vocabulary is 30,000 to 40,000 words.

A person builds his vocabulary throughout his life. Studies have shown that a child entering school may know only from 3,000 to 4,000 words. But by the time he has completed college, he may use or understand from 10,000 to 30,000 words.

It is important for a person to broaden his vocabulary. The range of a person's vocabulary is a clue to his culture, education, and general intelligence. Control over words is often the same as control over the ideas the words represent.

The dictionary is an important tool for increasing your vocabulary. If you encounter a word you do not know, look it up and find out what it means and how it is used. MARIO PEI

See also BASIC ENGLISH; DICTIONARY; READING.

VOCAL CORD. See LARYNX.

VOCAL MEMNON. See MEMNON.

VOCATION. See VOCATIONAL GUIDANCE.

337

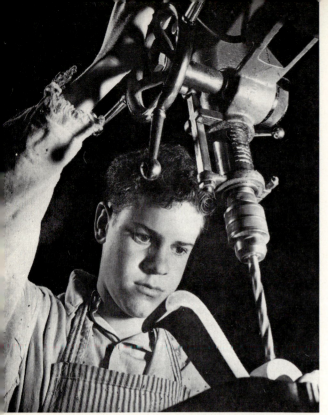

Vocational Education students receive basic training in mechanical crafts and trades by using machines in school workshops.

VOCATIONAL EDUCATION is any kind of training that helps a person to make a success of his job. A girl who takes courses in typing and shorthand may become a successful stenographer, department head, and even an executive, in her firm. A boy who learns how to operate a lathe may become a machine-shop foreman, and finally head of his own business. Vocational education—in school or on the job—can make a real difference in a person's life. It can also make a real difference in a nation's life. Knowledge, skill, and training often make up a country's greatest resource.

Kinds of Vocational Education

Apprenticeship teaches a young person all phases of a skilled trade, both on the job and in the classroom (see APPRENTICE). Suppose a young man decides on a job that calls for apprenticeship. He must usually join a labor union to become an apprentice. Union officials and the employer agree on a training schedule for apprentices. This schedule specifies the number of hours the apprentice must spend learning each basic process in the trade. It also specifies the order in which basic processes may be learned best and the amount of time needed to become a full-fledged craftsman. Apprenticeship often includes courses in technical schools. The employer pays for the apprentice's training. The apprenticeship agreement also specifies the wages the man will receive during his training. See LABOR.

Donald E. Super, the contributor of this article, is Professor of Psychology and Education at Columbia University and co-author of Appraising Vocational Fitness.

To qualify for apprenticeship in any skilled trade, a young man should have better than average ability to use his hands, as well as his head. Applicants must often take tests, and high-school graduates are usually preferred. The required age for an apprentice ranges from 16 to 24. But a war veteran over 24, or an older worker with unusual ability, may often win acceptance.

High Schools train young people for many different jobs. High-school training programs may be *comprehensive* or *specialized*. For example, a high-school program may give a youngster comprehensive training that will help him begin a career in bookkeeping. Or, it may give him specialized training in such subjects as electronics or mechanical drawing. Both programs operate in the belief that persons who have completed their high-school education will hold better jobs.

A high-school counselor usually assists each student to understand the facts about the student's interests and aptitudes. He helps the student to use these facts to his best advantage. With the help of the counselor, a student can choose his courses so that they form a sound basis for later job preparation.

This later preparation can take place on the job itself, at college, or in a vocational, technical, or professional school. The student may find that he needs training in English, mathematics, science, social studies, art, shop, or other subjects. He may find that knowledge of other related subjects will help him in his work.

A student who plans to go to work immediately after finishing high school may gain much by attending a *technical*, or *vocational*, *high school*. This kind of school combines courses in such general subjects as English and mathematics with special job training. A student learns by doing as well as by studying. The schools maintain well-equipped shops for teaching automobile repair, electronics, machine shop, carpentry, and other trades. They often have home economics departments and scientific laboratories. At the same time, a student does not lose a general education. He takes courses in such subjects as English, history, and social studies.

Apart from technical schools, a high-school student may often prepare for an occupation by participation in activities outside the classroom. Many high-school clubs and organizations help a student try out the kind of work he thinks he might like. For example, a high-school photography club can give a student practical experience in photography. Four-H clubs contribute much to the education of students interested in agriculture (see FOUR-H CLUB). Arts, crafts, hobbies, and other activities also help a student to find himself. They may give him new interests or broaden those interests he already has.

Night Schools. Many universities, colleges, high schools, and other institutions offer vocational courses in the evening. These courses meet the needs of men and women who work in the daytime. The courses may include such skilled subjects as electronics, fashion design, mechanical drawing, and toolmaking. These courses often help a person to obtain a better job or to improve his present skills. See NIGHT SCHOOL.

Business Colleges offer training in most of the larger cities in the United States and Canada. Most schools known as business colleges are private. Similar courses are offered by junior colleges and technical schools. They aim at giving a student a knowledge of business

English, bookkeeping, business arithmetic, commercial law, shorthand and typing, and the use of various office machines. They help a student to begin a career in business or to qualify for a better job.

Correspondence School Courses help many persons to use their leisuretime to prepare themselves for a chosen career. A man or a woman with a regular, full-time job may find it advisable to take a correspondence course to improve his chances of advancement.

Correspondence courses cover subjects in many different fields. They allow the student to progress as rapidly or as slowly as he chooses. His study, and sometimes his practical experience or experimental work, takes place at home. The correspondence school handles examinations, written work, and reports by mail. It takes considerable self-discipline to complete a correspondence course successfully. But this education has helped many persons to equip themselves for better jobs.

On-the-Job Training. Many larger business establishments and industrial plants provide on-the-job training for employees. This kind of training helps an employee to learn valuable skills and to become more efficient. It also gives him a chance to advance to a better job. Training programs vary widely. Many companies have regular teachers and a departmental director to organize and conduct the instruction program.

Technical Schools and Institutes. Many private and public schools offer highly specialized vocational training to students of high-school age or older. These institutions are called *technical schools, technical institutes,* or *trade schools.* This kind of training is often called *terminal training,* because many students have had several years of high school, and the training prepares them for immediate employment in a certain job. For example, a trade school might prepare a student for immediate employment as a television repairman. Technical and trade schools usually teach a student only the skills he needs for a certain job.

Many junior colleges offer terminal training programs. These programs resemble the instruction given in trade and technical schools, and equip a student for immediate employment. See JUNIOR COLLEGE.

Universities and Colleges offer many kinds of vocational training. A young man or woman who wishes to join such professions as engineering, law, or medicine must usually attend a university or college. Most universities contain regular schools for such subjects as art, architecture, business administration, journalism, and many others. Many universities and colleges—particularly state-supported schools—have special training programs for certain kinds of jobs; for example, police work or textile manufacturing. Apart from special programs, entrance to a university or college usually requires graduation from a high school or preparatory school. See UNIVERSITIES AND COLLEGES.

Teaching Methods

In vocational education, teachers find that both high-school and adult students learn best by actually doing work under job conditions. An atmosphere of reality makes learning and remembering easier. Doing the same task a number of times also helps in learning.

Teachers in vocational education usually specialize in teaching certain jobs. For example, teachers may specialize in automobile repair, basic electricity, cabi-

netmaking, or welding. They teach by means of lectures, discussions, demonstrations, and experiments. Perhaps of greater importance, they guide the students in actually doing work and in carrying out projects. A teacher must use many different methods to give his students the skill and knowledge they need.

Most teachers in this field have had experience in their trade prior to teaching. A good vocational teacher is never really parted from his occupation. He keeps abreast of changes and improvements in order to teach the latest methods. His students emerge into a world of now, not of the past.

History

In prehistoric times, parents and elders taught children all the skills they needed for everyday life. The custom of apprenticeship began in ancient times. By about 2500 B.C., boys in ancient Babylonia and Egypt were apprenticed to master craftsmen who taught them such trades as carpentry, pottery making, and weaving. Apprenticeship continued through the Middle Ages. A boy usually had to spend seven years with a master craftsman. Then he had to pass a test to become a *journeyman,* or skilled worker.

The Industrial Revolution of the 1700's and 1800's marked the decline of apprenticeship (see INDUSTRIAL REVOLUTION). The new factories did not need so many highly skilled workers. But a number of charitable organizations organized classes for men and women in factories. For example, in about 1800 George Birkbeck (1776-1841), an English physician, began lectures for mechanics. This became the *mechanics institute movement* in Great Britain and the United States. Many thousands of workers attended lectures on the arts and sciences, given by the mechanics institutes. Another movement, called the *lyceum movement,* sponsored lectures throughout the United States (see LYCEUM).

In the United States, the *academies* of the 1700's and 1800's introduced vocational education in a number of fields, such as navigation and surveying (see ACADEMY). After 1800, public high schools began to replace academies in popularity. Even the first high schools offered vocational training. After 1862, the federal government helped the states establish agricultural and mechanical colleges that specialized in vocational training. A whole series of federal acts extending from the 1900's to the 1950's helped agricultural education. Federal aid to veterans of World War II and the Korean War helped many young men to obtain on-the-job training. In 1963, a $1,500,000,000 bill expanding Federal aid to vocational education was passed. It was to help meet the need for skilled technicians created by machines that do the work of the unskilled worker and must be maintained by skilled workers. Vocational education is being changed to meet these needs.   DONALD E. SUPER

Related Articles in WORLD BOOK include:

VOCATIONAL EDUCATION ACT. See SMITH-HUGHES ACT.

VOCATIONAL GUIDANCE

VOCATIONAL GUID-ANCE includes a wide range of activities that are intended to help people be successful and happy at their work. These activities are primarily directed toward helping a person make wise occupational choices, but they also include the steps necessary to prepare for, enter upon, and make progress in a job.

A person considering a career must know, in general, what he wants from life. The job, or sequence of jobs, he holds will affect his happiness and influence the lives of people around him. But the selection of a job represents only one of many decisions that he must make in preparing for a career. Vocational guidance includes the vocational, social, personal, and educational aspects of helping a person help himself in his work.

Choosing a vocation is one of the most important and difficult decisions a person must face in his entire life. Each of us wants to reserve the right to select his own occupation. A child may dream of what he would like to become. As he grows up, he often discovers that his goals in life have changed and that his choice of a voca-

Ewing Galloway

the early settlers in America. Our forefathers usually had their vocations selected for them by their parents, by government decree, or by restrictions of religion or social class. They came to America in pursuit of freedom and happiness. They helped make the United States a land where everyone is free and has the right to choose his own career.

Today, the educated job-seeker has a wide choice of jobs and job conditions. If he cannot find work he likes in one part of the country, he can move to a place where his chances of finding it are better. Government support to local schools and payment for training of veterans have made it possible for more and more persons to continue their schooling and training for better jobs. Legislation and education have helped to break down racial and religious barriers to jobs.

In the United States, the number of kinds of jobs to choose from is increasing more rapidly each year. In the early 1960's, there were more than 40,000 different ways of earning a living throughout the nation. This rapid increase in vocations makes the selection of a career more complex than ever before.

Children in their early teens—and even younger—once made up a large proportion of the nation's working force. Today, child-labor laws have raised the age at which young persons can seek employment.

In earlier times, marriage was about the only career open to a girl. The young girl of today, unlike the girl of a few generations ago, should plan on being employable even though she may plan to marry eventually. In the United States, about four of every ten women are in the civilian labor force. Almost 60 per cent of the women workers today are married.

Men today can hope to live longer than their fathers did because of advances in medical science and the standard of living. But there is a trend toward lowering the age at which a person can retire from his job. Some experts predict that a man who will be 20 years old in the year 2000 can expect to spend $19\frac{1}{2}$ years between the time he retires and his death. Planning for the physical limitations that come with age is now becoming less important than finding satisfactory activities for a person who retires from his regular job.

Many of the methods used in choosing a vocation

Donald E. Super, the contributor of this article, is Professor of Psychology and Education at Columbia University and co-author of Appraising Vocational Fitness.

tion is affected by what it is possible for him to do. Each of us wants to enjoy what he does for a living. For a job to provide satisfaction, it must give the rewards a person wants. Rewards differ for different persons. Some persons want to be looked up to, others want a large salary. Others get satisfaction from a job well done, while some seek outlets for special talents.

Finding a satisfactory job does not just happen. Each person has the responsibility of planning his own future and taking steps to make sure that he reaches his goal. To plan wisely, he must use every tool available that can help him see more clearly both what he can and what he cannot achieve. Knowing how to choose a job wisely and well can help make the hours spent at work much more pleasant and profitable.

Jobs Yesterday and Today

Living in the United States today makes choosing a vocation a different kind of problem from that faced by are not new. The development of vocational guidance as a specific process has been credited to the work of Frank Parsons. In Boston in the early 1900's Parsons organized the training of counselors and the development of guidance tools. Through his efforts, schools and industry began to use improved vocational planning and selection methods. One of Parsons' major contributions came from his recommendation that occupational information be gathered and given to persons working in the vocational guidance field. His successors started using new methods of judging aptitudes and interests.

Choosing Your Vocation

To select the best kind of work, you will probably find it helpful to ask yourself questions like these:

1. How can I find out what I like to do? How can I discover the skills and abilities I possess?

2. What must a job offer to make me happy?

3. What help can my parents, my school, and my community give me in making my choice of a job?

4. How do I discover the jobs in which my interests and abilities will be most useful?

5. What kind of training will I need for the job I would like to get, and what are my chances for getting the job I seek?

6. Where can I find the job once I am trained?

7. If I find the decision difficult, how can a counselor help me? Where will I find a vocational counselor, in case I should need his help?

8. Once I get the job I want, what are the problems I must face to be promoted?

9. How will age or accidents affect what I do for a living?

10. If my present job should no longer be available, how can I find another which I might be qualified for and like?

Information About Yourself. Every person has a variety of specific abilities and traits that combine to make him the kind of person he is. Persons differ from one another because of their varying interests, skills, abilities, and personalities. A person does not have the same level of ability in all his skills. For example, the fact that a man can speak well does not mean he can run well. If he has a strong interest in fishing it does not follow that all his other interests will be equally strong. Neither does it mean that he can always do well the things he likes. In order to choose a vocation a person must know the kind of an individual he is and what he can do in comparison with other persons.

It is fortunate that we are not all alike in our abilities and interests. The jobs to be done in this world cover a wide range of possible working conditions and requirements for employment. These jobs require all kinds of people. It is important that a person choose the job that best fits his abilities and interests. Job happiness definitely depends upon being yourself and working where you enjoy the work.

There are many ways that a person can get a clearer picture of his likes and abilities. Tests, school achievement, leisuretime activities, part-time jobs, and conferences with a vocational counselor are but a few of the ways you can find out more about yourself.

Tests are given for admission to college, for deferment from the army, to get jobs, to be promoted, or, as in school, to measure what one has learned and can do.

Tests have become an important influence in vocational guidance. They represent a method of measuring to what extent a person possesses a certain character-

istic or ability. For a test to be of practical value, it must be able to do the following:

1. It must measure what it is claimed to measure. The title *mechanical-aptitude test* is an example of how a test title can be misleading. The term *mechanical work* can mean skills that require the ability to visualize spaces as in the work of the draftsman, the ability to have delicate finger control as in the work of the watchmaker, or the ability to co-ordinate hand and foot movements as in flying an airplane. Each illustration might be called mechanical aptitude. But a person who is skilled in one of these areas is not necessarily able to do well in the others. For a test to be valuable to the job-seeker it is important to know the jobs or training where this ability is to be used.

2. If a test is used several times, the answer, or "measure" obtained should be always about the same. Just as a scale should show a ten-pound block of wood as having the same weight no matter how many times it is weighed, so tests should give the same results.

3. Results should show how well a person measures up against other persons who have taken the test. It does no good to get a score of 80 on a test unless we know how well others did when taking the test.

Although tests have become very popular, taking a poor test, or one that measures something different from what you think it does, can give you only misinformation about yourself.

No test can measure exactly, but it should be devised so that it eliminates guessing as much as possible.

To be of value, tests need to be carefully selected, administered, and explained. This is one of the jobs in the guidance process that is done best by a specialist, who thoroughly understands the tests.

One of the most widely used tests is the *intelligence test*. Most intelligence tests measure how well we can read, write, work with numbers, and solve problems. Because these skills are needed to succeed at school and in many jobs, scores on intelligence tests help show a person how well he can compete in those places where these skills are important. Many intelligence tests today measure other capabilities, too, such as a person's ability to visualize how parts of a puzzle fit together. Intelligence tests try to measure what you can learn by determining how well you can do what you have learned so far. Your score will be affected by your previous education. A person's score on these tests may change as he makes better use of his abilities.

Many of us know persons who are skilled in working with their hands, but who have difficulty in expressing themselves. There are other persons who are top-notch speakers but are not able to do mechanical tasks. Both kinds of persons are able, but they are able in different ways, and will succeed at those jobs that call for their best abilities. In using test results, it is helpful to see them as clues to a person's strengths as well as his weaknesses. Tests help us see that we may not be the best person in a specific ability. But too often we lose sight of the other areas where our abilities could help us find success and satisfaction.

Tests help us estimate how much we can hope to achieve. Trying hard, and using every ounce of ability we have, can help us compete against those who may be smarter but are not using all their potential strength. But working hard will not alone guarantee success. The top level in any skill we might want to develop may be

VOCATIONAL GUIDANCE

partially limited by the body we are born with. One example of this can be seen in the field of sports, where the taller boys get on the basketball team, and the heavier fellows stand the best chance of getting on the football team. But few jobs depend on only one skill. The basketball player who is not tall, but can move fast, shoot the ball accurately, and get along with teammates, may still make the team.

We need several abilities on most jobs. Thus it usually is helpful to take a series of tests which can be fitted together to provide a better over-all picture than just one test would give. *Achievement tests* and *aptitude tests* can be helpful. See Tests and Measurements.

Interest inventories may help a person discover his interests. Generally, tests of this type list many activities either done on a job or frequently found among persons who are successful in a particular field. The individual taking interest inventories is given the opportunity to see what he likes as he goes about comparing many activities and selecting the one he likes best. Once a

can be helpful in showing which subjects are of greater interest to a person, and in showing how well an individual is doing as compared with his classmates studying the same subjects.

Difficulties with school work frequently arise from poor study habits or from lack of effort on the student's part. Ability to concentrate and to learn can be improved. Teachers and counselors can help a person discover the basis for the difficulty and may offer ways of improving study skills.

Many students do not know how the subjects they are studying can be applied in the world of work. The study of job descriptions helps relate school subjects to job demands.

Young persons facing service in the armed forces often have had difficulty in seeing the relationship between their studies and what they will do in service. There is a wide range of military jobs to which persons may be assigned, and staying in school may improve their chances for a better assignment. The armed services issue information on career fields to show the importance of school subjects to the jobs in the services.

LEADING FIELDS OF WORK

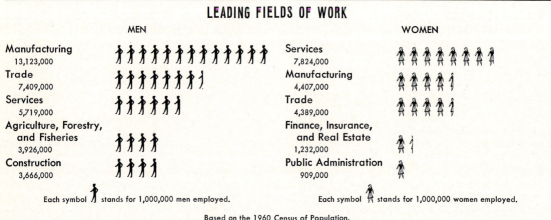

Each symbol stands for 1,000,000 men employed.

Each symbol stands for 1,000,000 women employed.

Based on the 1960 Census of Population.

person discovers the area of his interests, he can check his abilities and thus discover the jobs which he can do.

Jobs may be roughly grouped into three classes: those that call for working with *people*, those that require working with *ideas*, and those that involve working with *things*. The group that an individual selects is partly determined by the kind of person he is. *Personality tests* help provide a picture of how we get along with others and how we act when faced with problems.

Test results cannot be used alone in choosing a job. They are simply one way of getting needed information. Once the person knows more about himself and his goal he still must apply this information to the jobs that exist and the training they will require.

Academic Achievement. People do not always do well in the school subjects they enjoy. Generally, however, if a person is interested in a subject he will want to work harder. The greater the effort he puts into it, the more satisfying are the results. The more satisfaction a person gets from the results, the greater is the desire to work harder. This cycle works in reverse, too. A disliked subject tends to be the one that gets less attention, and less learning results. Grades in school subjects

Planning and selecting the subjects to take in high school are all-important. A person must determine the courses which will be helpful in a future career, or the subjects needed for entrance at the trade school or college he may wish to attend. Courses that will merely enable a person to graduate from high school do not always help in a future career. But today, knowledge of English and mathematics is helpful in preparation for all work.

A person's academic rank in his graduating class is one of the best indications of his chance of success at college. Similarly, the amount of schooling and training a person can get is closely related to his future earnings and where he will finally stand on the job ladder.

Hobbies and Extracurricular Activities. The young man who tears down his car and converts it into a hot-rod may be learning just as much as the individual who formally enters a trade school to pursue his interests. What a person does "for fun" can be very important in vocational guidance. Not everything that a person learns comes from schooling. Many persons are self-educated, because they have been stimulated into developing skills and knowledge in order to do some-

GETTING A JOB . . .
AND GETTING AHEAD

Choosing a vocation is one of life's most important decisions. Happiness in the years ahead depends partly on working at a job you like, and one that you can do well. Careful planning at the start will help you to make progress in the job you choose.

1. **"This Is What I Like, and Can Learn to Do."** First find out all you can about yourself, with the aid of a trained vocational counselor, if possible. He can help you determine what your special aptitudes are, and where they may be needed by an employer.

H. Armstrong Roberts

2. **"This Is What I Must Learn."** You may need special training to fill the job you choose. In many cases you can get this training as an apprentice on the job, or in an "after-hours" school.

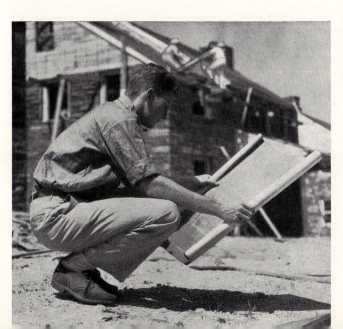

3. **"These Are the Working Conditions on the Job."** The old saying that "one man's meat is another man's poison" is particularly true in a vocation. The working conditions you prefer may be entirely different from those liked best by your friends or members of your family.

4. **"This Is Where My Job May Lead."** Every job can lead you into other similar kinds of work, or to positions of greater responsibility. The range and the nature of job advancement may vary greatly in the different occupations you are considering.

SOME PERSONS LIKE TO WORK WITH CHILDREN . . .

For such a person, teaching school offers tremendous satisfactions. Other ways of working with children include a wide range of jobs, from community recreation supervisor to the medical specialist for children, or *pediatrician.*

thing in which they were interested. We may not all succeed in getting jobs which provide all the satisfactions we seek. Leisuretime activities can often provide the rewards not available in our work.

A large number of persons have developed their hobbies into well-paying jobs. A typical example is the photography fan who begins to take portraits of the neighbors' children and soon discovers he can make enough money at this to have photography serve as his daily job.

As we grow older, and as we are physically less able to continue at our work, skills developed earlier through hobbies may provide a basis for changing occupations to either paid work or leisure activities better fitted to the interests and abilities of older persons.

Joining clubs, managing groups, and becoming active in service organizations all provide experiences that serve as training for future jobs and help a person test his interest in various types of activity. Writing on a school newspaper, organizing a fund-raising campaign, helping in a hospital—all are examples of skills that a person can develop in extracurricular activities and that can help in a future career.

The more varied experiences a young person can get, the better basis he may have for choosing the jobs he likes best or can do best. Similarly, the wider the range of training received in this way, the greater the experience he has to offer a future employer. See Hobby.

Exploratory Job Experiences. One of the most significant sources of training for a future career can come from the part-time jobs taken during school years. Working at any job can provide experience in getting along with others. It also can develop the habits and skills that are needed for advancement, and give a more realistic picture of both the range of occupations in a given field and the actual working conditions there.

To use these part-time experiences to greatest advantage, it is good sense to try to get jobs in those entry occupations which can lead to the career you want.

As a person becomes experienced on a beginning job, he is able to earn more salary. But the job may give the person little satisfaction aside from the pay check. Part-time or beginning jobs selected only in terms of the money they pay limit a person's chances for obtaining a broader picture of the satisfactions other work might provide. Most entry jobs are less challenging than the final, or end, jobs at which a person may plan to find employment eventually. It is helpful to measure the attractiveness of an occupation by asking oneself this question:

"Will I be happy doing the tasks called for in this work seven or eight hours a day, five days a week, for the next thirty years?"

Employers prefer to hire people who will stay on the job. When a person tries to determine the kind of work he likes by skipping from one job to another, he may injure his future employment possibilities. But most employers recognize that work done while attending school is limited by vacations and the hours at which a student is free. Holding a number of jobs while attending school is not considered "job-hopping" or an evidence of a lack of seriousness on the student's part.

In planning exploratory job experiences, it is helpful to consider the work-experience courses now being offered by many schools. Courses in diversified occupations, distributive occupations, and cooperative education frequently are designed to allow students to spend part of their school time working on the job they are preparing for in school. Some high school courses, and some colleges include work-experience programs as part of their requirements.

School counselors, placement offices, and state

... AND SOME LIKE TO WORK WITH OLDER PEOPLE

Your personality, as much as your aptitudes, should help determine your job choice. Some persons prefer to be associated with other adults, rather than with children, in performing their daily work.

employment services are prepared to help beginning workers use their job experiences constructively in planning for the future.

Counseling. Vocational counselors are trained to help persons think out solutions to their problems. Parents and teachers are helpful in providing the information and friendship a person may need when he has to make difficult decisions. But they generally lack training in counseling, and there are situations in which someone outside one's circle of friends can be more helpful. Those who are close to the person and feel strongly about him cannot always be as helpful as they would like. The things they may wish for him may not be the things he wishes for himself. In his efforts to decide what he wants to do, it is hard for him not to hurt their feelings. In coming to a decision for himself, he must be free to look at all the alternatives with someone whom he feels will not be affected by what he decides. Counselors can offer the kind of objective help a person may need to solve his problems.

Frequently counselors are thought of as persons who give a person advice about what to do. A counselor certainly will help the person to get any information he needs to make a decision, but he knows that the person himself must make the decision, because it is he who will be most affected by it. He helps the person seeking aid to see why certain courses of action make sense, and how he can take the necessary steps.

If a counselor is to help, the individual must be prepared to think about the things that are giving him trouble, and the ways he would consider solving them. A counselor can be particularly helpful when a person wants to talk to someone who will keep the conversation confidential.

It is important, however, to consult only a reputable trained counselor. Trained vocational counselors can commonly be identified in the following ways:

1. They have been certified or licensed to practice, in states where laws cover this kind of professional activity.

2. They have taken advanced college training in the tools and techniques of guidance and counseling.

3. They may be members of one of the professional societies, such as the American Psychological Association, the National Vocational Guidance Association, or the American Personnel and Guidance Association.

4. They are connected with a reputable public or private institution.

5. In helping a person, they can use and apply such tools as tests and job information. The tools used meet the standards discussed in previous sections of this article.

6. They make no claims about their ability to know *the* best job for any person.

Every person meets problems he cannot solve alone. Just as going to a doctor is the sensible thing to do when one is sick, going to a counselor is a normal and sensible way to meet confusing situations.

Planning the Selection of a Job. Knowing about yourself does not guarantee that you will be happy in your work. Counselors point out that persons selecting a career sometimes use techniques that appear to be sound but which actually can lead to unhappiness. Following are a few of the techniques to guard against:

1. *Do not* use *only* the advice of other persons as to what they think you ought to do. Although many people may make good guesses, you are the one who has to like the work and be able to succeed.

2. *Do not* select a job *primarily* because of the present need for workers. The demands of industry change. The field you select now may not have a shortage of workers when you have finished training. When workers are let out, only the best workers are kept. The fact that a job is available does not mean you can compete when conditions change.

3. *Do not* stay in a field where you have obtained some experience but where you may not be happy. Experience

VOCATIONAL GUIDANCE

helps a person to get more pay at first, but job satisfaction and adjustment will determine how long he will hold the job and the raises he will get in the long run.

4. *Do not* take a job you dislike, even if it pays well. Holding such a job forces a person to spend the major part of his life earning enough to enjoy the few remaining waking hours left each day. If the job provides satisfaction, work and play may be hard to separate.

To plan your selection of a suitable job most efficiently, be sure that you do these things:

1. Determine what work interests you most.
2. Determine which things you do best.
3. List the jobs which require your major interests.
4. Check job trends and the locations offering the greatest employment possibilities.
5. Plan your training to qualify for your area of interest.
6. Map out a job-hunting plan.
7. Find out about other jobs requiring similar interests and skills, so that you can seek new employment if a job is discontinued, or if you seek to get better jobs.
8. Know which persons are available to help you decide what you want to do, and how to do it.

The young person choosing a vocation may interview successful workers in various fields. He may also visit places where persons work, to observe working conditions. He may also get help from studying biographies of persons who achieved success in their vocations. But he must keep in mind that he himself, and not some other worker, must be satisfied with the job he finally chooses.

Where to Find Information About Jobs. Helping people get occupational information is one of the major jobs of persons working as vocational counselors, as librarians, and in the public employment services. These three groups usually keep files that include descriptions of jobs and reports of local and national employment trends. There are several sources for this information.

The current occupational books and pamphlets are described monthly in *The Guidance Index* (Science Research Associates, Chicago), and quarterly in the *Occupational Index* (Personnel Services, Peapack, N.J.), and in the *Vocational Guidance Quarterly* (American Personnel and Guidance Association, Washington, D.C.). About 3,000 occupational books and pamphlets are described in *Occupational Literature—An Annotated Bibliography*.

Government Sources. The most usable source of job information published by the federal government is called the *Occupational Outlook Handbook*. It gives an interesting and informative job survey for each of over 500 occupations. Each job survey includes a summary of the employment trends and outlook in that occupation at the time of publication. It describes the training and qualifications required and gives the range of earnings and working conditions. It also includes listings of the professional and trade groups and some of the available publications about the occupation. This handbook and the *Occupational Outlook Quarterly* are written for the general public and can be found in most schools, libraries, and employment offices. Copies can be purchased from the Superintendent of Documents, Washington, D.C. 20402.

The *Dictionary of Occupational Titles* is prepared by the Division of Occupational Analysis of the United States Employment Service and represents a major

H. Armstrong Roberts

SOME PERSONS LIKE TO WORK WITH IDEAS ...
They get their greatest satisfaction from organizing and writing down their thoughts, or from planning projects.

source of help for persons wanting to know about jobs. At first, the *Dictionary of Occupational Titles* may seem complicated, but it is worth learning how to use it because of the vast amount of information offered. A vocational counselor or a librarian can show the job-seeker how to use it.

Each of the government agencies has material covering jobs in the area over which it has control, and will mail it on request. A list of all material available can be obtained by writing for an Index of Government Publications and Documents, U.S. Government Printing Office, Superintendent of Documents, Washington, D.C. 20402

For information on:	Write to:
Apprenticeships	U.S. Department of Labor
Business and Retail Trade	U.S. Department of Commerce
Farms and Farming	U.S. Department of Agriculture
Government Jobs	U.S. Civil Service Commission
Military Jobs	U.S. Department of Defense
Occupational Trends	Bureau of Labor Statistics, U.S. Department of Labor
Physically Handicapped	U.S. Department of Health, Education, and Welfare
Public Health Careers	U.S. Department of Health, Education, and Welfare
Schools and Training Facilities	U.S. Department of Health, Education, and Welfare, Office of Education
Wildlife and Forestry	Fish and Wildlife Service, U.S. Department of the Interior
Women's Occupations	Women's Bureau, U.S. Department of Labor

Private and Industrial Sources of Job Information. Many industries and publishers issue pamphlets or monographs dealing with occupations. It is helpful to know how to judge whether the job information they contain is correct. Some monographs are designed to recruit people into a certain field or occupation. Such publications tend to point up the glamorous parts of the work and do not mention less desirable but equally important demands of the job. In order to have confidence in the publication you are reading, check it by questions such as these:

1. Who is the author? How qualified is he to present the correct information?

2. How recently was the information gathered? Has anything happened which might have changed the job possibilities since this information was published?

3. Does this source tell the number and kinds of workers employed? Does it also describe where in the country there are too many or too few workers?

4. How specifically is the job described? Does the publication include a description of the nature of the work and the tools or machines used to do the job?

5. Does the information include facts about government laws, licensing, and union requirements for admission to the job?

6. Does it include a careful description of the skills, interests, personality characteristics, and age or sex qualifications necessary for employment?

7. What training is indicated? Does the publication describe where and how the training can be obtained?

8. Does it give information about how to enter the field, and the requirements for promotion?

9. Does it show the beginning wages and the various wage scales in different parts of the country?

10. How many hours will a person work at the job described? Does the publication include information on the time of the day when people work? Does it tell about vacations?

... AND OTHERS LIKE TO WORK WITH THEIR HANDS. This skilled worker on a television assembly line gains personal satisfaction from the efficiency and care with which she fits together the delicate parts of a TV receiver.

Ewing Galloway

11. How much is told about the regularity of employment? Is the industry described a seasonal one?

12. Does the publication describe health or accident hazards on the job?

13. Are the places where people work in this job indicated?

14. Are you given leads as to other sources of information about the field?

See *Books to Read* section at the end of this article.

Training for Your Vocation

In School. One of the big problems facing a student is the selection of the school which will best prepare him for the field he wishes to enter. He should first get information about a school's reputation for sound training, and for placing the graduate in an appropriate job. Schools differ greatly in their teaching methods and graduation requirements. There are many differences between schools, such as those based upon size, cost, entrance requirements, housing facilities, courses of study available, location, and characteristics of the faculty and the student body. These and numerous other factors need to be considered carefully before a final selection is made.

There are several directories that provide descriptions of the schools available on the different training levels, and that list the individual characteristics of each school. These directories are found in every library, and help a person decide which schools he may wish to consider further. It is helpful to follow this first step by writing to the schools, requesting their catalogs and bulletins. These provide a more extensive picture of the school's training program and regulations. See *Books to Read* at the end of this article.

Many states have extensive lists of all their training facilities. These can usually be obtained by writing to the state Department of Education. The major professional organizations, too, can supply lists of institutions where training in their particular specialities can be obtained. The student should visit schools in which he is interested before making a selection.

On-the-Job Training. Industry itself does a large share of the training of workers. It is on the job that a worker usually learns to operate the machines peculiar to the industry, finds out the company's methods of working, and gets knowledge of his trade.

Much of the training workers get is informal instruction by the foreman or supervisor under whom they work. But many large industrial organizations train workers by more formal methods. Some companies have what are known as *vestibule schools*, where workers are taught to do their jobs. The new workers remain at these schools until they develop sufficient skill to take their place on an assembly line without slowing up production.

The need for managerial and executive employees who understand the many problems of the company, as well as the problems of the employees, has resulted in the rapid growth of executive-training programs. These programs often require the trainee to work at all levels and in all departments of the organization before he assumes an executive position.

One of the oldest forms of on-the-job training, dating back to the Middle Ages, is the apprenticeship pro-

MANY PERSONS PREFER TO WORK OUT OF DOORS . . .

This oil-field worker, soaking up the Louisiana sunshine as he checks gauges at an oil well, might not trade jobs with an office employee if he were given the opportunity. Such jobs as his sometimes have led to top administrative positions in business and industry.

gram. Under the modern apprenticeship arrangement, the company enters into a contract with the apprentice. This contract specifies the period of training, the pay, the kind of work, and the kind of supervision the apprentice will receive. Usually, a set number of hours a week at school is required, so that the apprentice can learn the theory and background knowledge of the trade. The length of training as an apprentice varies in the different trades. The conditions governing the hiring and training of apprentices are partly determined by the policies of the labor unions involved. See APPRENTICE.

Partly because of the worker's interest, and partly to train people who might qualify for promotion, some companies hire teachers to conduct classes for their workers during their off-duty hours. Subjects now being taught cover the entire range of skills people need on the job or may have as hobbies.

Paying the Bill. Apprenticeships are examples of a type of training where you earn as you learn. In the business fields, also, paying for your training through part-time employment is often possible. Some companies pay for an employee's education or training.

But when training demands full-time attendance at school, earning extra money is not easy. Some students are able to get part-time jobs to pay for room and board, but extensive time devoted to earning a living tends to limit what a person can achieve at school.

There are many scholarships, fellowships, and loans available to help students. Certain conditions have to be met in order for a person to qualify for help. These conditions range from high grades in school to those that require some rather unusual characteristic such as being born in a certain county or sharing the same

name as the original donor of the grant. Most people think of these subsidies only as rewards for academic achievement, and for this reason many of these sources of student help go unused each year, due to lack of applicants.

The student who will have to earn his way should discuss this problem with counselors or staff members at the school he plans to attend. The school officials may be able to tell him about local sources of financial help. At the same time, they will explain limitations that may exist as to where a student can work. School officials may also explain how many hours a day he is permitted to work when carrying a full- or part-time study load.

Many organizations and groups sponsor needy students. A list of over 300 of these organizations is to be found in a book entitled *Scholarships, Fellowships and Loans.* (See *Books to Read* at end of this article.) This book describes the nature of the organizations and the extent and nature of the financial aid they provide. It tells what qualifications are required, and how to apply for aid. An equally helpful catalog is *Your Opportunity to Help Yourself, to Help Others,* by Theodore S. Jones, Milton, Mass. A document covering almost 22,000 awards available from 72 countries, territories, or organizations is *Study Abroad: International Handbook of Fellowships, Scholarships and Educational Exchange,* UNESCO Vol. II, Columbia University Press, New York, N.Y. For further information, see SCHOLARSHIP.

Although the cost of schooling is rising rapidly, more and more people are continuing their training to higher levels. This increase in the average amount of training means that it is essential for each person to obtain as much schooling as he possibly can, so that he can meet the resulting higher standards set for employment.

How to Get the Job You Want

Planning a Job Hunt. Every person, regardless of the work he does, must be a salesman at least once in his life. He must sell himself to an employer as a person worth hiring.

One of the major principles in salesmanship is discovering what the person you are trying to sell needs and likes. After finding out what the customer wants, the saleman demonstrates in every possible way how his product will do the job.

Using this idea in a job hunt means that the first step required is a careful study of the characteristics and skills of successful workers in the field you wish to enter. Then, using sources such as the *Dictionary of Occupational Titles*, it is possible to check the school subjects, hobbies, job experiences, personality characteristics, and skills which you possess and which are necessary to the job you seek.

Employers realize that good workers are persons who are doing jobs they enjoy, and for which they are prepared. A prospective employee who requests "just any job" demonstrates that he has not considered seriously his own abilities and his future goals. Seeking "any job" does not enable a candidate for employment to show how his particular background will best serve the employer.

Three Ways to Get a Job. Basically there are three ways in which a person gets a job:

1. *The Job Is Made Available to You.* About half of all jobs are secured through recommendations by family and friends. They hear about vacancies that are going to develop, and they suggest possible candidates to the employer before the job is made available to the public. This is the easiest way to get a job, but it has its disadvantages. Jobs secured in this way do not always represent possibilities for satisfaction and a future. Often the work you really want may not be available in your local community or in fields where your family and friends are employed.

2. *You Seek the Job.* Going after the job demands knowing where to find it. Advertisements placed in the newspaper may call you to an employer's attention. Many companies review "situation wanted" advertisements when they have an immediate vacancy to fill. Your advertisement will let them know about you at the time a vacancy develops. Unexpected vacancies occur daily, and the person hired often tends to be a combination of the best person and the one most available.

Prepare a list of all companies that might employ you. Visit each one and discover the specific jobs available and their requirements. Develop a portfolio, or summary, of information, including how your background qualifies you for the job, letters of recommendation, and, if possible, samples of your work or achievements. Leave copies of this material with those companies to which you feel you have something to offer. After your visits, send follow-up letters thanking each company for its courtesy. This will indicate your interest, and also bring your name back to the company's attention.

3. *You May Make the Job.* A large portion of the population is self-employed. If you check the services in your community, you may discover that a new business is needed. Some companies make it possible for an individual to go into business for himself and sell their products. Thousands of automobile-service station owner-operators get their start as businessmen in this way.

... AND MANY OTHERS LIKE INDOOR WORK
The person who prefers "inside" work has an almost unlimited number of jobs from which to choose—in factories, offices, and stores. Such a person must be content to enjoy outdoor life only on weekends and during vacations.

SOME LIKE TO WORK WITH PEOPLE . . .

Personal service and selling jobs are rewarding vocations for such persons.

. . . AND OTHERS LIKE TO WORK WITH THINGS

Scientific and industrial laboratories are among the leading places of employment such persons usually prefer.

Some persons develop new inventions or ideas that will increase production in an existing industry. If they can convince a company of the value of their ideas or skills, new positions may be created for them so that they can develop their suggestions. This method of getting a job is probably the most difficult. Changes in an industry tend to be developed by persons at present employed on a job. Companies are reluctant to try the ideas of a person who may not understand the problems of the company.

Sources of Information About Job Vacancies. In professional and technical fields, most vacancies are filled by recommendations of established men in the field. In fields requiring advanced training, job vacancies are frequently reported to the teachers in the field who may then recommend qualified candidates.

Some employers do not wish to be bothered seeing a large number of job applicants. They may prefer that someone else screen out unfit candidates. These companies often list their vacancies with private or public employment agencies. Important public agencies include state employment service offices. A job applicant should seriously consider such private and public agencies as possible sources of jobs. Labor unions and government personnel offices also offer information about vacancies. Agencies operating on a national level report job opportunities outside the local community.

Notices of job vacancies in the "help wanted" section of the newspaper are immediate possibilities for the job hunter. Newspaper reports of plans for starting a new business or for the expansion of an old one are clues to job possibilities.

What Employers Look For. Being hired for a job is a two-way process. The job applicant is trying to convince the employer of his worth, while he is deciding if he would like the job. At the same time the employer is anxious to secure workers, provided they will be competent and stay on the job.

Employers evaluate a job candidate chiefly by his behavior and experience as revealed during the job interview. The employer asks himself:

Does this person seem to know what he wants from a job?

Does he have the ability to do the job and produce the kind of work we require?

Can he get along with other persons? Is he polite and tactful? Can he stand criticism?

What kind of appearance does he present? Is he neat, clean, and alert?

How long is he likely to stay on the job? Is he a likely candidate for promotion to better jobs in the company?

Will the job we have open provide a chance for him to succeed and be happy?

The interviewer gets answers to questions such as these by asking the job applicant about himself, including what he has done, and by weighing both what he says and how he says it. But many companies try to get a more objective picture of a person's abilities and personality. To do this, tests or sample jobs are often given to discover the applicant's ability.

What Makes a Job

Jobs and Job Descriptions. One of the most important steps in choosing a career is to have a clear picture of the vocation being considered. Most persons asked to describe a job do so in terms of the daily activities a worker performs, or of the place of employment. They say "Mr. Jones mends shoes" or "Miss Appleton works for Metropolitan." A sound selection of a vocation considers all the characteristics of the work and compares the prospective employee's skills, abilities, and

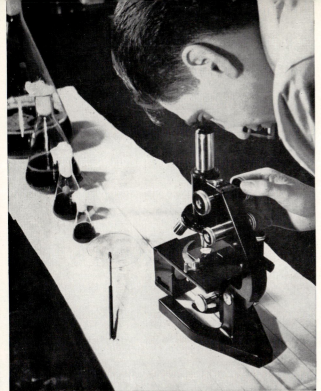

H. Armstrong Roberts

quires each of the following activities from the worker:

Walking	Crouching	Handling
Jumping	Kneeling	Fingering
Running	Sitting	Feeling
Balancing	Reaching	Talking
Climbing	Lifting	Hearing
Crawling	Carrying	Seeing
Standing	Throwing	Color vision
Turning	Pushing	Depth perception
Stooping	Pulling	Working speed

For example, here is a description of physical demands made on a television-service and repair man:

Climbing: Occasionally, when adjusting or installing television antennas.

Standing; Sitting: Continually, at bench in repair shop while testing and repairing television receivers.

Walking: Occasionally, about shop to use electrical testing equipment; frequently, while making service calls.

Turning; Stooping: Frequently, while picking up or setting down tools, equipment, and television chassis.

Lifting: Frequently, while moving and raising television receivers weighing up to 100 pounds.

Reaching: Continually, with both hands to adjust knobs on various electrical testing equipment and to plug and unplug wire connections.

Feeling, Fingering, Handling: Constantly, while handling delicate parts and receiver controls when testing, adjusting, and repairing television receivers.

Seeing: Continually, while observing and analyzing quality of television picture and making necessary adjustments to obtain clear picture.

Working conditions found in jobs include the following:

Inside	Dirty	High places
Outside	Odors	Exposure to burns
Hot	Noisy	Electrical hazards
Cold	Adequate lighting	Explosives
Sudden	Adequate ventila-	Radiant energy
temperature	tion	Toxic conditions
changes	Vibration	Working with
Humid	Mechanical	others
Dry	hazards	Working around
Wet	Moving objects	others
Dusty	Cramped quarters	Working alone

The working conditions of a television-service and repair man are described as follows:

Works inside shop or customer's home or establishment, usually adequately heated and ventilated. Works either alone or with an assistant, but usually around others. Occasionally works outdoors when adjusting antenna. Drives car from shop on service calls.

Hazards. In connection with hazards, the job analyst determines the possible injuries which might be involved in the occupation. He considers the following hazards:

Cuts	Sprains	Impairment of sight
Bruises	Hernia	Impairment of hearing
Burns	Fracture	Occupational diseases
Collapse	Loss of parts of body	Electric shock

Hazards to a television-service and repair man are: Possibility of electric shocks and burns from soldering iron, occasional injury from explosion of picture tubes when they are dropped, and falls from ladder or roof when adjusting antennas.

5. Relation to Other Jobs. It is helpful to a person to have information about the other jobs for which he qualifies. Such information describes jobs to which this job leads, and also indicates the major source of workers employed in the job being analyzed.

Occupational guides describing various jobs are pre-

interests with the demands of the job.

Each job must be carefully described, to give persons a basis for comparing their needs with job demands, and also to compare one job with another. The task of developing job descriptions is frequently given to a *job analyst.* An analyst observes many workers in a specific occupation and then reports what "makes the job" by writing a description of that job.

A summary of material generally found in detailed job descriptions is given below. A person seeking to choose a vocation might well review the categories described to determine what he can do or would like to find in the job of his choice.

1. Job Title, the name or names by which this job is called. Each job may have several titles. For example, the person who operates steam engines, air compressors, generator motors, ventilation equipment, and similar machines may be known by any of four job titles: stationary engineer, operating engineer, power-plant operator, and stationary-engine man. Information about job titles is frequently obtained from the *Dictionary of Occupational Titles.* This book also lists a specific *code number* for each job.

2. Job Description. A summary of the work performed on the job as well as a detailed description of each operation performed. The performance requirements for a worker on the job are usually covered under a definition of the (1) responsibility, (2) job knowledge, (3) mental application, and (4) the dexterity and accuracy required.

3. Training Requirements and Educational Background. The specific knowledge expected of workers in the field, as well as the experience required. People may train for jobs in several ways—by on-the-job training, vocational training, technical training, and general education, and through activities and hobbies.

4. Physical Demands, Working Conditions, and Hazards. *Physical demands* include the degree to which the job repared by the U.S. Department of Labor and can be obtained from the Superintendent of Documents, Washington, D.C. 20402.

Thus far jobs have been considered in terms of the requirements necessary to perform them satisfactorily. There are many jobs which each person could fill. But they include many jobs at which he would not care to work. Being happy and satisfied with a job comes from many characteristics of employment besides the work itself. Doing well in your work and being satisfied with your employment may depend on the answers to such questions as these:

1. Does the job give you prestige among the people who are important to you?
2. Do you like the people you work with?
3. How much do you earn?
4. What are your hours of work?
5. What are your opportunities for advancement?
6. Can you see the results of your efforts? Do you get satisfaction from a job well done?
7. What chance is there in the job for service to others?
8. What are the working conditions?
9. Are you free to live where you choose?
10. How much responsibility does the job demand from you? How much competition?
11. How does your religion affect your work?
12. How tiring is the work?
13. How much appreciation or criticism do you get?
14. How secure is the job?

The answers to questions like these will differ from one person to another, as well as from job to job. For example, a job might seem dull to one person and exciting to another. Many jobs provide some sources of satisfaction along with many unsatisfactory elements. For example, teaching is rated high in terms of prestige, but not in salary. Rarely is a job altogether pleasant. Happiness on the job requires that it include enough pleasant things to balance out those things that are unpleasant.

Grouping Jobs by Families. Describing jobs does more than provide information about a specific occupation. It permits the grouping of jobs into families. These families are developed by grouping together all those jobs which have something in common. The U.S. Census Bureau groups jobs in terms of social and economic levels. The United States Employment Service groups jobs similarly, except that it adds categories developed from the level of skills of people in the trades, and some categories which are based on the process, or the activity, where the job takes place. Job families exist which are based upon (1) belonging to the same industry, (2) working conditions, (3) training requirements, (4) interest, (5) intelligence, (6) prestige, or (7) occurrence in similar geographical settings.

Knowing about job families helps a person to discover jobs which are similar to the one he now holds or seeks. It is not true that there is only one job for a person. If depressions occur or industrial advances do away with certain jobs, many of the workers who have lost employment can find similar occupations through their knowledge of job families. Job families also point up the road for advancement from one job to the next one up the ladder.

Many young men and women who plan to transfer from civilian to military life, or who seek a civilian job after being in service, have found information about job families helpful in preparing for and adjusting to their new life.

People who can decide on an interest, an industry, or a field in which they would enjoy working have a helpful start toward selecting a vocation. Vocational charts such as those issued by the U.S. Bureau of Labor Statistics give the job-seeker a picture of the rising employment in the field, both the kinds and the percentages of workers employed at the different jobs available, and the cities which offer the best chances for employment.

Such charts are just a start, however, for they do not give a clear picture of the many specific jobs within the industry. Also, they do not describe the commodities that the industry produces. One of the major sources of employment in our country is in what is called the "Printing, Publishing, and Allied Graphic Arts Industry." The size of this industry does not become clear until a person considers which of the 21 processing services, the 73 product classifications, or the 200 occupations will offer most satisfaction to him.

Many people think of an industry in terms of one of its popular occupations. One of the most helpful results of exploring job families is to show the variety of jobs within an industry. See INDUSTRY; MANUFACTURING.

An industry contains a surprising number of occupations. Try this test on yourself. See how many jobs in the insurance field you can name. Then read the list below of just a few of the jobs found in this field.

Jobs in the Insurance Field

Accountant	Editor	Payroll Auditor
Actuary	Examiner	Personnel Manager
Agent	Field Man	Policy Checker
Auditor	File Clerk	Publicity Writer
Bookkeeper	Fire Prevention	Purchasing Agent
Broker	Engineer	Safety Engineer
Business-Machine	Inspector	Secretary
Operator	Lawyer	Solicitor
Cashier	Librarian	Special Agent
Chemical	Mail Clerk	Statistician
Engineer	Medical	Stenographer
Claim Adjuster	Technician	Training
Construction	Messenger	Supervisor
Engineer	Nurse	Underwriter
Dietitian	Office Manager	X-Ray Technician
Doctor		

Each of these jobs has been listed by insurance companies as being an occupation necessary to staff the insurance field. And there are many others.

The Chances of Getting the Kind of Job You Want are decided largely by how much competition exists. The job-hunter must find out (1) how many jobs are available, (2) how many applicants there are, and (3) how well qualified they are.

The development of the United States as an industrial nation is slowly changing the kinds of jobs. In 1910, about 30 out of every 100 people who worked for a living were farmers. By the early 1960's, only about 6 of every 100 workers listed their occupations as farmer or farm laborer.

Many parents urge their children to become professional men and women—such as doctors, lawyers, or engineers. The professions actually offer fewer jobs than other fields of employment do. Only 12 of every

ANNUAL INCOME IN THE UNITED STATES BY AMOUNT OF EDUCATION

Median income in 1964 (Median is the middle number in a group arranged according to size.)

EDUCATION COMPLETED   Elementary ▬▬   High School ▬▬   College ▬▬

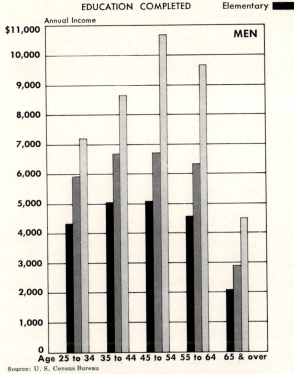

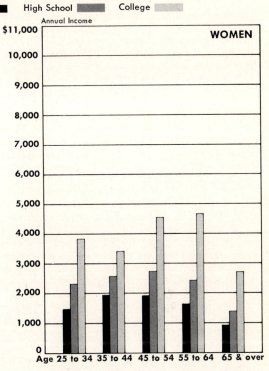

Source: U. S. Census Bureau

100 workers find employment at the professional level.

Figures about the number of people employed in the various types of jobs are important in vocational guidance. In planning for the future, it is usually wise to know the chances for employment at different job levels.

Occupational information helps a person planning for the future to get a clear picture of the changes which are taking place in the jobs which are available. If we compare the job picture obtained from the 1960 census with the results of the 1950 census, we can see that some important changes are taking place.

Most noticeable is the rapid decrease in farm jobs and the rise in professional and technical employment. Most people in 1960 worked as *operatives*. The term *operative* covers people who are working as apprentices, and such workers as assembly line workers, press operators, bus drivers, stationary firemen, weavers, and welders. The second largest occupational group consisted of *clerical workers*, including secretaries, stenographers, typists, bookkeepers, and office machine operators. The third largest group included *craftsmen and other skilled workers*, such as carpenters, machinists, and plumbers.

Jobs and opportunities for employment are closely related to geography, and to the movement of people from one state to another. Many industries, such as shipping and shipbuilding, obviously must be located near the water. Similarly, mining, farming, and other occupations which depend on our natural resources can be carried on only in certain parts of the country. Beyond these relatively fixed occupations, however, the demand for workers in different parts of the country is changing rapidly. Many textile firms have moved to the South to take advantage of favorable labor and

weather conditions. Irrigation techniques are being used to make farmland out of desert. A large part of the population of our country has migrated to the seacoasts, with the largest group heading toward the mild climate on the West Coast. The increased population in these areas has brought development of industries required to serve and maintain large communities. Houses need to be built, schools must be enlarged, and other necessities and luxuries of life must be provided. Often, employment possibilities are directly related to the size of population in the locality. Accounting, for example, offers better opportunities in a large community than in a small one.

Vocational Guidance as a Profession

Who Counselors Are, and Where They Work. Counselors are professional workers who have obtained training in helping people to live more effective lives. They assist a person in knowing himself better and in getting the information he may need to act on his decisions. People begin to develop their personalities, interests, and skills from childhood, so counselors are often found in elementary schools and junior high schools, as well as in high schools, vocational schools, social agencies, colleges, and universities.

Graduation from school does not mean the end of the need for counseling. Counselors to help adults, and special groups such as veterans or the handicapped, work in various public and social agencies. Follow-up and helping the person to adjust and progress on the job is one of the most important functions of the counselor.

Religious groups, for example, the YMCA and the Jewish Vocational Services, do a major job in helping

353

people in the community face their problems of vocational adjustment. There are growing employment possibilities in organizations serving people with specific handicaps, such as the National Tuberculosis Association and the American Foundation for the Blind. The U.S. government offers guidance jobs in such agencies as the Veterans Administration, the State Employment Services, and the Vocational Rehabilitation Administration (Department of Health, Education, and Welfare).

Industry is increasingly recognizing the relationship between production and good personnel selection and training procedures. Training in vocational guidance and counseling represents sound preparation for personnel work in industry.

The U.S. Department of Labor has issued reports covering employment possibilities for counselors in schools, in the rehabilitation field, and in employment offices.

Employment opportunities as counselors in schools and in other settings have become better as people have become more aware of the value of vocational guidance. The rise in the number of young persons in school has also increased the demand for school counselors. There is more concern today about employment of the handicapped and older workers. Employment possibilities are good for counselors who are trained to work with these groups.

Training Needed. Most counselors today have either the master's or doctor's degree in guidance or psychology. As a background for graduate professional preparation in counseling, students should possess a broad liberal education with courses in labor, economics, psychology, sociology, and statistics. Graduate training includes psychology or guidance courses devoted to understanding (1) the development of and type of problems people have, (2) techniques for identifying a person's strengths and weaknesses, and (3) methods of helping a person develop his potential. The counselor should know the sources of information his clients may need, and the people who are available to help persons find desirable employment.

Professional Organizations. The major professional organizations in guidance and counseling are the American Psychological Association, 1200 17th Street NW, Washington, D.C. 20036, and the American Personnel and Guidance Association, 1605 New Hampshire Avenue NW, Washington, D.C. 20036. Both groups have subdivisions working with special groups. For example, the American Personnel and Guidance Association includes the American College Personnel Association, the American Rehabilitation Counseling Association, the American School Counselor Association, the Association for Counselor Education and Supervision, the Association for Measurement and Evaluation in Guidance, the National Vocational Guidance Association, and the Student Personnel Association for Teacher Education.

Letters sent to either of the major organizations will bring further information about the function of each of the many divisions, training facilities in the field, current employment trends, and a detailed description of the many job titles under which persons trained in vocational guidance and counseling find employment.   DONALD E. SUPER

Related Articles in WORLD BOOK include:

CAREER OPPORTUNITIES

The following WORLD BOOK articles contain information helpful to a general understanding of a vocational field. Many of these articles include Career sections and other sections that give qualifications, training, and sources of further information.

Accounting	Marine Corps, United States
Advertising	Mathematics
Agriculture	Mechanical Drawing
Air Conditioning	Medicine
Air Force, United States	Merchant Marine
Airline Stewardess	Metallurgy
Airplane Pilot	Meteorology
Anthropology	Mining
Archaeology	Modeling
Architecture	Mortician
Army, United States	Motion Picture
Astronomy	Music
Atomic Energy	Navy, United States
Automobile	Nursing
Aviation	Occupational Therapy
Banks and Banking	Ocean
Biology	Office Work
Bookkeeping	Ophthalmology
Botany	Optometry
Building Trade	Osteopathy
Business	Patternmaker
Cartoon	Petroleum
Chemistry	Pharmacy
Chiropractic	Photography
Clothing	Physical Therapy
Coast Guard, United States	Physics
Commercial Art	Plastics
Conservation	Police
Criminology	Political Party
Dancing	Post Office
Dental Hygiene	Printing
Dentistry	Psychiatry
Dietitian	Psychology
Diving, Deep-Sea	Public Relations
Economics	Publishing
Electricity	Radio
Electronics	Railroad
Engineering	Real Estate
Engineering Technician	Recreation
Entomology	Religious Education
Federal Bureau of	Repairmen and Mechanics
Investigation	Research
Fire Fighting	Restaurant
Florist	Retailing
Forest and Forest Products	Salesmanship
Geology	Science
Government	Ship and Shipping
Hairdressing	Social Work
Handicapped	Sociology
Homemaking	Speech Therapy
Hospital	Surveying
Hotel	Taxidermy
Industrial Design	Teaching
Insurance	Telephone
Interior Decoration	Television
Iron and Steel	Theater
Journalism	Toolmaking
Labor	Veterinary Medicine
Law	Writing
Library	Zoology

OTHER RELATED ARTICLES

Apprentice	Health, Education, and
Civil Service	Welfare, Department of
Employment Agency	Letter Writing
Fellowship	Peace Corps
Foreign Service	Scholarship
Guidance	Vocational Education

Outline

Questions

What activities does the term *vocational guidance* include?

How many different kinds of jobs are there in the United States?

How should a person go about getting a job?

What are some possible sources for information about job vacancies?

How can a vocational counselor help the job-seeker?

In what ways can a person gain information about himself that will help him choose an occupation?

What is a job description? Why is it important to the job-seeker?

How does knowledge of job families help a worker?

What do employers look for in job applicants?

Where do vocational counselors work?

Books to Read

AMERICAN COUNCIL ON EDUCATION. *American Universities and Colleges.* Ed. by Allan M. Cartter. 9th ed. The Council, 1964.

BURT, JESSE C. *Your Vocational Adventure.* Abingdon, 1959.

COHEN, NATHAN M., comp. *Vocational Training Directory of the United States: A Directory of over 7,000 private and public schools, offering almost 700 semiprofessional, technical, and trade courses.* 3rd ed. rev. & enl. Potomac Press, 1958.

FORRESTER, GERTRUDE, comp. *Occupational Literature: An Annotated Bibliography.* H. W. Wilson Co., 1964.

HOROWITZ, ALICE H., ed. *The Outlook for Youth.* Wilson, 1962. Discusses the choice of college and career, employment trends, and participation in public affairs.

LOVEJOY, CLARENCE E. *College Guide: A Complete Reference Book to 2,834 American Colleges and Universities for Use by Students, Parents, Teachers . . .* Rev. ed. Simon & Schuster, 1966.

SPLAVER, SARAH. *Your Career If You're Not Going to College.* Messner, 1963.

UNITED STATES. BUREAU OF LABOR STATISTICS. *Occupational Outlook Handbook: Employment Information on Major Occupations for Use in Guidance.* 1966-67 ed. U.S. Govt. Ptg. Office.

WILSON, EUGENE S., and BUTCHER, C. *College Ahead! A Guide for High School Students, and Their Parents.* Harcourt, 1961.

ZAPOLEON, MARGUERITE W. *Occupational Planning for Women.* Harper, 1961.

ZAREM, LEWIS. *Careers and Opportunities in Astronautics.* Dutton, 1962. This book deals with job opportunities in space research. It includes college programs and information sources.

VOCATIONAL REHABILITATION ADMINISTRATION is an agency in the Department of Health, Education, and Welfare. It works with the states in vocational rehabilitation programs for civilians. These programs take care of persons who can no longer follow their occupations because of injury or disease. They also prepare them for new jobs. Services include medical treatment; artificial devices, such as limbs, braces, and hearing aids; training; and job placement.   JOHN C. BOLLENS

VODER is the name of a device that imitates the sounds of human speech by electrical and electronic means. The name came from the initials of its full name, which is **V**oice **O**peration **D**emonstrator. The voder has a keyboard. When the operator presses certain keys, various sound-producing devices in the voder create the effect of human speech. The voder can speak entire sentences, and can even master the pronunciation of such difficult words as *Albuquerque.* The voder can imitate the voice of a man, woman, or child. It can also imitate a sheep's bleat, a pig's grunt, and the tapping of a woodpecker. It uses two special vacuum tubes, and can make a total of 23 different and fundamental sounds, with hundreds of combinations of these sounds.   RAYMOND F. YATES

VODKA. See ALCOHOLIC DRINK (Distilled Liquors).

VODUN. See VOODOO.

VOGELWEIDE, WALTHER VON DER. See MINNESINGER.

VOGT, WILLIAM (1902-   ), is an American ecologist and ornithologist. He served as chief of the conservation section of the Pan American Union and became national director of the Planned Parenthood Federation in 1951. Vogt wrote *Road to Survival* (1948), a book dealing with the relationship between world populations and food supplies. Vogt was born in Mineola, N.Y. After he graduated from St. Stephens College (now Bard College), Vogt edited *Bird Lore Magazine.* ROGERS McVAUGH

VOICE. Almost all animals have voices. A few animals, like the giraffe, rarely use their voices. But most higher animals can bark, cry, howl, groan, growl, chirp, or make some other noise. Many of the animals use their voices to communicate with each other. Birds can make music with their voices. Dogs can express several feelings with their voices. They whimper when begging or when they feel guilty, they growl when angry, and bark eagerly when they are happy. Several of the zoo animals, such as the chimpanzee, also make various sounds to show different feelings. But no animal's voice is as highly developed as man's.

The Human Voice can express difficult ideas through a variety of arrangements of consonant and vowel sounds. It can also be used for singing. It can combine speech with music, and sing words. With his highly developed voice, man has developed elaborate languages. These allow us to tell each other the most exact details of our thoughts and actions.

The vocal cords are the main sound producers in

VOICE

man. These two small bands of tissue stretch across the *larynx* (voice box). One band stretches on each side of the windpipe opening. Muscles in the larynx stretch and relax the vocal cords.

When we breathe, we relax our vocal cords so they form a V-shaped opening that lets air through. When we speak, we pull the vocal cords by the attached muscles, narrowing the opening. Then, as we drive air from the lungs through the larynx, the air vibrates the tightened vocal cords and sound results.

Varying the Sound. The voice mechanism is so well organized that we use our vocal cords, muscles, and lungs in many combinations without thinking about it. The more tightly the vocal cords are stretched, the higher are the sounds produced. The more relaxed the cords, the lower the sounds. Even in normal speech we stretch and relax the cords to many degrees, producing variations in the sounds of our voice.

The pitch of the voice is determined by the size of the larynx. Women's voices are usually pitched higher than men's because their vocal cords are shorter. Boys and girls have vocal cords about the same size until the boys reach puberty. Then the voice boxes of the boys suddenly grow larger and their voices change.

The tongue, lips, and teeth also help shape the sounds of the voice. The nasal cavity gives resonance and color to the voice. When a person gets a cold and his nasal passages stop up, his voice changes.

Straining the Voice affects the vocal cords. So does a general muscular tension caused by nervousness. In the disease called *laryngitis* the larynx is inflamed, irritated, or infected. Sometimes the sick person cannot speak at all for a day or two. ARTHUR C. GUYTON

Related Articles in WORLD BOOK include:

Alto	Conversation	Soprano	Tenor
Baritone	Laryngitis	Stuttering and	Voder
Bass	Larynx	Stammering	Windpipe
Contralto	Singing		

VOICE, in grammar, is a feature of verbs. It tells whether the subject of the verb acts or is acted upon. English has two voices, *active* and *passive*.

A verb is in the active voice when its subject is the doer of the action. For example, the verb is in the active voice in *John sees the picture*, because the subject (*John*) performs the action (*sees*).

A verb is in the passive voice when its subject receives the action. In *The picture was seen by John*, the subject (*picture*) receives the action (*was seen*). The verb is therefore passive. In English, the passive voice consists of some form of the verb *be* (such as *is, was, were,* or *been*), plus the past participle (such as *seen*) of the main verb. Passive forms of *see* include *is seen, was seen, were seen, have been seen,* and *was being seen.* Only *transitive verbs* (verbs that take a direct object) can be in the passive voice. PAUL ROBERTS

VOICE OF AMERICA broadcasts information about the United States to a world-wide audience. It is the radio division of the United States Information Agency (see UNITED STATES INFORMATION AGENCY). The Voice of America broadcasts in English and in 37 other languages over a network of 87 transmitters.

The programs originate in Washington, D.C., and are broadcast from short-wave transmitters in the United States. Relay stations operate in Europe, the Middle East, South Asia, and the Far East.

A United States Coast Guard cutter in the Mediterranean also serves as a relay station to help overcome jamming by Russian broadcasting stations.

The broadcast time is divided almost evenly between news and such features as commentaries, discussions, drama, and music. The Voice of America began operating in 1942 to inform the world of America's role in World War II. LOWELL BENNETT

VOILE, *voil,* is a thin, open cloth made of silk, cotton, wool, rayon, or nylon. It gets its name from the French word *voiler* (to veil). Voile has a plain weave. It comes in white, in plain colors, or in printed designs. Widths vary from 36 inches for cotton to 54 inches for wool. Voiles are used in making dresses, curtains, and trimmings.

VOJVODINA. See YUGOSLAVIA (Government).

VOLAPÜK, *VOH luh pyook,* was the first widely used universal language. The name of the language comes from two of its words meaning *world* and *speak.* Johann Martin Schleyer (1831-1912), a German priest, introduced the language in his book *Volapük* (1880). By 1889, about 200,000 persons used Volapük, but no one uses it today. Volapük's vocabulary combined elements from English, German, Latin, and Romance languages such as French and Italian. But many Volapük words were difficult to learn, and the grammar was complicated. MARIO PEI

The Lips Help Form Sounds of the voice. They are fairly wide apart, *left,* to shape the sound "ah." They are drawn more closely together to form the long "o," *center,* and puckered with a small opening, *right,* to exclaim "Oo!"

AH   Ō   OO

VOLCANO, *vol KAY noh.* For hundreds of years volcanoes have struck terror and wonder into the heart of man. In ancient times they even moved man to worship. The word volcano comes from *Volcanus,* the name of the Roman god of fire (see VULCAN). The name was first used for Volcano, one of the Lipari Islands in the Mediterranean Sea, where the god was thought to live.

A volcano is an opening in the earth's surface. Through this opening has come rock so hot that it is in a liquid or gaseous state. This melted rock deep in the earth is called *magma* (see IGNEOUS ROCK). Philosophers once thought that volcanic eruptions came from the burning of natural fuel. Sir Charles Lyell and his associates later showed that volcanic mountains were piled up from the products of their own eruptions.

How Volcanoes Are Formed

Within the last 100 years, scientists have come to a better understanding of what causes volcanoes. But new questions arise with each new gain in knowledge. Even now many scientists doubt the most likely theories. Generally, they believe that chambers of extremely hot magma must lie 20 to 40 miles below the volcano. A passage called a *conduit* carries explosive gases and rock to the earth's surface. From observing hot springs, geysers, and volcanoes themselves, we know that extreme heat exists below the earth's surface. We know this also from the way the temperature rises as we go deeper and deeper into mine shafts and oil wells.

This increase in temperature at greater depths is called the *geothermal gradient.* But even these facts do not account for the intense heat of the magma in the deepest chambers. Assuming that this intense heat is in the chambers, the conduit to the surface could also be formed partly by the magma that melts the overlying layers of rock. Magma contains much gas, which is made up chiefly of steam, or water vapor. These gases are released as the magma pushes up against the melting roof of its chamber. The gases are so hot that they exert a tremendous explosive pressure on whatever surrounds them. They will sooner or later reach the weaker places in the earth's outer crust as a means of escape. A conduit is then blasted through the earth's surface by the great force of the gases. The magma cools as it comes to the top and becomes *lava,* which flows over the outside of the crater until it hardens.

The eruption at the mouth of a volcano is produced by action of the gas in the upper part of the conduit. From time to time the opening becomes choked by cooling magma. This again causes gases to build up pressure to blast the plugging material into the air.

For many years, scientists have studied volcanoes during eruptions, often under dangerous conditions. In many parts of the world, special laboratories investigate the nature and causes of eruptions. One of the most famous laboratories rests on the very slopes of Mt. Vesuvius. Another laboratory has been set up on the brink of Mt. Kilauea in Hawaii. Other laboratories have been established at Mont Pelée in the French West Indies, and in Java. The knowledge gained at these stations has saved many lives and much valuable property. Parícutin volcano in Mexico is famous because scientists have been able to watch its growth closely from its start in a field in February, 1943. Every known scientific method has been used to observe its gradual rise to

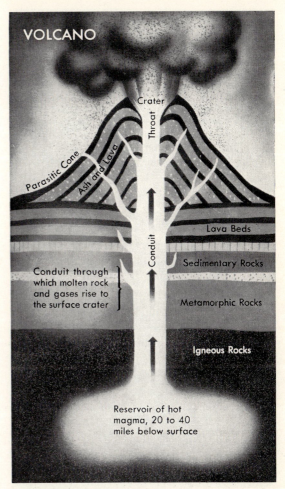

VOLCANO

Crater

Throat

Parasitic Cone

Ash and Lava

Conduit

Lava Beds

Sedimentary Rocks

Conduit through which molten rock and gases rise to the surface crater

Metamorphic Rocks

Igneous Rocks

Reservoir of hot magma, 20 to 40 miles below surface

Cross Section of a Volcano. This is the explosive type. It erupts violently, throwing out clouds of volcanic dust.

a height of 1,500 feet above the surrounding area. It is now dormant.

Products of Volcanic Eruption

The smoke that comes out of volcanoes is really a gaseous mixture made up chiefly of steam. At the time of the explosion it is made black by the great amount of extremely fine dust that is carried up with the steam. Other gases that come from erupting volcanoes are carbon dioxide, hydrochloric acid, hydrofluoric acid, and hydrogen. Some volcanoes throw off combinations of sulfur such as hydrogen sulfide and sulfur dioxide. *Solfataras* and *fumaroles* are volcanic vents from which only gases and magmatic vapors are expelled. See FUMAROLE.

Pieces of rock thrown into the air come either from the crust around the cone of the volcano or from deep within the conduit. Some of these pieces are called *volcanic ash,* which is rock hardened from a melted state. Others are called *lapilli* from the Latin word for *little stones. Volcanic bombs* are great pieces of molten lava. The outer surfaces of these harden when they reach cool air. Volcanic bombs are often fifteen feet long. *Bread-crust,* or spindle, bombs are several feet across. They get their

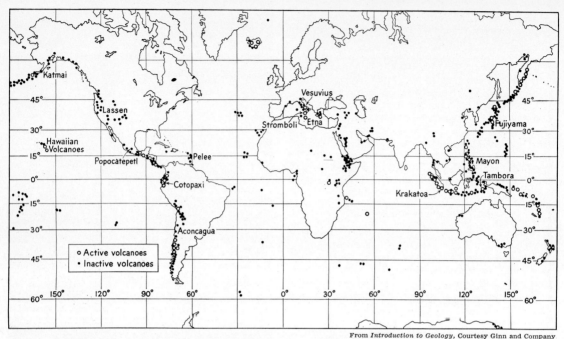

From *Introduction to Geology*, Courtesy Ginn and Company

The Dots on the Map Show the Location of Some of the World's Most Important Volcanoes.

name from the crusty appearance caused by gases escaping from the bomb while the outer surface is hardening. Volcanic cinders, ashes, and dust are all different kinds of hardened lava. Mudflows occur when rain accompanies the force of an explosive eruption, carrying the volcanic dust down in torrents of mud.

Many volcanoes do not throw lava high into the air but push it out in a quiet lava flow. On steep slopes, fluid lava moves quickly in a red-hot mass. As it hardens, the outer surface becomes sticky and dark and finally turns to the rocky stuff we see in lava beds. The two main kinds of lava are called *aa* (rough and scaly), and *pahoehoe* (smooth or ropy).

Spatter cones and *lava tubes* are among the interesting forms in which lava hardens. The spatter cones are shaped like volcanoes and are made up of clots of lava which pile up into steep-sloped cones from a few feet to a hundred feet high. Tubes are often found in pahoehoe lava flows. As the lava flows, the outer surface hardens on contact with the air. The inner lava keeps flowing, leaving a cave or tunnel in place of a molten river.

Kinds of Volcanoes

Scientists classify volcanoes in four general groups, Hawaiian, Strombolian, Vulcanian, and Peléean. These are further classified according to the lava material and the way in which it is thrown out, as well as the way gas is released from the magma. The *Hawaiian* volcanoes have a fluid magma which usually erupts without violence. The *Strombolian* volcano has thicker lava from which the gases are released with explosions. In the *Vulcanian* volcano, the magma is almost as thick as tar. Heavy clouds of volcanic dust rise from the violent explosions which come with each eruption. The *Peléean* volcano is the most violent of all. The clouds above its eruptions glow as though they were on fire.

Some volcanoes are constantly *active*. Stromboli, which is on an island in the Mediterranean Sea, erupts so regularly that it has been compared to a lighthouse. Other volcanoes can be called *intermittent* because they erupt at fairly regular periods. Many of these erupt in cycles, with the length of the cycle being fixed by the amount of time needed to make enough heat to produce an eruption. Mount Etna is this kind of volcano. Those that are quiet, but have not been dead long enough for us to know when they will break out again, are called *dormant* volcanoes. Volcanoes that have remained quiet since the beginning of recorded history and probably will not erupt again are called *extinct*.

There are also stages of eruption which vary with the kind of volcano. The life period of a volcano starts with light earthquake shocks. These become sharper and occur more often as the time for eruption nears. Warnings of an eruption can be seen in springs that become hot and contain volcanic salts, and in other signs. The first eruptions are usually the most violent, throwing great clouds of steam and other gases up with the lava. This part of the eruption may go on for some time with more or less violence, or the activity may stop altogether for short periods and then start again. After the main part of the eruption is over, gases and fumes may be quietly expelled for a long time. When the gas stages die out, the volcano is said to be extinct. Some extinct craters are occupied by lakes as in the famous Crater Lake in Oregon. Other cones, including the one at Auvergne, France, have rounded tops without craters.

Where Volcanoes Are Found

Most volcanoes are located in belts of weakness in the earth's crust near the great mountain chains. The volcanic mountain systems are generally near seacoasts.

The Circum-Pacific system, often called the "circle of

A Perfectly Proportioned, Fluted Cone Surrounds One of the Many Volcanic Craters on Java

Screen Traveler, Gendreau: Kurt Severin, Dever, Black Star

A Plume of Smoke Rises from the crater of towering Irazu volcano in Costa Rica. Irazu's eruptions have caused many earthquakes.

The Crater of Popocatepetl in Mexico as it looks from a high-flying airplane.

VOLCANO

fire," includes the volcanoes of the Falkland Dependency, the South American Andes, the West Indies, Central America, Mexico, western United States, the Alaskan peninsula, and the Aleutian Islands. West of the Pacific, this system includes the volcanoes of Japan, Kamchatka, the Kurils, the Philippines, and continues through the Indonesian islands to New Zealand.

In addition, there are many islands in the Atlantic, Indian, and Pacific oceans containing active volcanoes. A few volcanoes, such as Kenya and Kilimanjaro in Africa, lie inland. Erebus, which is still active, and Terror, formerly active, lie in the Antarctic.

Benefits of Volcanoes

Volcanoes are mostly thought of as the causes of some of the world's great disasters. But volcanic force has also brought its share of good to the world. Heat and power

FAMOUS VOLCANOES

Name	Location	Height (ft.)
Cotopaxi	Ecuador	19,344
Krakatoa	Sunda Strait	2,667
Lassen Peak	California	10,466
Mauna Loa	Hawaii	13,680
Mont Pelée	Martinique	4,800
Mount Aconcagua	Argentina	22,834
Mount Etna	Sicily	11,122
Mount Fujiyama	Japan	12,388
Mount Katmai	Alaska	6,715
Mount Mayon	Philippines	8,071
Mount Tambora	Indonesia	9,255
Parícutin	Mexico	9,213
Popocatepetl	Mexico	17,887
Stromboli	Tyrrhenian Sea	3,038
Vesuvius	Italy	3,842

come from plants run by volcanic steam in Italy, Sicily, Iceland, Chile, and Bolivia. The most successful of these plants is at Larderello in Tuscany. Hot springs are also used for medicinal, laundry, and bathing purposes.

Pumice, which comes from lava, has long been used for grinding and polishing, and for the building of roads. Sulfur, another volcanic product, is used in making chemicals. Lava is often used for building material. Lava beds are important sources of water supply because they are porous and allow fresh water to gather in underground reservoirs. Such reservoirs are the chief source of drinking water in Hawaii. Many countries have rich soils formed by decayed volcanic products.

Famous Volcanic Eruptions

The eruption of Vesuvius in A.D. 79 is the best known in history. When Skaptarjökul, Iceland, erupted in 1783, one fifth of the population was killed. One of the greatest known eruptions occurred in 1883, when Krakatoa, between the islands of Java and Sumatra, exploded. Nearly five cubic miles of material was thrown out, and more than 36,000 persons died.

When Mont Pelée, on Martinique, erupted in 1902, it destroyed the town of St. Pierre and took 38,000 lives. Mont Pelée erupted less severely in 1929 and 1932. Mount Katmai, in Alaska, erupted in 1912. Its area since has been made a national monument.

Other large eruptions occurred at Mauna Loa, in

1950; at Hibok Hibok, on a Philippine island, in 1950 and 1951. Ilha Nova erupted from the Atlantic Ocean in the Azores in 1957. Now 150 feet above sea level, it connects with the island of Fayal. In 1963, Mt. Agung on the Indonesian island of Bali erupted and killed about 1,500 persons.   FRANK PRESS

Related Articles in WORLD BOOK include:

VOLCANOES

Aconcagua	Ixtacihuatl	Mount Fuji
Alaska (Land Regions)	Kilauea	Mount Hood
Aniakchak	Kilimanjaro	Mount Kenya
Ararat	Krakatoa	Mount Rainier
Chimborazo	Lassen Peak	Mount Shasta
Cotopaxi	Mauna Kea	Parícutin
Diamond Head	Mauna Loa	Pichincha
El Boquerón	Mont Pelée	Popocatepetl
El Misti	Mount Apo	Stromboli
Hekla	Mount Etna	Vesuvius

OTHER RELATED ARTICLES

Cement and	Crater Lake	Geology	Hot Springs
Concrete	Dust	Geyser	Lava
(History)	Earthquake	Hawaii	Pumice
Crater	Fumarole	(picture)	

VOLCANO ISLANDS is a group of three small volcanic islands in the northwest Pacific Ocean. For location, see PACIFIC ISLANDS (map). The islands are located between the Bonin Islands and the Marianas, about midway between Saipan and Tokyo. They are called Kita-Iwo Jima (North Sulfur Island), Iwo Jima, and Minami-Iwo Jima (South Sulfur Island). Before World War II, Japanese farmers raised sugar cane on Kita-Iwo Jima. It has an area of 2 square miles and rises to 2,630 feet. The uninhabited southern island is a volcanic cone, 3,180 feet high. American Marines fought the Japanese on Iwo Jima, the middle island, in World War II. See also IWO JIMA.   EDWIN H. BRYAN, JR.

VOLE is a mouse-like animal. Voles have plump bodies about 5 inches long. They have short or medium-length tails, short legs, and tiny ears. Most voles have gray fur. The many *species* (kinds) of voles are usually named for their *habitats* (places where they live). For example, *meadow voles* live in grassy places. *Water voles* live near water. *Tundra voles* live in cold, swampy plains called *tundra*.

Meadow voles are the most common North American species. They live in fields and build their grassy nests on the ground. They eat grass, roots, and seeds.

Voles are closely related to lemmings. The vole population changes greatly every three or four years, as does the number of lemmings (see LEMMING). The number of voles may increase by 20 times in this period. Then, presumably because of enemies, diseases, and lack of food, it drops sharply to its original level.

Scientific Classification. Voles are in the New World rat and mouse family, *Cricetidae*. Meadow voles are genus *Microtus*; a common species is *M. pennsylvanicus*. DANIEL H. BRANT

VOLGA-BALTIC SEA CANAL. See CANAL (Canals of Europe).

VOLGA RIVER, *VAHL guh,* is the longest river in Europe. It flows entirely within Russia. The Volga and its branches provide more than 20,000 miles of water travel and transportation for a region in which about 50 million persons live. The Volga begins in the Valdai Hills, 200 miles southeast of Leningrad. The river flows in a winding course for 2,290 miles to its great delta mouth in the Caspian Sea. The Volga Delta is about

70 miles wide and has more than 200 outlets. It is 86 feet below sea level. The most important branches of the Volga are the Oka, the Kama, and the Unzha rivers. The Oka and the Kama are longer than any other western European rivers except the Danube. For location, see RUSSIA (physical map).

Commerce. The Volga is frozen for most of its length during three months of each year. Canals connect the river with the Baltic Sea, the Arctic Ocean, the Don River, and Moscow. They are important in bringing products of the Volga Valley to the Russian borders.

The fertile river valley is a great wheat-growing region and the center of a large petroleum industry. The Volga Delta and the nearby waters of the Caspian Sea make up one of the world's great fishing grounds. Astrakhan is the center of the caviar industry. Loading wharves along the Volga often have to be moved up higher, since the Volga River is always eating away its banks.

Volgograd (formerly Stalingrad) and Gorki are important manufacturing cities on the banks of the Volga. Saratov, Kazan, and Kuibyshev are other important cities on the river. Two of the world's largest dams block the Volga at Kuibyshev and Volgograd.

History. Ptolemy, the ancient Egyptian scholar, mentioned the Volga River in his *Geography*. The river basin was important in the history of the great movements of people from Asia to Europe. A powerful Bulgarian empire once flourished where the Kama River joins the Volga. Volgograd was the scene of the major Russian victory over the Germans during World War II. The deep feeling of the Russian people for the Volga River has been told again and again in their songs and literature. THEODORE SHABAD

See also OKA RIVER; RIVER (color chart, Longest Rivers).

VOLGOGRAD, *VAWL goh grahd* (pop. 684,000; alt. 180 ft.), is an important manufacturing city in Russia. It lies on the west bank of the Volga River, about 250 miles above the river's mouth (see RUSSIA [political map]). Volgograd factories make aluminum, and tractors and other heavy machinery.

Volgograd was founded in the 1200's. Its name was originally Tsaritsyn. In 1925, it was renamed Stalingrad in honor of the Soviet leader Joseph Stalin. In 1961, Stalin was downgraded and dishonored throughout Russia, and the city was renamed Volgograd. During World War II, the city was an important point in the German drive into Russia. Soviet armed forces defended the city and finally captured a large German army after a long battle. Following World War II, a large dam and a hydroelectric plant were built on the Volga River just north of the city. THEODORE SHABAD

See also STALINGRAD, BATTLE OF.

VOLLEYBALL is a popular team game that is simple enough to be played for general exercise, yet demanding enough to be played as a competitive sport. The game can be played either indoors or outdoors. Volleyball has spread throughout the world as a recreational and competitive sport, mainly because of the YMCA and the United States armed forces. The game is played in more than 60 countries and by more than 50 million people each year.

Volleyball is played on a court 30 feet wide and 60 feet long. A net 3 feet wide, the top of which is 8 feet from the floor for college and competitive play, runs

across the center of the court. The official ball is inflated to 8 pounds pressure, and has a white leather cover. It must be approximately 26 inches in circumference, and weigh not more than 10 ounces. Each team has six players, stationed in two rows of three each.

The Game starts with the serve, which is made by the right back player of the serving team. He serves by hitting the ball with one hand. The serve is good if it passes over the net into the opposing team's court. The first attempt must be good, because no second serve is allowed. The opposing players must return the ball by hitting or batting it in the air with their hands. The ball cannot be caught, thrown, or lifted. The receiving players may hit the ball no more than three times on their side before sending it back over the net. The ball is played back and forth over the net until one team fails to play the ball or return it legally. This occurs when one team allows the ball to drop in its court, or when either team hits the ball out of bounds. If the serving team fails to return the ball legally, a *side out* occurs, and the receiving team takes the ball for its serve.

After a side out, the players of the receiving team must rotate clockwise one position. The player in the left back position moves to the left front position, the

Chicago Public Schools

Volleyball Games provide spirited fun and exercise for young people and adults. The players bat a ball back and forth across a high net, and often leap high to *spike* a ball, or drive it downward. Volleyball can be played on both indoor and outdoor courts and by mixed teams of boys and girls. The diagram, *below*, shows the positions for six-man teams.

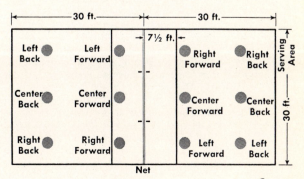

player in the left front position moves to the center front position, and so on around the court. If the receiving team fails to knock the ball back over the net legally, the serving team scores a point. The player in the right back position then serves again. He continues to serve until his team fails to return the ball legally. Only the serving team can score points. The game ends when one team scores 15 points, unless the score is 15 to 14. In that case, play continues until one team gains a two-point lead.

History. Volleyball was invented in 1895 by William G. Morgan, physical director of the Holyoke (Mass.) YMCA. Morgan developed it to provide recreation and competition for the members of his businessmen's classes. He used the bladder of a basketball for a ball, and stretched a tennis net across the gymnasium.

The Physical Directors Society of the YMCA adopted a set of rules for volleyball in 1900. The YMCA controlled the sport until 1928, when the United States Volleyball Association was organized. The association published a rule book and guide, and organized an annual series of regional and national tournaments for volleyball players.　　　　　WILLIAM T. ODENEAL

See also NET (picture, The Net Used in Water Volleyball).

VOLLMER, AUGUST (1876-1955), was a police administrator, consultant, author, and criminologist. He became famous for his contributions to police professionalization. As the police chief of Berkeley, Calif., from 1905 to 1932, he began practices which made his department internationally famous.

The "lie detector" was developed under his inspiration and guidance. He took an active part in many research projects. His interest in the welfare of Berkeley youth led to the formation of America's first community council in 1919. Vollmer also helped establish criminology courses at the University of California in 1916. They led to a School of Criminology in 1950. He served as professor of police administration at the University of Chicago from 1929 to 1931, and at the University of California from 1931 to 1938. He wrote four books on criminology, and advised many cities on reorganizing their police departments. Vollmer was born in New Orleans, La.　　　　　O. W. WILSON

VOLOS. See THESSALY.

VOLSCIANS. See CORIOLANUS, GAIUS MARCIUS.

VOLSTEAD, ANDREW JOHN (1860-1947), a Minnesota Republican congressman from 1903 to 1923, introduced the National Prohibition Act of 1919, better known as the Volstead Act (see VOLSTEAD ACT). He personally opposed saloons more than moderate drinking. He also wrote the Farmers' Co-operative Marketing Act as well as drainage and homestead laws. He was born in Goodhue County, Minnesota, and was graduated from St. Olaf's College. After his election defeat of 1923, he served as counsel to prohibition groups. LOUIS FILLER

VOLSTEAD ACT provided for the enforcing of national prohibition of the use of intoxicating liquors. It was passed by the Congress of the United States in 1919, over the veto of President Woodrow Wilson. Amendment 18 to the Constitution of the United States prohibited the manufacture, sale, or transportation of intoxicating liquors within the United States. The Vol-

stead Act provided the means to investigate and punish violators of the amendment. The act took its name from that of Representative Andrew J. Volstead of Minnesota, who introduced it. The act defined intoxicating liquors as beverages which contain "one-half of one per centum or more of alcohol by volume."

The Commissioner of Internal Revenue of the Treasury Department was made responsible for the enforcement of prohibition. Later, in 1930, that responsibility was transferred to the Department of Justice. The Volstead Act provided for strong enforcement of the prohibition amendment. It regulated strictly the distribution of liquor for a few special purposes. The act's critics say that its definition of intoxicating liquors was its main weakness, because it was stricter than many citizens thought it should be. As a result, the law was broken by many persons who might have obeyed it if it had been more lenient. In addition, the law provided for the arrest of violators by one governmental department and their prosecution by another. This made it more difficult to convict violators.

After the ratification of Amendment 21, which repealed prohibition, the Volstead Act expired automatically, except in the Territories.　　　JOHN A. KROUT

See also PROHIBITION; VOLSTEAD, ANDREW JOHN.

VOLSUNGA, SAGA vahl SOONG guh, is an old Icelandic tale written in the 1100's or 1200's. The material for this poem comes from the second, or poetic, portion of the Elder Edda, and deals with the exploits of King Volsung and his family. The hero of the saga is Sigurd, the last of the Volsungs. Richard Wagner used the poem as a basis for his opera The Ring of the Nibelungs.

VOLT, vohlt, is the unit of electromotive force that will drive a current of one ampere through a resistance of one ohm. The volt, also, is the unit of work done for each coulomb of charge moved through the circuit (see COULOMB). Voltage may be thought of as a "push" that moves or tends to move a current through a conductor. One volt is practically the electromotive force of a simple voltaic cell. A common dry cell has a voltage of about 1.5. The instrument used to measure voltage is called the voltmeter. These terms honor the memory of the great Italian scientist Alessandro Volta. See also AMPERE; ELECTRIC CURRENT; OHM; VOLTA, COUNT; VOLTMETER.　　　E. R. WHITEHEAD

VOLTA, VAHL tuh, **COUNT** (1745-1827), ALESSANDRO VOLTA, won fame as the inventor of the electric battery. His discovery of the decomposition of water by an electrical current laid the foundations of electrochemistry (see ELECTROCHEMISTRY). The volt, a unit of electrical measurement, is named for him (see VOLT). He also invented the electric condenser.

Count Volta
Culver

Volta was born in Como, Italy, a member of a noble family. By 1774, he had established a reputation by his research work in electricity.　　　SIDNEY ROSEN

See also BATTERY; ELECTRICITY (Flowing Electricity).

VOLTAIC CELL. See BATTERY.

VOLTAIRE, *VAWL TAIR* (1694-1778), was the pen name of François Marie Arouet, one of the greatest of all French writers. He was a philosopher, poet, historian, encyclopedist, satirist, novelist, and dramatist. His poems, artificial in style and rhythm, are noted chiefly for their wit. His histories are readable, but cannot be ranked with the work of leading historians. As a dramatist, Voltaire was clever and skillful, but he lacked a true sense of dramatic values. He is noted chiefly for his brilliant and witty prose style. Each sentence of his work is like a polished gem.

Voltaire's greatness is based on the influence of his writings. He was one of the social philosophers whose writings helped bring about the French Revolution. He bitterly attacked the political and social institutions of his time. His excellent romance, *Candide* (1759), was a satire against social wrongs (see Candide). But much of what he attacked has been corrected, and today some of his sharper satires have been dulled.

Voltaire was born in Paris on Nov. 21, 1694. He did his early studying under his father and the worldly Abbé de Châteauneuf. He later studied under the Jesuits at Collège Louis-le-Grand. In 1711, he joined the brilliant literary circle of Louis XIV's court. He then went to The Hague as the secretary of the French ambassador to The Netherlands, but was forced to return to Paris after an unfortunate love affair. In Paris he continually got into trouble by writing sharp satires mocking members of the court.

First Success. Voltaire's career as a writer began with the drama *Oedipe*. He revised the play while serving a prison term for one of his satires on the French regent, Philippe, Duke of Orléans. Voltaire was released after spending 11 months in the Bastille, and the play was first performed in public in 1718. *Oedipe* brought him lasting fame and much money.

His ambitious epic poem, *La Henriade*, appeared in 1724. This poem tells the story of Henry IV of France, and is a strong plea for religious toleration. Soon after the poem's publication, Voltaire quarreled with a powerful young nobleman, Chevalier de Rohan, and was again imprisoned in the Bastille.

Visits England. When Voltaire was released, he went to England for three years. There he made many friends among the literary great. But the most important result of this visit and contact with great minds was that Voltaire contrasted the freedom of thought in England with the lack of freedom in France. Deeply stirred by what he saw, Voltaire wrote *Letters Concerning the English Nation*, which he published in 1734. In this work, he advised France to copy English patterns. The work caused such an uproar that Voltaire left Paris.

Voltaire had made an enormous sum of money through a lucky business venture some time before, and he no longer needed to write to support himself. From 1734 to 1749, he lived at the Château of Cirey in Lorraine with Madame du Châtelet, a woman of great intellect. She encouraged him in his writing, and he worked steadily on his plays, on a history of Louis XIV, and on the translation into French of Sir Isaac Newton's *Principia* (see Newton, Sir Isaac). His fame spread rapidly, and in 1746 he was elected to membership in the French Academy.

Later Years. Voltaire went to live with Frederick the Great of Prussia in Potsdam in 1750. He and the king

Art Institute of Chicago

Statue of Voltaire is by the French sculptor, Jean Houdon. Voltaire gave the world a heritage of brilliant books and famous sayings. "I disapprove of what you say, but I will defend to the death your right to say it," is a statement credited to Voltaire.

got along well at first, but Voltaire was a difficult person to live with, and the two men finally began to quarrel. Voltaire fled to Paris in 1753. But he did not like living there, and settled at Ferney, an estate on French soil, four miles from Geneva, Switzerland. His niece kept house for him, and he lived here in freedom and comfort for the rest of his life.

Most of Voltaire's later writings were short attacks on the intolerance and narrow religious beliefs in France. He was actually a deist, and believed in God, but he was accused of atheism (see Deism). Voltaire also wrote his famous social philosophical articles for the *Encyclopédie* at this time. He had become the most famous and wealthiest author of his day. He was the champion of the common people against their rulers, and adopted for his slogan "Écrasez l'infâme!" (Wipe out the evil thing!) in his attacks on the Roman Catholic Church.

Voltaire visited Paris for the last time in 1778. He rode to Paris in triumph, and received a laurel crown in the theater where his play *Irène* was being performed. But the excitement of the trip was too much for him, and he died on May 30, 1778, in Paris.

Voltaire also wrote the tragedies *Brutus* (1730), *Zaïre* (1732), and *Mérope* (1743). His historical works include *Le Siècle de Louis XIV* (1751), and *Dictionnaire Philosophique* (1764). His novel *Zadig* appeared in 1747. Voltaire's poems include *Le Mondain* (1736), and *Discours sur l'Homme* (1738).

Francis J. Bowman

VOLTE. See DANCING (The Renaissance).

VOLTMETER is an instrument that measures the *volt-age* (difference in potential) between two points of an electric current. Most commercial voltmeters are gal-vanometers connected in series with a high resistance. They have scales that read in volts. A typical direct-current voltmeter has a magnet shaped like a horseshoe. To each *pole* (end) of the magnet is attached a semi-circular piece of soft iron that also becomes magnetized. These pieces of soft iron direct the magnetic field to-ward a small iron cylinder placed between the poles of the magnet. Since soft iron becomes highly magnetized, this cylinder concentrates the magnetic field.

Surrounding the cylinder is a coil of thin copper wire wound on a light, rectangular frame. This coil is the movable coil through which the electric current flows. Each end of the wire coil is connected to a small spiral spring. As the coil moves, a needle attached to the coil also moves. This needle moves across a dial and indi-cates the reading in volts. Another coil of very high re-sistance, up to several thousand ohms, is connected in series with the movable coil.

When the voltmeter is not in use, the frame does not move and the needle reads "zero." When a current passes through the movable coil, a magnetic field is set up around the coil. As a result, the magnetic field of the horseshoe magnet acts on the current-carrying wires of the coil to produce a force on the coil. This force causes the coil to turn. The springs oppose the motion of the coil and are adjusted so that the position of the needle indicates the correct voltage. In taking voltage readings, a voltmeter is always placed across the part of the circuit to be measured.　　　E. R. WHITEHEAD

See also GALVANOMETER; POTENTIOMETER; VOLT.

VOLTURNO RIVER, a stream in southern Italy, rises in the province of Campobasso. The Volturno flows southeast until it meets the Calore River. The joined streams then flow west past Capua. The total length of the Volturno is about 110 miles. The Volturno River empties into the Gulf of Gaeta on the Tyrrhenian Sea, a point about twenty miles southeast of Gaeta. In World War II, during the Allied drive north from Naples, an important battle was fought at the lower end of the river.　　　GEORGE KISH

VOLUME of a body is the amount of space it occupies. The unit of measurement for volume is the cube whose edges are of equal length. The volume of a box, for ex-ample, is usually indicated in cubic inches, cubic feet, or cubic yards.

There are several ways of measuring the volume of a substance, depending upon the shape of the substance and whether it is a solid or liquid. The volume of a rectangular solid, such as a box, is found by multiplying the length by the width by the depth. This could be stated in the formula, $v = lwd$. A cubic yard equals 27 cubic feet, and one cubic foot equals 1,728 cubic inches.

The volume of a cylinder is determined by multiply-ing the area of the base by the height, or $v = \pi r^2 h$. The area of the base is obtained by multiplying π (or about 3.1416) by the square of its radius. The volume of a sphere is computed by the formula $v = \dfrac{\pi D^3}{6}$ (or about .524 D^3), where D is the diameter.

Liquids are usually measured by special glass devices having a graduated scale. There are two systems of measurements, the English and metric systems. In the English system, the main units are the gallon, quart, pint, and fluid ounce. A gallon equals four quarts, a quart equals two pints, and a pint equals sixteen fluid ounces. In the metric system, liquids are measured mainly in cubic centimeters and liters. One liter is equal to 1,000 cubic centimeters.　　　E. G. STRAUS

Related Articles in WORLD BOOK include:

Barrel	Hogshead	Pint
Bushel	Liter	Quart
Density	Minim	Weights and Measures
Gallon	Peck	

VOLUNTEER STATE. See TENNESSEE.

VOLUNTEERS OF AMERICA is a religious social-welfare organization which provides spiritual and ma-terial services to the needy. It has 471 program centers throughout the United States. Its spiritual services in-clude missions, Sunday Schools, Bible study groups, and spiritual counseling and guidance.

The organization operates maternity homes and child placement services, summer camps, homes and clubs for the aged, rehabilitation services for the handicapped, residences for working girls, day nurseries, and emer-gency shelters for the homeless. The Volunteers also gather clothing and household goods for needy families, and assist prisoners and parolees and their families.

Ballington Booth and his wife, Maud Ballington Charlesworth Booth, founded the Volunteers in New York City in 1896 (see BOOTH [family]). The organiza-tion operates on a semimilitary basis, and its officers wear uniforms and hold rank. National headquarters are at 340 W. 85th St., New York, N.Y. For member-ship, see RELIGION (table).　　　JOHN F. McMAHON

VOLUTE. See COLUMN (The Greek Orders).

VOLVOX. See PROTOZOAN (Flagellates).

VOMER. See FACE.

VOMITING, *VAHM it ing*, is the forceful expulsion of the contents of the stomach and intestines through the mouth. In digestion, the muscles of the stomach and small intestine contract and push the stomach con-tents down through the alimentary canal. In vomiting, these muscles reverse their contractions and push up-ward. A person usually has a feeling of nausea before he vomits. The medulla of the brain controls vomiting (see BRAIN [The Medulla Oblongata]).

Vomiting may be merely an occasional annoyance, or it may be a sign of serious illness. Unpleasant sights or odors sometimes cause vomiting in a nervous indi-vidual. Vomiting may also result from diseases such as blockage of the coronary arteries of the heart, enlarge-ment or obstruction of the gastrointestinal tract, or inflammation of parts of the abdomen. Nausea and vomiting that occur in the early stages of pregnancy are known as *morning sickness*.

Retching is an attempt to vomit. It occurs when the *diaphragm*, a flat muscle between the abdomen and chest, contracts in spasms. However, this action alone does not move the stomach contents. Neither vomiting nor retching empty the stomach completely. If a person vomits uncontrollably for any length of time, a physician should be called.　　　E. CLINTON TEXTER, JR.

See also ANTIDOTE; CHLORPROMAZINE; EMETIC; NAUSEA; STOMACH.

VON is a German word that frequently precedes personal names to indicate nobility or rank. The word means *of* or *from*. It was originally used before names of places or estates.

VON BÉKÉSY, *vahn BAY keh shee,* **GEORG** (1899-), an American physicist, won the 1961 Nobel prize in medicine for his research on the *cochlea* (the spiral canal of the inner ear). Von Békésy was born in Budapest, Hungary. He received his Ph.D. from the University of Budapest in 1923. He became a senior research fellow in psychophysics at Harvard University in 1949.

VON BRAUN, *vawn brown,* **WERNHER** (1912-), is considered the foremost rocket engineer in the world. He directed the team that successfully launched the *Explorer,* the first United States earth satellite, on Jan. 31, 1958. At the age of 20, he took charge of the German army's rocket station. There, during World War II, he developed the V-2 rocket used by the Germans to bombard London. When Hitler took personal control of rocket work, Von Braun resigned and was put in jail.

After the war, Von Braun was invited to the United States to build rockets for the U.S. Army, and became director of the George C. Marshall Space Flight Center at Huntsville, Ala. He became a U.S. citizen in 1955. He was born in Wirsitz, Germany.   IRA M. FREEMAN

See also GUIDED MISSILE (In World War II); SPACE TRAVEL.

VON KÁRMÁN, *vahn CAR man,* **THEODORE** (1881-1963), became one of the outstanding scientists of the 1900's. His primary interest was aeronautics, but he wrote nearly 150 books and articles on many aspects of engineering, physics, and mathematics. Von Kármán helped found important aeronautical institutions and agencies, including the Guggenheim and Jet Propulsion Laboratories at the California Institute of Technology, the Aerojet Engineering Corporation, the U.S. Air Force Scientific Advisory Board, and the Advisory Group for Aeronautical Research and Development in NATO. Von Kármán was born in Budapest, Hungary. He became a U.S. citizen in 1936.   CLARK B. MILLIKAN

See also HELICOPTER (Pioneer Inventors).

VON NEUMANN, *fohn NOI mahn,* **JOHN** (1903-1957), was an outstanding mathematician. He wrote *The Mathematical Foundations of Quantum Mechanics* (1944), a treatise which showed that two different theories, Erwin Schrödinger's wave mechanics and Werner Heisenberg's matrix mechanics, were equivalent. Perhaps his best known book was *The Theory of Games and Economic Behavior* (1944), written with Oskar Morgenstern. He also helped organize the first research group in numerical weather prediction.

Von Neumann made major contributions to the design of high-speed electronic computers. They were important in the development of the hydrogen bomb. He was appointed to the U.S. Atomic Energy Commission in 1955. Von Neumann was born in Budapest, Hungary. He became an American citizen in 1937.   PHILLIP S. JONES

VOODOO, or VODUN, is the name given to the religious beliefs and the practice of magic of certain African Negro tribes. The word is a West African word which means *god* or *spirit*. The beliefs and practices of voodoo have spread to many parts of the West Indies, and to a few parts of the United States. Voodooism often has a powerful influence on those who practice it.

According to voodooism, the spirits of the dead live

---

in a world of ghosts, but can visit the world of the living to bless or curse people. The chief magicians bring the living into touch with the dead. A medicine man may talk with a wooden image and say that a spirit answers him through the image. If a man makes a wax image of his enemy and sticks pins into it, he is practicing voodooism to injure his enemy.   JOHN MULHOLLAND

VOORTREKKERS. See SOUTH AFRICA (British Occupation).

VOR. See RADIO BEACON.

VORARLBERG, *FOHR AHRL berk,* was a province of the Austro-Hungarian Empire before 1918. After 1918, it was a province of the Austrian republic. In 1938, Germany took over the territory. After World War II, the French Zone of Occupation included Vorarlberg. It again became part of the Republic of Austria in 1955. The province is a popular tourist center because of its beautiful mountain scenery. Farmers raise beef and dairy cattle, and crops of corn and potatoes.

VORINGFOSS, *VUH ring faws,* is a waterfall on Hardanger Fiord in southwestern Norway. It is located in Hordaland County, near the village of Eidfjord. The waterfall, which measures 535 feet in height, has become a popular tourist attraction.

VOROSHILOV, *voh roh SHIH lawf,* **KLIMENT EFREMOVICH** (1881-), was a Russian marshal. He fought in the Red army in the civil war following the Bolshevik revolution of 1917. Joseph Stalin liked him, and made him commissar of defense from 1925 to 1940. During World War II, Voroshilov led his troops poorly, and lost his command. He headed the Allied Control Commission in Hungary in 1945, but soon lost favor with Stalin. He was about to be purged in early 1953, but Stalin's death saved him, and he became chairman of the Presidium of the Supreme Soviet. Voroshilov kept this job, which actually had little power, until 1960. In 1961, he was dropped as a member of the Presidium. He was born in Verkhneye, in the Ukraine, and went to work in a mine at the age of 7. At 18, he became a revolutionary.   ALBERT PARRY

VORTICELLA. See PROTOZOAN (The Ciliates).

VORTIGERN, *VAWR tih gurn,* was the British king who invited the Jutes to come to Britain to help him fight the Picts about A.D. 449. This event began the Anglo-Saxon conquest of England. Later he fought with Hengist, leader of the Jutes, whose victory led to the founding of the kingdom of Kent. According to some ancient legends, Vortigern married Hengist's daughter, Rowena.   ROBERT S. HOYT

VOSGES MOUNTAINS, *vohzh,* form a short, low mountain range that extends for about 150 miles along the western side of the Rhine River Valley. The Vosges form the border between France's provinces of Alsace and Lorraine. The highest peak is Sulzer Belchen (4,672 ft.). The mountains, largely granite and sandstone, contain copper, lead, silver, coal, and rock salt.

VOSGES TUNNEL. See LUSSE TUNNEL.

VOSTOK ISLAND is a tiny, uninhabited coral island in the Pacific Ocean, about 580 miles north-northwest of Tahiti. A Russian explorer, Fabian von Bellingshausen, discovered the island in 1820. Both Great Britain and the United States claim it. For location, see PACIFIC OCEAN (color map).   EDWIN H. BRYAN, JR.

365

Voting Officials in Ghana Bring Filled Ballot Boxes from the Country's Interior to Counting Stations by Boat.

VOTING is a democratic method by which the people decide issues and choose their leaders and governments. Freedom to vote (suffrage) is essential to self-government, whether carried on directly or through elected representatives of the people. The United States will be a republic only so long as its people can vote freely for the candidates they think will govern best.

A citizen who is too lazy or indifferent to vote is throwing away one of his most precious rights. He is abandoning his right to have a voice in his own government. But many voters are so indifferent that they do not vote. This indifference could permit unscrupulous persons to gain control of a government.

There are about 109 million United States citizens of voting age. Many of these have never voted. The presidential elections have brought out the highest total vote, but it has never exceeded two-thirds of the number of voters. Such public indifference has caused some countries, such as Costa Rica and Uruguay, to compel every qualified citizen to vote. Citizens who do not vote are fined or given a prison sentence.

Voting goes on throughout the United States all year long. Local judges and officials come up for election at various times. Once every four years the people of the United States vote to elect a President (though indirectly), and once every two years they vote for members of the Congress. Some states hold preferential primaries to select delegates to the national political conventions. Voting is used for other purposes than the choice of public officers or the decision of political issues. Clubs and societies vote on their officers and programs, and children vote for school leaders and dele-gates. Company and corporation stockholders elect directors and vote on important business matters.

Who May Vote. The Constitution of the United States does not specify the qualifications necessary for a person who is to vote for members of Congress or of the Electoral College (see ELECTORAL COLLEGE). The states set up their own qualifications, which vary greatly. But all states require that a voter be a citizen of the United States. He must also have lived for a certain length of time in the state, the county, and the precinct, where his vote is to be cast. Most states also require that voters be registered in the precinct for a certain length of time before they are permitted to vote. Women of the United States won the right to vote with the adoption of the Nineteenth Amendment to the Constitution in 1920, although several states had permitted woman suffrage before that time. Most states require that a voter be at least 21 years old, but Georgia and Kentucky have reduced this age to 18, Alaska to 19, and Hawaii to 20.

The citizens of United States territories, such as Guam, may vote for local officials. The people of the Commonwealth of Puerto Rico elect a Resident Commissioner to the United States Congress. He may take part in the discussions in Congress, but he has no vote.

Voting laws in Canada are much like those in the United States. Canadian citizens and British subjects may vote after they have lived in Canada for a year. Voters must be 21 years old in all but three provinces. In Alberta and British Columbia, a voter must be at least 19 years old. In Saskatchewan, voters must be 18.

Restrictions on Voting. Some citizens of the United States are not permitted to vote. Because of their tribal

366

membership, American Indians have often been disfranchised. Since 1948, however, Indians in all states have had the right to vote. Idiots and insane persons are not permitted to vote. Persons convicted of serious crimes may lose their voting rights. Members of the armed forces dishonorably discharged for wartime desertion lose the right to vote in national elections. In Canada, mentally incompetent persons are not allowed to vote, and certain criminals may lose their voting rights.

In the past, some states made the payment of a poll tax and the passing of literacy tests voting requirements. But Amendment 24 to the United States Constitution, ratified in 1964, prohibits poll taxes as voting requirements in national elections. A voting rights law passed in 1965 allows federal examiners to suspend state literacy tests if the tests are used to deny a citizen his right to vote because of his race or color. In 1966, the Supreme Court of the United States outlawed poll taxes in state and local elections. See POLL TAX.

Methods of Voting. Many different methods of voting are used throughout the world. The United States and Canada use the Australian ballot, except where voting machines are used. The Australian ballot allows a voter to mark his ballot inside a screened booth, in secret and accompanied "only by his conscience." See BALLOT.

Many states have begun to use voting machines. Voting machines speed up the process of casting and counting votes, reduce the possibility of error, and make it possible to determine the election results very shortly after the polls are closed. See VOTING MACHINE.

Many persons are away from their home precincts on election day. Since a person can vote only in his own precinct, he would lose his vote if some provision were not made for *absentee voting*. So a number of states have passed election laws which allow a voter who expects to be away on election day to cast his vote at a central election office before the election. In other cases, ballots are mailed to absentee voters to be marked and returned. Absentee ballots are held by the authorities until election day, when they are counted with the total vote cast.

During World War II, special voting arrangements were made for members of the armed forces who were away from home. Servicemen received the standard ballots used in their home districts. The completed ballots were returned to the servicemen's home precincts and were counted with the other votes cast there.

Voting Districts. The smallest voting unit is called the *precinct*. The precinct is a subdivision of a county or ward, and is set up for voting purposes. A state may have several thousand precincts. The residents of a certain precinct must cast their votes in that precinct. After the polls have closed, the election officials in each precinct count the total of votes cast for each candidate and report these figures to election headquarters.

Each polling place is under the supervision of a group of election officials. These officials are usually volunteers who serve without pay. Each polling place has an election judge, a staff of clerks, and several "watchers." The watchers represent all of the opposing political parties, and watch for attempts at fraud.

Fraud. Attempts at fraudulent voting are common. Different methods are tried and used. Dishonest party workers may try to buy the votes of vagrants. Ballot boxes may be "stuffed" with fraudulent votes, or one

voter may try to vote several times. In a district controlled by a dishonest political machine, the total vote is sometimes fraudulently counted and reported.

Voting in Legislative Bodies. Voting in lawmaking bodies is carried on in much the same way that it is in neighborhood social clubs. Each legislator has a single vote. Any bill before the Congress of the United States can be passed by a simple majority vote. But a two-thirds vote is required to pass a bill over the President's veto, to propose an amendment to the Constitution, or to convict an impeached officer by vote of the Senate.

A member of Congress or of a state legislature may vote on a measure or abstain from voting, as he chooses. Sometimes he may wish to avoid placing his vote on record. Then, if he is opposed to a certain measure, he and a Congressman who favors the measure may agree that neither will vote on it. This is called *pairing*, and the result is the same as if both had voted.

The United States Senate has a *cloture* rule. It provides that an overlong debate may be shut off by a vote of two-thirds of the members present and voting. Cloture limits each Senator to one hour of debate on the floor of the Senate. See CLOTURE.

Related Articles in WORLD BOOK include:

Absentee Voting	Election	Initiative and
Congress of the U.S.	Fifteenth	Referendum
(Passing a Bill)	Amendment	Logrolling
Democracy (pictures,	Gerrymander	Plebiscite
Voting Around	Grandfather	Recall
the World)	Clause	Woman Suffrage

VOTING IN PRESIDENTIAL ELECTIONS. See ELECTORAL COLLEGE (color diagram); VOTING.

VOTING MACHINE is a mechanical device for recording and counting votes at an election. It provides an absolutely secret ballot and records it automatically, with total accuracy and with maximum speed and economy. More than half of the people in the United States cast their ballots on voting machines.

Operation. Voting machines may differ in some details, but they all work in much the same way. The voter stands in front of the machine and moves a master lever to close a set of curtains around him and unlock the mechanism. Before him are the names of all the candidates, arranged in rows according to their political party. The candidates are listed next to the titles of the offices they seek. The voter turns a pointer next to the name of each candidate he chooses for an office. In some states, he may vote a *straight ticket* by pulling a *party lever* at one end of the party's row of candidates. The machine will then register a vote for each candidate in the row. The machine does not register or count any votes until the voter moves the master lever back. This registers and counts the vote, and opens the curtains.

Voting machines also provide for ballots on bond issues or other proposals. The machine registers a *yes* or *no* vote. Modern voting machines have one row of voting pointers for questions, and nine party rows of voting pointers for candidates. They are built in sizes to accommodate 270, 360, 450, or 540 candidates.

Advantages. A voting machine is both automatic and impartial. Dishonest officials cannot change it or tamper with its records, although they might "stuff" a ballot box with paper ballots. Fewer election officials

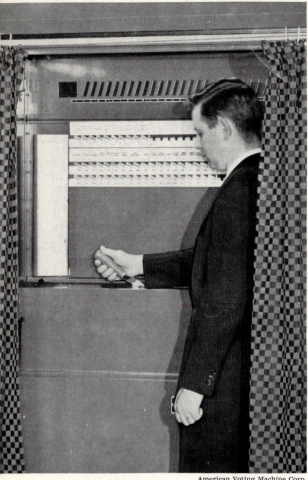

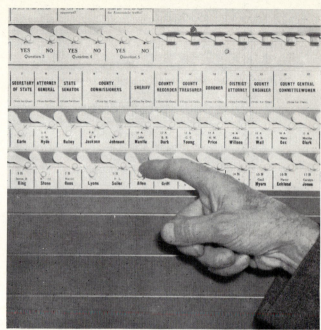

Using a Voting Machine, *above,* a voter must push down a pointer next to the name of each candidate he chooses. The machine then will automatically tabulate each selection he makes.

The Voting Machine Provides Privacy. The voter must pull a lever, *left,* that closes the curtain before he can vote. After voting, he pushes the lever back to open the curtain.

are needed, and the cost of printing paper ballots is reduced. The machine also eliminates the need for expensive and inaccurate recounts of hand-counted paper ballots. The savings resulting within a few years from these and other items often equals the machine's cost. The useful life of a voting machine is often as much as 50 years.

Legislative Voting Machines record the votes for and against proposals in many state legislatures. These electric and mechanical devices reduce the time needed for a roll-call vote of the legislators. Each lawmaker has buttons on his desk with which he can vote either *yes* or *no.* When he presses the button of his choice, his vote appears on a counting device at the clerk's or speaker's desk. Many legislatures also have a counting board on one wall of the chamber. As each legislator casts his vote, he lights a colored light opposite his name on this board. Many legislative voting machines provide a permanent record for the clerk, showing the total votes cast and the vote of each legislator on each roll-call.

History. Thomas Edison invented the first legislative voting machine in 1868 (see EDISON, THOMAS ALVA [Early Inventions]). Election voting machines developed more slowly. The first practical voting machine used in an actual election was put into service in Lockport,

New York, in 1892. Manufacture and distribution of voting machines has continued steadily since that time. The machines are in use in more than three-fourths of the states. Many states now require the use of voting machines in all elections, including primaries.

The United States was the first country to conduct elections by machine. Several other countries began using voting machines in the 1960's. Still other countries are engaged in research on their use. R. E. HORROCKS

VOTING TRUST. See TRUST (The Voting Trust).

VOUSSOIR. See ARCH (diagram).

VOWEL. When a person opens his mouth and says "ah" for the doctor, he makes an open sound with free passage of breath. This sound is a vowel, as are all the other open and freely breathed sounds in speech. In English, the vowel sounds are represented by the letters, *a, e, i, o, u,* and sometimes *w* and *y* (as in *now, city*). But each letter stands for several sounds. The open quality of vowels distinguishes them from *consonants.* Consonants are formed with the organs of speech more or less closed. A vowel may be a syllable in itself, or it may be joined with one or more consonants to produce a syllable. See also CONSONANT; PRONUNCIATION.   CLARENCE STRATTON

VOYAGES AND TRAVELS. See EXPLORATION AND DISCOVERY.

VTOL. See CONVERTIPLANE.

VULCAN, *VUL kun,* was the god of fire in Roman mythology. His Greek name was Hephaestus. He was patron of blacksmiths and metalworkers.

Two stories are told of his life. One says that he was the son of Jupiter (Zeus) and Juno (Hera), and was born lame and ugly (see JUNO; JUPITER). Juno was shocked at the sight of him, and threw him from Olympus. He was saved and reared by some nymphs and Nereids in a cave beneath the ocean. They taught him his wonderful skill in making things from metal.

The other story says that Vulcan angered Zeus and was punished. Zeus had a quarrel with Hera, and Vulcan tried to help his mother. Zeus became furious, and threw the young god out of Olympus. Vulcan fell for a whole day and landed on the island of Lemnos, in the Aegean Sea. The fall made him lame.

Vulcan, according to some accounts, never went back to live on Olympus. He built palaces for the other gods, and made thunderbolts for Zeus. His assistants were the Cyclopes. Vulcan also made weapons for the gods and the famous armor for Achilles. He created Pandora out of earth and water (see PANDORA). He caught Venus and her lover Mars in a net of iron. Vulcan married Venus, but she grew tired of him (see VENUS). According to another account, he married Charis. He helped at the birth of Athena by splitting the head of Zeus with an ax (see MINERVA).

Vulcan was served in his own home by maidens he had made from gold. They could move, talk, and think.

In art, Vulcan is shown as a vigorous old man with strong shoulders. He is usually dressed in a short leather garment and stands at a forge.   VAN JOHNSON

VULCANIZATION. See RUBBER (Discovery of Vulcanization; Vulcanization).

VULGATE is the name of a Latin translation of the Bible. The word is Latin in origin and means *commonly received translation.* The Vulgate is a revision of the earlier, Old Latin versions of the Bible. It was completed in A.D. 405 by Saint Jerome.

By a decree of the Council of Trent the Vulgate translation was made the standard Bible of the Roman Catholic Church. Pope Sixtus V appointed scholars to revise the Vulgate in 1587, but after his death in 1590 many alleged errors were found in the work. Under Pope Clement VIII there were further revisions in 1592 and 1598. The last one became the official text for use in the Roman Catholic Church.

The Vulgate and the English versions of the Bible differ in the order of the books and the divisions of chapters. The Vulgate also contains certain books which Protestants consider part of the Apocrypha. The English translation of the Vulgate is called the Douai, or Douay, Bible, after the town of Douai, France, in which it was first published.

In 1941 a new Catholic English version of the New Testament was published in America. Later, Pope Pius XII declared that scholars should now take account of the "original languages" (Hebrew and Greek) as well as the Latin, in interpreting the Scriptures.

A revision of the Vulgate was undertaken by Catholic scholars in 1908, and is now in progress. An important translation of the Bible from the Vulgate into the English language was published in three volumes, from 1944 to 1950.   EDGAR J. GOODSPEED

See also BIBLE (How the Bible Developed).

Charles Phelps Cushing

Vulcan, the Roman God of Fire, was also the blacksmith for the gods. He made the scepter of Jupiter. Vulcan also made the shield of Achilles and the arrows of Apollo and Diana.

VULTURE, *VUL tyoor,* is the name of several large birds of prey. They eat *carrion,* or dead animals. Other birds of prey have feathers on their heads, but vultures do not. They have slightly hooked bills and blunt claws which are poor weapons for seizing and carrying off their food. Vultures live in the temperate and tropical regions of America. The vultures of Europe and Asia look like American vultures and have similar habits. But their bodies are different. The Old World vultures belong to a different family, the hawk family.

Vultures are ugly birds, with their naked heads and dark feathers. They not only eat carrion, but they often vomit when they are disturbed. But they are useful, because they eat dead bodies which otherwise might decay and become dangerous to health. Generally, vultures do not carry disease.

Vultures have a graceful, easy, soaring flight. They sail in broad circles, high in the sky. They have sharp eyes and a keen sense of smell. They can see dead animals from great distances.

Vultures are usually seen in large, mixed flocks, except during breeding season. Then they pair off and nest on the ground under overhanging cliffs, in logs, and in caves. They build no nests. The female lays from 1 to 3 eggs on bare surfaces. The parents bring food in their throats and empty it directly into the young bird's mouth.

New World Vultures. There are six species of American vultures. Three live in North America. The

369

turkey vulture, sometimes called *buzzard* or *turkey buzzard*, lives in the southern United States and northern Mexico. It grows about 30 inches long.

The *black vulture* is about 6 inches shorter than the turkey vulture. It lives from Central America to the southwestern United States. This bird is entirely black except for white underwings.

The largest land bird in North America is the vulture called the *California condor*. It is 45 to 50 inches long and has a wingspread of 8 to 11 feet.

The *king vulture* is the most striking of the three South American vultures. It has a feather ruff around its neck, and its head is yellow, scarlet, white, and blue, with fleshy growths of rich orange. Its bill is orange and black.

The *South American condor* is about as large as the California condor. It lives high in the Andes of Chile and Peru, and appears on the coats of arms of Bolivia, Chile, Colombia, and Ecuador. The *yellow-headed turkey vulture* of northern South America and Brazil resembles such North American vultures as the turkey buzzard.

Old World Vultures. There are 14 vultures in the Old World. The *cinereous vulture* is about 42 inches long

African White-Rumped Vultures use their claws and beaks to fight each other for food. They live in big-game areas.
American Museum of Natural History

Santa Catalina Island Co.

The South American King Vulture is a bird of the forests and deep swamps. Like other vultures, it has keen eyesight and can spy out dead animals from as high as 5,000 feet.

with a bare, pinkish head and black feathers. It lives in southern Europe, northwestern Africa, and central Asia.

The *griffon vulture* is about the same size and appearance, and has about the same range. The *Egyptian*, or *white*, *vulture* is about 25 inches long with a naked yellow head and whitish feathers except for the black wings. It lives in the Mediterranean area, as far east as India.

Scientific Classification. New World vultures belong to the family *Cathartidae*. The turkey vulture is genus *Cathartes*, species *C. aura;* the black vulture is *Coragyps atratus;* and the California condor is *Gymnogyps californianus*. The king vulture is *Sarcoramphus papa;* the South American condor is *Vultur gryphus;* and the yellow-headed turkey vulture is *Cathartes urubitinga*. Old World vultures belong to the family *Accipitridae*. The cinereous vulture is *Aegypius monachus*, the griffon vulture is *Gyps fulvus*, the Egyptian is *Neophron percnopterus*, and the white-rumped is *Gyps africanus*. OLIN SEWALL PETTINGILL, JR.

See also ANIMAL (color picture, Animals of the Grasslands); BUZZARD; CONDOR; LAMMERGEIER.